SEXUAL DEVIANCE

SEXUAL DEVIANCE

Theory, Assessment, and Treatment

Edited by

D. Richard Laws
William O'Donohue

THE GUILFORD PRESS
New York London

Library of Congress Cataloging-in-Publication Data

Sexual deviance: theory, assessment, and treatment / D. Richard Laws,
William O'Donohue.
   p. cm.
  Includes bibliographical references and index.
  ISBN 1-57230-241-0
  1. Sexual deviation. 2. Sex therapy.   I. Laws, D. Richard.
II. O'Donohue, William T.
  RC556.S4765 1997
  616.85'83—dc21   97-25929
                                      CIP

CONTRIBUTORS

GWEN ADSHEAD, MRCPSYCH, trained in forensic psychiatry at St. George's Hospital, London, England. She worked for two years in the Trauma Clinic at the Maudsley Hospital, London, and now works at Broadmoor maximum security hospital, Crowthorne, England. She has run treatment groups for sex offenders and carried out research into the use of repertory grids in monitoring change in such groups. She has also assessed and treated victims of sexual assault. Dr. Adshead holds a master's degree in medical law and ethics, and has a particular interest in the ethical dilemmas raised in the assessment and treatment of sexually deviant or offending patients.

HOWARD E. BARBAREE, PHD, is head of the Forensic Division at the Clarke Institute of Psychiatry, Toronto, Ontario, and head of the Forensic Psychiatry program at the University of Toronto, Ontario. He is also the founding director of the Warkworth Sexual Behaviour Clinic, a Canadian penitentiary treatment program for sex offenders. Dr. Barbaree was a professor of psychology at Queen's University in Kingston, Ontario, for over 13 years. He has published numerous articles and book chapters on sexual aggression and sexual deviance.

ROY F. BAUMEISTER, PHD, holds the Elsie B. Smith Professorship in the Liberal Arts at Case Western Reserve University, Cleveland, Ohio. He received his PhD in social psychology from Princeton in 1978 and has taught at Case Western since 1979, with visiting appointments at the Universities of California (Berkeley), Texas (Austin), and Virginia (Charlottesville), and at the Max-Planck-Institute (Munich, Germany). He has published 10 books and over 160 articles.

RAY BLANCHARD, PHD, received his doctoral degree in psychology from the University of Illinois, Champaign–Urbana, in 1973. He was a Killam Postdoctoral Fellow at Dalhousie University from 1973 to 1976, and then worked as a clinical psychologist at the Ontario Correctional Institute, Brampton, Ontario. In 1980, he was appointed research psychologist at the Gender Identity Clinic of the Clarke Institute of Psychiatry, Toronto, Ontario, and, in 1995, was named head of the Clinical Sexology Programme at that institute. Dr. Blanchard is on the editorial board of *Archives of Sexual Behavior* and was a member of the DSM-IV Subcommittee on Gender Identity Disorders.

JOHN BRADFORD, MD, is clinical director of the Forensic Program and the Sexual Behaviours Clinic at the Royal Ottawa Hospital, Ottawa, Ontario, and professor of

psychiatry and head of the Division of Forensic Psychiatry, Faculty of Medicine, University of Ottawa, Ottawa, Ontario. He is involved in research in forensic psychiatry and has published a large number of papers on this subject, particularly in the area of the assessment and treatment of the paraphilias. Dr. Bradford is also the editor of *Clinical Aspects of Forensic Psychiatry* (Saunders, 1992). He founded the Canadian Academy of Psychiatry and the Law, is a fellow of the American Psychiatric Association, past president of the American Academy of Psychiatry and the Law, past president of the Canadian Academy of Psychiatry and the Law, a fellow of the Royal College of Psychiatrists in England, a member of the American College of Psychiatrists, and has recently been appointed as a member of the Task Force on Sexually Dangerous Persons by the President of the American Psychiatric Association. He was an international adviser to DSM-IV and was appointed to the Sexual Disorders Work Group and the Impulse Control Work Group.

JENNIFER L. BUTLER, MA, is a graduate student in the social psychology program at Case Western Reserve University, Cleveland, Ohio. Her research interests include the self, interpersonal relations, and performance.

CYNTHIA A. DOPKE, MA, received her master's degree in psychology from Northern Illinois University, DeKalb, Illinois, where she is currently working on her PhD in clinical psychology. Her current research focuses on the effects of stress on social information processing in individuals at risk for child physical abuse.

KURT FREUND, MD, DSC (deceased), was head of the Department of Behavioural Sexology, Clarke Institute of Psychiatry, Toronto, Ontario, until his retirement in 1995, and was an associate professor in the Department of Psychiatry, University of Toronto, Toronto, Ontario. He introduced the phallometric procedure for the assessment of erotic preferences and published extensively on homosexuality and the paraphilias, particularly pedophilia.

DON GRUBIN, MD, MRCPSYCH, is a consultant forensic psychiatrist and a senior lecturer in forensic psychiatry at the University of Newcastle, Newcastle, England. He has a BA in philosophy from Oxford University, Oxford, England. He did his medical training at the University of London and his psychiatric training at the Maudsley Hospital, both in London, England.

R. KARL HANSON, PHD, received his doctoral degree in clinical psychology from the University of Waterloo, Waterloo, Ontario, in 1986. He conducted clinical work with sex offenders for the Ontario Ministry of Correctional Services and the Clarke Institute of Psychiatry before obtaining the position of senior research officer with the Department of the Solicitor General Canada in 1991. His research has focused on the prediction of sexual offender recidivism and the development of new assessment measures for sexual offenders and male batterers. Dr. Hanson is also an adjunct research professor at Carleton University and is frequently invited to present to professional and governmental organizations in Canada, the United States, and abroad.

ANDREW J. R. HARRIS, MSC, works as a sex offender researcher at the Penetanguishene Mental Health Centre, Penetanguishene, Ontario. Presently on educational leave to complete a PhD in forensic psychology, his thesis explores the intersection of Hare's (1995) conception of psychopathy and measures of sexual deviance. Mr. Harris specializes in managing large field-team research projects, having led the field teams of the Survey of Mentally Disordered Offenders for the Province of Ontario (in 1992) and the Dangerous Offender Review Project

for the Solicitor General Canada (in 1996). He presently leads the nationwide survey of Dynamic Predators of Sexual Re-offense for the Solicitor General Canada. Mr. Harris lectures extensively on prison history and design, the assessment of sexual preference, and managing the developmentally handicapped sex offender.

CLIVE R. HOLLIN, PHD, currently holds the joint post of reader in psychology at the University of Leicester, Leicester, England, and consultant forensic psychologist at Rampton Hospital Authority, Nottinghamshire, England. He is a fellow of the British Psychological Society and a chartered forensic psychologist. The author or editor of 14 books, including *Psychology and Crime* (Routledge, 1989), he has published over 100 academic articles, particularly on delinquency. He is coeditor of the journal *Psychology, Crime, and Law.*

STEPHEN J. HUCKER, FRCPC, FRCPSYCH, is currently professor of psychiatry, psychology, and law at Queen's University in Kingston, Ontario. He is also chairman of the Division of Forensic and Correctional Psychiatry and vice chairman of the Department of Psychiatry. Prior to this, he spent 20 years at the Clarke Institute of Psychiatry in Toronto, Ontario, where he was head of the forensic program for much of that time. His professional interests have included psychiatric aspects of crime in the elderly and in female offenders, but most of his research has involved sexual disorders, both criminal and noncriminal. He has published a number of articles on fatal and living cases of autoerotic asphyxsia and has recently begun a large study of sexual sadists and sexually motivated homicides.

STEPHEN M. HUDSON, PHD, is currently director of clinical training at the University of Canterbury, Christchurch, New Zealand, and is the consultant psychologist to the Kia Marama Sex Offender Treatment Program at Rolleston Prison, Rolleston, New Zealand. He has been treating and carrying out research in the area of sexual aggression since 1982. He is coeditor of *The Juvenile Sex Offender* (with H. E. Barbaree and W. L. Marshall; Guilford, 1993).

JOHN A. HUNTER, JR., PHD, is a clinical psychologist with over 20 years experience working in the child sexual abuse field as a clinician, clinical administrator, and researcher. He is currently the vice president and director of research and outcomes for Alternative Behavioral Services at First Hospital Corporation, Norfolk, Virginia, and research associate professor in the Department of Psychology at the University of Arizona, Tucson, Arizona.

JOHN JUNGINGER, PHD, received his doctoral degree in clinical psychology from Indiana University, Bloomington, Indiana. His research interest is experimental psychopathology, especially the association between psychosis and "symptom-consistent" violence. Dr. Junginger is director of training, Adult Mental Health Division, Hawaii Department of Health, Honolulu, Hawaii. He also is an associate professor in the Department of Psychology at the University of Hawaii, Manoa, Hawaii.

MEG S. KAPLAN, PHD, a clinical psychologist, is currently the director of the Sexual Behavior Clinic at the New York State Psychiatric Institute, New York, New York, and an associate professor of clinical psychology in psychiatry at the Columbia University College of Physicians and Surgeons, New York, New York. She received her PhD in human sexuality and has conducted clinical research in psychosexual disorders since 1979. Dr. Kaplan is on the board of the Association for the Treatment of Sexual Abusers and is a board member of the Special Classification Review Board at Avenyl Correctional Facility in Rahway, New

Jersey. She reviews for numerous publications and has over 35 publications in the sexual disorders field.

RICHARD B. KRUEGER, MD, is a psychiatrist at the New York State Psychiatric Institute, New York, New York, and medical director of its Sexual Behavior Clinic, and is in private practice in New York City. He is an assistant professor of psychiatry at the Columbia University College of Physicians and Surgeons, New York, New York, and is active in the teaching of medical students and residents. He received his MD from Harvard Medical School in 1977 and has treated sex offenders since 1985. For three years, he was a psychiatric consultant to the Sexual Treatment Center in Bridgewater, Massachusetts. He is a board certified forensic psychiatrist. He has an expertise in psychopharmacology and has over 16 publications in the area of biological psychiatry.

MICHAEL KUBAN, MA, is the program coordinator of Clinical Sexology, formerly known as the Department of Behavioural Sexology, at the Clarke Institute of Psychiatry, Toronto, Ontario. He is presently a graduate student at the Institute of Medical Science, University of Toronto, Toronto, Ontario. His research interests include the paraphilias and the use of phallometric procedures.

D. RICHARD LAWS, PHD, received his doctoral degree from Southern Illinois University in 1969. He is presently a psychologist with Adult Forensic Psychiatric Community Services in Victoria, British Columbia, and coordinator of the Victoria Adult Sex Offender Management Program. Dr. Laws is well known in the field of sexual deviation as an innovator in the development of assessment procedures and in program development and evaluation. He is the author of 50 articles and book chapters and an equal number of professional presentations. He currently serves on the editorial boards of the *Journal of Interpersonal Violence* and *Sexual Abuse: A Journal of Research and Treatment*. He is a past president of the Association for the Treatment of Sexual Abusers and has served on their executive board since 1991. Dr. Laws is the editor of *Relapse Prevention with Sex Offenders* (Guilford, 1989) and coeditor with W. L. Marshall and H. E. Barbaree of *Handbook of Sexual Assault* (Plenum, 1990). With coeditors S. H. Hudson and T. Ward, he is currently preparing two new volumes: *Rethinking Relapse Prevention* and *Containing Evil: Sex Offending as a Public Health Issue*.

BARRY M. MALETZKY, MD, is currently professor of clinical psychiatry at the Oregon Health Sciences University, Portland, Oregon; director of the Sexual Abuse Clinic, an organization devoted to the treatment of the sexual offender; and editor-in-chief of the scholarly journal *Sexual Abuse: A Journal of Research and Treatment*. Although specializing in the treatment of the sexual offender, Dr. Maletzky has published three books and more than 60 papers, and has delivered numerous presentations in the United States and abroad on a variety of topics. His areas of specialization and publication include treatment of refractory affective disorders and forensic and management aspects of crimes of violence.

RUTH MANN, MSc, is head of HM Prison Service's Sex Offender Treatment Programme, London, England. She is currently studying for a doctorate in the role of cognition in sexual offending. She has also authored publications about motivational interviewing with sex offenders.

W. L. MARSHALL, PHD, is a professor of psychology and psychiatry at Queen's University in Kingston, Ontario. He has been conducting research and treating sexual offenders for 26 years. In addition to his other research interests, Dr. Marshall has published over 90 journal articles, 36 book chapters, and three books on sexual offending. He has been involved in establishing four treatment programs in Canadian penitentiaries and a community program in Kingston, Ontario, and has assisted in establishing similar programs in six other countries.

DEBBIE MASON, MB, CHB, MPHIL, MRCPSYCH, is a senior registrar in forensic psychiatry at the University of Newcastle, Newcastle, England. She studied for her medical degree and a master's degree in law and ethics in medicine at the University of Glasgow, Glasgow, Scotland, and trained as a psychiatrist at the University of Glasgow as well.

FIONA L. MASON, MBBS, MRCPSYCH, DSP, is a consultant forensic psychiatrist at the Broadmoor Hospital, Crowthorne, England. Her interest in sexual deviation stems both from her work with sex offenders and her particular interest in cycles of violence and abuse. In addition, she has worked extensively with adolescent offenders and trained at the Portman Clinic in London in forensic psychotherapy.

RUTH MATHEWS, PHD, is a licensed psychologist working as the clinical supervisor at Northland Therapy Center, codirector of the Adult Female Sexual Offenders Program at Transition Place, and clinical consultant and researcher at the Program for Healthy Adolescent Sexual Expression (PHASE), all in St. Paul, Minnesota. Her expertise is in the assessment and treatment of female and adolescent sexual offenders, sexual victimization, and sexual identity issues.

JULIE MCCORMACK, BSC, is a postgraduate student in clinical psychology at the University of Canterbury, Christchurch, New Zealand. Her research interests include the relapse process and intimacy deficits in sex offenders. She has an interest in the combined use of qualitative and quantitative research methods.

JOEL S. MILNER, PHD, is professor of psychology, Presidential Research Professor, and director of the Family Violence and Sexual Assault Research Program at Northern Illinois University, DeKalb, Illinois. His current research focuses on the description and screening of child physical and sexual abusers.

WILLIAM D. MURPHY, PHD, received his doctoral degree in 1976 in clinical psychology from Ohio University, Athens, Ohio. Dr. Murphy is currently a professor in the Division of Clinical Psychology, Department of Psychiatry, at the University of Tennessee, Memphis, Tennessee. He is director of the Special Problems Unit, a sex offender evaluation and treatment program.

WILLIAM O'DONOHUE, PHD, is an associate professor of psychology at the University of Nevada, Reno. His research specialities include sexual behavior, behavior therapy, and the philosophy of science. He has also coedited *Theories of Human Sexuality* (Plenum, 1987), *The Sexual Abuse of Children* (Erlbaum, 1992), *Handbook of Sexual Dysfunction* (Allyn & Bacon, 1993, with James Geer); and *Sexual Harassment: Theory, Research, and Practice* (Allyn & Bacon, 1997).

DEVON POLASCHEK, MA, is a lecturer in criminal justice psychology and clinical psychology at Victoria University, Wellington, New Zealand. Formerly a clinical psychologist with the New Zealand Department of Justice, her research interests include sexual and violent offenders, investigative psychology, and correctional intervention design and evaluation. Her PhD research is on the offense process in rapists.

PAUL A. SCHEWE, PHD, received his doctoral degree from Northern Illinois University, DeKalb, Illinois. His research has emphasized designing and evaluating programs for the primary prevention of rape among high-risk males. He is currently completing postdoctoral training in prevention research at the University of Illinois at Chicago.

MICHAEL C. SETO, MA, is a research scientist with the Impulse Control Disorders Programme, Forensic Division, Clarke Institute of Psychiatry, Toronto, Ontario. He is a doctoral candidate in clinical psychology at Queen's University in Kingston, Ontario. His research interests include psychopathy, sexual deviance, and sexual preferences.

DAVID THORNTON, PHD, received his doctoral degree from Exeter University, Exeter, England. He is currently head of HM Prison Service's Programme Development Section, London, England, with overall responsibility for the development, managment, and evaluation of correctional programs. He specializes in risk assessment and program design.

TONY WARD, PHD, is currently director of clinical training at the University of Canterbury, Christchurch, New Zealand, and is a research consultant to the Kia Marama Sex Offender Treatment Program at Rolleston Prison, Rolleston, New Zealand. His research interests include the area of attachment and intimacy deficits in sex offenders, cognitive distortions, and the offense process in sexual and violent offenders.

KENNETH J. ZUCKER, PHD, received his doctoral degree in psychology from the University of Toronto, Ontario, in 1982. Dr. Zucker is head of the Child and Adolescent Gender Identity Clinic and psychologist-in-charge in the Child and Family Studies Centre, Clarke Institute of Psychiatry, Toronto, Ontario. He currently serves as the director of training of the joint American Psychological Association and Canadian Psychological Association internship program in clinical psychology at the Clarke Institute. Dr. Zucker is the book review editor of *Archives of Sexual Behavior* and was a member of the DSM-IV Subcommittee on Gender Identity Disorders.

CONTENTS

SEXUAL DEVIANCE

1

INTRODUCTION

Fundamental Issues in Sexual Deviance

D. Richard Laws
William O'Donohue

One fact about human behavior that is so obvious that it needs no research program to establish its truth is that humans judge some sexual practices to be undesirable and changeworthy. The number of prohibitions and the importance attached to sexual behavior is one of the most distinctive features of human sexuality. Breaches of sexual prohibitions are regarded as one of the more serious infractions an individual can commit. We believe that the large amount of valuation that occurs with human sexuality is a reflection of the importance of human sexuality to the well-being of the individual and of the species, as well as the potential of sexual misbehavior to result in serious harm to others.

This book is devoted to explicating what we know about those kinds of sexual deviance that are currently regarded by most mental health professionals as the major ones. The particulars surrounding these negative judgments made by mental health professionals about some sexual practices are, unfortunately, not so clear. For example, it is not clear on what grounds humans in general, or mental health professionals in particular, either do evaluate or should evaluate sexual practices. That is, should sexual practices be evaluated on the grounds of whether they harm others (If so, what kinds of harm, and how much harm, are necessary for the behavior to be regarded as a mental disorder?), or whether the sexual practices are unhealthy (utilizing this criterion is clearly problematic as it simply pushes the question to how properly healthy practices can be distinguished from unhealthy ones), or whether the behaviors deviate from a statistical norm, or whether the behaviors seem to be maladaptive in some evolutionary sense? The lack of well-supported criteria upon which to distinguish permissible or healthy sexual behavior from unhealthy, deviant, and proscribed behavior probably is related to the inability of mental health professionals to provide clear demarcations of what distinguishes normal from abnormal behavior. We are not, however, arguing that because there are no clear demarcation criteria, there is no such thing as abnormal sexual behavior. We claim that there is sexual behavior that is deviant, and that it is an important intellectual task to explicate a sound case for criteria that accurately make this demarcation.

Currently, it appears that most professionals show some, perhaps reasonable, temerity in making these judgments. Many scholars are concerned about what lessons we should learn from the case of homosexuality. For many years, mental health professionals, among others, regarded this as a disease. However, in DSM-III, the American Psychiatric Association (1980) reversed itself so that it regarded only *ego-dystonic* homosexuality as a mental disorder. Homosexuality accepted by the individual now is regarded as a sexual interest and practice that is not disordered.

What is most interesting from this case is that it is not very clear what evidence or arguments resulted in this change. The vast majority of professionals cannot point to some landmark study or influential theoretical article that influenced professional thinking about this issue. (It also is interesting that the members of the American Psychiatric Association resolved this matter by a vote. Moreover, the vote indicated that a very sizable percentage of the membership voted to continue to classify homosexuality as a mental disorder.) However, the fact remains that before 1980, homosexuality was regarded as a mental disorder, and post-1980 it was not. Moreover, it is not at all clear from this example what caused this rather significant change.

Most troubling about this development is that some have suggested that the major influence on the APA was the political advocacy by the gay liberation movement (Bayer, 1981). That is, their protests, disruption of certain talks at mental health association meetings, and other actions may have had a considerable influence in affecting this change. This is troubling because as scientists we do not want to have a taxonomy of disordered sexual behavior that is a function of how effective or ineffective certain subgroups are in using political tactics to influence or intimidate the American Psychiatric Association. Rather, it would be a more desirable state of affairs if we could define changeworthy sexual interests and practices on explicit criteria justified by sound argumentation. Currently, this is not the case; thus, it raises the specter that we may be missing certain classes of problematic sexual behavior which ought to be classified as paraphilic, or that we are including as disordered sexual behavior and that actually is not.

This book utilizes the classificatory scheme of DSM-IV (American Psychiatric Association, 1994) for its general organization. We did this because, despite its many flaws, the DSM has been accepted as the standard taxonomy by the vast majority of professionals. DSM-IV defines a mental disorder as

> a clinically significant behavioral or psychological syndrome or pattern that occurs in an individual and that is associated with present distress (e.g., a painful symptom) or disability (i.e., impairment in one or more important areas of functioning) or with a significantly increased risk of suffering death, pain, disability, or an important loss of freedom. In addition, this syndrome or pattern must not be merely an expectable and culturally sanctioned response to a particular event, for example, the death of a loved one. Whatever its original cause, it must currently be considered a manifestation of a behavioral, psychological, or biological dysfunction in the individual. Neither deviant behavior (e.g., political, religious, or sexual) nor conflicts that are primarily between the individual and society are mental disorders unless the deviance or conflict is a symptom of a dysfunction in the individual, as described above. (pp. xxi–xxii)

It is fortunate for us that the authors of the DSM explicitly mentioned sexual deviance in their definition of a mental disorder, because it allows certain issues to be clearer. Deviant sexual behavior is regarded as a mental disorder by these authors because this behavior is *a symptom of a dysfunction in the individual.* Further, this definition tells us that there are three types of dysfunction: behavioral, psychological, and biological. Although the definition states that the dysfunction is "described above," it is unclear exactly where it is described. If we take this description to be found in the first sentence, then the dysfunction in the individual may be either (1) distress; (2) disability; or (3) a significantly increased risk of suffering death, pain, disability, or an important loss of freedom.

To clarify our understanding of the basis for considering certain sexual behavior to constitute a mental disorder, let us take a look at the general structure of the diagnostic criteria for the paraphilias. The general structure used in diagnosing each paraphilia is similar across the specific kinds of paraphilia. Criterion A specifies the specific fantasies, urges, or behaviors that characterize the paraphilia (e.g., young children for pedophilia, exposing one's genitals for exhibitionism). Criterion B also is constant across the individual paraphilia categories and states:

> B. The fantasies, sexual urges, or behaviors cause clinically significant distress or impairment in social, occupational, or other important areas of functioning. (e.g., p. 528)

Because we have seen already that according to the DSM, the dysfunction needs to be *in the individual,* it appears that the individual (as opposed to others) must be distressed by his or her sexual fantasies, urges, or behavior for the distress criterion to be met. Thus, if a mental health professional comes across a contented member of the North American Man Boy Love Association (NAMBLA), who clearly has sexual fantasies and urges toward children but is not distressed by these, then the mental health professional, according to DSM-IV, would not diagnose this individual as having pedophilia. It is not uncommon for mental health professionals to encounter individuals who, for a variety of reasons, are not distressed by their deviant sexual interests. Thus, the criterion of distress of the individual is met in some cases, but in cases when it is not we must look for additional criteria to make the diagnosis. Marshall (Chapter 5, this volume) also discusses this issue.

However, the syntactical structure of Criterion B is that of a disjunction. The second half of the disjunct suggests that a diagnosis also can be made if "impairment in social, occupational, or other important areas of functioning" is found. But how do we determine this impairment? Although the magnitude and kind of impairment is an important question (and makes a valid attribution that the impairments that the individual is experiencing are caused by his sexual urges, behavior, or fantasies, as opposed to something else about the individual), the more important question is, what if this impairment is due largely or solely to the reactions of others? In this case, several paradoxes arise.

First, if the argument is based on the claim that if others find out an individual has these sexual interests, then they will tend to not socialize with, or will divorce or fire the individual, and the like, then this seems, based on the DSM's definition of mental disorders, to be an unacceptable basis for attributing a mental disorder (remember the explicit disavowal of deviant sexual behavior in the DSM's definition of mental disorder). First, given the negative attitudes toward homosexuality in society and the stigmatization that occurs, it appears that if Criterion B defines what should be regarded as sexual mental disorders, then homosexuality should, by this criterion, still be regarded as a mental disorder because it can result in "impairments in social or occupational functioning" (resulting from the reactions of others). The problem stems from a poor elucidation of behaviors that *inherently* produce impairments versus behaviors that produce impairments due to the prejudicial, irrational *reactions of others.* Being of color in a racist society produces impairments due to the later case (and thus clearly should not be a mental disorder), whereas being psychotic produces impairments in the former case (and thus clearly is an acceptable candidate for a mental disorder). Parenthetically, it is interesting to note that DSM-IV does not allow the reactions of others to count as an impairment in social functioning. It is clear in some cases why this is reasonable (e.g., in the case of prejudices). However, in other cases it is not. It the case of a conduct-disordered child, the reactions of others seems to be essential to making the diagnosis. Many have claimed that mental disorders are not so much rather *disturbed* behavior but *disturbing* behavior and have developed plausible theories of mental disorders as social deviance (Szasz, 1970; Ullmann & Krasner, 1975).

Second, what if we made the argument that a sexual orientation toward children, far from causing an impairment in social and occupational functioning, actually enhances it? For example, what if a second-grade teacher were to *accurately* claim the following:

1. I will never act in an abusive manner toward children, for example by actually touching them. (The teacher may bolster this claim by pointing out that it is a common experience for an individual's job to place them in contact with people they become sexually attracted to, but many of these individuals never act on this attraction.)
2. I enjoy my job more and perform better in my job because of my sexual attraction to these children. Thus, my occupational functioning actually is enhanced.
3. I socialize and become better acquainted with children (which also enhances my job) because of my strong sexual attraction toward, and interest in, children. Thus, my social life (because of my enhanced relationships with children) is enriched by my pedophilic sexual orientation.

It seems that we can make a good argument that a sexual orientation toward children actually can enhance social and occupational functioning, and "impairments" will occur in such cases mainly because of the reactions of others to the individual's interests. However, this is not sufficient to meet the DSM's criterion of the dysfunction occurring *within the individual*.

A core problem is that the construct, "dysfunction within the individual," is dependent upon an accurate understanding of what factors within the individual are responsible for proper or healthy sexual functioning. The DSM fails to describe what these factors are and, given that our understanding of human sexuality still is in its infancy, it is fair to say that currently we do not know what these are. However, even if we knew these factors, it is another question whether we can assess them. Without the ability to accurately, directly, and independently assess whether these are functioning properly, it is impossible to make a reasonable attribution of dysfunction.

At a minimum, the DSM should be consistent. That is, it should apply whatever criteria it uses consistently so that all behaviors falling on one side of the demarcation are included and all behaviors falling on the other are excluded. Although the failure to explicate the exact criteria used to make the demarcation between paraphilic and nonparaphilic behavior makes this process difficult, it seems that the DSM fails to be consistent. For example, it is entirely unclear why fetishism currently is included as a mental disorder and homosexuality is not. It appears that any criterion which would exclude homosexuality also should exclude fetishism. If all parties are consenting, it hurts no one. (Also, many individuals engage in their fetishism when they are alone.) It does not appear to inherently cause impairments in social or occupational functioning, and so on. We suggest that future editions of the DSM more clearly explicate (1) what factors within the individual are responsible for healthy sexual functioning; (2) how to assess each of these factors; (3) what criteria to use to demarcate proper from improper sexual behavior; (4) what kind and how much impairment in social or occupational functioning is required for something to be considered a disorder; (5) how to assess such impairments; and (6) how to validly attribute any impairments to sexual variables as opposed to some other cause.

Thus, we argue that a problem plaguing the current classification system is a failure to explicate a set of criteria that can accurately and clearly demarcate changeworthy from "normal" sexual behavior and interests. This in all likelihood is due to ambiguities regarding the "proper" nature of sexual behavior. The DSM refers vaguely to disorders as stemming from "dysfunctions within the individual," but it clearly fails to specify what the insides of a properly functioning individual ought to look like. Moreover, it states that the problematic sexual behavior, urges, and fantasies cause impairments in "social or occupational functioning or in other important areas of functioning" but fails to explicate what is normative social or occupational functioning, how to clarify exactly what is causing any putative impairments, or what "other important areas of functioning" are.

Moreover, we found the current taxonomy of sexual deviancy in DSM-IV glaringly incomplete in one regard. That is, we regard attraction to rape as a paraphilia; thus, we have included chapters on rape. Although some rapists can be classified as sadists, not all can; thus, we believe that there ought to be a category which captures males who can be aroused by coerced sex. We can raise questions about whether other classes of paraphilias have been omitted. Is bisexuality a paraphilia? Is an attraction to sex in public places? Is a preference for masturbation over intercourse a paraphilia?

Finally, when attempting to accurately and comprehensively classify what constitutes disordered sexual behavior, there are some interesting ambiguities regarding what constitutes sexual behavior. One interesting question concerns what are the boundaries of sexual behavior in the general behavioral stream. For example, is the purchase of a flashy car sexual behavior, given that the buyer is making this purchase solely to attract sexual partners? Or more relevant, is the purchase of child pornography sexual behavior? This was not clear in DSM-III-R, but it seems to be regarded as sexual behavior in DSM-IV. For a pedophile, is practicing a profession that puts one in close contact with children sexual behavior?

Another point that we must make is that the study of sexual deviance is largely the study of males. This is not to say that females never act in a sexually deviant manner. We have included a chapter by Hunter and Mathews that nicely summarizes what we know about female sexual deviance. However, we must make the point that sexual deviance is gendered: The vast majority of paraphiles are males and the large majority of their victims are females.

GAPS IN OUR KNOWLEDGE AND METHODS

Assessment Problems

Measurement is basic to any scientific field, as all questions regarding a phenomenon are predicated upon the scientist being able to measure that phenomenon. Thus, questions such as Does x cause y?; or, Is the frequency of x increasing?; or, Does x correlate with y? all presume that x can be measured. Clinically, the picture is much the same. Questions such

---

Note. With regard to the use of nonsexist language we wish to state the following. Most of the subjects in this book are males, so changing text to read "he or she" is not really appropriate. Therefore, the generic "he" is used throughout the book except in Chapter 24, which deals with female sexual deviance.

as Is x present?; Is it related to y? (say, in a functional analysis); or, Is x improving? all presume that x can be measured.

Psychological constructs are notoriously difficult to measure. Constructs related to sexual deviance are among the most difficult to measure. Part of this difficulty stems from the general human tendency to present misinformation about sexual matters, particularly about sexual matters that are stigmatized. Another part of the measurement problem is due to the fact that some key sexual behavior is private (e.g., fantasies, masturbation) or semiprivate (e.g., most sex acts). A final part of the measurement problem is due to ethical constraints on measurement. Individuals have legitimate rights to keep much of their sexual behavior private, and some sexual behavior is difficult to study because of ethical considerations (e.g., the development of sexual fantasies in children and adolescents).

It is clear that we have few psychometrically sound measurement methods to address even the most basic questions in the field. For many of the disorders discussed in this book we do not currently have sound measurement methodologies to detect their presence or absence. Moreover, we do not have measurement technologies to assess some of the constitutive constructs associated with these disorders. For example, the diagnosis of each of the paraphilias calls for the measurement of sexual fantasies. However, there currently does not exist a psychometrically sound way of measuring sexual fantasies (O'Donohue, Letourneau, & Dowling, 1997).

We cannot overemphasize the importance of these lacunae. Hypotheses cannot be adequately tested, criterion groups cannot be properly formed, diagnoses cannot accurately be made, and treatment progress (or lack thereof) cannot be tracked unless we can overcome these measurement gaps. We strongly suggest that test construction and test validation work be a priority in this field. The field will not progress if it relies upon borrowed measurement methodologies for slightly related issues or on measurement techniques of unknown validity.

Therapy Problems

Finding effective therapies requires a sustained research program utilizing rigorous research designs. Although, the minimal experimental tests a therapy needs to pass to be considered effective are not clear, some have suggested that a reasonable criterion would be a randomized clinical trial utilizing double-blind procedures and placebo and no-treatment control groups (e.g., McFall, 1991). Some have suggested that other, less stringent criteria can bestow at least an appellation of "probably effective." However, it is clear from the following chapters that despite the centuries-old concern about deviant sexual behavior, there have been few reasonably designed outcome or process studies of therapies for the paraphilias.

This is consistent with the conclusion reached in a recent review of the sex offender outcome literature (Furby, Weinrott, & Blackshaw, 1989). These authors argued that, because of numerous design flaws, extant research does not show that there are treatments that cause long-term change in pedophiles over what would be expected from placebo effects or from spontaneous remission. This is a field in which practical concerns affect research design. How can subjects ethically and practically be randomly assigned to a no-treatment control group? What is a sensitive and specific measure of paraphilic behavior? How long can follow-up periods be?

The lack of clear evidence for the efficacy of treatments of sexual deviance raises a number of concerns. First, many individuals with paraphilias are being treated; thus, we can raise ethical and practical questions about the cost effectiveness of these efforts. One must remember that simply calling something "therapy" does not actually make the endeavor therapeutic. Second, how much false confidence is being instilled by these interventions of dubious merit? That is, a commonly accepted progressive view about these matters is that individuals engaging in sexually deviant should not "just be locked up," but rather, they should at least be in therapy for their problems. We think that the basic intention behind this notion is acceptable. However, the problem currently is that if there is little evidence that these therapies actually work, then placing the individual in an intervention actually may do little to change the individual. Individuals with an unwarrantedly high notion of the effectiveness of therapy can make problematic judgments that can lead to further harm (e.g., premature parole, premature family reunification, etc.). Finally, we have argued elsewhere (e.g., O'Donohue & Szymanski, 1995) that research provides needed criticism that we can use to help interventions be more effective. Without this program evaluation/criticism function, the power of therapies can stagnate. This is a particular problem in this field when the social costs of failure can be so high.

We believe that the field can profit from the following two initiatives. First, making a very strong commitment to research-based therapy development and evaluation is crucial. We refer readers to McFall (1991) for a more detailed exposition of this perspective. Second, we realize that this philosophical commitment is not sufficient, as there are serious practical difficulties in conducting well-designed research in this field. In the foreseeable future many of these will get worse, not better. However, we believe that another important initiative is the pooling and coordination of resources in multisite studies of therapy effectiveness. There are important precedents for this established for the study of depression and anxiety, as well as for other clinical problems. We think that this model can usefully be extrapolated to the study of sexual deviance, and it can help with problems such as insufficient subject and therapist samples, blindness of raters, random assignment, and the like. Many of the paraphilias have low base rates or there are other practical barriers to gathering samples adequate for sufficient statistical power. Multisite collaborative studies are a vital tool for studying these groups.

Another problem involved in the treatment of the paraphilia concerns the question of whether sexual orientation can be modified. There is very little data suggesting that it can be. It may be the case that sexual orientation is not modifiable, particularly in adults. It appears that the field has been acting on the assumption that a deviant sexual orientation is more plastic than is a normal one. That is, male heterosexuals think that they share with other male heterosexuals an immutable attraction to intercourse with adult females. No amount of hours discussing this with a therapist, or even aversive conditioning trials, would change this. However, it seems that psychotherapists have believed that deviant attractions are somehow "weaker" or more susceptible to change, that is, that "explorations" of these, or counterconditioning trials, could replace these "weaker" orientations with a "normal," more permanent set of attractions.

However, because of our skepticism regarding changing our own orientations and the lack of evidence that paraphilic orientations somehow are more modifiable, we believe that these problems are not "curable." That is, there is little evidence suggesting that a paraphilic orientation can be reliably and permanently replaced by a normal orientation. Rather, we believe that the assumptions associated with a relapse prevention model (Laws, 1989) are the most tenable. The client may for his entire life have a paraphilic orientation, but the goals are to decrease the intensity of these interests and most importantly to learn skills to decrease the likelihood that he will act on this orientation. Thus, the goal of therapy is not a "cure," but rather the maintenance of abstinence from acting on the interest.

A further problem stems from the tendency of paraphiles to not fully and honestly report information about their situations. It is essential that the therapist receive accurate and complete information. This allows the therapist to devise the most appropriate treatment, to accurately monitor progress, and to make revisions in the treatment plan.

Some have suggested that paraphiles are particularly good at lying because they have lived lives which necessitated their hiding their interests and actions. Though we are not sure that this is accurate, we can understand how difficult it is for an individual to fully disclose information about their sexual interests and behaviors about which there is so much stigma. Moreover, because the sexual offender often has much to gain by treatment progress (e.g., freedom, family reunification), there is added incentive to minimize problems and to exaggerate treatment gains. Finally, reporting laws, other laws, and social stigma contrive to make it difficult for the sexual offender to report lapses and relapses. Thus, the state of the art of psychotherapy is such that progress is difficult to come by and all too easy to lose, and the forces that serve to minimize the flow of accurate and complete information in the treatment of sex offenders further conspire against treatment progress.

Another way in which treating paraphiliacs has grown more complicated than treating many other problems is that in recent years, there has been an emphasis on the treatment of adolescent sexual offenders. The rationale for this emphasis is quite plausible: (1) There have been recent data (e.g., Abel & Rouleau, 1991; Barbaree, Marshall, & Hudson, 1993) suggesting that many sexual offenders begin offending in early adolescence, thus in the course of the problem this is the point at which the problem first presents; (2) intervening early in the careers of sexual offenders decreases the harm done to others and minimizes the harm the offender does to himself; and (3) intervening early may increase the chances for successful outcome as, in general, intervening before problems have become well practiced increases the chance that they may be modifiable.

Despite the sound rationale for intervention with adolescents, this approach results in serious problems for the practitioner. The foremost problem concerns adolescents' status as legal minors. As the following chapters will show, treating the paraphilia involves discussions of sex, measurement involving sex (e.g., penile plethysmography), and sexual interventions (e.g., masturbatory reconditioning). Some practitioners have faced legal and ethical charges because others have construed the treatment of adolescent sex offenders to be objectionable (and perhaps even constituting sexual abuse of children) because it involves such explicit sexual content with clients who are children.

This is a difficult problem to sort out. Certainly, all would agree that such practices with the average child clearly would be inappropriate. The central question involves whether the past behavior of adolescent sexual offenders justifies their admittedly extraordinary treatment. We believe that if these therapies are found to be the most effective at lowering the rates at which these adolescents relapse, then the therapists are justified in delivering these therapies. However, we must give careful scrutiny to other methods of assessment and treatment which are sensitive to the age of these individuals.

Another problem therapists face in treating paraphilic clients is that a large number of these clients are not optimally motivated to seek or to cooperate with treatment. Many paraphiliacs are referred to therapy because of some legal problem or because of an agreement with a significant other (e.g., wife or boss). Because treatment of a paraphilia is not short-term and because the most successful treatment places numerous demands on the client over a prolonged period of time, poor motivation and compliance can be particular impediments with these clients. Thus, as discussed above, clinicians face not only a problem in attempting to deal with a problem of sexual attraction, which is a powerful force and which may not in itself be modifiable, but they also must do this with clients who may be poorly motivated to participate in therapy.

Another reality that adds complication to paraphilia treatment is that much treatment takes place in a forensic context. This adds numerous complications. First, it can complicate who actually is the therapist's client: the legal system paying the bills, or the sex offender. Second, it can add complication to conducting therapy, for example, regarding confidentiality and exceptions to it (e.g., does a probation officer receive periodic progress reports?). Third, it can define artificial but nonetheless important limitations affecting therapy (e.g., when treatment can be outpatient, when treatment ends, etc.). Fourth, it can create unwilling and unmotivated clients (e.g., when treatment is legally mandated.) Fifth, it easily can result in the client and even the therapist having a legalistic orientation in which legal issues take precedence over psychological issues. Thus, forensic issues which do not intrude in the treatment of many other problems often are a factor in the management of paraphilia treatment and can greatly complicate case management.

Also, the high cost of treatment failure makes therapy more difficult. Although it is always disappointing when therapy fails, in many others cases the cost of failure is much less. A client having another panic attack when these have been in remission for many months is disappointing, but the costs of this do not compare with those of a rapist committing another act of rape. Because we know that no therapy will be perfectly effective, we know that at best we can lower the rate of relapse in the population of clients we treat. However, some will reoffend or relapse and do serious harm to others and to themselves. This realization makes therapy with this population difficult.

Finally, individuals who have problems with a paraphilia have high incidences of comorbid problems. Substance abuse, marital problems, social problems, anxiety problems, depression, personality disorders, and anger control problems are quite common with these individuals and they vastly complicate treatment. It often is the case that the therapist must pay as much attention, or more, to these comorbid problems as they do to the paraphilia. Because there are not effective therapies for many of these comorbid problems, and because these are related in direct ways to the paraphilia, treatment becomes more difficult and the prognosis less optimistic.

Research Problems

We can evaluate a scientific field by the rate of progress it is making. In the last few decades there have been some important developments in the study of sexual deviance. We believe that the development of psychophysiological testing, cognitive-behavioral interventions, and relapse prevention are examples of these developments. However, we are concerned about the rate of progress of this field in the foreseeable future. We have observed that the field has grown increasingly litigious. Working with adolescents, using penile plethysmography, treatment failures, and incorrect predictions have resulted in lawsuits. It is understandable that practitioners need to be held accountable for malpractice. However, many of these suits essentially claim that the acceptable standards of practice within the field constitute malpractice. This is a troubling development and can cause some to leave the field and others to practice in an overly defensive manner, or to do research is an overly conservative manner.

The second reason why we are concerned about the immediate future of this field is that funding for research is in jeopardy; the picture is grim. This field is hampered by researchers needing to bootstrap resources to meet minimal design requirements. However, far too much research tells us very little because of these compromises. Test development and validation are plagued by small sample sizes, poor criterion measures, and a lack of appropriate matching, among other problems. Small sample sizes, nonrandom assignment of subjects to conditions, poor sampling of therapists, problematic outcome measures, lack of treatment fidelity measures, and insufficient length of follow-up all hamper therapy research.

These problems, we believe, are not due to intellectual limitations; researchers in the field are well aware of these design criteria. The problems stem from insufficient resources.

We believe that a new generation of high-quality research is possible if the U.S. National Institutes of Health or the National Institute of Justice will fund multisite studies.

STRUCTURE OF THE WORK

As we indicated above, our intention was to organize this work *around* DSM-IV but not to religiously follow that taxonomic structure. In the first section of this chapter we described our central concerns about DSM-IV, problems which we believe to be unresolvable within that taxonomy. Therefore, in conceiving this book, we decided to take a different approach. Readers will note that 19 of the first 21 chapters of this book follow the general outline of DSM-IV. Included here are exhibitionism, fetishism, frotteurism, pedophilia, sexual sadism, sexual masochism, transvestic fetishism, voyeurism, and paraphilias not otherwise specified. However, to give a more rounded view of sexual deviance, we added chapters. Above, we mentioned that we believe that rape deserves treatment outside the context of sexual sadism, and we included it in the preceding list. Because most of our authors are of a distinctly cognitive-behavioral persuasion we decided that, in fairness, we should include information on medical interventions. Therefore, readers will find a chapter that simply describes sexual deviance from a medical perspective, and one which describes biological interventions. We know little and very little has been written about sexual deviance among females, so we included a chapter summarizing current knowledge. Finally, because this is a field of endeavor which never seems to stop growing, we included a closing chapter which details very clearly how much there remains to do.

With the exception of the chapters on medical interventions, female sexual deviance, and future directions, we asked all authors to follow a specific set of guidelines in preparing their chapters. Examination of the table of contents shows that for each of the paraphilias we have included two chapters, one on psychopathology and theory, and one addressing assessment and treatment. We thought that, proceeding in this manner, we could best summarize and criticize what is currently known about each.

We asked authors writing on psychopathology and theory to do the following:

1. Provide a description of the disorder (diagnostic criteria, age of onset, course, etc.).
2. State the epidemiological factors (prevalence, incidence, risk).
3. Describe any associated features (concomitant problems, correlated factors).
4. Describe any associated juvenile or developmental issues.
5. Identify the forensic issues (details of interest to the court, issues in expert witnessing).
6. Provide a critical review of theories of etiology.
7. Make an assessment of future directions.

We asked authors writing on assessment and treatment to address the following:

1. How is the problem diagnosed? How do we know that the client has this problem?
   a. What are the psychometric considerations (reliabilities and validities of relevant measurement strategies)?
2. How is the client assessed for treatment? What does the therapist need to know to perform treatment?
   a. What are the psychometric considerations (reliabilities and validities of relevant measurement strategies)?

   b. What are the nuts and bolts of assessment? Contrast behavior-specific measures such as plethysmography, card sorts, questionnaires, and inventories with more traditional global measures of psychopathology.

3. State the theories of therapy with a critical review of outcome and process research.
4. What are the recommended treatment interventions for this disorder? Critique from most to least effective.
5. What are the forensic issues (details of interest to the court, issues in expert witnessing)?
6. Make an assessment of future directions for assessment and treatment.

We recognized from the outset that these guidelines represented a tall order for any author. We therefore asked the authors to follow the guidelines to the best of their ability, but not to feel overly constrained by them. We recognized that, for some paraphilias, there simply is not very much past research. For this reason we reminded the authors that part of their task would be to specify research priorities. We recommended that, in all cases, it would be necessary to strike a balance between the reality of clients needing immediate treatment and the present paucity of substantial research data.

OVERVIEW OF THE WORK

Exhibitionism

Murphy (Chapter 2) notes that exhibitionism is a disorder of males, has an early onset, and is directed primarily at females, including children and adolescents. About one third of identified offenders are exhibitionists. There is no personality profile for exhibitionists, no good evidence that they are shy or unassertive, and no good evidence of a disordered family background. There also is no clear evidence of a deviant sexual arousal profile in these men. Although the data vary, a substantial number of these offenders recidivate. The major theories underlying exhibitionism are psychoanalytic, cognitive-behavioral, and courtship disorder. The latter currently seems to show the most promise (see Freund, Seto, & Kuban, Chapter 6, this volume).

Maletzky (Chapter 3) is widely recognized as one of the outstanding practitioners, treating exhibitionists for the past 25 years. Initially, he recommends a lengthy and sophisticated diagnostic assessment including a review of supporting information; a sexual history; a mental status examination; corroborating interviews; the offender's self-report; a variety of psychological tests, rating scales, and questionnaires; a neuropsychological assessment; penile plethysmography (although many exhibitionists are unresponsive to this test); the possible use of polygraphy; and evaluation of hormonal levels. Clearly, only a clinic as well equipped as Maletzky's would have all these capabilities. Although a psychiatrist, Maletzky always has been solidly within the behaviorist tradition of treatment. He describes and discusses the treatment of exhibitionists using aversion techniques such as electrical shock, covert sensitization, assisted covert sensitization (which he developed), minimal arousal conditioning (an excellent but underused procedure), aversive behavior rehearsal (a quite controversial technique), and vicarious sensitization (one of the new behavior therapies). On the positive conditioning side, he considers social skills training and alternative behavior completion, a little-used technique. He also describes some standard behavior therapies including plethysmographic feedback, masturbation techniques, fantasy change, satiation, and impulse-control training. More cognitive approaches include cognitive restructuring, relapse prevention, and empathy training. He also considers biological interventions such as antiandrogenic and psychotropic medications. Few of us have worked with as many exhibitionists as has Maletzky, and most of us who have had any contact with this population would note that they seem very difficult to reach and refractory to treatment. Maletzky's chapter is an excellent reply to the question, "What do I do now?"

Fetishism

Mason (Chapter 4) notes at the outset that, given the nature of fetishism—sexual attraction to inanimate objects or parts of a human person, it is extremely difficult to specify what is normal and what is abnormal. For example, much present-day advertising relies heavily upon sexual fetishism to sell products which have nothing to do with sex. Etiologically speaking, fetishism has been examined from sociocultural, sociobiological, ethological, biological, behavioral, and psychodynamic perspectives. Apparently, none of these has been particularly helpful. There are no good epidemiological data for this paraphilia. It appears to be more common in males than in females, possibly because males are more easily conditioned to objects associated with sexual experience. From Krafft-Ebing to the present, the description of fetish objects has been remarkably similar. Despite this, such etiological theories as exist are virtually impossible to test empirically. Of the biological theories, that of temporal lobe dysfunction seems predominant. From a psychological perspective, Pavlovian conditioning has been considered, but social learning offers a better account. The only other major competitor is psychoanalytic theory, featuring sufficient detail to satisfy everyone.

Junginger (Chapter 5), on the other hand, is very single-mindedly behaviorist. Abreast of the times, he consulted the USENET groups of the Internet, specifically the alt.sex forums, to get an indication of the variety of interest in fetishism. Not surprisingly, the most frequently mentioned body parts or inanimate objects were exactly what has been reported in the literature for decades. Unlike most clinical writers in this area, Junginger goes on to propose a two-process learning theory account of the development of fetishism. Although not essential to performing treatment, this account provides the rationale for the use of behavioral assessment (penile plethysmography) to assess, and behavior therapy to treat fetishism. Again reverting to the conditioned suppression model as a paradigm to treat fetishism, he describes techniques such as counterconditioning by electric shock, covert sensitization, and masturbatory satiation. Additionally recommended to increase appropriate sexual interest and arousal are techniques such as orgasmic reconditioning. Junginger convincingly winds up the chapter with an extensive case study in which he demonstrates the use of his theoretical model to treat a client with an extremely unusual fetish.

Frotteurism

The late Kurt Freund and his colleagues Seto and Kuban (Chapter 6) weigh in with the latest installment of their empirical validation of the construct of courtship disorder. They do not make a sharp distinction between frotteurism (rubbing the penis against a stranger) and toucheurism, erotic preference for touching a (usually female) stranger's crotch or breasts. These authors selected the clinical records of 743 individuals seen at the Clarke Institute of Psychiatry in Toronto over a period of 20 years. Because this was a courtship disorder study, included in this group were voyeurs, exhibitionists, frotteurs/toucheurs, nonsadistic rapists, sadists, and masochists. The authors note that there are no etiological theories of frotteurism, but there are various theories of voyeurism, exhibitionism, and the paraphilias in general. Their research is based on Krafft-Ebing's notion that there are mutual affinities between the paraphilias. Their interest is in the mutual relationship between voyeurism, exhibitionism, frotteurism, and "preferential" rape. These disorders, they argue, are distortions of the normal courtship sequence (e.g., Havelock Ellis referred to exhibitionism as a "symbolic act based on a perversion of courtship"). The chapter goes on to state several hypotheses and describes the evaluation of the relationships between the various paraphilias. In general, the authors conclude that, of the courtship disorders, exhibitionism is most likely to appear on its own and in combination with other paraphilias. Frotteurism and its equivalent, toucheurism, appear to be closely related to voyeurism, exhibitionism, and the preferential rape pattern. While this chapter departs from the recommended guidelines, it is very interesting in that it provides impressive organizing evidence for a presently little-used but highly useful construct.

Highly similar to Maletzky's approach, Krueger and Kaplan (Chapter 7) recommend a comprehensive intake assessment. They recommend examining all records obtainable and, in particular, conducting a structured interview including a sexual history, a medical history, and a mental status examination. They suggest using a wide range of psychometric instruments including a history questionnaire, an inventory of sexual functioning, a cognition scale, and card sorts, as well as physiological measures such as penile plethysmography and polygraphy. As treatment modalities, Krueger and Kaplan suggest cognitive-behavioral, relapse prevention, or biological approaches. Cognitive-behavioral treatments include masturbatory satiation, covert sensitization, cognitive restructuring, sex education, and training in social skills and assertiveness. Relapse prevention strategies, on the other hand, offer a method for organizing an individual's typical pattern(s) of approaching and engaging in deviant behavior. This approach essentially teaches coping strategies to avoid lapses and relapses. Biological interventions that are *not* specifically antiandrogenic have become popular in recent years, and the authors consider several of these. Interestingly, the authors note that frotteurism is rarely considered to be a serious crime, and few consequences usually are attached to it. We find this distressing, as frotteurism/toucheurism contains many of the elements of rape. Indeed, the work of Freund et al. (Chapter 6, this volume) suggests that, as part of the courtship disorder sequence, we should take it very seriously.

Pedophilia

Marshall (Chapter 8) is the only author in the text to take serious issue with what he views as the inadequacies of DSM-IV's description of the paraphilias. It is a brilliant and devastating analysis. Prevalence and incidence reports and estimates are faulted, Marshall argues; pedophilia, he says, is pandemic. In discussing risks for engaging in pedophilia, he makes the interesting observation that risk factors are not "out there" but are products, not causes, of child molestation. Marshall notes that the associated feature of pedophilia that has received the most attention has been sexual preferences. He also considers drug and alcohol abuse, sexual "addiction," psychopathology, personality problems, empathy and intimacy deficits (areas in which he has considerable expertise), and distorted cognitions. Unlike other authors, Marshall considers theories of etiology according to explanatory levels: (1) a macrolevel wherein an attempt is made to explain all aspects of deviant behavior, (2) a midlevel which attempts to explain just one type of deviant behavior, and (3) a microlevel which tries to explain just one aspect of one type of deviant behavior. With Hudson and Ward (Chapter 18, this volume) Marshall also has made significant contributions to midlevel theory.

As have other authors, Barbaree and Seto (Chapter 9) recommend assessing a child molester's self-report about his fantasies, urges, and behavior using psychometrics specific to sexual deviation. Barbaree is well known as a strong advocate of sexual preference testing (phallometry), and he emphasizes this in the chapter. Regarding treatment, unlike many clinicians, these authors make the critical distinction between within-treatment and long-term outcome goals and the importance of determining the functional relationship (if any) between the two. They show little enthusiasm for general psychotherapy. Unlike many clinicians, they are equally unenthusiastic about pharmacotherapy, citing its uncertain effects (see also Bradford, Chapter 23). They are clear in their review of behavior therapies and recommend only three: electrical aversion, covert sensitization, and masturbatory satiation. They are mildly enthusiastic about the popular relapse prevention approach and they point also to some of its shortcomings. Comprehensive programs, they argue, are superior to any of these single interventions. Finally, we must credit these authors with producing a long section on evaluation of treatment outcome, the most neglected area in the sexual deviance literature.

Sexual Sadism

Once again we can appeal to early researchers such as Krafft-Ebing and Schrenck-Notzing for careful descriptions of a disorder that persist to this day. In terms of prevalence, says Hucker (Chapter 10), sexual sadism (if we exclude rape) is fairly rare. He notes, however, that it commonly co-occurs with other paraphilias, notably masochism. It is a broadly described paraphilia and includes necrophilia, sadistic and lust murders, and sadistic rape, possibly the most common type. As with other paraphilias, etiology is uncertain and has been variously explained by psychoanalytic, behavioral, and endocrine and brain abnormalities. Forensic issues tend to get muddied because of the sensational nature of sexually sadistic crimes, particularly murders. It appears that a large proportion of sexually motivated killers may be judged unfit for trial or be acquitted for reasons of insanity.

Hollin (Chapter 11) describes several elements of the diagnostic assessment of sexual sadism: fantasy (the scenario for the offense), symbolism (fetishes associated with sadism), ritualism (repetitive behavior), and compulsion (the drive to enact the fantasy). Assessment, he says, should be based upon these key indices. He recommends several self-report assessments specific to aggressive sexuality. Penile plethysmography, he says, will enable the clinician to determine the types of images and/or behaviors that the individual finds arousing. To the extent that the client is cooperative, one may also gain information on fantasies that precede the act, as well as the nature of the act. Hollin states that there are at least nine theories of sexual aggression which could identify theories of treatment. Echoing Barbaree and Seto (Chapter 9) Hollin urges a focus upon process (within-treatment) measures and outcome of treatment measures. As for a focus on treatment strategies, he recommends covert sensitization, olfactory/gustatory aversion, masturbatory satiation, and masturbatory reconditioning to treat sexual arousal problems. On a more psychotherapeutic level he recommends increasing victim empathy and changing cognitive distortions.

Sexual Masochism

Given Baumeister's earlier work (*Masochism as Escape from Self, Escaping the Self*), it is not surprising that he does not consider consensual sadomasochism to be a pathological state. As he and Butler (Chapter 12) say, it "rests at the borderline of convention" and, further, is "a fairly innocuous activity that is entirely compatible with an otherwise healthy, normal, successful approach to life." While he appreciates its inclusion in DSM-IV (e.g., some masochists might inadvertently go too far), he believes that these probably are the extreme cases. In discussing the function of masochism Baumeister and Butler restate the theory of masochism as a voluntary loss of control, a letting go, an escape from the self.

This is an altogether fascinating chapter which views a very unusual sexual, or quasisexual, behavior from an accepting, humanistic viewpoint.

More in the tradition of experimental psychopathology is the assessment and treatment chapter by Thornton and Mann (Chapter 13). Like Baumeister and Butler, these authors recognize that sexual masochism lies on the borderline between paraphilia and "harmless expressions of human diversity." They believe that individuals rarely present with sexual masochism as a problem, so they opt to deal with it as it occurs in the context of male sexual offending. Thornton and Mann acknowledge Baumeister's contribution to theorizing about masochism. However, they consider the "escape from self" as a possible enhancer of deviant sexual experience which may serve to stimulate even further paraphilic experimentation. These authors operate a large, nationwide, prison-based sex offender treatment program in England and their approach to assessment and treatment derives from those programs. For assessment purposes Thornton and Mann recommend sexual deviance card sorts, the Wilson Sexual Fantasy Questionnaire, and the Clarke Sexual History Questionnaire. For investigation of the paraphilia itself, they recommend carefully introducing the topic in a comprehensive interview after rapport is well established. Their treatment approach involves first using motivational interviewing to encourage modification of masochistic interests. Specific treatment techniques would include verbal satiation, directed masturbation, risk management by relapse prevention procedures, and finally, antiandrogenic drugs or fluoxetine hydrochloride treatment. An alternative approach they recommend is *not* attempting to modify masochistic interests, but rather working to break the links between those interests and sexual offending.

Transvestic Fetishism

One might question as well whether this behavior belongs in a taxonomy of paraphilias. As Marshall did in his critique of the DSM-IV description of pedophilia (Chapter 8), Zucker and Blanchard (Chapter 14) compare the varying definitions of transvestic fetishism across DSM-III, DSM-III-R, and DSM-IV and find them wanting, nor are they pleased with its inclusion under gender dysphoria in DSM-IV. To put transvestic fetishism in proper perspective they clarify the above problems by describing Blanchard's categorization of *autogynephilia*. Not surprisingly, then, Zucker and Blanchard echo Baumeister and Butler (Chapter 12) in arguing at some length the issues of mental illness, distress, and disability. The authors go to considerable lengths to describe the etiology and developmental course of transvestic fetishism. In all, this is an extremely well-written chapter on an obscure subject which attracts little professional interest.

Adshead (Chapter 15) notes that there is no agreed-upon diagnostic method for the identification and assessment of transvestic fetishism. Because of this, obtaining a comprehensive and accurate sexual history is extremely important. In addition to the client's self-report of sexual history, she recommends use of the Multiphasic Sex Inventory and the Clarke Sexual History Questionnaire. To assess gender identity she recommends Freund's Gender Identity Scale, the Mf scale of the Minnesota Multiphasic Personality Inventory, or the Bem Sex Role Inventory. Fantasy life can be explored by interview as well as with the Wilson Sexual Fantasy Questionnaire. Although she notes that there is essentially no description in the literature of physiological assessment of transvestic fetishism, there seems no reason not to use penile plethysmography. Past or present mental disorder may be assessed by the Brief Symptom Inventory, the Beck Depression Inventory, or the Symptom Checklist–90. Of some interest is Adshead's treatment of forensic issues in assessment, as transvestic fetishists ordinarily are not considered dangerous. Following Thornton and Mann (Chapter 13), she recommends assessing dangerousness when transvestic fetishism

co-occurs with other, readily identifiable dangerous behaviors (e.g., sadomasochistic practices and rape). Regarding treatment she notes that early efforts used aversive techniques
(electric shock, shame aversion) in an attempt to extinguish the behavior. In recent years
the emphasis has been on more benign behavior therapies such as masturbatory reconditioning or covert sensitization. Psychodynamic therapy, on the whole, has not been successful
with this population. She also considers antiandrogenic agents and psychotropic medication
as possible treatments for this disorder. Efficacy of treatment for this problem has proven
extremely difficult to assess.

Voyeurism

Kaplan and Krueger (Chapter 16) note that voyeurism is most commonly considered as
becoming sexually aroused while viewing some form of nudity or sexual activity. The definition, they say, is broader than this and includes "scopophilia" (watching others undress),
"scoptophilia" (watching others have sex), or "triolism" (observing one's partner having sex
with another person). The onset of voyeurism is before age 15 and it lasts a lifetime. As noted
above, Freund and his colleagues (Chapter 6) argued that voyeurism plays a central role in the
syndrome of courtship disorder. The initial theorizing in this area was psychoanalytic and
entirely speculative, and this has not changed even in recent times. Voyeurism is far more easily
explained by social learning theory or from an evolutionary perspective by sociobiology.
Money's description of voyeurism as a truncated form of conventional sexual attraction bears
close similarity to Freund et al.'s notions of courtship disorder.

Hanson and Harris (Chapter 17) note, as have other authors, that voyeurism is not
always defined in terms of psychopathology. They state that sexual interest in viewing
becomes a paraphilia when it is overemphasized in the repertoire of sexual behaviors and
it is this exaggeration on which the DSM-IV diagnosis focuses. Hanson and Harris state
that their approach to voyeurism is consistent with Freund et al.'s (Chapter 6) construct of
courtship disorder, which means that it is highly likely that voyeurs engage in other sexually
deviant behaviors, typically exhibitionism or frottage/toucheurism. Due to this co-occurrence, a very comprehensive assessment is necessary, as voyeurism may not be the major
paraphilia. They recommend that clinicians consider four central issues: (1) the extent of
voyeuristic interests and impulses, (2) the extent of voyeuristic activities, (3) the personal
distress caused by voyeurism, and (4) the impairment in social and occupational functioning.
Additional assessments would include the little-used Erotic Preferences Examination Scheme,
the Multiphasic Sex Inventory, the Clarke Sexual History Questionnaire, the Sexual Behavior
Inventory, and several sexual deviance card sorts. Phallometric testing of voyeurs, the
authors note, is hampered by the lack of stimulus materials specific to this paraphilia. There
is very little information on the treatment of voyeurs, and all accounts are single-case studies.
If one were to design a more comprehensive treatment, Hanson and Harris say, it should
address two broad concerns: (1) setting up blocks or obstacles to continued voyeuristic
activities, and (2) finding alternative, socially acceptable means of meeting the needs and
desires that the voyeur has been attempting to fulfill through peeping. If the latter criteria
are met, therapy is likely to be successful.

Rape

Both chapters in this section (Chapter 18 and 19) were prepared by Hudson, Ward, and
their colleagues, clinicians–researchers–theoreticians from New Zealand. As we noted above,
rape is not included as a paraphilia in DSM-IV, but it is included here because of the
enormous clinical and forensic interest in the behavior. In the initial chapter (Chapter 18)

Hudson and Ward first review the various classificatory schemes that have been advanced over the years, most notably that of Knight and Prentky. The interesting thing about rapists is that, whereas they are much like the rest of prison inmates in terms of low socioeconomic status, high school-dropout rates, and unstable employment, in terms of other demographic variables they are very much like the rest of us. Early phallometric studies clearly differentiated rapists from nonrapists; as more studies accumulate, this difference is disappearing. In terms of etiology, there are at least six different theories. There are several psychodynamic theories but, in common with other such approaches, they have failed to be useful in either treatment or prevention. Behavioral theories initially were based on the presence of deviant sexual arousal. More recently, a six-model theory has appeared which shows considerably more promise. Feminists theorize that rape is a violent, nonsexual act motivated by male dominance. The really useful feature of the feminist approach has been the sharpening of focus upon date rape and sexual harassment in general. A new approach is social-cognitive theory, the study of social knowledge and cognitive processes to understand social behavior. In the present context this would involve such issues as the way in which offenders' expectancies and beliefs bias the way they process sex-related information. Sociobiological theory arguably is the most controversial (e.g., males who engage in forced copulation with many partners maximize their reproductive possibilities). Comprehensive theories, on the other hand, attempt to integrate a number of variables from various domains to account for behavior. In conclusion, the authors note that a complex phenomenon such as rape is very unlikely to be explained by single-factor theories.

Ward, McCormack, Hudson, and Polaschek (Chapter 19) approach the assessment and treatment of rape with equal thoroughness. In assessing rapists for treatment, Ward et al. recommend focusing first upon developmental factors, specifically family, educational, occupational, social, and sexual histories. Next, psychological characteristics such as denial/perception of responsibility, cognitive processes, empathy, social competence, sexual preference/sexual arousal, psychopathology, and religious beliefs should be the focus. Other variables include offense antecedents, offense planning, victim characteristics, and nature of the offense. This information can be obtained from a variety of sources, beginning with a comprehensive clinical interview. They then recommend a huge battery of measures which encompass sexual behavior, cognitions, denial, empathy, intimacy, anger, personality, and psychopathy. Finally, they note that there is a vast literature on the use of phallometric measures with rapists, but they show rather diminished enthusiasm for its use. In approaching treatment of rapists, the authors first review what the literature has told us in recent years. Then, in a very carefully written section, the authors discuss the various issues that must be considered in treating rapists. Like many writers in this area, they recommend group treatment which focuses upon denial and minimization, hostility, sexual boundaries, cognitive distortions, inappropriate attitudes, anger management, stress management, intimacy deficits, and impulse control.

Paraphilia Not Otherwise Specified (NOS)

This category was created in recognition of the fact that there are some sexual disorders that occur so infrequently or have been so inadequately described in the literature that a separate category for them cannot be justified. These paraphilias have had an unusual history in that there seems to have been a continuing uncertainty as to where to put them. The current title—paraphilia NOS—emerged as recently as DSM-III-R (American Psychiatric Association, 1987). In Chapter 20, Milner and Dopke go well beyond the list of paraphilias specified in DSM-IV. They divide paraphilia NOS into four categories: (1) nonhuman objects (animals, enemas, filth, urine, feces, and blood), (2) suffering or humiliation of oneself or one's partner (obscene telephone calls, obscene language with partner, being charged or forced to pay, soiling/damaging of clothing or body, and vomiting), (3) children or other nonconsenting persons (corpses, sleeping partner, and stage-managed disaster), and (4) atypical focus involving human objects (self and others; 23 individual paraphilic behaviors). This is simply a descriptive and utterly fascinating chapter.

In his chapter on assessment and treatment, Schewe (Chapter 21) acknowledges that there is very little or no information available. Therefore, the information in this chapter comes from case studies and analysis of existing data. Specifically, Schewe discusses the treatment of telephone scatologia, necrophilia, zoophilia, coprophilia, urophilia, partialism, and klismaphilia, a list far shorter than Milner and Dopke's. Given the obscure nature of these paraphilias, it is difficult to know how to assess them. Schewe, like other authors in this volume, recommends the Wilson Sexual Fantasy Questionnaire and the Multiphasic Sex Inventory, but he acknowledges that these touch upon only a few paraphilias. He also suggests that penile plethysmography may be used, but special audiotaped narratives may have to be constructed virtually on a case-by-case basis. Areas of assessment information, in Schewe's view, should be matched to specific treatment interventions—that is, (1) deviant and nondeviant sexual fantasies (covert sensitization, aversion therapy, orgasmic reconditioning), (2) sources of sexual anxiety (systematic densensitization), (3) cognitions surrounding deviant and nondeviant behavior (cognitive restructuring, relapse prevention, empathy training), (4) social–sexual skills (social skills training), (5) early sexual development (psychodynamic therapy), and (6) motivation to change (all of the preceding). Schewe notes that the bizarre nature of the minor paraphilias, the infrequency with which clients present for treatment, and the lack of findings published in the literature do not bode well for finding out very much about paraphilia NOS in any general sense.

Medical Models of Sexual Deviance

Grubin and Mason (Chapter 22) note that, in recent years, medical models of sexual deviance have grown unpopular. They often are seen as patronizing or as providing physical excuses for socially deviant or simply bad behavior. This is a rather philosophical chapter which discusses issues such as the nature of health and disease. They recognize that psychiatrists often are placed in a difficult position forensically when they are asked to forecast recidivism based on symptoms that fall well short of psychosis. Additionally, they say, psychiatrists become even more uncomfortable when the presenting problem is one of unusual or socially deviant behavior rather than of psychological symptoms. They tell us that physicians tend to view human sexuality on a continuum rather than categorically; therefore, the boundaries between "socially acceptable" and "deviant" may be somewhat indistinct. From the medical point of view, a person's sexual behavior is just part of that individual's personality. It is not a medical problem until it becomes more globally dysfunctional (i.e., when sexual fantasies impair functioning, a diagnosis is possible). The balance of the chapter is devoted to a description of medical approaches to deviant sexuality (e.g., hormonal intervention, surgical castration, specialized serotonin reuptake inhibitors) as well as to general discussions of pedophilia and sexual aggression toward women.

Medical Interventions in Sexual Deviance

Bradford is one of the foremost proponents of the use of antiandrogenic preparations with sexual deviants. His opening sentence (Chapter 23) essentially states his position on medical interventions: "The importance of medical interventions in the treatment of sexual deviance is that they can be used regardless of the type of paraphilia or how many paraphilias are present." In his view, pharmacology is destiny. In examining sexual deviance from this perspective Bradford considers the mechanism of action of surgical castration, the role and mechanism of action of neurotransmitters in sexual behavior and sexual arousal, and the role of serotonin reuptake inhibitors in the treatment of sexual deviance.

He concludes with lengthy discussions of the role of antiandrogens and hormonal agents in sexual deviance treatment. This is a comprehensive account of treatment from a particular point of view. It will not be an easy read for those unfamiliar with the basics of psychopharmacology.

Female Sexual Deviance

Deviant sexual behavior perpetrated by females has been and remains a controversial topic. Though it certainly is true that the vast majority of sexual offenders are male, it has been recognized in recent years that substantial numbers of females are also involved. The authors initially note, not surprisingly, that there is a dearth of published literature devoted to this topic. Although they consider the full spectrum of female sex offending, the bulk of the chapter is devoted to child molestation, as this is the most frequent offense perpetrated by females. Sexual aggression in females may have a prepubertal or juvenile onset. Adolescent offenders are most frequently reported; their victims are usually relatives or acquaintances. Female offenders report a higher incidence of childhood sexual victimization than do their male counterparts. Adult female offenders account for about 5% of female child molestations and 20% of male child molestations. The authors discuss at length the possible relationship of posttraumatic stress disorder (PTSD) and sexual offending. Unlike past practice, Hunter and Mathews (Chapter 24) state that female offenders are increasingly being referred for treatment. In assessing for treatment, the authors recommend extreme caution in approaching these offenders. They suggest that a comprehensive intake include the following: early development including history of maltreatment, the nature and quality of past and present familial and peer relationships, history of academic functioning, history of employment, exposure to pornography, being a witness of domestic violence, history of nonsexual delinquent behavior and substance abuse, and sexual history, including deviant and nondeviant behaviors. They also recommend a mental status examination with attention to a history of past psychological difficulties. The authors note that there are no psychological instruments currently available that are specific to female sexual offending. They recommend gender-specific treatment, although many of the methodologies are commonly used with men as well. Some areas of treatment focus with adolescents and adults include sex education, self-esteem and improvement of social competence, improvement of family communication, prior victimization, problems associated with PTSD, increasing empathy, relationship issues, and psychotropic medication. It is our view that female sex offenders will be identified in increasing numbers in coming years. It is therefore essential to have reliable and valid assessment procedures and treatment interventions to meet this need.

Future Directions

Hudson and Ward (Chapter 25) close the volume with their recommendations for how the field should proceed, based on what we know today. They believe that the lack of an integrated approach to theory building in sexual deviance is a serious problem. They then offer a more detailed discussion of what they call Level I, II, and III theories, each of which describes different behavioral phenomena (see also Marshall, Chapter 8). We do not know how vulnerability to sexual offending develops, what turns vulnerability into an initial offense, or the importance of situational variables. Classification, they say, is limited by the lack of integration with risk assessment and treatment outcomes. Additionally, they recommend that we (the field) should stop being so parochial and import theories and models from other areas of psychopathology.

The single greatest problem with assessment, they say, is the heavy reliance on self-report measures. Phallometry, while it has not met the initial hope of a truly objective measure that would replace self-report, clearly distinguishes deviants from nondeviants and from subclasses of deviants, and reliably predicts recidivism; it has not been a total failure. Work remains to be done in the area of interpersonal competence, on beliefs and attitudes that predispose men to be sexually assaultive. In recent years there have been great leaps in risk assessment; static predictors are effective, but much remains to be done with dynamic predictors.

Who gets to be treated is a continuing problem. The authors recommend that offenders be classified according to risk and appropriate expectations for treatment interventions, with considerations of harm reduction rather than absence of reoffending. Thus, the most cost-effective (and most risky) approach is treating those with the highest risk of reoffense. They conclude the chapter with discussions of various areas in treatment that remain unresolved. These include treatment structure, expectations of treatment, relapse prevention, and treatment evaluation. That these kinds of central issues can be recognized clearly and feasible solutions can be described suggests to us not how much there is left to do, but rather how far we have come.

CONCLUSIONS

This is a handbook in the truest sense of that word. We believe that we have put together a volume which appeals broadly to two audiences: clinicians and researchers. Careful use of these materials will provide both groups with information that will help them better understand the various forms of sexual deviance and better to address those problems in assessment and treatment. In all cases, the deficiencies in knowledge of psychopathology, theory, assessment, and treatment are there for all to see. Inevitably, this work raises far more questions than it answers. That, we feel, is the proper function of a comprehensive, descriptive, and critical work. It has often been said that people write and edit books in areas where they wished there had been knowledge when *they* needed it. Both of us wish that such a resource had been available to us when we entered this field.

REFERENCES

Abel, G. G., & Rouleau, J. L. (1990). The nature and extent of sexual assault. In W. L. Marshall, D. R. Laws, & H. E. Barbaree (Eds.), *Handbook of sexual assault* (pp. 9–21). New York: Plenum Press.

American Psychiatric Association. (1980). *Diagnostic and statistical manual of mental disorders* (3rd ed.). Washington, DC: Author.

American Psychiatric Association. (1987). *Diagnostic and statistical manual of mental disorders* (3rd ed., rev.). Washington, DC: Author.

American Psychiatric Association. (1994). *Diagnostic and statistical manual of mental disorders* (4th ed.). Washington, DC: Author.

Barbaree, H. E., Marshall, W. L., & Hudson, S. M. (Eds.). (1993). *The juvenile sex offender.* New York: Guilford Press.

Bayer, R. (1981). *Homosexuality and American psychiatry: The politics of diagnosis.* New York: Basic Books.

Furby, L., Weinrott, M., & Blackshaw, L. (1991). Sex offender recidivism: A review. *Psychological Bulletin, 105,* 3–30.

Laws, D. R. (Ed.). (1989). *Relapse prevention with sex offenders.* New York: Guilford Press.

McFall, R. (1991). Manifesto for a science of clinical psychology. *Clinical Psychologist, 44,* 75–88.

O'Donohue, W., Letourneau, E., & Dowling, H. (1997). The measurement of sexual fantasy. *Sexual Abuse: A Journal of Research and Treatment, 9,* 167–178.

O'Donohue, W., & Szymanski, J. (1995). How to win friends and not influence people: Popular but false ideas that impair treatment effectiveness. *Behavior Therapist, 17,* 29–33.

Szasz, T. (1970). *Ideology and insanity.* New York: Doubleday.

Ullmann, L., & Krasner, L. (1975). *A psychological approach to abnormal behavior.* New York: Prentice Hall.

2

EXHIBITIONISM
Psychopathology and Theory

William D. Murphy

The study of exhibitionism has shown somewhat of an uneven course compared with that of other paraphilias. There were numerous early descriptive studies from forensic psychiatric/court clinics which provided basic descriptive information regarding this population. Many of these studies were conducted between 1940 and 1960, and research decreased after that time. In reviewing the literature, it appears that the focus shifted to violent sex offenses, especially rape and pedophilia, and there was less focus on what at times are considered nuisance or hands-off offenses. With these limitations in mind, the purpose of this chapter will be to present our basic knowledge regarding this disorder and our current theoretical understanding of its etiology.

DESCRIPTION AND EPIDEMIOLOGY

Diagnostic Criteria

Most investigators have attributed the introduction of the term "exhibitionism" to the literature on psychopathology to Lasgue in 1877 (cited in Cox, 1980). DSM-IV (American Psychiatric Association, 1994) criteria for the diagnosis of exhibitionism actually differs little from this early description. The DSM-IV criteria for the diagnosis of exhibitionism require that (1) for at least 6 months an individual has recurrent, intense, sexually arousing fantasies or behaviors of exposing their genitals to an unexpecting stranger, and (2) the fantasies, urges, or behaviors cause clinically significant distress or impairment in social, occupational, or other important areas of functioning. There is limited controversy regarding the diagnostic criteria for exhibitionism itself, except that at times patients' denial and minimizations make it difficult to apply the 6-month criteria. However, the major problem with the current official criteria is that they have little usefulness.

The diagnosis of exhibitionism by DSM-IV criteria tells us little about the etiology, risk, or treatment needs of the individual. As this chapter will show, individuals who expose themselves are heterogeneous and current official nomenclature do not capture this heterogeneity. In other areas of psychopathology, for example, the affective disorders, the ability to more narrowly define diagnostic groups improves the ability to understand etiology and more clearly guides treatment choice. Within the paraphilias, there has been significant research attention to the development of classification systems for child molesters and rapists (Knight & Prentky, 1990). Unfortunately, there have been few systematic attempts to more rationally and empirically understand the heterogeneity within the population of individuals who expose themselves.

Description

Exhibitionism, like many paraphilias (Abel & Rouleau, 1990), has an early onset. Mohr, Turner, and Jerry (1964) found a bimodal distribution of onset in the midteens and mid-20s. Similar ages of onset were reported by Smukler and Schiebel (1975). Abel and Rouleau (1990), in a study involving 142 exhibitionists seen in an outpatient clinic who were promised confidentiality, found that 50% of the exhibitionistic subjects reported the onset of their sexual interest before age 18. Although many exhibitionists appear to begin in adolescence, their first charges and convictions are generally in their mid-20s (Berah & Myers, 1983; Gebhard, Gagnon, Pomeroy, & Christenson, 1965; Mohr et al., 1964).

Although no studies have followed a group of exhibitionists over a long period of time, most descriptive studies show a steady decline of onset after age 40. The frequency of offenders being identified after age 40 ranges from 6% (Mohr et al., 1964) to 27% (Radzinowicz, 1957), with most of the early descriptive studies reporting between 14% and 16% (Arieff & Rotman, 1942; East, 1924; MacDonald, 1973; Taylor, 1947). Note, however, that these early descriptive clinical studies involved subjects who were in prison or who were seen in specific forensic clinics that were usually court affiliated. The extent to which this relatively select population is an unbiased representation of exhibitionists is unknown. The natural history of the disorder in individuals not identified by the legal or mental health systems is unknown.

Exhibitionism is primarily a male disorder and victims are primarily female. There are limited case reports of female exhibitionism (Freund, 1990; Grob, 1985; Hooshmand & Brawley, 1969) and basically no reports of exposure to males. MacDonald (1973) did briefly describe one case in his Denver sample and we have seen one case of preferential exposure to males at the University of Tennessee, Memphis program.

It also appears that a significant proportion of victims are children or adolescents, although data vary. In MacDonald's (1973) sample, 28% of the victims were between 5 and 13 years of age, whereas Mohr et al. (1964) in their surveys from Toronto reported that 17 of their 55 subjects exposed to children only and an additional six exposed to adults and children. Gittleson, Eacott, and Mehta (1978), in a sample of British nurses, found that 57% were exposed to before age 16, whereas 66% of Cox and MacMahon's (1978) college student sample reported being exposed to before age 16. A critical question is whether those subjects exposing themselves to prepubertal children are actually pedophilic in interest, or if their arousal is actually linked to the exhibitionism per se. There are few data to answer this question.

Many of the earlier studies also presented data on marital status, education, employment, and intelligence. Blair and Lanyon (1981) reviewed these data thoroughly. Recognizing the limitations of basically forensic populations, the data suggest that one half to two thirds of subjects were married and that their education, vocation, and intelligence did not differ from the general population's.

Prevalence and Incidence

The incidence and prevalence of exhibitionism are unknown. A number of early studies cite data suggesting that exhibitionists account for approximately one third of the sex offenders who come to the attention of authorities (Arieff & Rotman, 1942; East, 1924; Ellis & Brancale, 1956; Mohr et al., 1964; Taylor, 1947). Abel and Rouleau (1990) reported that of 565 offenders seen in their outpatient clinic, 25% had some history of exhibitionism, although most of their subjects had also engaged in other paraphilic behaviors.

However, as with most sex offenders, those officially reported represent only a small percentage of cases. Cox and Maletzky (1980) reported that only 17% of incidences are ever reported. Among reports from adolescent-based programs, there appears to be more variability in the frequency of exhibitionists in their populations. Fahrenbach, Smith, Monastersky, and Deisher (1986) reported that 11% of their over 290 subjects seen in the adolescent clinic had some history of exhibitionism. Similarly, Saunders, Awad, and White (1986) reported that 4 of their 63 subjects seen in Toronto were there for exhibitionism and that six additional subjects had a history of at least two courtship disorders (exhibitionism, obscene phone calls, or toucheurism).

It appears that the frequency of exhibitionism among adult clinical populations is greater than that found among adolescent populations, although adolescent data are limited. Note that except for the Abel and Rouleau (1990) and Abel and Osborne (1992) data, the adolescent and adult data were collected during different time periods. Currently, it may be that with an increased focus on rape and child sexual abuse, there is less attention to exhibitionism in clinical programs for both adults and adolescents. There is some support for this notion. Maletzky (1991) reported that between 1973 and 1978 57% of the offenders seen in his Portland clinic were exhibitionists, whereas 32% were heterosexual pedophiles. From 1978 to 1990, however, this decreased to 15% for exhibitionists and increased to 68% for heterosexual pedophiles. Additionally, there may be a tendency to treat exhibitionism among adolescents lightly and to not refer for treatment.

There are a number of other sources of data that also suggest that exhibitionism occurs frequently. Gittleson et al. (1978), in a survey of British nurses with a mean age of 37, found that 44% reported they had been exposed to outside of work. Cox and MacMahon (1978) found that 32% of 405 female college students sampled from general psychology courses at four universities across the United States had been victims of exhibitionism. Templeman and Stinnett (1991) reported that 2% of a sample of 60 college males admitted to a history of exhibitionism. Abel and Rouleau (1990), in their sample, pointed to the extensiveness of exhibitionistic behavior. The 142 subjects in that sample who exposed themselves reported a total of 72,974 victims, a number that represented approximately 38% of all victims reported by their cohort of 561 paraphiliacs.

In summary, from a descriptive and epidemiological standpoint, exhibitionism appears to be an early-onset disorder of males whose victims are overwhelmingly females, including a significant number of children and adolescents. Although the natural history of this disorder is unknown, identified new cases drop considerably after age 40. True prevalence and incidence are unknown but exhibitionists may represent approximately one third of identified offenders and account for a large number of victims, and limited community and college samples suggest that 40% to 60% of females report being exposed to. There are no current data to suggest a difference between exhibitionists and the general population in terms of IQ, education, or vocational status. Given that the mean age of most offenders identified is in the mid-20s, there is no evidence that their marital rates would differ from a population of this age.

ASSOCIATED FACTORS/CLINICAL CHARACTERISTICS

In this section I attempt to review relevant clinical descriptions and empirical experimental studies of characteristics associated with exhibitionism. At times, the distinction between associated factors and theories of etiology is unclear. Factors that could be considered to have etiological significance are discussed in this section, and more general theories that are broader in scope are in the section on theories of etiology.

Personality and Psychopathology

Many of the earlier studies reported a variety of psychological disorders associated with exhibitionism and described the exhibitionist as shy, inhibited, and nonassertive (see Blair & Lanyon, 1981, for review). Reports of psychotic illness, usually poorly defined within exhibitionists, have ranged from none in Mohr et al.'s (1964) series, up to 16% (Arieff & Rotman, 1942; East, 1924; Henninger, 1941; Taylor, 1947). There is wide variance in reports of exhibitionists as "psychoneurotic," again not defined by any specific criteria, ranging from 7% to 72% (Blair & Lanyon, 1981). There have also been wide variations in descriptions of personality disorders, with Ellis and Brancale (1956) describing 63% of their sample as having inadequate personalities, whereas Smukler and Schiebel (1975) reported basically normal personality patterns.

Most of these early studies are severely flawed by today's research standards. No structured psychiatric interviews were employed and diagnoses appeared to be guided by psychodynamic formulation rather than by modern diagnostic criteria. Also, as noted, many of these samples were very selective and probably not representative of exhibitionists in general.

Studies using more standardized assessment instruments do not necessarily suggest severe psychopathology, and there is even some suggestion that general personality disturbance may be more related to general criminality than to exhibitionism per se. Smukler and Schiebel (1975), in a group of approximately 40 exhibitionists in an outpatient clinic, found subclinical elevations (scores below 60 and 70) on the psychopathic Deviant scale of the MMPI (Dahlstrom, Welsh, & Dahlstrom, 1972) and scores on the Comrey Personality Scale (Comrey, 1970) suggesting a tendency toward social conformity. Using a wide variety of standardized, objective personality and interpersonal scales Langevin, Paitich, Freeman, Mann, and Handy (1978) and Langevin et al. (1979) did not find any specific personality characteristics of exhibitionists. It is also of interest that the Langevin et al. (1979) study found basically no differences between exhibitionists and controls on a number of standardized measures of heterosocial skills and assertiveness.

McCreary (1975) found that degree of disturbance on the MMPI correlated with the number of previous convictions. The subjects with six or more prior arrests evidenced elevations on the Psychopathic Deviant and Schizophrenic subscales, those with no prior arrests evidenced basically normal profiles, and those with one to five arrests were intermediate between these two groups. Forgac and Michaels (1982) and Forgac, Cassel, and Michaels (1984), however, showed that the MMPI elevations indicating increases in psychopathology were correlated not with exhibitionistic reoffenses but with nonexhibitionistic criminal behavior. The McCreary (1975) study included both exhibitionistic and nonexhibitionistic offenses, and when Forgac and colleagues (Forgac & Michaels, 1982; Forgac et al., 1984) separated these, it was clear that the elevations were most related to repeat, nonexhibitionistic criminal behavior.

Two studies of adolescent offenders (Saunders & Awad, 1991; Saunders et al., 1986) presented a mixed picture of adjustment. Both studies are somewhat difficult to interpret because they described a group of courtship disorders that included exhibitionists, but was not a pure exhibitionistic group. Saunders et al. (1986) compared the courtship disorder with rapists and pedophile subjects. Data for the study included standardized IQ scores, results from the projective test, and results from clinical interviews with the adolescents and the adolescents' families. The results suggested that the courtship-disordered subjects came from less disorganized families, were better adjusted, and were less severely disturbed than were members of the other two groups. However, over 60% were described as socially isolated and 60% were described as having at least a moderate level of maladjustment. Saunders and Awad (1991) reported on 19 exhibitionists and obscene phone callers using similar data collection procedures. They reported high levels of psychopathology in this group. However, only eight of the subjects had committed only hands-off offenses, and 58% had histories of antisocial behavior in general.

In general, studies reveal that the rate of psychopathology in exhibitionists is similar to rates in other offender groups (Murphy, Haynes, & Worley, 1991; Murphy & Peters, 1992). Although there are numerous clinical descriptions of a variety of psychological difficulties in exhibitionists, these in general are not replicated when standardized tests are used. As with other offender groups, a certain percentage appear to have psychological difficulties. However, there does not appear to be any one specific personality pattern or psychological difficulty, and there is no clear indication of a link between personality and/or psychopathology in the etiology of the development of exhibitionism.

General Criminology

The above suggests that some of the disturbances seen in exhibitionists are related to general criminality rather than to exhibitionism per se. Trying to determine the actual incidence of nonsexual criminal behavior in this population is difficult because of the selective samples. Blair and Lanyon (1981), reviewing a number of studies which reported data regarding arrest and conviction for nonexhibitionistic offenses, found rates ranging from 17% to 30%. Berah and Myers (1983), however, found higher rates in a group of 151 convicted exhibitionists. In this sample, only 31% of their sample had never been convicted of offenses other than indecent exposure at the time of the study. Twenty-five percent had one or more convictions for offenses other than indecent exposure before their first arrest for exhibition-ism, 17% had convictions only after their first conviction for exhibitionism, and 26% had other convictions both before and after their first offense of exhibitionism. As might be expected, they also found that the more frequent the convictions for exhibitionism, the greater the probability of having convictions for other offenses. This suggests some correlation between chronicity of exhibitionists and general antisocial behavior.

Studies of adolescent populations show somewhat mixed patterns and as noted previously, they are difficult to interpret because of a tendency to combine various categories of hands-off offenses. Saunders et al. (1986) found that their courtship disorder group, which included exhibitionists, had the lowest level of prior delinquent behaviors compared with other offender groups. Fahrenbach et al. (1986), in their study of 293 adolescent offenders, found that subjects referred for hands-off offenses were more likely to have prior sexual and nonsexual offenses (40%) than were subjects referred for indecent liberties or for rape (approximately 20%). However, it appears that the prior sex offenses for the hands-off group included hands-on offenses; therefore, this was not a group who had only engaged in exhibitionistic behavior.

Given the limitations in terms of sample selection, it is difficult to draw any firm conclusions of actual incidence of general criminality in an exhibitionistic population. However, it is clear that not all exhibitionists are "solid citizens" who tend to be rule abiding and there appear to be at the least a significant minority who are generally criminal. The relationship of this general criminality to treatment outcome is not clear, but is an important variable for investigation.

Relationship to Other Paraphilias

Although early psychoanalytic theorists (Karpman, 1948) posited relationships between exhibitionism and voyeurism, there has been a tendency to perceive exhibitionists as rather harmless. Mohr et al. (1964) stated that other deviations are rare in exhibitionism. However, there are now a number of data sources that raise some questions about this assumption. Rooth (1973), in an early study of a small number of exhibitionists (n = 30), suggested that those who expose preferentially to children are at risk for pedophilia, hebephilia, and incest. Gebhard et al. (1965) reported in their study of sex offenders in custody that 1 in 10 exhibitionists had attempted or seriously contemplated rape, whereas approximately 20% had previous convictions for sexual offenses that involved some use of force. Longo and McFadin (1981), in a study of 43 incarcerated rapists and 41 incarcerated child molesters, found that 31% had a history of exhibitionism and 62% had histories of voyeurism or exhibitionism as juveniles. In a second study of 128 incarcerated child molesters and 107 incarcerated rapists, Longo and Groth (1983) found that 28% of the child molesters and 15% of the rapists had histories of exposure as juveniles.

Freund and colleagues (Freund, 1990; Freund, Scher, & Hucker, 1983) have also presented extensive data on the relationship of exhibitionism with other paraphilias. Freund (1990) reported data on 241 exhibitionists. Thirty-two percent engaged in voyeuristic activities, 30% in toucheurism or frottage, and 15% had raped. Abel and Osborn (1992) also reported extensive data on the co-occurrence of paraphilias in a large sample of outpatient offenders. Of the 118 whose primary diagnoses were exhibitionism, data on their secondary diagnosis were presented. Twenty-seven percent had a secondary diagnosis of voyeurism, 39% had molested children, 17% had engaged in frottage, and 14% had a secondary diagnosis of rape. Abel and Rouleau (1990) indicated that 93% of the exhibitionistic subjects had more than one paraphilic diagnosis, whereas approximately 73% had over three paraphilic diagnoses. In general, the more recent data by Freund suggests a significant frequency of crossover between paraphilic diagnoses. The Abel and Rouleau data included a significant minority who had engaged in pedophilic behavior and aggressive sexual behavior toward adults. Abel and Rouleau, however, did not present data that allow one to determine whether the exhibitionists who molested children had also exposed preferentially to children. We need more data to determine whether those exposing preferentially to children comprise the subgroup that molests and is at risk for molesting children.

Neurological Correlates

There have been a number of attempts to link sexually deviant behavior to brain dysfunction (see Langevin, 1990, for review). Specific attention has been paid to the temporal lobe area given the association between sexual behavior and the temporal lobe that was revealed in the early animal studies of Kluver and Bucy (1939). These early studies indicated that the removal of the temporal lobes of primates led to fairly indiscriminate sexual behavior and what was described as hypersexuality. Early studies of humans with temporal lobe abnormalities indicated, however, that over one half of individuals with temporal lobe disorders actually displayed hyposexuality, although there appears in some cases to be a relationship between temporal lobe dysfunctions and paraphilias (Blumer, 1970; Blumer & Walker,

1967). The most frequent paraphilias are fetishes; however, there are case reports of temporal lobe disorders associated with exhibitionism (Hooshmand & Brawley, 1969; Kolarsky, Freund, Machek, & Polak, 1967). For exhibitionists, the most extensive data with objective measures come from Flor-Henry and colleagues (Flor-Henry, 1987; Flor-Henry & Lang, 1988). Flor-Henry (1987) found significant differences in paraphilias in general and exhibitionism specifically on neuropsychological tests measuring left frontal temporal dysfunction. Similarly, in a second study comparing 50 community controls with 50 exhibitionists on computer-analyzed EEG frequencies during rest, verbal tests, and nonverbal tests, results indicated left hemispheric dysfunction (Flor-Henry & Lang, 1988). Hucker et al. (1986) also described neuropsychological deficits in similar areas in pedophiles.

Two studies, although not with exhibitionists, showed no neuropsychological deficits in a small group ($n = 11$) of mixed paraphiliacs seen in an outpatient clinic (O'Carroll, 1989) and a group of outpatient adolescent sex offenders (Tarter, Hegedus, Alterman, & Katz-Garris, 1983). Even though these were not exhibitionists per se, the fact that many exhibitionists have multiple paraphilias makes these data relevant. Again, the two studies cited above raise one of the major issues of this chapter; subject selection. The subjects studied by Kolarsky and colleagues (1967) were recruited from a neurology clinic, and this population may be quite different than that seen in general mental health settings. The Flor-Henry (1987) subjects were recidivists, incarcerated offenders averaging five to six convictions (O'Carroll, 1989). In contrast, those reports using outpatients (O'Carroll, 1989; Tarter et al., 1983) showed limited neurological impairment. As with any behavioral disorder, there is probably a subset of individuals with some sign of neurological/cognitive impairment. It also appears that most individuals with temporal lobe epilepsy are not exhibitionists; the most frequent finding is hyposexuality. Therefore, it appears premature to view temporal lobe disorders as being causative of exhibitionism in general. However, some of the findings are intriguing and suggest that further investigations with more sophisticated measures, such as magnetic resonance imaging or positron emission tomography scans, may be valuable in investigating temporal lobe disorders and in determining whether temporal lobe disorders may be related to some subset of exhibitionism.

Early Childhood and Family Functioning

For sex offenders in general, there has been a significant clinical focus on family dysfunction and early histories of abuse as being causative of sexual offending. However, there are generally limited empirical data with objective measures and adequate control groups to support specific family dysfunction in sex offenders or any difference between sex offenders and most other clinical groups (Murphy, Haynes, & Page, 1992; Murphy & Smith, 1996). Even history of sexual abuse among child molesters, although higher than the 16% expected in nonclinical populations (Finkelhor, Hotaling, Lewis, & Smith, 1990) is probably only 30% to 35% (Hanson & Slater, 1988). When focusing specifically on exhibitionists, the data are even more meager. The early descriptive studies as summarized by Blair and Lanyon (1981) indicated a number of reports of high frequency of fathers absence and poor relationships with fathers during childhood. However, most of these data are based on nonstructured clinical interviews with rather unclear definitions of what constitutes a poor relationship.

More recent data with adolescent offenders also do not provide a very clear picture. In adolescent populations, Saunders and colleagues (1986) presented mixed results, reporting that courtship disorders are associated with the lowest rates of family discord, whereas Saunders and Awad (1991) reported high levels of family discord in their group of exhibitionists and obscene phone callers. However, as noted previously, the Saunders and

Awad (1991) sample appeared to include many subjects with hands-on offenses and a high number with general antisocial behavior. In terms of histories of personal abuse, Saunders and Awad (1991) reported that 13% had histories of being physically abused and 17% had histories of sexual victimization. Fahrenbach et al. (1986) found that hands-off offenders had low rates of abuse (7.5% having histories of sexual and 9.4% with histories of physical victimization), whereas their group of child molesters and rapists had rates of sexual and physical victimization ranging from 20% to 30%.

As with paraphilic groups in general, there are numerous clinical descriptive studies of family discord, but little empirical data with objective measures and adequate clinical control groups. Although the data are limited, it also does not appear that rates of physical and sexual victimization are any higher in the exhibitionistic group than might be expected in any psychiatric population, and in fact the Fahrenbach et al. (1986) data reported relatively low rates, even lower than might be expected in the general population.

FORENSIC ISSUES

There appear to be three primary questions that clinicians may be asked by the judicial system. These include: (1) "Did he do it?" or "Does he fit the profile of an exhibitionist?"; (2) "Is he dangerous?" (i.e., is he likely to progress to more serious offenses?); and (3) "Is he treatable," or "What is the likelihood of reoffense?" Unfortunately, limited empirical data exist to answer any of these questions.

Smith (1980) reviewed legal issues related to exhibitionists. Relevant to the discussion are the basic criminal law principles that for exposure to be a crime, the individual must have engaged in the behavior and the act must be intentional. As many clinicians are aware, exhibitionists will at times totally deny their behavior, but they also may very often deny the sexual intent. A common presentation by exhibitionists is that they were urinating and were "accidentally seen." Defense attorneys, prosecuting attorneys, and judges may ask the mental health professional to provide evidence as to whether the person exposed themselves intentionally, or of their state of mind at the time, or more frequently, he or she may be asked if the individual fits the profile of an exhibitionist. Mental health professionals can review victim statements and histories of past behavior, and they also can attempt to explore inconsistencies in the patient's descriptions of events. However, it is not clear that a mental health professional examining such information is in any better a position to determine intent than is a jury.

It is probably more common for a mental health professional to present psychological data that an individual does or does not have characteristics similar to exhibitionists. Murphy and Peters (1992) and Peters and Murphy (1992) reviewed the data related to profiling issues for offenders against children. The conclusion from those reviews, courts have generally supported, is that there is no one profile for offenders. Even physiological measures of sexual arousal, where significant data exist for child molesters, have large error rates that limit their use in the guilt-determining phase of the criminal proceedings.

The preceding section on personality disorders in exhibitionists supports similar cautions as raised by Murphy and Peters (1992) for child molesters. As data indicate, there is no one personality profile for exhibitionists, there is no clear evidence that all exhibitionists are shy and nonassertive, and there is no clear evidence that exhibitionists have any one type of family background. Although I will review arousal measures in the context of behavioral theories in the next section, I can state that there is no clear evidence of a specific deviant arousal pattern in exhibitionists. Basically, there are no data that support statements by mental health professionals that someone does or does not fit a profile of an exhibitionist.

As most mental health professionals are well aware, prediction of dangerousness in general is fraught with difficulties (Monahan, 1993). For exhibitionists, the question of dangerousness generally is a question of whether the offender is likely to progress to more serious sexual offenses, for example, rape or child molestation. Among incarcerated populations of rapists and child molesters, that a significant number have prior histories of exhibitionism (Longo & Groth, 1983). In addition, Abel and Osborn's (1992) sample of outpatient offenders also suggests that a significant number of exhibitionists have additional serious hands-on offenses. Most exhibitionists, however, are never apprehended, and of those reported, few probably end up in specialized sex offender programs. The actual base rate of hands-on offenses among exhibitionists is unknown. However, the base rate is probably much lower than that among populations represented in the literature, which tends to include subjects with more chronic histories.

Another major problem is that there are no data that would allow one to predict which exhibitionists are likely to engage in more serious offenses. Rooth (1973) presented limited data suggesting blurred boundaries between exhibitionism, hebephilia, and pedophilia for those who expose preferentially to children. However, this study was based on only 30 subjects. In this study, 6 of 30 subjects exposed themselves regularly to prepubertal children and three of those (or 50%) had some history of pedophilia. In addition, of the eight subjects in the series who had some history of pedophilia or hebephilia, they exposed at least at times to prepubertal children or teenagers. These data are suggestive, but they require further replication.

From a forensic standpoint, the data are probably too limited to make strong statements within the judicial system. However, clinicians should probably take a conservative approach to exhibitionists who expose preferentially to children. They should at least entertain the possibility that these individuals are at risk for actual molestation of children and should probably make the same types of restrictions in terms of access to children on these individuals as they would for any pedophilic subject.

The final forensic question generally is related to amenability to treatment, which in reality is the likelihood of reoffending. Unfortunately, data are limited and specifically there are limited data regarding who is and who is not at risk to reoffend. Early recidivism data by Frisbee and Dondis (1965), in a forensic psychiatric population, suggested very high rates of recidivism (40%) among exhibitionists. Marshall and Barbaree (1990) reviewed more recent data from outpatient programs with a cognitive-behavioral approach. Recidivism data for these programs ranged from 6% (Maletzky, 1987) to 48% (Marshall & Barbaree, 1988) for treated offenders. Data from Marshall's clinic in Kingston indicated that treated offenders had approximately 47% recidivism, whereas untreated offenders showed an approximately 66% rate with a mean follow-up of 57 weeks. In another, later report from his Portland clinic, Maletzky (1991) reported a 93% success rate in a sample of 770 exhibitionists followed between 1 and 17 years with 65% followed over 3 years.

Marshall, Eccles, and Barbaree (1991), in a group of 44 exhibitionists, found recidivism rates of 39% for treated offenders and a rate of approximately 57% for untreated offenders followed for approximately 143 months. Treatment for these subjects involved procedures for reducing deviant arousal and some behavioral treatments to improve social skills and to reduce deviant arousal. It is not clear whether some of the subjects included in the 1991 study were also those reported by Marshall and Barbaree (1988). Because of these high rates of offenses, Marshall et al. (1991) described treatment for an additional 17 patients who received more focus on cognitive and relationship variables than on sexual arousal. The subjects received a version of covert sensitization used as a self-management skill and treatment focused on cognitive factors such as the need to be perfect. In addition, treatment focused on assisting the offender to achieve more intimacy in relationships. This revised treatment program led to a recidivism rate of 24% for subjects followed for 47 months. Although follow-up was shorter, Marshall et al. (1991) pointed out that in their previous series over 91% of the subjects had relapsed by the 47-month mark.

In general, the question of risk of reoffending is difficult to answer. The most promising results appear to come from Maletzky's clinic in Oregon and, as Marshall and Barbaree (1990) pointed out, Maletzky has a long history of research in the area of the treatment of exhibitionists which may somehow impact the results. The revised treatment program described by Marshall et al. (1991) seems to hold promise, although it only includes a small number of subjects and needs replication. We may cautiously assume, based on the limited data, that a cognitive-behavioral treatment incorporating self-management skills can reduce recidivism over a nontreated group. However, we must recognize that even in this case, 23% to 30% of subjects relapsed.

At this time, there are few data among exhibitionistic groups regarding prediction of who will and who will not reoffend. Hanson and Bussière (1996) reviewed a number of studies of prediction of reoffenses among child molesters. In most of these studies, the most significant predictors were state variables, such as past sexual and nonsexual criminal behavior, which cannot be changed. Rice, Quinsey, and Harris (1991) and Malcolm, Andrews, and Quinsey (1993) have also found significant relationships between arousal measures and recidivistic behavior, but no such data exist for exhibitionists. There are also no data available for any of the paraphilic groups to determine whether these more static historical variables maintain predictive power for treated offenders.

Basically, there are limited empirical data for clinicians to use to predict who will be responsive in treatment. Until better data are available, the clinician will be better served by attempting to structure environmental controls to prevent relapse than by attempting to predict relapse. This is more consistent with current relapse prevention models (Pithers, 1990) of offender treatment.

THEORETICAL MODELS

This section will focus on general theoretical models which have been proposed to explain the development of paraphilic behavior in general and of exhibitionism specifically. This section will include a brief description of psychoanalytic theory because of its historical significance. Although analytic models are less frequently mentioned in the sex offender literature, at the current time certain clinical descriptions from this literature, such as feelings of inadequacy and issues of masculinity, still are part of clinical lore regarding exhibitionists. The second major model I address is the cognitive-behavioral model, which tends to be one of the major organizing forces of treatment programs for exhibitionists at this time. Finally, I review Freund's (1990) courtship disorder model as one of the few sex offender-specific models for exhibitionists.

Psychoanalytic Models

Psychoanalytic thought and theory dominated early views of exhibitionism (Allen, 1980; Gillespie, 1955; Karpman, 1948). Core to many of the psychoanalytic theories is the oedipal complex and castration anxiety (Allen, 1980; Enelow, 1969). As with many psychoanalytic conceptualizations, the child's relationship with the mother is given dominant significance. Allen (1980), summarizing the analytic literature, describes the predisposition to exhibitionism as coming from the child interacting with a flirtatious, controlling, and seductive mother. Analytic literature also posits fathers of exhibitionists as emotionally absent and unable to provide adequate nurturance and limit setting (Allen, 1980). In its simplest form, exhibitionism is seen as a defense against castration anxiety, with the reaction of the female proving to the exhibitionist that his penis does exist.

Also inherent in analytic theories is the role of narcissism as a defense against feelings of inadequacy and fragile masculine identity. Within this psychoanalytic framework, exhibitionistic acts are likely to be triggered when the individual suffers "a narcissistic or emotional hurt" which may involve rejection by a significant other or a failure or perceived failure in a masculine role (Allen, 1980). Within this framework, the exhibitionistic act not only proves that one "has a penis" but also it is a way of asserting one's masculine identity and establishing a sense of power and dominance, and on many occasions it is an expression of anger toward females (Allen, 1980; Fenichel, 1945).

Although conceptions such as castration anxiety are not frequently seen in the literature on sex offenders, a number of the concepts derived from the analytic theorists are not uncommon in the current literature on paraphilias. For example, that exhibitionism is triggered by certain interpersonal stressors is not inconsistent with the general relapse prevention treatment model (Pithers, 1990). The notion that the act of exhibitionism is a means of expressing power, dominance, and hostility toward women is also fairly consistent with feminist views of sexual offenders.

However, the empirical literature supporting these notions is relatively limited. Analytic theorists suggest that there should be histories of dysfunctions in families and the previous review of this issue and the summary of this literature by Blair and Lanyon (1981) did not provide any evidence that families, of exhibitionists are any more dysfunctional than are the families seen in any clinical or forensic population. And, as we have noted, most of these studies are severely flawed by the lack of adequate control groups and nonstandardized data collection procedures. Paitich and Langevin (1976) presented one of the only controlled studies of parent–child relationships in offenders with a standardized measure (the Clarke Parent–Child Interaction Questionnaire). Results indicate that exhibitionists did not differ significantly from controls in terms of their relationships with mothers, but they saw their fathers as more strict. However, their scores on family relationships tended to fall between those of controls and other offender groups, suggesting that if there were disturbances in families of origin or parent–child interactions, they were much less serious than for other paraphilic groups.

Langevin et al. (1979) also presented an interesting attempt to investigate the role of narcissism using penile plethysmography. They hypothesized that exhibitionists would show increased responsiveness to audiotaped stimuli describing the female as admiring the subject's penis. Basically, there were no differences between exhibitionists and normal controls. Langevin and colleagues (Langevin et al., 1978, 1979) also failed to find deficits in male role identity using structured self-report inventories in a group of exhibitionists.

The analytic literature provides rich clinical description that does not lend itself to easy empirical testing. The limited studies available do not necessarily support some of the conceptualizations. However, some of the hypotheses regarding the exhibitionistic act as having a component related to power, dominance, and expression of hostility have received little testing and appear to be worthy of further follow-up. The fact that exhibitionistic behavior shares some components with other sexual offenses directed against adult females is consistent with the courtship disorder model, which I review later.

Behavioral/Cognitive-Behavioral Models

Early behavioral theories of paraphilias were primarily focused on the development of deviant sexual arousal patterns through either operant or classical conditioning. Early laboratory studies (Rachman, 1966; Rachman & Hodgson, 1968) provided initial support for the role of conditioning. These studies basically showed that pairing pictures of boots to nude pictures of adult females led to an increase in penile responding to what could be a fetishistic stimuli. Others have found it more difficult to produce such conditioning (Herman, Barlow, & Agras, 1974; Marshall, 1974). McGuire, Carlisle, and Young (1965) stressed the importance of masturbation in developing paraphilic arousal patterns. They hypothesized that it is the repeated pairing of orgasm with the paraphilic stimuli through masturbation that leads to the conditioned arousal. Evans (1968) found that among a group of 52 mixed offenders (16 were exhibitionists), 79% reported the use of deviant fantasies during masturbation. Evans (1970) found that subjects who were unsuccessfully treated with electrical aversion comprised the group which had the highest rate of using deviant masturbatory fantasies. This provides some indirect support to conditioning theories in that those subjects who masturbated more frequently to exhibitionistic fantasies would have the strongest conditioned response and therefore would be the most difficult to decondition.

Laws and Marshall (1990) presented one of the more sophisticated conditioning theories on the etiology and maintenance of deviant sexual preference. They not only focused on operant and classical conditioning of deviant arousal patterns, but also integrated the role of higher-order conditioning, extinction processes, social learning processes, and maintenance processes. Although the presentation is quite sophisticated, consistent with the current literature on learning processes in general and with clear testable hypotheses, many of these have not been empirically validated.

Inherent in behavioral theories, even the more sophisticated processes described by Laws and Marshall (1990), is the role of the development of deviant arousal in the etiology of the offense. Although there is in general support for the role of deviant arousal in a significant subgroup of pedophiles (Murphy & Barbaree, 1994), there are very limited data related to deviant sexual arousal patterns in exhibitionists. Langevin et al. (1979), in a study already described, found no differences between exhibitionists and controls on laboratory arousal measures, and both groups responded more to descriptions of intercourse than to exhibitionistic stimuli. Fedora, Reddon, and Yeudall (1986) did find that exhibitionists responded more to pictures of clothed females in a public area than did normal controls or nonexhibitionist sex offender controls. However, the exhibitionists' responses to explicit adult female slides were five times greater than were their responses to slides of females in public places. Very similarly, Marshall, Payne, Barbaree, and Eccles (1991) found that exhibitionists did show more arousal to scenes of exhibitionism and lower arousal to consenting intercourse than did non-sex-offenders. However, for the exhibitionists, arousal to consenting intercourse was over two times that of arousal to exhibitionistic scenes. These studies suggest that exhibitionists may respond more to exhibitionistic stimuli than do controls. However, in terms of a preference hypothesis, their arousal is more to intercourse, and their responsiveness to exhibitionistic stimuli might suggest a deficit in inhibition to those stimuli, but not necessarily a preference for them.

Recognizing this, Marshall, Payne, et al. (1991) looked at the ability to diagnose exhibitionism using a deviance quotient, which is basically the ratio of arousal to deviant and nondeviant stimuli. They found that among the exhibitionists only 13.6% had a quotient above 0.8, which has usually been used as a cutoff in studies of child molesters and rapists (Murphy & Barbaree, 1994). They also present data using combined criteria that they have found in other studies to be more sensitive, including deviant arousal being 70% of nondeviant arousal, or an absolute criterion of 30% of a full erection in response to deviant stimuli. With these criteria, 34% of the exhibitionists could be classified as having a deviant preference. It appears that only a small proportion of exhibitionists actually display deviant sexual arousal patterns, therefore; a strict conditioning model may at best only account for a third or less of the exhibitionists.

Marshall, Eccles, et al. (1991) proposed a more cognitive-behavioral model which focuses less on deviant sexual arousal but more on (1) what they label as "subtle assertive deficits" leading to others taking advantage of the exhibitionist, (2) a need to be perfect, and (3) an inability to achieve a sense of intimacy in adult relationships. As previously reviewed, the introduction of these components to a treatment program appeared to improve treatment outcome significantly (Marshall, Eccles, et al., 1991). However, there are no data available that actually suggest that these specific deficits occur in exhibitionists. In fact, previously reviewed studies by Langevin et al. (1979) did not suggest severe deficits among exhibitionists in specific assertiveness skills.

In general, cognitive-behavioral theories appear to have had significant heuristic value in generating treatment approaches. However, the evidence suggesting that conditioned deviant sexual arousal accounts for a large percentage of the variance is rather weak and to date there has been no testing of more sophisticated models such as that proposed by Laws and Marshall (1990).

Courtship Disorders

A final theoretical model views exhibitionism as an expression of a more general disorder, namely, courtship disorder (Freund, 1990; Freund & Blanchard, 1986; Freund, Scher, & Hucker, 1983; Freund, Scher, & Hucker, 1984). Freund (1990) proposed that normal human sexual interactions can roughly be divided into four phases: (1) location of a partner, (2) pretactile interactions, (3) tactile interactions, and (4) genital union. The courtship disorders consist of voyeurism, exhibitionism, toucheurism/frottage, and the preferential rape pattern. Each is seen as a distorted or intensified version of one of these normal phases, wherein other phases are admitted or minimized. Exhibitionism is seen as a disturbance of normal pretactile interactions. The value of this conceptualization is that it provides a theoretical rationale for the co-occurrence of a group of paraphilic behaviors. This organizational framework could also have potential heuristic value in terms of suggesting etiological hypotheses. Data to date regarding this theoretical model have been basically limited to co-occurrence of the various expression of courtship disorders. As reviewed earlier, Freund (1990) reported what he considered substantial histories of co-occurrence between exhibitionism, voyeurism, toucheurism, and frottage. This has also been reported by Abel and colleagues (Abel & Osborn, 1992) and has been observed by Lang, Langevin, Checkley, and Pugh (1987).

Because of the offender's tendency to deny various erotic preferences, Freund (1990) postulated that the actual co-occurrence may be higher than suggested by patient's self-report. This may be especially true among the co-occurrence with rape because of the possible consequences to subjects for admitting to rape. To provide data related to this, Freund et al. (1983) presented two studies using phallometric measures. In study 1, 17 patients with mixed courtship disorders, but who denied voyeuristic activity, and 20 controls underwent phallometric measures to verbal descriptions of (1) neutral stimuli, (2) voyeuristic stimuli, (3) normal tactile interactions, and (4) intercourse. Results indicated that the courtship-disorder patients who denied voyeuristic arousal showed higher levels of arousal to the voyeuristic stimuli than did the controls, whereas controls showed higher levels of arousal to tactile interactions, with no differences seen for neutral stimuli or for intercourse stimuli. In a second, similar study, a group of 15 exhibitionists who denied toucheurism/frottage activities were compared with controls on neutral, exhibitionistic, toucheuristic, normal tactile, and intercourse stimuli. Exhibitionists who denied toucheurism or frottage showed significantly more responsiveness to both exhibitionistic and toucheuristic stimuli as compared with controls. These two studies suggest that even when denying the specific behavior, a subject with one courtship disorder tends to respond more to another courtship disorder than do controls. Freund et al. (1984) provided further data that the results of the previous study, wherein ipsative *z* scores were used, were not artifacts of a lack of arousal to normal sexual interactions. In this study, exhibitionistic subjects were compared with controls and the stimuli involved audio descriptions of what they termed the "normal phases of sexual interactions." With these stimuli, there were no differences between exhibitionists and normals.

There are a number of potential criticisms of this model. Marshall, Payne, et al. (1991) pointed out that the exhibitionists in the Freund et al. (1984) study, as has been found in other erectile studies, evidenced more arousal to normal heterosexual intercourse than they did to what was described as "normal pretactile interactions." However, it is not clear if the exhibitionistic stimuli in the Freund et al. (1983) study, wherein exhibitionists were more responsive than were normals, differed in some way from what Freund et al. (1984) described as the "normal pretactile stimuli." Another potential problem is uncertainty as to whether certain groups of paraphilias tend to co-occur or whether there is a tendency for an individual with any one paraphilia to be generally sexually anomalous. Freund (1990) found relatively low rates of overlap between two other disorders included for comparison purposes: transvestism and sadism. Lang et al. (1987), however, found that 41% of their exhibitionistic subjects were transvestites. As reviewed previously, Abel and Osborn (1992) found high rates of victimizing children among their exhibitionistic sample. However, they did not exclude subjects who exposed preferentially to children or adolescents, which may have impacted their figures.

The courtship disorder model, like theories of deviant sexual arousal, is a sex offender-specific model. At this time, the data are limited on the courtship disorder model, with at least some suggestions that it may have some useful organizational value, although further empirical studies are needed. Also, we need studies focusing on possible precursors that might disrupt normal courtship patterns in humans.

FUTURE DIRECTIONS

Langevin et al. (1979), in the discussion section of their extensive study, stated that "the results provide more information on what the exhibitionist is not than what he is" (p. 327). This statement appears still to hold true today. Research to date suggests that exhibitionism is probably a heterogeneous disorder with multiple causes. A primary direction for future research is to unravel some of this heterogeneity through the development of more refined subclassification systems or the use of more multidimensional scaling techniques. Primary variables on which exhibitionists appear to vary are degree of concomitant psychopathology, age of onset, degree of general criminality, and degree of co-occurrence with other paraphilias. Future studies need to take these variables into account during both theory development and in attempting to look at specific etiological factors.

A second important area for future research is the potential overlap between those exhibitionists who expose preferentially to children or adolescents and pedophilia and incest. Whether this subgroup of exhibitionists should be more clearly defined as pedophiles or whether there are two coexisting disorders in the same person needs further exploration. Also, studies that have indicated rather high rates of exhibitionistic behaviors in incarcerated rapists suggest a need to further subidentify this population.

Finally, there is a strong need for more outcome studies and continued refinement of treatment techniques. Although Maletzky's (1991) results are very promising, the results were rather unique and not achieved by other treatment programs. The refinements described by Marshall, Eccles, and Barbaree (1991) of their treatment program are promising but need further follow-up. We also need many more studies that examine both factors that may predict recidivism, especially factors amenable to treatment, and procedures that we can implement to prevent relapse, not just to predict it.

REFERENCES

Abel, G. G., & Osborn, C. (1992). The paraphilias: The extent and nature of sexually deviant and criminal behavior. *Psychiatric Clinics of North America, 15,* 675–687.

Abel, G. G., & Rouleau, J. L. (1990). The nature and extent of sexual assault. In W. L. Marshall, D. R. Laws, & H. E. Barbaree (Eds.), *Handbook of sexual assault: Issues, theories, and treatment of the offender* (pp. 9–21). New York: Plenum Press.

Allen, D. W. (1980). A psychoanalytic view. In D. J. Cox & R. J. Daitzman (Eds.), *Exhibitionism: Description, assessment and treatment* (pp. 59–82). New York: Garland.

American Psychiatric Association. (1994). *Diagnostic and statistical manual of mental disorders* (4th ed.). Washington, DC: Author.

Arieff, A. J., & Rotman, D. B. (1942). One hundred cases of indecent exposure. *Journal of Nervous and Mental Disease, 96,* 523–528.

Berah, E. F., & Myers, R. G. (1983). The offense records of a sample of convicted exhibitionists. *Bulletin of the American Academy of Psychiatry and Law, 11,* 365–369.

Blair, C. D., & Lanyon, R. I. (1981). Exhibitionism: Etiology and treatment. *Psychological Bulletin, 89,* 439–463.

Blumer, D. (1970). Changes of sexual behavior related to temporal lobe disorders in man. *Journal of Sex Research, 6,* 173–180.

Blumer, D., & Walker, A. E. (1967). Sexual behavior in temporal lobe epilepsy. *Archives of Neurology, 16,* 37–43.

Comrey, A. L. (1970). *Comrey Personality Scales: Manual.* San Diego, CA: Educational and Industrial Testing Service.

Cox, D. J. (1980). Exhibitionism: An overview. In D. J. Cox & R. J. Daitzman (Eds.), *Exhibitionism: Description, assessment and treatment* (pp. 3–10). New York: Garland.

Cox, D. J., & Maletzky, B. M. (1980). Victims of exhibitionism. In D. J. Cox & R. J. Daitzman (Eds.), *Exhibitionism: Description, assessment and treatment* (pp. 289–293). New York: Garland.

Cox, D. J., & MacMahon, B. (1978). Incidence of male exhibitionism in the United States as reported by victimized female college students. *National Journal of Law and Psychiatry, 1,* 453–457.

Dahlstrom, W. G., Welsh, G. S., & Dahlstrom, L. E. (1972). *An MMPI handbook: Vol. 1. Clinical interpretation.* Minneapolis: University of Minnesota Press.

East, W. N. (1924). Observations on exhibitionism. *Lancet, 2,* 370–375.

Ellis, A., & Brancale, R. (1956). *The psychology of sex offenders.* Springfield, IL: Charles C Thomas.

Enelow, M. L. (1969). Public nuisance offenses: Exhibitionism, voyeurism, and transvestism. *Sexual Behavior and the Law, 37,* 478–486.

Evans, D. R. (1968). Masturbating fantasies and sexual deviation. *Behaviour Research and Therapy, 6,* 17–19.

Evans, D. R. (1970). Subjective variables and treatment effects in aversion therapy. *Behaviour Research and Therapy, 8,* 147–152.

Fahrenbach, P. A., Smith, W., Monastersky, C., & Deisher, R. W. (1986). Adolescent sexual offenders: Offender and offense characteristics. *American Journal of Orthopsychiatry, 56,* 225–233.

Fedora, O., Reddon, J. R., & Yeudall, L. T. (1986). Stimuli eliciting sexual arousal in genital exhibitionists: A possible clinical application. *Archives of Sexual Behavior, 15,* 417–427.

Fenichel, O. (1945). *The psychoanalytic theory of neurosis.* New York: Norton.

Finkelhor, D., Hotaling, G., Lewis, I. A., & Smith, C. (1990). Sexual abuse in a national study of adult men and women: Prevalence, characteristics, and risk factors. *Child Abuse and Neglect, 14,* 19–28.

Flor-Henry, P. (1987). Cerebral aspects of sexual deviation. In G. D. Wilson (Ed.), *Variant sexuality: Research and theory* (pp. 49–83). Baltimore, MD: Johns Hopkins University Press.

Flor-Henry, P., & Lang, R. (1988). Quantitative EEG analysis in genital exhibitionists. *Annals of Sex Research, 1,* 48–62.

Forgac, G. E., Cassel, C. A., & Michaels, E. J. (1984). Chronicity of criminal behavior and psychopathology in male exhibitionists. *Journal of Clinical Psychology, 40,* 827–832.

Forgac, G. E., & Michaels, E. J. (1982). Personality characteristics of two types of male exhibitionists. *Journal of Abnormal Psychology, 91,* 287–293.

Freund, K. (1990). Courtship disorders. In W. L. Marshall, D. R. Laws, & H. E. Barbaree (Eds.), *Handbook of sexual assault: Issues, theories, and treatment of the offender* (pp. 195–207). New York: Plenum Press.

Freund, K., & Blanchard, R. (1986). The concept of courtship disorder. *Journal of Sex and Marital Therapy, 12,* 79–92.

Freund, K., Scher, H., & Hucker, S. (1983). The courtship disorders. *Archives of Sexual Behavior, 12,* 369–379.

Freund, K., Scher, H., & Hucker, S. (1984). The courtship disorders: A further investigation. *Archives of Sexual Behavior, 13,* 133–139.

Frisbee, L. V., & Dondis, E. H. (1965). *Recidivism among treated sex offenders* (California Mental Health Research Monograph No. 5). Sacramento, CA: Department of Mental Hygiene.

Gebhard, P. H., Gagnon, J. H., Pomeroy, W. B., & Christenson, C. V. (1965). *Sex offenders: An analysis of types.* New York: Harper & Row.

Gillespie, W. H. (1955, July). *The general theory of sexual perversion.* [Contribution to the Panel on Perversions]. Paper presented at the 19th International Psycho-Analytical Congress, Geneva.

Gittleson, N. L., Eacott, S. E., & Mehta, B. M. (1978). Victims of indecent exposure. *British Journal of Psychiatry, 132,* 61–66.

Grob, C. S. (1985). Single case study: Female exhibitionism. *Journal of Nervous and Mental Disease, 173,* 253–256.

Hanson, R. K., & Bussière, M. T. (1996). *Predictors of sexual offender recidivism: A meta-analysis.* Public Works and Government Services of Canada, Ottawa, Ontario.

Hanson, R. K., & Slater, S. (1988). Sexual victimization in the history of sexual abusers: A review. *Annals of Sex Research, 1,* 485–499.

Henninger, J. M. (1941). Exhibitionism. *Journal of Criminal Psychopathology, 2,* 357–366.

Herman, S. H., Barlow, D. H., & Agras, W. S. (1974). An experimental analysis of classical conditioning as a method of increasing heterosexual arousal in homosexuals. *Behavior Therapy, 5,* 33–47.

Hooshmand, H., & Brawley, B. W. (1969). Temporal lobe seizures and exhibitionism. *Neurology, 19,* 1119–1124.

Hucker, S., Langevin, R., Wortzman, G., Bain, J., Handy, L., Chambers, J., & Wright, S. (1986). Neuropsychological impairment in pedophiles. *Canadian Journal of Behavioural Science, 18,* 440–448.

Karpman, B. (1948). The psychopathology of exhibitionism: Review of the literature. *Clinical Psychopathology, 9,* 179–225.

Kluver, H., & Bucy, P. (1939). Preliminary analysis of functions of the temporal lobes in monkeys. *Archives of Neurological Psychiatry, 42,* 979–1000.

Knight, R. A., & Prentky, R. A. (1990). Classifying sexual offenders: The development and corroboration of taxonomic models. In W. L. Marshall, D. R. Laws, & H. E. Barbaree (Eds.), *Handbook of sexual assault: Issues, theories, and treatment of the offender* (pp. 23–52). New York: Plenum Press.

Kolarsky, A., Freund, K., Machek, J., & Polak, O. (1967). Male sexual deviation: Association with early temporal lobe damage. *Archives of General Psychiatry, 17,* 735–743.

Lang, R. A., Langevin, R., Checkley, K. L., & Pugh, G. (1987). Genital exhibitionism: Courtship disorder or narcissism? *Canadian Journal of Behavioural Science, 19,* 216–232.

Langevin, R. (1990). Sexual anomalies and the brain. In W. L. Marshall, D. R. Laws, & H. E. Barbaree (Eds.), *Handbook of sexual assault: Issues, theories, and treatment of the offender* (pp. 103–113). New York: Plenum Press.

Langevin, R., Paitich, D., Freeman, R., Mann, K., & Handy, L.(1978). Personality characteristics and sexual anomalies in males. *Canadian Journal of Behavioural Science, 10,* 222–238.

Langevin, R., Paitich, D., Ramsey, G., Anderson, C., Kamrad, J., Pope, S., Geller, G., Pearl, L., & Newman, S. (1979). Experimental studies of the etiology of genital exhibitionism. *Archives of Sexual Behavior, 8,* 307–331.

Laws, D. R., & Marshall, W. L. (1990). A conditioning theory of the etiology and maintenance of deviant sexual preference and behavior. In W. L. Marshall, D. R. Laws, & H. E. Barbaree (Eds.), *Handbook of sexual assault: Issues, theories, and treatment of the offender* (pp. 209–229). New York: Plenum Press.

Longo, R. E., & Groth, A. N. (1983). Juvenile sexual offenses in the histories of adult rapists and child molesters. *International Journal of Offender Therapy and Comparative Criminology, 27,* 150–155.

Longo, R. E., & McFadin, J. B. (1981). Sexually inappropriate behavior: Development of the sexual offender. *Law and Order, 29,* 21–23.

MacDonald, J. M. (1973). *Indecent exposure.* Springfield, IL: Charles C Thomas.

Malcolm, P. B., Andrews, D. A., & Quinsey, V. L. (1993). Discriminant and predictive validity of phallometrically measured sexual age and gender preference. *Journal of Interpersonal Violence, 8,* 486–501.

Maletzky, B. M. (1987, May). *Data generated by an outpatient sexual abuse clinic.* Paper presented at the 1st annual Conference on the Assessment and Treatment of Sexual Abusers, Newport, Oregon.

Maletzky, B. M. (1991). *Treating the sexual offender.* Newbury Park, CA: Sage.

Marshall, W. L. (1974). The classical conditioning of sexual attractiveness: A report of four therapeutic failures. *Behavior Therapy, 5,* 298–299.

Marshall, W. L., & Barbaree, H. E. (1988). The long-term evaluation of a behavioral treatment program for child molesters. *Behaviour Research and Therapy, 26,* 499–511.

Marshall, W. L., & Barbaree, H. E. (1990). Outcome of comprehensive cognitive-behavioral treatment programs. In W. L. Marshall, D. R. Laws, & H. E. Barbaree (Eds.), *Handbook of sexual assault: Issues, theories, and treatment of the offender* (pp. 363–385). New York: Plenum Press.

Marshall, W. L., Eccles, A., & Barbaree, H. E. (1991). The treatment of exhibitionists: A focus on sexual deviance versus cognitive and relationship features. *Behaviour Research and Therapy, 29,* 129–135.

Marshall, W. L., Payne, K., Barbaree, H. E., & Eccles, A. (1991). Exhibitionists: Sexual preferences for exposing. *Behaviour Research and Therapy, 29,* 37–40.

McCreary, C. P. (1975). Personality profiles of persons convicted of indecent exposure. *Journal of Clinical Psychology, 31,* 260–262.

McGuire, R. L., Carlisle, J. M., & Young, B. G. (1965). Sexual deviations as conditioned behavior: A hypothesis. *Behaviour Research and Therapy, 2,* 185–190.

Mohr, J. W., Turner, R. E., & Jerry, M. B. (1964). *Pedophilia and exhibitionism.* Toronto: University of Toronto Press.

Monahan, J. (1993). Limiting therapist exposure to Tarasoff liability: Guidelines for risk containment. *American Psychologist, 48,* 242–250.

Murphy, W. D., & Barbaree, H. E. (1994). *Assessments of sexual offenders by measures of erectile response: Psychometric properties and decision making.* Brandon, VT: Safer Society Press.

Murphy, W. D., Haynes, M. R., & Page, I. J. (1992). Adolescent sex offenders. In W. O'Donohue & J. H. Geer (Eds.), *The sexual abuse of children: Clinical issues* (Vol. 2, pp. 395–429). Hillsdale, NJ: Erlbaum.

Murphy, W. D., Haynes, M. R., & Worley, P. J. (1991). Assessment of adult sexual interest. In C. R. Hollin & K. Howells (Eds.), *Clinical approaches to sex offenders and their victims* (pp. 77–92). West Sussex, England: Wiley.

Murphy, W. D., & Peters, J. M. (1992). Profiling child sexual abusers: Psychological considerations. *Criminal Justice and Behavior, 19,* 24–37.

Murphy, W. D., & Smith, T. A. (1996). Sex offenders against children: Empirical and clinical issues. In L. Berliner, J. Briere, J. Bulkley, & C. Jenny (Eds.), *APSAC handbook on child maltreatment*. Thousand Oaks, CA: Sage.

O'Carroll, R. (1989). A neuropsychological study of sexual deviation. *Sexual and Marital Therapy, 4*, 59–63.

Paitich, D., & Langevin, R. (1976). The Clarke Parent–Child Relations Questionnaire: A clinically useful test for adults. *Journal of Consulting and Clinical Psychology, 44*, 428–436.

Peters, J. M., & Murphy, W. D. (1992). Profiling child sexual abusers: Legal considerations. *Criminal Justice and Behavior, 19*, 38–53.

Pithers, W. D. (1990). Relapse prevention with sexual aggressors: A method for maintaining therapeutic gain and enhancing external supervision. In W. L. Marshall, D. R. Laws, & H. E. Barbaree (Eds.), *Handbook of sexual assault: Issues, theories, and treatment of the offender* (pp. 343–361). New York: Plenum Press.

Rachman, S. (1966). Sexual fetishism: An experimental analogue. *Psychological Record, 16*, 293–296.

Rachman, S., & Hodgson, R. J. (1968). Experimentally induced "sexual fetishism": Replication and development. *Psychological Record, 18*, 25–27.

Radzinowicz, L. (1957). *Sexual offenses: A report of the Cambridge Department of Criminal Science*. London: Macmillan.

Rice, M. E., Quinsey, V. L., & Harris, G. T. (1991). Sexual recidivism among child molesters released from a maximum security psychiatric institution. *Journal of Consulting and Clinical Psychology, 59*, 381–386.

Rooth, G. (1973). Exhibitionism, sexual violence and paedophilia. *British Journal of Psychiatry, 122*, 705–710.

Saunders, E. B., & Awad, G. A. (1991). Male adolescent sexual offenders: Exhibitionism and obscene phone calls. *Child Psychiatry and Human Development, 21*, 169–178.

Saunders, E. G., Awad, G. A., & White, G. (1986). Male adolescent sexual offenders: The offender and the offense. *Canadian Journal of Psychiatry, 31*, 542–549.

Smith, S. R. (1980). Legal stand toward exhibitionism. In D. J. Cox & R. J. Daitzman (Eds.), *Exhibitionism: Description, assessment and treatment* (pp. 11–38). New York: Garland.

Smukler, A. J., & Schiebel, D. (1975). Personality characteristics of exhibitionists. *Diseases of the Nervous System, 36*, 600–603.

Tarter, R. E., Hegedus, A. M., Alterman, A. I., & Katz-Garris, L. (1983). Cognitive capacities of juvenile, violent, nonviolent, and sexual offenders. *Journal of Nervous and Mental Disease, 171*, 564–567.

Taylor, F. H. (1947). Observations on some cases of exhibitionism. *Journal of Mental Science, 93*, 631–638.

Templeman, T. L., & Stinnett, R. D. (1991). Patterns of sexual arousal and history in a "normal" sample of young men. *Archives of Sexual Behavior, 20*, 137–150.

3

EXHIBITIONISM
Assessment and Treatment

Barry M. Maletzky

Although we may not at present be able to determine the origins of many paraphilias, references to exhibitionism extend back to biblical times. Had the serpent been less wily or the apple more sour, exhibitionism might never have been deemed a crime. From fig leaves through tunics to tuxedos, civil societies have prohibited genital exposure, asserting that it is offensive, if not harmful, and should be grouped among a score of paraphilias, some blatant and others subtle, but all producing victims embarrassed, outraged, and possibly damaged by such exposure.

No other member of the animal kingdom purposefully hides its genitals, or even seems to take much notice of them. However, at times of sexual arousal, some species focus on their genitals. Scientists, hunters, and zoo attendees all have witnessed exhibitionism in several closely affiliated species:

> Then at midcycle the male [orang-utan] performed a display. . . . [He] reclined supine . . . with an erection and directed his penis toward the female . . . until the female approached and examined his penis. The female then mounted the male's penis and initiated thrusting. (Nadler, 1988, p. 158)

Such displays are common among the great apes, having been witnessed in groups of chimpanzees, gorillas, and orangutans, and in the baboon, a lesser ape.

An animal model of human behavior is not a duplication of, as much as a template for, understanding the wellsprings of human pathology (Bailey, 1991). Because our species shares approximately 99% of its DNA architecture with chimpanzees, and 97% with gorillas, it is prudent to question social scientists' theories about the origins of exhibitionism; does a chimpanzee exposing his erection to a midestral-phase female really feel inadequate socially? Is he guilty of abusing masculine power in trying to dominate his chimp world? These questions do not belittle social and psychological contributions to understanding sexual human aberrations; rather, they suggest that we not lose sight of the powerful evolutionary forces shaping human behavior. Recent findings in psychiatry suggest the importance of considering biological elements in the determination of causes: receptor sensitivities in obsessive–compulsive disorder (Barr et al., 1994), panic disorder (Papp, Klein, & Gorman, 1993), paranoid states (Hollister, Mednick, Breman, & Cannon, 1994), and bipolar disorder (Debruyn et al., 1994) may be too finely tuned, causing overreaction in various central nervous system sites, examples of evolutionary mechanisms gone awry. We should not underestimate the power of phylogenetic continuity in motivating raw behavior.

In this view, some paraphilias can be considered as sexual drives displaced, malimprinted, or disinhibited and, by and large, committed by males (Bailey, 1991). Once, millennia ago, public nudity might not have caused concern. Forbidden fruit, perhaps a metaphor for carnal knowledge, may have caused in our species over millennia the capacity for shame. With erect posture and the possibility of face-to-face sexual interactions, frontal elements assumed increasing importance. Many men were attracted to women's pubic hair and breasts, many women to a larger penis—human females have the largest breast:body size ratio in the entire animal kingdom, males the largest penis:body size ratio (Singer, 1985). With self-knowledge and attraction, and our capacity for embarrassment, exhibitionism changed from a sexual signal to an aggressive and detested act; with the development of empathy, it became a crime.

ASSESSMENT

Diagnostic Assessment

Arriving at the diagnosis of exhibitionism does not appear at first glance to be complex. An offender either exposes or does not. However, some ambiguities exist:

A 42-year-old married man often parked his vehicle in a shopping center complex in the evening. When a woman walked from or to her car, he would watch her and masturbate. If he was discovered, however, he would lose his erection and flee.

A 19-year-old college student enjoyed watching female students enter and leave a sorority house. He would hide behind a sign located nearby and masturbate when an attractive female walked by. On several occasions, however, a girl would notice him. He was frightened at first, but gradually began to enjoy his victims' responses, particularly those of surprise and laughter. He began to expose from his car and in a dimly lit and brushy park nearby.

Is public masturbation a precursor to exhibitionism? Are there fundamental differences between the above cases? Some research indicates that not all men who expose begin by masturbating in public (Maletzky & Price, 1984). However, among those who do, men who do so most boldly and pay particular attention to the victim's face will go on to expose in public (Maletzky, 1980). Although much has been intelligently written about the response an exhibitionist most anticipates, the data are still not easily summarized. Although a common axiom among clinicians asserts that the exhibitionist wants to induce fear or shame in his victim(s), over 50% of exhibitionists interviewed in a recent survey cited a potential sexual approval from the victim as the best possible response (Freund, Watson, & Rienzo, 1988).

Are all exhibitionists motivated by frustrated sexual and social urges, unfulfilled due to their own inadequacies? Data indicate that most exhibitionists are either married or living with a woman, and enjoy a normal sexual relationship within that bond (Langevin & Lang,

1987; Maletzky, 1991a). In assessing an exhibitionist, a thorough history of sexual relationships is essential; of equal importance, an interview with the sexual partner can uncover crucial information.

Every clinician is familiar with the minimization or denial demonstrated by most sexual offenders demonstrate. Frequently, an exhibitionist has committed many repetitions of his standard method of exposing. An estimate by one observer asserts that we have probably learned about just 1% of the crimes of exhibitionists (G. G. Abel, personal communication, January 13, 1995). To add yet more confusion, a diagnosis of exhibitionism markedly increases the chances that the offender has associated paraphilias, particularly voyeurism, frotteurism, and obscene telephone calling (Freund et al., 1988; Freund & Watson, 1990). These associations prompted Freund and coworkers to propose that exhibitionism lies on a continuum of sexual activity that is appropriate in limited circumstances (e.g., preparing for intercourse), but is inserted inappropriately early in the sexual chain. These authors proposed a four-part continuity in normal sexual behavior which could be subverted by an offender at various times. Table 3.1 depicts these reformulated phases and possible aberrations in sexual offending related to each phase. In this paradigm, sexual offending represents an anomaly, or a caricature, of normal sexual behavior. In exhibitionism, the patient attempts a sexual behavior, exposing, before appropriate partner choice. Freund bolstered this hypothesis with data demonstrating the co-occurrence of other paraphilias common in exhibitionists. However, the power of these findings is diminished somewhat by a heavy reliance on self-report and the lack of any independent means of verifying these histories. In addition, Freund and colleagues did not evaluate a simpler hypothesis—that these men had either heightened sexual arousal or diminished sexual control.

Although the determination of whether an individual has exposed or not appears straightforward, the diagnostic assessment does not end at that point. The clinician will need to determine the duration and extent of offending, against whom it has occurred, how the crimes have been perpetrated, what meanings they may have for the offender, and, of even greater practical significance, how he might best be treated. The steps in a comprehensive assessment form the foundation upon which to base a treatment plan.

Review of Materials

Every effort should be made to obtain all information about an offender *before* the first interview. Materials usually available to the clinician include police and victim reports, a presentence investigation, prior psychological and psychiatric evaluations, psychological testing, children's agency reports, depositions, and any testimony recorded. Because offenders often distort information about their sexual activities, reviewing these background documents is an essential element in assessment. Records about the present offense are crucial, but records of prior sexual and nonsexual crimes are relevant as well. Of particular

TABLE 3.1. Phases of Sexual Interaction and Possible Aberrations

Phase	Possible aberrations
Location, appraisal, and sanction of a partner	Excessive cruising, searching, and staring Voyeurism
Pretactile interaction	Excessive flirting and pestering Exhibitionism Obscene telephone calling, scatologia
Tactile interaction	Aggressive sexuality, frotteurism
Genital interaction	Abuse of prostitutes, male prostitution, rape

interest are histories of drug and alcohol use and any prior psychological or psychiatric treatment.

The Clinical Interview

Obtaining a History

Clinicians are uncommonly skilled at extracting information from patients, yet we often underestimate the value of clinical history taking and mental status examinations. Most clinicians possess not only years of experience with these assessment tools, but also great skill in eliciting relevant information as well, not an easy task in evaluating the sexual offender who often is not the most cooperative of patients.

Although structured clinical interviews of psychiatric patients have appeared in the literature, none have been directed toward the sexual offender. Most clinicians favor an unstructured interview to elicit as much information as possible while enhancing trust in the therapist–patient relationship. Flexibility makes sense when evaluating an offender to both assess his condition and to modify the nature of the interaction in an appropriate fashion.

Although information may be gained at various times during the interviews, it should be organized into a concise, yet comprehensive report. Most clinicians have developed their own systems for reporting results of assessment interviews. In many cases, 2 to 3 hours of interviewing, perhaps separated into several sessions, should prove sufficient to gain and report an understanding of the offender's problem areas, sexual and nonsexual, and some indication of early treatment goals. Offenders often come to these evaluations at their lowest point, defensive, isolated, angry, and with self-reproach and fears of financial loss. They deserve and will appreciate the clinician's support not for what they have done but for who they are. These early sessions will serve well the twin goals of trust building and self-disclosure necessary to begin the work of treatment.

Of special importance in obtaining a history from clients with exhibitionism is the clinician's awareness that a single act of exposing might be the only tangible bit of evidence upon which to construct a plan for treatment. Yet, this act may have been simply the title page of a volume filled with an assortment of pathologies, not only sexual but psychological and interpersonal as well. It is unrealistic to expect that the therapist could predict the ending after reading just the first few pages.

The Mental Status Examination

Rather than being a series of questions and replies, the mental status is the therapist's organized report of behavioral "vital signs," a series of behavioral observations reported in a systematic fashion but obtained over the course of the initial interview and modified in subsequent sessions as necessary. Categorizations within the mental status examination should follow standard psychological and psychiatric texts; however, several elements can be particularly important in the assessment of the exhibitionist:

1. *Appearance*: Is the client ill kempt? Is his posture open or closed? Does he maintain eye contact?
2. *Sensorial assessment*: Is the client aware of his behavior? Is he oriented and able to participate in court proceedings? Is he able to give informed consent for treatment?
3. *Affective display*: Is the offender's affect appropriate? How much understanding and empathy can he show toward the victim(s)? To what extent is a false display of

emotion shown? How have the incidents surrounding the exposing affected his mood? Is there some measure of remorse?

4. *Thought processes*: Are any signs of a thought disorder present, such as loosening of associations or ideas of reference? If so, are they related to the exposing? Is there any suicidal or homicidal ideation?

5. *Thought content*: Does the exhibitionist know his behavior is wrong? Does he know why? Are there assumptions and distortions? What does he think, and how does he feel, about treatment?

Corroboration Interviews

It is no surprise that sexual offenders sometimes distort, minimize, or lie about their activities. Aside from reviewing the materials mentioned above, the therapist would do well to seek the observations and opinions of partners, parents, friends, and relatives to obtain other views; few of us are perceptive self-observers. While such individuals may be swayed by their own loyalties or antagonisms, other points of view can be illuminating:

> When several high school girls complained about a male student opening the door of a girls' restroom at school and exposing his erect penis, the boy explained that he was urged to do so as a joke and would receive money if he dared to carry out the act. Vague about the details, he pled with an interviewer not to report this to his parents. School policy demanded otherwise; his parents reported that he had been apprehended at his last school in a similar incident and used the same story to evade treatment.

Self-Reports

Aside from eliciting the exhibitionist's story of his offenses, the therapist can ask the client to keep track of sexual urges, fantasies, dreams, and actual behaviors (exposing or masturbating to fantasies of exposing). Are these reports of any value, however, given the sexual offender's predisposition to misreport data based on self-interest?

There is a long history and a detailed literature about the relevance of self-reports in a variety of conditions, but only two comprehensive studies of the accuracy of self-report and exhibitionism have appeared (Freund et al., 1988; Maletzky, 1980). In an exhaustive review of 437 exhibitionists, voyeurs, frotteurs, and men predisposed toward rape (Freund et al., 1988), the exhibitionists revealed a good deal more information than was required in their treatment sessions. Almost half admitted to masturbating while exposing, while more than two thirds experienced the act as either an invitation to intercourse or as a substitute for it. While extrapolation from other studies of paraphilia leads to the conclusion that self-reports are undoubtedly biased (Abel & Rouleau, 1990), the offender's perceptions of his crimes are always of interest. Moreover, an offender's own evaluations of progress in treatment often parallel plethysmograph data in depicting trends (Maletzky, 1974, 1980, 1991a).

Although many therapists grow cynical about their clients' observations and recollections of their own exposing behaviors, we can distill some general principles from the literature and from clinical experience:

1. Exhibitionists are *more* likely than other offenders to underreport their frequency of offending behaviors (McConaghy, 1993).

2. They are *less* likely than other offenders to believe that their exposing has harmed a victim (Cox & Maletzky, 1980).

3. They are *more* likely than other offenders to deny the coexistence of other paraphilias (Freund & Blanchard, 1986; McConaghy, Blaszczynski, & Kid, 1988).
4. They are *more* likely than other offenders to have committed other sexual crimes (Freund & Blanchard, 1986; Langevin & Lang, 1987).

Psychological Tests, Rating Scales, and Questionnaires

Psychological Tests

Despite gigabytes of information about psychological testing with sexual offenders, no study has isolated exhibitionists as a separate category with a clearly defined set of characteristic responses on any single, or any combination of, reliable and validated psychological tests (Marshall & Hall, 1995). As a corollary, an evaluator is not yet justified in making public conclusions about the probability of future acts based upon any combination of tests alone. The personal history and clinical presentation of the offender form the foundation upon which a diagnosis, treatment plan, and prognosis are built. The lack of a strong correlation among test results, diagnoses, and future predictions of treatment response may stem from a heterogeneity in sexual offenders in general (Hall, 1989; Schlank, 1995) and exhibitionists in particular (Hall, 1990).

Among psychological tests commonly employed, the second edition of the Minnesota Multiphasic Inventory (MMPI-2; Butcher, Dahlstrom, Graham, Tellegen, & Kassmer, 1989)) has received the widest use. However, it never was designed as a test of sexual proclivities; rather, its purpose was to provide a general measure of psychological functioning. The wide range of responses of sexual offenders on the MMPI-2 stems not only from its design but from the inclusion of a variety of offenders (pedophiles, exhibitionists, rapists) to generate a statistical average (Graham, 1993; Kalichman, 1991). When data are extracted for an exhibitionist group, the number of subjects is usually too small to be significant. In addition, broad overlap often occurs, with many exhibitionists producing lower pathology scores than do nonoffenders (Langevin, Wright, & Handy, 1990).

Several other tests have been employed in attempts to distinguish a specific sexual offender profile although, again, the majority of these offenders were pedophiles, incest offenders, and rapists. Although the Multiphasic Sex Inventory (MSI; Nichols & Molinder, 1984) appeared superior to the MMPI-2 in a recent sampling of incarcerated offenders in defining clinical subtypes, no validating data were offered (Schlank, 1995). A Sexual Offender Treatment Rating Scale (SOTRS) has been proposed by Anderson, Gibeau, and D'Amora (1995) to assess initial factors of insight, risks, motivations, victim empathy, and offense disclosure. Pairs of rater-therapists produced acceptable levels of reliability on this index, which the researchers employed sequentially during treatment. Only 9% of subjects were exhibitionists. No individual data for this subgroup were reported and no validity conclusions could be offered, but this multidimensional instrument, as presented, could prove useful in measuring improvement.

The lack of assessment studies on exhibitionism alone is surprising because exhibitionists comprise the first- (McConaghy, 1993) or second-largest (Maletzky, 1991a) diagnostic group treated as sexual offenders. This lack may be a reflection of a common belief that exhibitionism is a trifling matter compared with hands-on crimes; hence, the need to ferret out common characteristics of exhibitionists may not be seen as politically urgent, as interesting, or as easily funded, when compared with more aggressive crimes. However, victims of exhibitionism may be as deeply affected as victims of more newsworthy crimes: Such women may suffer phobias, generalized anxieties, nightmares, difficulty trusting men, and reduced libido, symptoms similar to those of victims of child abuse and rape (Cox & Maletzky, 1980).

Summarizing a thorough review of the utility of personality tests in sexual offenders, Marshall and Hall (1995) concluded that such tests "however they are scored or represented do not satisfactorily distinguish any type of sexual offender from various other groups of subjects including, most particularly, nonoffenders" (pp. 216–217).

Rating Scales

When sexual offenders are asked to state the intensity of their sexual drive or attraction to a set of stimuli, the same set of biases arises as in self-reports. Exhibitionists have good reasons to underreport their sexual fantasies and actions: They are in a legal predicament and need to deflect attention away from their crimes.

Moreover, offender rating scales may offer an illusion of objectivity with numerical scores standing in for nebulous characteristics, such as sexual impulse control, maturity, and integrity. Conte (1983), in a review of self-report scales, found disappointing test–retest reliability, and offered no data about validation. Schiavi, Derogatis, Kuriansky, O'Connor, and Sharpe (1979) reported no evidence of test validity in a review of over 50 self-rated instruments presented to a variety of sexual offenders. Therapist-generated scales have not warranted any greater confidence. Often, such scales have been employed to evaluate pre- and posttreatment results by statistical comparisons of experimental and control group averages (Jacobsen, Follette, & Revenstorf, 1984). At times, statistically significant differences are discovered without any relevance to clinically meaningful events. For example, LoPiccolo and Steger (1974) constructed a sexual interaction inventory utilizing global therapist assessments such as "much improvement," "improved," and the like. Thus, reliability was improved but clinical advances were trivial.

Card Sorts

A type of rating scale frequently used to assess sexual preferences employs user-friendly card sorts (Brownell & Barlow, 1977). Offenders are asked to read a series of sexual scenes on cards and then rate how much sexual arousal those scenes generate. Whereas a number of preprinted cards have been employed (Farrenkopf, 1984), some clinicians print their own, varying content to match their patient's idiosyncratic responses. Unfortunately, no test–retest reliability or inherent validity studies have been reported in evaluating this interesting and labor-nonintensive device.

In a different but related technique the therapist asks offenders to keep a daily log of sexual events, including fantasies, urges, acts of masturbation, or other sexual releases. The offender is then asked to rate the sexual pleasure of these events; these ratings can subsequently be used to construct a hierarchy of scenes for treatment. However, offenders' unreliability in self-reports can erode confidence in such techniques.

A novel assessment technique bearing some elements in common with card sorts asks a client to view computer-driven deviant slides, rating his interest in each one. A physiological measure of slide viewing is, however, being taken outside the client's awareness. This innovative approach, the Abel Screen II (G. G. Abel, personal communication, January 13, 1995), awaits independent validation.

Neuropsychological Assessment

Early studies of sexual offenders in general and exhibitionists in particular have led to suggestions on the part of several authors that brain pathology might play a role in some cases of exhibitionism (Baker, 1985; Flor-Henry, Lang, Koles, & Frenzel, 1988). An extensive body of literature had implicated temporal lobe and limbic area abnormalities in patients with sexual deviations, including exhibitionism (Cummings, 1985; Hucker et al., 1988; Langevin, Lang, Wortzman, Frenzel, & Wright, 1989). Among samples of patients with developmental disabilities, the rate of exhibitionism is higher than that among matched normal males (Langevin et al., 1989). However, the majority of exhibitionists lacked evidence of lesions when computed tomography (CT) and magnetic resonance scans were compared (Hucker et al., 1988). Baker (1985) administered the Halstead–Reitan battery to 23 exhibitionists and found deficiencies in each one. However, these findings were not characteristic but rather scattered, although there was a suggestion of left fronto-temporal localization.

An ongoing research project at the Clarke Institute of Psychiatry (Langevin et al., 1989) compared 15 exhibitionists with 36 nonsexual offenders on the WAIS-R and the Halstead–Reitan battery. Findings included some significant differences on various subtests. Global differences between the two groups, however, were not found; CT scans did not distinguish one group from another.

Physiological Assessment

The Penile Plethysmograph

The most widely used physiological assessment of sexual preferences measures penile circumference changes. Although measurements of penile volume changes historically preceded circumference changes, the latter have risen to dominate physiological assessment because the methodology was available, the technique feasible, its reliability reasonable, and its validity now demonstrated (Marshall, Barbaree, & Butt, 1988; Nagayama Hall, Proctor, & Nelson, 1988).

Technical details in the application of the plethysmograph (Jensen, Laws, & Wolfe, 1994) point toward a practitioner consensus, now codified in guidelines for those using the instrument for assessment and treatment (Association for the Treatment of Sexual Abusers, 1993). I will not review the development of this device and its technical application here. Rather, I will review its use specific to exhibitionism, and problems stemming from that use.

When the therapist uses plethysmography to assess deviant sexual arousal, he or she presents a variety of stimuli to the patient, including graphic depictions of sexual activity in the form of slides, movies, videotapes, scenes read by a therapist, and scenes spoken by the offender. There is little disagreement about appropriate stimulus materials when assessing and treating men who have molested children or raped women. But what stimuli might differentiate exhibitionists from nonexhibitionists or from other sexual offenders?

Clinicians have used slides of exposing situations, such as a photograph of a female walking down an empty street (Freund & Watson, 1990; McGrath, 1991). A number of researchers have reported some arousal among exhibitionists viewing such scenes, but the results are less than clear cut (Maletzky, 1991a; Marshall & Barbaree, 1988; Marshall, Payne, Barbaree, & Eccles, 1991). To complicate matters, most exhibitionists demonstrate similar sexual arousal patterns when compared with nonoffenders (Langevin & Lang, 1987; Maletzky, 1980). However, many exhibitionists demonstrate some arousal upon hearing exhibitionist scenes (Maletzky, 1980); nonexhibitionists have demonstrated only rare arousal to such scenes, enhancing slightly the validity of the test, especially if a criterion of 20% of full erection is used as a threshold below which the instrument cannot validly measure arousal.

An additional problem in evaluating plethysmographic data stems from sampling bias. We evaluate only those exhibitionists who get caught. Often exhibitionists enter a treatment program only after numerous successful exposing incidents without detection. Other deviant acts, such as voyeurism, may have occurred without detection as well. To further complicate matters, some exhibitionists may expose only to prepubescent females because of deviant sexual interests or because the risk of being reported is lower. Some of these men may require treatment for pedophilia as well as for exhibitionism.

Perhaps partly as a result of these problems, no large-scale study of the utility of the plethysmograph in exhibitionists has been reported. When the vagaries of stimulus selection are combined with the lack of normative data, the test itself comes under close scrutiny. Some findings indicate the likelihood that the plethysmograph has validity in the measurement of the relative degree of arousal for most offenders (McAnulty & Adams, 1992), but it is only weakly related to the absolute strength of sexual interests (Marshall et al., 1988; Marshall & Barbaree, 1988).

An additional problem arises in exhibitionism because of its frequent association with other paraphilias, whether admitted by the offender or suspected by the clinician. Data are convincing that many exhibitionists (we lack a clear percentage) are polymorphously perverse. The incidence of voyeurism, frotteurism, and obscene telephone calling range from an estimated 20% to over 80% in exhibitionists (Freund & Watson, 1990; McConaghy, 1993). Some clinicians suspect that heterosexual pedophilia may be present in some exhibitionists as well, especially those who expose to females below the age of 18. While some of these offenders will be revealed by the plethysmograph, many (up to 50% in some estimates) will show a false negative reaction—they either suppress erections (using a variety of well-documented evasions) or simply cannot become aroused under the artificial conditions of the laboratory. One saving grace of the instrument, however, is its tendency to infrequently show false positives. Nonetheless, even these can occur; some offenders may have a high level of arousal to many stimuli. Indeed, adolescent offenders showed their greatest response on the plethysmograph to scenes connected with exposing (Kaemingk, Koselka, Beeker, & Kaplan, 1995).

The very real problem of false negatives, reported in 33% of admitted offenders (Maletzky, 1991a; Marshall et al., 1986; Nagayama Hall et al., 1988), has been attacked in a variety of ways: accommodation to the laboratory setting; frequent shifting of stimulus materials, such as the use of slides, movies, and tapes in sequence or in combination; and the use of idiosyncratic stimulus materials. Sexual arousal is rarely predictable; of all our pleasures, sexual behavior is the most idiosyncratic. Often, researchers are pulled between the need for results reproducible in other settings and the need to generate clinically significant levels of arousal (Howes, 1995). Therefore, many therapists are relying increasingly upon audiotaped stimuli (Marshall, Payne, et al., 1991). An exhibitionist listening to a scene is not constrained visually. In his mind's eye, close-to-perfect scenarios can unfold. Most males are visually excitable; exhibitionists especially may require a detailed scenario, yet one in which their imaginations are allowed the freedom to visualize ideal situations. It is no surprise that clinical reports indicate greater arousal in exhibitionists to verbal presentations of scenes of exposing than to slides of exposing situations (Howes, 1995; Maletzky, 1991a).

Many offenders are suspected of suppressing deviant sexual arousal and, conversely, of increasing normal arousal on the plethysmograph. However, several remedies may be helpful. Time of last sexual release should be ascertained and recorded. In addition, comparison of serial recordings taken over a span of weeks can sometimes be enlightening. In the experience of seasoned clinicians, offenders may have more natural skills in suppressing deviant sexual arousal than in inducing detumescence once it has occurred. Hence, an exhibitionist may be presented with a scene of normal sexual activity with a female. Upon reaching a state of full erection, he can be presented with an audiotaped scene of exposing. Many nonexhibitionists lose 50% to 100% of their erections within the first 60 seconds of such a presentation. An exhibitionist, however, may be unable to detumesce as rapidly, if at all.

In summary, the plethysmograph remains controversial in determining the presence of deviant sexual arousal in exhibitionists, even among respected clinicians and researchers. Indeed, its most important use for the exhibitionist may not be in assessment at all, but rather as a biofeedback device in treatment (Maletzky, 1991a). If some deviant arousal is reliably present in association with exhibitionist stimuli, however, the instrument can often be used to measure improvement (or lack of it) as treatment progresses, an ability not as true of paper-and-pencil tests, self-reports, checklists, card sorts, and questionnaires.

The Polygraph

If possible, even more controversy surrounds the use of the poorly named "lie detector" than the plethysmograph. The public and many professionals regard the test with skepticism, although it has been clinically helpful in several ways. During the polygraph examination, an offender is asked, among a number of questions, whether or not he has engaged in any sexually deviant acts at critical time periods based on his offending history, while recordings are made of his pulse, blood pressure, EKG, and galvanic skin response. As with the plethysmograph, the offender is in an artificial and potentially hostile environment; he is aware of the purpose of the test and that the major reason for the test itself is because he is suspected of not telling the truth. As with the plethysmograph, the polygraph is intrusive, and not accorded full validity in the scientific and popular press. Yet, again in similarity to the plethysmograph, its use is ubiquitous. Polygraphy, a field with its own literature, has been accorded a measure of respect in recent years, partly due to its value in working with sexual offenders (Abrams, 1991).

Yet the polygraph is different than the plethysmograph in important ways. The plethysmograph measures a physiological change, both more specific and focused than the polygraph. We do not conclude from a reading of deviant sexual arousal that an offender has or has not committed a crime; no statements about the past can be made from measurements of penile circumference, although projections into the future can be made with some research support (Abel, Becker, Murphy, & Flanagan, 1981). The results of a polygraph, in contrast, can lead to conclusions, at times quite expansive: that an offender is being deceitful *in general,* that he may continue to try to deceive, and that bodily measures of general anxiety and arousal can be relied upon to excavate truth and deception with scientific accuracy.

Experience with polygraph examinations of exhibitionists is mixed: Many such offenders fail the test and then admit culpability for some or all of their crimes. Many others pass who may have conquered the machine and their own anxiety, at least for the present. Although it is said that the more sociopathic offenders often do better on the test, as they are adept at unimpassioned trickery, no study in exhibitionists has attempted to prove that assertion. However, in one attribute the polygraph and plethysmograph share an important similarity: They are equally important as devices for treatment as well as assessment.

A 27-year-old construction worker often stayed at his job site for lunch breaks, or even after work. Complaints from female tenants in an apartment building across the parking lot revealed the reason—he was exposing to them from hiding spots within the half-finished building. Although he was identified by several witnesses, he steadfastly maintained that this was a case of mistaken identity. On a plethysmograph assessment, he demonstrated 40% to 50% of full erection with scenes depicting exposing situations when compared with 70% to 80% with normal stimuli and zero to 10% to stimuli depicting sexual activities with youngsters. When confronted with these results, he admitted these crimes. The plethysmograph was then employed in subsequent treatment sessions as a biofeedback device in helping him to learn better control of sexual arousal and to track reductions in deviant arousal throughout treatment.

A 20-year-old college student who frequented a campus laundromat at odd hours was charged with exposing himself to several female students. He denied culpability and several plethysmograph evaluations failed to demonstrate any deviant sexual arousal. Following a "no contest" plea to charges of indecent exposure, he entered an outpatient sexual abuse clinic. As part of ongoing individual treatment, his therapist told him of a requirement for regular polygraphs. Several weeks before his first examination, his therapist explained that the staff wanted him to succeed on the polygraphs, and to help him do so, he needed to think very hard about his recent activities and tell the entire truth before undergoing the test. In a subsequent session, he confessed to several additional acts of exposing, peeking into women's dormitory windows and rubbing up against women on escalators on campus.

Ethical objections can certainly be raised against such practices, although they are now commonplace in helping to prevent future victimizations. Most well-meaning clinicians have adopted similar techniques. It remains for future ethicists to judge whether these means justify those ends.

In summary, the polygraph has proven increasingly useful to clinicians, not just as an assessment device, but for the purposes of treatment as well. The ethics of its use, however, will, in all likelihood, continue to be debated by philosophers of the next millennium.

Biological Assessments

Despite extensive evidence that testosterone levels in males contribute to sexual aggression (Bradford & McLean, 1984; Langevin et al., 1988), no replicated abnormalities of any sexual hormone levels have been found in the majority of any type of male sexual offender (Langevin et al., 1988). The call for evidence of any relationship between any hormone level and exhibitionism has provoked an extraordinary silence. Most such work centers on sexual aggression: Exhibitionism has rarely been mentioned in studies of a variety of sexual hormones. Levels of circulating hormones such as luteinizing hormone, follicle stimulating hormone, and testosterone measure just one side of a two-sided coin: Variable cell receptor sensitivities and intracellular abnormalities of receptor density may be of greater clinical significance. A single prospective study examined hormone levels in exhibitionists and nonsexual offender controls (Lang, Langevin, Bain, Frenzel, & Wright, 1989). Offenders yielded lower estradiol and testosterone levels but higher free-circulating testosterone. This study begs replication.

Even were such individual differences correlated with measures of sexual aggression or offending, knowledge would be advanced only part way. Researchers would also need to examine the causes of these individual differences. Yet such research is virtually nonexistent in North America, partly a reflection of the widely accepted notion that deficits in social and behavioral learning cause sexual abnormalities. Exhibitionism is particularly singled out as an example of the hydraulic paradigm of psychopathology: The exposer's unrequited social and sexual feelings are dammed up, leading to intense back pressure and eventual flooding of side valleys. As a corollary, exhibitionists should be less likely to offend based either upon the frequency of prior exposing incidents, or the success of prior social and sexual contacts, conclusions unsupported by evidence in the scientific literature (Maletzky, 1980, 1991a; McConaghy, Armstrong, & Blaszczynski, 1981; McConaghy et al., 1988).

Currently, biological factors are not only unimportant in theories of sexual offending, but also they are believed to be dangerous because no offender should be able to excuse his behavior based upon unchangeable quirks of biological selection, such as genetic heritage and cell receptor sensitivities. It is possible, however, that a greater danger would be the unquestioned acceptance of axioms framed in socially acceptable terms. Complex behaviors may be multidetermined. Even if biological factors figure into the etiologic equation, no behavior is inevitable based upon a relative's genotype. None is excusable based upon a biological predisposition.

TREATMENT

Literature on the maladaptive sexual approach disorders such as pedophilia, exhibitionism, and rape has contained more references to theoretical, etiological, and epidemiological concerns than to issues of treatment. This disparity may reflect simply the state of our science, more descriptive than curative. However, a trend toward treatment-oriented studies is occurring. Much of the treatment literature in the 1970s and early 1980s consisted of case reports and retrospective analyses of treatment outcomes. Over the past half decade, however, many researchers have constructed more closely controlled studies, including some prospective and well-conceived efforts that attempt to isolate crucial treatment factors comprising the cognitive and behavioral treatment approaches to sexual offending.

Institutional versus Community-Based Treatment

While many aggressive offenders receive long-term prison sentences, especially in our day of media attention devoted to sexual abuse, most exhibitionists are not sent to prison and only a slight majority are sentenced to jail for a period longer than 1 week. Even in an era of outrage over sexual offending, exhibitionists have, by and large, escaped restrictions of their freedom for several reasons: Their crimes are deemed less harmful than those of other offenders, institutional space is limited, and many people believe that, because their crimes are regarded as mere peccadillos, exhibitionists should be easier to treat. Only the second reason is true:

> A 26-year-old unemployed drifter exposed himself in downtown areas late at night to women leaving office buildings at the end of their 3:00–11:00 P.M. shifts. Frequent complaints about him were treated lightly by local police officers, who perceived him as an amusing nuisance. One night he gained access to an office building, hid in an elevator, and attempted a rape of a woman maintenance worker at knife point.

> Several teenage girls waiting at a school bus stop noticed one morning that a man across the street, dressed only in pajamas, opened his garage door, stood in the middle of the garage and began masturbating, while smiling at the girls. While two of the girls, after reporting the incident, believed it had no ill effects, a third girl, not previously a victim of sexual abuse, had nightmares and panic attacks for many months after the episode. She finally convinced her concerned and frightened parents to move to a different neighborhood.

While no comprehensive survey of sentences for indecent exposure has been published, clinical experience indicates lower rates of incarceration, shorter periods of custody and supervision, imposition of lesser sanctions, and less concern for safety in local communities. As more information becomes available about the harm that can occur to victims of exhibitionism (Cox & Maletzky, 1980), community pressure may lead to more serious sentences for men who expose, especially with the growing awareness that exhibitionism may represent but one of an offender's deviant and harmful behaviors.

The decision to treat an offender in the community or within an institutional program is usually only affected by a clinician if she or he is asked to testify at sentencing or to submit recommendations about dangerousness to be at large. Because any of the following treatment techniques could be employed within either inpatient or outpatient treatment settings, this decision will usually be made on the basis of safety rather than on availability of treatment methods (Maletzky, 1993).

Behavioral Approaches

A flurry of activity in the 1960s and 1970s led to the application, at times exclusive, of therapy based upon a strict interpretation of behaviorism. With advances in research and experience, behavioral approaches are, today, employed as part of a comprehensive program utilizing a broad range of empirically and clinically tested techniques.

Aversive Conditioning

Electroshock

Aversive therapy is based upon classical conditioning paradigms attempting to pair an unconditioned aversive stimulus with a deviant response to reduce the likelihood of that response occurring in the future. Therapists hope to produce a conditioned aversive response to the deviant stimuli that would generalize to such cues in the patient's real-life experience. The earliest work employed electroshock as the aversive stimulus, usually at a level unpleasant but not harmful (MacCulloch & Feldman, 1967; MacCulloch, Waddington, & Sanbrook, 1978; Evans, 1970). Although shock received the most publicity, foul odors (Kennedy & Foreyt, 1968; Levin, Barry, Gambero, Wolfinsohn, & Smith, 1977) or tastes (Maletzky, 1991a; Sajwaj, Liberti, & Agras, 1974) were also employed. Details of such devices can be found in Maletzky (1991a).

At times, this method was employed in combination with plethysmograph monitoring. If sexual arousal rose to a predetermined level in response to deviant stimuli, a shock would be delivered, administered either by the therapist or by automated equipment. Many therapists also provided for the opportunity to avoid the punishment: If the patient showed no deviant arousal, or if he showed appropriate arousal, he could avoid shock (Maletzky, 1991a).

A detailed literature already exists about the merits of the plethysmograph in determining deviant arousal, especially in cases of exhibitionism (Kaemingk et al., 1995; Maletzky, 1980, 1991a; Marshall, Payne, et al., 1991). It is disingenuous, however, to employ this device as the only factor leading to punishment or its avoidance. Many offenders show no deviant arousal or they show variations in sexual arousal based upon a host of factors outside the conditions of treatment. Yet the occurrence of deviant arousal on the plethysmograph is still employed as the sole criterion determining punishment in many clinics.

Other problems with the simple punishment model and its applications have arisen. While there is convincing evidence that aversive procedures can reduce deviant arousal (Maletzky, 1991a; Marshall, Earls, Segal, & Darke, 1983) and reduce recidivism (Maletzky,

1993), some scholars disagree. McConaghy (1993), citing evidence from the 1960s and 1970s, criticized single-case reports and the inclusion of attempts to change ego-syntonic homosexuality. Expansive conclusions based upon small numbers of subjects, retrospective uncontrolled data, and the use of questionable stimulus materials are suspect. Indeed, several studies from this author's group demonstrated that such simple conditioning procedures could reduce the occurrence of sexual crimes without directly altering deviant arousal (McConaghy et al., 1981; McConaghy, 1993). It is possible that these techniques increased an offender's ability to control behavior rather than to eliminate the behavior through classical conditioning.

Clinicians have discovered additional practical and political limitations to the use of shock:

1. It causes negative reactions in patients' families and the media, who equate it with torture.
2. Some patients refuse to undertake shock aversion regardless of the consequences and, hence, may drop out of treatment.
3. Its flexibility is limited, as it can only be induced for extremely brief durations, from 0.1 to 0.5 second per stimulus. Thus, it cannot use stimuli that require longer intervals to build sexual arousal, such as slides and stories.
4. It increases nonspecific aggression in some patients.
5. It requires expensive technical equipment.
6. It may reduce the chances of a good patient–therapist relationship (Maletzky, 1980).

Despite these shortcomings, electroshock is still employed in some cognitive and behavioral programs today (Maletzky, 1991a). However, its importance has diminished. In one protocol, the avoidance of shock has been said to reduce deviant arousal: The patient has the option of avoiding shock if he turns off the deviant stimulus in time, an "anticipatory avoidance" paradigm. An escape is available: By disarming shock, the patient avoids the punishment while, at the same time, an appropriate sexual stimulus is displayed (MacCulloch & Feldman, 1967).

Unfortunately, no recent study has separated the different components of therapy with exhibitionists to determine which parts are the most effective. Much of the recent literature describes these procedures for men who molest children or rape. Exhibitionism may be regarded not only as less serious, but atypical as well; it is difficult to define and present the deviant stimuli. Whereas stimuli can be modeled after real-life situations, this is a difficult task when compared with the more aggressive offenses. Slides, videotapes, and scenes of exposing may not trigger arousal in many exhibitionists, especially in a laboratory setting (Maletzky, 1980; Marshall, Eccles, & Barbaree, 1991; Marshall, Payne, et al., 1991). Even worse, the stimuli arousing to an exhibitionist may not be deviant at all, such as coming upon an attractive woman at night in an isolated location. Here, the behavioral response of exposing is deviant, but the arousal itself is not. Moreover, most exhibitionists report fantasizing about normal sexual relationships when they expose (Freund et al., 1988), a situation that might make aversive deconditioning procedures hazardous.

With multiple problems, electroshock aversion has not been cited in the literature extensively since the mid-1980s. Nonetheless, nationwide surveys of current clinical practice give indications that therapists continue to employ it in combination with a variety of other techniques (Knopp, Freeman-Longo, & Stevenson, 1992). One large outpatient clinic reports the use of electroshock as a random substitute for an aversive odor on an average ratio of 10 presentations of odor to 1 of shock (Maletzky, 1991a).

Covert Sensitization

By the mid-1970s, adverse publicity about electric shock aversion and problems with equipment forced many therapists to devise aversive procedures that were less intrusive and easier to administer and which would not alienate the sensitivities of patients' families and the public. While a number of techniques were implemented, covert sensitization emerged as a hopeful replacement for physically aversive procedures.

In this technique the patient first learns relaxation, an optional step designed to increase the likelihood of reliable visualization. In a relaxed state, the patient is then asked to visualize his usual scenes of exposing, followed by an adverse event. For example, a patient who typically exposed to schoolgirls from his car in the early morning was asked to imagine driving by groups of girls on their way to school:

> "As you see their young faces, you start to get hard. You can feel your penis stiffening as you rub it. They notice you! You call the girls over to the car. They don't know what's waiting for them. As they approach, you take it out and begin to jerk off violently. The girls are shocked. They don't know what to do. They're just staring at it as you're about to come, but suddenly there's a pain—you've got your penis stuck in your pants zipper. You try to yank it free but it only catches more. It's starting to bleed and you go soft. The kids are laughing and a policeman is coming over. . . . "

In such scenes the therapist usually adds an escape associated with nonoffending:

> "You're able finally to get your penis back in your pants. You drive off and, as you get away from the kids and exposing, you begin to relax and breath easier now that you've gotten away."

Such scenes commonly contain three elements: (1) the build up of deviant sexual arousal; (2)–an adverse consequence; and (3) an escape associated with not exposing. The elements of aversive conditioning are augmented by the obvious suggestions of escape. There are no data to help us know if all three components are necessary or to what extent each of these contributes to the outcome.

Covert sensitization has won a place in almost all treatment programs professing to treat offenders with a cognitive-behavioral approach (Knopp et al., 1992) because it is easy to implement, requires no expensive or cumbersome equipment, and enjoys the blessing of community approval. Despite multiple advantages, however, covert sensitization has not produced as robust a response as desired (Maletzky, 1991a; McConaghy, 1990). Some patients demonstrate reduction in deviant arousal but no actual behavior change. Others have modest responses and complain that the procedure lacks sufficient power.

Assisted Covert Sensitization

For such patients, an augmented procedure was devised (Maletzky, 1973). After the build up of sexual arousal in an exposing scene, and at the point where aversive imagery begins, a foul odor is also introduced and is continuously presented until the escape portion is reached:

> "As you hide in the bushes you see a woman walking her dog. You see her face and body—she is really well built. You are jerking off as she comes closer. She sees

you and she doesn't know what to do—she is paralyzed, just staring. As you move toward her [foul odor is introduced], you step in some dog crap; it's smeared on your shoes and socks. It's slimy and smelly and it's making you sick. You go soft and try to get out of there but you slip on it and more crap gets on you. You're gagging and the odor is driving you crazy. Chunks of vomit come up in your throat. You try to gag them down but you can't. You vomit all over yourself. Chunks of vomit dribble down your chin and you get some on your clothes. You run home as fast as you can and clean off [foul odor removed]. You can finally breath again. That horrible odor is gone and now that you have gotten away from exposing you can breathe the fresh air again."

As can be seen, this procedure is not simply aversive olfactory conditioning, because no actual conditioned stimulus is employed, such as a slide or a description of exposing. The conditioned stimulus, the scene, is imaginal, although the consequences, the unconditioned stimuli, are real.

The choice of an olfactory stimulus can contribute to the power of this technique. Most commonly, ammonia is used by holding crushable packets of smelling salts under a patient's nose. However, ammonia produces a painful response rather than a nauseous one. It is mediated by the fifth (trigeminal) cranial nerve. Rotting tissue has proven more effective (Maletzky, 1980), perhaps because it travels directly via the first (olfactory) cranial nerve to limbic areas thought to be important in the perception of sexual pleasure. A number of studies have demonstrated that the response of nausea is more powerful than that of pain for reducing harmful consummatory behaviors such as eating, smoking, and sexual response (Franks, Fried, & Ashem, 1966; Foreyt & Kennedy, 1971; Maletzky, 1974, 1993; Maletzky & George, 1973; Morganstern, 1974).

Refinements of this technique in recent years have included the manufacture of odor pumps and automated equipment connecting plethysmograph response to delivery of foul odor (Maletzky, 1991a). However, most presentations of deviant stimuli should be followed by aversion. For effective treatment, one cannot wait for a plethysmographic response, as often, especially for exhibitionists, it may not occur.

Minimal Arousal Conditioning

In a novel use of aversive conditioning principles, Gray (1995) and Jensen and colleagues (1994) found sexual arousal too powerful for deconditioning in some patients and placed the aversive stimulus earlier in the response chain, when minimal arousal was present and before intense sexual pleasure was attained. If possible, this point can then be advanced in the sexual chain increasingly closer to sexual release. While this procedure has not enjoyed extensive experience clinically or in the literature, it is promising for offenders whose arousal levels are too high to follow typical aversion paradigms. Unfortunately, it has not been systematically applied to exhibitionists thus far.

Aversive Behavior Rehearsal

Sometimes inaccurately called *shame therapy* (Serber, 1970), this technique has enjoyed fame and notoriety, as much for its reported efficacy as for its apparent simplicity (Wickramaserka, 1980). It is one of the few techniques especially designed for exhibitionism, although reports indicate its effective use with other paraphilias as well (Maletzky, 1991a). While reported to be markedly effective, its present-day use is considered insensitive, and possibly unethical, although not absolutely contraindicated:

A 23-year-old student could not stop his compulsive exposing to attractive coeds on campus. Arrested twice by security police, he was threatened with expulsion from school unless he obtained therapy. He gave consent for a procedure in which he exposed in a hospital psychiatric setting to male and female staff for a period of three minutes on each of three occasions. The staff was instructed to make no response but merely to watch silently. Following the first session, he reported he lost all urges to expose.

A 62-year-old retired grocer and grandfather frequently exposed from his truck to young girls in the neighborhood. He agreed to expose from his truck to male and female hospital staff who offered no response. He achieved no erection. The procedure was debriefed immediately thereafter. He had not re-exposed at a 9-year follow-up.

Although attractive because of its reported efficacy, drawbacks include the difficulty in obtaining consent, the problems in soliciting staff to participate, the possibility of an adverse effect upon staff, and, in the main, its terribly aversive nature. While submitting exhibitionists to mental anguish might be considered by some as due reward, if other less aversive, yet equally effective techniques exist, it would be difficult to condone its use, a paradox in that its major advances are also its unfortunate drawbacks.

Therapists can employ variations on this theme, however, which still might be of help in a comprehensive treatment program for exhibitionism. The therapist may ask the patient to expose to himself in a mirror and record his observations on tape. He may videotape typical exposing incidents and then view the tape in private. Faced with the reality of their own behaviors, some exhibitionists may recoil at the images of their offenses (Wolfe, 1989).

Vicarious Sensitization

A novel technique recently introduced for the treatment of a variety of sexual offenses contains elements of cognitive restructuring, empathy training, and aversive conditioning. In this procedure, originally crafted for adolescent offenders (Maletzky, 1994; Weinrott & Riggan, in press), an exhibitionist views a series of videotapes depicting adverse outcomes of offending, both likely and improbable. Table 3.2 gives summaries of typical scenarios, depicted on screen by actresses and actors. Although it may appear that this technique is cerebral, a form of cognitive therapy, the effect upon a viewer is often visceral. Many offenders suffer queasy stomachs and a pervasive nausea throughout the tapes and for a variable time thereafter. This result can be enhanced by having the offender view the tapes

---

TABLE 3.2. Vicarious Sensitization Videotaped Vignettes

An experienced inmate describes the brutal rape of a young male sexual offender in prison; the offender is chased across the prison yard.

Neighbors, outraged about an offender's sexual abuse of several girls in their community, chase, then corner him, force him to undress, and subject him to cruel ridicule.

A victim describes the revenge she would like to extract from her offender while, on-screen, scenes are shown of an actual surgical castration and phallectomy.

An adolescent offender is shunned by several groups of high-school girls who whisper about him, point, and make jokes; he complains to friends, who remain unsupportive, that he cannot get a date.

Several victims are shown in various stages of psychological disarray because of their sexual abuse; a young girl attempts suicide; an older woman mourns her life traumatized by the sequelae of the abuse.

alone, rather than in a group. Vicarious sensitization has been applied mainly to adolescents (Weinrott & Riggan, in press) or to men who molest children or rape (Maletzky & McFarland, in press). Its scenarios flow naturally from such aggressive crimes, yet may still have some impact upon exhibitionists, particularly those who expose to children, those whose exposing is frequent enough to warrant incarceration, or those who have some tendency to graduate to hands-on crimes.

Positive Conditioning

While therapists commonly employ the positive reinforcement of arousal as described in some of the techniques above, a variety of positive approaches stand on their own as important contributions to the treatment of exhibitionism.

Social Skills Training

Most therapists believe that the large array of techniques called social skills training are crucial components of a treatment program for the exhibitionist. McFall (1990) has outlined an assessment procedure for social skills deficits and proposed an individualized treatment approach based upon an information-processing analysis of social skills. A variety of such techniques has been helpful for offenders and nonoffenders alike. Female therapists may be particularly effective in applying these approaches to male offenders. Although not easily researched, methods such as cue-assisted learning, psychodrama, assertive training, and the use of *in vivo* relaxation techniques are important parts of most treatment programs' therapeutic arsenals.

Alternative Behavior Completion

Based upon work with the treatment of compulsive gamblers, McConaghy (1993) outlined a procedure reported as helpful to a variety of offenders, including exhibitionists. An offender listens to descriptions of typical exposing situations, including entry into the behavioral chain; however, he successfully tolerates the stimuli evoking urges to expose and completes the chain without exposing, and then leaves the situation in a relaxed state:

> "As you drive home one night you notice an attractive woman driver on your right in a van. She can see right into your car. You slow down and drive parallel with her as you begin to get aroused. You want to rub your penis and take it out to show her. However, the urge this time is weaker than before and you drive past her quickly without exposing. You feel good about yourself for being able to exert control."

This technique is similar to an approach others have termed *success imagery* (Maletzky, 1991a) and is based upon techniques of desensitization already shown to be effective in reducing social anxieties. If proven effective in larger trials, it may indicate that exposing carries with it not only pleasant feelings, but anxious ones as well.

Reconditioning Techniques

A number of techniques appear to stand midway between aversive conditioning and purely cognitive approaches, and perhaps they combine elements of both:

Plethysmographic Biofeedback

While debate swirls around the plethysmograph as an assessment technique, its use in treatment is both less controversial and less publicized. Nonetheless, several authors (Maletzky, 1991a; McConaghy, 1993) mention this potentially important and innovative approach. In this technique, if the exhibitionist shows deviant arousal (not as usual in pure exhibitionists as in other paraphiliacs), the plethysmograph can be automatically or manually connected to an external light or sound device to provide feedback to the patient about his arousal level. Commonly, a bank of colored vertical lights is employed, although an escalating sound can be used as well (Maletzky, 1991a). Red lights can be used to denote higher levels of arousal, orange intermediate levels, and green low levels. The exhibitionist's task during any session might be to keep out of the red area when exposed to deviant stimuli or to keep in the red area with normal stimuli.

Ingenious though it may be, this technique may not be applicable to many exhibitionists, who, as a group, show arousal to exposing scenes at a lower rate than do other offenders to their particular deviant stimuli (Marshall, Payne, et al., 1991). Take care in giving instructions and selecting stimuli for exhibitionists, due to their greater rate of associated paraphilias. Case examples of the successful application of this technique have been published (Maletzky, 1991a), although no controlled studies have been performed.

Masturbation Techniques

Many clinicians believe that pleasure in masturbation and climax are important reinforcers of sexual behavior. Pairing fantasies of deviant sexual imagery with these pleasures repeatedly stamps in deviant arousal. Simple admonitions to offenders to discontinue these pairings probably go unheeded. Additional techniques are needed to decondition the powerful arousal associated with exposing.

Fantasy Change. In this procedure (Maletzky, 1986), an exhibitionist is asked to masturbate to deviant fantasies until the point of ejaculatory inevitability, and at that moment to switch to a nondeviant fantasy. As treatment progresses, the patient is asked to make that switch earlier and earlier in the masturbatory chain until he is masturbating exclusively to nondeviant fantasies. Many therapists request that the offender tape record these sessions aloud to (partially) guarantee compliance.

Satiation. In this technique (Laws & Marshall, 1991; Maletzky, 1986), the offender is asked to masturbate to ejaculation using only nondeviant fantasies; *following* climax, he is asked to masturbate to deviant fantasies again, for lengths of time varying from 30 to 60 minutes. Again, many therapists request that tape recordings are made to ensure that this homework is completed. Actual observations of masturbatory behavior are contraindicated as overly intrusive and quite likely ineffective due to lack of privacy.

This seemingly simple technique has ignited a controversy about why this approach is helpful. Behavior therapists believe that aversive conditioning is the crucial element, as it is clearly unsatisfying to masturbate immediately after ejaculation and, indeed, it may be highly aversive (Maletzky, 1980). In addition, this technique pairs deviant imagery with the point of minimal sexual arousal. Laws (1995) has argued that the important part of this technique is the satiation element. Indeed, some data indicate that simple verbal satiation, with an exhibitionist repeating the same deviant scenes, produces results equal to such repetitions associated with forced masturbation (Laws, 1995). Boredom, fatigue, and deconditioning may all play some active role.

Redirection

As simple as it sounds, merely asking the exhibitionist to refrain from masturbating to fantasies of exposing should probably be a standard request, particularly early in treatment.

An unspoken assumption in these techniques is that deviant arousal exists in exhibitionists and must be deconditioned, a premise which never has been convincingly demonstrated, although apparently most therapists accept it. In addition, it again appears that techniques such as masturbatory satiation, so pertinent and clearly applied to pedophiles and rapists, may not easily transfer to the treatment of exhibitionists. Nonetheless, most clinicians believe that such patients will benefit from these techniques, regardless of theoretical consistency.

Sexual Impulse Control Training

Regardless of its origins, exhibitionist behavior is the end result of a journey of many steps. Constructing obstacles early in this chain may be more effective than designing interventions closer to the sexual pleasure of release. Under the rubric of sexual impulse control training (Maletzky, 1991a), a loose band of techniques attempts to construct such obstacles.

For example, the exhibitionist might be asked to begin masturbating to exposing fantasies, and then stop before ejaculation; or to read about and look at pictures of exposing situations, and then abstain from masturbation or intercourse for at least 24 hours. Partial verification of completing these homework assignments can occur either by asking the offender to tape record masturbation sessions or by interviewing a partner (neither are proof positive). Some therapists might edge out ever further on this limb by asking the exhibitionist to seek out exposing situations, fantasize exposing, and then leave the scene. A bit safer might be the standard homework assignment of approaching these situations, then smelling a foul odor or chewing a bitter tablet. Needless to say, these latter methods are best used after there is verification that arousal has been reduced or that the patient has advanced well in his program.

Cognitive Approaches

Therapists apply a diverse and disparate collection of cognitive techniques widely to offenders to reduce the likelihood of repeated exposing. Because many of these methods appear to be at least somewhat effective, Quinsey and Earls (1990) suggested that all of them may act in a general rather than a specific fashion. At present, it appears unlikely that any one such technique can be isolated and tested in a prospective double-blind study; equally unlikely is a test of cognitive versus behavioral methods, due to ethical concerns in withholding treatment from offenders whose crimes can harm victims in so many ways.

Cognitive therapies are not easily categorized and broad overlap between subcategories exists. Most providers, however, agree that within the cognitive approaches three domains can be identified: recognition and correction of cognitive distortions, relapse prevention, and empathy training. Although many specific reviews describing these approaches can be found (e.g., Laws, 1989), a decided minority focus on exhibitionism. Nonetheless, cognitive therapies can be applied to the treatment of men who expose, often with gratifying results.

Restructuring Cognitive Distortions

Based in part on the work of Yochelson and Samenow (1977), and unfortunately described as "thinking errors," a set of typical distortions, actually assumptions and justifications, has come to be widely recognized in many offenders. For the exhibitionist, examples of frequently used distortions are presented in Table 3.3. Simply labeling these as "errors" rarely leads to significant behavioral change. Incorporating the corrections to these distortions into a *habit of thinking* by frequent, conscious repetition can be helpful. In discussing these, the therapist encourages the offender to practice repetitively giving himself corrective messages often enough for them to become innate, reflexive, automatic responses:

> A middle-aged offender would expose to grade school girls from his front porch. He had practiced several distortions to provide a cognitive approval for his actions:
>
> PATIENT: These girls are too young to be harmed by my exposing.
> THERAPIST: The younger they are, the worse the harm.
>
> PATIENT: Many girls find this amusing.
> THERAPIST: These victims do not know how to respond at the time; later, damage can occur.
>
> PATIENT: I never touched a child, therefore, I didn't molest anyone.
> THERAPIST: Sexual and emotional harm can occur to these victims, affecting some the rest of their lives.

A 15-year-old boy often exposed himself and masturbated in a parking structure when women were returning to their cars. He rationalized the behavior as justifiable:

> PATIENT: These women are older than me and, therefore, cannot be harmed.
> THERAPIST: Women of any age can be traumatized by witnessing an exposure.
>
> PATIENT: These women are enjoying it because they often smile.
> THERAPIST: Many victims are not sure how to respond; smiling does not guarantee lack of adverse impact.

Identification of a distortion is only the first part of treatment. The next, and perhaps more difficult step, is skillfully presenting it as such to the offender. Many exhibitionists are reluctant to endorse a distortion once it is pointed out, as, to most, it is patently false.

TABLE 3.3. Examples of Assumptions and Justifications among Men Who Expose

Category	Self-statement
Attributing blame	"The way she was dressed, she was just asking for it." "I wouldn't have done it if I hadn't been drinking."
Minimizing, or denying, sexual intent	"I was just looking for a place to pee."
Debasing the victim	"She was a slut anyway." "She was always a liar."
Minimizing consequences	"I never touched her, so I couldn't have hurt her." "Exposing is no big deal." "She smiled, so she must have liked it."
Deflecting censure	"It's not like I raped (or molested) anyone." "This happened months (years) ago; why can't everyone forget about it?"
Justifying causes	"If I wasn't molested, I wouldn't have exposed." "If my partner gave in to my sexual demands, I never would have exposed."

The therapist must avoid battering the patient with confrontations, especially at first. Often, these battles hinge on semantics. It is best to accumulate several examples of distortions and urge the patient to make the jump from the specific to the general case. The therapist can help the patient identify and explore faulty cognitions and the role they play in maintaining offensive behaviors. It appears that cognitive distortions may not initiate, as much as they perpetuate, offending behaviors.

A number of scales have been devised to measure distortions, including the Abel and Becker Cognition Scale (Abel et al., 1984) and several subscales (Schlank, 1995) on the Multiphasic Sex Inventory (Nichols & Molinder, 1984). However, these scales have been developed for and tested mainly on men who molest children or rape; no test or combination of tests has been rendered specific for exhibitionism.

There is no reason, however, why these assessment and treatment approaches cannot be applied to the exhibitionist. Question and answer techniques, psychodrama, illustration by example, and role reversal have all been helpful in treatment (Maletzky, 1980). Overlap of exhibitionism with other paraphilias necessitates the identification and inclusion of any other deviant activities as well.

Relapse Prevention

Based upon a treatment approach for addictive behaviors (Marlatt & Gordon, 1985), relapse prevention has been extended to include treatment for many sexual offenders (Pithers, 1990). Although these techniques of relapse prevention have been employed for more aggressive sexual behaviors, exhibitionism is quite suitable for these methods as well.

Central to the use of relapse prevention is the concept of behavior chains and cycles. Exposing is conceived as the culmination of a chain beginning with seemingly innocuous behavior, but gathering momentum in a cascade of behaviors, resulting in the exposing act. Nonoffending behavior can be categorized in this way as well: It is more difficult to recite the national anthem if one has to start in the middle. In chains ending with a strongly pleasurable act, it is much more likely that interventions with optional choices will be successful early, rather than late in the behavioral chain.

A number of antecedents and assumptions comprise the behavioral chain leading to exposing. Taking a walk on a sunny summer day, going to a community pool, and driving around dark parking lots, all can be high-risk behaviors. Simply being in that setting may slightly increase sexual arousal and create a lapse, a desire to expose. If left unchecked at this point, exposing, a relapse, becomes increasingly likely.

Relapse prevention begins with self-awareness and self-scrutiny. The offender is asked to keep a record of lapses and their triggers to be better able to identify dangerous situations early on. Next, stimulus control procedures are put into place:

> A young married exhibitionist would often "forget" something at his office and return at night after supper to retrieve it. Often, when doing so, he would drive through several parking lots and look for isolated women. As part of treatment, he was required to always notify his wife of his whereabouts; she would call him toward the end of the day to remind him to be sure to take any work he needed home with him.

A lapse is not a defeat, but rather an opportunity to learn which stimuli control which behaviors. A relapse is a failure, although that does not preclude learning from it as well.

Therapy incorporating relapse prevention can be provided in a group format. However, individual sessions should be considered as each exhibitionist's patterns may be sufficiently unique to warrant individual study. In addition, the task of problem solving is most powerfully accomplished in one-to-one sessions. The patient and therapist need to review situations of heightened risk and problem solve alternative escape strategies, resulting in the accumulation of sufficient skills to avoid exposing in the future.

If many events predisposing a lapse can be anticipated, they may be circumvented. But identification, while necessary, is not sufficient to prevent a relapse. Discussion must be supplemented with practice. Many therapists demonstrate problem-solving techniques to help the exhibitionist consider his options and to make safe choices. The therapist can review what difficulties the patient has encountered recently, how he handled those situations, and what else he could have done. The steps of brainstorming, evaluation, and option selection are crucial. Repeated practice of this *process* is essential, as these steps must become behavioral habit, rather than intellectual concepts the offender has studied and can repeat by rote but that he rarely practices. Several workbooks, complete with exercises and homework assignments, have proven of benefit in internalizing these concepts (Freeman-Longo & Bays, 1989).

Advocates of relapse prevention have recognized that internal self-management may not prove entirely adequate in halting all sexual offending (Pithers, 1990). The power of sexual reinforcement can be so seductive, and the promise of sexual release so strong, that every conceivable cognition pales in comparison. Measures of *external control* are often necessary as well. Members of the exhibitionist's family, and possibly even those in his workplace, should be informed about high-risk situations and efforts he is making to change. Their reinforcement of these attempts is important—it is often better to reinforce effort and approximations of the final goal than to await ultimate success.

The patient himself can provide a locus of control by equipping himself with reminders of his therapy, such as his particular cognitive distortions, risky situations, and options when temptation appears. Failsafe cards have often proven helpful for such purposes. These commonly list early warning signs and options when urges to expose occur. However, consequences of offending should also be included. Photographs of family members have proven helpful as well when urges to expose occur. While there is no guarantee an offender will employ the cards at moments of intense allure or extreme risk, they can provide a tangible extension of the therapeutic hour.

Some of the strongest allies the therapist has in working with most men who expose are their corrections officers. Many programs now go beyond the routine monthly written reports and incorporate joint sessions with the offender and his parole or probation officer to review situations of risk, signs of lapse, and predictors of imminent relapse (Maletzky & Prueitt, in press).

Empathy Training

Although much has been written about empathy training for the sexual offender (Murphy, 1990), the literature has been largely silent about application of these techniques for exhibitionists. It may be especially important in this group of offenders, however, because of the common misperception that exhibitionism is a victimless crime. Among victims of exhibitionism, predominantly women from prepubertal age to their mid-30s, a host of sequelae can be seen: higher levels of background anxiety, specific phobias of venturing out unaccompanied or at night, nightmares, mistrust of strangers, and trouble relaxing during sexual relations (Cox & Maletzky, 1980).

Although rarely conceptualized as a series of therapies, empathy training can be divided arbitrarily into five segments: (1) identification of the victim; (2) identification of the victimizing act; (3) identification of the harm; (4) role reversal; and (5) development of empathy.

Although *identification of the victim* seems apparent, this is not always so in exhibitionism because many people, including the exhibitionist himself, may not conceive of exhibitionism as creating a victim. The therapist might provide some materials to initiate this process: testimonials from victims of exhibitionism; letters by victims to their exhibitionists; case histories and videotapes of victims describing the trauma due to being victimized; and, in a group setting, face-to-face discussions with several victims.

These techniques can lead naturally to discussions of exhibitionism as *a victimizing act,* in some ways especially traumatic due to its occurrence in public settings outside of specific discriminative stimuli, such as within the confines of a home. Safe settings may turn to ones of menace. In some cases, an approach of a male, even during the day or even with others present, may elicit fear that neither respects cognition nor allows reassurance.

These discussions and techniques can also be employed in *identification of the harm.* Exhibitionists need to become aware of some of the long-term effects of exposing, not only in general, but also specifically associated with their own acts. However, these messages cannot be bludgeoned into a patient; an interchange in therapy is important to allow the offender to arrive at his own conclusion that harm has occurred due to his own acts. Guilt induction is not the primary method nor goal; rather, emotional acceptance, as opposed to intellectual awareness, can be obtained in many men who expose.

Psychodramatic techniques are often employed in treating exhibitionists, especially during several forms of *role reversal.* The offender might be asked how a victim might feel, not only during the act, but thereafter, as the residue of victimization often persists for longer than the exhibitionist realizes. These approaches can often best be applied in group settings in which offenders are asked to portray victims' responses in situations reminiscent of the exposing act, at first in a generalized exposing setting, and then in scenes specifically tailored to each offender. Offenders might also be asked to view an exposing scene on videotape or to expose into a mirror, techniques close to the aversive conditioning approaches already discussed.

From these methods the *development of empathy* can hopefully emerge. While some scales have been developed to measure this domain in a cross-section of offenders (Parker & Parker, 1986; Stermac & Quinsey, 1986), data have by and large been collected only from questionnaires typically given to populations of aggressive offenders (Overholser & Beck, 1986; Segal & Marshall, 1985). Nonetheless, in clinical practice, it is not uncommon to recognize an offender becoming aware that his exposing has hurt others. Flashes of sudden insight are to be mistrusted, but often a therapist sees the exhibitionist not only lip serving the ritual of self-blame, but assuming a more responsible lifestyle, as reflected in his nonsexual behavior as well.

A taxi driver who exposed from his cab to women isolated at night on residential streets would often pull up to them, ostensibly to ask for directions. It was no surprise when he was identified and arrested. As part of treatment, he was asked to write out, and then describe, things that he had gotten away with which no one knew about. He identified a number of acts of pilferage and shoplifting, as well as multiple exposing incidents. He began to talk about cheating on his meter, often inflating customers' bills. He seemed relieved to confess and went on to make specific changes in his lifestyle quite apart from sexual offending.

Empathy training should be seen as not only an adjunctive technique. It forms one foundation upon which treatment rests, especially because many offenders regard exposing as at best, a trivial offense, and at worst, an amusing inconvenience for victims.

Biological Approaches

Based upon work demonstrating some biological abnormalities in sexual offenders in general (Jones & Frei, 1979; Lang et al., 1989) and in some exhibitionists specifically (Bain et al., 1988; Gourmani & Dwyer, 1986), therapists have expressed the hope that somatic treatments might be helpful in this area. Despite promising leads, no controlled study of the use of medications in exhibitionists has been published. Surgical approaches (Heim & Hursch, 1979) are too drastic to be considered in North America. However, several medications have been demonstrated to reduce sexual drive in males and, hence, to afford some protection against reoffending in exhibitionists treated in community settings.

Hormonal Treatment

Medroxyprogesterone acetate (MPA), also known as Depo-Provera, and cyproterone acetate (CPA) are the two medications most studied for the treatment of sexual offenders. Each may act at different points in normal male hormonal functioning to reduce circulating testosterone by increasing its metabolism in the liver (Southern, Gordon, Vittek, & Altman, 1977) and by blocking cellular binding of normal circulating testosterone (Monti, Brown, & Corriveau, 1977). MPA is used in the United States, while CPA, not approved by the Food and Drug Administration (FDA) due to rare liver reactions, enjoys wide use in Canada and the European continent. Both reduce circulating testosterone levels, but researchers do not agree upon how to measure effective doses. Some authors aim to reduce testosterone to prepubertal levels (less than 50 ng/100 ml; Walker, Meyer, Emory, & Robin, 1964), whereas others report a goal of reducing testosterone to 30% to 50% of pretreatment levels (Gagne, 1981). Clinical studies find both criteria adequate in markedly reducing the risk of reoffense in general (Wincze, Bansal, & Malamud, 1986), and with exhibitionists more specifically (Laschet & Laschet, 1975; Langevin et al., 1979; Maletzky, 1991b). Both substances can be administered in a long-acting *depot* form, especially necessary for offenders in mandated treatment. Intramuscular doses have ranged from 400 mg per week to 200 mg twice per month for MPA and 300 mg to 600 mg every 10 days to 3 weeks for CPA. There is little debate about the ability of both hormones to reduce male sexual drive, as demonstrated by a reduction in frequency of erections, self-initiated sexual behaviors, and sexual fantasies as well, with a consequent decrease in masturbation. Although most studies find overall drive to be reduced (Walker & Meyer, 1981; Wincze et al., 1986), some controversy about this point continues (Bradford & Pawlak, 1987). Most offenders studied commented parenthetically that both hormones tend to reduce aggression, a welcome result only for selected offenders. Side effects of both agents have included mild weight gain, headaches, muscle cramping, and rarely, venous clots. Discontinuation due to side effects, however, is infrequent—less than 1% in two large clinical populations of mixed offenders (Maletzky, 1991b; Walker & Meyer, 1981).

As expected, most offenders treated with hormones show a rapid return of deviant drive following the discontinuance of medication, although some dispute this belief (Bradford, 1990). The majority of treatment centers using hormones in North America now combine hormonal treatment with cognitive and behavioral methods in a multimodal approach (Knopp et al., 1992). In such programs the hormone is tapered, then discontinued, while the offender is still under supervision to monitor progress without the drug. The use of hormones remains controversial, with fears that coercion will reduce the therapeutic alliance. In the majority of programs, medication is seen as a necessary stop-gap measure to reduce the chances of reoffending for men in the community who are unlikely to control deviant urges on their own. An unusually high percentage of exhibitionists treated hormonally have suffered prior pre- or postnatal central nervous system damage or as a result of head trauma, and hence may have impaired impulse control (Maletzky, 1991b).

There may be some sexual offenders for whom seasoned clinicians might wish perpetual hormonal care. In Western societies, this wish cannot be converted into reality. We are still not aware of long-term effects, although a number of exhibitionists reportedly have been treated for over 10 years (Walker & Meyer, 1981). Few of these individuals, however, have been pure exhibitionists. Many have had a multitude of paraphilias, with an associated reduction in impulse control and a high rate of offending regardless of consequences, yet they had free access to the community and experienced difficulty participating fully in cognitive and behavioral programs.

Psychotropic Medications

A number of other medications have been proposed for treatment of sexual offenders. These drugs share one trait—they reduce sexual drive. While neuroleptic medications, particularly thioridazine (Mellaril), have been employed (Comings & Comings, 1982), newer serotonin reuptake inhibitors are most often mentioned for the use of treatment-resistant paraphilias. Although the drug most discussed is fluoxetine (Prozac) (Kafka, 1991), clomipramine (Anafranil) was actually the medication first used to reduce deviant sexual arousal (Casals-Ariet & Cullen, 1993).

Both thioridazine and clomipramine reduce sexual drive in the majority of patients taking them, but they also produce side effects ranging from barely tolerable to frankly dangerous (Burnstein, 1983). On the other hand, fluoxetine produces very few side effects and has been used as an antidepressant in psychiatric settings for the past 15 years without any permanent harm. It reduces sexual drive in over 70% of patients (Burnstein, 1983). Because depression of several types, such as dysthymia and major depressive disorder, is not unknown among sexual offenders (Kafka & Prentky, 1994), and because antidepressants reduce depression, they may also reduce the impulsivity that may accompany it (McElroy, Hudson, & Pope, 1992). Moreover, fluoxetine and clomipramine have both been remarkably successful in the treatment of obsessive–compulsive disorder (Jenike, 1990). As sexual offending is often both obsessive in thought and compulsive in deed, some authors have expressed the hope that such agents can reduce the pressure of deviant fantasies and preoccupations (Kafka, 1991; Kreusi, Fine, & Valladares, 1992).

However, no psychotropic medication is as powerful as hormones for reducing sexual drive. Because some pyschotropic agents also produce difficult side effects, at present the use of hormones should be considered the first medical approach for treating exhibitionists dangerous to be at large on a temporary basis until, hopefully, cognitive and behavioral methods take hold.

Efficacy of Treatment Techniques

The literature on treatment for the sexual offender is not impoverished by a lack of outcome studies. Although an earlier review of such studies reached the pessimistic conclusion that inadequate controls and variable rating instruments precluded any judgment about efficacy (Furby, Weinrott, & Blackshaw, 1989), a more recent report offers a differing view—that sufficient documentation and clinical experience warrant a less gloomy outlook (Marshall & Barbaree, 1990). Problems noted in such reviews include short duration of follow-up and varying inclusion criteria. No-treatment control groups are, arguably, unethical, but an ongoing project in California (Marques, 1994, 1996) hopes to avoid this problem through the use of both untreated offender volunteers and nonvolunteers.

Outcome studies of exhibitionists alone are few; this is unfortunate because exhibition-ism counts for between one third (Smulker & Scheibel, 1975) and two thirds (Gebhard, Gagnon, Pomeroy, & Christenson, 1965) of all sexual crimes. In the absence of treatment, by 6 years after discovery, 41% of all exhibitionists had reoffended, and 57% of repeat offenders had (Frisbie & Dondis, 1965). Reviews of individual programs revealed efficacy rates (variably defined) from 5% to 71%. Rooth and Marks (1974) reported high rates of recidivism, up to 67%, for exhibitionists using electric shock aversion alone. Using similar techniques, Evans obtained somewhat better rates: 29% over 1 year (1967) and 14% over 3 years (1970). Covert sensitization alone proved effective in the majority of patients treated by Callahan and Leitenberg (1973). Adding aversive odor to covert sensitization ("assisted covert sensitization") reduced relapse rates to under 25% in 155 exhibitionists (Maletzky, 1974, 1980). The data from California (Marques, 1996) unfortunately were not reported for subtype of offender.

There have been no outcome evaluations using *single*-treatment techniques for exhibi-tionist patients. Multifaceted approaches, however, have been described for a variety of programs for exhibitionists. Two large private clinics have reported repeat offending in 15% (Wolfe, 1989) and 14% (Maletzky, 1987) of exhibitionists over a range of between 1 and 14 years. However, some programs have published relapse rates of 41% (Langevin et al., 1979) and 48% (Marshall & Barbaree, 1990). These latter authors contrasted techniques designed to reduce deviant arousal, such as electric shock aversion, orgasmic reconditioning, masturbatory satiation, and ammonia aversion, with techniques to foster self-control, such as relapse prevention, assertiveness training, social skills training, general cognitive restruc-turing, and anxiety management training. Although their report stressed the superiority of the latter regimen, careful reading dilutes this assertion, as patient numbers were small (21 and 17, respectively), numbers relapsed were even smaller (9 and 4), and the latter group, whose focus of treatment was cognitive and social, also received covert sensitization and ammonia aversion.

Among the approaches attempted to treat exhibitionists, medical treatment, at first ignored in the psychological literature, appears both intriguing and limited. The antiandro-gens MPA and CPA have long been employed in sexual offenders deemed dangerous to be at large. Placebo-controlled studies have not been reported due to ethical concerns, but large case reports (Maletzky, 1991b) indicate a very low rate of recidivism among offenders while taking these medications. These hormones are most often administered under some duress, usually as a condition of probation or parole, and in long-acting intramuscular preparations. The legal and ethical implications of such administration are well-reviewed by Dempsky (1984). Unfortunately, recidivism after termination of antiandrogens is high (Berlin & Meinecke, 1981; Maletzky, 1991b). Therefore, hormones might best be employed in a comprehensive treatment program for exhibitionists, reserved for those at highest risk to reoffend and in the main, for a period of time during which behavioral and cognitive elements in treatment are beginning to take hold. While long-term treatment with these agents has been reported occasionally (Cordoba & Chapel, 1983; Laschet & Laschet, 1975), uncertainties still exist about the possibility of damaging side effects (Neumann, 1977; Walker & Meyer, 1981).

FUTURE DIRECTIONS AND CONCLUSIONS

Estimates of the prevalence of exhibitionism are so variable that epidemiological studies would be helpful to assess the scope of the problem. Of equal import, we need to assess the co-occurrence of a variety of paraphilias and to understand how each might be a part of, distinct from, or preparatory to, the others.

Special populations of exhibitionists have not enjoyed much attention in the scientific literature. Female exposers are not unheard of (McConaghy, 1993), and further reports would be welcomed. While exhibitionism is often the initial crime for adolescent offenders (Saunders & Awad, 1991), exposing behavior is part of a not-uncommon triumvirate, along with voyeurism and pedophilia, in the offender with central nervous system damage (Langevin et al., 1989; Maletzky, 1991b). There are no reports of comparative treatment efficacies for these special populations.

A variety of factors impedes our ability to generalize about treatment effectiveness for exhibitionists. For example, inclusion criteria vary, yet we know that they influence outcome: Exhibitionists with central nervous system damage have greater rates of reoffending (Langevin, 1990), yet many programs exclude such patients. In addition, treatment refusals and high dropout rates are not uncommon. One study reported refusal rates of 67% for electric aversion and 63% for aversive behavior rehearsal (Maletzky, 1980). If a patient begins treatment, then drops out, his next victim may not be cheered by the fact that he is not counted among a clinic's failures. It is imperative that statistics on success tally dropouts as failures.

Sometimes statistics tell just half the tale. Practical issues of treatment expense, refusal and dropout rates, sources of referral, program reputation, ease of access, and inclusion criteria all combine to contribute to patient outcome. If a comprehensive cognitive-behavioral treatment program directed by doctoral-level clinicians treats one exhibitionist for $3,000 and reports a success rate of 95%, is it to be preferred over a simpler program using a single treatment technique (such as covert sensitization, for example) costing $1,000 and yielding a 75% success rate? If 100 exhibitionists are treated with a 75% success rate, at least 75 victims are saved; if 10 are treated with a 90% success rate, just nine victims are spared.

Present assessment techniques frankly are inadequate. Psychological measurement tools are based on conjecture, not on empirical studies of their reliabiity and validity with this population. Confidential surveys should not be a substitute for objective measurement, but our sole physiological device, the plethysmograph, is faulty in several directions—it produces too many false negatives to be useful diagnostically, and occasional but sufficient false positives to render it suspect for forensic purposes. Novel assessment measures, such as the Stroop color test (Greco, 1993) and the Hanson Sex Attitudes Questionnaire (Hanson, Gizzarelli, & Scott, 1994) are unlikely to offer robust validity. The Abel Screen II (G. G. Abel, personal communication, January 13, 1995) offers a promising venue for further research.

There is sufficient biological drift in psychiatry and psychology these days to suggest that physiological reactions may, in the future, detect sexual intent. Biochemical changes occur upon arousal, although rapid and inexpensive detection is problematic. Patterns of central nervous system activity may, in the future, reveal sexual excitement. This is no longer far-fetched fantasy. Work at several medical centers reveals that imagery techniques such as positron emission tomography may be able to detect a specific neural firing pattern upon sexual arousal (R. D. Watson, personal communication, January 12, 1995). It may be best to leave to future ethicists how such biological "mindreading" could be deployed with sufficient sensitivity to protect individual liberties.

It is unlikely that large, controlled, double-blind studies on treatment outcome will occur soon. The pragmatics and ethics of present-day treatment preclude such investigations. Government and private funding of outcome studies for sexual offenders will not be a high priority. Large, clinically based studies, however, can be as valuable as those tightly controlled and can point the way to ever-improving technologies. In addition, making treatment affordable should be a priority, perhaps by teaching, encouraging, and exhorting government agencies to staff and maintain sexual offender treatment programs. Fewer than 10% of county and state community-based mental health treatment facilities now offer sexual offender treatment programs (Damon, 1994). The majority of exhibitionists will, in all likelihood, never be treated, even if their crimes are disclosed, because of lack of funding. Many may be punished and released, never to test how effective treatment might have been. This policy guarantees that there will be no shortage of exhibitionists or victims upon which to conduct future studies.

Clinicians and researchers also have both obligation and opportunity to provide education to a variety of audiences to reduce the damage that exposing causes. Chief among these is the real trauma suffered by a victim, harm often treated lightly, even by victim advocate groups. In addition, we need to address the *prevention* of exhibitionism as thoroughly as we advocate for its treatment. Although public education is not a panacea, it could inform potential exhibitionists and victims of the harm exposing causes, document the numbers of otherwise law-abiding individuals who carry it out, and explain the potential of treatment to reduce its likelihood. Perhaps this will increase the motivation of some offenders to obtain treatment who otherwise are too afraid or too ashamed, or who wish to stop exposing but who cannot. With an increase in the population of exhibitionists entering treatment, hopefully we will be better able to understand the behavior of exposing and, hence, the nature of one of humankind's more unusual passions.

REFERENCES

Abel, G. G., Becker, J. V., Cunningham-Rathner, J., Rouleau, J. L., Kaplan, M., & Reich, S. (1984). *The treatment of child molesters*. Unpublished manuscript. (Available from G. G. Abel, Behavioral Medicine Institute, 3280 Howell Mill Road, Altanta, GA 30327-4101.)

Abel, G. G., Becker, J. V., Murphy, W. D., & Flanagan, F. (1981). Identifying dangerous child molesters. In R. B. Stuart (Ed.), *Violent behavior: Learning approaches to prediction, management, and treatment* (pp. 81–97). New York: Brunner/Mazel.

Abel, G. G., & Rouleau, J. L. (1990). The nature and extent of sexual assault. In W. L. Marshall, D. R. Laws, & H. E. Barbaree (Eds.), *Handbook of sexual assault: Issues, theories, and treatment of the offender* (pp. 9–21). New York: Plenum Press.

Abrams, S. (1991). The use of polygraphy with sex offenders. *Annals of Sex Research, 4*, 239–263.

Anderson, R. D., Gibeau, D., & D'Amora, D. A. (1995). Psychometric characteristics of the Sex Offender Treatment Rating Scale. *Sexual Abuse: A Journal of Research and Treatment, 7*, 221–227.

Association for the Treatment of Sexual Abusers. (1993). *The ATSA practitioner's handbook*. Lake Oswego, OR: Author.

Bailey, K. G. (1991). Human paleopsychopathology: Implications for the paraphilias. *New Trends in Experimental and Clinical Psychiatry, 7*, 5–16.

Bain, S., Langevin, R., Hucker, S., Dickey, R., Wright, P., & Schonberg, C. (1988). Sex hormones in pedophiles: 1. Baseline values of six hormones. 2. The gonadotropin releasing hormone tests. *Annals of Sex Research, 1*, 443–454.

Baker, L. (1985). *Neuropsychological and power spectral EEG characteristics of exhibitionists: A model of sexual deviation*. Unpublished doctoral dissertation, University of Alberta, Edmonton, Canada.

Barr, L. C., Goodman, W. K., McDougle, C. J., Delgado, P. L., Heninger, G. R., Charney, D. S., & Price, L. H. (1994). Tryptophan depletion in patients with obsessive compulsive disorder who respond to serotonin reuptake inhibitors. *Archives of General Psychiatry, 51*, 309–317.

Berlin, F. S., & Meinecke, C. G. (1981). Treatment of sex offenders with antiandrogenic medication: Conceptualization, review of treatment and modalities, and preliminary findings. *American Journal of Psychiatry, 138*, 601–607.

Bradford, J. M. W. (1990). The antiandrogen and hormonal treatment of sex offenders. In W. L. Marshall, D. R. Laws, & H. E. Barbaree (Eds.), *Handbook of sexual assault: Issues, theories, and treatment of the offender* (pp. 297–310). New York: Plenum Press.

Bradford, J. M. W., & McLean, D. (1984). Sexual offenders, violence and testosterone: A clinical study. *Canadian Journal of Psychiatry, 29,* 335–343.

Bradford, J. M. W., & Pawlak, A. (1987). Sadistic homosexual pedophilia: Treatment with cyproterone acetate. *Canadian Journal of Psychiatry, 29,* 335–343.

Brownell, K. D., & Barlow, D. H. (1977). The behavioral measurement and treatment of sexual deviation. In E. Foa & A. Goldstein (Eds.), *The handbook of behavioral interventions* (pp. 302–309). New York: Wiley.

Burnstein, J. G. (1983). *Handbook of drug therapy in psychiatry* Boston: John Wright, PSG.

Butcher, J. N., Dahlstrom, W. G., Graham, J. R., Tellegen, A., & Kassmer, B. (1989). *Minnesota Multiphasic Personality Inventory—2 (MMPI-2): Manual for administration and scoring.* Minneapolis: University of Minnesota Press.

Callahan, E. J., & Leitenberg, H. (1973). Aversion therapy for sexual deviation: Contingent shock and covert sensitization. *Journal of Abnormal Psychology, 81,* 60–73.

Casals-Ariet, C., & Cullen, K. (1993). Exhibitionism treatment with clomipramine. *American Journal of Psychiatry, 150,* 1273–1274.

Comings, D. E., & Comings, B. G. (1982). A case of familial exhibitionism successfully treated with haloperidol. *American Journal of Psychiatry, 139,* 913–915.

Conte, J. R. (1983). Development and use of self-report techniques for assessing sexual functioning: A review and critique. *Archives of Sexual Behavior, 12,* 555–576.

Cordoba, O. A., & Chapel, J. L. (1983). Medroxyprogesterone acetate antiandrogen treatment of hypersexuality in a pedophilic sex offender. *American Journal of Psychiatry, 140,* 1036–1039.

Cox, D. J., & Maletzky, B. M. (1980). Victims of exhibitionism. In D. J. Cox & R. J. Daitzman (Eds.), *Exhibitionism: Description, assessment, and treatment* (pp. 289–293). New York: Garland Press.

Cummings, J. L. (1985). *Clinical neuropsychiatry.* New York: Grune and Stratton.

Damon, P. P. (1994). *Tough issues, hard facts: The report of the National Council on Crime and Delinquency.* Washington, DC: U.S. Government Printing Office.

Debruyn, A., Mandelbaum, K., Sandkujil, L. A., Delvenne, V., Hirsch, D., Staner, L., Mendlewicz, J., & Van Broeckhaven, C. (1994). Nonlinkage of bipolar illness to tyrosine hydroxylase. *American Journal of Psychiatry, 151,* 102–106.

Dempsky, L. S. (1984). The use of Depo-Provera in the treatment of sex offenders. *Journal of Legal Medicine, 5,* 295–322.

Evans, D. R. (1967). An exploratory study into the treatment of exhibitionism by means of emotive imagery and aversive conditioning. *Canadian Psychologist, 8,* 162.

Evans, D. R. (1970). Subjective variables and treatment effects in aversive therapy. *Behaviour Research and Therapy, 8,* 141–152.

Farrenkopf, T. (1984, March). *Assessment techniques for the sexual offender.* Paper presented at the Research Symposium on Sexual Aggression, Simon Fraser University and the Correctional Services of Canada, Vancouver, BC.

Flor-Henry, P., Lang, R. A., Koles, Z. J., & Frenzel, R. R. (1988). Quantitative EEG investigations of genital exhibitionism. *Annals of Sex Research, 1,* 49–62.

Foreyt, J. P., & Kennedy, W. (1971). Treatment of overweight by aversive therapy. *Behaviour Research and Therapy, 9,* 29–34.

Franks, C., Fried, R., & Ashem, B. (1966). An improved apparatus for the aversive conditioning of cigarette smoking. *Behaviour Research and Therapy, 4,* 301–308.

Freeman-Longo, R. E., & Bays, L. (1989). *Who am I and why am I in treatment?* Orwell, CT: Safer Society Press.

Freund, K., & Blanchard, R. (1986). The concept of courtship disorder. *Journal of Sex and Marital Therapy, 12,* 79–92.

Freund, K., & Watson, R. (1990). Mapping the boundaries of courtship disorder. *Journal of Sex Research, 27,* 589–606.

Freund, K., Watson, R., & Rienzo, D. (1988). The value of self-reports in the study of voyeurism and exhibitionism. *Annals of Sex Research, 1,* 243–262.

Frisbie, L. U., & Dondis, E. H. (1965). *Recidivism among treated sex offenders* (California Mental Health Research Monograph No. 5). Sacramento, CA: Department of Mental Hygiene.

Furby, L., Weinrott, M. R., & Blackshaw, L. (1989). Sex offender recidivism: A review. *Psychological Bulletin, 105,* 3–30.

Gagne, P. (1981). Treatment of sex offenders with medroxyprogesterone acetate. *American Journal of Psychiatry, 138,* 644–646.

Gebhard, P. H., Gagnon, J. H., Pomeroy, W. B., & Christenson, C. V. (1965). *Sex offenders.* New York: Harper and Row.

Gourmani, P. D., & Dwyer, S. M. (1986). Serum testosterone levels in sex offenders. *Journal of Offender Counseling Services and Rehabilitation, 11,* 39–45.

Graham, J. R. (1993). *MMPI-2: Assessing personality and psychopathology* (2nd ed.). New York: Oxford University Press.

Gray, S. R. (1995). A comparison of verbal satiation and minimal arousal conditioning to reduce deviant arousal in the laboratory. *Sexual Abuse: A Journal of Research and Treatment, 7,* 143–153.

Greco, E. (1993). The Emotional Stroop Test: A review of the literature. *Psichiatrica e Psicoterapia Analitica, 12,* 219–223.

Hall, G. C. N. (1990). Prediction of sexual aggression. *Clinical Psychology Review, 10,* 229–245.

Hall, G. C. N. (1989). WAIS-Rs and MMPIs of men who have sexually assaulted children: Evidence of limited utility. *Journal of Personality Assessment, 53,* 404–412.

Hanson, R. K., Gizzarelli, R., & Scott, H. (1994). The attitudes of incest offenders: Sexual entitlement and acceptance of sex with children. *Criminal Justice and Behavior, 21,* 187–202.

Heim, N., & Hursch, C. J. (1979). Castration of offenders: Treatment or punishment? A review and critique of recent European literature. *Archives of Sexual Behavior, 8,* 281–304.

Hollister, J. M., Mednick, S. A., Breman, P., & Cannon, T. D. (1994). Impaired central nervous system habituation in those at genetic risk for schizophrenia. *Archives of General Psychiatry, 51,* 552–558.

Howes, R. J. (1995). A survey of plethysmographic assessment in North America. *Sexual Abuse: A Journal of Research and Treatment, 7,* 9–24.

Hucker, S., Langevin, R., Dicky, R., Handy, L., Chambers, J., & Wright, S. (1988). Cerebral damage and dysfunction in sexually aggressive men. *Annals of Sex Research, 1,* 33–47.

Jacobsen, N. S., Follette, W. C., & Revenstorf, D. (1984). Psychotherapy outcome research: Methods for reporting variability and evaluating clinical significance. *Behavior Therapy, 15,* 336–352.

Jenike, M. A. (1990). Drug treatment of obsessive–compulsive disorder. In M. A. Jenike, L. Baer, & W. E. Minichiello (Eds.), *Obsessive–compulsive disorders: Theory and management* (pp. 249–282). Chicago: Year Book Medical Publishers.

Jensen, S., Laws, D. R., & Wolfe, R. (1994, November). *Reduction of sexual arousal: What to do and not do.* Symposium conducted at the 13th annual Research and Treatment Conference of the Association for the Treatment of Sexual Abusers, San Francisco, CA.

Jones, I. H., & Frei, D. (1979). Exhibitionism: A biological hypothesis. *British Journal of Medical Psychology, 52,* 63–70.

Kaemingk, K., Koselka, M., Becker, J. V., & Kaplan, M. S. (1995). Age and adolescent sexual offender arousal. *Sexual Abuse: A Journal of Research and Treatment, 7,* 249–257.

Kafka, M. P. (1991). Successful antiandrogen treatment of nonparaphilic sexual addictions and paraphilias in men. *Journal of Clinical Psychiatry, 52,* 60–65.

Kafka, M. P., & Prentky, R. A. (1994). Preliminary observations of DSM-III-R Axis I comorbidity in men with paraphilias and paraphilia-related disorders. *Journal of Clinical Psychiatry, 55,* 481–487.

Kalichman, S. C. (1991). Psychopathology and personality characteristics of criminal sexual offenders as a function of victim age. *Archives of Sexual Behavior, 20,* 187–197.

Kennedy, W. A., & Foreyt, J. (1968). Control of eating behavior in an obese patient. *Psychological Reports, 23,* 571–573.

Knopp, F. H., Freeman-Longo, R. E., & Stevenson, W. F. (1992). *Nationwide survey of juvenile and adult sex offender treatment programs and models.* Orwell, VT: Safer Society Press.

Kreusi, M. J. P., Fine, S., & Valladares, L. (1992). Paraphilias: A double-blind crossover comparison of clomipramine versus desipramine. *Archives of Sexual Behavior, 21,* 587–593.

Lang, R. A., Langevin, R., Bain, J., Frenzel, R., & Wright, P. (1989). Sex hormone profiles in genital exhibitionists. *Annals of Sex Research, 2,* 67–75.

Langevin, R. (1990). Sexual anomalies and the brain. In W. L. Marshall, D. R. Laws, & H. E. Barbaree (Eds.), *Handbook of sexual assault. Issues, theories, and treatment of the sexual offender* (pp. 103–113). New York: Plenum Press.

Langevin, R., Bain, J., Wortzman, G., Hucker, S., Dickey, R., & Wright, P. (1988). Sexual sadism: Brain, blood, and behavior. In R. A. Prentky & V. L. Quinsey (Eds.), *Human sexual aggression: Current perspectives* (pp. 163–171). New York: New York Academy of Sciences.

Langevin, R., & Lang, R. A. (1987). The courtship disorders. In G. O. Wilson (Ed.), *Variant sexuality: Research and theory* (pp. 202–228). London: Croom Helm.

Langevin, R., Lang, R. A., Wortzman, G., Frenzel, R. R., & Wright, P. (1989). An examination of brain damage and dysfunction in genital exhibitionists. *Annals of Sex Research, 2,* 77–87.

Langevin, R., Paitich, D., Hucker, S., Newman, S., Ramsay, G., Pope, S., Geller, G., & Anderson, C. (1979). The effect of assertiveness training, Provera and sex of therapist in the treatment of genital exhibitionism. *Journal of Behavior Therapy and Experimental Psychiatry, 10,* 275–282.

Langevin, R., Wright, P., & Handy, L. (1990). Use of the MMPI and its derived scales with sex offenders: II. Reliability and criterion validity. *Annals of Sex Research, 3,* 453–486.

Laschet, U., & Laschet, L. (1975). Antiandrogens in the treatment of sexual deviations of men. *Journal of Steroid Biochemistry, 6,* 821–826.

Laws, D. R. (Ed.). (1989). *Relapse prevention with sex offenders.* New York: Guilford Press.

Laws, D. R. (1995). Verbal satiation: Notes on procedure with speculations on its mechanism of effect. *Sexual Abuse: A Journal of Research and Treatment, 7,* 155–166.

Laws, D. R., & Marshall, W. L. (1991). Masturbatory reconditioning with sexual deviates: An evaluative review. *Advances in Behavior Research and Therapy, 13,* 13–25.

Levin, S. M., Barry, S. M., Gambero, S., Wolfinsohn, L., & Smith, A. (1977). Variations of covert sensitization in the treatment of pedophilic behavior: A case study. *Journal of Consulting and Clinical Psychology, 10,* 896–907.

LoPiccolo, J., & Steger, J. C. (1974). The sexual interaction inventory: A new instrument for assessment of sexual dysfunction. *Archives of Sexual Behavior, 3,* 585–595.

MacCulloch, M. J., & Feldman, M. P. (1967). Aversion therapy in the management of 43 homosexuals. *British Medical Journal, 2,* 594–597.

MacCulloch, M. J., Waddington, J. L., & Sanbrook, J. E. (1978). Avoidance latencies reliably reflect sexual attitude during aversive therapy for homosexuality. *Behavior Therapy, 9,* 562–577.

Maletzky, B. M. (1973). "Assisted" covert sensitization: A preliminary report. *Behavior Therapy, 4,* 117–119.

Maletzky, B. M. (1974). Assisted covert sensitization in the treatment of exhibitionism. *Journal of Consulting and Clinical Psychology, 42,* 34–40.

Maletzky, B. M. (1980). Assisted covert sensitization. In D. J. Cox & R. J. Daitzman (Eds.), *Exhibitionism: Description, assessment, and treatment* (pp. 187–251). New York: Garland Press.

Maletzky, B. M. (1986). Orgasmic reconditioning. In A. S. Bellack & M. Hersen (Eds.), *Dictionary of behavior therapy techniques* (pp. 57–58). New York: Pergamon Press.

Maletzky, B. M. (1987, October). *Data generated by an outpatient sexual abuse clinic.* Paper presented at the annual conference of the Association for the Treatment of Sexual Abusers, Newport, OR.

Maletzky, B. M. (1991a). *Treating the sexual offender.* Newbury Park, CA: Sage.

Maletzky, B. M. (1991b). The use of medroxyprogesterone acetate to assist in the treatment of sexual offenders. *Annals of Sex Research, 4,* 117–129.

Maletzky, B. M. (1993). Factors associated with success and failure in the behavioral and cognitive treatment of sexual offenders. *Annals of Sex Research, 6,* 239–247.

Maletzky, B. M. (1994, November). *Advanced techniques in behavioral conditioning for the sexual offender.* Workshop presented at the annual conference of the Association for the Treatment of Sexual Abusers, San Francisco, CA.

Maletzky, B. M., & George, F. S. (1973). The treatment of homosexuality by "assisted" covert sensitization. *Behaviour Research and Therapy, 11,* 655–657.

Maletzky, B. M., & McFarland, B. (in press). Vicarious sensitization in the treatment of adult nonparaphilic sexual offenders: A pilot study. *Sexual Abuse: A Journal of Research and Treatment.*

Maletzky, B. M., & Price, R. C. (1984). Public masturbation in men: Precursor to exhibitionism? *Journal of Sex Education and Therapy, 10,* 131–136.

Maletzky, B. M., & Prueitt, M. A. (in press). A sexual offender's orientation group: Introduction to therapy. *Sexual Abuse: A Journal of Research and Treatment.*

Marlatt, G. A., & Gordon, J. R. (Eds.). (1985). *Relapse prevention: Maintenance strategies in the treatment of addictive behaviors.* New York: Guilford Press.

Marques, J. K. (1994, November). *New outcome data from California's Sex Offender Treatment and Evaluation Project.* Paper presented at the annual conference of the Association for the Treatment of Sexual Abusers, San Francisco, CA.

Marques, J. K. (1996, November). *The California Sex Offender Treatment and Evaluation Project: New data.* Paper presented at the annual conference of the Association for the Treatment of Sexual Abusers, San Francisco, CA.

Marshall, W. L., & Barbaree, H. E. (1988). *Erectile responses of exhibitionists to the act of exposing.* Unpublished manuscript, Queen's University, Kingston, Ontario.

Marshall, W. L., & Barbaree, H. E. (1990). Outcome of comprehensive cognitive-behavioral treatment programs. In W. L. Marshall, D. R. Laws, & H. E. Barbaree (Eds.), *Handbook of sexual assault: Issues, theories, and treatment of the offender* (pp. 363–385). New York: Plenum Press.

Marshall, W. L., Barbaree, H. E., & Butt, J. (1988). Sexual offenders against male children: Sexual preferences. *Behaviour Research and Therapy, 29,* 37–40.

Marshall, W. L., Earls, C. M., Segal, Z., & Darke, J. (1983). A behavioral program for the assessment and treatment of sexual aggressors. In K. D. Craig & R. J. McMahon (Eds.), *Advances in clinical therapy* (pp. 148–174). New York: Brunner/Mazel.

Marshall, W. L., Eccles, A., & Barbaree, H. E. (1991). The treatment of exhibitionists: A focus on sexual deviance versus cognitive and relationship features. *Behaviour Research and Therapy, 29,* 129–135.

Marshall, W. L., & Hall, G. C. N. (1995). The value of the MMPI in deciding forensic issues in accused sexual offenders. *Sexual Abuse: A Journal of Research and Treatment, 7,* 205–219.

Marshall, W. L., Payne, K., Barbaree, H. E., & Eccles, A. (1991). Exhibitionists: Sexual preferences for exposing. *Behaviour Research and Therapy, 29,* 37–40.

McAnulty, R. D., & Adams, H. E. (1992). Validity and ethics of penile circumference measures of sexual arousal: A reply to McConaghy. *Archives of Sexual Behavior, 21,* 177–186.

McConaghy, N. (1990). Sexual deviation. In A. S. Bellack, M. Hersen, & P. E. Kazdin (Eds.), *International handbook of behavior therapy and modification* (2nd ed., pp. 565–580). New York: Plenum Press.

McConaghy, N. (1993). *Sexual behavior: Problems and management.* New York: Plenum Press.

McConaghy, N., Armstrong, M. S., & Blaszczynski, A. (1981). Controlled comparisons of aversive therapy and covert sensitization in compulsive homosexuality. *Behaviour Research and Therapy, 19,* 425–434.

McConaghy, N., Blaszczynski, A., & Kidson, W. (1988). Treatment of sex offenders with imaginal desensitization and/or medroxyprogesterone. *Acta Psychiatrica Scandinavica, 77,* 199–206.

McElroy, S., Hudson, J. I., & Pope, H. G. (1992). The DSM-III-R impulse control disorders not otherwise classified: Clinical characteristics and relationship to other psychiatric disorders. *American Journal of Psychiatry, 149,* 318–327.

McFall, R. M. (1990). The enhancement of social skills. In W. L. Marshall, D. R. Laws, & H. E. Barbaree (Eds.), *Handbook of sexual assault: Issues, theories, and treatment of the offender* (pp. 311–330). New York: Plenum Press.

McGrath, R. J. (1991). Sex-offender risk assessment and disposition planning: A review of empirical and clinical findings. *International Journal of Offender Therapy and Comparative Criminology, 35,* 328–350.

Monti, P. M., Brown, W. A., & Corriveau, D. D. (1977). Testosterone and components of aggressive and sexual behavior in man. *American Journal of Psychiatry, 134,* 692–694.

Morganstern, K. (1974). Cigarette smoking as a noxious stimulus and self-managed aversion therapy for compulsive eating. *Behavior Therapy, 2,* 255–260.

Murphy, W. D. (1990). Assessment and modification of cognitive distortions in sex offenders. In W. L. Marshall, D. R. Laws, & H. E. Barbaree (Eds.), *Handbook of sexual assault: Issues, theories, and treatment of the offender* (pp. 331–342). New York: Plenum Press.

Nadler, R. D. (1988). Sexual aggression in the great apes. In R. A. Prentky & V. L. Quinsey (Eds.), *Human sexual aggression: Current perspectives* (pp. 154–162). New York: New York Academy of Sciences.

Nagayama Hall, G. C., Proctor, W. C., & Nelson, G. M. (1988). Validity of physiological pedophilic sexual arousal in a sexual offender population. *Journal of Consulting and Clinical Psychology, 56,* 118–122.

Nichols, H. R., & Molinder, I. (1984). *Multiphasic Sex Inventory manual.* Tacoma, WA: Authors.

Neumann, F. (1977). Pharmacology and potential use of cyproterone acetate. *Hormones and Metabolic Research, 9,* 1–13.

Overholser, J. C., & Beck, S. (1986). Multimodal assessment of rapists, child molesters, and three control groups on behavioral and psychological measures. *Journal of Consulting and Clinical Psychology, 54,* 682–687.

Papp, L., Klein, D. F., & Gorman, J. M. (1993). Carbon dioxide hypersensitivity, hyperventilization and panic disorder. *American Journal of Psychiatry, 150,* 1149–1157.

Parker, H., & Parker, S. (1986). Father–daughter sexual abuse: An emerging perspective. *American Journal of Orthopsychiatry, 56,* 531–549.

Pithers, W. D. (1990). Relapse prevention with sexual aggressors. In W. L. Marshall, D. R. Laws, & H. E. Barbaree (Eds.), *Handbook of sexual assault: Issues, theories, and treatment of the offender* (pp. 343–361). New York: Plenum Press.

Quinsey, V. L., & Earls, C. M. (1990). The modification of sexual preference. In W. L. Marshall, D. R. Laws, & H. E. Barbaree (Eds.), *Handbook of sexual assault: Issues, theories, and treatment of the offender* (pp. 219–295). New York: Plenum Press.

Rooth, G., & Marks, I. M. (1974). Persistent exhibitionism: Short-term response to aversion, self-regulation, and relaxation treatments. *Archives of Sexual Behavior, 8,* 227–248.

Sajwaj, T., Libert, J., & Agras, S. (1974). Lemon-juice therapy: The control of life-threatening rumination in a six-month old infant. *Journal of Applied Behavior Analysis, 7,* 557–563.

Saunders, E. B., & Awad, G. A. (1991). Male adolescent sexual offenders: Exhibitionism and obscene phone calls. *Child Psychiatry and Human Development, 21,* 169–178.

Schiavi, R. C., Derogatis, L. R., Kuriansky, J., O'Connor, D., & Sharpe, I. (1979). The assessment of sexual function and marital interaction. *Journal of Sex and Marital Therapy, 5,* 169–224.

Schlank, A. M. (1995). The utility of the MMPI and the MSI for identifying a sexual offender typology. *Sexual Abuse: A Journal of Research and Treatment, 7,* 185–194.

Segal, Z. V., & Marshall, W. L. (1985). Self-report and behavioral assertion in two groups of sexual offenders. *Journal of Behavior Therapy and Experimental Psychiatry, 16,* 223–229.

Serber, M. (1970). Shame aversion therapy. *Journal of Behavior Therapy and Experimental Psychiatry, 1,* 213–215.

Singer, B. (1985). A comparison of evolutionary and environmental theories of erotic response: Part I. Structural features. *Journal of Sex Research, 21,* 229–257.

Smulker, A. J., & Schneibel, D. (1975). Personality characteristics of exhibitionists. *Diseases of the Nervous System, 36,* 600–603.

Southern, A. L., Gordon, G. G., Vittek, J., & Altman, K. (1977). Effect of progestogens on androgen metabolism. In L. Martini & M. Motta (Eds.), *Androgens and antiandrogens* (pp. 263–279). New York: Raven Press.

Stermac, L. E., & Quinsey, V. L. (1986). Social competence among rapists. *Behavioral Assessment, 8,* 171–185.

Walker, P. A., & Meyer, W. J. (1981). Medroxyprogesterone acetate treatment for paraphilic sex offenders. In J. R. Hays, T. K. Roberts, & K. S. Solway (Eds.), *Violence and the violent individual* (pp. 353–373). New York: S. P. Medical and Scientific Books.

Walker, P. A., Meyer, W. J., Emory, L. E., & Robin, A. L. (1964). Antiandrogenic treatment of the paraphilias. In H. C. Spencer, R. E. Garfinkel, & V. M. Ranoff (Eds.), *Guidelines for the use of psychotropic drugs* (pp. 318–327). Jamaica, NY: Spectrum Publications.

Weinrott, M. R., & Riggan, M. (in press). Vicarious sensitization: A new method to reduce deviant arousal in adolescent sex offenders. *Archives of Sexual Behavior.*

Wickramaserka, I. (1980). Aversive behavior rehearsal: A cognitive-behavioral procedure. In D. J. Cox & R. J. Daitzman (Eds.), *Exhibitionism: Description, assessment, and treatment* (pp. 123–149). New York: Garland Press.

Wincze, W. P., Barsal, S., & Malamud, M. (1986). Effects of medroxyprogesterone acetate on subjective arousal, arousal to erotic stimulation, and nocturnal penile tumescence in male sex offenders. *Archives of Sexual Behavior, 15,* 293–305.

Wolfe, R. (1989, October). *Novel techniques in treating the sexual offender.* Workshop presented at the annual conference of the Association for the Treatment of Sexual Abusers, Seattle, WA.

Yochelson, S., & Samenow, S. E. (1977). *The criminal personality: Vol. II. The change process.* New York: Jason Aronson.

4

FETISHISM

Psychopathology and Theory

Fiona L. Mason

> *Fetish,* a natural or artificial object (as an animal tooth or a wood
> carving) believed among a primitive people to have a preternatural
> power to protect or aid its owner often because of ritual
> consecration or animation by a spirit; broadly: any material object
> regarded with superstitious or extravagant trust or reverence.
> *Webster's Third New International Dictionary Unabridged (1986)*

The term "fetish," as defined above, is derived from the Portuguese, *fetiço.* Scholars believe that this word originated after the discovery by Portuguese explorers in the 15th century of the worship of carved wooden figures or stones by the indigenous people of West Africa (Greenacre, 1979). In 1760 the French anthropologist, Charles de Brosses, conducted a study of the role of such figures, and the word "*fetiço*" was subsequently incorporated into general use (Nagler, 1957; Wise, 1985). A century later the word "fetishism" was applied to sexually motivated behaviors by both Binet (1887) and Krafft-Ebing (1886/1965). The latter, in his celebrated book *Psychopathia Sexualis,* defined a "fetich" [*sic*] as "an object, or parts or attributes of objects, which by virtue of association to sentiment, personality, or absorbing ideas, exert a charm . . . or at least produce a peculiar individual impression which is no wise connected with the external appearance of the sign, symbol or fetich" (p. 11). He went on to describe "fetishism" as "the individual valuation of the fetich extending even to unreasoning enthusiasm" (p. 11).

In common with other sexual disorders, the term "fetishism" encompasses a spectrum of thoughts and behaviors from the normal to the abnormal. Knowledge of the patterns of normal sexual behavior is extremely limited, and without accurate details regarding normality it is almost impossible to clearly define the "abnormal." Kinsey, Pomeroy, and Martin (1948) attempted to describe sexual behavior in men, and later in women (Kinsey, Pomeroy, Martin, & Gebhard, 1953), although, in fact, it is in the latter publication that they examined the concept of fetishism in more detail. Unfortunately, however, they provided no data to support their statement that "persons who respond only to objects which are remote from the sexual partner, or remote from the overt sexual activities with a partner, are not rare in the population" (pp. 678–679).

Krafft-Ebing (1886/1965) recognized the existence of "normal" patterns of fetishistic behavior, and described "physiological fetichism" [sic] in addition to various forms of "pathological fetishism," speculating that these forms represented opposite ends of a spectrum rather than distinct entities. He applied the former term to the sexual preferences expressed by "normal" men and women that lead to a partiality for those with, for example, a particular hair color or body shape. Krafft-Ebing stated that these preferences were not pathological "so long as [their] leading qualities represent the integral parts, and so long as the love engendered by [them] compromises the entire mental and physical personality" (p. 12; i.e., there was not the "unreasoning enthusiasm" described above, which by its nature would preclude an appreciation of the whole). This concept, although delineated over 100 years ago, has persisted and is now incorporated into modern diagnostic criteria as will be seen below.

Many cultures now tolerate expression of fetishistic preferences, and organizations exist which cater to those with such preferences. Gosselin and Wilson (1980) undertook research designed to examine the sexual variations in fetishism, sadomasochism, and transvestism and were able to contact and investigate 125 fetishists through two such organizations. In contrast, Chalkley and Powell (1983), who examined the discharge register of a large London teaching hospital, found only 48 cases of clinical sexual fetishism in a 20-year period.

Given the proliferation of organizations of the kind contacted by Gosselin and Wilson, and the relative scarcity of fetishists presenting to professionals, we can safely assume that clinicians will only see a small proportion of the total population. We also recognize that those with sexual "disorders" present for help only when the disorder is causing either themselves or their partners distress or difficulty (Christie-Brown, 1983). It follows that those fetishists who are seen by clinicians will be uncharacteristic of fetishists in the population (Wise, 1985) and that current knowledge of the psychopathology of fetishism will therefore have been drawn from an unrepresentative sample. However, these biases may be less of a concern to clinicians, as they tend to want information that is applicable to clinical samples.

It also follows that, as information is gained for the most part from single, detailed case reports or a single author's clinical experience, the descriptions of psychopathology and proposed etiologies will also be limited by the relative rarity of fetishism in clinical practice.

This chapter reviews the psychopathology and theories postulated to explain fetishism and will concentrate on the abnormal or pathological forms. In the last 100 years authors from many disciplines have examined the concept of fetishism from many perspectives, including the sociocultural, sociobiological, ethological, biological, behavioral, and psychodynamic, I review all of these, although placing theoretical models of etiology in context is somewhat difficult, as little epidemiological evidence has been published.

DIAGNOSTIC CRITERIA

Before examining the disorder of fetishism in further detail, bearing in mind that not all fetishistic thought or behavior constitutes a disorder, it is essential to describe and define what is meant by fetishism in diagnostic terms. Both the *International Classification of Diseases 10* (ICD-10) of the World Health Organization (1988), and the fourth edition of the *Diagnostic and Statistical Manual of Mental Disorders* (DSM-IV) of the American Psychiatric Association (1994) include fetishism as a subcategory. ICD-10 lists fetishism under "disorders of sexual preference" (F 65.0), while DSM-IV places this disorder in the category of "paraphilias" (302.81).

Despite this difference in terminology, both classification systems define fetishism in terms of the use of, or reliance on, nonliving objects as a stimulus for sexual arousal and gratification. ICD-10 states that the disorder should only be diagnosed if the fetish is the most important source of sexual stimulation or essential for satisfactory sexual response, and that fetishistic fantasies amount to a disorder only if they lead to rituals that are so compelling and unacceptable as to interfere with sexual intercourse and cause the individual distress. DSM-IV stipulates similar diagnostic criteria (see Table 4.1).

As seen in Table 4.1, modern diagnostic criteria exclude body parts from the definition of fetishism. DSM-IV denotes a separate category of "partialism" (exclusive focus on parts of the body) under "302.9 paraphilia not otherwise specified." Similarly, ICD-10, although not specifying partialism, would allow for classification under "F65.8 other disorders of sexual preference." Necrophilia (corpses), and other conditions such as zoophilia (animals), coprophilia (feces), and urophilia (urine), are also regarded by some authors as fetishisms (e.g., Stoller, 1986), and although modern diagnostic criteria also categorize these conditions under 302.9 and F65.8, I will not give them further specific consideration in this chapter. The theoretical models are outlined below are, however, applicable to these.

Note also that separate categories exist for transvestic fetishism (DSM-IV, 302.3 transvestic fetishism, and ICD-10, F65.1 fetishistic transvestism). While this latter category is generally accepted as being a separate entity, the exclusion of partialism has provoked much debate and is in contrast to operational definitions of fetishism given by many authors who include part-objects (e.g., Langevin, 1983; Wise, 1985). Bancroft (1989) argued that partialism should be considered part of fetishism in the broadest sense and De Silva (1993) argued that the exclusion of partialism unnecessarily narrows the range of fetishistic urges and behaviors. Marks (1972) also argued that understanding of this subject will only improve if a loose concept of fetishism is adopted and larger samples thus are studied.

As most authors include body parts as fetishes, I will follow a similar principle in this text and will include partialism. I will not, however, consider transvestic fetishism in any detail, as it is covered elsewhere (Zucker & Blanchard, Chapter 14, this volume; Adshead, Chapter 15, this volume).

EPIDEMIOLOGY

Prevalence and Incidence

As is the case with many other sexual disorders, there is no sound epidemiological data for fetishism. However, it is widely accepted that pathological fetishism is rare. Curren (1954) found only five cases with fetishism as the primary problem out of a series of 4,000 patients seen in private practice.

Crepault and Couture (1980) interviewed 94 men about their sexual fantasies. Unfortunately, although their questionnaire contained some references to partialistic fantasy, there

---

TABLE 4.1. DSM-IV Diagnostic Criteria for Fetishism

A. Over a period of at least 6 months, recurrent, intense sexually arousing fantasies, sexual urges, or behaviors involving the use of nonliving objects (e.g., female undergarments).

B. The fantasies, sexual urges, or behaviors cause clinically significant distress or impairment in social, occupational, or other important areas of functioning.

C. The fetish objects are not limited to articles of female clothing used in cross-dressing (as in Transvestic Fetishism) or devices designed for the purpose of tactile genital stimulation (e.g., a vibrator).

Note. From American Psychiatric Association (1994, p. 526). Copyright 1994 by the American Psychiatric Association. Reprinted by permission.

were no specific questions about inanimate objects. They reported that 77.7% of their subjects admitted to having used the fantasy "scene where you imagine part of a female body" (p. 570), and 50% admitted to having used the fantasy "scene where you are with a woman wearing exciting clothing and accessories" (p. 570).

Gosselin and Wilson (1980) found that fetishistic fantasies were common in all groups that they examined (64% of sadomasochists and 59% of transvestites) and reported that 18% of their control sample also reported having fetishistic fantasies. Chalkley and Powell (1983) identified fetishists from the discharge register of a psychiatric hospital. Only 0.8% of all patients over a 20-year period were identified as fetishists.

Given the discrepancies in the findings of Gosselin and Wilson (1980; 18% of the control group reporting fetishistic fantasies) and Chalkley and Powell (1983; 0.8% of patients identified as fetishists), it is reasonable to conclude that only a small minority of fetishists present for treatment.

Sex Differences

Evidence relating to the development of sexual preferences in women is generally more limited than that relating to men, and this is particularly true of fetishism. We know that fetishism is significantly more common for males than for females; however, given the lack of any sound epidemiological evidence, exact proportions are unknown. Although rare, female fetishists are reported in the literature (e.g., Krafft-Ebing, 1886; Zavitzianos, 1971), but some authors (e.g., Greenacre, 1979) argue that the frequency of occurrence in women is not as low as was previously thought. In Chalkley and Powell's (1983) group of 48 fetishists only one was a woman, a lesbian with a fetish for breasts. Given her homosexual orientation and the nature of the fetish (a secondary sexual characteristic) it could in fact be argued that this subject was not a true fetishist.

Various authors have postulated theoretical models to explain these differences, some of which are worthy of review. Kinsey et al. (1953) noted that they saw only one or two cases of fetishism in their female cohort. They suggested that the difference in incidence between males and females depended upon the fact that the male is more easily conditioned by his sexual experiences and by objects that were associated with those experiences. Bancroft (1989) stated that there is some evidence in mammals of innate sexual preferences being confined to females, and speculated therefore, that as women have less learning to do than men in establishing their sexual preferences, there is less scope for "error." He also postulated that the lack of a clear genital signal (i.e., an erect penis) in women protects against learning sexual responses to abnormal stimuli.

Gosselin and Wilson (1980) also explained the predominance in males by pointing out the visual nature of fetishism, the sensitivity of men to visual stimuli, and the strong biofeedback supplied by the penis. Wilson (1987) examined the issue from an ethological standpoint, arguing that sexual drive is predominantly determined by the need to ensure

TABLE 4.2. Sources of Referral

Referral initiated by	Number of patients
Legal sources (e.g., courts, probation, or police)	13
Patient (through GP)	14
Family or close friends (through GP)	5
Reasons other than fetishism (through GP)	10

Note. GP = general practitioner. From Chalkley & Powell (1983).

TABLE 4.3. Number of Fetishes per Patient

Number of fetishes	Number of patients
1	17
2	9
3	12
4	6
5	1
6	1
7	1
9	1

Note. From Chalkley & Powell (1983).

gene survival. Therefore, as females have a limited number of eggs, the identification of an appropriate sexual partner gets greater priority.

Flor-Henry (1987) examined the role of prenatal factors in determining the differential cerebral organization of men and women, suggesting that testosterone-dependent neuro-chemical interactions determine the organization of lateralized cognitive systems in males and females. Male specialization hinges on interactions between the left hemisphere and testosterone, which slows the rate of development of this dominant hemisphere. Flor-Henry proposed that this process renders the male more susceptible to aberrant sexual programming and that the gender differences in sexual deviations can be accounted for by the combination of this increased vulnerability and men's more lateralized patterns of verbal and visuospatial cognitive functioning. Pitcher (1990) also alluded to the possible sensitizing effects of prenatal hormones on brain development as a possible explanation for gender differences in fetishism.

Welldon (1992) argued that the difference between male and female perversion lies in the aim of the act of perversion. She concluded that, whereas for men the act is aimed at an external part-object, for women it is aimed against themselves. Zavitzianos (1971) reviewed the analytic view of fetishism, and presented a case of the analysis of a 20-year-old female psychopath who showed several perverse tendencies including fetishism. He argued that this patient used the fetishes as penis substitutes to deny the female genitalia and to gratify her incestuous wishes for her father. Zavitzianos (1971) concluded by offering analytically based theoretical models to explain the relatively low incidence of fetishism in females.

These theoretical models may, in part, explain the different incidence of fetishism in men and women. However, as information is almost entirely based on the rare, single-case

TABLE 4.4. Psychiatric Diagnoses in Addition to Fetishism

Additional diagnosis	Number of patients
Paranoid schizophrenia	3
Depression/reactive depression/depressive neurosis	7
Anxiety neurosis	2
Personality disorder	13
Sexual dysfunction or deviation (excluding fetishism and homosexuality)	9

Note. From Chalkley & Powell (1983).

reports of female fetishists and on extrapolations of theoretical models relating to the development of sexuality in general, we must regard any conclusions drawn as speculative.

CLINICAL FEATURES

As indicated above, the clinical features described in the literature may not be representative of the disorder as a whole, given the limitations in the sampling methods used. Two studies have attempted to overcome the considerable lack of data on this topic by describing larger populations (Chalkley & Powell, 1983; Gosselin & Wilson, 1980). Chalkley and Powell (1983) identified 48 subjects with "clinical sexual fetishism" from a teaching hospital's discharge register. Note that although the sample included those who wore their fetishistic object, and thus could be classified as transvestic fetishists, much of the data provided by Chalkley and Powell remains relevant. These authors found that 47 of the subjects were males with a median age of 28 years (range, 12–59 years). Ten patients stated a homosexual sexual preference. Other results from this study, examining the sources of referral of the patients and the number of fetishes for each patient, are presented below (Tables 4.2 and 4.3, respectively).

Chalkley and Powell (1983) found that the subjects in their sample utilized a variety of fetishes (including parts of the body, clothes, soft material and fabrics, footwear, leather, and rubber) in a variety of ways (e.g., fondling, sucking, stealing, rolling in, burning, cutting, gazing at, and seeing someone dressed in). Of the 48 patients, 16 had one additional psychiatric classification and 13 had more than one (see Table 4.4).

Gosselin and Wilson (1980) examined a nonclinical population of 125 fetishists, 87 of whom were "rubberites" and 38 of whom were "leatherites." They compared these samples with male controls, sadomasochists, and transvestites; each group completed the Eysenck Personality Questionnaire (EPQ; Eysenck & Eysenck, 1975) and the Wilson Sexual Fantasy Questionnaire (WSFQ; Wilson, 1978). Although methodologically flawed in parts (e.g., different versions of the EPQ were used for different fetishism groups), the study nevertheless provided some useful insights into fetishism as it exists outside of a clinical setting. Some of the findings included:

1. There was considerable overlap in fantasy material between the sadomasochistic and fetishistic groups (especially the "leatherites").
2. Fetishists scored higher than did controls on measures of impersonal sexual fantasy.
3. "Leatherites" were indistinguishable from controls in terms of personality.
4. Noting that "rubberites" completed a slightly different version of the EPQ, they scored higher than did controls on measures of introversion and emotionality.
5. Fewer "leatherites" than controls rated their mothers as good women (37% versus 95% for controls). Data were not available for "rubberites."

Both the study outlined above and the case reports scattered throughout the literature note the early onset of interest in the fetish and the persistence of that interest throughout life. McConaghy (1993) reported on his clinical experience with fetishists and noted that most recall a strong interest in the fetish in childhood, the interest becoming sexually arousing at puberty.

ASSOCIATED FEATURES

The links between fetishism, transvestism, and homosexuality have been commented on in the literature for many years. However, scientific evidence for links between fetishism and

TABLE 4.5. Percentage of Patients with a Secondary Diagnosis, When the Primary Diagnosis Is Fetishism (*n* = 12)

Secondary diagnosis	%
Pedophilia (all types) (*n* = 5)	41
Rape (*n* = 1)	8
Exhibitionism (*n* = 1)	8
Voyeurism (*n* = 1)	8
Frottage (*n* = 1)	8
Obscene mail (*n* = 1)	8
Transvestism (*n* = 4)	33
Sadism (*n* = 2)	17
Masochism (*n* = 4)	33
Public masturbation (*n* = 2)	17

other sexual variations, has only been produced more recently. Both Crepault and Couture (1980) and Gosselin and Wilson (1980) noted the considerable overlap in fantasy material in their subjects. As noted above, of particular interest is the latter study, in which the authors found considerable overlap between the sadomasochistic and fetishistic groups (especially the "leatherites").

Langevin (1983,1985) reviewed the evidence indicating that the presence of one sexual deviation in an individual increased the likelihood of other sexual deviations occurring in the same individual and concluded that this was in fact the case. Abel and Osborn (1992), in their paper examining all paraphilic behavior, reported the percentages of cross-diagnosis. They examined their data in terms of the subjects' perceptions of a single primary diagnosis and one or more secondary diagnoses. Although all the subjects came from treatment programs and thus are unrepresentative of the population in general, the data remain of interest. The results are presented below. Table 4.5 shows the secondary paraphilias when fetishism was identified by the subject as the primary paraphilia, and Table 4.6 presents the

TABLE 4.6. Percentage of Patients with Fetishism When the Primary Diagnosis Is of Another Paraphilia

Type	Secondary diagnosis of fetishism (%)
Pedophilia (all types)	22
Rape	1
Exhibitionism	4
Voyeurism	15
Frottage	11
Transvestism	20
Masochism	8
Ego-dystonic homosexuality	7
Obscene phone calling	25
Public masturbation	18
Bestiality	33

Note. From Abel & Osborn (1992).

range of primary paraphilias in which the subject said that one of their secondary paraphilias was fetishism.

Although somewhat complex, these data clearly demonstrate the overlap in paraphilic behaviors in this somewhat extreme, clinic-based sample.

In addition, fetishistic behavior has also been linked with kleptomania and "borderline personality organization" (Wise, 1985), although the strength of such associations has not been clearly delineated.

THE CHOICE OF FETISH, SIGNIFICANCE, AND CLASSIFICATION

Although there are case reports of bizarre fetishes (e.g., De Silva & Pernet, 1992), certain types of objects tend to be used by the majority of fetishists and, as can be seen in Chalkley and Powell's study (1983), these objects tend to cluster into specific groups.

Authors have attempted to explain why some objects become fetishes more frequently than others, and a variety of classifications of fetishes have been developed. These classifications, although not founded in sound epidemiology, do provide an often useful overview of the diversity and nature of fetishistic objects, and as they link closely with theoretical models of fetishism will be examined in brief below.

Krafft-Ebing (1886/1965) delineated pathological erotic "fetichism" and divided it into: "a) The Fetich is a Part of the Female Body, b) The Fetich is an Article of Female Attire, c) The Fetich is Some Special Material, d) Beast-fetichism" (pp. 147, 162, 176, 185). Proceeding on from this early classification, Balint (1935) also proposed a model to describe fetishistic objects, stating that many were either hollow or used as receptacles, thus representing the vagina and the womb. Gebhard (1969) in his typology of fetishes divided them into two major groups: inanimate objects and physical attributes of a person (partialism). He further subdivided inanimate objects into media (the substance of the object; e.g., leather, rubber) and form (the shape of the object; e.g., shoes, girdles), thus incorporating features of both Krafft-Ebing's and Balint's models.

Epstein (1969, 1975) highlighted certain characteristics of fetishistic objects, for example, glistening, shining, texture, shape, and smell, and examined these qualities in terms of phylogenicity and perceptual preference. He stated that many of the qualities described evoke an intense response in the individual, and that there is often a strong associative link with the mother or other significant person. He notes that many fetishes bear a relationship to body parts, or the person as a whole, and have the capacity to be applied to the body. He concluded from this that the object symbolizes the identification with, or incorporation of, the desired person and that often this object is encountered at a crucial stage of development. Wilson (1987) reached similar conclusions, linking the choice of fetish to imprinting theories (see below). He noted that fetish objects have strong gender associations, are worn close to sexually arousing parts of the body, and have striking visual attributes that mimic genital signals.

Bancroft (1989) delineated three principal categories of sexual stimulus in the fetishist: (1) a part of the body; (2) An inanimate extension of the body (e.g., article of clothing); and (3) a source of specific tactile stimulation (e.g., the texture of a particular form of material). It may be seen that this latter classification closely follows that developed by Krafft-Ebing (although excluding "beast fetishism") written over 100 years earlier. Interestingly, although the categories of fetish have remained relatively constant over time, the objects within those categories have changed. Thus, in the 19th century, popular textures for fetishists were velvets and silks, and these have nowadays been largely replaced by materials such as rubber and leather. In addition to the effects of availability on object choice, cultural factors have also been noted to be influential. Money (1977) noted the special sexual appeal of the bound or "lotus" foot widespread in China until recently.

Note also that a number of authors commented upon the role of the smell of the fetish (e.g., Balint, 1935; Epstein, 1969; Money, 1984), and that although many theoretical models emphasize the importance of visual stimuli, other sensory modalities also can be of importance in determining the choice of fetish.

DEVELOPMENTAL ISSUES

The development of an individual's sexuality is a complex and relatively poorly understood field. In addition to the comprehensive review of sexual arousal provided by Dekker and Everaerd (1989), Bancroft (1989) developed a clear and useful "Eclectic Interactional Model" of sexual development that has two dimensions, strands and stages. The strands of sexuality (differentiation into male or female and development of gender identity, sexual responsiveness, and the capacity for close dyadic relationships) coalesce as the individual proceeds through the life stages from prenatal to midlife. The other concepts fundamental to this model are the functions of sexual behavior and sexual preference. It is this latter concept that is most distorted in the fetishist.

Sexual development is without doubt influenced by many factors. It is likely to be determined in a multifactorial manner, including the influences of both inborn and environmental determinants. Although we consider the etiological theories proposed for the development of fetishism in more detail below, we will consider a brief overview of the development of sexuality at this stage (with reference to the possible developmental mechanisms that may contribute to the development of fetishism) to provide a framework in which to place the specific etiological proposals.

Money (1980, 1984) based his theoretical model on the notion of templates, which he called "lovemaps." He talked of "schemas implanted in the brain," stating that the lovemaps are not complete at birth, but require input from the social environment. Money argued that in paraphiliacs the imagery constituting the lovemap goes awry. Perper (1985) continued the theme of templates, and proposed the existence of "pre-figured gestalts" of the ideal partner. He suggested that these were not encoded in the genes, but were created by a slow developmental process involving genetic regulation of neural development and later neuro physiological construction of an increasingly detailed and recognizable image. Bancroft (1989) argued that although these concepts may provide a useful framework for thought, they are impossible to test scientifically.

Freund and Blanchard (1993) reported Blanchard's finding that one class of paraphilia in heterosexual men (including fetishism, transvestism, and related cross-gender phenomena) resulted from developmental errors in locating sexual targets in the environment, which Blanchard categorized as errors of erotic target location. These errors lead to sexual orientation toward nonessential features of the desired object in the fetishist, for example, the underwear of the women instead of the actual woman.

Gosselin and Wilson, (1980), on questioning their sample of "rubberites," found that the interest in rubber began between the ages of 4 and 10. As many of the sample were children during the Second World War, they speculated that the combination of anxiety-provoking circumstances, an absent father, an overprotective mother, and the common use of rubber in gas masks at this time in the United Kingdom all contributed to the development of a rubber fetish in these individuals.

FORENSIC ISSUES

Krafft-Ebing (1886) emphasized the "great forensic importance" of fetishism, noting that it could lead to theft and robbery. Although not considered to be of such importance nowadays, the association between fetishism and stealing the fetish object still persists. In all, 25% of the group studied by Chalkley and Powell (1983) stole their fetish object, and in 13 out of 48 cases, referral was initiated by a legal source. Although it is clear that not all fetishists steal, it seems likely that if a fetishist commits a crime linked to his sexual disorder, the crime is usually one of theft.

Apart from this link with stealing, fetishism and its associated behaviors rarely brings the fetishist into contact with the law (Grubin, Gudjonsson, Gunn, & West, 1993). There are, however, cases of violent criminal acts in which it was argued that fetishism was central to the crime (Snow & Bluestone, 1969). Snow and Bluestone presented three case histories of fetishists; in two of these the patient has killed someone. They propose that fetishism is a defense against the fetishist's desire to mutilate or kill, and that when this defense breaks down, the fetishist does in fact kill. Nagler (1969), in his commentary on the Snow and Bluestone paper, raised the vital question: "Were these two murderers who happened to be fetishists, or two fetishists who happened to be murderers?" (p. 99). Distinguished forensic psychiatrists such as J. Gunn (personal communication, 1995) would argue that, in such cases, comorbid factors such as other paraphilias, personality disorder, psychiatric illness, or criminality are of far more significance in the violent act than is the fetishism itself. Langevin (1983) agreed with this viewpoint. In reviewing the paper by Snow and Bluestone, he argued that there is little convincing evidence that fetishism per se is associated with violence.

Thus, it is likely that the fetishist who commits a violent criminal act is not driven solely by the desire to express or satisfy his fetishistic urges, although expression of the disorder may be a feature in the offense. Kunjukrishnan, Pawlak, and Varan (1988) reported such a case; a fetishist committed indecent assault. After thorough assessment, dual diagnoses of fetishism and inadequate personality disorder were made, thus supporting the view that it was not the fetishism alone that led to the commission of the offense.

PROPOSED ETIOLOGICAL FACTORS

Etiological models of fetishism have incorporated ideas from many disciplines. Although many treatment techniques encompass behavioral and other psychological theories (Junginger, Chapter 5, this volume), many of the early theoretical models describing fetishism developed from the work of the psychoanalysts. Attention has also focused on possible biological mechanisms, ethological explanations, and sociocultural and sociobiological factors.

In considering possible etiological mechanisms, Wise (1985) argued that clinical models of fetishism must be viewed from multiple perspectives, such as those listed above. This viewpoint is also supported by Huws, Shubsachs, and Taylor (1991) and Stoller (1986), who, despite a firm conviction in the psychoanalytical viewpoint, stated: "We still know too little about what affects the unfolding of sexuality after the essential inputs of heredity, constitution and early environment" (p. 45). It follows from this that much remains unknown and our understanding at this stage is limited.

The Biological Perspective

A number of authors have given consideration to broad biological factors and their relevance to fetishism. Pitcher (1990) noted that nonbiological (e.g., psychoanalytic and behavioral) theories of fetishism fail to account for possible "heritable and constitutional factors (probably neuroendocrine in nature) affecting the personality . . ." (p. 685) and thus, presumably sexual behavior. Flor-Henry (1987) reviewed with clarity the embryonic, biological aspects of the development of sexuality and sexual deviation, and although his review is of relevance, and I commented on it above in relation to the gender differences in fetishism, I will not consider the organic basis for the development of normal sexuality further here. However, in addition to the work on normal cerebral function and the mechanisms for development of sexuality, the literature also considers the relevance of brain injury (from, for example, accidents, surgery, and toxic substances) and other neurological abnormalities such as epilepsy, in the development of sexually anomalous behaviors such as fetishism (Langevin, 1990). Although it is essential to be cautious in extrapolating the findings from this body of work, which consists largely of case reports, it still may give important clues to the pathogenic causes of sexual deviance; I will, therefore, review it at this stage.

The association between temporal abnormalities and fetishism has been noted by a number of authors. Mitchell, Falconer, and Hill (1954) reported a now much-quoted case of a man presenting with a fetish for safety pins which was relieved by temporal lobectomy. The patient reported that thinking about safety pins would precipitate seizures, and that he had strong urges to look at them when aroused or anxious. Thoughts about safety pins gradually replaced coitus as the preferred sexual activity. After left temporal lobectomy the patient regained his desire for sexual intercourse and lost both his seizures and the desire to look at safety pins. Ball (1968) reported a similar case in which fetishism emerged with the onset of a temporal lobe tumor. Despite these reports, it is interesting to note that Shukla, Srivastava, and Katiyar (1979) found no cases of sexual deviation in their study of 70 cases of temporal lobe epilepsy. The authors themselves commented on the discrepancy between their findings and those of others and postulated that these differences arose as a result of culturally determined taboos which prevented their subjects from divulging the true facts about their sexuality.

Epstein (1960, 1961, 1969) wrote extensively about the links between brain pathology and fetishism. In 1960, he reviewed the psychopathology of fetishism, with particular reference to brain mechanisms as an etiological factor. He concluded the review by arguing that fetishism demonstrated two characteristic types of behavioral phenomena: those representing a state of increased orgasmic excitability (resulting from cerebral pathophysiology) and those representing attempts to maintain orgasmic control. In 1961 and 1969, he extended these arguments, relating the behavioral characteristics of fetishism to the manifestations of temporal lobe dysfunction. He also suggested that the limbic system played a role in sexual disorders such as fetishism and transvestism, arguing that it subserves mechanisms concerned with sexual arousal. He postulated that dysfunction could prevent proper subordination and integration of sexually arousing stimuli during sexual development, so that the "sign and symbol" aspects of sex became more dominant.

Langevin (1983) was critical of many of the case reports in the literature, stating that the sexual behavior was often inadequately assessed. He was, however, impressed by two studies conducted by Epstein (1969) and Kolarsky, Freund, Machek, and Polak (1967), both of which he briefly reviewed. Langevin argued that both of these studies demonstrated a link between fetishism and temporal lobe abnormalities, although McConaghy (1993), in commenting on the latter study, concluded that the authors were unable to demonstrate a particular association between temporal lobe epilepsy and fetishism and transvestism.

More recent papers have also commented on the link with temporal lobe abnormalities, although noting the presence of more diffuse pathology. Huws, Shubsachs, and Taylor (1991) presented the case of a man who developed hypersexuality and a foot fetish after the onset of multiple sclerosis. They reported that although the patient had diffuse brain damage, the main features were those of frontal lobe syndrome with damage to the temporal regions. Cases of fetishism have also been documented subsequent to head injury with generalized abnormalities on electroencephalogram (Pandita-Gunawardena, 1990). This latter case, however, clearly demonstrates the problematic nature of inferring etiology from single case reports. In addition to presenting the possible relationship between the head injury and fetishistic behavior, the author accepts that the behavior presented could equally be viewed from behavioral or psychoanalytic viewpoints.

We can see from the above review that clinicians still have a poor understanding of the links between brain mechanisms and sexuality in general and specifically regarding fetishism. To date there has been little research into the presence or absence of brain abnormality in fetishism, with the majority of existing work focusing on those known to have brain abnormalities with secondary sexual abnormalities. As Langevin (1983) suggested, if we are to further our understanding of the biological components of etiology, future work should focus on examining fetishists to determine the incidence of brain pathology. He concludes that it would be premature to accept that brain dysfunction causes fetishism, as we know that temporal lobe damage is not always associated with fetishism.

The Psychological Perspective

As early as 1897, Binet offered a conditioning model as an explanation for fetishism. He postulated that if a vulnerable individual was paired with "fortuitous circumstances," a fetishistic arousal pattern could develop.

Classical Conditioning

Conditioning theorists propose that the sexual response system becomes conditioned to respond to various kinds of stimuli which usually are physical characteristics of the potential partner. In the fetishist the sexual response is conditioned to a particular, somewhat unusual stimulus or stimuli, such as rubber, handbags, or feet. The fetishist has become sexually preoccupied with a particular body part or object and thus is less interested in the associated partner.

A variety of authors have demonstrated the capacity in men to develop erections in response to unusual stimuli (i.e., to be conditioned) under experimental conditions (Bancroft, 1974; Rachman, 1966; Rachman & Hodgson, 1968). In Rachman's (1966) work five subjects were conditioned to give a sexual response to a photograph of a pair of boots, but the response was easily extinguished. Attempting to relate this experimental phenomenon to fetishism occurring in the population, Bancroft (1989) argued that a simple conditioning model is not sufficient and does not account for the maintenance of such responses throughout an individual's life. Although McGuire, Carlisle, and Young (1965) proposed that the mechanism of maintenance may be the reinforcement obtained through masturbation and orgasm, Bancroft still questioned a purely learning theory model. His doubts arose particularly when considering the lack of generalization of learning and the discriminate reinforcement of certain stimuli and not others. Wilson (1987) also questioned the conditioning theories, highlighting not only the points raised by Bancroft, but also the lack of explanation for why certain individuals develop fetishism and others do not. O'Donohue and Plaud (1994) questioned the internal validity of many of the studies of male sexual arousal.

Social Learning

The development of fetishism may also, in part, be understood in terms of experiences in which the subject is rejected by others in sexually tense situations. La Torre (1980) neatly illustrated the potential for the development of fetishistic responses in an experiment in which 60 males were exposed to potential girlfriends by photograph and were then asked to select one. Thirty of the men were told that they had been rejected by the woman of their choice and 30 were told that their interest had been reciprocated. All 60 were then asked to rate the attractiveness of a range of pictorial stimuli, including an abstract design, a whole woman, parts of a woman (e.g., feet), and women's garments (e.g., underwear). The 30 rejected males rated the whole woman and the design as being less attractive than the garments and body parts relative to the "accepted" men. This study raises interesting questions about the role of self-esteem, previous experiences, perceived inadequacy, and failure in the generation of fetishistic fantasy and possibly behavior. Gebhard (1969) also examined issues relating to social learning and argued that the pubertal or adolescent male is more vulnerable to associating sex with "symbols," which he encounters before experiencing the actuality of sociosexual gratification.

Ethology

Wilson (1987) neatly summarized ethological models for the development of fetishism. In brief, ethologists, who examine the role of instinct on our behavior and that of other species, argue that as sex drive evolved to promote gene survival, the behavioral strategies that serve sexual instincts became driven by powerful, inflexible emotions that are deep seated within ancient parts of the brain.

Wilson (1987) identified the two major instinctual mechanisms involved. First, he outlined the role of innate releasing mechanisms in which the organism responds sexually to the sexual signals of the opposite sex even if reared in isolation. He went on to consider the role of imprinting (a form of learning during a critical period of development), whereby the range of stimuli that are to become sexually exciting later in life are delineated (Bateson, 1978). To some extent this depends on the visual stimuli that the animal is exposed to at the critical period, which is in early infancy. As with other neurological mechanisms, errors may occur in either of these instincts. Thus, when considering fetishism, the imprinting mechanism leads to an excessively narrow and incorrect specification of the sex object.

Sociobiological Factors

Both Wilson (1987) and Epstein (1987) gave consideration to sociobiological factors in their examination of evolution and phylogenicity. Epstein examined the topic from a phylogenetic viewpoint, concluding that:

1. Fetishistic behavior is seen not only in humans, but also in other primates.
2. Fetishism may represent a high primate automatic behavioral response (sexual arousal) evoked by an exciting object. This response may have a reflex component based within the tempero-limbic region of the brain.

3. The mechanism may have a genetic component, and is usually inhibited in the maturing human, but may be released in several contexts including brain damage.
4. Forces other than sexual drive, for example, the strong human interest in external objects, may also play a role.

Sociocultural Factors

Wise (1985) noted that paraphilic behavior may also be influenced by sociocultural factors. Certain cultures, for example, the Chinese, give erotic significance to particular body parts, whereas others, such as industrialized societies, do not tolerate childhood sexual activity. Both Gebhard (1969) and Money (1984) speculated that such cultures promote sexual interest and play in other, more acceptable forms, and thus contribute to the development of fetishism. Epstein (1969) examined the normal, culturally determined, role of sexual "signs" and images to which many males respond and argued that in the fetishist, the sign assumes complete dominance.

The Psychoanalytic Perspective

In psychoanalytical considerations of fetishism, the representation of the fetish takes a central role. Freud (1905/1962a) stated that the selection of the fetish was determined by traumatic experiences that occurred in childhood. Greenacre (1979) reached the same conclusion, considering the child who, feeling overwhelmed, resorts to fantasy or denial of reality to deal with their panic. Freud later developed the concept of "castration anxiety" (Freud, 1927/1962b). He argued that the fetish object represented a penis, protecting the male from his fear of castration, and was denial of the penis-less state of the woman. The fetishist thus allows a denial of the true nature of the female genitalia, while at the same time being aware that the woman does not in reality have a penis. An ego split thus develops. Greenacre (1979) also considered fetishism to be invariably associated with an extraordinarily severe castration complex. Bak (1953) emphasized the role of the separation from the mother and the subsequent anxiety produced (prephallic stage). In linking the development of fetishism with pregenital stages, psychoanalysts offer explanation for the interest in smells that can accompany or play an important part in fetishism (see above).

Nagler (1957), in his review of the psychoanalytic contribution to the understanding of fetishism, conceptualized the fetishist as an individual who tries to overcome low self-esteem and feelings of inadequacy through the use of an inanimate object—the fetish. Extrapolating from the Freudian concept of an ego split, Zavitzianos (1971), in hypothesizing about the patient described earlier, postulated that the woman was utilizing the fetish as a transitional object to maintain a sense of ego identity. Stoller (1979) regarded the fetishistic act as one of cruelty and triumph over the trauma of an early parental humiliation. He argued that to create a fetish a person must (1) want to punish someone (object) who has harmed them (role of childhood trauma); (2) strip the object of humanity; (3) endow a nonhuman object (fetish) with the stolen humanness; and (4) choose the fetish because it has some quality that represents the loved, needed traumatizing object.

Many other psychoanalysts have postulated theoretical models of fetishism, for example, Balint (1935), and the literature continues to grow. Wise (1985) argued that the diversity of the psychoanalytic contributions to this subject should be considered in the context of the evolution of psychoanalytic theory that has taken place since Freud. It should be noted, however, that in similarity with much of the work in this field, experimental testing of these hypotheses is severely lacking.

FUTURE DIRECTIONS

> No other variation of the sexual instinct that borders on the pathological can lay so much claim to our interest as this one [fetishism]. . . .
>
> —*Freud (1905/1962a)*

Throughout this review the difficulty of extrapolating from clinical populations, single case reports, and small series of cases has been highlighted. It may be that, given the increasing relaxation in attitudes toward sexual matters and the subsequent growth in the freedom of expression of peoples' sexuality, we can gain access to larger "normal" populations, and that through such access, we can increase our understanding of the etiology of fetishism.

Bak (1968) argued that fetishism could be used as a model for all perversions, stating that the main defensive position in these disorders was the reinvestment by the individual in the fantasy of the phallic woman. This is most clearly demonstrated in fetishism, where the castration anxiety produced at the recognition of the penis-less woman leads to the establishment of the fetish object as a replacement. Stoller (1986) expanded and clarified these arguments, identifying the central themes of splitting, dehumanization, and idealization that occur in fetishism and relating these themes to all other perversions. If one accepts this theory, then the study of the phenomenology and psychopathology of fetishism is of even greater importance, in that through understanding fetishism, knowledge of the mechanisms underlying other sexual deviations will increase. If we accept the need to investigate this topic further, any such investigation should attempt to overcome the problems highlighted above, and should draw inferences from large, population-based, representative samples.

REFERENCES

Abel, G. G., & Osborn, C. (1992). The paraphilias: The extent and nature of sexually deviant and criminal behavior. *Psychiatric Clinics of North America, 15,* 675–686.

American Psychiatric Association. (1994). *Diagnostic and statistical manual of mental disorders* (4th ed.). Washington, DC: Author.

Bak, R. C. (1953). Fetishism. *Bulletin of the American Psychoanalytic Association, 1,* 285–294.

Bak, R. C. (1968). The phallic woman: The ubiquitous fantasy in perversions. *Psychoanalytic Study of the Child, 23,* 15–36.

Ball, J. R. B. (1968). A case of hair fetishism, transvestism and organic cerebral disorder. *Acta Psychiatrica Scandinavica, 44,* 249–254.

Balint, M. (1935). A contribution on fetishism. *International Journal of Psycho-Analysis, 16,* 481–483.

Bancroft, J. (1974). *Deviant sexual behaviour: Modification and assessment.* Oxford: Clarendon Press.

Bancroft, J. (1989). *Human sexuality and its problems* (2nd ed.). Edinburgh: Churchill Livingstone.

Bateson, P. (1978). Early experience and sexual preferences. In J. Hutchinson (Ed.), *The biological determinants of sexual behaviour.* Chichester: Wiley.

Binet, A. (1887). Le fetishisme dans l'amour. *Revue Philosophique, 24,* 143–167, 252–274.

Chalkley, A. J., & Powell, G. E. (1983). The clinical description of forty-eight cases of sexual fetishism. *British Journal of Psychiatry, 142,* 292–295.

Christie-Brown, J. R. W. (1983). Paraphilias: Sadomasochism, fetishism, transvestism and transsexuality. *British Journal of Psychiatry, 143,* 227–231.

Crepault, C., & Couture, M. (1980). Men's erotic fantasies. *Archives of Sexual Behavior, 9*(5), 565–581.

Curren, D. (1954). Sexual perversion. *Practitioner, 172,* 440–445.

Dekker, J., & Everaerd, W. (1989). Psychological determinants of sexual arousal: A review. *Behaviour Research and Therapy, 27*(4), 353–364.

De Silva, P. (1993). Fetishism and sexual dysfunction: Clinical presentation and management. *Sexual and Marital Therapy, 8*(2), 147–155.

De Silva, P., & Pernet, A. (1992). Pollution in "Metroland": An unusual paraphilia in a shy young man. *Sexual and Marital Therapy, 7*(3), 301–306.

Epstein, A. W. (1960). Fetishism: A study of its psychopathology with particular reference to a proposed disorder in brain mechanism as an etiological factor. *Journal of Nervous and Mental Disease, 130,* 107–119.

Epstein, A. W. (1961). Relationship of fetishism and transvestism to brain and particularly to temporal lobe dysfunction. *Journal of Nervous and Mental Disease, 133,* 247–253.

Epstein, A. W. (1969). Fetishism: A comprehensive review. In J. H. Masserman (Ed.), *Science and psychoanalysis* (Vol. 15). New York: Grune & Stratton.

Epstein, A. W. (1975). The fetish object: Phylogenetic considerations. *Archives of Sexual Behavior, 4*(3), 303–308.

Epstein, A. W. (1987). The phylogenetics of fetishism. In G. Wilson (Ed.), *Variant sexuality: Research and theory.* London: Croom Helm.

Eysenck, H. J., & Eysenck, S. B. G. (1975). *Manual of the Eysenck Personality Questionnaire.* London: Hodder and Stoughton.

Freud, S. (1962a). Three essays on the theory of sexuality. In J. Strachey (Ed. and Trans.), *The standard edition of the complete psychological works of Sigmund Freud* (Vol. 7). London: Hogarth Press. (Original work published 1905)

Freud, S. (1962b). Fetishism. In J. Strachey (Ed. and Trans.), *The standard edition of the complete psychological works of Sigmund Freud* (Vol. 3). London: Hogarth Press. (Original work published 1927)

Freund, K., & Blanchard, R. (1993). Erotic target location errors in male gender dysphorics, paedophiles, and fetishists. *British Journal of Psychiatry, 162,* 558–563.

Gebhard, P. (1969). Fetishism and sado-masochism. *Science and Psychoanalysis, 15,* 71–80.

Gosselin, C., & Wilson, G. (1980). *Sexual variations.* London: Faber & Faber.

Greenacre, P. (1979). Fetishism. In I. Rosen (Ed.), *Sexual deviation.* Oxford: Oxford University Press.

Grubin, D., Gudjonsson, G., Gunn, J., & West, D. (1993). Disordered and offensive sexual behaviour. In J. Gunn & P. J. Taylor (Eds.), *Forensic psychiatry: Clinical, legal and ethical issues.* Oxford: Butterworth-Heinemann.

Huws, R., Shubsachs, A. P. W., & Taylor, P. J. (1991). Hypersexuality, fetishism and multiple sclerosis. *British Journal of Psychiatry, 158,* 280–281.

Kinsey, A. C., Pomeroy, W. B., & Martin, C. E. (1948). *Sexual behavior in the human male.* Philadelphia: Saunders.

Kinsey, A. C., Pomeroy, W. B., Martin, C. E., & Gebhard, P. H. (1953). *Sexual behaviour in the human female.* New York: Simon & Schuster.

Kolarsky, A., Freund, K., Machek, J., & Polak, O. (1967). Male sexual deviation: Association with early temporal lobe damage. *Archives of General Psychiatry, 17,* 735–743.

Krafft-Ebing, R. von. (1965). *Psychopathia sexualis* (12th ed., F. S. Klaf, Trans.). New York: Stein & Day. (Original work published 1886)

Kunjukrishnan, R., Pawlak, A., & Varan, L. (1988). The clinical and forensic psychiatric issues of retifism. *Canadian Journal of Psychiatry, 33,* 819–825.

Langevin, R. (1983). *Sexual strands.* Hillsdale, NJ: Erlbaum.

Langevin, R. (1985). *Erotic preference, gender identity, and aggression in men: New research studies.* Hillsdale, NJ: Erlbaum.

Langevin, R. (1990). Sexual anomalies and the brain. In W. Marshall, D. Laws, & H. Barbaree (Eds.), *Handbook of sexual assault.* New York: Plenum Press.

La Torre, R. (1980). Devaluation of the human love object: Heterosexual rejection as a possible antecedent of fetishism. *Journal of Abnormal Psychology, 89,* 295–298.

Marks, I. M. (1972). Phylogenesis and learning in the acquisition of fetishism. *Danish Medical Bulletin, 19,* 307–310.

McConaghy, N. (1993). *Sexual behaviour: Problems and management.* New York: Plenum Press.

McGuire, R. J., Carlisle, J. M., & Young, B. G. (1965). Sexual deviations as conditioned behaviour: A hypothesis. *Behaviour Research and Therapy, 2,* 185–190.

Mitchell, W., Falconer, M., & Hill, D. (1954). Epilepsy with fetishism relieved by temporal lobectomy. *Lancet, ii,* 626–630.

Money, J. (1977). Peking: The sexual revolution. In J. Money & H. Mustaph (Eds.), *Handbook of sexology.* Amsterdam: Excerpta Medica.

Money, J. (1980). *Love and love sickness: The science, gender difference, and pair bonding.* Baltimore: John Hopkins University Press.

Money, J. (1984). Paraphilias: Phenomenology and classification. *American Journal of Psychotherapy, 38,* 164–179.

Nagler, S. H. (1957). Fetishism: A review and a case study. *Psychiatric Quarterly, 10,* 713–770.

Nagler, S. H. (1969). Discussion. In J. H. Masserman (Ed.), *Science and psychoanalysis* (Vol. 15). New York: Grune & Stratton.

Pandita-Gunawardena, R. (1990). Paraphilic infantilism: A rare case of fetishistic behaviour. *British Journal of Psychiatry, 157,* 767–770.

Perper, T. (1985). *Sex signals: The biology of love.* Philadelphia: ISI Press.

Pitcher, D. (1990). Fetishism. In R. Bluglass & P. Bowden (Eds.), *Principles and practice of forensic psychiatry.* Edinburgh: Churchill Livingstone.

Rachman, S. (1966). Sexual fetishism: An experimental analogue. *Psychological Record, 16,* 293–296.

Rachman, S., & Hodgson, R. (1968). Experimentally induced "sexual fetishism": Replication and development. *Psychological Record, 18,* 25–27.

Shukla, G. D., Srivastava, O. N., & Katiyar, B. C. (1979). Sexual disturbances in temporal lobe epilepsy. *British Journal of Psychiatry, 134,* 288–292.

Snow, E., & Bluestone, H. (1969). Fetishism and murder. In J. H. Masserman (Ed.), *Science and psychoanalysis* (Vol. 15). New York: Grune & Stratton.

Stoller, R. J. (1979). *Sexual excitement: Dynamics of erotic life.* London: Maresfield Library.

Stoller, R. J. (1986). *Perversion: The erotic form of hatred.* London: Maresfield Library.

Webster's third new international dictionary, unabridged. (1986). London: G. Bell & Sons.

Welldon, E. V. (1992). *Mother, madonna, whore: The idealization and denigration of motherhood.* New York: Guilford Press.

Wilson, G. (1978). *The secrets of sexual fantasy.* London: J. M. Dent.

Wilson, G. (1987). An ethological approach to sexual deviation. In G. Wilson (Ed.), *Variant sexuality: Research and theory.* London: Croom Helm.

Wise, T. N. (1985). Fetishism: Etiology and treatment. A review from multiple perspectives. *Comprehensive Psychiatry, 26*(3), 249–257.

World Health Organization. (1988). *International classification of diseases* (Version 10). Geneva: WHO Division of Mental Health.

Zavitzianos, G. (1971). Fetishism and exhibitionism in the female and their relationship to psychopathology and kleptomania. *International Journal of Psycho-Analysis, 52,* 297–305.

5

FETISHISM

Assessment and Treatment

John Junginger

Fetishism is a type of paraphilia (deviant attraction) in which a person has a strong and recurrent sexual attraction to inanimate objects, or to specific body parts—a variation of fetishism known as "partialism." Fetishism is almost exclusively a male disorder, although there have been isolated reports of females with fetishes, especially in the later psychoanalytic literature (e.g., Raphling, 1989; Richards, 1990; Zavitzianos, 1982). Ironically, in an odd twist on the feminist mandate for equality, Gamman and Makinen (1995) specifically criticized analysts for enforcing a "taboo" against fetishism in women.

Whether or not fetishism is deliberately ignored in women as Gamman and Makinen (1995) claimed, the actual incidence of fetishism in the general population is difficult to determine. The major difficulty with establishing a base rate for the disorder is that persons with fetishes rarely seek treatment unless their deviant attraction greatly interferes with daily functioning. Chalkley and Powell (1983) described what probably is the largest sample of fetishists in the psychiatric literature. They reviewed the discharge records of London's Bethlem, Royal, and Maudsley Hospitals over a 20-year period and estimated that the incidence of fetishism in the psychiatric population is 0.8%. Although we might correctly assume that these patients represented a more severely disturbed sample of persons with fetishes, it is interesting to note that only three of the 48 subjects (6.3%) identified in the discharge records were described as markedly dependent on their fetish object for sexual excitement. Furthermore, for only 14 subjects (29.2%) was the patient's concern about the fetish the major factor in seeking treatment, and in only 18 cases (37.5%) was treatment instigated by others, such as the courts, police, friends, or relatives. So, even with this presumably more disturbed sample, Chalkley and Powell (1983) were probably correct in characterizing their subjects' fetishes as "distressing rather than disabling" (p. 294).

The variety of objects, or body parts, that may become sexual fetishes most likely is unlimited. However, the vast majority of fetishes do seem to involve articles of clothing (especially underwear), rubber products, and the feet and their coverings. In the relatively large sample of patients described by Chalkley and Powell (1983), for example, 58.3% had clothing fetishes including knickers (long, lacy women's undergarments), panties, stockings, dresses, corsets, girdles, slips, and "suspenders" (which I take to mean "women's garter belts"); 22.9% had fetishes involving rubber and rubber items such as raincoats; 14.6% had footwear fetishes; and 14.6% had fetishes for parts of the body, with the leg being the part most often noted. (Gosselin & Wilson, 1980, and Wise, 1985, described what appears to be a similar distribution of fetish objects.) It is also interesting to note that whereas the largest percentage of Chalkley and Powell's subjects were described in the discharge records as having only one fetish (35.4%), collectively an even larger percentage had three or more (45.8%), and one patient was described as having 9!

As with a host of other human interests such as sports, music, and celebrity gossip, fetishism has found its way onto some of the nation's newsstands in the form of a new magazine, "Fetish Times." The stated purpose of this magazine is to focus on the "resurgence of fetishism in sexual behavior." A possible indication of this resurgence is the popularity of fetish interest groups on the modern equivalent of the corner newsstand: The ever-expanding alliance of computer networks known as the Internet.

Table 5.1 lists several sexual newsgroups or forums that were available on the Internet in midyear 1995. The so-called "alternative" forums such as those listed in Table 5.1 bypass the formal Usenet procedures for organizing Internet newsgroups and typically are not moderated. Consequently, these types of forums tend to have more of a freewheeling nature. The alternative sex forums were organized so that persons with various sexual preferences can post and reply to messages on topics of shared interest. Some of the forums, such as *alt.sex.fetish.feet* and *alt.sex.fetish.diapers,* deal almost exclusively with fetishes. They can be thought of as the modern equivalent of organizations such as the Mackintosh Society, an England-based group of rubber fetishists with members in more than 20 countries. (In England, a rubberized raincoat is called a "mackintosh.") Others forums, such as *alt.sex.erotica,* are of a more general nature.

A fairly random sampling of posts on the alternative sex forums listed in Table 5.1 during the months of April and May 1995 revealed numerous references to or depictions of fetish-like behavior or interests. In keeping with the general theme of fetishes as "unusual" objects of attraction, my sampling was deliberately biased toward the inclusion of objects

TABLE 5.1. Alternative Sex Forums Available on the Internet with Primarily Fetish Themes or Occasional Fetish Themes, April and May 1995

alt.pantyhose	alt.binaries.multimedia.erotica
alt.personals.fetish	alt.binaries.pictures.erotica
alt.sex.anal	alt.binaries.pictures.lingerie
alt.sex.bestiality	alt.binaries.pictures.breasts
alt.sex.exhibitionism	alt.sex.fetish.amputee
alt.sex.fat	alt.sex.fetish.diapers
alt.sex.jp	alt.sex.fetish.fashion
alt.sex.masturbation	alt.sex.fetish.feet
alt.sex.pictures	alt.sex.fetish.hair
alt.sex.services	alt.sex.fetish.orientals
alt.sex.spanking	alt.sex.fetish.redheads
alt.sex.stories	alt.sex.fetish.tickling
alt.sex.stories.d	alt.sex.fetish.watersports
alt.sex.swingers	alt.sex.erotica.marketplace
alt.sex.underwear	alt.binaries.pictures.erotica.bondage
alt.sex.voyeurism	alt.binaries.pictures.erotica.d
alt.sex.wanted	alt.binaries.pictures.erotica.fetish
alt.sex.wizards	alt.binaries.pictures.erotica.furry
alt.support.jock-strap	

and body parts not normally considered to be within the usual realm of sexual interests. Consequently, frequent references to or depictions of the female breast and buttocks were excluded, even though the preoccupation with these body parts apparent in some of the posts was clearly fetish-like (cf. Wise, 1985). Also, because many of the posts were sent to more than one forum at a time, I took care not to count individual posts more than once, although I undoubtedly made that error on occasion.

TABLE 5.2. Fetish Objects, Body Parts, and Behavior Mentioned or Depicted on the Alternative Sex Forums (Table 5.1), April and May 1995

Objects/body parts	Behavior with fetish object
Underwear	Wearing (87)
Panties (45)	Looking at, fondling, or spanking someone else wearing (47)
Diapers (32)	Looking at (13)
Bra (18)	Fondling (12)
Pantyhose (15)	Collecting/hoarding (11)
Silk stockings (11)	Lying on (9)
Silk slips (10)	Inserting up rectum (7)
Other underwear (5)	Rubbing up against (5)
	Sucking (4)
Rubber objects (48)	Stealing (4)
Rubber/plastic underwear (12)	Lying underneath (3)
Enemas (8)	Sitting on (3)
Rubber raincoats/rain hats (8)	Sleeping with/in (2)
Rubber sheets/mattress pads (7)	
Rubber galoshes (6)	
Rubber mats (2)	
Rubber "wet suit" (2)	
Other rubber (3)	
Body parts (46)	
Foot/toes (29)	
Leg (7)	
Red hair (4)	
Long, curly hair (4)	
Ear/ear lobe (2)	
Outer clothing (45)	
Silk blouse (18)	
Silk shirt (15)	
Silk scarves (8)	
Other clothes (4)	
Leather objects (45)	
Leather shoes/boots (30)	
Leather pants (4)	
Leather purse/brief case (4)	
Leather jacket/coat (3)	
Leather dress (2)	
Other leather (2)	
Miscellaneous (18)	
Feathers/feather duster (6)	
Baby crib (6)	
Catheter (4)	
Silk handkerchief (2)	

The most frequently mentioned or depicted objects or body parts from the sampling of the alternative sex forums are listed in Table 5.2. In spite of the admittedly unscientific method of this sampling, the distribution of fetish objects and body parts was similar to that found in the sample described by Chalkley and Powell (1983). Again, note the frequent occurrence of articles of clothing (especially underwear), feet/toes and footwear, and rubber objects. The ear also makes an appearance, as does hair color—red apparently is the color of choice, probably because of its relative rarity. The frequent occurrence of diapers is consistent with some speculations that the "choice" of many fetish objects has its origins in early childhood, when a person may first learn the pleasurable association between baby accessories, such as diapers, and genital stimulation (Gosselin & Wilson, 1980). A similar explanation may account for the consistent appearance of rubber objects on lists of common fetishes; these also, presumably, are first encountered in early childhood in the form of rubber pants, sheets, and pacifiers. Of course, if this were true, the current reliance on disposable diapers, training pants, and crib sheets may signal the beginning of a decrease in the number of rubber fetishes as the more "rubber-oriented" baby-boom generation dies off.

Persons with fetishes engage in a variety of behaviors with the fetish object to achieve sexual arousal and orgasm. They may stroke, fondle, or even suck on the object while masturbating. In the case of clothing fetishes, the article of clothing is often worn, either by the person with the fetish or by his sexual partner. Referring again to the relatively sizable sample of patients described by Chalkley and Powell (1983), 21 of 48 patients (43.8%) wore fetish articles of clothing, 11 (22.9%) apparently enjoyed seeing someone else wear fetish clothing, 6 (12.5%) enjoyed "gazing" at the fetish object, 6 (12.5%) inserted rubber fetish objects or shoes up their rectums, and 10 (21%) either fondled, sucked, burned, or "rolled in" the fetish object.

The Internet sampling of fetish behavior was similar to that found by Chalkley and Powell (1983). As shown in Table 5.2, the overwhelming percentage of posts on the alternative sex forums described or depicted either wearing or seeing someone else wear fetish clothing. References to or depictions of looking at, fondling, collecting/hoarding, lying on, and inserting the fetish object up the rectum were less frequent, but still were relatively common.

An interesting side development on the Internet is the increasing variety of "goods and services" available to "fetters." You may have already guessed from my description of the sampling of the alternative sex forums that it is possible to post pictures on the text-based Usenet newsgroups. With the proper software and a little ingenuity (both available on the 'Net), subscribers to the alternative sex forums can decode and display encoded text files featuring pictures, sounds, and even multimedia (sound and video) of fetish objects and behavior. In fact, the newer web browsers accomplish this automatically. Occasionally, provocative catalog covers from commercial outlets of fetish paraphernalia are posted. Just a bit more outlandish is the fairly regular offering by a few enterprising females to sell their worn underwear "for a reasonable price," usually about $25. In keeping with this infectious spirit of entrepreneurship, underwear "specially prepared" can be obtained for an additional charge of $5.[1]

Several authors have commented on the compulsivelike behavior often exhibited by persons with fetishes (e.g., Gosselin & Wilson, 1980; Wise, 1985). This type of behavior is particularly evident in the person's attempt to acquire the fetish object. Stealing or hoarding the object of attraction is not uncommon (Chalkley & Powell, 1983; Gosselin & Wilson, 1980)—for example, fetishists have been known to commit burglary merely to obtain footwear or underwear ("Legal Shoe Drops," 1994). Less often, a fetishist may compulsively follow a person who is wearing fetish articles, or even attack someone to have contact with fetish body parts ("Parents Guard Girls," 1992). It is this compulsivelike urge to acquire access to the fetish object, among other characteristics of the disorder, that suggests similarities with obsessive–compulsive disorder and a conceptualization of fetishism within the two-process learning theory of avoidance.

Mowrer (1947), Miller (1948), and Schoenfield (1950) were among the first to propose that two processes are involved in the acquisition and maintenance of avoidance behavior: classical conditioning and instrumental (or operant) learning. Within this framework, known as two-process learning theory, a former neutral stimulus acquires the potential to elicit a conditioned emotional response of fear after being paired with an aversive event; this is the classical conditioning process. Fear is an aversive emotional state that motivates the organism to behave. Behavior that terminates the "warning signal" for the aversive event (Mowrer, 1947), or that avoids an expected aversive event (Herrnstein, 1969), reduces fear and so is negatively reinforced; this is the operant learning process.

The two learning processes just described can be illustrated with symbols that are often used to represent classical and operant procedures or phenomena. The first schematic depicts a standard experimental-type pairing of a neutral stimulus (S; tone) with an aversive unconditioned stimulus (UCS; electric shock), which elicits an unconditioned response (UCR; fear or anxiety):

$$S\text{———}UCS\text{———}UCR$$
$$\text{tone}\quad\text{shock}\quad\text{fear/anxiety}$$

After some number of pairings of the tone and the shock, the tone is "conditioned" (CS) and acquires the potential to elicit a conditioned response (CR) of fear or anxiety:

$$CS\text{———}CR$$
$$\text{tone}\quad\text{fear/anxiety}$$

As already mentioned, fear motivates the organism to behave. Behavior (R) that terminates the warning signal (CS; tone), or that avoids the aversive event (UCS; shock), will lead to a reduction in fear and so will be negatively reinforced (S^{R-}):

$$CS\text{———}CR\text{———}R \longrightarrow S^{R-}$$
$$\text{tone}\quad\text{fear/}\quad\text{escape/}\quad\text{negative}$$
$$\text{anxiety}\quad\text{avoidance}\quad\text{reinforcement}$$

Although some of its predictions have proved difficult to verify (see Mineka, 1979), two-process theory is generally accepted as the standard against which other theories of avoidance behavior are measured (Domjan & Burkhard, 1986). The two-process framework seems especially useful for conceptualizing obsessive–compulsive disorder (OCD). In the case of compulsive handwashing, for example, some form of contamination, such as dirt or germs, is a CS, which elicits a CR of fear or anxiety. Handwashing is an operant response (R) that is negatively reinforced because it removes contamination, thus reducing anxiety.

What may not be as obvious is that the two-process framework is also useful for conceptualizing fetishism, resulting in some interesting contrasts with its depiction of OCD. In the case of fetishism, the CS is the fetish object, which at one time, presumably, was a neutral stimulus. The fetish object elicits a CR not of fear or anxiety, as in OCD, but rather of sexual arousal. The fetish object acquired the potential to elicit sexual arousal, following from two-process theory, because it was previously paired with sexual stimulation, a UCS that elicits a UCR of sexual arousal. The operant response R is not one of escape or avoidance, as in OCD, but rather of approach and masturbation, which is positively and negatively reinforced (S^{R+-}) by an increase in sexual arousal and orgasm:

$$\text{CS}\text{———}\text{CR}\text{———}\text{R} \longrightarrow \text{S}^{R+-}$$

fetish	sexual	approach/	positive and negative
object	arousal	masturbation	reinforcement

In fact, two-process theory may be better suited for conceptualizing fetishism than it is for avoidance learning. The appetitive nature of the operant response in fetishism ensures that the UCS, sexual stimulation, is constantly readministered in the form of masturbation. This is not the case with avoidance, wherein the operant response ensures that the UCS is not encountered. Thus, the difficulties in accounting for the persistence of avoidance behavior in the absence of the UCS, and in the apparent absence of conditioned fear (see Mineka, 1979), are not a concern with fetish behavior. The fetishist continuously self-administers the UCS and by doing so maintains the motivating properties of the CR: sexual arousal.

As previously mentioned, there has been some speculation that early childhood associations between baby accessories and genital stimulation may account for the relatively frequent occurrence of fetish objects such as diapers and rubber items (Gosselin & Wilson, 1980). The learned association between these types of objects and sexual stimulation presumably is a product of classical conditioning. In two studies that now would be considered marginally ethical at best, Rachman (1966) and Rachman and Hodgson (1968) showed that a clinical analogue of fetishism, in fact, could be classically conditioned in the laboratory.[2]

In the first of these two studies, Rachman (1966) used a modification of a penile plethysmograph first developed by Freund (1963, 1965) to measure sexual arousal in three "young unmarried psychologists"(!) (p. 294). After determining that no penile response occurred to a colored slide of a pair of black, knee-length women's boots (i.e., boots were a neutral stimulus), the boots slide was presented again, this time followed by one of six slides of attractive, naked females—the UCS. All three subjects acquired a CR of sexual arousal to the slide of the boots after some number of pairings of boots with slides of naked females. In addition, stimulus generalization was evident in that each subject showed some minimal level of sexual arousal to stimuli similar to the boots CS, such as slides of high-heeled black shoes, sandals, and so on. Rachman was careful to extinguish the subjects' arousal to boots at the conclusion of the experiment by repeatedly presenting the boots slide alone until the CR extinguished. However, in light of what we now know about the tendency for extinction to be context specific, and conditioning to be much less so (Bouton & Bolles, 1985), it would be interesting to speculate whether the subjects' "mini" boot fetish later resurfaced on occasion.

The demonstration by Rachman (1966) and by Rachman and Hodgson (1968) that a clinical analogue of fetishism can be conditioned in the laboratory is not, of course, proof that fetishism necessarily develops along similar lines. What seems reasonably certain, however, is that at some point in the life of a fetishist some type of association is made between the fetish object and sexual stimulation or sexual arousal. In spite of its limitations, two-process theory does seem to provide a useful framework for describing how this association is made, and how it might be suppressed.

Identifying the objects of attraction for a fetishist is fairly straightforward in most cases. If the patient has a well-defined masturbation routine, which is often the case with fetishists, then a detailed account of the objects and behaviors involved in the routine could provide a fairly complete picture of the patient's deviant sexual arousal pattern.

Another strategy that may provide additional, or even unexpected information about the patient's deviant arousal pattern is to obtain a reasonably accurate record of the situations encountered in his natural environment that elicit sexual arousal. This can be accomplished by asking the patient to carry a small notebook with him at all times and to note in some detail the situations that cause at least a minimum level of sexual arousal; the patient should also note his specific response to the arousal, such as approaching the object or masturbating. Other information, such as his perceived level of sexual arousal, might also be useful, but the patient obviously should not be overburdened with too much detailed recording. The goal is to maintain a fairly noninvasive approach to collecting information about the patient's pattern of sexual arousal in his natural environment. This type of approach could be thought of as a "general assessment" in the sense that we are getting a general idea about the objects and situations that the patient finds sexually arousing, and about his behavior when these objects and situations are encountered.

What we might call "specific assessment" involves an assessment of the actual pattern and level of sexual arousal to the objects and situations described for the masturbation routine or identified in the general assessment. Specific assessment should include both self-report measures and more objective or direct measures, such as actual penile response. Although there have been opinions to the contrary (McConaghy, 1988), measures of penile circumference as indicated by various modifications of Freund's (1963, 1965) penile plethysmograph, or of Barlow, Becker, Leitenberg, and Agras's (1970) penile strain gauge, generally have been accepted as objective, reliable, and valid measures of male sexual arousal (Barlow, 1977). The procedure for measuring penile response has been somewhat formalized and was first described in detail by Barlow (1977), and by Tollison and Adams (1979, Table 2-2).

A typical assessment of penile response to presumed fetish objects involves the use of a polygraph to record simultaneously at least three measures of interest: (1) penile circumference as indicated by some type of penile plethysmograph; (2) body movement as indicated by a device sensitive to movement along any axis of the chair in which the patient is seated; and (3) time, measured in seconds.

In the actual procedure, the patient enters the assessment room, sits in a comfortable chair, and a penile plethysmograph is properly placed. After a 20- to 30-minute habituation period to allow the patient to become at least somewhat comfortable with the unusual surroundings, a baseline of "0% full erection" is marked on the polygraph chart. The patient is then asked to self-stimulate to a fully erect penis, at which point the coincident pen deflection on the polygraph chart is marked as "100% full erection." The penile response is allowed to return to baseline and the planned presentation of stimulus conditions begins.

The penile response to each stimulus is scored as a percentage of full erection; the movement channel on the polygraph is carefully monitored to ensure that the patient is not manually stimulating himself during the presentations. Between presentations of the stimuli of interest, a neutral stimulus is presented until the penile response returns to baseline, at which point the next stimulus of interest is presented. To minimize the effect of fatigue on responses to stimuli presented late in the assessment period, the duration of presentation of each stimulus is limited to about three minutes. A self-report measure of sexual arousal can be obtained during assessment simply by asking the patient to estimate his level of arousal along some continuum, such a 10-point scale ranging from 1, "no arousal," to 10, "extreme arousal."

There are a few other considerations in the assessment of penile response to fetish stimuli. Abel, Blanchard, and Barlow (1981), for example, found that videotaped presentations of paraphilic stimuli generally resulted in greater penile responses than did audiotape, colored slides, or "free fantasy" presentations. With the notable exception of some cases of partialism, this should not be an issue in the assessment of fetishism where the fetish object itself should simply be "presented." In those cases of partialisms where the presentation of the actual body part is not feasible, videotape presentations probably should be used.

Abel et al. (1981) also found that the instructions given to patients influenced the subsequent penile response to paraphilic stimuli. Patients who were asked to voluntarily suppress their erections to the paraphilic stimuli showed significant decreases in penile response, although it should be noted that no patient was able to suppress his erections completely. Nevertheless, the authors reaffirmed the caution that the voluntary control of sexual arousal must be taken into account during assessment of penile response. A true picture of the patient's pattern of deviant sexual arousal, or at least of the actual levels of arousal, cannot be obtained without the full cooperation of the patient. Patients who consciously try to suppress their arousal, for whatever reason, will succeed to some extent.

A final consideration for assessment is the possibility of summated arousal. Some models of classical conditioning, such as those by Grings (1972), Hull (1943), and Rescorla and Wagner (1972), allow for the summation of conditioned responses—that is, the CR elicited by two CSs presented together will be some additive function of the individual CRs of each CS presented alone. That being the case, the possibility exists that for some patients there is a combination of fetish stimuli that would be particularly "motivating." One could imagine, for example, that the patient in the sample described by Chalkley and Powell (1983) who was reported to have had nine fetishes would have been extremely aroused had he encountered all nine fetish objects at once. Obviously, if one of the goals of assessment is to identify potential conditions under which sexual arousal may become unmanageable, then we must investigate the phenomenon of summated arousal. Such an investigation would involve presenting various combinations of stimuli during specific assessment to determine which combinations elicit the highest levels of arousal. A full appreciation of the forces behind some patients' fetish behavior may not be possible unless their response to combinations of fetish stimuli is determined.

Of course, fetish objects are not really "encountered" as much as they are "sought out"; as has already been described, a fetishist may go to great lengths to acquire his object of attraction. If we accept that summation of arousal occurs, and there is, in fact, some evidence for this phenomenon (Junginger, 1988), then we might also guess that a fetishist will seek out these stimuli to enhance his sexual arousal. A reasonable conclusion is that for each case of fetishism there is some combination of fetish stimuli and possibly other, more appropriate stimuli that the fetishist finds most arousing. Accordingly, the fetishist will tend to seek out these particular stimulus combinations, some of which may lead to unmanageable levels of sexual arousal and its unfortunate consequences.

Experimental psychology has a long tradition of the use of aversive techniques to suppress appetitive behavior (e.g., Estes and Skinner's [1941] "conditioned suppression" technique). It is not surprising, then, that behavior therapists initially adopted these techniques to treat fetishism. Although there are variations on the actual method, as will be seen, the basic strategy is to pair the fetish object with an aversive UCS (e.g., electric shock) that elicits a UCR that is incompatible with sexual arousal:

CS———	(CR)———	UCS———	UCR
fetish	sexual	shock	fear/
object	arousal		anxiety

The general term for this type of procedure is "counterconditioning." The aversive UCS, in this case electric shock, is used to condition the CS in a manner counter to its original conditioning; that is, the prior CR of sexual arousal is "countered" by a subsequently learned CR of fear or anxiety. "Covert sensitization" (Cautela, 1967) is a term that formerly was reserved for counter-conditioning procedures in which both the CS and UCS are presented imaginally. Current usage, however, applies the term to any procedure in which either the CS or the UCS is presented in that mode. Marks and Gelder (1967), for example, presented electric shocks to the forearm or leg of their patients while the patients were engaged in deviant behavior, and during "fantasy trials"—that is, while the patients were imagining their deviant behavior. The treatment appeared extremely effective in reducing the deviant behavior of a variety of paraphiliacs, including fetishists. A 2-year follow-up (Marks, Gelder, & Bancroft, 1970) found a continued reduction in deviant behavior compared with both pretreatment levels and the deviant behavior of a group of patients who refused treatment.

As in Marks and Gelder (1967), most treatments of fetish arousal follow from the same basic counterconditioning model. However, researchers have been very creative in their choice of aversive UCSs. Marshall and Lippens (1977), for example, paired their patient's deviant fantasies with conditions that created "boredom." Their patient was instructed to masturbate to orgasm while verbalizing his deviant fantasies about panty hose. After reaching orgasm, he was to continue masturbating for the remainder of the 90 minute session while verbally fantasizing about panty hose, even if it became difficult or even uncomfortable to do so.

Marshall and Lippens (1977) reported that after nine sessions the patient had lost almost all interest in panty hose as indicated by penile response, self-report, and by the verbal content of his masturbation fantasies; from a conditioning perspective, the newly acquired CR of satiation had countered the prior CR of sexual arousal. Furthermore, the patient's penile response and self-report of arousal to an appropriate sexual stimulus—an erotic description of a naked woman without panty hose—dramatically increased, an outcome Marshall and Lippens attributed to the patient's subsequent use of appropriate fantasies during masturbation. (Although, as we will see, there may be another explanation for such increases in appropriate arousal.) Interestingly, the patient apparently could not be taught to use appropriate fantasies during masturbation before his arousal to deviant fantasies was reduced.

In one of the earliest reports of the use of aversive techniques to treat fetishism, Raymond (1956) described a more traditional counterconditioning procedure, but one also having elements similar to the "stimulus satiation" approach to counterconditioning used by Marshall and Lippens (1977). Raymond's patient was referred for prefrontal leukotomy after attacking a perambulator (baby carriage), the twelfth such attack reported to police. The patient reported that he had experienced sexual urges to attack baby carriages and women's handbags since the age of 10, and actually carried out these attacks on an average of two or three times a week.

Several handbags, baby carriages, and colored illustrations of these objects were gathered in the hospital and were shown to the patient after he was injected with a nausea-inducing drug. This treatment was given every 2 hours, day and night, for a week, after which the patient was allowed to go home for 8 days. When he returned to the hospital, he reported that for the first time he was able to have intercourse with his wife without fantasizing about handbags and baby carriages. The treatment continued and, in addition, the patient was asked to write about the objects, which he did at great length. After 5 more days of treatment, he reported that the mere sight of baby carriages and handbags made him sick. At that point, he was confined to bed and handbags and baby carriages were piled around him. Treatment continued at irregular intervals and the patient was finally discharged from the hospital, seemingly cured of his fetishes. A 19-month follow-up found no fetish behavior or fantasies. Again, from a conditioning perspective, the newly acquired CR of nausea and satiation had countered the prior CR of sexual arousal.

In spite of the straightforward formulation provided by two-process theory, there is not general agreement that the moderate success of conditioning approaches to the treatment of fetishism is due, in fact, to conditioning. McConaghy (1990), for example, claimed that aversive counterconditioning may not actually eliminate deviant arousal, but it may give the patient some control over his deviant overt behavior. The mechanism through which this control is achieved is unknown.

In any case, treatments narrowly focused on the patient's attraction to unusual sexual objects appear less likely to be successful than those that also encourage appropriate arousal. Davidson (1968) was among the first to describe a specific technique to train appropriate sexual arousal. In his procedure, now referred to as orgasmic reorientation or reconditioning, the patient is encouraged to use his deviant fantasies during masturbation to become sexually aroused. At a point just short of orgasm, however, he is to switch his attention to more appropriate sexual stimuli. The patient is allowed to return to his deviant fantasies if he loses his arousal prior to orgasm, but orgasm itself must be associated with appropriate sexual stimuli. As treatment progresses, the patient learns to associate sexual arousal and orgasm with the more appropriate sexual stimuli.

Orgasmic reconditioning is thought to be somewhat effective at conditioning (presumably) sexual arousal to appropriate real-world stimuli and fantasies (Abel, Mittelman, & Becker, 1985; Brownell, Hayes, & Barlow, 1977). The moderate success of this approach highlights the importance of the patient's masturbatory practices in determining his sexual arousal pattern. A developing view among researchers seems to be that sexual fetishes are originally established through a process best conceptualized by classical conditioning. However, the deviant arousal pattern is maintained through the patient's masturbatory practices, which may be a consequence of the unavailability of an appropriate sexual partner. In other words, the patient substitutes an item associated with women through classical conditioning—thus, the common fetish of women's undergarments—in lieu of the actual woman herself. A woman may be unavailable as a sexual partner because the patient lacks the necessary skills to establish a heterosexual relationship (cf. LaTorre, 1980).

Several authors have noted the apparent ineptitude of many paraphiliacs; they are often characterized as timid and lacking social skills (Gosselin & Wilson, 1980). They may even perceive women as threatening. It is increasingly clear, then, that all of these various aspects of fetishism must be addressed in therapy. Aversion therapy may lessen the patient's arousal to inappropriate sexual stimuli, or at least allow him to control his overt behavior toward these stimuli (McConaghy, 1990), but gaining access to more appropriate sexual outlets may involve social skills training and possibly procedures to reduce the anxiety associated with women. Without access to more appropriate sexual outlets, the patient could be expected to return to deviant masturbatory practices and to reestablish his deviant sexual arousal pattern.

The case study I have chosen to illustrate some of the major issues discussed in this chapter has been described elsewhere (Junginger, 1985, 1988). Although it could hardly be characterized as a successful treatment of fetishism, it does raise a number of collateral issues, such as summated arousal and other conditioning phenomena, which are rarely given much consideration.

The patient, whom we will call "Mark," was a 26-year-old white male whose disruptive behavior was often brought to the attention of local authorities. Mark was arrested on a number of occasions for "acting out" in public, which typically involved his making a nuisance of himself with women. Mark would confront women and act "in a peculiar manner." Although he was never reported to have assaulted anyone, his behavior was threatening enough so that the police often became involved. In the most recent incident, Mark was arrested and subsequently reprimanded to the local mental health center after continually harassing a young girl at a public swimming pool.

At the mental health center, Mark claimed that his "problem with women" was that they made him "hot" (sexually aroused). He claimed that he would never harm anyone, but that sometimes he just couldn't help himself and had to get close to a woman. Getting close to a woman made him even more aroused, which often led to the disruptive behavior that now landed him in the hands of mental health officials. He denied anything unusual about his behavior, but admitted that he was somewhat "preoccupied" with women and sex.

As a general assessment, Mark was asked to carry a small notebook with him at all times and to make note of the situations that made him "hot" and how he dealt with this arousal. Over a 4-week period, Mark recorded an average of three to four orgasms a day in situations that always involved the presence of a woman and a second, very unusual stimulus—radio static.

When asked about his attraction to radio static, Mark reported that he had found it sexually arousing since he was a child. He recalled vigorously rocking on a toy rocking horse at the age of six while listening to his mother's old vacuum-tube radio blaring out music and static. Sometime later, he became aware that radio static alone could make him become sexually aroused:

$$S\text{————}UCS\text{————}UCR$$
radio static   rocking   sexual arousal

Sometime after that, in early adolescence, he began to notice that static in the presence of a woman made him become particularly aroused and he would often seek out women when he heard static; occasionally, he would masturbate in their presence:

$$CS\text{————}CR\text{————}R\text{ ——————→ }S^{R+-}$$

radio	sexual	approach	positive and negative
static	arousal	women/	reinforcement
		masturbation	

Over the years, Mark had established a fairly set masturbation routine in which he would turn on a radio, tune it between stations so that it would blare static, and then masturbate while he looked at some of his favorite pictures of women from a collection he kept locked in a small strong box. Mark never had a girlfriend, but claimed that he often would pay prostitutes at a local truck stop to have sex with him in his car while the radio blared static. Socially he appeared extremely inept (again, an observation often made of paraphiliacs [Gosselin & Wilson, 1980]).

Specific assessment of Mark's deviant sexual arousal pattern involved assessing his penile response and report of arousal to the stimuli used in his masturbation routine: static and pictures of women from his collection. In addition, we should be interested in his response to the combination of static and pictures of women because of the possibility that the individual CRs may summate and lead to unmanageable sexual arousal. Mark brought in two pictures from his collection, neither of which were very provocative, for use in the specific assessment. The specific assessment followed the procedure recommended by Tollison and Adams (1979, Table 2-2), which was briefly described earlier.

Mark was seated in a comfortable chair, and a penile-plethysmograph was properly placed. A motion-sensitive device located under his chair recorded any movement during the assessment. Penile response, movement, and time were recorded on the moving chart of a Grass Model 7 polygraph. At 1-minute intervals during the 3-minute stimulus presentations, Mark was asked to report his level of sexual arousal on a 10-point scale.

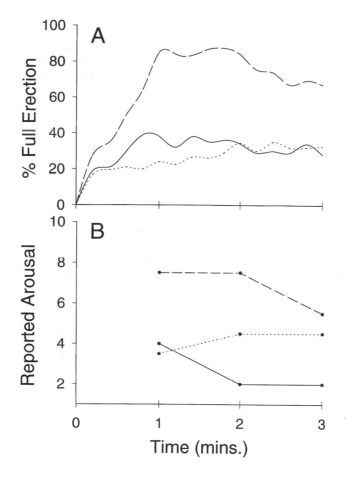

FIGURE 5.1. (A) Mean penile response to stimuli of interest. (B) Mean self-report of sexual arousal to stimuli of interest. Adapted from Junginger (1988). Copyright 1988 by Elsevier Science Ltd. Adapted by permission.

Figure 5.1(A) shows Mark's penile response to the stimuli of interest. His mean penile response to the two pictures of women was slightly less than his response to static, both hovering around 35–40% full erection. Note, however, that when the two types of stimuli were presented together, the response appears to be a summation of the responses to the individual stimuli presented alone. This resulted in extremely high levels of arousal peaking around 85% of full erection. Figure 5.1(B) shows that Mark's self-report of sexual arousal followed a similar pattern, except that he reported slightly more arousal to pictures of women than to static. Once again, however, the combination of static and pictures of women resulted in high levels of summated arousal, in this case indicated by self-report. Clearly, in Mark's case, static in the presence of a woman could lead to unmanageable levels of sexual arousal.

Supporting this conclusion was Mark's description of his most recent brush with the law at the public swimming pool. He reported that the employees at the pool had placed a radio next to the public address microphone so that swimmers could listen to music. The combination of poor radio reception and an open mike resulted in a great deal of static being broadcast though the public address system. This caused Mark to become sexually aroused, and his arousal was intensified by the presence of numerous women in swimsuits.

He focused his attention on a young girl sunning in a chair next to him, and the police were called when he ignored her father's repeated requests to leave her alone.

Treatment initially was narrowly focused on removing Mark's deviant sexual arousal to static. This was to be followed by a social skills training program to establish at least a minimal level of social competence that I hoped would give him access to more appropriate sexual outlets. I considered several aversive stimuli for use as a UCS in a counterconditioning procedure. Mark had made several references to his enjoyment of the "smells of sex," so I decided that this might be a particularly sensitive mode of presentation. He was brought back into the assessment laboratory to test first the effectiveness of a noxious smell for countering his arousal to static, and then to begin treatment.

Figure 5.2 shows Mark's penile response to static, and to the noxious smell: lavender smelling salts. Not only did the smell fail to suppress his arousal to static, it actually dramatically increased it! When asked about his unusual response to a smell that I and several others found almost unbearable, Mark explained that the lavender smelling salts reminded him of the smell of urinals, which he found very arousing. This was an element of his sexual arousal pattern that I had completely missed in the general and specific assessments.

After some further experimentation, I found that a mild electric shock (really more annoying than painful) presented to the underside of Mark's right wrist was an effective counter to his arousal to static. I quickly set up a procedure in which static was presented for 30 minutes, during which Mark would receive a mild electric shock every 5 seconds that his penile response was above 20% of full erection; he would receive no shocks as long as his arousal stayed below 20%. The 30-minute presentation of static was followed by a 30-minute presentation of one of the pictures of a woman from his collection. During the presentation of the picture, Mark was not shocked and was allowed to become as aroused as he liked, as long as he did not manually stimulate himself. Three treatment periods, each consisting of one 30-minute presentation of static followed by one 30-minute presentation of a picture of a woman, were planned for each therapy session. This was a fairly rigorous schedule in which Mark would be undergoing treatment for 3 hours in each of the daily therapy sessions.

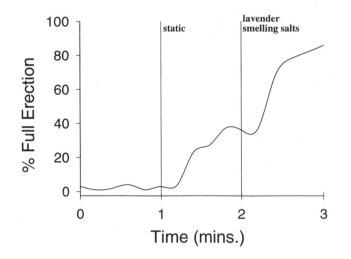

FIGURE 5.2. Penile response to static and to potential aversive UCS (lavender smelling salts).

Mark completed 4 days of treatment before the psychiatrist in charge of his case had a change of heart and pulled him out of treatment. She was concerned that the apparent effectiveness of the procedure at eliminating his attraction to static may lead to his behaving aggressively toward women. That is, in her original formulation of the case, she believed that Mark's attraction to static was the result of the action of two ego defense mechanisms: reaction formation and displacement. According to her hypothesis, Mark hated women, but his ego changed this hatred to sexual attraction and then displaced it onto static.

Be that as it may, Mark's response to the treatment conditions in the 4 days that he was in treatment was encouraging. Figure 5.3 shows his penile response to a picture from his collection, and, indirectly, to static as indicated by the number of shocks he received in each treatment period when his penile response was above 20%. (The first period of Thursday's session is not shown because it was in that period that the failed experiment with lavender smelling salts occurred.)

In the last two treatment periods within each session, there was a dramatic decrease in penile response to both static and a picture of a woman, which was probably attributable to habituation (cf. O'Donohue & Geer, 1993). However, the obvious decrease in the number of shocks across daily sessions was probably the result of extinction, or of learned suppression. In the last session, Tuesday, Mark received practically no shocks and reported that for the first time in his memory he was losing his interest in static.

Just as interesting is Mark's penile response to the picture of a woman. Across sessions, Mark showed a gradual but very noticeable increase in penile response to the picture, even as his arousal to static was decreasing. This apparently was not the result of orgasmic reconditioning in that Mark reported that, for the most part, he was following instructions

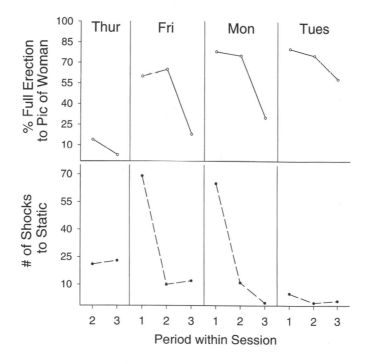

FIGURE 5.3. Penile response to picture of a woman, and number of shocks to static within and across therapy sessions.

to refrain from any masturbatory behavior between sessions. At the very least, he was not engaged in any concerted effort to pair pictures of women with masturbation in the absence of static.

Mark's increase in arousal to a picture of a woman may have been a consequence (in some sense) of his decrease in arousal to static. Pavlov (1927) was the first to demonstrate that when two or more stimuli are presented in compound and paired with a UCS, the stronger or more salient of the stimuli appears to acquire most of the conditioning; in other words, the stronger or more salient stimulus "overshadows" the other stimuli. Furthermore, other researchers (e.g., Kaufman & Bolles, 1981; Matzel, Schachtman, & Miller, 1985) have found that when the CR to the dominant stimulus is extinguished, the CR to the overshadowed stimulus is somehow facilitated. This appears to have occurred in Mark's case; as his CR of sexual arousal to static was being extinguished, his CR of sexual arousal to the picture of a woman was being facilitated. The mechanism behind this phenomenon is unknown. Nevertheless, it would be interesting to speculate how often it is misattributed to other causes. As noted earlier, Marshall and Lippens (1977) described practically the same phenomenon, but attributed their patient's subsequent increase in appropriate arousal to orgasmic reconditioning because the patient claimed that he was now masturbating to appropriate sexual stimuli. Mark's case certainly suggests that "recovery from overshadowing" (Matzel et al., 1985) is another plausible explanation.

There are other classical conditioning phenomena that also may play a part in fetishism. "Blocking," for example, is a phenomenon in which the prior conditioning of one stimulus of a compound "blocks" subsequent conditioning of the other stimuli of the compound (Kamin, 1968, 1969). A patient, therefore, who continuously pairs a fetish object with masturbation would not be expected to develop sexual arousal to new, possibly more appropriate sexual stimuli when they are paired with the fetish object during masturbation; prior conditioning of the fetish object would block subsequent conditioning to the new, more appropriate stimuli. As with recovery from overshadowing, we might wonder how often blocking is a consideration in the development and maintenance of fetish arousal and its treatment.

Within the two-process framework, we might also wonder why the standard treatment for OCD, exposure and response prevention (Rachman & Hodgson, 1980), is not typically used with fetishism. As has already been noted, the popularity of aversive counterconditioning approaches to the treatment of fetishism probably comes out of a long tradition in experimental psychology of the use of aversive techniques to suppress appetitive behavior. However, an approach more consistent with a view of fetishism as essentially a variant of OCD would involve exposing the patient to the fetish object (the CS) while preventing genital stimulation (the UCS), thus extinguishing sexual arousal (the CR). Of course, assurances must also be made that the patient is not engaging in deviant masturbation outside of therapy.

In some ways, Mark's treatment could be thought of as a type of exposure and response prevention—he was continuously exposed to static while his arousal was prevented or suppressed by mild, distracting shocks, and his movement was monitored by a motion-sensitive device to ensure that he was not masturbating. Unfortunately, the inclusion of electric shocks somewhat complicates conceptualizing the treatment as exposure and response prevention (it might more accurately be called "punishment"), but the basic approach would seem to have merit. Treatments based more directly on Pavlovian extinction might be worth investigating.

There are several conclusions to be drawn from this review of fetishism that may be helpful to researchers and therapists. First, a number of classical conditioning phenomena potentially may be at play in the development and maintenance of fetish arousal. The possibility of summated arousal must be investigated to obtain a more accurate picture of the forces behind the compulsivelike behavior often seen in fetishism. For any fetishist, the possibility exists that there is some combination of stimuli, both fetish and appropriate, that may result in unmanageable levels of sexual arousal. These unmanageable levels of arousal may not be obvious in more cursory assessments of responses to individual fetish stimuli.

In fact, the seemingly abnormal *level* of sexual arousal in fetishism is another characteristic that may distinguish it from normal sexual arousal patterns. At present, it is unclear whether fetishists actually have higher absolute levels of sexual arousal (cf. Abel et al., 1981; Bailey, 1991) or whether they may possess a greater capacity for conditioned arousal (see, for example, Rescorla and Wagner's [1972] concept of *lambda,* the highest level of conditioning that can be supported by a particular UCS). In any case, the type of family study that has linked, for example, an inherited potential for general anxiety with the development of a variety of specific anxiety disorders (Black, Noyes, Goldstein, & Blum, 1992) has yet to be done for fetishism. Such a study could tell us something about the biological predisposition to develop the disorder.

Recovery from overshadowing (Matzel et al., 1985), on the other hand, is a phenomenon that may become obvious only after treatment, when arousal to dominant fetish stimuli has been extinguished. Accordingly, it may be worthwhile to redo a general and specific assessment after treatment to determine if arousal to "latent" fetish stimuli has been facilitated. I should add, however, that the probability of this occurring, and its clinical significance, are unknown. At least in theory, the extinction of arousal to dominant fetish stimuli could lead to problematic arousal to other stimuli that went unnoticed during the initial assessments.

The importance of social skills training is obvious, if only to ensure that the patient has access to other sexual outlets after his deviant arousal is suppressed. Without such access, we would be unreasonable to think that the patient would not return to deviant masturbatory practices and thus reestablish his fetish arousal. Of course, this is a rather narrow view of the potential benefits of social skills training. We might also hope that such training would result in the kind of life that is less favorable to the development of psychological problems, of which fetishism is only one.

The effectiveness of treatments of fetishism more directly based on Pavlovian extinction probably should be investigated, if only to decrease the general use of aversive techniques. With the proper consideration given to masturbatory practices outside of therapy, straightforward exposure and response prevention would seem to be an obvious approach to eliminating fetish arousal and the compulsivelike fetish behavior it motivates.

Finally, I have to wonder how often this "disorder" really warrants treatment. With the current climate of increasing acceptance of almost all forms of sexual expression, we might again ask the fundamental question of who, exactly, thinks fetishism is a disorder? Obviously, if a person consistently experiences unmanageable levels of sexual arousal in situations where that arousal cannot be expressed, then something should be done. However, it appears that the overwhelming majority of fetishists have adjusted to their "disorder" by creating more situations where their arousal can be expressed, such as on the Internet "alternative sex" forums.

My guess is that fetishism, narrowing defined as attraction to unusual or atypical objects, will become less of a concern for psychology and psychiatry as these alternative outlets of expression proliferate. Global forums such as the Internet may allow the assimilation of fetishism into the mainstream of sexual interests in a way that is much more effective than the old social groups such as the Mackintosh Society. Fetishists who cannot assimilate will be those with other, more serious deficits, and they will become the concern of the mental health professions.

NOTES

1. As I proofread this in midyear 1997, most of the "fetish action" on the Internet is taking place on the alternative sex forums. However, some fetish groups are just now establishing "home pages" on the World Wide Web—a network of file servers on the Internet that can instantly display (unlike the text-based Usenet newsgroups) both text and picture files, and in some cases, sound and video. Even as the alternative sex groups seem to be moving to "the Web," it is impossible to predict where on the Internet they will be a few years from now. With the initial attempts at censorship of the Internet now being debated in the U.S. Congress, the alternative sex groups may move and regroup several times in the months ahead.
2. Letourneau and O'Donohue (1997) generally failed in their efforts to classically condition sexual arousal in females. When considered with the positive results in males reported by Rachman (1966) and by Rachman and Hodgson (1968), this failure may provide some clues to the overwhelming imbalance in the fetishism sex ratio.

REFERENCES

Abel, G., Blanchard, E., & Barlow, D. (1981). Measurement of sexual arousal in several paraphilias: The effects of stimulus modality, instructional set and stimulus content on the objective measurement of sexual arousal in several paraphilias. *Behaviour Research and Therapy, 19,* 25–33.

Abel, G., Mittelman, M., & Becker, J. (1985). Sexual offenders: Results of assessment and recommendations for treatment. In M. Ben-Aron, S. Hucker, & C. Webster (Eds.), *Clinical criminology: The assessment and treatment of criminal behavior.* Toronto: M & M Graphics.

Bailey, K. (1991). Human paleopsychopathology: Implications for the paraphilias. *New Trends in Experimental and Clinical Psychiatry, 7,* 5–16.

Barlow, D. (1977). Assessment of sexual behavior. In A. Ciminero, K. Calhoun, & H. Adams (Eds.), *Handbook of behavioral assessment.* New York: Wiley.

Barlow, D., Becker, R., Leitenberg, H., & Agras, W. (1970). A mechanical strain gauge for recording penile circumference change. *Journal of Applied Behavior Analysis, 3,* 73–76.

Black, D., Noyes, R., Goldstein, R., & Blum, N. (1992). A family study of obsessive–compulsive disorder. *Archives of General Psychiatry, 49,* 362–368.

Bouton, M., & Bolles, R. (1985). Contexts, event-memories, and extinction. In P. Balsam & A. Tomie (Eds.), *Context and learning.* Hillsdale, NJ: Erlbaum.

Brownell, K., Hayes, S., & Barlow, D. (1977). Patterns of appropriate and deviant sexual arousal: The behavioral treatment of multiple sexual deviations. *Journal of Consulting and Clinical Psychology, 45,* 1144–1155.

Cautela, J. (1967). Covert sensitization. *Psychological Reports, 20,* 459–468.

Chalkley, A., & Powell, G. (1983). The clinical description of forty-eight cases of sexual fetishism. *British Journal of Psychiatry, 142,* 292–295.

Davidson, G. (1968). Elimination of a sadistic fantasy by a client-controlled counterconditioning technique: A case study. *Journal of Abnormal Psychology, 73,* 84–90.

Domjan, M., & Burkhard, B. (1986). *The principles of learning and behavior* (2nd ed.). Pacific Grove, CA: Brooks/Cole.

Estes, W., & Skinner, B.F. (1941). Some quantitative properties of anxiety. *Journal of Experimental Psychology, 29,* 390–400.

Freund, K. (1963). A laboratory method for diagnosing predominance of homosexual and heterosexual interest in the male. *Behaviour Research and Therapy, 1,* 85–93.

Freund, K. (1965). Diagnosing heterosexual pedophilia by means of a test for sexual interest. *Behaviour Research and Therapy, 3,* 229–234.

Gamman, L., & Makinen, M. (1995). *Female fetishism.* New York: New York University Press.

Gosselin, C., & Wilson, G. (1980). *Sexual variations.* New York: Simon & Schuster.

Grings, W. (1972). Compound stimulus transfer in human classical conditioning. In A. Black & W. Prokassy (Eds.), *Classical conditioning II: Current theory and research*. New York: Appleton-Century-Crofts.

Herrnstein, R. (1969). Method and theory in the study of avoidance. *Psychological Review, 76*, 49–69.

Hull, C. (1943). *Principles of behavior*. New York: Appleton-Century-Crofts.

Junginger, J. (1985). Atypical psychosis and fetishism. In J. Neal, T. Oltmanns, & G. Davidson (Eds.), *Case studies in abnormal psychology*. New York: Wiley.

Junginger, J. (1988). Summation of arousal in partial fetishism. *Journal of Behavior Therapy and Experimental Psychiatry, 19*, 297–300.

Kamin, L. (1968). "Attention-like" processes in classical conditioning. In M. Jones (Ed.), *Miami symposium on the prediction of behavior: Aversive stimulation*. Miami: University of Miami Press.

Kamin, L. (1969). Predictability, surprise, attention and conditioning. In B. Campbell & R. Church (Eds.), *Punishment and aversive behavior*. New York: Appleton-Century-Crofts.

Kaufman, M., & Bolles, R. (1981). A nonassociative aspect of overshadowing. *Bulletin of the Psychonomic Society, 18*, 319–320.

LaTorre, R. (1980). Devaluation of the human love object: Heterosexual rejection as a possible antecedent to fetishism. *Journal of Abnormal Psychology, 89*, 295–298.

Legal shoe drops for Marla Maples aide with foot fetish. (1994, February 17). *The Boston Globe*, p. 3.

Letourneau, E., & O'Donohue, W. (1997). Classical conditioning of female sexual arousal. *Archives of Sexual Behavior, 26*, 63–78.

Marks, I., & Gelder, M. (1967). Transvestism and fetishism. Clinical and psychological changes during faradic aversion. *British Journal of Psychiatry, 113*, 711–729.

Marks, I., Gelder, M., & Bancroft, J. (1970). Sexual deviants two years after electric aversion. *British Journal of Psychiatry, 117*, 173–185.

Marshall, W., & Lippens, K. (1977). The clinical value of boredom: A procedure for reducing inappropriate sexual interests. *Journal of Nervous and Mental Disease, 165*, 283–287.

Matzel, L., Schachtman, T., & Miller, R. (1985). Recovery of an overshadowed association achieved by extinction of the overshadowing stimulus. *Learning and Motivation, 16*, 398–412.

McConaghy, N. (1988). Sexual dysfunction and deviation. In A. Bellack & M. Hersen (Eds.), *Behavioral assessment* (3rd ed.). Needham Heights, MA: Allyn & Bacon.

McConaghy, N. (1990). Sexual deviation. In A. Bellack, M. Hersen, & A. Kazdin (Eds.), *International handbook of behavior modification and therapy* (2nd ed.). New York: Plenum Press.

Miller, N. (1948). Studies of fear as an acquirable drive. *Journal of Experimental Psychology, 38*, 89–101.

Mineka, S. (1979). The role of fear in theories of avoidance learning, flooding, and extinction. *Psychological Bulletin, 86*, 985–1010.

Mowrer, O. (1947). On the dual nature of learning—a reinterpretation of "conditioning" and "problem solving." *Harvard Educational Review, 17*, 102–148.

O'Donohue, W., & Geer, J. (1993). Research issues in sexual dysfunction. In J. Geer & W. O'Donohue (Eds.), *Handbook of the assessment and treatment of sexual dysfunction*. New York: Allyn & Bacon.

Parents guard girls from jogger with toe fetish. (1992, March 6). *St. Louis Post-Dispatch*, p. A12.

Pavlov, I. (1927). *Conditioned reflexes*. Oxford: Oxford University Press.

Rachman, S. (1966). Sexual fetishism: An experimental analogue. *Psychological Record, 16*, 293–296.

Rachman, S., & Hodgson, R. (1968). Experimentally-induced "sexual fetishism": Replication and development. *Psychological Record, 18*, 25–27.

Rachman, S., & Hodgson, R. (1980). *Obsessions and compulsions*. Englewood Cliffs, NJ: Prentice Hall.

Raphling, D. (1989). Fetishism in a woman. *Journal of the American Psychoanalytic Association, 37*, 465–491.

Raymond, M. (1956). Case of fetishism treated by aversion therapy. *British Medical Journal, 2*, 854–857.

Rescorla, R., & Wagner, A. (1972). A theory of Pavlovian conditioning: Variations in the effectiveness of reinforcement and nonreinforcement. In A. Black & W. Prokassy (Eds.), *Classical conditioning II: Current theory and research*. New York: Appleton-Century-Crofts.

Richards, A. (1990). Female fetishes and female perversions: Hermine Hug-Hellmuth's "A case of female foot or more properly boot fetishism" reconsidered. *Psychoanalytic Review, 77,* 11–23.

Schoenfeld, W. (1950). An experimental approach to anxiety, escape and avoidance behavior. In P. Hock & J. Zubin (Eds.), *Anxiety*. New York: Grune and Stratton.

Tollison, D., & Adams, H. (1979). *Sexual disorders*. New York: Gardner Press.

Wise, T. (1985). Fetishism-etiology and its treatment: A review from multiple perspectives. *Comprehensive Psychiatry, 26,* 249–257.

Zavitzianos, G. (1982). The perversion of fetishism in women. *Psychoanalytic Quarterly, 51,* 405–425.

6

FROTTEURISM

Frotteurism and the Theory of Courtship Disorder

Kurt Freund
Michael C. Seto
Michael Kuban

THE PARAPHILIAS

The paraphilias—a term coined by Stekel (1923)—are pathological erotic preferences. They can be broadly divided into two categories, pathological erotic *target* preferences, and pathological erotic *activity* preferences. In the former, the preferred targets of erotic cognitions (masturbation fantasies) or activities are objects other than physically mature persons. In the latter, the preferred activities are highly atypical for individuals who erotically prefer physically mature persons. Differentiating between pathological target and activity preferences—without ignoring the fact that both may occur in the same individual—may have certain advantages for analyzing the mutual relationships between paraphilias.

Our knowledge about the paraphilias has not yet reached the level of development in other areas of psychopathology. Moreover, relatively little progress has been made in the organization of paraphilias since Binet (1887) and Krafft-Ebing (1886/1978).

Etiology

Among the neurologically oriented theories of the paraphilias is that of Kolarsky, Freund, Machek, and Polak (1967), who concluded that some paraphilic behavior may be caused by early lesions or similar abnormalities of the left temporal lobe. Such patients were more likely to exhibit paraphilic behavior than those patients whose epileptic focus had a different brain localization, or whose seizures started much later in life. There are many other consistent clinical observations in the literature. Their validity has been recently discussed, together with the findings of other relevant neurophysiological studies, by Langevin (1994).

Binet (1887) was the first to point out the possibility of pathological imprinting in early childhood (the first mention of the imprinting hypothesis with regard to humans), an application of which still appears to be plausible as one of a number of etiological factors. In Binet's implicit conditioning theory, the primary object is a person to whom the child is attached and the mediators between the child and the fetish are the senses of touch and smell. Schrenck-Notzing (1899) elaborated on Binet's hypothesis, heading in the direction of later learning theorists by suggesting that association of activated sexual emotion with an external experience could be used for therapeutic purposes. McGuire, Carlisle, and Young (1965) argued that conditioning contributes to the development and maintenance of paraphilias, but is not a sufficient cause. More elaborate conditioning and social learning theories have been discussed by Laws and Marshall (1990).

Probably the most representative psychoanalytic theory is by Gillespie (1964), who characterized the paraphilias as remnants of childhood sexuality. Langevin (1994) has recently reviewed a number of psychoanalytic theories regarding the paraphilias. A related example of etiological hypothesizing is a paleoethologist's suggestion that the paraphilias represent some degree of phylogenetic regression, "whereby the older repressed and suppressed once-adaptive material is recovered and made accessible to the motivational system and possibly to behavior and consciousness as well" (Bailey, 1991, pp. 5–6). At least in the near future, it will not be easy to gather observations to test any of these etiological hypotheses.

AN ALTERNATIVE APPROACH

Krafft-Ebing (1886/1978), the most comprehensive early researcher of paraphilias, examined the mutual affinities between paraphilic expressions. This inquiry has served as a starting point for later etiologically oriented analyses. Abel and Rouleau (1990) did not address the possible existence of particular patterns of affinities, although they demonstrated that the same individual can have a substantial number of paraphilic interests. However, Abel and Rouleau interpreted their results as indicating that "*irrespective of the category of specific paraphilia,* members in any one category were concurrently involved, or had been involved in other specific categories of paraphilic behavior [emphasis added]" (p. 16).

The Investigated Group of Paraphilic Patterns

The study reported here was conducted under the supposition that Krafft-Ebing's approach may provide a convenient basis for research on the etiology of paraphilias. The analysis concerned the mutual relations between a specific group of pathological activity preferences: voyeurism, exhibitionism, frotteurism, and the "preferential rape pattern" (Freund, 1990). The preferential rape pattern can be defined as a pathological, nonsadistic preference for committing rape (i.e., having sex with a nonconsenting person). With the exception of the preferential rape pattern, these paraphilias appear in the latest edition of the *Diagnostic and Statistical Manual of Mental Disorders* (DSM-IV; American Psychiatric Association, 1994) as specific diagnostic categories. We argue that these types of paraphilias are closely related, possibly representing expressions of the same underlying disorder. They will be referred to as types of "courtship disorder," an abbreviation of "disorder of phasing of courtship behavior" (see Freund, 1990). This name reflects the use of the term "courtship" by students of avian behavior (Morris, 1970; Tinbergen, 1965) for all precopulatory reproductive activities. This name is also used by students of the sexual behavior of *Drosophila melanogaster,* the fruit fly (Greenspan, 1995; Hall, 1994).[1]

The idea of paraphilia as a disturbance in the realm of courtship was originally put forward by Ellis (1933/1978, p. 190), who referred to exhibitionism as a "symbolic act based on a perversion of courtship."

The mutual relatedness of some of these types of courtship disorder was observed by early authors in sexology. Krafft-Ebing (1886/1978) called frotteurism a form of exhibitionism, and Freud (1905/1925) coined the term "scoptophilia" to indicate his belief that voyeurism and exhibitionism were intrinsically related. More recent authors have also noted associations between these paraphilic patterns. Taylor (1947) noted a co-occurrence of exhibitionism and frotteurism. Yalom (1960) described cases of co-occurrence of voyeurism, exhibitionism, and rape. Grassberger (1964) found that 12% of subjects arrested for indecent exposure had committed other sexual offenses, especially rape. According to Gebhard, Gagnon, Pomeroy, and Christenson (1965), 1 in 10 incarcerated exhibitionists had also committed rape; these authors also reported an association between exhibitionism and toucheurism. Abel, Becker, Cunningham-Rathner, Mittelman, and Rouleau (1988) found a high degree of co-occurrence in paraphilic behaviors for a group of 561 male outpatients. For example, 28% of the 142 men reporting exhibitionistic activity also reported voyeuristic activity; conversely, 63% of the 62 men reporting voyeuristic activity also reported exhibitionistic activity. Finally, Bradford, Boulet, and Pawlak (1992) have also reported on the co-occurrence of these paraphilias in a sample of 443 men undergoing a forensic psychiatric assessment. Of the 115 men reporting voyeuristic activity (the largest single paraphilic category in their study), 66% had engaged in frotteuristic activity, 52% had engaged in exhibitionistic activity, and 47% had committed rape.

Three Basic Hypotheses

The idea that certain paraphilic patterns are closely related is based mainly on two hypotheses. First, that *normal human sexual interaction (courtship) is regulated by a set of preferences for a certain sequence of erotic sensory stimuli and erotic activities.* Second, *in courtship disorder, sexual interactions deviate from this normative sequence in a characteristic way.* Freund and Kolarsky (1965) described an idealized courtship sequence consisting of four phases: (1) a finding phase, consisting of locating and appraising a potential partner; (2) an affiliative phase, characterized by nonverbal and verbal overtures such as looking, smiling, and talking to a potential partner; (3) a tactile phase, in which physical contact is made; and (4) a copulatory phase, in which sexual intercourse occurs. The theory of courtship disorder views the paraphilic types as extreme intensifications or distortions of one of these four phases, wherein the remaining phases are entirely omitted or retained in a vestigial way.

A third explanatory hypothesis is that *distortions in the normal courtship sequence reflect the preference of these patients for a virtually instant conversion of sexual arousal into orgasm,* either at the time or later when the event is recalled in a masturbation fantasy. This third hypothesis may explain typical paraphilic activity features such as the preference for strangers as targets (as observed for exhibitionism by Mohr, Turner, & Jerry, 1964), and the relatively indiscriminate choice of target with regard to attractiveness and age.

The present formulation of the instant conversion hypothesis is based on the theorizing of Madlafousek, Zantovsky, Hlinak, and Kolarsky (1981). They suggested that men who target unknown and unsuspecting women may do so because they experience difficulty in making the transition from an initial state of low sexual arousal to states of higher sexual arousal. They therefore tend to skip over lower sexual arousal states. The erotic preference for unknown women, as it occurs in courtship disorder, can also be observed less frequently in predatory sadism.

In support of Madlafousek et al.'s (1981) hypothesis, Kolarsky and Madlafousek (1983) offered experimental evidence using phallometric testing, a method which measures penile volume changes while a subject watches erotic stimuli on a screen. They compared responses of exhibitionists and normal volunteers to two videotaped scenes. In one scene an actress made a gesture of explicit sexual invitation (raising her miniskirt, lifting one leg while spreading her knees, and pointing to her exposed genitals), and in the other this explicit invitation was preceded by coy erotic signaling (unbuttoning her blouse and turning away from the camera in order to avoid exposing her breasts). As predicted, the responses of the exhibitionists were greater when the explicit scenes were not preceded by any coy erotic signaling, whereas the normal volunteers responded more to the explicit gestures when they were preceded by coy erotic signaling.

The following analyses were restricted to the existence of courtship disorder in males who erotically prefer women (gynephiles). Courtship disorder also occurs in homosexual men. Whether courtship disorder also occurs in pedophiles is unclear. Among pedophiles, exposing is the only topographically similar paraphilic activity. Whether pedophilic versions of voyeurism, frotteurism/toucheurism, or preferential rape exist has not been demonstrated. An argument against the existence of courtship disorder in pedophiles is that the typical sequences of sexual interaction between adult and child is different from the normative courtship sequence between adults. However, this kind of argument is countered by a case of zoophilic voyeurism and exhibitionism described by McNally and Lukach (1991). This mildly mentally retarded patient would masturbate in front of large dogs that he abducted from their owners (and then let go), found in an owner's backyard, or observed through windows; however, he never tried to have sexual intercourse with a dog.

Only a few cases of otherwise mentally healthy women who exposed themselves have been published (see Gayford, 1981; Grob, 1985; Hermann & Schroder, 1936; Hollender, Brown, & Roback, 1977). There appear to be female versions of courtship disorder, although the senior author has diagnosed only one such patient.

REORGANIZING THE CLINICAL PRESENTATIONS

In the course of time, we found courtship disorder to include a much broader range of paraphilic behavior than first envisaged. We now believe there is a multitude of clinical presentations of courtship disorder, but most of them rarely come to the attention of professionals. To organize this diversity the clinical presentations were divided into "proto-types" and "variants." This division follows Thagard's (1992) differentiation between two types of representations of a category: prototypes, which are the "best examples" of the category, and variants, which constitute less obvious examples of a category. In the present context prototypes are clinical presentations which can easily be recognized as distortions of a particular phase in the normal courtship sequence. Voyeurism, exhibitionism, frotteur-ism, and the preferential rape pattern can be viewed as prototypes of courtship disorder. It further seemed appropriate to differentiate between two types of variants, those which appear to represent a combination of two or more prototypes of courtship disorder, and those which appear to represent a combination of a prototype of courtship disorder and other paraphilias.

Notes on the Typical Patterns

Voyeurism

Voyeurism, according to DSM-IV, involves

> the act of observing unsuspecting individuals (usually strangers) who are naked, in the process of disrobing, or engaging in sexual activity. The act of looking (peeping) is for the purpose of achieving sexual excitement, and generally no sexual activity with the observed person is sought. Orgasm, usually produced by masturbation, may occur during the voyeuristic activity or later while the person remembers what he has witnessed. (American Psychiatric Association, 1994, p. 532)

As conceived in the present discussion, voyeurism is an erotic preference for an activity other than normal sexual interactions. Sexually frustrated men may, for the purpose of achieving sexual excitement, engage in opportunistic peeping, but they are not voyeurs because these are not preferred activities. Similarly, preferential rapists and predatory sadists may engage in nonvoyeuristic peeping when trying to locate a suitable victim alone in a home.

An example of an equivalent voyeuristic prototype is an erotic preference for masturbating to pornographic videos or photographs when attractive sexual partners of the individual's preferred age and sex are readily available and there are no social conditions that would prevent sexual interaction. Another example is a preference for masturbating when listening by telephone to a woman describing sexual activities. These activities are usually substitute activities that take place during periods when attractive, willing partners are unavailable. Their persistent presence when a sexual partner is available is indicative of paraphilia.

A relatively common voyeuristic variant is a preference for observing women or fantasizing about women engaging in nonsexual activities, most frequently urination. This pattern appears to be a combination of voyeurism with a pathological target preference (see below). Such voyeurs often intrude or find ways to look into women's bathrooms.

An example of a clinical presentation which may occur as a voyeuristic prototype or variant involving the combination of voyeuristic and masochistic prototypes is triolism. In males, triolism is an erotic preference for viewing or listening to one's partner interacting sexually with another man, having her disrobe where other men might observe her, or asking her to speak during intercourse about her sexual experiences with other men. This paraphilia appears to be an transposition where the triolist pretends he is a male stranger, thus placing himself in a voyeuristic role, while his partner plays the role of an unknown woman.

Exhibitionism

According to DSM-IV, exhibitionism

> involves the exposure of one's genitals to a stranger. Sometimes the individual masturbates while exposing himself (or while fantasizing about exposing himself). If the person acts on these urges, there is generally no attempt at further sexual activity with the stranger. (American Psychiatric Association, 1994, p. 525)

There are a number of equivalent prototypes and variants of exhibitionism. Hirschfeld (1921, cited in Haire, 1966) suggested that obscene telephone calls should be considered an equivalent of exhibitionism. A variant with a masochistic component is a preference for exposing the buttocks, as described in "The Confessions of Jean Jacques Rousseau" (Rousseau, 1783/1985). A number of researchers have investigated the biological aspects of exhibitionism, so we will not discuss these here (e.g., Lang, Langevin, Bain, Frenzel, & Wright, 1989).

Frotteurism/Toucheurism

Frotteurism is a pathological erotic activity preference for rubbing the penis against an unknown person. According to DSM-IV, frotteuristic behavior "usually occurs in crowded places (e.g., busy sidewalks or in public transportation vehicles)" (American Psychiatric Association, 1994, p. 527). The most often encountered equivalent clinical presentation is toucheurism, an erotic preference for touching a female stranger's crotch region or breasts, usually from behind.[2] Frotteurism has at least one variant. One of our patients who was voyeuristic and exhibitionistic did not practice frotteurism or toucheurism himself but became sexually excited by viewing other men engaging in frotteurism in public transportation facilities.

The Preferential Rape Pattern

Rapists are a heterogeneous group. At least some of them are probably not paraphiliacs but have social or other kinds of deficiencies. In their review of the literature on rape proneness, Prentky and Knight (1991) described their most recent classification scheme for rapists. The group of "sexual nonsadistic" offenders is likely to overlap or to be very similar to our group of preferential rapists (see also Barbaree, Seto, Serin, Amos, & Preston, 1994). The preferential rape pattern is a distortion in the normal sequence of sexual interaction in a similar way to the other prototypes of courtship disorder. Freund and Watson (1990) demonstrated that the preferential rape pattern co-occurs more often with other posited types of courtship disorder than with other pathological erotic activity preferences.

A number of authors believe that phallometric testing can contribute to a diagnosis of the preferential rape pattern and sadism. Seto and Kuban (1996) used this method for comparing responses of self-referred sadists, accused or charged sadistic rapists, nonsadistic rapists, men with types of courtship disorder other than the preferential rape pattern, and community controls. The combined group of men reporting sadistic fantasies, accused or charged sadistic rapists, and nonsadistic rapists showed significantly larger penile responses to narratives describing sadistic rape or nonsexual violence directed at females than did the combined group of men showing a courtship disorder (other than preferential rape) and community controls. Further analyses found no differences between the fantasizers, sadists, or nonsadistic rapists in their relative responses to sexually or nonsexually violent stimuli; however, men with courtship disorder responded more to these narratives than did community controls. This latter finding agrees with two earlier phallometric studies of men with courtship disorder (Freund, Scher, & Hucker, 1983, and Freund, Scher, Racansky, Campbell, & Heasman, 1986, using overlapping samples).

At present the most reliable basis for the differential diagnosis between various types of rape appears to be a clinical evaluation of offender characteristics and the circumstances in which the rape occurred. In their paper, Prentky and Knight (1991) indicated that the criteria most frequently used for differentiating among rapists are the "amount of aggression, the presence or absence of antisocial personality, the presence or absence of sadism, and the degree of 'sexualization' " (p. 644).

We have used the amount of victim maltreatment as one of the criteria for differentiating between sadism and the preferential rape pattern, on the assumption that the preferential rapist uses only as much physical force as required to subdue the victim (Freund

& Watson, 1990). What is considered to be sufficient force, however, depends on an assessment of the offender's judgment (an extreme example is what a mentally handicapped man may consider to be sufficient force). Although offense characteristics can be used to classify some offenders as nonparaphilic rapists, preferential rapists, or sadistic rapists, there are many individuals for whom a differential diagnosis cannot be made.

An innocuous equivalent prototype of the preferential rape pattern is an erotic preference for prostitutes when attractive partners would be easily available. Interaction with a prostitute is similar to the preferential rape pattern in the sense that there is no preliminary sexual interaction, that is, courtship. A number of the senior author's patients have complained that they invest excessive amounts of money and time frequenting prostitutes, while at the same time they avoid intercourse with their attractive partners.

Epidemiology

It would be very difficult to arrive at a realistic estimate of the prevalence of the various patterns of courtship disorder in the general population. Cox, Tsang, and Lee (1982) attempted such an assessment with regard to exhibitionism. The next best epidemiological approach is to focus on those cases subjects come to the attention of professionals because they request help or are required to do so by legal authorities.

We selected as subjects 743 individuals who demonstrated or admitted having an activity paraphilia from the Clarke Institute's data bank of 5,189 male sexology patients between 17 and 55 years of age. Excluded from this selection were any men who were below borderline intelligence (based on clinical impression), psychotic, homosexual, or who had offended against children and did not demonstrate some form of paraphilic activity directed at adults. Subjects were voyeurs, exhibitionists, frotteurs/toucheurs, nonsadistic

TABLE 6.1. Proportions of Mandated and Self-Referred Subjects Demonstrating One or More Paraphilic Diagnoses

		V	E	F	R no S	S	M no S
Total	N	183	333	163	124	193	91
Mandated	Single	16 (15%)	94 (40%)	42 (31%)	62 (54%)	85 (56%)	3 (23%)
	Multiple	89 (85%)	138 (60%)	94 (69%)	52 (46%)	47 (44%)	10 (77%)
	(Binom)	***		**			
Self-referred	Single	18 (23%)	39 (39%)	4 (15%)	2 (18%)	23 (59%)	60 (87%)
	Multiple	60 (77%)	62 (61%)	23 (85%)	9 (82%)	16 (41%)	9 (13%)
	(Binom)	***		**			***
t test				**			

Note. V, voyeurism; E, exhibitionism; F, frotteurism/toucheurism; R no S, nonsadistic multiple rape; S, sadism; M no S, masochism; Binom, binomial tests comparing the proportion of subjects in each group, mandated or self-referred, with single versus multiple diagnoses. *t* tests compared the mandated and self-referred groups in terms of their ratio of single to multiple diagnoses. Percentages of single versus multiple diagnoses, for mandated or self-referred groups separately, are given in parentheses.

**p < .01; ***p < .001.

rapists who had attempted or completed two or more rapes (or who had raped one victim but also had another paraphilic disorder), sadists, and masochists. Individuals who had attempted or completed one rape only were excluded because of the difficulty in determining whether the rape was due to social or other deficiencies rather than a pathological preference for rape. Table 6.1 shows the total number of subjects who had each paraphilia (individuals can contribute to more than one category), and the number of subjects who demonstrated only one paraphilia.

All subjects described in this chapter were interviewed by the senior author at the sexology clinic of a metropolitan psychiatric hospital between 1974 and 1994. The reliability of diagnoses is uncertain because a single clinician made the diagnostic judgments; however, we argue that poor reliability is likely to attenuate rather than inflate effect size by increasing within-group variance. There were 516 individuals who were accused, charged, or on parole at the time they were seen (mandated group) and 227 individuals who voluntarily came to the clinic asking for help (self-referred group). We made a further division within each of these two groups according to whether an individual demonstrated one or more than one type of activity paraphilia.

In the mandated group, 302 individuals ($M = 28.0$ years, $SD = 7.5$) demonstrated only one type of paraphilia and 214 men ($M = 27.3$ years, $SD = 7.3$) demonstrated more than one type. In the self-referred group, 146 individuals ($M = 32.7$ years, $SD = 8.3$) demonstrated only one paraphilic type and 81 individuals ($M = 32.0$ years, $SD = 7.2$) demonstrated more than one type. There was no overall difference between the mandated and self-referred groups in the proportion of men showing more than one paraphilia, $\chi^2(1) = 2.32$, ns. Self-referred individuals who demonstrated only one paraphilic type had a median level of education of grade 12, whereas the remaining groups had a median education of more than grade 8 but less than grade 12.

As shown in Table 6.1, there were very few self-referred perpetrators of nonsadistic rape and very few mandated masochists. There was a significantly greater proportion of voyeurs and frotteurs/toucheurs who were judged to have other types of paraphilias compared with those who did not; exhibitionists showed a nonsignificant tendency in the same direction. In contrast, sadists showed the reverse pattern, with a greater proportion exhibiting sadism only. These differences held for both the self-referred and mandated groups, suggesting that mandated subjects were not as likely to deny other paraphilias as might be expected by their legal situation. The only exception was a difference between the mandated and self-referred groups in the proportion of multiple rapists who had exhibited another kind of paraphilia. This result is not surprising given that rapists faced the most severe legal sanctions for their behavior.

Paraphilic versus Opportunistic Activities

Judging whether an anomalous erotic target or activity is *preferred to the normative courtship sequence* is sometimes difficult. As mentioned above, behavior that is characteristic of courtship disorder may sometimes occur in nonparaphilic men. We discuss the validity of this observation here.

Two volunteer groups, one consisting of 69 university students and the other of 35 men from the community, most of whom had between a 9th and 11th grade education, completed the Erotic Preferences Examination Scheme (EPES; Freund, 1965). This questionnaire includes the following item: "Since age 16, have you ever masturbated while watching or trying to observe a girl or woman who was unaware of your presence?" Twelve percent of the university student volunteers answered this question in the affirmative, whereas 22.9%

of the less educated community volunteers did so. In comparison, 85% of a sample of 60 voyeurs admitted to masturbating while peeping.

The control subjects also answered the following set of questions pertaining to exhibitionism: (1) "Since age 16 have you ever shown your penis (from a distance) to a female who was almost or totally a stranger to you?"; and (2) "Since age 16 have you ever shown your naked buttocks (from a distance) to a female who was almost or totally a stranger to you?" None of these volunteers answered yes to exposing their penis to a female stranger, although 11.1% of the students and 17.1% of the less educated volunteers had shown their buttocks, and approximately 5% of both samples said they had shown both their penis and buttocks (in this context the showing of the buttocks as a prank, i.e., "mooning," has to be considered). In contrast, 49.3% of 150 exhibitionists admitted that they had exposed their penis to a female stranger, less than 1% admitted showing their buttocks only, and 31.3% admitted showing both their penis and buttocks. These estimates do not agree with Radzinowiez's (1957) and MacDonald's (1973) estimates. According to Radzinowiez, 80% of exhibitionists expose only the penis, while according to MacDonald about 15% expose their entire body.

We also examined the responses of 63 university students and 186 less educated volunteers to the following two questions contained in the EPES: (1) "Since age 16, have you ever attempted to fondle the breasts or crotch of an unsuspecting female who was almost or totally a stranger?"; and (2) "Since age 16, have you ever stood behind an unsuspecting female who was almost or totally a stranger to you and pressed (intentionally) your penis against her buttocks?" Thirty percent of the less educated men and 31.7% of the university students answered yes to one or both questions. In contrast, 79% of 77 frotteurs/toucheurs admitted to this behavior.

It cannot be expected that volunteers would be willing to admit to rape, so a parallel investigation of the preferential rape pattern is not possible. It is known that in times of social instability (e.g., in a protracted war) a substantial proportion of soldiers will commit rape. A large anonymous survey of male college students found that 7.7% admitted to attempting or committing acts that would meet the legal definition of rape (Koss, Gidycz, & Wisniewski, 1987); however, the proportion of these subjects who were paraphilic rapists is unknown.

Overall, the data suggest that, in adult men, intentional exposing of the penis to a unknown woman occurs almost exclusively as a paraphilia. Given the virtual absence of penile exhibitionism in nonparaphilic, heterosexual men without gross brain pathology, and its high rate of occurrence as a chronic activity pattern in some clinical patients, penile exhibitionism appears to be the hub of courtship disorder.

CO-OCCURRENCE OF CLINICAL PRESENTATIONS

The various putative types of courtship disorder differ in regard to their patterns of co-occurrence (see Table 6.2). Each type of courtship disorder appears to have a characteristic pattern. Exhibitionism and multiple nonsadistic rape are the most likely to occur without another clinical presentation. In contrast, voyeurism was usually accompanied by another type of courtship disorder. Equal proportions of individuals with frotteurism showed one or two other types, and very few individuals (*n* = 8) demonstrated all four types of courtship disorder.

An earlier study investigated the coherence of the clinical presentations of courtship disorder (Freund & Watson, 1990). Their most notable finding was the high percentage of co-occurrence between exhibitionism, voyeurism, toucheurism/frotteurism, and (to a lesser

TABLE 6.2. Proportions of Mandated versus Self-Referred Voyeurs, Exhibitionists, Frotteurs/Toucheurs, and Nonsadistic Multiple Rapists with Another Type of Courtship Disorder

	Voyeurism	Exhibitionism	Frotteurism	Rape
Mandated	99	220	122	114
Self-referred	71	90	22	10
0[a]	16 (16.2%)	94 (42.7%)	42 (34.4%)	62 (54.4%)
	18 (25.4%)	39 (43.3%)	4 (18.2%)	
1	42 (42.4%)	79 (35.9%)	42 (34.4%)	29 (25.4%)
	38 (53.5%)	36 (40.0%)	6 (27.3%)	2 (20.0%)
2	36 (36.4%)	42 (19.1%)	33 (27.0%)	18 (15.8%)
	12 (16.9%)	12 (13.3%)	9 (40.9%)	3 (30.0%)
3	5 (5.1%)	5 (2.3%)	5 (4.1%)	5 (4.4%)
	3 (4.2%)	3 (3.3%)	3 (13.6%)	3 (30.0%)

[a]Number of other types of courtship disorder diagnosed; upper row represents mandated patients; lower row represents self-referred patients.

degree) nonsadistic rape, in contrast to the lower degrees of co-occurrence between these putative types of courtship disorder and sadism or masochism. The weaker affinity between the courtship expressions and rape was most likely due to the difficulty of determining whether a particular case of rape was sadistic, an expression of the preferential rape pattern, or nonparaphilic.

Measuring the Degree of Co-occurrence

Using a larger sample than reported by Freund and Watson (1990), we calculated phi and other measures of association to replicate the finding of stronger affinities between the posited expressions of courtship disorder compared with the affinities between these expressions and other activity paraphilias, that is, sadism and masochism.

The sample consisted of 847 clinical subjects ($M = 28.8$ years, $SD = 8.02$) and 162 control subjects ($M = 30.5$ years, $SD = 6.89$) recruited from the community. Subjects were included if they were not psychotic and were clinically judged to be at a borderline level of intellectual functioning or higher. The control group was significantly older than the clinical group, $t(1007) = 2.61$, $p < .01$. The groups did not differ in marital status, $\chi^2 (1)$ 1.00, ns, but did differ in their level of education, $\chi^2 (3) = 10.17$, $p < .05$. A greater proportion of the clinical subjects had less than an eighth grade level of education and a smaller proportion of these subjects had some postsecondary education. Subjects were included in the clinical sample if they had engaged in at least one act of exhibitionism, voyeurism, frotteurism/toucheurism, or rape as judged by the senior author. Control subjects indicated that they had not engaged in any of these activities.

As shown in Table 6.3, the results for phi supported our hypothesis, with the strongest association between voyeurism and exhibitionism. We also calculated Jaccard, Ochiai, and Kulczynski 2 similarity coefficients because, unlike phi, these measures of association do not include joint absences (i.e., when neither paraphilia is present) in their calculations. We wanted to exclude joint absences because we were primarily interested in the co-occurrence of paraphilias, and the inclusion of joint absences would "inflate" the apparent degree of association.[3]

TABLE 6.3. Phi Coefficients for the Activity Paraphilias

	Voyeur	Exhib	Touch	Rape	Sad
Exhib	.35				
Touch	.16	.17			
Rape	−.14	−.25	−.12		
Sad	−.20	−.30	−.14	−.04	
Mas	−.11	−.16	−.08	−.20	−.01

Note. Voyeur, voyeurism; Exhib, exhibitionism; Touch, toucherism; Sad, sadism; Mas, masochism. Values on and above the diagonal are omitted.

The results for the Jaccard, Ochiai, and Kulczynski 2 similarity coefficients all supported the hypothesis that the courtship disorder expressions are more closely connected with each other than with other activity paraphilias (see Table 6.4). All three measures of association showed that there were stronger relationships between voyeurism, exhibitionism, and toucherism than between these paraphilias and rape, sadism, or masochism. The magnitude of associations between rape and voyeurism, exhibitionism, or toucherism were larger than those involving rape and sadism or masochism, providing some support for the inclusion of rape as a type of courtship disorder. The results for rape are presumably less clear because of the heterogeneity of rapists (see Barbaree et al., 1994; Prentky & Knight, 1991; Seto & Barbaree, 1997).

TABLE 6.4. Similarity Coefficients for the Activity Paraphilias

	Voyeur	Exhib	Touch	Rape	Sad
		(A) Jaccard			
Exhib	.33				
Touch	.19	.21			
Rape	.07	.09	.07		
Sad	.02	.03	.04	.12	
Mas	.02	.03	.03	.01	.06
		(B) Ochiai			
Exhib	.52				
Touch	.32	.37			
Rape	.14	.16	.13		
Sad	.04	.05	.08	.22	
Mas	.05	.06	.06	.01	.13
		(C) Kulczynski 2			
Exhib	.54				
Touch	.32	.40			
Rape	.14	.16	.14		
Sad	.04	.05	.08	.22	
Mas	.05	.08	.06	.01	.14

Note. Voyeur, voyeurism; Exhib, exhibitionism; Touch, toucherism; Sad, sadism; Mas, masochism.

The Kulczynski 2 similarity coefficients are particularly interesting because they represent the average of the conditional probabilities that one paraphilia is present given that the other paraphilia is present. As shown in (C) of Table 6.4, individuals with an expression of courtship disorder had a relatively high probability of having another expression. The results were less clear for rape, although the conditional probabilities of having voyeurism, exhibitionism, or frotteurism/toucheurism were higher for rape than for sadism or masochism. Finally, there were intermediate levels of association between rape and sadism (representing sadistic rapists), and between sadism and masochism (representing sadomasochists).

Accuracy of Diagnosis

The sensitivity and specificity of the paraphilic diagnoses are unknown at this time. Some paraphilias obviously remained undetected, and the proportions of ostensibly "normal" subjects who have engaged in voyeuristic or frotteuristic/toucheuristic acts that could be deemed paraphilic illustrate the difficulty of making an accurate, specific diagnosis. Although it is not presently possible, selection of only paraphilic subjects using an objective, reliable, and valid measure would provide a stronger test of the courtship disorder hypothesis. One potential candidate that is still in its experimental stages is phallometric testing for activity preferences. There have been relatively few phallometric investigations of activity preferences other than rape.[4] For example, Marshall, Payne, Barbaree, and Eccles (1991) found a significant difference between exhibitionists and controls in their relative responses to depictions of exposing. In contrast, Freund, Scher, and Hucker (1984) found no difference between exhibitionists and controls in their responses to consenting sex.

One possible contributor to the difficulties of developing tests for activity preferences is the deliberate suppression of responses to the preferred stimuli by clinical subjects (i.e., faking). We are currently interested in developing a phallometric test for masochism using subjects solicited from the community to evaluate this possibility. These self-referred subjects would be willing to admit having a paraphilic preference for masochistic activities, and would subsequently be very unlikely to fake their responses because there are no legal sanctions for such activities (if it is mutually consenting). Failure to strongly discriminate between masochists and controls would suggest that faking is not a sufficient explanation, at least on its own, for the difficulty in achieving high sensitivities and specificities in tests for activity preferences. Other possible contributing factors to the difficulty in developing tests for activity preferences are the characteristics of the stimuli used. For example, Lalumière and Quinsey (1994) found that studies using stimulus sets with more exemplars per category and more brutal descriptions of rape were better able to discriminate between rapists and controls.

Combinations of Courtship Disorder with Other Paraphilias

The organization of the paraphilias involves dividing the paraphilias into target and activity preferences (omitting at this time an analysis of target preferences); dividing the activity paraphilias into courtship disorder, sadism, or masochism; and dividing courtship disorder into a number of prototypes (omitting at this time sadism and masochism).

This organization demonstrated that combinations of prototypes sometimes occur. This brought up the possibility that some overlap may also occur between courtship disorder, masochism, and sadism, as well as between activity and target preferences. Furthermore, it appeared that *all of these paraphilic combinations may involve common features of the paraphilias* (hypothesis 4).

Combining Activity Preferences

As we have mentioned, the evidence for the existence of the preferential rape pattern is mixed. Our data were re-analyzed to examine the connection of the preferential rape pattern with the remaining putative types of courtship disorder and assess the closeness and nature of the connections of courtship disorder with sadism and masochism (see Table 6.5).

The first re-analysis involved a comparison between sadistic and nonsadistic rapists for the presence of other types of courtship disorder. A t test of proportions demonstrated that there were significantly more nonsadistic than sadistic rapists who were also judged to show voyeurism, exhibitionism, or frotteurism, $t(242) = 2.691$, $p < .01$. This comparison omitted 16 sadomasochistic rapists, but their inclusion did not change the pattern of results. Table 6.5 also shows that the association of courtship disorder with sadism or masochism is relatively weak. Only 17.1% of the 175 sadists and 13.5% of the 89 masochists exhibited one or more expressions of courtship disorder, in contrast to the degrees of co-occurrence between voyeurism, exhibitionism, and frotteurism/toucheurism. Table 6.5 also shows the distributions of types of courtship disorder that co-occurred with sadism, sadomasochism, or masochism. Only 6.4% of the 264 sadists, sadomasochists, or masochists who also had a paraphilic expression of courtship disorder did not show exhibitionism. This result also supports the idea that exhibitionism is the hub of courtship disorder.

Combining Activity and Target Preferences

As mentioned above, the most frequent paraphilic target preference in courtship disorder is a preference for a stranger as victim. This combination is almost always present. A less frequent combination is the choice of both adults and children as targets of paraphilic activities. The connection between voyeurism and fetishism for bodily excretions has also been already mentioned (i.e., peeping at women who are urinating). Fetishism involving bodily excretions also occurs in nonpredatory sadism and sadomasochism (see Spengler, 1977).

An earlier study assessed the affinities of heterosexual nontransvestic fetishists for female attire, transvestic fetishism, gender identity disorder of adolescence and adulthood

TABLE 6.5. Co-occurrence of Types of Courtship Disorders, or Combinations of These Types, with Sadism, Rape, or Masochism

Courtship disorder(s)	N^a	Voy	Exhib	Touch	V + E	V + T	E + T	V + E + T
Sad no R	18/125 (14.4%)	2	6	6	0	0	4	0
Sad + Rape	10/50 (20.0%)	4	2	3	1	0	0	0
Rape no S	60/124 (48.4%)	4	18	9	13	1	7	8
Mas no S	10/73 (13.7%)	0	3	0	3	0	2	2
Mas + Sad	2/16 (12.5%)	0	0	1	0	1	0	0

Note. Voy (V), voyeurism; Exhib (E), exhibitionism; Touch (T), frotteurism/toucheurism; Sad (S), sadism; Mas, masochism.

[a]Number of subjects diagnosed with a type of courtship disorder over the total number of subjects in the category; percentage given in brackets.

of a nontranssexual type (GIDAANT), and heterosexual transsexualism with the various prototypes of courtship disorder (Freund, Watson, & Dickey, 1991). Using data from new subjects, we replicated and extended this comparison of paraphiliacs' target preferences with regard to their connections with the various types of courtship disorder (see Table 6.6). Because more subjects were available, the usual age restriction of 18 to 55 years could be used, consistent with other analyses presented here.

As can be seen in Table 6.6, *t* tests of proportions showed that nontransvestic fetishists for female attire and transvestic fetishists were overrepresented among the 58 subjects who demonstrated fetishism or gender identity disorder and also had a type of courtship disorder; in contrast, transsexuals were underrepresented in this group. Table 6.7 shows the distribution of types of courtship disorder for these 58 individuals. Again, the most common type of courtship disorder was exhibitionism.

Variations of Clinical Presentation

Another issue which we should not overlook is variation in clinical presentations. Paraphilic patterns can vary from patient to patient and can vary in the same patient over time. Abel and Rouleau (1990) characterized the longitudinal variation in clinical presentation by the remark that "as an initial paraphilia fades, a second paraphilia begins to accelerate in frequency and may overtake the initial paraphilia as the most common deviant behavior" (p. 14). Between-patient variation in clinical presentation may be explained by a fifth hypothesis: *The prototypes are a result of underlying disturbances that vary in strength.* Within-patient variation may reflect fluctuations in these disturbances due to changes in endocrinological or environmental conditions.

SUMMARY AND CONCLUSIONS

This chapter demonstrated, primarily by pointing out a common explanatory scheme (see Thagard, 1992, pp. 122–123), that voyeurism, exhibitionism, frotteurism/toucheurism, and the preferential rape pattern are closely related and can be conceived as expressions of a common disorder. This corresponds to the seventh of Thagard's (1992) nine degrees of conceptual change: "Collapsing part of a kind of hierarchy, abandoning a previous distinction" (pp. 34–35). We further attempted to demonstrate that the four paraphilic prototypes are the core of a much larger number of expressions of courtship disorder.

TABLE 6.6. Proportions of Fetishists and Gender Identity Disorder Patients with or without Courtship Disorder (CD)

Courtship disorder status	N	NTF	TF	GIDAANT	TS
No CD	274	41 (15.0%)	92 (33.6%)	59 (21.5%)	82 (29.9%)
CD	58	19 (32.8%)	31 (53.4%)	6 (10.3%)	2 (3.5%)
t test[a]		*	*		**

Note. NTF, nontransvestic fetishism for female attire; TF, transvestic fetishism; GIDAANT, gender identity disorder of adolescence or adulthood of a nontranssexual type; TS, transsexualism; CD, courtship disorder. Percentage of group (no CD or CD) is in parentheses.

[a]*t* tests of proportions; using extreme splits for GIDAANT and TS.

*p < .01; **p < .001.

TABLE 6.7. Distribution of Paraphiliac Types across Fetishists and Gender Identity Disordered Patients with a Courtship Disorder

Patient type	Voy	Exhib	Touch	V + E	V + T	E + T	V + E + T
NTF	2	4	0	6	3	0	4
TF	3	12	3	4	2	1	6
GIDAANT	0	3	1	1	0	1	0
TS	1	0	0	1	0	0	0

Note. Voy (V), voyeurism; Exhib (E), exhibitionism; Touch (T), frotteurism/toucheurism; NTF, nontransvestic fetishm for female attire; TF, tranvestic fetishism; GIDAANT, gender identity disorder of adolescence or adulthood of a nontranssexual type; TS, transsexualism.

The assumption that a typical succession of courtship behavior exists and that some persons may display defects in this succession might be seen as unnecessary speculation. However, there is reason to think otherwise. Within the context of modern evolutionary theory, David Buss and his colleagues have demonstrated that human mate preferences are important psychological mechanisms that determine sexual behavior (for a review, see Buss, 1994). They have also argued that the function of these mechanisms cannot be fully understood without identifying the acts generated by each mechanism and the adaptive significance of these acts. The existence of a set of mechanisms regulating the courtship process does not seem far-fetched. Interestingly, from a Darwinian perspective, the clinical observation that men exhibiting a courtship disorder are relatively indiscriminate in their choice of female victims according to age and attractiveness suggests that courtship disorder is pathological (see Wakefield, 1992).

The degree of coherence between various clinical presentations, as previously demonstrated by Freund and Watson (1990), and replicated in this chapter using a different statistical approach, supports the courtship disorder hypothesis. However, the earlier studies also showed that the concept of courtship disorder should be restricted to the activity paraphilias (see Freund, 1990).

We reviewed five post hoc hypotheses to explain the characteristic features of the types of courtship disorder. The first hypothesis (that normative interaction is regulated by a set of preferences for a certain succession of sensory erotic stimuli and erotic activities) is derived from everyday experience. One possible means of assessing the feasibility of this hypothesis is to carry out a content analysis of open-ended interviews with men regarding the kinds of erotic experiences they have had and how they enjoyed them. Other methods for identifying mating preferences have been described by Buss (1994).

The feasibility of the second and third hypotheses, explaining the characteristic features of courtship disorder and proposing that the disorder reflects a pathological need for a rapid conversion of arousal into orgasm (usually brought about by masturbation) was partly demonstrated. This need for rapid conversion may be secondary, however, to the fact that the hypothesized defects in the normative courtship sequence reduce erotic valence. Note that the instant conversion hypothesis presented here is less specific than the original version proposed by Madlafousek et al. (1981).

The fourth hypothesis asserted that paraphilias co-occur not by chance but according to particular mutual affinities. The differential patterns of co-occurrence between types of courtship disorder and other paraphilias demonstrated the feasibility of this hypothesis. The fifth hypothesis—that the prototypes are the results of underlying disturbances that vary in strength—has been proposed without testing its feasibility.

The arguments in this chapter for the existence of courtship disorder and the five hypotheses regarding the main features of courtship disorder are crude and necessarily omit many details. Species vary widely in this regard. We do not know in what directions and to what degree gynephilic males are able to normally adjust their courtship behavior to variations in partner behavior and situational factors. In contrast, fruit flies (*Drosophila melanogaster*) seem to exhibit a rigidly controlled sequence of courtship behavior. Greenspan (1995, p. 73) has described this courtship sequence:

> This process consists of a series of actions, each of which is accompanied by the exchange of visual, auditory and chemosensory signals between males and females. The male is the more active of the dancers in this intricate ballet and has therefore been the focus of much of the research.
>
> The ritual begins with a step called orientation. The male, who needs no instruction in this process, stands facing the female, about 0.2 millimeter away. Then he taps her on the abdomen with a foreleg and follows her if she moves away. Next, he displays one wing and flutters it to execute his form of a "love song." Depending on the female's level of interest at this point, he may go back and repeat his actions. But if all is going well, he unfurls his proboscis (a tubular appendage carrying the mouthparts at the tip) and licks the female's genitals. He may then mount her and, if she is receptive, copulate with her. Fruit flies will not mate unless the males have gone through this entire routine and the female has become receptive.

According to Hall (1994, p. 1702), the female is not passive either:

> When she is in principle "receptive" to the male's advances . . . she nevertheless performs some rather subtle (and mild) rejection behaviours, which are considered to represent "female coyness." Eventually, she indicates receptivity by slowing down her general locomotor activity, apparently to make her a better target for the male's copulation attempts. For an attempt to succeed, it appears as if the female must assume a particular posture and manipulate her external genitalia appropriately.
>
> If a female of this species is not inherently receptive to courtship because she had mated recently, then she produces a more overt rejection response to male courtship. A fertilized female extrudes her ovipositor in the face of a male who tries to mate with her; this blocks most copulation attempts.

The relative simplicity of fruit fly courtship might facilitate the development of models to explain the components of courtship behavior. Hall (1994) has argued that fruit fly courtship is influenced by a variety of genes because specific defects in courtship behavior appear to be results of different pleiotropic mutations (i.e., mutations having more than one phenotypic effect). Hall compared behavioral defects with abnormalities in central nervous system structures, whereas Greenspan continued this analysis to compare behavioral defects with physical defects in various genes.

In contrast to what we know about the fruit fly, we do not know what brain structures or genetic mechanisms are involved in the different expressions of courtship disorder in human males. It may someday be possible to use a sophisticated modeling method to assess the feasibility of the theory of courtship disorder. Neuropsychologists who analyze reading impairments (dyslexia) in patients with brain lesions have found regularities in the kinds of reading mistakes these patients make. These regularities serve as the basis of current models of neural processing of language (e.g., Caramazza & Hillis, 1990). These models suggest that the brain processes features of written text in parallel rather than in sequence, and that different kinds of mistakes are caused by errors in different paths.

A relatively recent and exciting development in this area is connectionist modeling or neural networking (Hinton & Shallice, 1991), which uses computer simulations of idealized networks involving large numbers of relatively simple processing elements. Hinton and his colleagues have used neural networking to generate sophisticated models for understanding dyslexia and providing insights into the neural architecture underlying certain language functions. In contrast to traditional linear statistical approaches, the nonlinear modeling available through neural networking can control hypothesis building in a much more complex way. This approach appears to be the method of choice for a future analysis of the feasibility of the different hypotheses regarding courtship disorder.

Similar to the work in language processing, this kind of computer simulation might begin with a hypothetical reconstruction of pathways activated in the course of normative sexual arousal and activities. Speculations about missing or faulty components (i.e., processing pathways) that result in the various paraphilic expressions could inform hypotheses about how components are related in normal courtship. For example, some components may be involved in regulating reward during the various courtship phases that increases the probability of progressing to the next phase. Another example is the influence of a female's actions on a male's behavior in terms of staying in a particular courtship phase, advancing to the next phase, retreating to the previous phase, or breaking off from any further sexual interaction. There may be several components involved in the processing of female signals and determining the male's ability to respond appropriately and effectively.

In the future, the neuropsychological analysis of cognitive processes may also utilize magnetic source imaging (e.g., Gallen et al., 1993), a technology combining magneto-encephalographic scanning and magnetic resonance imaging. Magnetic source imaging permits inferences about the spatial locations of neural regions associated with normal and pathological activity patterns. It will, however, likely be a long time before this technology is fully realized and subcortical and cortical models of paraphilias can be adequately explored.

NOTES

1. We will discuss animal models later, in the Summary and Conclusions section.
2. The manifestation of the activity paraphilias in men who erotically prefer males (androphiles) is poorly understood. This chapter focuses exclusively on the paraphilias as they appear in men who erotically prefer women (gynephiles).
3. These additional measures of association were available through the PROXIMITIES procedure in SPSS-X.
4. A meta-analysis of 16 published and unpublished studies concluded that rapists can be discriminated from controls by their relative responses to depictions of nonconsenting sex (Lalumière & Quinsey, 1994). However, the overall sensitivity and specificity of phallometric testing for rapists is distinctly lower than has been found for phallometric testing for pedophilia (cf. Lalumière & Quinsey, 1993, and Freund & Watson, 1991).

REFERENCES

Abel, G. G., Becker, J. V., Cunningham-Rathner, J., Mittelman, M., & Rouleau, J. L. (1988). Multiple paraphilic diagnoses among sex offenders. *Bulletin of the American Academy of Psychiatry and the Law, 16*, 153–168.

Abel, G. G., & Rouleau, J. L. (1990). The nature and extent of sexual assault. In W. L. Marshall, D. R. Laws, & H. E. Barbaree (Eds.), *Handbook of sexual assault: Issues, theories, and treatment of the offender* (pp. 9–21). New York: Plenum Press.

American Psychiatric Association. (1994). *Diagnostic and statistical manual of mental disorders* (4th ed.). Washington, DC: Author.

Barbaree, H. E., Seto, M. C., Serin, R. C., Amos, N. L., & Preston, D. L. (1994). Comparisons between sexual and non-sexual rapist subtypes: Sexual arousal to rape, offense precursors and offense characteristics. *Criminal Justice and Behavior, 21,* 95–114.

Bailey, K. G. (1991). Human paleopsychopathology: Implications for the paraphilias. *New Trends in Experimental and Clinical Psychiatry, 7,* 5–16.

Binet, A. (1887). Le fetichisme dans l'amour [Fetishism in love]. *Revue Philosophie, 24,* 143–167.

Bradford, J. M. W., Boulet, J., & Pawlak, A. (1992). The paraphilias: A multiplicity of deviant behaviours. *Canadian Journal of Psychiatry, 37,* 104–108.

Buss, D. M. (1994). *The evolution of human desire.* New York: Basic Books.

Caramazza, A., & Hillis, A. E. (1990). Where do semantic errors come from? *Cortex, 26,* 95–122.

Cox, D. J., Tsang, K., & Lee, A. (1982). A cross-cultural comparison of the incidence and nature of male exhibitionism among female college students. *Victimology, 7,* 231–234.

Ellis, H. (1978). *The psychology of sex* (2nd ed.). New York: Harcourt Brace Jovanovich. (Original work published 1933)

Freud, S. (1925). *Drei Abhandlungen zur Sexultheorie [Three essays on the theory of sexuality].* Leipzig: Psychoanalytischer Verlag. (Original work published 1905)

Freund, K. (1965). *Erotic Preferences Examination Scheme.* Unpublished manuscript.

Freund, K. (1990). Courtship disorder. In W. L. Marshall, D. R. Laws, & H. E. Barbaree (Eds.), *Handbook of sexual assault: Issues, theories, and treatment of the offender* (pp. 195–207). New York: Plenum Press.

Freund, K., & Kolarsky, A. (1965). Grundzuge eines einfachen Bezugsystems fur die Analyse sexueller Deviationen [A simple reference system for the analysis of sexual of sexual dysfunctions]. *Psychiatrie, Neurologie, und medizinische Psychologie, 17,* 221–225.

Freund, K., Scher, H., & Hucker, S. (1983). The courtship disorders. *Archives of Sexual Behavior, 12,* 369–379.

Freund, K., Scher, H., & Hucker, S. (1984). The courtship disorders: A further investigation. *Archives of Sexual Behavior, 13,* 133–139.

Freund, K., Scher, H., Racansky, I. G., Campbell, K., & Heasman, G. (1986). Males disposed to commit rape. *Archives of Sexual. Behavior, 15,* 23–35.

Freund, K., & Watson, R. (1990). Mapping the boundaries of courtship disorder. *Journal of Sex Research, 27,* 589–606.

Freund, K., & Watson, R. (1991). Assessment of the sensitivity and specificity of a phallometric test: An update of phallometric diagnosis of pedophilia. *Psychological Assessment, 3,* 254–260.

Freund, K., Watson, R., & Dickey, R. (1991). Sex offenses against female children perpetrated by men who are not pedophiles. *Journal of Sex Research, 28,* 409–423.

Gallen, C. C., Sobel, D. F., Lewine, J. D., Sanders, J. A., Hart, B. L., Davis, L. E., & Orrison, W. W., Jr. (1993). Neuromagnetic mapping of brain function. *Radiology, 187,* 863–867.

Gayford, J. J. (1981). Indecent exposure: A review of the literature. *Medicine, Science, and the Law, 21,* 233–242.

Gebhard, P., Gagnon, J., Pomeroy, W., & Christenson, C. (1965). *Sex offenders.* New York: Harper & Row.

Gillespie, W. H. (1964). The psychoanalytic theory of sexual deviation with special reference to fetishism. In I. Rosen (Ed.), *The pathology and treatment of sexual deviation: A methodological approach.* Oxford: Oxford University Press.

Grassberger, R. (1964). Der Exhibitionismus [Exhibitionism]. *Kriminalistik in Osterreich, 18,* 557–562.

Greenspan, R. J. (1995, April). Understanding the genetic construction of behavior: Studies of courtship and mating in the fruit fly offer a window on the ways genes influence the execution of complex behaviors. *Scientific American,* 72–78.

Grob, C. S. (1985). Single case study: Female exhibitionism. *Journal of Nervous and Mental Disease, 173,* 253–256.

Haire, N. (1966). *Sexual anomalies and perversions* (2nd ed.). London: Sidders & Sons.

Hall, J. C. (1994, June 17). The mating of a fly. *Science, 264,* 1702–1714.

Hermann, K., & Schroder, G. E. (1936). Un cas d'exhibitionisme chez une femme [A case of exhibitionism in a woman]. *Acta Psychiatria et Neurologia Scandinavica, 10,* 547–564.

Hinton, G., & Shallice, T. (1991). Lesioning an attractor network: Investigations of acquired dyslexia. *Psychological Review, 98,* 74–95.

Hollender, M. H., Brown, C. W., & Roback, H. B. (1977). Genital exhibitionism in women. *American Journal of Psychiatry, 134,* 436–438.

Kolarsky, A., Freund, K., Machek, J., & Polak, O. (1967). Male sexual deviation: Association with early temporal lobe damage. *Archives of General Psychiatry, 17,* 735–743.

Kolarsky, A., & Madlafousek, J. (1983). The inverse role of preparatory erotic stimulation in exhibitionists: Phallometric studies. *Archives of Sexual Behavior, 12,* 123–148.

Koss, M. P., Gidycz, C. A., & Wisniewski, N. (1987). The scope of rape: Incidence and prevalence of sexual aggression and victimization in a national sample of higher education students. *Journal of Consulting and Clinical Psychology, 55,* 162–170.

Krafft-Ebing, R. (1978). *Psychopathia sexualis.* New York: Stein and Day. (Original work published 1886)

Lalumière, M. L., & Quinsey, V. L. (1993). The sensitivity of phallometric measures with rapists. *Annals of Sex Research, 6,* 123–138.

Lalumière, M. L., & Quinsey, V. L. (1994). The discriminability of rapists from non-sex offenders using phallometric measures: A meta-analysis. *Criminal Justice and Behavior, 21,* 150–175.

Lang, R. A., Langevin, R., Bain, J., Frenzel, R. R., & Wright, P. (1989). Sex hormone profiles in genital exhibitionists. *Annals of Sex Research, 2,* 67–76.

Langevin, R. (1994). Genital exhibitionism and voyeurism: Theories and treatment. In J. J. Krivacska & J. Money (Eds.), *The handbook of forensic sexology: Biomedical and criminological perspectives* (pp. 126–154). New York: Prometheus.

Laws, D. R., & Marshall, W. L. (1990). A conditioning theory of the etiology and maintenance of deviant sexual preference and behavior. In W. L. Marshall, D. R. Laws, & H. E. Barbaree (Eds.), *Handbook of sexual assault: Issues, theories, and treatment of the offender* (pp. 209–229). New York: Plenum Press.

MacDonald, J. M. (1973). *Indecent exposure.* Springfield, IL: Charles C Thomas.

Madlafousek, J., Zantovsky, M., Hlinak, Z., & Kolarsky, A. (1981). Sexual behavior as a communicative process by which the system of partial motivational states is executed. *Czechoslovakian Psychiatry, 77,* 377–384.

Marshall, W. L., Payne, K., Barbaree, H. E., & Eccles, A. (1991). Exhibitionists: Sexual preferences for exposing. *Behaviour Research and Therapy, 29,* 37–40.

McGuire, R. J., Carlisle, J. M., & Young, B. G. (1965). Sexual deviations as conditioned behaviour: A hypothesis. *Behaviour Research and Therapy, 2,* 185–190.

McNally, R. J., & Lukach, B. M. (1991). Behavioral treatment of zoophilic exhibitionism. *Journal of Behavioral Therapy and Experimental Psychiatry, 22,* 281–284.

Mohr, J., Turner, R. E., & Jerry, M. (1964). *Pedophilia and exhibitionism.* Toronto: University of Toronto Press.

Morris, D. (1970). *Patterns of reproductive behaviour: Collected papers by Desmond Morris.* London: Jonathan Cape.

Prentky, R. A., & Knight, R. A. (1991). Identifying critical dimensions for discriminating among rapists. *Journal of Consulting and Clinical Psychology, 59,* 643–661.

Radzinowiez, L. (1957). *Sexual offenses: A report of the Cambridge Department of Criminal Science.* London: Macmillan.

Rousseau, J. J. (1985). *Confessions.* London: Penguin. (Original work published 1783)

Schrenck-Notzing, A. (1899). Zur suggestiven Behandlung des kondtraren Geschlechtsriebes und der Masturbation [Suggestion therapy for contrary sex drive and masturbation]. *Zentralblatt fur Nervenheulkunde und Psychiatrie, 12,* 257–260.

Seto, M. C., & Barbaree, H. E. (1997). Sexual aggression as antisocial behavior: A developmental model. In D. Stoff, J. Breiling, & J. D. Maser (Eds.), *Handbook of antisocial behavior* (pp. 524–533). New York: Wiley.

Seto, M. C., & Kuban, M. (1996). Discriminant validity of a phallometric test for paraphilic rape and sadism. *Behaviour Research and Therapy, 34,* 175–183.

Spengler, A. (1977). Manifest sadomasochism of males: Results of an empirical study. *Archives of Sexual Behavior, 6,* 441–456.

Stekel, W. (1923). *Onanie und Homosexualitat* [*Onanism and homosexuality*]. Berlin: Wien.

Taylor, F. H. (1947). Observations on some cases of exhibitionism. *Journal of Mental Science, 93,* 681–683.

Thagard, P. (1992). *Conceptual revolutions.* Princeton, NJ: Princeton University Press.

Tinbergen, N. (1965). Some recent studies of the evolution of sexual behavior. In F. A. Beach (Ed.), *Sex and behavior* (pp. 1–33). New York: Wiley.

Wakefield, J. M. (1973). The concept of mental disorder: On the boundaries between biological facts and social values. *American Psychologist, 47,* 373–388.

Yalom, I. D. (1960). Aggression and forbiddenness in voyeurism. *Archives of General Psychiatry, 3,* 305–319.

7

FROTTEURISM

Assessment and Treatment

Richard B. Krueger
Meg S. Kaplan

Sexual crimes are commanding more media attention in our society. Whether there is an increase in crime or an increase in reporting has not been empirically established. However, the focus on sexually "deviant" interests has led to increased public interest in the paraphilias. More specifically, the lesser paraphilias, traditionally described as "nuisance" behaviors, have become more prominent in the public's eye. The public is fearful that these "nuisance" acts might lead to more violent sexual acts, and women upon whom these nuisance acts are usually perpetrated are more apt to speak out against them and to prosecute their perpetrators. Therefore individuals with these behaviors seem to be coming to treatment now more frequently than in the past. This chapter will concern itself with the assessment and treatment of one of these paraphilias, frotteurism.

Frotteurism is a paraphilia that involves the touching, usually in a crowd or place from which the perpetrator could easily escape if detected, of an unsuspecting person. According to the fourth edition of the *Diagnostic and Statistical Manual of Mental Disorders* (DSM-IV; American Psychiatric Association, 1994, p. 527), the diagnostic criteria for frotteurism consist of "A. Over a period of a least 6 months, recurrent, intense sexually arousing fantasies, sexual urges, or behaviors involving touching and rubbing against a nonconsenting person," and "B. The fantasies, sexual urges, or behaviors cause clinically significant distress or impairment in social, occupational, or other important areas of functioning."

Although there is literature on the paraphilias, the available literature on frotteurism is minimal. For example, a computer search by the reference department of the New York State Psychiatric Institute library, using the search title "frotteurism" in *Psychlit* from 1974 to March 1997, and in *Medline* from 1966 May 1997, resulted in only 17 sources. Accordingly, many of recommendations regarding the assessment and treatment of frotteurism derive from the clinical experiences of ourselves and our colleagues in evaluating and treating individuals with multiple paraphilias. Furthermore, although sex offenses are committed by both males and females, there are no published accounts which we know of involving female frotteurs; therefore we will refer to a frotteur as "he."

DIAGNOSTIC ASSESSMENT

As with all psychiatric disorders, diagnostic assessment must begin with a comprehensive initial history and mental status examination. Sexual offenders are notorious for being poor historians, and often they have great incentives to deliberately minimize or deny any history of offenses that they might have. Furthermore, individuals may have cognitive distortions or rationalizations which come into play due to shame, guilt, or fear of consequences. Accordingly, it is very important at the onset of an evaluation to arrange for collateral sources of information to supplement a patient's history and account of events.

For instance, if an attorney refers an individual for assessment and/or treatment, all relevant court documents, including arrest reports, victims' statements, and prior psychiatric evaluations should be available, if at all possible, to the examining clinician by the time of the initial interview, so that he or she can question the patient on the basis of sources of information other than self-report. Often this involves reading verbatim from various records and challenging a patient's own version of events. Any sources of information that exist should be used to develop the history as fully as possible. If possible, interview family members regarding their observations and knowledge of the patient. For instance, in the case of a frotteur, ask them how often does he ride the subway or bus? Are there periods in his schedule during the day that are unaccounted for and that may allow him time or opportunity for frotteuristic activity? In addition, ask the frotteur if he has disclosed his activity to significant others or to family members. The degree of disclosure to family members becomes important later in treatment in the creation of a monitoring network, consisting of family or friends or significant others who agree to observe the patient for signs or evidence of relapse and to report their observations to the treating clinician.

Regarding interviewing technique, it is our practice to conduct an ordered, comprehensive evaluation. In addition to recording the identifying data, source and purpose of referral, and/or the chief complaint, a thorough history of the paraphilic behavior and criminal history is important, focusing on the most recent events but then obtaining information on all prior aspects of the patient's paraphilic and criminal histories. We take a thorough history probing for prior psychiatric/psychological therapy, prior psychiatric hospitalizations or incarcerations, and any symptoms suggestive of major psychiatric syndromes. We obtain a thorough sexual history, including both deviant and nondeviant behavior and any history of sexual dysfunction that might be present. Ask about every paraphilia regardless of self-report.

Abel (1989) cites a number of factors affecting prognosis and treatment considerations which are important to include in the initial history and assessment. These include the age of onset of the paraphilic interest and behavior (earlier onset correlates with greater ingraining of the paraphilia); age of the paraphilic patient (paraphilic behaviors tend to decrease spontaneously with age); frequency of the paraphilia (greater frequency usually is associated with greater recidivism); anxiety or guilt related to the paraphilic behavior (guilt is crucial to gaining insight and motivating the offender); concomitant drug and/or alcohol diagnosis (which should be treated); environmental surveillance (significant others who can help monitor the individual); and the presence or absence of concomitant appropriate sexual arousal.

Obtain a medical history with a focus on any endocrinological or neurological abnormalities, including any history of head injury.

Finally, describe and perform a full mental status examination with special attention to any stigmata of psychosis, major affective disorder, or cognitive abnormalities.

Psychometric Considerations in Diagnostic Assessment

There are numerous tools, including structured interviews and other psychometric tests, that clinicians can use to obtain information on both deviant and nondeviant behavior. Conte (1983) reviewed numerous scales developed to assess sexual functioning, most of which were intended to focus on nondeviant sexual behavior. She described two instruments, the Clarke Sexual History Questionnaire for Males (Clarke SHQ; Paitich, Langevin, Freeman, Mann, & Handy, 1977) and the Derogatis Sexual Functioning Inventory (Derogatis, 1980; Derogatis & Melisaratos, 1979). She concluded that the Clarke SHQ appeared to be clinically useful for the assessment of deviant sexual behaviors and preferences in males, and that it could be used to assess sex offenders and sexually anomalous individuals. It is a 190-item sexual history questionnaire which inquires about the frequency and age of occurrence of a wide range of sexual behaviors, including paraphilias. This questionnaire has been used effectively in studies and surveys to identify paraphiliacs. In a recent survey, Bradford, Boulet, and Pawlak (1992) used this instrument to study 443 adult males consecutively admitted to the Sexual Behaviours Clinic at the Royal Ottawa Hospital for a forensic psychiatric assessment. A large portion of the sample was excluded from the final analysis, but the 274 subjects retained for analysis admitted to a combined total of 7,677 sexually deviant incidents. The authors noted that, whereas the agreement between actual and self-reported activity is always suspect, this instrument could be used to estimate the overall level of paraphilic activity.

In another recent study of 60 college-aged men, Templeman and Stinnett (1991) used the Clarke SHQ and the Farrenkopf Arousal Portfolio and Cardsort (Farrenkopf, 1986) to better evaluate the role of sexual arousal in individuals usually used as controls in sex research. They found, strikingly, that 65% had engaged in some form of sexual misconduct in the past, although only 2 subjects reported an arrest history. Interestingly, 35% of this sample of 60 had engaged in frottage.

We have found the Clark SHQ to be clinically useful. It can be used in conjunction with a clinical history to look for inconsistencies between the written and oral histories and to further question the individual, or to pick up details which may have been omitted in the verbal history. There is also a computerized, self-administered version available.

The Derogatis Sexual Functioning Inventory focuses more on current and nondeviant functioning (Derogatis, 1980; Derogatis & Melisaratos, 1979). It is a 258-item, self-administered instrument which reflects sexual functioning in 10 areas: information, experience, drive, attitudes, psychological symptoms, affects, gender role definition, fantasy, body image, and satisfaction. Scores are derived from each of the subtests and an overall score of sexual functioning is then computed. A major disadvantage is its length and complexity.

Another instrument, the Abel Screen, was developed by Dr. Gene Abel (Abel, 1994). It is a computer-driven, self-report instrument which initially presents slides of various sexual stimuli and then prompts the patient to endorse in a graded way his or her preference for the stimuli presented. The client then completes questionnaire which, in a very comprehensive fashion, queries about his or her sexual and paraphilic history. Dr. Abel is in the process of validating this instrument, and presented at the 1995 annual meeting of the Association for the Treatment of Sexual Abusers (ATSA) (Abel, 1995) some preliminary reliability and validity data concerning it, but as yet there are no published articles that describe it.

The Adult Cognition Scale was developed by the group at the New York State Psychiatric Institute (Abel et al., 1984). This is a 29-item self-report questionnaire, in which adults endorse statements according to a 5-point Likert-type scale ranging from "strongly agree" to "strongly disagree." These statements describe various false cognitions that child molesters have. Abel et al. (1989) reported that child molesters endorsed significantly more distorted thoughts about molesting children than did other non-child-molesting paraphiliacs or community controls.

A second instrument developed by Abel (1984) and his colleagues is called the Adult Sexual Interest Cardsort. It consists of 75 items which are statements describing various forms of sexual activity, such as "A 25-year-old man and I are lying side by side naked touching each other all over." Individuals are asked to endorse one of 7 items about the statement ranging from –3, "extremely sexually repulsive," to 0, "neutral," to +3, "extremely sexually arousing." The items cover a wide range of sexual activities and preferences. This is used routinely by clinicians in the field, but its utility is weakened by the lack of published standardizations or validation.

The use of self-report techniques for assessment has raised the issue of whether some sexual behaviors and fantasies are under- or overreported during interviews or on questionnaires. In recent years researchers have developed objective physiological measures of sexual arousal (Abel, Blanchard, & Barlow 1981; Pithers & Laws, 1988). Although *The ATSA Practitioner's Handbook* (Association for the Treatment of Sexual Abusers, 1993, p. 5) states that "plethysmography cannot be used to prove an individual did or did not, or will or will not commit a sexual offense," it is useful as an aid for diagnosis, for pre- and posttreatment, and for assessment. A research study by Abel, Cunningham-Rathner, Becker, and McHugh (1983) examined the validity of traditional clinical interviews by confronting paraphiliacs with the results of subsequent evaluations. These confrontations revealed that 50 subjects (55.5 %) admitted to an additional 92 paraphilic diagnoses. The results demonstrated that at least 55.5% of traditional clinical interviews with paraphiliacs are invalid, as various confrontation procedures (cardsort, 18.9%; reinterview, 20.0%; erection measures, 62.9%) can lead subjects to reveal a large number of new additional acts.

Although the research evidence supports penile erection measures as the most systematic and reliable measure of male sexual arousal, one criticism is the ability of some individuals to suppress penile erections. Some studies have indicated that subjects can intentionally influence their penile responses to visual stimuli in varying degrees (Freund, Watson, & Rienzo, 1988; Laws & Holman, 1978). Nevertheless, although there are difficulties, the objective measurement of sexual arousal is an important assessment technique with this population.

Some clinicians have used lie detector tests as an aid to help the individual admit to paraphilic acts. Lie detectors have been used in the assessment and treatment of pedophiles (Abrams & Abrams, 1993). Lie detector tests are not, for the most part, admissible in a court of law and their predictive value has been demonstrated to be poor (Brett, Phillips, & Beary, 1986). However, they are very intimidating and, not infrequently, they can induce individuals into admitting wrongdoing; some clinicians use them with this strategy in mind. In this regard, it is helpful to meet with the individual being tested before any such test and review his history in such a way that the individual is clearly confronted with a situation of lying or not. Often, his story might change and/or new details might emerge, and when confronted with this an individual may admit to deviant acts.

ASSESSMENT FOR TREATMENT

Abel et al. (1987) reported from their assessments of nonincarcerated paraphiliacs that frottage was a common paraphilic act. The mean number of acts of the 62 adult males they found with a primary diagnosis of frottage was 849.5. Accordingly, to fully quantify an individual's frotteuristic and paraphilic histories, it is important to ascertain the frequency and number of occurrences. Clinicians should elicit further details which will be particularly relevant in subsequent treatment, such as the frotteur's usual location for committing his acts (a train, a subway, a crowded street?). What is his usual *modus operandi*? Does he engage in his activity on his way to or from work or school? Does he engage in such an act impulsively or with planning? What is the frequency of the act? Which sex is his target? Are they old or young? Is there a particular appearance or body type that arouses him? Are their antecedents, for example, alcohol or drug ingestion, stress at work, or disappointment, to the frotteur's offenses?

Incarcerated offenders also report a high occurrence of nonsexual crimes. Weinrott and Saylor (1991) obtained self-reports from 99 incarcerated sexual offenders and found that this sample reported that they committed nearly 20,000 nonsexual crimes in the year prior to incarceration. Accordingly, it is important to ask not only for a paraphilic history, but also for an overall criminal history. This also can have an obvious bearing on assessment and treatment.

In an early study Rooth (1973) reported that of 30 exhibitionists whom he examined, 12 had engaged in frottage. Abel, Becker, Cunningham-Rathner, Mittelman, and Rouleau (1988) demonstrated that individuals rarely have only one paraphilia. Interviewing 561 nonincarcerated paraphiliacs who were seeking voluntary evaluation and/or treatment for possible paraphilia under the protection of a certificate of confidentiality, they found that only 21% of frotteurs had frotteurism as a sole diagnosis and that on average, individuals with frotteurism had 4.8 paraphilias. Freund, Scher, and Hucker (1983) likewise reported on self-report data of a sample of patients referred for evaluation of paraphilia. Of the 22 patients referred for "toucheurism" (touching breasts or genital area of a female stranger without her consent), five reported voyeuristic activity, five exhibitionistic activity, two obscene calls, and none, rape. Likewise, Bradford et al. (1992), using the Clarke SHQ (Paitich et al., 1977) to study 443 adult males consecutively admitted to the Sexual Behaviors Clinic at the Royal Ottawa Hospital for a forensic psychiatric assessment, found a high occurrence of multiple paraphilias in the same individual. They found that, of individuals who reported frotteurism as a paraphilia, 24% also admitted heterosexual pedophilic activity, 35% heterosexual hebephilic activity, 21% homosexual pedophilic activity, 17% homosexual hebephilic activity, 17% cross-dressing, 66% voyeurism, 29% scatologia, 31% attempted rape, 16% rape, and 31% exhibitionism.

Other authors (Freund, 1988, 1990; Freund & Blanchard, 1986) have hypothesized that voyeurism, exhibitionism, toucheurism–frotteurism, and preferential rape patterns are all part of the same disorder, namely courtship disorder. In a more recent publication, Freund and Watson (1990) demonstrated that the preferential rape pattern co-occurred with voyeurism, exhibitionism, and toucheurism–frotteurism to a higher degree than did other paraphilic patterns.

Abel and Rouleau (1990) on the basis of their earlier work, recommended that sex offenders who present with one paraphilia should be evaluated with the possibility in mind that the individual may have multiple paraphilias, as clearly suggested by the other studies mentioned above. The occurrence of multiple or even one additional paraphilia(s) in the same individual is a finding which has not been replicated by Marshall and Eccles (1991), and they take issue with Abel and Rouleau's (1990) recommendations for the comprehensive evaluation of individuals with one paraphilia for other paraphilias, saying that it could be too time consuming. In our experience, we frequently come across individuals with the coexistence of multiple paraphilias and we recommend asking specifically about additional paraphilias.

Additionally, the concomitant occurrence of a history of physical and/or sexual abuse (Hanson & Slater, 1988), conduct and attention deficit disorder in adolescent sex offenders (Kavoussi, Kaplan, & Becker, 1988), and depressive symptoms (Becker, Kaplan, Tenke, & Tartaglini, 1991; Grossman & Cavanaugh, 1990; Kafka & Prentky, 1994) have been documented and clinicians should ask about these in any evaluation.

Psychometric Considerations in Assessment for Treatment

Once the clinician has obtained a clinical history with details as noted above, then he or she can obtain additional information from psychometric assessment to supplement the self-report.

Testing specific to the paraphilias can aid in treatment recommendations by revealing information which unstructured self-reports cannot provide. The Clarke SHQ (Paitich et al., 1977), mentioned earlier, provides an excellent instrument to probe for multiple paraphilias. The Derogatis Sexual Functioning Inventory (Derogatis, 1980; Derogatis & Melisaratos, 1979), surveys the individual's sexual functioning.

Penile plethysmography for an individual who admits to his deviant behavior can be a valuable instrument to assess the individual's arousal to deviant and nondeviant sexual stimuli. Plethysmography was introduced into the study of sexual deviance by Freund (1963, 1965, 1967). Zuckerman (1971) reviewed various physiological and possible biochemical measures of sexual arousal in humans and concluded that the most specific measure of sexual arousal in the male involves penile plethysmography. Simon and Schouten (1991) recently reviewed the use of plethysmography in the assessment and treatment of sexual deviance and concluded that its validity and clinical utility remain to be demonstrated. There are numerous problems with the use of plethysmography in treatment, including lack of a standardized stimulus set, lack of standardized protocols in terms of order of presentation of stimuli and length of exposure to stimuli, the possibility of test–retest learning, and the possibility of faking or suppressing responses. Nevertheless, we find this assessment useful. For instance, for frotteurs the presentation of various verbal scenarios and establishment of high arousal to frotteuristic stimuli seems to be good corroborative evidence that this activity is arousing to them. One could then administer behavioral or other treatments and reassess after a period of time to determine if there has been an objective decrease in arousal as measured by the plethysmograph. However, plethysmography is time consuming and should be used discriminately; caution in the use of plethysmographic assessment seems warranted. One can contrast the above psychometric tests, which more specifically probe for paraphilic psychopathology, with more general instruments, which may yield other psychiatric diagnoses.

There are well-accepted standard diagnostic instruments that probe for major mental illness, such as the Schedule for Affective Disorders and Schizophrenia (Endicott & Spitzer, 1978) or the National Institute of Mental Health Diagnostic Interview Schedule (Robins, Helzer, Croughan, & Ratcliff, 1981), which could be used if aspects of the history require a more careful examination and confirmation of the diagnoses of major mental disorder.

The Personal Diagnostic Questionnaire (Hyler, 1995) is a self-report questionnaire designed to assess an individual and generate appropriate personality disorders from the 10 available in DSM-IV. Various versions of this have been described and validated (Hyler et al., 1990; Hyler, Skodol, Kellman, Oldham, & Rosnick, 1990; Trull & Larson, 1994). We see the utility of this instrument, as with all psychological testing, as an aid in confirming diagnoses or as a screen which can suggest further areas to explore.

Fagan et al. (1991) reported on the use of an instrument called the NEO Personality Inventory (NEO-PI; Costa & McCrae, 1985, 1989), comparing personality profiles generated from 51 men with sexual dysfunction with those of 51 age-matched men with a primary diagnosis of paraphilia. Men from the sexual dysfunction group had an average personality profile comparable to a normative sample whereas the paraphilic men had a distinctive personality profile characterized by high scores in the neuroticism domain and low scores on the agreeableness and conscientiousness domains. A second study by Wise, Fagan, Schmidt, Ponticas, and Costa (1991) examined 24 men diagnosed with transvestic fetishism utilizing DSM-III-R (American Psychiatric Association, 1987) criteria and found this group to be similar on most dimensions of the NEO-PI to the group of paraphiliacs studied earlier.

Erickson, Luxenberg, Walbek, and Seely (1987) reported on a study of 568 convicted sex offenders who had been referred for a presentence evaluation and who were given the Minnesota Multiphasic Personality Inventory (MMPI; Dahlstrom, Welsh, & Dahlstrom, 1972). They concluded that their findings did not support descriptions of any MMPI profile as typical of any sort of sex offender, and they condemned any attempts to identify individuals as likely sex offenders on the basis of their MMPI profiles. They posited that the MMPI could be better used to monitor long-term treatment progress. Hall, Graham, and Shepherd (1991) applied the MMPI to a sample of 261 sexual offenders in a state hospital and found that the offenders comprised a very heterogeneous population. In a broad review of the literature of personality correlates of pedophilia, Okami and Goldberg (1992), reviewing studies using the MMPI and other tests to examine numerous clinical contentions about pedophiles, concluded that "relatively little may be stated about the personality or phenomenology of pedophiles and sex offenders against minors" (p. 320).

Eysenck (1971) administered a personality inventory measuring psychoticism, extroversion, and neuroticism and a 19-question sexual questionnaire to approximately 800 male and female students and found that personality scores were correlated with some of the sexual attitude factors. Wilson and Cox (1983) administered the Eysenck Personality Questionnaire (Eysenck & Eysenck, 1975) to 77 members of a self-help club for pedophiles and found that, compared with control males, the pedophiles were more significantly introverted and higher on the psychoticism and neuroticism scales.

The Rorschach (Exner, 1974) has been used in individuals with paraphilias. For example, Meloy and Gacono (1992) presented a case study involving detailed Rorschach testing of a 33-year-old male with a history of sexual assault. They used these responses to develop a dynamic portrait which to them suggested a psychotic level of organization and great dangerousness.

The Hare Psychopathy Checklist—Revised (Hare, 1991) has been used to obtain a broad survey of an individual's sociopathy. This is a 20-item rating scale for assessing psychopathy in male forensic populations. Scores on the Psychopathy Checklist were predictive of violent recidivism in a maximum security psychiatric setting (Harris, Rice, & Cormier, 1989) and in a sample of adult rapists (Rice, Quinsey, & Harris, 1991). The Buss–Durkee Hostility Inventory (BDHI; Buss & Durkee, 1957) is a widely accepted instrument that can be used to assess impulsivity and aggression. Hall (1989) used this instrument to examine a sample of 239 sexual offenders and found that BDHI scores were higher in sexual offenders against adolescents and adults compared with those of sexual offenders against children. However, Overholser and Beck (1986), comparing incarcerated child molesters, rapists, and three control groups, found that the BDHI and other instruments used to assess hostility were not useful in distinguishing child molesters and rapists from the three control groups.

Hucker et al. (1986) reported on the neuropsychological assessment of 41 pedophiles, which included the Reitan neuropsychological test battery (Reitan, 1979), the Luria–Nebraska Neuropsychological Battery (Golden, Hammeke, & Purisch, 1981), the WAIS-R (Wechsler, 1981), and the Michigan Alcohol Screening Test (Selzer, 1971). They found that pedophiles tended to have lower IQs than controls and were significantly more impaired on all measures. Scott, Cole, McKay, Golden, and Liggett (1984) compared sexually anomalous men with normal controls using the Luria–Nebraska Neuropsychological Battery and found that 36% of pedophiles showed impairment. O'Carroll (1989), however, using different neuropsychological tests and a group of only 11 sexually deviant subjects, did not find differences compared with control groups of anxious patients or normal subjects. These studies suggest that there may well be neuropsychological abnormalities in some paraphiliacs. Although we do not routinely do neuropsychological testing, if there is a reason to suspect brain injury or damage from the clinical history, then we use the mini-mental status examination, with modifications (Folstein, Folstein, & McHugh, 1975; Dick et al., 1984), to screen and decide if further evaluation is indicated. It has been used mainly in the study of dementias.

Still another instrument which has been used by some clinicians is the MicroCog (Powell et al., 1993), which is a computer-administered method of assessing adults with mild to moderate levels of cognitive impairment. It is a self-administered instrument which assesses functioning in 9 areas of brain functioning and which can be used as a screen to determine if further neurological or neuropsychiatric assessment is warranted. Head injury or neurological illness can be associated with decreased impulse control in individuals with paraphilias, and a clinical history and the above instruments can screen for these.

Substance abuse is an important area to assess. Erickson et al. (1987) reported that over 50% of the subjects of their sample of 568 convicted sex offenders were chemically dependent. Bradford and McLean (1984) found that the high violence subgroup in their survey of 50 male sex offenders was significantly associated with a history of serious alcohol abuse and dependence. Hucker et al. (1986), in a survey of pedophiles completing the Michigan Alcoholism Screening Test, found that 38% of pedophiles were alcoholics. The Short Michigan Alcoholism Screening Test (Selzer, 1971; Selzer, Vinokur, & Van Rooijan, 1975) is an excellent self-administered instrument which can screen for problems with alcohol.

Finally, the Beck Depression Inventory (Beck, Ward, Mendelson, Mock, & Erbaugh, 1961) is a self-administered, brief screen for depression.

The Multiphasic Sex Inventory (MSI; Nichols & Molinder, 1984, 1992) is another instrument that has been administered to sexual offenders. It contains scales of sexual knowledge, sexual deviance, validity, and sexual dysfunction. Data have been published on the utility of the MSI in predicting treatment progress and therapy outcome (Simpkins, Ward, Bowman, & Rinck, 1990).

The Millon Clinical Multiaxial Inventory–III (Millon, 1983) is another instrument that has been used with pedophiles; however, there are no published studies involving its use with frotteurs.

Medical Aspects of Assessment for Treatment

Some clinicians incorporate as a usual part of their treatment a physical examination, screening laboratory tests (including a complete blood count with differential), a complete chemistry screen, an electrocardiogram, a urinalysis, and endocrinological measures including testosterone level, follicle stimulating hormone level, and luteinizing hormone level. Although we do not routinely do this, we will refer the patient for a medical or neurological workup if specific aspects of a patient's history suggest its utility. For example, a history of a head injury antedating paraphilic behavior suggests a possible relationship between the two, and we would refer an individual to a neuropsychologist and/or a neurologist for a more detailed assessment. The development of frotteurism abruptly in a man in his 50s or 60s with headaches might suggest a brain tumor, and that individual should be referred to a neurologist. If an individual is to be placed on tricyclic antidepressants, a treatment which has been used for some frotteurs, then a careful history regarding an individual's cardiovascular health, any family history of cardiovascular disease, and a baseline electrocardiogram to rule out conduction defects in the heart's electric system (which can be exacerbated by tricyclics) is indicated. We usually refer the patient to an internist or to his family doctor for this.

Rada, Laws, and Kellner (1976) reported that plasma testosterone was significantly higher in sadistic compared with nonsadistic rapists, but failed to replicate this (Rada et al., 1983). Gaffney and Berlin (1984) studied hypogonadal–pituitary function in seven pedophiles, five nonpedophilic paraphiles, and five controls and found a significant difference between the pedophilic group and the other two groups in the luteinizing hormone response to luteinizing hormone releasing hormone, with the pedophiles responding with a marked elevation of luteinizing hormone to luteinizing hormone releasing hormone compared with the two other groups. However, Bradford and McLean (1984), examining morning testosterone levels of 50 consecutive male sexual offenders presenting for an evaluation, found no relation between violent sexual offenders and plasma testosterone levels. Accordingly, it is not our usual practice to perform gonadotropin or endocrinological assessments of individuals unless so guided by other data.

THEORIES OF THERAPY WITH REVIEW OF OUTCOME AND PROCESS RESEARCH

Again, we must emphasize that, aside from a few case reports, therapy suggestions have been developed from a heterogeneous group of paraphiliacs in general and not derived specifically from the treatment of frotteurs, as far as the published literature is concerned. Furthermore, as we have pointed out, frotteurism often occurs along with other paraphilias in the same individual, and therapy must be designed to target multiple paraphilias. Additionally, because the patient may have personality, medical, and other individual factors that require attention and create a unique situation, therapy must be individualized to the needs of the specific frotteur.

That said, major current treatment therapies for frotteurs can be divided into cognitive-behavioral, biological, and relapse prevention modalities.

Cognitive-Behavioral Therapies

Cognitive-behavioral therapy has been widely used in the treatment of the paraphilias, and is well described in several reviews (Abel, Osborn, Anthony, & Gardos, 1992; Abel, Rouleau, & Cunningham-Rathner, 1983; Hawton, 1985). This treatment views sexual fantasy as an independent variable (Abel & Blanchard, 1974) that can be altered by behavioral interventions, including techniques of covert sensitization that link deviant urges with negative consequences by having the patient mentally and verbally pair the two (Abel et al., 1984), olfactory aversion (pairing the smell of ammonia with paraphilic images and urges; Laws, Meyer, & Holmen, 1978; Laws & Osborn, 1983), masturbatory satiation wherein a patient masturbates in a certain prescribed way designed to decrease his arousal to the deviant stimuli (Laws & Marshall, 1991; Abel et al., 1984), and cognitive restructuring (encountering a paraphile's rationalizations and cognitive distortions; Abel et al., 1984; Murphy, 1990). It is very practically oriented, focusing most on the here and now and on improving an individual's control of his deviant impulses and decreasing his arousal.

An earlier review by Kilmann, Sabalis, Gearing, Bukstell, and Scovern (1982) examined outcome research on the treatment of patients with paraphilias; they noted that there was a reliance upon verbal self-reports in the evaluation of outcome and concluded that the literature tentatively supported a multiple behavioral package specifically tailored to the patient's sexual arousal pattern. Marshall, Jones, Ward, and Johnston (1991) published a more recent review which concluded that comprehensive cognitive-behavioral programs and combined hormonal and psychological treatments were effective in treating child molesters and exhibitionists, but not rapists. Quinsey, Harris, Rice, and Lalumière (1993) challenged this review, expressing the opinion that the effectiveness of treatment in reducing sexual offender recidivism had not yet been scientifically demonstrated and that more well-controlled outcome research was necessary. Marshall (1993) responded to their criticism regarding outcome data. Marshall and Barbaree (1990) reviewed outcomes of comprehensive cognitive-behavioral treatment programs and concluded that these approaches had a positive future, but that indices for treatment effectiveness needed to be developed. Laws and Marshall (1991) reviewed the literature on employing various sorts of masturbatory satiation. They reviewed four methods of masturbatory reconditioning and noted that there were few controlled studies and no group comparison studies. They indicated that directed masturbation and satiation might be most effective and suggested that more careful, larger studies would be required to develop a solid empirical basis for these techniques.

Many programs identified and described in the survey of treatment programs and models of the Safer Society Program (Freeman-Longo, Bird, Stevenson, & Fiske, 1994) employ a cognitive-behavioral approach. This treatment approach utilizes techniques such as masturbatory satiation, covert sensitization, cognitive restructuring, sexual education, social skills training, and assertiveness training. These are administered primarily in a group therapy setting, with augmentation as needed with individual or couple sessions, and with medications. Relapse prevention is also an important component of these programs.

In recent years there has been a great deal of controversy over whether to treat men who deny a sexual behavior problem (Maletzky, 1996). Several approaches have shown positive results in working with offenders who deny (Hoke, Sykes, & Winn, 1989; Maletzky, 1996; O'Donohue & Letourneau, 1993; Schlank & Shaw, 1996; Winn, 1996).

Biological Therapies

Biological therapies specific for the paraphilias have by and large consisted of antiandrogen therapy and antidepressant therapy. There are several reviews of antiandrogen therapy (Berlin & Meinecke, 1981; Bradford, 1985; Cooper, 1986). These have focused on the use in the United States of depot or oral Provera, which lowers testosterone and in Canada the use of cyproterone acetate, which acts through competitive inhibition of androgen receptors, blocking the actions of testosterone and dihydrotestosterone. Cyproterone acetate is not approved for use in the United States. Bradford and Pawlak (1993) reported on a double-blind, placebo-controlled, crossover study involving 19 paraphilic men referred for a pretreatment assessment, one of whom had the exclusive diagnosis of frotteurism. Results showed a significant reduction of testosterone and follicle stimulating hormone (FSH) along with a reduction in sexual arousal, activity, and fantasy, compared with placebo. Meyer, Cole, and Emory (1992) reported on a series of 40 men with heterogeneous diagnoses who were treated weekly with intramuscular medroxyprogesterone acetate (MPA) in durations lasting from 6 months to 12 years (usually more than 2 years); the follow-up period lasted from 2 to 12 years. Whereas the control group was not randomized and it consisted of individuals who had refused the therapy, 18% reoffended while receiving MPA therapy, compared with 58% of control patients. Main side effects included weight gain, malaise, migraine headaches, leg cramps, elevated blood pressure, gastrointestinal complaints, gallbladder stones, and diabetes mellitus. Gottesman and Schubert (1993) described the use of low-dose oral MPA in doses of 60 mg per day in seven men who were outpatients with heterogeneous diagnoses, none of which included frotteurism. All patients reported significantly fewer paraphilic fantasies, and none reported engaging in paraphilic incidents during MPA treatment.

Recently there have been several reports on the use of long-acting gonadotropic hormone-releasing hormone agonists (e.g., Lupron) to treat paraphilias, with excellent results (Dickey, 1992; Thibaut, Cordier, & Kuhn, 1993; Rousseau, Couture, Dupont, Labrie, & Couture, 1990). These agonists result in the continued stimulation of the gonadotrope cells in the anterior pituitary, which secrete luteinizing hormone (LH) and FSH, desensitizing these cells and leading, after a week or two, to suppression of the secretion of LH and FSH; this in turn leads to a decrease in gonadal testosterone secretion. They are unrelated to steroid hormones and adverse effects such as gynecomastia, thromboembolism, edema, and liver and gallbladder problems are less common than with other antiandrogen agents (American Medical Association, 1995; Tolis, Mehta, Comaru-Schally, & Schally, 1981). They are also available in a depot form, which can be given as a monthly injection.

A possible relationship between paraphilias and obsessive–compulsive disorder (OCD) has been suggested (Cryan, Gutcher, & Webb, 1992; Jenike, 1989; Stein et al., 1992), and accordingly, it has been further suggested that agents used to treat OCD might be useful in the treatment of paraphilias. Furthermore, marked side effects on sexual functioning exist for the agents used to treat OCD, including both clomipramine, a tricyclic (Monteiro, Noshirvani, Marks, & Lelliott, 1987), and other serotonergic medications such as fluoxetine, paroxitine, and sertraline (American Medical Association, 1995). Kruesi, Fine, Valladares, Phillips, and Rapoport (1992) reported on a double-blind, crossover comparison of clomipramine versus desipramine in 15 patients with paraphilias; this sample included three individuals with frotteurism. Four subjects were placebo responders and were dropped from the study and three subjects failed to complete the study. Both drugs decreased the severity of paraphilic symptoms relative to placebo and there was no difference between the two drugs. Side effects noted during this 5-week trial were greater with clomipramine than with desipramine and included delayed ejaculation, erectile dysfunction, and pain on ejaculation. The authors noted no apparent relation between these side effects and improvement in paraphilia while on the antidepressant; they reported that sexual functioning often improved without return of the paraphilic behavior. Selective serotonin reuptake inhibitors have also been tried successfully. Kafka (1991a) reported that 9 of 10 men with either nonparaphilic sexual addiction or paraphilia improved while taking fluoxetine, imipramine or lithium. He also reported on the successful treatment of a rape assailant with fluoxetine (Kafka, 1991b). Perilstein, Lipper, and Friedman (1991) reported on the apparently successful treatment of three individuals, including one with voyeurism/frotteurism, with fluoxetine. Bradford and Gratzer (1995) offered a case report of the successful use of sertraline in a patient diagnosed with pedophilia, major depression, and trichotillomania. The monoamine oxidase inhibitor phenelzine has also been reported to influence sexual behavior (Golwyn & Sevlie, 1993; Warnecke, 1994).

Relapse Prevention Therapies

Relapse prevention strategies have been described and employed recently with paraphiliacs (Freeman-Longo & Pithers, 1992; Laws, 1989; Pithers, 1990; Pithers, Kashima, Cumming, & Beal, 1988). This therapeutic modality emphasizes helping individuals to identify the chain of antecedent thoughts, situations, and behaviors that lead to a relapse and offers strategies to an individual to avoid lapses. These strategies include interrupting the chain of events leading to lapses, avoiding precipitating stimuli, avoiding or escaping from situations of risk, enhancing interpersonal skills, and anger and stress management.

RECOMMENDED TREATMENT STRATEGIES

As with any patient with a psychiatric disorder, effective treatment must be based on a thorough assessment and diagnosis. Often this will include a report to the patient's lawyer and/or to the court. Although a patient's legal situation can remain uncertain for a long period of time, we attempt to help them resolve it with a clear-cut recommendation from the court or from parole or probation agencies specifying that individuals continue in therapy.

Given the often very poor motivation of paraphiles, it is imperative to, if possible, get the legal system and/or significant others involved to insist on therapy. It is also important to have the individual acknowledge guilt and accept responsibility. This is sometimes accomplished by the time the individual enters treatment, by admitting his wrongdoing or having pled guilty in court. Many offenders deny at the beginning of treatment but admit responsibility during the course of treatment; some continue to deny. Some clinicians will work with individuals who deny, but only for limited periods of time and with the principal goal of helping them to admit. Recently, clinicians have been successful in this area (Maletzky, 1996).

With respect to treatment modality, unless a patient is dangerously out of control, the first treatment attempted would involve verbal and cognitive-behavioral methods because these avoid the side effects of medication. If an individual has another Axis I disorder, such as alcohol or substance abuse or dependence, bipolar disorder, or depression, then it is important to treat the Axis I disorder in the conventional fashion initially, initiating appropriate medications and recommending Alcoholics Anonymous or Narcotics Anonymous, family member participation, toxic screens of blood and/or urine, and hospitalization if indicated.

If an individual is unable to achieve control of his deviant urges, then the clinician might consider medication using one of the serotonin-reuptake inhibitors, which might diminish and give the individual more control over his frotteuristic urges. If these interventions are not successful, then antiandrogen agents might be indicated. Whereas either oral or depot Provera could be used, we have found that depot Lupron given at monthly intervals is superior; it is better tolerated, requiring monthly as opposed to weekly injections, and causes markedly fewer side effects than does Provera. When initiating a course of depot Lupron, treatment with flutamide, a nonsteroidal antiandrogen, to commence on the day of Lupron injection and to continue for 2 weeks is indicated to counteract any surge in testosterone which may occur with the onset of Lupron. The antiandrogens are, in our experience, markedly effective in suppressing sexual urges. The problem with them is that they significantly truncate an individual's sexual life and sooner or later an individual wishes to stop them. Prior to this happening, and while someone is on a course of Lupron therapy, we initiate and continue cognitive-behavioral treatment as well.

Following completion of an acute group of weekly sessions which generally lasts from 1½ to 2 years, if ready, patients are referred to an ongoing relapse prevention group for indefinite continuation. When family members have been educated regarding the individual's problem, clinicians enjoin them to help monitor the patient and report any worrisome activity to the therapist. For instance, if an individual's frotteurism has been associated in the past with alcohol intoxication and his wife sees him intoxicated, then she is to notify his treating clinician. Periodically, the therapist will have individual meetings with the family member or individual patient.

FORENSIC ISSUES

Individuals with paraphilias most of the time do not enter treatment of their own volition, and this is also true of frotteurs. Their paraphilic behavior is pleasureful and reinforcing and patients do not like to relinquish it; often arrest and involvement of the legal system are required to bring the individual to treatment. Frotteurism is often viewed as a "nuisance" crime; furthermore, cases are frequently very difficult to prove because a frotteur's contact may be ambiguous and there need to be many complainants to successfully prosecute a case. Accordingly, any pleas or sentencing may involve a reduction to a misdemeanor (frotteurism is in some states a felony), with sentencing to outpatient therapy and with no jail time. Indeed, it is extremely unlikely that frotteurs will be incarcerated for their frotteuristic activity.

Referral sources often include legal entities with numerous interests, such as defense attorneys, who may wish to have a forensic defense prepared, if possible, or who may wish to have their client assessed and involved with treatment before sentencing or as an aid in sentencing. Some prosecutors may wish to have a second opinion regarding diagnosis and treatment from a psychiatrist or psychologist other than those, usually hired by the patient's defense lawyer, who may have already assessed the patient. Judges may wish to have an independent evaluation as an aid in adjudicating the case. Less often, a significant other (spouse or girlfriend) will discover the behavior and insist that the individual come to evaluation. Occasionally other entities, such as medical boards, hospital administrations, or corporations will become aware of complaints from patients or employees and refer the individual for therapy.

Accordingly, given the numerous sources of referral and reasons for an evaluation, it is paramount to inform the individual, even before the clinician sees him or her, of concerns regarding confidentiality and duty. Usually, because frotteurs do not have an identifiable target who is predictably at risk, there is no duty to report any activity or crimes to the authorities. If an individual is referred from a prosecutor or lawyer, then one should additionally say to the individual just who has ordered the assessment and for what reason. We caution patients that the usual patient–physician confidentiality does not apply, and that whatever they might say could be included in a report to the referring entity. Furthermore, if they have not made admissions prior to the evaluation, then whatever they admit in an evaluation session could be potentially used to incriminate them, and we advise individuals of this. If the clinician interviews family members such as a husband, wife, or child, then we give them the same warning. Wherever there is the possibility of legal or criminal involvement (which is most of the time), we always ask individuals if they have an attorney, and we advise them to get one if they do not have one already. Clearly, there are numerous purposes for evaluations and confidentiality is not at all assured; we tell the perpetrator involved about the ground rules. Laws and practices regarding confidentiality vary from state to state and between different countries, and the clinician should check with his or her professional organization or lawyer for applicable guidelines.

The lack of confidentiality clearly can have a dramatic effect on the extent and truthfulness of the history. Kaplan, Abel, Rathner, and Mittelman (1990) studied offenders who were interviewed about their paraphilic histories, first by their parole officer in a correctional setting, and then at a setting within the mental health system with elaborate safeguards to their confidentiality. Offenders reported only 5% of the sexual offenses in the criminal justice setting that they did in the mental health setting. However, Weinrott and Saylor (1991) reported on a study which used computer-administered interviews to examine self-reports of criminal behavior from 99 institutionalized sex offenders, who were told that their responses would be "confidential but not anonymous." They found that offenders disclosed an enormous number of offenses, both sexual and nonsexual, and argued that self-report instruments were a valid method of collecting data. It is never possible to completely ascertain truthfulness. However, it is our experience that individuals range in the admissions that they make from complete denial to a seemingly extensive acknowledgment of acts committed under the circumstances of warning.

At the onset of treatment, when the legal system is involved the clinician should have the patient sign a release of information which will allow the clinician to speak with his parole officer, probation officer, or other supervising entity at any point regarding attendance, motivation, or dangerousness. We tell individuals when they sign such a release that by and large we will not reveal details of their treatment or verbalizations, but rather we will tell the supervising official only of the attendance rate, the degree of motivation in sessions, and the reported degree of control over sexual impulses. For individuals who have a probation officer, we often develop a sheet, which the patient is instructed to carry with him at all times, which includes a record of the date and time of the session scheduled, the time the patient arrived, the degree of motivation he manifested, any other comments, and the date and time of the next session. The treating clinician initials each completed session. In our initial contact with parole or probation officers we inform them of the existence of such a sheet. This then allows the official to check with the patient at any time regarding their attendance without necessitating frequent written reports from the therapist. This also allows the parole or probation officer to make spot checks or home visits and have immediately available documentation of attended sessions.

Regarding the use of plethysmography, the Association for the Treatment of Sexual Abusers (ATSA) has published standards and guidelines (Association for the Treatment of Sexual Abusers, 1993). According to these guidelines the use of plethysmography as a vehicle for determining the guilt or innocence of an individual is unethical. The determination of guilt or innocence should be left to the judicial system.

Regarding risk assessment, clinicians are frequently asked to make predictions. However, according to Monahan (1981, 1984), the track record of clinicians' use of intuitive judgments in predicting violence is quite poor. There are no known empirically validated instruments that we know of which are predictive. There is no "profile" that can be constructed reliably with standard psychometric tests that will predict dangerousness. Clinicians must rely on their experience, and factors of relevance include the coexistence of multiple paraphilias, the existence of other diagnoses, the amount of violence involved, the number of victims involved, and the severity of the offense.

With respect to informed consent, the issue of freedom of choice is a significant one, particularly if antiandrogen agents are given. Generally speaking, if an individual does not come to treatment, it could have repercussions for him should his probation or parole officer become aware of this. Accordingly, there exists a subtle or not-so-subtle coercion for the individual to come to therapy, or, as an alternative, to be incarcerated.

We recommend that clinicians have an individual sign an informed consent which lists the risks and benefits of any specific assessment and the risks and benefits of specific treatment modalities. Principally, the main risks of both evaluation and treatment are sexual dysfunction and mild symptoms of anxiety and/or depression. Obviously, medications have their own specific effects; side effects and risks and benefits and should be dealt with separately.

FUTURE DIRECTIONS

The problem of nonconsenting sexual behavior is widespread in our society. Although the literature on frotteurism is sparse, there is a great deal of research on paraphilias in general. What is known is that men who engage in frotteurism have large numbers of victims, are not often arrested, and, when apprehended, do not serve long sentences. Although frottage is usually considered merely a "nuisance," future research needs to ascertain what percentage and which of these individuals are at risk to commit more violent sexual offenses. Further research also needs to address the early onset of this behavior.

There are numerous assessment and treatment modalities which have worked with other paraphilias and should work as well with frotteurs. Research needs to address specific areas of treatment needs with frotteurs, and what treatments frotteurs respond to.

Psychophysiological assessment is a valuable method of eliciting information which may not be available in other self-report assessments. Because this method of assessment is time consuming and expensive, the development of reliable and valid alternative assessments of sexual interest would be a valuable contribution to the field.

The evidence presented on medication seems especially promising; medications will have an important role to play in conjunction with other treatments. Any case reports or small studies of successful treatment with frotteurs would be an important contribution to the field.

REFERENCES

Abel, G. G. (1984). *The Adult Sexual Interest Cardsort.* (Available from G. G. Abel, Behavioral Medicine Institute of Atlanta, 3280 Howell Mill Road, Atlanta, GA 30327-4101.)

Abel, G. G. (1989). Paraphilias. In H. I. Kaplan & B. J. Sadock (Eds.), *Comprehensive textbook of psychiatry* (5th ed., pp. 1069–1085). Baltimore: Williams & Wilkins.

Abel, G. G. (1994). *Abel Assessment for Interest in the Paraphilias.* Atlanta: Abel Screening, Inc.

Abel, G. G. (1995). *Reliability and validity of Abel assessment.* Paper presented at the 1995 Association for the Treatment of Sexual Abusers meeting, New Orleans, LA.

Abel, G. G., Becker, J. B., Cunningham-Rathner, J., Rouleau, J. L., Kaplan, M., & Reich, J. (1984). *Treatment manual: The treatment of child molesters.* (Available from G. G. Abel, Behavioral Medicine Institute of Atlanta, 3280 Howell Mill Road, Atlanta, GA 30327-4101.)

Abel, G. G., Becker, J. B., Cunningham-Rathner, J., Mittelman, M., & Rouleau, J. L. (1988). Multiple paraphilic diagnoses among sex offenders. *Bulletin of the American Academy of Psychiatry and the Law, 16*(2), 153–168.

Abel, G. G., Becker, J. B., Mittelman, M., Cunningham-Rathner, J., Rouleau, J. L., & Murphy, W. D. (1987). Self-reported sex crimes of nonincarcerated paraphiliacs. *Journal of Interpersonal Violence, 2*(1), 3–25.

Abel, G. G., & Blanchard, E. B. (1974). The role of fantasy in the treatment of sexual deviation. *Archives of General Psychiatry, 30,* 467–475.

Abel, G. G., Blanchard, E. B., & Barlow, D. H. (1981). The effects of stimulus modality, instructional set and stimulus content on the objective measurement of sexual arousal in several paraphilias. *Behaviour Research and Therapy, 19,* 25–33.

Abel, G. G., Cunningham-Rathner, J., Becker, J. V., & McHugh, J. (1983, December). *Motivating sex offenders for treatment with feedback of their psychophysiologic assessment.* Paper presented at the World Congress of Behavior Therapy, Washington, DC.

Abel, G. G., Gore, D. K., Holland, C. L., Camp, N., Becker, J. B., & Rathner, J. (1989). The measurement of the cognitive distortions of child molesters. *Annals of Sex Research, 2,* 135–153.

Abel, G. G., Osborn, C. A., Anthony, D., & Gardos, P. (1992). Current treatments of paraphiliacs. *Annual Review of Sex Research, 3,* 255–290.

Abel, G. G., & Rouleau, J. L. (1990). The nature and extent of sexual assault. In W. L. Marshall, D. L. Laws, & H. E. Barbaree (Eds.), *Handbook of sexual assault: Issues, theories and treatment of the offender* (pp. 9–21). New York: Plenum Press.

Abel, G. G., Rouleau, J. L., & Cunningham-Rathner, J. (1986). Sexually aggressive behavior. In W. J. Curran, A. L. McGarry, & S. Shah (Eds.), *Forensic psychiatry and psychology* (pp. 289–313). Philadelphia: Davis.

Abrams, S., & Abrams, J. (1993). *Polygraph testing of the pedophile.* Portland, OR: Ryan Gwinner Press.

American Psychiatric Association. (1987). *Diagnostic and statistical manual of mental disorders* (3rd ed., rev.). Washington, DC: Author.

American Psychiatric Association. (1994). *Diagnostic and statistical manual of mental disorders* (4th ed.). Washington, DC: Author.

American Medical Association. (1995). *Drug evaluations, Annual 1995.* Chicago: Author.

Association for the Treatment of Sexual Abusers. (1993). *The ATSA practitioner's handbook.* Beaverton, OR: Author.

Beck, A. T., Ward, C. H., Mendelson, M., Mock, J., & Erbaugh, J. (1961). An inventory for measuring depression. *Archives of General Psychiatry, 4,* 561–567.

Becker, J. V., Kaplan, M. S., Tenke, C. E., & Tartaglini, A. (1991). The incidence of depressive symptomatology in juvenile sex offenders with a history of abuse. *Child Abuse and Neglect, 15,* 531–536.

Berlin, F. S., & Meinecke, C. F. (1981). Treatment of sex offenders with antiandrogenic medication: Conceptualization, review of treatment modalities, and preliminary findings. *American Journal of Psychiatry, 138*(5), 601–607.

Bradford, J. M. W. (1985). Organic treatments for the male sexual offender. *Behavioral Sciences and the Law, 3*(4), 355–375.

Bradford, J. M., Boulet, J., & Pawlak, A. (1992). The paraphilias: A multiplicity of deviant behaviors. *Canadian Journal of Psychiatry, 37*(2), 104–108.

Bradford, J. M., & Gratzer, T. G. (1995). A treatment for impulse control disorders and paraphilia: A case report. *Canadian Journal of Psychiatry, 40*(1), 4–5.

Bradford, J. M., & McLean, D. (1984). Sexual offenders, violence and testosterone: A clinical study. *Canadian Journal of Psychiatry, 29,* 335–343.

Bradford, J. M., & Pawlak, A. (1993). Double-blind placebo crossover study of cyproterone acetate in the treatment of the paraphilias. *Archives of Sexual Behavior, 22*(5), 383–402.

Brett, A. S., Phillips, M., & Beary, J. F. (1986, March 8). Predictive power of the polygraph: Can the "lie detector" really detect liars? *Lancet,* 544–547.

Buss, A. H., & Durkee, A. (1957). An inventory for assessing different kinds of hostility. *Journal of Consulting and Clinical Psychology, 21,* 343–349.

Conte, J. R. (1983). Development and use of self-report techniques for assessing sexual functioning: A review and critique. *Archives of Sexual Behavior, 12*(6), 555–576.

Cooper, A. J. (1986). Progestogens in the treatment of male sex offenders: A review. *Canadian Journal of Psychiatry, 31,* 73–79.

Costa, P. T., & McCrae, R. R. (1985). *The NEO Personality Inventory manual.* Odessa, FL: Psychological Assessment Resources.

Costa, P. T., & McCrae, R. R. (1989). *The NEO-PI/NEO-FFI manual supplement.* Odessa, FL: Psychological Assessment Resources.

Cryan, E. M. J., Gutcher, G. J., & Webb, G. T. (1992). Obsessive–compulsive disorder and paraphilia in a monozygotic twin pair. *British Journal of Psychiatry, 161,* 694–698.

Dahlstrom, W., Welsh, G., & Dahlstrom, L. (Eds.). (1972). *An MMPI handbook* (rev. ed.). Minneapolis: University of Minnesota Press.

Derogatis, L. R. (1980). Psychological assessment of psychosexual functioning. *Psychiatric Clinics of North America, 3,* 113–131.

Derogatis, L. R., & Melisaratos, N. (1979). The DSFI: A multidimensional measure of sexual functioning. *Journal of Sexual and Marital Therapy, 5,* 244–281.

Dick, J. P., Guiloff, R. J., Stewart, A., Blackstock, J., Bielawska, C., Paul, E. A., & Marsden, C. D. (1984). Mini mental state examination in neurological patients. *Journal of Neurology, Neurosurgery and Psychiatry, 47,* 496–499.

Dickey, R. (1992). The management of a case of treatment-resistant paraphilia with a long-acting LHRH agonist. *Canadian Journal of Psychiatry, 37,* 567–569.

Endicott, J., & Spitzer, R. L. (1978). A diagnostic interview: The schedule for affective disorders and schizophrenia. *Archives of General Psychiatry, 35,* 837–844.

Erickson, W. D., Luxenberg, M. D., Walbek, N. H., & Seely, R. K. (1987). Frequency of MMPI two-point code types among sex offenders. *Journal of Consulting and Clinical Psychology, 55*(4), 566–570.

Exner, J. E. (1974). *The Rorschach: A comprehensive system.* New York: Wiley.

Eysenck, H. J. (1971). Personality and sexual adjustment. *British Journal of Psychiatry, 118,* 593–608.

Eysenck, H. J., & Eysenck, S. B. G. (1975). *Manual of the Eysenck personality questionnaire.* London: Hodder & Stoughton.

Fagan, P. J., Wise, T. N., Schmidt, C. W., Ponticas, Y., Marshall, R. D., & Costa, P. T. (1991). A comparison of five-factor personality dimensions in males with sexual dysfunction and males with paraphilia. *Journal of Personality Assessment, 57*(3), 434–448.

Farrenkopf, T. (1986). Comprehensive arousal pattern assessment. In *Treating the juvenile sexual abuse perpetrator.* Minneapolis: University of Minnesota Press.

Folstein, M. F., Folstein, S. E., & McHugh, P. R. (1975). "Mini-mental state": A practical method for grading the cognitive state of patients for the clinician. *Journal of Psychiatric Research, 12,* 189–198.

Freeman-Longo, R. E., Bird, S., Stevenson, W. F., & Fiske, J. A. (1994). *1994 Nationwide survey of treatment programs and models serving abuse-reactive children and adolescent and adult sex offenders.* Brandon, VT: Safer Society Press.

Freeman-Longo, R., & Pithers, W. D. (1992). *Client's manual. A structured approach to preventing relapse: A guide for sex offenders.* Brandon, VT: Safer Society Press.

Freund, K. (1963). A laboratory method for diagnosing predominance of homo- and hetero-erotic interest in the male. *Behaviour Research and Therapy, 1,* 85–93.

Freund, K. (1965). Diagnosing heterosexual pedophilia by means of a test for sexual interest. *Behaviour Research and Therapy, 3,* 229–234.

Freund, K. (1967). Diagnosing homo- and heterosexuality and erotic age preference by means of a psychophysiological test. *Behaviour Research and Therapy, 5,* 208–228.

Freund, K. (1988). Courtship disorder: Is the hypothesis valid? *Annals of the New York Academy of Science, 528,* 172–182.

Freund, K. (1990). Courtship disorder. In W. L. Marshall, D. R. Laws, & H. E. Barbaree (Eds.), *Handbook of sexual assault: Issues, theories and treatment of the offender* (pp. 195–207). New York: Plenum Press.

Freund, K., & Blanchard, R. (1986). The concept of courtship disorder. *Journal of Sex and Marital Therapy, 12*(2), 79–92.

Freund, K., Scher, H., & Hucker, S. (1983). The courtship disorders. *Archives of Sexual Behavior, 12*(5), 369–379.

Freund, K., & Watson, R. (1990). Mapping the boundaries of courtship disorder. *Journal of Sex Research, 27*(4), 589–606.

Freund, K., Watson, R., & Rienzo, D. (1988). Signs of feigning in the phallometric test. *Behaviour Research and Therapy, 26*(2), 105–112.

Gaffney, G. R., & Berlin, F. S. (1984). Is there hypothalamic–pituitary–gonadal dysfunction in paedophilia? A pilot study. *British Journal of Psychiatry, 145,* 657–660.

Golden, C. J., Hammeke, T. A., & Purisch, A. D. (1981). *Luria–Nebraska Neuropsychological Battery manual*. Los Angeles: Eastern Psychological Services.

Golwyn, D. H., & Sevlie, C. P. (1993). Adventitious change in homosexual behavior during treatment of social phobia with phenelzine. *Journal of Clinical Psychiatry, 54*(1), 39–40.

Gottesman, H. G., & Schubert, D. S. (1993). Low-dose oral medroxyprogesterone acetate in the management of the paraphilias. *Journal of Clinical Psychiatry, 54*(5), 182–188.

Grossman, L. S., & Cavanaugh, J. L. (1990). Psychopathology and denial in alleged sex offenders. *Journal of Nervous and Mental Disease, 178*, 739–744.

Hall, G. C. (1989). Self-reported hostility as a function of offense characteristics and response style in a sexual offender population. *Journal of Consulting and Clinical Psychology, 57*(2), 306–308.

Hall, G. C. N., Graham, J. R., & Shepherd, J. B. (1991). Three methods of developing MMPI taxonomies of sexual offenders. *Journal of Personality Assessment, 56*(1), 2–13.

Hanson, R. K., & Slater, S. (1988). Sexual victimization in the history of sexual abusers: A review. *Annals of Sex Research, 1*, 485–499.

Hare, R. D. (1991). *The Hare Psychopathy Checklist—Revised*. Toronto: Multi-Health Systems.

Harris, G., Rice, M. E., & Cormier, C. P. (1989). Violent recidivism among psychopaths treated in a therapeutic community. *Penetangvishene Mental Health Centre Research Reports, 6*(1), 315–335.

Hawton, K. (1983). Behavioural approaches to the management of sexual deviations. *British Journal of Psychiatry, 143*, 248–255.

Hoke, S. L., Sykes, C., & Winn, M. (1989). Systemic/strategic interventions targeting denial in the incestuous family. *Journal of Strategic and Systemic Therapies, 8*, 44–51.

Hucker, S., Langevin, R., Wortzman, G., Bain, J., Handy, L., Chambers, J., & Wright, S. (1986). Neuropsychological impairment in pedophiles. *Canadian Journal of Behavioural Science, 18*(4), 440–448.

Hyler, S. E. (1995). *The PDQ-4*. Scarsdale, NY: NiJo Software.

Hyler, S. E., Lyons, M., Rieder, R. O., Young, L., Williams, J. B. W., & Spitzer, R. L. (1990). The factor structure of self-report DSM-III Axis II symptoms and their relationship to clinician's ratings. *American Journal of Psychiatry, 147*, 751–757.

Hyler, S. E., Skodol, A. E., Kellman, H. D., Oldham, J., & Rosnick, L. (1990). The validity of the personality diagnostic questionnaire: A comparison with two structured interviews. *American Journal of Psychiatry, 147*, 1043–1048.

Jenike, M. A. (1989). Obsessive–compulsive and related disorders: A hidden epidemic. *New England Journal of Medicine, 321*(8), 539–541.

Kafka, M. P. (1991a). Successful antidepressant treatment of nonparaphilic sexual addictions and paraphilias in men. *Journal of Clinical Psychiatry, 52*(2), 60–65.

Kafka, M. P. (1991b). Successful treatment of paraphilic coercive disorder (a rapist) with fluoxetine hydrochloride. *British Journal of Psychiatry, 158*, 844–847.

Kafka, M. P., & Prentky, R. A. (1994). Preliminary observations of DSM-III-R Axis I comorbidity in men with paraphilias and paraphilia-related disorders. *Journal of Clinical Psychiatry, 55*(11), 481–487.

Kaplan, M. S., Abel, G. G., Rathner, J., & Mittelman, M. (1990). The impact of parolees' perceptions of confidentiality on self-reported sex crimes. *Annals of Sex Research, 3*(3), 293–305.

Kavoussi, R. J., Kaplan, M., & Becker, J. V. (1988). Psychiatric diagnoses in adolescent sex offenders. *Journal of the American Academy of Child and Adolescent Psychiatry, 27*, 241–243.

Kilmann, P. R., Sabalis, R. F., Gearing, M. L. II, Bukstell, L. H., & Scovern, A. W. (1982). The treatment of sexual paraphilias: A review of the outcome research. *Journal of Sex Research, 18*(3), 193–252.

Kruesi, M. J., Fine, S., Valladares, L., Phillips, R. A. J., & Rapoport, J. L. (1992). Paraphilias: A double-blind crossover comparison of clomipramine versus desipramine. *Archives of Sexual Behavior, 21*(6), 587–593.

Laws, R. D. (Ed.). (1989). *Relapse prevention with sex offenders*. New York: Guilford Press.

Laws, D., & Holman, M. (1978). Sexual response faking by pedophiles. *Criminal Justice and Behavior, 5*, 343–356.

Laws, D. R., & Marshall, W. L. (1991). Masturbatory reconditioning with sexual deviates: An evaluative review. *Advances in Behavior Research and Therapy, 13,* 13–25.

Laws, D. R., Meyer, J., & Holmen, M. I. (1978). Reduction of sadistic sexual arousal by olfactory aversion: A case study. *Behaviour Research and Therapy, 16,* 281–285.

Laws, D. R., & Osborn, C. A. (1983). How to build and operate a behavioral laboratory to evaluate and treat sexual deviance. In J. G. Greer & I. R. Stuart (Eds.), *The sexual aggressor: Current perspectives on treatment* (pp. 293–335). New York: Van Nostrand Reinhold.

Maletzky, B. M. (1996). Denial of treatment or treatment of denial? *Sexual Abuse: A Journal of Research and Treatment, 8*(1), 1–5.

Marshall, W. L. (1993). The treatment of sex offenders: What does the outcome data tell us? A reply to Quinsey, Harris, Rice and Lalumière. *Journal of Interpersonal Violence, 8*(4), 524–530.

Marshall, W. L., & Barbaree, H. E. (1990). Outcome of comprehensive cognitive-behavioral treatment programs. In W. L. Marshall, D. R. Laws, & H. E. Barbaree (Eds.), *Handbook of sexual assault: Issues, theories and treatment of the offender* (pp. 363–385). New York: Plenum Press.

Marshall, W. L., & Eccles, A. (1991). Issues in clinical practice with sex offenders. *Journal of Interpersonal Violence, 6*(1), 68–93.

Marshall, W. L., Jones, R., Ward T., & Johnston, P. (1991). Treatment outcome with sex offenders. *Clinical Psychology Review, 11,* 465–485.

Meloy, J. R., & Gacono, C. B. (1992). A psychotic (sexual) psychopath: "I just had a violent thought. . . . " *Journal of Personality Assessment, 58*(3), 480–493.

Meyer, W. J. III, Cole, C., & Emory, E. (1992). Depo Provera treatment for sex offending behavior: An evaluation of outcome. *Bulletin of the American Academy of Psychiatry and the Law, 20*(3), 249–259.

Millon, T. (1983). *Millon Clinical Multiaxial Inventory* (3rd ed.). Minneapolis: Interpretive Scoring Systems.

Monahan, J. (1981). *The clinical prediction of violent behavior.* Beverly Hills, CA: Sage.

Monahan, J. (1984). The prediction of violent behavior: Toward a second generation of theory and policy. *American Journal of Psychiatry, 141,* 10–15.

Murphy, W. D. (1990). Assessment and modification of cognitive distortions in sex offenders. In W. L. Marshall, D. R. Laws, & H. E. Barbaree (Eds.), *Handbook of sexual assault: Issues, theories, and treatment of the offender* (pp. 331–342). New York: Plenum Press.

Nichols, H. R., & Molinder, I. (1984). *Multiphasic Sex Inventory manual: A test to assess the psychosexual characteristics of the sexual offender.* Tacoma, WA: Author.

Nichols, H. R., & Molinder, I. (1992, October). *Research finding and clinical use of the Multiphasic Sex Inventory II.* Paper presented at the 11th Annual Research and Treatment Conference of the Association for the Treatment of Sexual Abusers, Portland, OR.

O'Carroll, R. (1989). A neuropsychological study of sexual deviation. *Sexual and Marital Therapy, 4*(1), 59–63.

O'Donohue, W., & Letourneau, E. (1993). A brief group treatment for the modification of denial in child sexual abusers: Outcome and follow-up. *Child Abuse and Neglect, 17,* 299–304.

Okami, R., & Goldberg, A. (1992). Personality correlates of pedophilia: Are they reliable indicators? *The Journal of Sex Research, 29*(3), 297–328.

Overholser, J. C., & Beck, S. (1986). Multimethod assessment of rapists, child molesters, and three control groups on behavioral and psychological measures. *Journal of Consulting and Clinical Psychology, 54*(5), 682–687.

Paitich, D., Langevin, R., Freeman, R., Mann, K., & Handy, L. (1977). The Clarke SHQ: A clinical sex history questionnaire for males. *Archives of Sexual Behavior, 6*(5), 421–436.

Perilstein, R. D., Lipper, S., & Friedman, L. J. (1991). Three cases of paraphilias responsive to fluoxetine treatment. *Journal of Clinical Psychiatry, 52*(4), 169–170.

Pithers, W. E. (1990). Relapse prevention with sexual aggressors. A method for maintaining therapeutic gain and enhancing external supervision. In W. L. Marshall, D. R. Laws, & H. E. Barbaree (Eds.), *Handbook of sexual assault* (pp. 343–361). New York: Plenum Press.

Pithers, W. D., Kashima, K. M., Cumming, G. F., & Beal, L. S. (1988). Relapse prevention: A method of enhancing maintenance of change in sex offenders. In A. C. Salter (Ed.), *Treating child sex offenders and victims: A practical guide* (pp. 131–170). Newbury Park, CA: Sage.

Pithers, W. D., & Laws, D. R. (1988). The penile plethysmograph. In B. K. Schwarts & H. R. Cellini (Eds.), *A practitioner's guide to treating the incarcerated male sex offender* (pp. 85–94). Washington, DC: U.S. Government Printing Office.

Powell, D. H., Kaplan, E. F., Whitla, D., Weintraub, S., Catlin, R., & Fundenstein, H. H. (1993). *MicroCog assessment of cognitive functioning.* San Antonio, TX: Psychological Corporation.

Quinsey, V. L., Harris, G. T., Rice, M. E., & Lalumière, M. L. (1993). Assessing treatment efficacy in outcome studies of sex offenders. *Journal of Interpersonal Violence, 8*(4), 512–523.

Rada, R. T., Laws, D. R., & Kellner, R. (1976). Plasma testosterone in the rapist. *Psychosomatic Medicine, 38,* 257–268.

Rada, R. T., Laws, D. R., Kellner, R., Srivistava, L., & Peake, G. (1983). Plasma androgens in violent and non-violent sex offenders. *Bulletin of the American Academy of Psychiatry and the Law, 11,* 149–158.

Reitan, R. (1979). *Manual for administration of neuropsychological test batteries for adults and children.* Tuscon, AZ: Author.

Rice, M., Quinsey, V., & Harris, G. (1991). Sexual recidivism among child molesters released from a maximum security psychiatric institution. *Journal of Consulting and Clinical Psychology, 59*(3), 381–386.

Robins, L. N., Helzer, J. E., Croughan, J., & Ratcliff, S. (1981). National Institute of Mental Health diagnostic interview schedule: Its history, characteristics, and validity. *Archives of General Psychiatry, 38,* 381–389.

Rooth, G. (1973). Exhibitionism, sexual violence and paedophilia. *British Journal of Psychiatry, 122,* 705–710.

Rousseau, L., Couture, M., Dupont, A., Labrie, F., & Couture, N. (1990). Effect of combined androgen blockage with an LHRH agonist and flutamide in one severe case of male exhibitionism. *Canadian Journal of Psychiatry, 35,* 338–341.

Schlank, A., & Shaw, T. (1996). Treating sexual offenders who deny their guilt: A pilot study. *Sexual Abuse: A Journal of Research and Treatment, 8*(1), 17–25.

Scott, M. L., Cole, J. K., McKay, S. E., Golden, C. J., & Liggett, K. R. (1984). Neuropsychological performance of sexual assaulters and pedophiles. *Journal of Forensic Sciences, 29,* 1114–1118.

Selzer, M. (1971). The Michigan Alcoholism Screening Test: The quest for a new diagnostic instrument. *American Journal of Psychiatry, 127,* 1653–1658.

Selzer, M., Vinokur, A., & Van Rooijan, L. (1975). A self-administered Short Michigan Alcoholism Screening Test (SMAST). *Journal of Studies on Alcohol, 36,* 117–126.

Simon, W. T., & Schouten, P. G. W. (1991). Plethysmography in the assessment and treatment of sexual deviance: An overview. *Archives of Sexual Behavior, 20*(1), 75–91.

Simpkins, L., Ward, W., Bowman, S., & Rinck, C. M. (1990). Characteristics predictive of child sex abusers' response to treatment: An exploratory study. *Journal of Psychology and Human Sexuality, 3*(1), 19–55.

Stein, D. J., Hollander, E., Anthony, D. T., Schneier, F. R., Fallon, B. A., Liebowitz, M. R., & Klein, D. F. (1992). Serotonergic medications for sexual obsessions, sexual addictions, and paraphilias. *Journal of Clinical Psychiatry, 53*(8), 267–271.

Templeman, T. L., & Stinnett, R. D. (1991). Patterns of sexual arousal and history in a "normal" sample of young men. *Archives of Sexual Behavior, 20*(2), 137–150.

Thibaut, F., Cordier, B., & Kuhn, J. (1993). Effect of a long-lasting gonadotropin hormone-releasing hormone agonist in six cases of severe male paraphilia. *Acta Psychiatrica Scandinavica, 87,* 443–450.

Tolis, G., Mehta, A., Comaru-Schally, A. M., & Schally, A. V. (1981). Suppression of androgen production by d-tryptophan-6-luteinizing hormone-releasing hormone in man. *Journal of Clinical Investigation, 68,* 819–822.

Trull, T. J., & Larson, S. L. (1994). External validity of two personality disorder inventories. *Journal of Personality Disorders, 8*(2), 96–103.

Warneke, L. (1994). Phenelzine and sexuality. *Journal of Clinical Psychiatry, 55*(5), 216–217.

Wechsler, D. (1981). *Wechsler Adult Intelligence Scale—Revised.* New York: Psychological Corporation.

Weinrott, M. R., & Saylor, M. (1991). Self-report of crimes committed by sex offenders. *Journal of Interpersonal Violence, 6*(3), 286–300.

Wilson, G. D., & Cox, D. N. (1983). Personality of paedophile club members. *Personality and Individual Differences, 4*(3), 323–329.

Winn, M. (1996). The strategic and systemic management of denial in the cognitive/behavioral treatment of sexual offenders. *Sexual Abuse: A Journal of Research and Treatment, 8*(1), 25–37.

Wise, T. N., Fagan, P. J., Schmidt, C. W., Ponticas, Y., & Costa, P. T. (1991). Personality and sexual functioning of transvestitic fetishists and other paraphilics. *Journal of Nervous and Mental Disease, 179*(11), 694–698.

Zuckerman, M. (1971). Physiological measures of sexual arousal in the human. *Psychological Bulletin, 5*, 297–320.

8

PEDOPHILIA
Psychopathology and Theory

W. L. Marshall

DIAGNOSTIC ISSUES

The term "pedophilia" has been, and still is, consistently used in two somewhat opposing and certainly confusing ways: either as a specific and restrictive description, or as a generic term for all persons who sexually molest children. In the American Psychiatric Association's *Diagnostic and Statistical Manual of Mental Disorders* (DSM) the term was first used in DSM-III (American Psychiatric Association, 1980) to describe a specific subset of child molesters who displayed particular characteristics. However, the nature of these defining characteristics has changed with the successive revisions of the manual and this has also caused problems which I will return to shortly. For the moment, let me note that, at least until the most recent version (i.e., DSM-IV; American Psychiatric Association, 1994), the diagnostic manual defined pedophilia in such a way that it excluded a substantial number of child molesters; this is where the confusion in the use of the term arose. On the other hand, many reports in the literature have used the term as a generic descriptor for all child molesters without any apparent concern for whether or not these offenders met the diagnostic criteria for pedophilia. As most clinicians recognize a need to evaluate and treat all child molesters, it is reasonable to assume that this is why many have chosen to not rigorously apply DSM criteria. However, it might have been more helpful if they had used the more diagnostically neutral term "child molesters" rather than describing these offenders as pedophiles. To add to this confusion, Abel, Mittelman, and Becker (1985) declared that 100% of child molesters could be diagnosed as pedophiles, although they did not make clear whether or not they meant this in terms of DSM criteria. Indeed, their declaration in the absence of data is puzzling.

In DSM-III and DSM-III-R (American Psychiatric Association, 1987), pedophilia was defined as involving "recurrent intense sexual urges and sexually arousing fantasies involving sexual activity with a prepubescent child or children" (1987, p. 285). Because these criteria did not include necessarily acting on these urges or fantasies, pedophilia, according to DSM-III and DSM-III-R, could be applied to persons who had never committed an offense, yet it could not be applied to those persons who had molested a child but who were not plagued by deviant urges and fantasies. In fact, in a review of my files (from both our prison and outpatient clinics) we could find no clear evidence of *recurrent* urges or fantasies in almost 60% of our nonfamilial child molesters and in over 75% of incest offenders. Apparently recurrent urges and fantasies are not diagnostic of all child molesters. Consequently, DSM-III and DSM-III-R criteria for pedophilia excluded a significant number of identified child molesters. This, of course, could have caused problems, were I to have believed that to qualify for treatment, the client had to meet DSM diagnostic criteria. Not surprisingly, many therapists working with child molesters choose to ignore DSM diagnostic issues and to respond simply as though all persons who committed sexual offenses against children had, by the nature of their behavior, problems in need of treatment. As opposed to some other clinicians, I decided to use the term "child molesters" rather than "pedophiles" to describe these clients. I did this not only to avoid diagnostic problems but also because I consider the term "pedophile" to be a misnomer. Translated from the Greek, it means approximately "child lover." My view is that these offenders do things to children that contradicts what most people mean by love. In any event, the result of this decision means that we define the need for treatment primarily in terms of behavior rather than any possible, but elusive, mental events.

One of the main problems with DSM-III and DSM-III-R criteria for pedophilia is that child molesters are understandably typically reluctant to admit having thoughts or feelings that could be construed by clinicians as deviant. One way around this problem is to employ a technology (which I will refer to collectively as "phallometry") that allows an assessment of sexual preferences. Advocates of these procedures assume that if a man displays deviant arousal during phallometric testing then he almost certainly has deviant urges or fantasies. As a result, phallometric testing has been seen as a way of addressing the diagnosis of pedophilia (Freund & Blanchard, 1989; Freund & Watson, 1991). Pedophiles, according to advocates of this view, are those child molesters who display sexual preferences for children during phallometric evaluation. Those child molesters who display nondeviant preferences during phallometric assessment are said not to be pedophiles. Whether or not one accepts that this is a satisfactory solution to the diagnostic problem, phallometric evaluations have provided a rather more meaningful way to distinguish among child molesters those who are and are not strongly attracted to sex with children. These findings regarding phallometric responses have implications for both treatment (Marshall & Fernandez, 1997) and risk assessment (Quinsey, Harris, & Rice, 1995; Quinsey, Lalumière, Rice, & Harris, 1995). I will raise the relevance and meaning of phallometric data again in later sections of this chapter.

The most recent version of the DSM, DSM-IV (American Psychiatric Association, 1994), defines the diagnostic criteria for pedophilia as "recurrent, intense sexually arousing fantasies, sexual urges, or behaviors involving sexual activity with a prepubescent child or children (generally age 13 years or younger)" (p. 528). These fantasies, sexual urges, or behavior are said to indicate pedophilia only if they "cause clinically significant distress or impairment in social, occupational, or other important areas of functioning" (p. 528). The pedophile also has to be 16 years of age or older and at least 5 years older than the child, although for late adolescents this age discrepancy is not specified and the diagnosis in those cases is left to the clinician's judgment.

Other than these diagnostic criteria, DSM-IV makes other claims about pedophiles. For instance, it posits that those pedophiles who are "attracted to females usually prefer 8 to 10-year olds, whereas those attracted to males usually prefer slightly older children" (American Psychiatric Association, 1994, p. 527). Furthermore, some pedophiles are said to be exclusively attracted to children whereas others are sometimes attracted to adults. The disorder is also assumed to usually begin in adolescence. DSM-IV also claims that the recidivism rate for pedophiles who are attracted to boys "is roughly twice that" for those attracted to girls. Finally, although gender differences are not mentioned in the section of DSM-IV that specifically describes pedophilia, in the introduction to the paraphilias it is claimed that other than sexual masochism, the paraphilias "are almost never diagnosed in females" (p. 524).

These diagnostic criteria and the associated claims present problems for researchers and clinicians alike. For example, the majority of men identified as having sexually molested a child at least initially deny recurrent fantasies or urges involving children. Although some subsequently admit such fantasies, it is not always clear that they are telling the truth or simply complying with the therapist's or researcher's demands. Certainly some maintain that they do not have recurrent fantasies or urges. If we believe these men, are they, on the basis of an absence of fantasies and urges to be judged as not pedophilic? The diagnostic criteria of DSM-IV, unlike those stated in DSM-III-R, have added to these requirements of recurrent fantasies and urges, the criteria "*or* behavior" (italics added). Previously there was no mention of sexual behavior involving children, so that if a man had molested many children, or only one child repeatedly, as long as he denied urges or fantasies (and there was no other evidence of deviant fantasies or urges) he was not diagnosed as a pedophile. The present criteria go some way toward overcoming this, but it appears that clinical practice in applying diagnostic criteria to child molesters tends to persist unless it is very clear that the addition of this reference to behavior is meant to significantly alter the application of the diagnosis of pedophilia. DSM-IV does not make clear why this additional criterion was added or what clinicians are to do as a consequence. If clinicians change their diagnostic practice accordingly, then more child molesters will be identified as pedophiles. The problem with this is that previous and future research on pedophiles will not be comparable in terms of the subjects employed. This, however, is a minor problem and by allowing diagnosticians to identify most child molesters as having a mental disorder, DSM-IV criteria should encourage more appropriate legal and administrative actions to deal with most child molesters and not just with those meeting the previous criteria for pedophilia. However, we still are left with a significant number of child molesters who may have offended too few times to meet any particular diagnostician's judgment of recurrent acts. It would improve things if future diagnostic manuals were to specify what "recurrent" means with respect most particularly to behavior, but also for fantasies and urges.

That pedophilia should be diagnosed only if it causes significant distress or impairment of functioning seems an odd caveat to add to the diagnostic criteria. Does this mean that if a person repeatedly molests children and is driven to do so by recurrent urges and fantasies, but is never detected and is undisturbed by his behavior, then he is not a pedophile? Such qualifications to the diagnostic criteria seem absurd if they are meant to apply to the offender. If they are meant to apply to the victims then the absurdity is hardly reduced, as most victims do suffer and for those who do not this is fortuitous and not a product of the offender's behavior or character.

The age specified for the child identified as the object of the pedophile's fantasies, urges, or behavior also presents problems. Whereas there must be some cutoff age, defining pedophilia as an attraction to or involvement with prepubescent children, and defining pubescence as typically age 13 years, seems arbitrary. Is the diagnostician supposed to determine the age of the victim independently of the offender's claim? Many child molesters claim either that the victim pubesced early or that, contrary to the victim's claim, they did not molest them until they were over age 13 years. Also, a significant number of offenders molest victims who are postpubescent but still quite young. Does this mean that these offenders do not have a mental disorder when those who molest younger children do? Of course, if DSM-IV had a category for sexual assault (i.e., for what most people call "rape") then the problem would be solved, as the age of the victim would not be relevant to whether or not the offender had a mental disorder but would rather indicate which sort of disorder he had.

Similar problems arise when dealing with adolescent offenders. As I noted, DSM-IV leaves the diagnoses in these cases to the judgment of the clinician. No age discrepancy between victim and offender is specified, but there appears to be a suggestion that the diagnosis of pedophilia should not be applied if the offender's age is less than late adolescence. As an increasing number of juvenile sexual offenders have been identified in recent years (Barbaree, Marshall, & Hudson 1993; Ryan & Lane, 1991), and as a reasonable proportion of these offenders persistently engage in abusive attacks, the failure of DSM-IV to address this issue is puzzling and will not help diagnosticians working with these youthful offenders.

As for the additional, nondiagnostic remarks in DSM-IV, it is difficult to know on what source the authors base these comments. For instance, I could find nothing in our extensive clinical files suggesting that child molesters attracted to female victims typically prefer 8 to 10-year-olds. We (Marshall, Barbaree, & Butt, 1988) also found that when we examined in detail our sample of those men who molested male children, two thirds were heterosexual in their orientation to adults, yet they almost exclusively attacked boys in the age range of 5 to 10 years; the remaining homosexually oriented one third of the group preferred postpubescent boys. DSM-IV also declares that pedophilia usually begins in adolescence, yet in one of our studies (Marshall, Barbaree, & Eccles, 1991), over half of the child molesters did not first offend until they were adults, and most of these adult-onset offenders denied fantasizing prior to adulthood. The claim made in DSM-IV that the recidivism rate for male-victim offenders is approximately twice that for female-victim offenders also does not fit with all of the literature. Furby, Weinrott, and Blackshaw's (1989) extensive review of recidivism rates suggested that reoffense rates were higher for male-victim offenders but not anything close to double the rate for female-victim offenders. Furthermore, in our (Marshall & Barbaree, 1988) long-term follow-up of treated and untreated child molesters, we found remarkably similar rates of reoffending among those who had molested boys and those who had molested girls. Finally, DSM-IV's indication that paraphilias are almost never diagnosed in females appears to ignore the wealth of recent reports revealing the extent of child sexual molestation by women (Cavanaugh-Johnson, 1988; Johnson & Shrier, 1987; Knopp & Lackey, 1987; Lane, 1991; Matthews, Matthews, & Speltz, 1989).

Obviously, DSM-IV has serious shortcomings for those working with offenders who abuse children. As noted, our response to this has been to ignore the diagnosis of pedophilia and to describe all such clients as simply child molesters. The use of this latter term derives from a straightforward analysis of the situation. If a person has sexually abused a child, unless both are similarly aged children between whom the acts were consensual, then the person is a child molester. Whether this represents a persistent behavioral pattern or not is irrelevant to the use of the label and although it may have implications for judicial disposition and for the duration or difficulty of treatment, a history of repeated offending does not suggest either differential treatment or a likely differential response to treatment. This is quite important because whatever DSM-IV says or does not say on the matter, it is widely believed among psychiatrists in particular that pedophilia is untreatable, yet there is no evidence to support this view. Indeed, a detailed analysis of our patients has revealed no difference in response to treatment among child molesters who did or did not meet DSM criteria.

In our clinical practice we also employ different age-of-victim criteria than does DSM-IV, although this certainly is one issue on which researchers should attempt to come to some agreement. In Canada the legal age of consent is 16 years, meaning that anyone over that age having sex with someone under that age is guilty of a criminal offense and may end up in a treatment program. In an early study, we (Baxter, Marshall, Barbaree, Davidson, & Malcolm, 1984) found that men who sexually molested victims aged 16 to 17 years differed in terms of their sexual preferences from those who molested younger children, but did not differ from men who sexually assaulted adults. We found no such differences between those child molesters who had offended against prepubescent versus younger postpubescent children. Accordingly, we have always used age 14 years as the upper limit for defining a victim as a child. This also is consistent with our findings from phallometric studies of sexual preferences wherein all subjects (offenders and nonoffenders) respond to persons displaying full secondary sexual features (i.e., teenagers over age 14 years) in the same way as they do to adults. Once again, if the diagnostic manual had a category for those offenders who sexually assault adults, we could set age 14 years of the victims as the diagnostic discriminator between child molesters and rapists. These are the criteria we have adopted in our clinical practice and the ones I follow, as best I can, in this chapter.

Unfortunately, as I noted, the unsatisfactory nature of the diagnostic manual's criteria for pedophilia has apparently caused many researchers to adopt their own bases for defining their patient population, and disagreement is common. This, of course, makes it difficult to compare studies and this problem will not be eliminated until there is a greater consensus on these taxonomic issues. As long as the official diagnostic manuals attempt to maintain the fiction that some child molesters suffer from a mental disorder called "pedophilia" while the rest do not, such manuals will not be very helpful to practitioners working with these offenders. As DSM-III-R was interpreted, for example, a person who had molested several children over several years was not properly diagnosed as a pedophile unless it could be determined that he had recurrent intense sexual urges and sexually arousing fantasies of sex with children. Of course, most clinicians would probably assume that such a person had deviant fantasies, but that does not mean that they necessarily do. A person who, on the other hand, had molested one child but had recurrent sexual fantasies involving children would be diagnosed properly as a pedophile. In fact, according to DSM-III-R criteria, even if a person had never touched a child, if he had recurrent fantasies of children then he would be a pedophile. Whether the changed wording of DSM-IV will have any impact on diagnostic practice remains to be seen, but certainly adding to the criteria of "recurrent urges and fantasies" the phrase "or behavior involving sexual activity with a prepubescent child" should lead diagnosticians to label as a pedophile all persons who sexually touch a child, even if only briefly on a single occasion. This might be seen in the eyes of some as overinclusive, but it will certainly reduce confusion and allow clinicians to consider all child molesters as having a disorder in need of treatment.

The proper concerns of diagnosis should be the specification of features that either determine risk or indicate a need for treatment. I will discuss these more meaningful issues when I turn to the associated features of child molesters, developmental and etiological factors, and forensic issues. They are also addressed more thoroughly in the chapter on the assessment and treatment of pedophiles (see Barbaree & Seto, Chapter 9, this volume).

One other related diagnostic issue has been raised in particular by Abel (Abel, Becker, Cunningham-Rathner, Mittelman, & Rouleau, 1988; Abel & Rouleau, 1990). He suggests that sexual offenders, including child molesters, typically are multiply paraphilic. In Abel's (Abel et al., 1988) study he found, for example, that among nonfamilial child molesters 61.4% of those who had molested girls and 54.2% of those who had molested boys reported having three or more paraphilias, as did 46% of incest offenders. However, Abel's diagnostic approach in defining the presence of various paraphilias differed from that of DSM-III-R (the manual in use at that time). For example, he counted as a paraphilia a sexual interest that was not enduring (i.e., it did not have to be present for at least 6 months, as required by DSM-III-R). It is difficult to know precisely what this meant in practice but it does allow the researcher to include as an additional paraphilia a reported transitory sexual interest or activity that took place years ago. In our study (Marshall et al., 1991) we carefully excluded such transitory inclinations and as a result, very few of our child molesters (12%) reported more than one additional paraphilia and only one had three additional paraphilias.

EPIDEMIOLOGY

Prevalence and Incidence

The incidence and prevalence of child molestation is difficult to determine, although a reasonable estimate might be obtained by multiplying the number of official reports by a figure suggested to reflect the rate of underreporting. At best this estimate of incidence is crude and we have no way of determining the degree to which it approximates reality. In addition, the official reports of sexual offenses frequently obscure the age of the victim and the relationships of victim to offender. For example, data from the Crime Analysis Unit of the New York City Police Department revealed only two identified cases of incest in Bronx County for each of the years 1981, 1982, and 1983 (cited in Travin & Protter, 1993), which seems absurd given that there are over 1 million residents of the Bronx. Perhaps other identified offenders pleaded guilty to a lesser charge or were convicted under another code. Jaffe, Dynnesson, and Bensel (1975), for example, found that for the 291 crimes described simply as sexual offenses that were reported in Minneapolis in 1970, one third involved child victims. On the basis of a similarly detailed analysis of the reports describing officially identified rapes in Britain, Wells (1958) found that 58% of the victims were under age 13 years.

The American Humane Association's (1988) National Reporting Study identified over 2 million children in the United States as having been abused or neglected and of these, 16% were found to be victims of sexual abuse. This results in an incidence estimate of over 300,000 cases of child sexual abuse per year. The victims were predominantly females (77%) whose average age was 9.2 years. The offenders were predominantly male (82%). In that same year, the New York State Division of Criminal Justice Services (1988) identified 1,750 arrests for sexual offenses against children.

Research commissioned by the Committee on Sexual Offenses against Children and Youths (1984) revealed that one third of Canadian males and over one half of Canadian females reported that they had been sexually victimized, with over four fifths of these incidents occurring before age 18 years. In identified cases of childhood sexual abuse, the National Hospital Survey and the National Police Survey, both of which were commissioned and reported by the Canadian Committee, indicated that 62% of the female victims were under age 12 years, as were 70% of the male victims.

It is generally acknowledged that official records underestimate the actual frequencies of child molestation due to underreporting and other process errors. Accordingly, surveys of the population (usually the adult population) have attempted to provide more accurate estimates. These surveys are, however, beset by their own problems (Haugaard & Reppucci, 1988). For example, in surveys examining sexual experiences we can expect significant numbers of possible participants to refuse to cooperate, and often we have no way of estimating this from the reports. Those reports that provide this information have indicated up to 90% participation in response to a questionnaire survey of a college sample (Finkelhor,

1979), and as low as 64% (Russell, 1984) and 61% (Wyatt, 1985) in interview surveys of the general population. Haugaard (1987) found that when he ensured complete participation, the percentage of respondents who identified themselves as victims of child sexual abuse was significantly lower than among low participation (25% and 42%) surveys. To confuse matters even further, Haugaard found that in a survey with participation levels somewhere between these two extremes (78% participation), the reports of sexual abuse were lower than those found in the entire group. Clearly, participation rates affect the reported proportion of child sexual abuse in ways that are not at all straightforward.

Researchers have also sampled quite different populations. Some have examined rates among university students (Finkelhor, 1979; Haugaard, 1987) and some have randomly sampled community populations, but without any attempt to obtain demographically representative samples (e.g., Russell, 1984; Wyatt, 1985). Obviously, we cannot pool results from these various surveys to estimate prevalence rates. Then there is the ever-present problem of such surveys concerning the honesty of the respondents' replies. Abused individuals may be reluctant to admit abuse while some nonabused individuals may be motivated to falsely report abuse. In the absence of independent confirmation of reported abuse, we can never know the true rates.

Despite these caveats, a consistent impression from all surveys and from an examination of official records is that child sexual abuse is far more widespread than was once thought. Clearly, many children are being sexually abused and few such crimes are reported. This means that we have an extensive and very serious social problem that must be appropriately addressed. It is a shame that our societies have taken so long to deal with this issue, and even now our response is far from adequate.

Risk Factors

We know very little about the factors that put people at risk for becoming child molesters. In fact, the only thing that can be said with confidence is that males are at greater risk to offend than are females. Beyond that, we can only guess based on theory and what is known about the features displayed by identified child molesters. There are problems with this strategy, however. For example, in Finkelhor's (1984) model a lack of empathy is said to disinhibit whatever constraints a child molester may have about sexually abusing a child. However, we have found that child molesters are significantly deficient in empathy toward their own victims, somewhat more empathic toward the child victims of other molesters, and normally empathic toward all other children (Marshall, Fernandez, Lightbody, & O'Sullivan, 1994). These data are consistent with the idea that child molesters effortfully restrain feelings of empathy toward their own victims and distort the way they perceive their victims so that they may molest the child. Repeated practice at this would result in an entrenched lack of empathy toward their own victims with some generalization to other child victims, but no effect on the child molesters' view of children in general.

If this analysis of the meaning of empathy deficits in child molesters is correct, then a lack of empathy in general, or a specific lack of empathy toward children, may not necessarily be a risk factor for child molestation among men who have not yet offended. If child molesters make an effort to suppress feelings of concern for their victims, then a lack of victim empathy may be more likely associated with the maintenance of the behavior, and therefore a factor in the risk to reoffend, but not a factor in the etiology of child molestation. The same may be true of speculations about the etiological meaning of other factors. For example, we (Marshall, Champagne, Brown, & Miller, in press; Marshall & Mazzucco, 1995) found that child molesters suffer from extremely low self-esteem and Pithers, Beal, Armstrong, and Petty (1989) reported that 61% of their child molesters experienced a significant drop in self-confidence immediately prior to offending. Of course, the social opprobrium these men face upon detection and incarceration is such that our finding of low self-esteem is not surprising and may simply reflect the consequences of detection rather than telling us anything about what these men were like before they began to offend. Similarly, in the case of Pithers et al.'s (1989) data, identified offenders may feel so poor about themselves that when asked to recall they project current feelings onto previous behavior.

Although conditioning theories suggest that child molesters are driven to offend by having developed deviant sexual preferences prior to their first offense, the evidence in support of this relies on the self-reports of these men, which are of dubious accuracy. In any case, there are contradictory results from studies that have inquired about the onset of sexual fantasies involving children and whether or not these fantasies preceded the child molester's first offense. Over 40% of Abel et al.'s (1987) nonfamilial child molesters reported that they developed deviant sexual fantasies prior to their first offense, whereas only 21% of our nonfamilial offenders said that they had sexual fantasies of children before offending (Marshall et al., 1991). Once again, it is necessary to distinguish risk to begin offending (etiology) from risk to keep offending (maintenance or risk to recidivate). Child molesters do fantasize about sex with children, although our guess is that this is far more of a risk factor once offending has commenced, whereas it is an indication of risk to begin offending in only a few cases. Furthermore, Pithers et al. (1989) found that deviant fantasizing was an immediate precursor of child molestation in only 51% of their offenders, so the usual assumption that deviant fantasizing always precedes offending does not appear to be tenable. Of course one reasonable response to these inconsistencies would be to suggest that child molesters are simply reluctant to tell the truth and because Abel et al. (1987) had elaborate procedures to protect their clients' confidentiality, their data are more likely to be accurate. However, we took similar steps to assure our clients of the confidentiality of their reports, although perhaps these attempts were not as convincing as those of Abel et al. (1987).

Another significant immediate precursor detected by Pithers et al. (1989) was cognitive distortions. Authors have used this term to cover a variety of the features of child molesters' thinking, including issues having to do with denial and minimization, a shift of responsibility toward others or to situational factors, and various attitudes and beliefs that are pro-of-fending in nature. No doubt, these are important features that facilitate offending, and there is some evidence (e.g., Marshall, 1994) that a substantial proportion of child molesters deny or minimize their offenses and avoid responsibility for their crimes. Inappropriate attitudes and beliefs have not been investigated sufficiently among child molesters, although Abel et al. (1989) identified some offense-facilitating beliefs held by child molesters. These include the ideas that children enjoy sex with adults, that they actively seek out sex with adults, and that they are not harmed by such behaviors. However, it is difficult to distinguish these attitudes/beliefs from the distorted perceptions regarding their victims that so often characterizes child molesters. For example, if a child innocently and without awareness sits in a manner that reveals their genitals or underwear, an offender may very likely construe this as an intentional sexual invitation by the child. These perceptions obviously arise out of the offender's desire to have sex with the child and it is this desire that is the significant precursor, not the distorted perception. These sort of distorted interpretations of children's behavior are likely to lead to inappropriate beliefs, rather than the beliefs determining the perceptions.

I could go on examining various identified or suggested risk factors, but the fact remains that most are a consequence of a desire to offend or a consequence of well-practiced offending. Thus, with the exception of a persistent desire to molest children, many of the immediate risk factors are in fact a product of, not a cause of, child molestation. It is among early factors in a person's life that we may discern etiologically significant risk factors, and it is among transitory emotional, situational, and state factors that we can identify immediate precursors to offending. Persistent drunkenness, for example, reduces inhibitions that might otherwise constrain offending, although many men abuse alcohol and do not offend. Similarly, being emotionally upset (angry, anxious, depressed, etc.) or under stress appears to increase the immediate risk to offend (Pithers et al., 1989). But perhaps the most important factor immediately preceding offending is being in a situation where offending can readily occur (e.g., being alone with a child, particularly one over whom the man has authority).

In their research Pithers et al. (1989) also identified what they called early precursors to offending. They found that the parent–child relationships of offenders were particularly disruptive and we (Marshall, Hudson, & Hodkinson, 1993) reviewed extensive research pointing to these same experiences as etiologically significant in child molestation. Along with many other researchers, Pithers et al. (1989) also noted the significance of childhood sexual victimization in the histories of these offenders. Depending upon the definition of what constitutes child sexual abuse, Hanson and Slater (1988) found from their review of the literature that anywhere from 0% to 67% of child molesters reported themselves to be childhood victims. In addition, it is difficult to determine the accuracy of these findings because in all cases researchers have relied on the self-reports of the offenders, who may be assumed to have a vested interest in, and a strong tendency to, attribute their offending to factors outside their control. In an attempt to overcome some of these difficulties, we (Dhawan & Marshall, 1996) distinguished contact from noncontact abuse and we employed both questionnaires and detailed interviews conducted by two independent judges. In terms of physical contact sexual abuse, 50% of our incarcerated child molesters reported experiencing this type of abuse as children, whereas only 20% of incarcerated nonsex offenders reported such abuse. This latter observation with nonsex offenders is similar to, although slightly higher than, data reported on nonoffender males (see Hanson & Slater [1988] for a review). It seems very likely, despite the obvious motivation to distort and the impossibility of ever eliminating such distortions, that a disproportionate number of child molesters experienced sexual abuse during their childhood. The question remains, however, why such abuse would lead to offending rather than a complete inhibition of such tendencies. If childhood sexual abuse is experienced as distressing, why would an abused person abuse someone else?

Quinsey and his colleagues (Quinsey, Harris, et al., 1995; Quinsey, Lalumière, et al., 1995) completed some of the best research in the area of identifying risk to reoffend among men convicted of sexual crimes. Before I list the factors Quinsey's groups have identified, however, it is important to note that their research subjects were all housed in a mental health unit devoted to the assessment and treatment of sexual offenders whose sanity was in doubt or who had been found to be insane. Insanity here means that the offender had an Axis I major disorder and that this affected his judgment to the degree that he either could not tell right from wrong or he did not realize that what he was doing was wrong. Furthermore, sadists appear to be disproportionately represented in this population. Both of these factors suggest that these subjects do not constitute a representative sample. It may be that the factors predicting risk in these unusual offenders are not the same as those predicting risk in more typical child molesters.

Quinsey's group found that features of the men's prior offense histories (both sexual and nonsexual offending) were factors in predicting risk, as were poor work and relationship histories and the abuse of alcohol. Scores on Hare's (1991) Psychopathy Checklist (Revised) also contributed to the prediction of risk, as did a younger age (i.e., higher Psychopathy scores and a younger age were related to greater increases in risk). However, even when combined, these factors were not powerful predictors. Furthermore, these factors, as the reader will observe, are all static and do not allow for any modification by treatment or as a result of incarceration. There is an urgent, but as yet unfulfilled, need to discern indices of change that predict future success or failure in these offenders.

ASSOCIATED FEATURES

The associated feature that has received the most extensive attention over the past 20 years concerns the sexual preferences of child molesters. It has been claimed (Abel & Blanchard, 1974; McGuire, Carlisle, & Young, 1965) that all types of sexual deviants engage in their eccentric or offensive behaviors as a result of having learned (through conditioning processes) to prefer these particular acts over more normative sexual practices. More specifically, it was suggested that child molesters, through some fortuitous pairing (probably at or around pubescence) of sexual arousal and the image of a child and subsequent masturbation to these images, develop an entrenched sexual attraction to children. I will examine some of the implications of this theory in more detail in the section on theories, but for the moment let me note that the clear implication is that men who engage in sex with children should be characterized by equal or stronger sexual arousal to children than to adults.

There are, in fact, several possible variants on this implication depending on how the theory is expressed (see Marshall & Eccles, 1993, and O'Donohue & Plaud, 1994, for an analysis of conditioning theories), but few conditioning theorists make their position sufficiently definitive. It could be that all child molesters are more aroused by children than adults (i.e., they all sexually prefer children). This is essentially the sexual preference hypothesis (Barbaree, 1990). In another variant it could be that child molesters do not discriminate for age. In either variant, it is not clear from the theories whether all or only some child molesters should have deviant sexual preferences. In the final analysis the issue is an empirical one, but unfortunately the available evidence does not permit a clear conclusion.

There are many reasons to expect the results of the various studies of the sexual preferences of child molesters to differ. First, there are clear sample differences across studies. Some studies mix familial and nonfamilial offenders, some do not distinguish male-victim from female-victim offenders, most do not make clear whether the sample consists of first or repeat offenders, and it is possible that in some studies admitters are mixed with deniers. In addition, some studies sampled child molesters held in secure psychiatric facilities (Quinsey, Chaplin, & Carrigan, 1979; Quinsey, Steinman, Bergersen, & Holmes, 1975), others have assessed prison populations (Avery-Clark & Laws, 1984), and still others have evaluated outpatient child molesters (Abel, Becker, Murphy, & Flanagan, 1981; Marshall et al., 1988; Marshall, Barbaree, & Christopher, 1986). These all are factors likely to be related to differential sexual preferences. Second, different instrumentation has been used which some authors, at least, believe importantly influences measured responding (see McConaghy, 1989, 1993, for a thorough review of this issue). Third, quite different stimuli have been employed to elicit responding and we can be certain that this influences arousal patterns. There are, no doubt, other factors that vary across studies that may influence responding.

In terms of group differences the results with nonfamilial child molesters are reasonably consistent despite these evident methodological differences. Compared with other groups (either other sexual offenders, nonsex offenders, or community controls), nonfamilial child molesters display greater sexual arousal to children (Freund, 1981; Freund, Heasman, & Roper, 1982; Marshall et al., 1986; Quinsey et al., 1975, 1979). Some studies of incest offenders find them to be nondeviant in that their responses reveal essentially the same arousal patterns as do comparison groups (Freund, 1987; Marshall et al., 1986; Quinsey et al., 1979). Other researchers (Abel et al., 1981; Murphy, Haynes, Stalgaitis, & Flanagan, 1986), however, have found incest offenders to be as deviantly aroused to children as are nonfamilial offenders. In addition, a few reports have examined the responses of child molesters to forced sex with children and have found equal or greater responding to coercive than to consenting sex between an adult and a child (Abel et al., 1981; Avery-Clark & Laws, 1984; Marshall & Christie, 1981).

While these studies are informative and have relevance for some aspects of various theories, they may not be as helpful to the clinician, and, indeed, group differences may be misleading. For example, we (Barbaree & Marshall, 1989) conducted a detailed analysis of the individual sexual preference profiles of nonfamilial child molesters (female victims only), father–daughter incest offenders, and matched nonoffenders. The results revealed that only 48% of the nonfamilial offenders and 28% of the incest offenders produced deviant profiles (i.e., arousal to children was approximately equal to or greater than their arousal to adults). Unfortunately, 15% of the supposedly normal men also displayed strong arousal to children, yet we had carefully screened them to exclude any who reported feeling attracted to children (by this procedure we have in our studies excluded between 38% and 62% of "normal" volunteers). In addition to these observations, 22% of the nonfamilial child molesters and 34% of the incest offenders produced such negligible arousal at assessment that we were unable to make any interpretation of their responding. We think these results present problems not only for clinicians in making sense of sexual preference assessments, but also for theories about child molestation that rely on some version of the sexual preference hypothesis.

Perhaps the most consistently observed associated problem among child molesters is the abuse of or the offense-facilitative use of an intoxicant of one kind or another, most often alcohol (Christie, Marshall, & Lanthier, 1979; Langevin & Lang, 1990; Lightfoot & Barbaree, 1993; Rada, 1976; Travin & Protter, 1993). In their detailed study of (among other sexual offenders) 123 child molesters, Langevin and Lang (1990) found that 55.8% scored above the alcoholic cutoff on the Michigan Alcoholism Screening Test (Selzer, 1971) and 17.8% had a drug abuse problem according to their scores on the Drug Abuse Screening Test (Skinner, 1982). In addition, the use of intoxicants (alcohol and other substances) has been found to immediately precede sexual offending in 30% of cases where the victim was a child (Pithers et al., 1989). When offenders are identified as addicted this indicates a significant risk to reoffend and should be a target in treatment. Furthermore, even when the offender is not an addict, if he uses intoxicants to disinhibit himself (either deliberately or without forethought) in order that he may offend, then this fact must also be addressed in treatment.

It has also been suggested that sexual offenders may be addicted to sex (Carnes, 1983) and that their offending is simply one manifestation of this. Certainly, most child molesters have quite inappropriate attitudes toward sex and they do seem to have some difficulty in resisting urges to offend. However, the notion of sexual addiction has been called into question (Coleman, 1987; Levine & Troiden, 1988) and this view is not popular with most clinicians working in this field. In fact, there is little in the way of sound research on this controversial concept.

Evidence suggests that very few child molesters suffer from either any form of psychopathology or disturbances in personality functioning. Fewer than 5% of child molesters appear to be psychotic (Abel, Rouleau, & Cunningham-Rathner, 1986; Mohr, Turner, & Jerry, 1964), and, in fact, antisocial personality disorder seems to be the only diagnosis applied to sex offenders with any consistency. In their studies of child molesters held in a Canadian mental health facility, Quinsey and his colleagues (Quinsey, Harris et al., 1995; Quinsey, Rice, & Harris, 1990; Rice, Quinsey, & Harris, 1991) evaluated both the incidence of psychopathy among child molesters (as defined by the earlier version of Hare's [1985] Psychopathy Checklist) and its power in predicting recidivism. Quinsey and his colleagues found an incidence of psychopathy among their subjects, who were all housed in a Canadian maximum security psychiatric facility, above 30%, and Prentky and Knight (1986) found similar figures in a similar American institution. However, these data may not reflect the incidence of psychopathy in other sex offender populations. For example, Abel et al. (1985) reported that only 12% of their outpatient child molesters met the criteria for antisocial personality disorder, and Serin, Malcolm, Khanna, and Barbaree (1994), in examining child molesters held in a medium security prison, found that only 7.5% scored above the cutoff for psychopathy on Hare's (1985) measure. As for the power of Hare's measure to predict recidivism in released child molesters, Quinsey's group has made much of its value (see Quinsey, Harris et al., 1995) but in fact, they found that the correlation between Hare's Checklist scores and sexual recidivism was only $r = .18$. Although this correlation is statistically significant at better than the 1% level, it obviously accounts for only a trivial percentage of the variance. Quinsey and his colleagues apparently recognized this and used a combination of 13 factors (unfortunately, all were static factors) to more satisfactorily predict relapse. Nevertheless, psychopathy apparently is not a remarkably common feature of child molesters.

As far as other personality problems are concerned, numerous authors (Kalichman, 1991; Panton, 1978, 1979; Toobert, Bartelme, & Jones, 1959) have claimed that the responses of child molesters to the Minnesota Multiphasic Personality Inventory (MMPI) reveal consistent deviations from the normative data. Our review of the literature on deviant responding to the MMPI revealed inconsistent results, with few studies showing group responses outside normal limits (Marshall & Hall, 1995). The use of other personality inventories has likewise produced contradictory results across studies (see Levin & Stava, 1987, for a review).

It has frequently been suggested that child molesters are deficient in empathy and this is a deficit that is integral to the notion of psychopathy. In fact, 94% of programs in North America include empathy enhancement as a treatment target (Knopp, Freeman-Longo, & Stevenson, 1992). Our review of this literature (Marshall, Hudson, Jones, & Fernandez, 1995), however, revealed little support for the idea that sex offenders of any type lacked empathy toward all other people. Our subsequent experimental analyses indicated that child molesters had little empathy for their own victims and were to some extent deficient in empathy toward victims of other child molesters (Marshall et al., 1994). These child molesters, however, displayed appropriate empathy toward distressed children who were not victims of sexual abuse.

One issue that we have been particularly interested in recently, and that seems to have relevance for the etiology and maintenance of child molestation, is a lack of intimacy and marked loneliness arising from inadequate attachment styles. We have found sex offenders to lack intimacy and to report themselves to be lonely (Garlick, Marshall, & Thornton, 1996; Seidman, Marshall, Hudson, & Robertson, 1994), and to have adopted dysfunctional styles of attachment (Ward, Hudson, & Marshall, 1996). We have tied these deficiencies theoretically to specific forms of child sexual molestation (Ward, Hudson, Marshall, & Seigert, 1995) and have obtained data consistent with these theoretical predictions (Ward et al., 1996). Once again, unless these problems are addressed in treatment, we can expect the child molester to have future problems and perhaps remain at risk to reoffend. Other possible deficits in social problems, although commonly thought of as being relevant, have not been consistently demonstrated to distinguish child molesters from other males (Marshall, in press; Stermac, Segal, & Gillis, 1990).

Distorted cognitions also appear to typify child molesters. This descriptor, however, is used inconsistently in the literature, with some authors including denial and minimization within the concept, whereas others restrict it to distorted perceptions of children's behavior, and yet others include more general attitudes about children's sexuality. It must be said that although it appears clinically obvious that many child molesters distort information in a self-serving way, the empirical demonstration of such distortions is not extensive, nor are the observed results always consistently supportive of the view that child molesters have distorted cognitions. For example, Abel et al. (1989), using the Cognitions Scale developed by Abel, Becker, and Cunningham-Rathner (1984), found clear evidence of distorted views among child molesters (e.g., children were perceived as interested in sex with adults, as seeking out sex with adults, and as enjoying and benefiting from the experience). Gore (1988), however, using the same scale found only small differences between child molesters and other sexual offenders. Other researchers (Cortoni, Gordon, Malcolm, & Ellerby, 1991; Hodkinson, 1990; Stermac & Segal, 1989) have identified distortions in child molesters in cognitions but have noted problems with the assessment procedures. As Hanson, Gizzarelli, and Scott (1994) point out, the present scales for measuring distortions are so transparent that they lend themselves readily to dissimulation. These problems may be the cause of the inconsistent findings as well as the frequent clinical observation that reports on questionnaires of minor distortions seem to underestimate what is evident at clinical interviews or during therapy. Hanson et al. (1994) attempted to overcome these difficulties by developing a less transparent scale and including in their assessment a measure of social desirability. Surprisingly, they found no evidence of differential dissimulation on the Marlowe–Crowne Social Desirability Scale (Crowne & Marlowe, 1960) between their incest offenders, male batterers, and community controls. Hanson et al. (1994) did find, however, that the child molesters differed from the other two groups in perceiving children to be sexually attractive and sexually motivated. The incest offenders also endorsed the view that males had a special privilege that essentially entitled them to be sexual with children.

JUVENILE/DEVELOPMENTAL ISSUES

There are essentially two related aspects to these issues: the inescapable fact that there are juveniles who sexually molest younger children, and the developmental characteristics of all child molesters. Both are important issues.

It is only in recent years that clinicians and researchers alike have come to acknowledge that many juveniles who sexually molest children are genuine offenders and not just youths engaging in some momentary experiment or satisfying some fleeting curiosity. There is now, in fact, a considerable body of literature dealing with juvenile child molesters (Ageton, 1983; Awad & Saunders, 1989; Barbaree et al., 1993; Becker, Cunningham-Rathner, & Kaplan, 1986; Cavanaugh-Johnson, 1988; Davis & Leitenberg, 1987; Ferenbach, Smith, Monastersky, & Deischer, 1986; National Adolescent Perpetrator Network, 1988; Ryan & Lane, 1991). For the most part, research with juvenile offenders has revealed much the same patterns of responding, on whatever measures are employed, as for adult child molesters. One area, however, that is bound to become even more contentious than it already is concerns the assessment of sexual preferences among juvenile sexual offenders. Several studies have reported the use of phallometric evaluations of juveniles (Becker, 1988; Becker, Hunter, Stein, & Kaplan, 1989; Becker & Kaplan, 1988; Saunders & Awad, 1988), but the application of such procedures to young males is fraught with potential problems and concern about the ethics of these assessments has been expressed (Marshall, 1996). Some clinicians who phallometrically evaluate juveniles have tested boys as young as 10 years old or have set their age criterion as *"usually* between the ages of 13 and 18 years old" (Becker & Kaplan, 1993, p. 266, italics added). It seems to me that presenting such young boys with clearly sexually erotic images of younger children might actually encourage deviance. In any case, I believe that, at best, the phallometric assessment of juveniles is of dubious ethical merit.

There is considerable speculation about the developmental features of boys who later grow up to be child molesters. Some suggest a cycle of abuse wherein childhood sexual victimization among males provides a model for adult abuse of children or in some other way entrenches a deviant sexual disposition that later manifests in offending (see Hanson & Slater, 1988, for a critical appraisal of this point of view). The evidence certainly supports the notion that a disproportionate number of child molesters were themselves sexually abused as children, although another way to view this is to suggest that child sexual victimization is but one aspect of the more general abuse or neglect that these offenders experience as children (Marshall, Hudson, et al., 1993). Indeed, the childhood of sexual offenders is characterized by family instability (Awad, Saunders, & Levene, 1984) and disturbed family relations (Saunders, Awad, & White, 1986). Child molesters report neglect by their parents (Davidson, 1983) and many claim that their parents were hostile and physically abusive toward them (Finkelhor, 1979, 1984).

We (Marshall, Hudson, et al., 1993) have taken this evidence to suggest that the attachment bonds between the parents and the young boy who grows up to be a sexual offender are dysfunctional and that these dysfunctional bonds serve as unfortunate templates for future relationships. Accordingly, the young male will develop distrust or ambivalence regarding peer-aged romantic relationships and this will serve to encourage him to seek out children who are nonthreatening and can be readily controlled. In the context of growing up with abusive parents, the child will learn (through modeling) to be abusive to those persons whom he can readily dominate and he will have little concern (empathy) for the rights and needs of others. Most social skills (particularly those to do with intimate relationships) are acquired as a result of affectionate and effective relations with parents (Marshall, 1989). When such relationships are of a poor quality, the child will not only fail to learn relationship skills, but he will be untrusting of others and lack self-confidence as well, all of which will interfere with the establishment of appropriate adult relationships. With these deficits and his lack of concern for others, along with his need to dominate, such a young male at or after pubescence is likely to turn to children in an attempt to meet not only his sexual needs, but also his needs for intimacy. We see these features of the developmental history of child molesters as critical to understanding why these males become offenders (Marshall 1989; Marshall, Hudson, et al., 1993; Ward et al., 1995).

FORENSIC ISSUES

There are many forensic issues relevant to child molesters, but the primary ones have to do with the contribution that psychological/psychiatric assessments can, or should, have on judicial or parole decisions. There are, no doubt, some areas in which these assessments can add valuable information, but there are others for which our evaluations should not be used. In terms of the court processes meant to lead to decisions of guilt or innocence, I do not believe that we have anything to contribute. Not everyone, however, shares this view. Some psychologists and psychiatrists are prepared to assist defense lawyers by doing an evaluation of their accused clients which is meant (at least in the mind of the lawyer and his client) to demonstrate that the accused is not the sort of person who would have sexually molested a child. These assessments may involve various evaluative procedures; among the most commonly employed instruments are the MMPI and the phallometric test. We (Marshall & Hall, 1995) have reviewed the value of the MMPI for these purposes and concluded that it cannot assist the triers of fact. Barbaree and Peacock (1995) evaluated the phallometric test and came to the same conclusion. The fact is, of course, that child molesters have few distinctive features, and on those few features that distinguish them as a group there is considerable overlap with non-child molesters. Certainly we are not in a position as a result of an assessment, however thorough it may be, to say much at all about the likelihood that a particular individual did or did not sexually molest a child. It would, in fact, serve well the reputation of our professions to decline the invitations of lawyers to assist them in such cases.

However, assessments can assist the court when it comes to sentencing and we can help parole boards in their release decisions. We are in a position on the basis of research to estimate the likelihood of a person with certain features committing a further sexual offense and the possibility of them being violent (Prentky, Knight, Sims-Knight, et al., 1989; Quinsey, Lalumière, et al. , 1995). Prentky et al. (1989), for instance, found that childhood experiences (constancy of caregiver and sexual deviation in the family) predicted the severity of sexual aggression among 82 incarcerated sexual offenders. Quinsey, Lalumière, et al. (1995) found that a combination of 12 factors allowed the categorization of offenders into six levels of increasing potential risk. In an analysis of the predictive value of these factors, Quinsey, Harris, et al. (1995) found that with 76% accuracy they could correctly classify 178 sexual offenders as recidivists or nonrecidivists. Employing these identified risk factors and taking into account the offender's response to treatment may permit us to estimate any particular offender's likely risk, and this information might enhance the accuracy of parole decisions and assist the courts in defining appropriate sentences aimed at protecting society.

Assessment also assists treatment providers in prisons and forensic psychiatric settings to determine the level of treatment needs and the specific targets that need to be changed to reduce risk before release. Such assessments also, of course, help determine whether or not treatment has been successful. In these circumstances quite comprehensive evaluations essential.

THEORIES OF ETIOLOGY

Any theory concerned to explain deviant human behavior can be aimed at one of three levels: (1) the macrolevel, where an attempt is made to explain all aspects of deviant behavior (e.g., how an individual becomes a sexual offender); (2) the midlevel, where the theory tries to explain just one type of deviant behavior (e.g., child molestation); or (3) the microlevel, where the effort is directed at elucidating one aspect of the behavior of one type of deviance (e.g. the role of empathy in child molesters).

Some theories of sexual offending have been aimed at the macrolevel. For example, most conditioning theories (Abel & Blanchard, 1974; McGuire et al., 1965; Quinn, Harbison, & McAllister, 1970) claim that fortuitous associations of particular deviant stimuli and sexual arousal may initiate masturbatory practices that entrench through conditioning processes a strong sexual attraction to the deviant acts. In these theories the nature of the particular deviant acts that become attractive is the result simply of the original accidental pairing of the stimuli and sexual arousal, so that all deviant practices are the result of essentially the same processes. One straightforward implication of these theories is that all sexual offenders should display deviant arousal. As we have seen, the results of phallometric assessments do not support this claim, although such tests may represent a limited test of the hypothesis, as erectile responses are but one aspect of sexual arousal. If conditioning theories are to be maintained we must prove that these processes of acquisition occur only in those sexual offenders who display deviant arousal. This is what Laws and Marshall (1990) proposed, but subsequent analyses of the relevant evidence do not appear to support even this limited version of a conditioning account (Marshall & Eccles, 1993; O'Donohue & Plaud, 1994). However, we must say that methodological problems in research with humans make an appropriate appraisal of conditioning theories very difficult. Considered in this light, it is accurate to say that research has not so much shown that conditioning of human sexual responses does not occur as it has not yet demonstrated the action of such processes. As O'Donohue and Plaud (1994) put it "Currently, the strength of the data suggesting the conditioning of sexual arousal is inadequate to support the vast weight of the diverse theories dependent upon the role of learning in sexual behavior" (p. 329).

We (Marshall, 1984a, 1984b, 1989; Marshall & Barbaree, 1984, 1990) have over the years integrated various processes into a comprehensive theory of the etiology and maintenance of sexual offending. The various forms of Marshall's theory are aimed at examining the relevance of particular aspects of the general theory and generating testable hypotheses. While these features of a theory are advantageous, Marshall's general account is strained by attempting to accommodate all sexual offenders within a single theory. The clear heterogeneity of sexual offenders, and indeed of even specific subtypes (e.g. child molesters) is so considerable that the best a macrolevel theory can do is point to likely features that need to be experimentally pursued. Such hypotheses can best be pursued by delineating more specific midlevel or microlevel theories.

Finkelhor (1984) has described a model for examining various processes in child molesters (a mid-level theory). He has identified four factors that he believes explain why child molesters sexually abuse children: (1) "Emotional congruence" concerns the reasons why child molesters find children sexually satisfying (e.g., mastery of their own victimization; the offender himself is childlike); (2) "sexual arousal to children" refers to the origins of a preference for children (e.g., conditioning, being themselves victims of childhood sexual abuse); (3) "blockage" identifies the factors preventing the offender from meeting his needs with adults (e.g., fear, poor social skills); and (4) "disinhibitions" which describe the conditions (e.g., intoxication, distorted perceptions of the child's desires) that overcome whatever inhibitions the offender might have as well as strategies (e.g., grooming) to overcome the child's reluctance. Finkelhor's model has been widely accepted as a useful framework for thinking about the important issues and has encouraged research into these various facets of offending.

We have turned, in recent years, to outlining the role that particular characteristics may have in facilitating child molestation (microlevel analyses). For example, we (Marshall, Hudson, Jones, & Fernandez, 1995) have proposed a role for empathy deficits in child molestation and have subsequently examined the implications of this account. We (Hudson et al., 1993) found that child molesters were deficient at recognizing the emotions that might trigger an empathic response. We also found that child molesters had limited deficiencies in general empathy (Marshall, Jones, Hudson, & McDonald, 1993, Marshall & Maric, 1996) but were quite deficient in empathy toward their own victims, and to a lesser extent, toward the victims of other abusers (Marshall et al., 1994). This sort of microlevel theorizing is more likely to generate directly testable hypotheses than are higher level theories, although the results of experimental tests of microtheories can feed in to more general theories at the mid- and macrolevels.

FUTURE DIRECTIONS

Perhaps the major stumbling block to continued progress in this field is the problem of the heterogeneity of child molesters. A priority for future research, therefore, ought to be on reducing this heterogeneity to manageable proportions. The work of Knight and Prentky (Knight, 1988, 1989; Knight & Prentky, 1990; Prentky, Knight, Rosenberg, & Lee, 1989) exemplifies a sophisticated approach to this issue. However, one objection that I could level at their classification system is that the proliferation of so many subtypes renders quite difficult the task of identifying the appropriate classification for individual offenders. Furthermore, some of the various types (4 on Axis I and 6 on Axis II) inevitably have so few subjects that research is hindered unless the investigator has access to an almost limitless number of subjects. Nevertheless, we must attempt some solution to the heterogeneity of child molesters.

Related to this is the need for researchers to consistently define their subject sample. Readers need to know the specific types of child molesters (nonfamilial vs. familial, victim gender; within familial offenders we need to know the relationship, i.e., father, brother, etc.), their offense histories (number of victims, duration of offending, use of force, degree of sexual intrusiveness), treatment histories, and whether or not they are incarcerated (and if so, for how long and under what circumstances—forensic psychiatric setting or prison, and level of security), to name some of the most important features. It is possible that the typical incest–nonincest dichotomy characteristically used in the literature is inappropriate; perhaps *modus operandi* would provide more valuable information. For example, many child molesters use their position of authority (e.g., father, teacher, scoutmaster, priest, etc.) to gain sexual access to children, whereas others seek out children at parks, playgrounds, video arcades, and the like. These differential persistent styles may be related to differential psychological characteristics.

In relation to research topics, the ones that appear to be yielding the most promising results at the present time and seem full of future possibilities are empathy, intimacy, and childhood attachments; self-efficacy and self-esteem; and identifying risk factors. On this latter issue, the value of risk factor research will be markedly increased when researchers turn to an examination of changeable features so that intervention can reduce risk. At the present, the outcome of this research has been the identification of high-risk offenders who we then deal with by excessively restrictive and costly means. This is not particularly productive even if, at the moment, child molesters are universally viewed with unsympathetic repugnance.

Finally, what I hope will happen over the next several years is a reduction in research attention to, and clinical use of, phallometric evaluations. Clearly, many child molesters (particularly incest offenders and those nonfamilial offenders who are at low risk to reoffend) do not have deviant sexual preferences, so evaluating them phallometrically is a waste of limited resources. Furthermore, subjecting all child molesters to sexual preference testing necessarily conveys to them that we believe sexual motivation is the primary, if not exclusive, factor causing their offensive behavior. Given the array of other factors addressed in treatment (see Marshall & Fernandez, 1997, for a review) this is a misleading and countertherapeutic message. In any case, far too much research (and assessment and treatment) energy has been spent on this issue despite the fact that phallometric testing procedures have not been demonstrated to have the psychometric properties so essential to proper assessment and research. Not all reviewers, however, agree with this claim that phallometric testing lacks a sound psychometric bases (Murphy & Barbaree, 1994), so the issue remains open to interpretation.

REFERENCES

Abel, G. G., Becker, J. V., & Cunningham-Rathner, J. (1984). Complications, consent, and cognitions in sex between children and adults. *International Journal of Law and Psychiatry, 7,* 89–103.

Abel, G. G., Becker, J. V., Cunningham-Rathner, J., Mittelman, M. S., & Rouleau, J. L. (1988). Multiple paraphilic diagnoses among sex offenders. *Bulletin of the American Academy of Psychiatry and the Law, 16,* 153–168.

Abel, G. G., Becker, J. V., Mittelman, M. S., Cunningham-Rathner, J., Rouleau, J. L., & Murphy, W. D. (1987). Self-reported sex crimes of nonincarcerated paraphiliacs. *Journal of Interpersonal Violence, 2,* 3–25.

Abel, G. G., Becker, J. V., Murphy, W. D., & Flanagan, B. (1981). Identifying dangerous child molesters. In J. R. Stuart (Ed.), *Violent behavior: Social learning approaches to prediction, management and treatment* (pp. 116–137). New York: Brunner/Mazel.

Abel, G. G., & Blanchard, E. B. (1974). The role of fantasy in the treatment of sexual deviation. *Archives of General Psychiatry, 30,* 467–475.

Abel, G. G., Gore, D. K., Holland, C. L., Camp, N., Becker, J. V., & Rathner, J. (1989). The measurement of the cognitive distortions of child molesters. *Annals of Sex Research, 2,* 135–152.

Abel, G. G., Mittelman, M. S., & Becker, J. V. (1985). Sexual offenders: Results of assessments and recommendations for treatment. In M. H. Ben-Aron, S. J. Hucker, & C. D. Webster (Eds.), *Clinical criminology: Current concepts* (pp. 191–205). Toronto: M & M Graphics.

Abel, G. G., & Rouleau, J. L. (1990). The nature and extent of sexual assault. In W. L. Marshall, D. R. Laws, & H. E. Barbaree (Eds.), *Handbook of sexual assault: Issues, theories, and treatment of the offender* (pp. 9–21). New York: Plenum Press.

Abel, G. G., Rouleau, J. L., & Cunningham-Rathner, J. (1986). Sexually aggressive behavior. In W. Curran, A. L. McGarry, & S. A. Shah (Eds.), *Forensic psychiatry and psychology: Perspectives and standards for interdisciplinary practice* (pp. 289–313). Philadelphia: F. A. Davis.

Ageton, S. (1983). *Sexual assault among adolescents.* Lexington, MA: Lexington Books.

American Humane Association (1988). *Highlights of official child neglect and abuse reporting, 1986.* Denver, CO: Author.

American Psychiatric Association. (1980). *Diagnostic and statistical manual of mental disorders* (3rd ed.). Washington, DC: Author.

American Psychiatric Association. (1987). *Diagnostic and statistical manual of mental disorders* (3rd ed., rev.). Washington, DC: Author.

American Psychiatric Association. (1994). *Diagnostic and statistical manual of mental disorders* (4th ed.). Washington, DC: Author.

Avery-Clark, C., & Laws, D. R. (1984). Differential erection response patterns of sexual child abusers to stimuli describing activities with children. *Behavior Therapy, 15,* 71–83.

Awad, G. A., & Saunders, E. (1989). Adolescent child molesters: Clinical observations. *Child Psychiatry and Human Development, 19,* 195–206.

Awad, G. A., Saunders, E., & Levene, J. (1984). A clinical study of male adolescent sex offenders. *International Journal of Offender Therapy and Comparative Criminology, 28,* 105–116.

Barbaree, H. E. (1990). Stimulus control of sexual arousal. In W. L. Marshall, D. R. Laws, & H. E. Barbaree (Eds.), *Handbook of sexual assault: Issues, theories, and treatment of the offender* (pp. 115–142). New York: Plenum Press.

Barbaree, H. E., & Marshall, W. L. (1989). Erectile responses among heterosexual child molesters, father–daughter incest offenders and matched nonoffenders: Five distinct age preference profiles. *Canadian Journal of Behavioural Science, 21,* 70–82.

Barbaree, H. E., Marshall, W. L., & Hudson, S. M. (Eds.). (1993). *The juvenile sex offender.* New York: Guilford Press.

Barbaree, H. E., & Peacock, E. J. (1995). Phallometric assessment of sexual preferences as an investigative tool in cases of alleged child sexual abuse. In T. Ney (Ed.), *Allegations of child sexual abuse: Assessment and case management* (pp. 242–259). New York: Brunner/Mazel.

Baxter, D. J., Marshall, W. L., Barbaree, H. E., Davidson, P. R., & Malcolm, P. B. (1984). Differentiating sex offenders by criminal and personal history, psychometric measures, and sexual response. *Criminal Justice and Behavior, 11,* 477–501.

Becker, J. V. (1988). Adolescent sex offenders. *Behavior Therapist, 11,* 185–187.

Becker, J. V., Cunningham-Rathner, J., & Kaplan, M. S. (1986). Adolescent sexual offenders: Demographics, criminal and sexual histories, and recommendations for reducing future offenses. *Journal of Interpersonal Violence, 1,* 431–445.

Becker, J. V., Hunter, J. A., Stein, R. M., & Kaplan, M. S. (1989). Factors associated with erection in adolescent sex offenders. *Journal of Psychopathology and Behavioral Assessment, 11,* 353–362.

Becker, J. V., & Kaplan, M. S. (1988). The assessment of adolescent sexual offenders. In R. Prinz (Ed.), *Advances in behavioral assessment of children and families* (pp. 97–118). Greenwich, CT: JAI Press.

Becker, J. V., & Kaplan, M. S. (1993). Cognitive behavioral treatment of the juvenile sex offender. In H. E. Barbaree, W. L. Marshall, & S. M. Hudson (Eds.), *The juvenile sex offender* (pp. 264–277). New York: Guilford Press.

Carnes, P. (1983). *The sexual addiction.* Minneapolis: CompCare.

Cavanaugh-Johnson, T. (1988). Child perpetrators: Children who molest children. *Child Abuse and Neglect: The International Journal, 12,* 219–229.

Christie, M. M., Marshall, W. L., & Lanthier, R. D. (1979). *A descriptive study of incarcerated rapists and pedophiles.* Report to the Solicitor General of Canada, Ottawa.

Coleman, E. (1987). Sexual compulsivity: Definition, etiology and treatment considerations. *Journal of Chemical Dependency Treatment, 1,* 189–204.

Committee on Sexual Offenses against Children and Youths. (1984). *Report on the Committee on Sexual Offenses against Children and Youths: Vols. 1–11, and summary* (Badgley Report; Cat. No. J2-50/1984/E, Vols. 1–11, H74-13/1984-1E, Summary). Ottawa: Department of Supply and Services.

Cortoni, F., Gordon, A., Malcolm, B., & Ellerby, L. (1991). The Attitudes Toward Sex with Children Scale: Preliminary results. *Canadian Psychology, 23,* 229.

Crowne, D. P., & Marlowe, D. (1960). A new scale of social desirability independent of psychopathology. *Journal of Consulting Psychology, 24,* 349–354.

Davidson, A. T. (1983). Sexual exploitation of children: A call to action. *Journal of the National Medical Association,75,* 925–927.

Davis, G. E., & Leitenberg, H. (1987). Adolescent sex offenders. *Psychological Bulletin,101,* 417–427.

Dhawan, S., & Marshall, W. L. (1996). Sexual abuse histories of sexual offenders. *Sexual Abuse: A Journal of Research and Treatment, 8,* 7—15.

Ferenbach, P. A., Smith, W. R., Monastersky, C., & Deischer, R. W. (1986). Adolescent sexual offenders: Offender and offense characteristics. *Journal of Orthopsychiatry, 56,* 225–233.

Finkelhor, D. (1979). *Sexually victimized children.* New York: Free Press.

Finkelhor, D. (1984). *Child sexual abuse: New theory and research.* New York: Free Press.

Freund, K. (1981). Assessment of pedophilia. In M. Cook & K. Howells (Eds.), *Adult sexual interest in children* (pp. 139–179). London: Academic Press.

Freund, K. (1987). Erotic preference in paedophilia. *Behaviour Research and Therapy, 25,* 339–348.

Freund, K., & Blanchard, R. (1989). Phallometric diagnosis of pedophilia. *Journal of Consulting and Clinical Psychology, 57,* 100–105.

Freund, K., Heasman, G. A., & Roper, V. (1982). Results of the main studies on sexual offenses against children and pubescents (a review). *Canadian Journal of Criminology, 24,* 387–397.

Freund, K., & Watson, R. J. (1991). Assessment of the sensitivity and specificity of a phallometric test: An update of phallometric diagnosis of pedophilia. *Psychological Assessment: A Journal of Consulting and Clinical Psychology, 3,* 254–260.

Furby, L., Weinrott, M. R., & Blackshaw, L. (1989). Sex offender recidivism: A review. *Psychological Bulletin, 105,* 3–30.

Garlick, Y., Marshall, W. L., & Thornton, D. (1996). Intimacy deficits and attribution of blame among sexual offenders. *Legal and Criminological Psychology, 1,* 251–288.

Gore, D. K. (1988). *Measuring the cognitive distortions of child molesters: Psychometric properties of the cognition scale.* Unpublished doctoral dissertation, Georgia State University, Atlanta.

Hanson, R. K., Gizzarelli, R., & Scott, H. (1994). The attitudes of incest offenders: Sexual entitlement and acceptance of sex with children. *Criminal Justice and Behavior, 21,* 187–202.

Hanson, R. K., & Slater, S. (1988). Sexual victimization in the history of child sexual abusers: A review. *Annals of Sex Research, 1,* 485–499.

Hare, R. D. (1985). *The Psychopathy Checklist.* Unpublished manuscript, University of British Columbia, Vancouver.

Hare, R. D. (1991). *Manual for the Revised Psychopathy Checklist.* Toronto: Multi-Health Systems.

Haugaard, J. J. (1987). *The consequences of child sexual abuse: A college survey.* Unpublished manuscript, University of Virginia, Charlottesville.

Haugaard, J. J., & Reppucci, N. D. (1988). *The sexual abuse of children: A comprehensive guide to current knowledge and intervention strategies.* San Francisco: Jossey-Bass.

Hodkinson, S. M. (1990). *The perception of consent to sexual contact in children: Child molesters versus non-offenders.* Unpublished master's thesis, York University, Toronto.

Hudson, S. M., Marshall, W. L., Wales, D., McDonald, E., Bakker, L. W., & McLean, A. (1993). Emotional recognition skills of sex offenders. *Annals of Sex Research, 6,* 199–211.

Jaffe, A. C., Dynnesson, R. N., & Bensel, R. W. (1975). Sexual abuse of children. *American Journal of Diseases of Children, 129,* 689–692.

Johnson, R. L., & Shrier, D. (1987). Past sexual victimization by females of male patients in an adolescent medicine clinic population. *American Journal of Psychiatry, 144,* 650–652.

Kalichman, S. C. (1991). Psychopathology and personality characteristics of criminal sexual offenders as a function of victim age. *Archives of Sexual Behavior, 20,* 187–197.

Knight, R. A. (1988). A taxonomic analysis of child molesters. *Annals of the New York Academy of Sciences, 528,* 2–20.

Knight, R. A. (1989). An assessment of the concurrent validity of a child molester typology. *Journal of Interpersonal Violence, 4,* 131–150.

Knight, R. A., & Prentky, R. A. (1990). Classifying sexual offenders: The development and corroboration of taxonomic models. In W. L. Marshall, D. R. Laws, & H. E. Barbaree (Eds.), *Handbook of sexual assault: Issues, theories, and treatment of the offender* (pp. 23–52). New York: Plenum Press.

Knopp, F. H., Freeman-Longo, R. E., & Stevenson, W. (1992). *Nationwide survey of juvenile and adult sex-offender treatment programs.* Orwell, VT: Safer Society Press.

Knopp, F. H., & Lackey, L. B. (1987). *Female sexual abusers: A summary of data from forty-four treatment providers.* Orwell, VT: Safer Society Press.

Lane, S. (1991). The sexual abuse cycle. In G. D. Ryan & S. L. Lane (Eds.), *Juvenile sexual offending: Causes, consequences, and correction* (pp. 103–141). Lexington, MA: Lexington Books.

Langevin, R., & Lang, R. A. (1990). Substance abuse among sex offenders. *Annals of Sex Research, 3,* 397–424.

Laws, D. R., & Marshall, W. L. (1990). A conditioning theory of the etiology and maintenance of deviant sexual preference and behavior. In W. L. Marshall, D. R. Laws, & H. E. Barbaree (Eds.), *Handbook of sexual assault: Issues, theories, and treatment of the offender* (pp. 209–229). New York: Plenum Press.

Levin, S. M., & Stava, L. (1987). Personality characteristics of sex offenders: A review. *Archives of Sexual Behavior, 16,* 57–79.

Levine, M. P., & Troiden, R. R. (1988). The myth of sexual compulsivity. *Journal of Sex Research, 25,* 347–363.

Lightfoot, L. O., & Barbaree, H. E. (1993). The relationship between substance use and abuse and sexual offending in adolescents. In H. E. Barbaree, W. L. Marshall, & S. M. Hudson (Eds.), *The juvenile sex offender* (pp. 203–224). New York: Guilford Press.

Marshall, W. L. (1984a). L'avenir de la thérapie béhaviorale: Le béhaviorisme bio-social (illustré à partir d'une théorie sur le voil). *Revue de Modification du Comportement, 14,* 136–149.

Marshall, W. L. (1984b, March). *Rape as a socio-cultural phenomenon.* The J. P. S. Robertson Annual Lecture, Trent University, Peterborough, Ontario.

Marshall, W. L. (1989). Invited essay: Intimacy, loneliness and sexual offenders. *Behaviour Research and Therapy, 27*, 491–503.

Marshall, W. L. (1994). Treatment effects on denial and minimization in incarcerated sex offenders. *Behaviour Research and Therapy, 32*, 559–564.

Marshall, W. L. (1996). Assessment, treatment, and theorizing about sex offenders: Developments over the past 20 years and future directions. *Criminal Justice and Behavior, 23*, 162–199.

Marshall, W. L. (in press). Enhancing social skills and relationship skills. In M. S. Carich & S. Mussack (Eds.), *Handbook of sex offender treatment*. Orwell, VT: Safer Society Press.

Marshall, W. L., & Barbaree, H. E. (1984). A behavioral view of rape. *International Journal of Law and Psychiatry, 7*, 51–77.

Marshall, W. L., & Barbaree, H. E. (1988). An outpatient treatment program for child molesters: Description and tentative outcome. *Annals of the New York Academy of Sciences, 528*, 205–214.

Marshall, W. L., & Barbaree, H. E. (1990). Outcome of comprehensive cognitive-behavioral treatment programs. In W. L. Marshall, D. R. Laws, & H. E. Barbaree (Eds.), *Handbook of sexual assault: Issues, theories, and treatment of the offender* (pp. 363–385). New York: Plenum Press.

Marshall, W. L., Barbaree, H. E., & Butt, J. (1988). Sexual offenders against male children: Sexual preferences. *Behaviour Research and Therapy, 26*, 383–391.

Marshall, W. L., Barbaree, H. E., & Christophe, D. (1986). Sexual offenders against female children: Sexual preferences for age of victims and type of behaviour. *Canadian Journal of Behavioural Science, 18*, 424–439.

Marshall, W. L., Barbaree, H. E., & Eccles, A. (1991). Early onset and deviant sexuality in child molesters. *Journal of Interpersonal Violence, 6*, 323–336.

Marshall, W. L., Champagne, F., Brown, C., & Miller, S. (in press). Empathy, intimacy, loneliness, and self-esteem in nonfamilial child molesters. *Journal of Child Sexual Abuse*.

Marshall, W. L., & Christie, M. M. (1981). Pedophilia and aggression. *Criminal Justice and Behavior, 8*, 145–158.

Marshall, W. L., & Eccles, A. (1993). Pavlovian conditioning processes in adolescent sex offenders. In H. E. Barbaree, W. L. Marshall, & S. M. Hudson (Eds.), *The juvenile sex offender* (pp. 118–142). New York: Guilford Press.

Marshall, W. L., & Fernandez, Y. M. (1997). Cognitive-behavioral approaches to the treatment of the paraphilias. In V. E. Caballo & R. M. Turner (Eds.), *International handbook of cognitive/behavioral treatment of psychiatric disorders* (pp. 299–331). Madrid, Spain: Siglio XXI.

Marshall, W. L., Fernandez, Y. M., Lightbody, S., & O'Sullivan, C. (1994). *Victim-specific empathy in child molesters*. Manuscript submitted for publication.

Marshall, W. L., & Hall, G. C. N. (1995). The value of the MMPI in deciding forensic issues in accused sexual offenders. *Sexual Abuse: A Journal of Research and Treatment, 7*, 205–219.

Marshall, W. L., Hudson, S. M., & Hodkinson, S. (1993). The importance of attachment bonds in the development of juvenile sex offending. In H. E. Barbaree, W. L. Marshall, & S. M. Hudson (Eds.), *The juvenile sex offender* (pp. 164–181). New York: Guilford Press.

Marshall, W. L., Hudson, S. M., Jones, R., & Fernandez, Y. M. (1995). Empathy in sex offenders. *Clinical Psychology Review, 15*, 99–113.

Marshall, W. L., Jones, R., Hudson, S. M., & McDonald, E. (1993). Generalized empathy in child molesters. *Journal of Child Sexual Abuse, 2*, 61–68.

Marshall, W. L., & Maric, A. (1996). Cognitive and emotional components of generalized empathy deficits in child molesters. *Journal of Child Sexual Abuse, 5*, 101–110.

Marshall, W. L., & Mazzucco, A. (1995). Self-esteem and parental attachments in child molesters. *Sexual Abuse: A Journal of Research and Treatment, 7*, 279–285.

Matthews, R., Matthews, J. K., & Speltz, K. (1989). *Female sex offenders: An exploratory study*. Orwell, VT: Safer Society Press.

McConaghy, N. (1989). Validity and ethics of penile circumference measures of sexual arousal: A critical review. *Archives of Sexual Behavior, 18*, 357–369.

McConaghy, N. (1993). *Sexual behavior: Problems and management* New York: Plenum Press.

McGuire, R. J., Carlisle, J. M., & Young, B. G. (1965). Sexual deviations as conditioned behavior: A hypothesis. *Behaviour Research and Therapy, 2*, 185–190.

Mohr, J. W., Turner, R. E., & Jerry, M. B. (1964). *Pedophilia and exhibitionism.* Toronto: University of Toronto Press.

Murphy, W. D., & Barbaree, H. E. (1994). *Assessments of sex offenders by measures of erectile response: Psychometric properties and decision making.* Brandon, VT: Safer Society Press.

Murphy, W. D., Haynes, M. R., Stalgaitis, S. J., & Flanagan, B. (1986). Differential sexual responding among four groups of sexual offenders against children. *Journal of Psychopathology and Behavioral Assessment, 8,* 339–353.

National Adolescent Perpetrator Network. (1988). Preliminary report from the National Task Force on Juvenile Sexual Offending. *Juvenile and Family Court Journal, 39,* 1–67.

New York State Division of Criminal Justice Services. (1988). *The investigation and prosecution of crimes against children in New York State.* Albany, NY: Author.

O'Donohue, W., & Plaud, J. J. (1994). The conditioning of human sexual arousal. *Archives of Sexual Behavior, 23,* 321–334.

Panton, J. H. (1978). Personality differences appearing between rapists of adults, rapists of children and non-violent sexual molesters of female children. *Research Communications in Psychology, Psychiatry and Behavior, 3,* 385–393.

Panton, J. H. (1979). MMPI profile configurations with incestuous and non-incestuous child molesting. *Psychological Reports, 45,* 335–338.

Pithers, W. D., Beal, L. S., Armstrong, J., & Petty, J. (1989). Identification of risk factors through clinical interviews and analysis of records. In D. R. Laws (Ed.), *Relapse prevention with sex offenders* (pp. 77–87). New York: Guilford Press.

Prentky, R. A., & Knight, R. A. (1986). Impulsivity in the lifestyle and criminal behavior of sexual offenders. *Criminal Justice and Behavior, 13,* 141–164.

Prentky, R. A., Knight, R. A., Rosenberg, R., & Lee, A. (1989). A path analytic approach to the validation of a taxonomic system for classifying child molesters. *Journal of Quantitative Criminology, 5,* 231–257.

Prentky, R. A., Knight, R. A., Sims Knight, J. E., Strauss, H., Rokous, F., & Cerce, D. (1989). Developmental antecedents of sexual aggression. *Development and Psychopathy, 1,* 153–169.

Quinn, J. T., Harbison, J., & McAllister, H. (1970). An attempt to shape human penile responses. *Behaviour Research and Therapy, 8,* 27–28.

Quinsey, V. L., Chaplin, T. C., & Carrigan, W. F. (1979). Sexual preferences among incestuous and nonincestuous child molesters. *Behavior Therapy, 10,* 562–565.

Quinsey, V. L, Harris, G. T., & Rice, M. E. (1995). Actuarial prediction of sexual recidivism. *Journal of Interpersonal Violence, 10,* 85–105.

Quinsey, V. L., Lalumière, M. L., Rice, M. E., & Harris, G. T. (1995). Predicting sexual offenses. In J. C. Campbell (Ed.), *Assessing dangerousness: Violence by sexual offenders, batterers, child abusers* (pp. 114–137). Thousand Oaks, CA: Sage.

Quinsey, V. L., Rice, M. E., & Harris, G. T. (1990). Psychopathy, sexual deviance, and recidivism among sex offenders released from a maximum security institution. *Penetanguishine Research Report, 7,* (1).

Quinsey, V. L., Steinman, C. M., Bergersen, S. G., & Holmes, T. F. (1975). Penile circumference, skin conductance, and ranking responses of child molesters and "normals" to sexual and nonsexual visual stimuli. *Behavior Therapy, 6,* 213–219.

Rada, R. T. (1976). Alcoholism and the child molester. *Annals of the New York Academy of Science, 273,* 492–496.

Rice, M. E., Quinsey, V. L., & Harris, G. T. (1991). Predicting sexual recidivism among treated and untreated extrafamilial child molesters released from a maximum security psychiatric institution. *Journal of Consulting and Clinical Psychology, 59,* 381–386.

Russell, D. E. H. (1984). *Sexual exploitation: Rape, child sexual abuse, and workplace harassment.* Newbury Park, CA: Sage.

Ryan, G. D., & Lane, S. L. (Eds.). (1991). *Juvenile sexual offending: Causes, consequences, and correction.* Lexington, MA: Lexington Books.

Saunders, E. B., & Awad, G. A. (1988). Assessment, management, and treatment planning for male adolescent sexual offenders. *American Journal of Orthopsychiatry, 58,* 571–579.

Saunders, E. B., Awad, G. A., & White, G. (1986). Male adolescent sex offenders: The offenders and the offense. *Canadian Journal of Psychiatry, 31,* 542–549.

Seidman, B. T., Marshall, W. L., Hudson, S. M., & Robertson, P. J. (1994). An examination of intimacy and loneliness in sex offenders. *Journal of Interpersonal Violence, 9,* 518–534.

Selzer, M. (1971). The Michigan Alcoholism Screening Test: The quest for a new diagnostic instrument. *American Journal of Psychiatry, 127,* 1653–1658.

Serin, R. C., Malcolm, P. B., Khanna, A., & Barbaree, H. E. (1994). Psychopathy and deviant sexual arousal in incarcerated sexual offenders. *Journal of Interpersonal Violence, 9,* 3–11.

Skinner, H. A. (1982). The Drug Abuse Screening Test. *Addictive Behaviors, 7,* 363–371.

Stermac, L. E., & Segal, Z. V. (1989). Adult sexual contact with children: An examination of cognitive factors. *Behavior Therapy, 20,* 573–584.

Stermac, L. E., Segal, Z. V., & Gillis, R. (1990). Social and cultural factors in sexual assault. In W. L. Marshall, D. R. Laws, & H. E. Barbaree (Eds.), *Handbook of sexual assault: Issues, theories, and treatment of the offender* (pp. 143–159). New York: Plenum Press.

Toobert, S., Bartelme, K. F., & Jones, E. S. (1959). Some factors related to pedophilia. *International Journal of Social Psychiatry, 4,* 272–279.

Travin, S., & Protter, B. (1993). *Sexual perversion: Integrative treatment approaches for the clinician.* New York: Plenum Press.

Ward, T., Hudson, S. M., & Marshall, W. L. (1994). The abstinence violation effect in child molesters. *Behaviour Research and Therapy, 32,* 431–437.

Ward, T., Hudson, S. M., & Marshall, W. L. (1996). Attachment style in sex offenders: A preliminary study. *Journal of Sex Research, 33,* 17–26.

Ward, T., Hudson, S. M., Marshall, W. L., & Seigert, R. (1995). Attachment style and intimacy deficits in sex offenders: A theoretical framework. *Sexual Abuse: A Journal of Research and Treatment, 7,* 317–335.

Wells, N. H. (1958). Sexual offenses as seen by a woman police surgeon. *British Medical Journal, 5109,* 1404–1408.

Wyatt, G. E. (1985). The sexual abuse of Afro-American and White-American women in childhood. *Child Abuse and Neglect, 9,* 507–519.

9

PEDOPHILIA

Assessment and Treatment

Howard E. Barbaree
Michael C. Seto

Western society increasingly recognizes the individual and social costs of child molestation. International surveys, some using national probability samples, have found that at least 7% of females and 3% of males have experienced some form of sexual abuse as children (see Finkelhor, 1994, for a review). The negative consequences for the victims of childhood sexual abuse can be serious and long lasting, including substance abuse, sexual acting out, and suicidal behavior (Beitchman et al., 1992; Conte, 1988). Child molesters underreport the number of children they have victimized, and many of these crimes remain undetected (Abel et al., 1987). Moreover, child molesters are likely to commit new offenses even after involvement in the criminal justice system. Hanson, Steffy, and Gauthier (1993) found that 42% of a total sample of 197 child molesters released between 1958 and 1974 committed a new sexual or violent offense during an average follow-up period of 19 years. The effective management of child molesters is therefore of obvious importance. This chapter is a review of the existing assessment and treatment approaches for sexual deviance in men who have molested or sexually assaulted children.

There are two subgroups of the child molester population which deserve special attention. First, juvenile offenders are a special subgroup because antihormonal treatments may be contraindicated for those who have not yet reached physical maturity, and use of explicit and violent stimulus materials during phallometric assessments of deviant sexual arousal is contentious. Also, gathering developmental and family information may play a greater role in the clinical assessment. Other aspects of treatment described here, however, are equally applicable to juvenile offenders (see Barbaree & Cortoni, 1993; Ryan, Lane, Davis, & Isaac, 1987; Saunders & Awad, 1988). Second, mentally handicapped offenders may not benefit from cognitive therapy and may require more direct supervision to prevent reoffense, although the other elements of treatment described here can still be important (Griffiths, Hindsburger, & Christian, 1985).

CATEGORIZING CHILD MOLESTERS

Child molesters are usually categorized rationally according to victim sex and the offender's relationship to the victim. A distinction is therefore made between incest offenders who have offended against their own children (primarily their daughters or stepdaughters) and nonfamilial child molesters, who molest children with whom they have no biological or legal family relationship. We also can make a theoretical distinction between offenders against biologically related children versus offenders against legally related children, in accordance with evolutionary theories about incest avoidance (e.g., Seto, Lalumière, & Kuban, 1997; Welham, 1990). Nonfamilial child molesters typically are further divided according to the gender of their victims. These subgroups usually are referred to as heterosexual or homosexual child molesters; however, this designation may be confusing because classifying men who molest boys according to their relative sexual arousal to adult male and female stimuli results in heterosexuals outnumbering homosexuals by a ratio of 2:1 (Marshall, Barbaree, & Butt, 1988).

A distinction typically is also made between pedophilic and nonpedophilic child molesters. Unfortunately, the terms "pedophile" and "child molester" are sometimes used interchangeably in the popular and scientific literature, creating unnecessary confusion. In this chapter, a child molester is any individual who has committed a sexual offense against a child victim, and is therefore identified according to legal definitions of "sexual offense" and "child victim." The upper age limit of the "child" designation depends on the legal age of consent and varies across jurisdictions. The conventional research definition of a child molester also requires that the offender is at least 16 years of age and 5 years older than the victim. A pedophile, in contrast, is a clinically identified individual with a sexual preference for prepubescent children rather than adults. Pedophilia is a paraphilia as defined in the latest edition of the *Diagnostic and Statistical Manual of Mental Disorders* (DSM-IV), and therefore requires the presence of "recurrent, intense sexually arousing fantasies, sexual urges, or behaviors involving sexual activity with a prepubescent child or children" over a period of 6 months (American Psychiatric Association, 1994, p. 528).

Not all child molesters are pedophiles, and some pedophiles may not have molested children (i.e., there may be men who prefer sex with prepubescent children rather than adults but who have not acted on their desires). Pedophilic and nonpedophilic child molesters probably have different motivations for their offenses. Pedophiles are motivated by their sexual interest in children (Freund, 1991), whereas nonpedophiles may have sex with children because an adult partner is not available (Freund, McKnight, Langevin, & Cibiri, 1972), as a result of intellectual handicap or psychopathology, or as part of a chronic pattern of antisocial behavior. Current research suggests that the proportion of pedophiles is higher among nonfamilial child molesters compared with incest offenders, homosexual compared with heterosexual child molesters, and offenders with multiple victims compared with offenders with one victim only (Freund & Watson, 1991; Freund, Watson, & Dickey, 1991; Quinsey, Chaplin, & Carrigan, 1979).

OBJECTIVES OF THIS CHAPTER

This chapter provides an overview of the literature on the assessment, treatment, and treatment outcome of child molesters. We pay particular attention to the assessment and treatment of deviant sexual interests because this is the defining characteristic of pedophiles. Finally, we review the existing treatment outcome research on sex offenders and discuss some of the current controversies regarding treatment evaluations.

PRETREATMENT ASSESSMENT

The diagnosis of pedophilia can be made from (1) the individual's self-report about his sexual fantasies, urges, and behavior; (2) psychometric testing using scales that measure sexual interests; and (3) phallometric testing, which provides a psychophysiological measure of sexual arousal to targets from different stimulus categories (e.g., depictions of nude children, adolescents, and adults).

We usually assess sexual histories through clinical interviews and questionnaires. Variables of particular interest include whether the offender has experienced physical or sexual abuse, the number and duration of consensual, age-appropriate sexual relationships in which he has participated, the age of onset of his deviant sexual interests, including other paraphilias, and a detailed description of the offender's sexual offenses and criminal history (Abel, Becker, Cunningham-Rathner, & Mittelman, 1988; Longo & Groth, 1983.

Several published scales have been used to assess sexual interest in children, including the Abel Child Cognitions Scale (Abel et al., 1989), the Clarke Sexual History Questionnaire (Paitich, Langevin, Freeman, Mann, & Handy, 1977), and the Multiphasic Sex Inventory (Nichols & Molinder, 1984). There are some data regarding reliability and validity of these scales, but none have been rigorously evaluated in terms of their psychometric properties and utility with child molesters (see review by Hanson, Cox, & Woszczyzna, 1991). Although self-report measures can be clinically useful, they are vulnerable to dissimulation because of the obvious nature of the questions and the legal or social sanctions that offenders may face; in responding to questions, offenders will often deny sexual interest in children. As a consequence, more emphasis is usually given to phallometric testing, which may be less vulnerable to faking (however, see Lalumière & Earls, 1992; Laws & Rubin, 1969; and Quinsey & Chaplin, 1988).

Sexual Preferences

The behavioral assessment and treatment of sex offenders has depended a great deal on phallometric measures of sexual arousal. A number of detailed reviews of this methodology are available (Earls & Marshall, 1983; Murphy & Barbaree, 1994; O'Donohue & Letourneau, 1992). In phallometric assessment procedures, the offender's sexual arousal is monitored through direct measurement of his penile erection in terms of change in volume or circumference while he is presented with stimuli varying in content of sexual and nonsexual cues.

There is consistent evidence for the discriminant validity of phallometric assessment for child molesters (e.g., Freund, 1967, 1981; Freund & Watson, 1991; Malcolm, Andrews, & Quinsey, 1993; Murphy, Haynes, Stalgaitis, & Flanagan, 1986; Quinsey, Steinman, Bergersen, & Holmes, 1975). Typically, nonoffenders respond with strong arousal to adult females but show decreasing arousal to stimuli depicting persons who appear to be younger than age 14 or 15. As a group, nonfamilial child molesters show stronger arousal to children than they do to adults; some of these men show exclusive responding to children of a very young age. Incest offenders are more likely to show a more normal pattern of arousal, with greater arousal to adults than to adolescents or children, but they show less arousal to the adult females than do the nonoffenders.

Child molesters, however, are heterogeneous in their sexual responding. Barbaree and Marshall (1989) sorted the response patterns of a group of child molesters and nonoffenders according to profile shape. Five distinct profile shapes were found. An "adult" profile was characterized by strong responses to adults and minimal responding to children. The teen–adult profile was similar to the adult profile except that responsiveness to the adolescent targets was higher than for those with the adult profile. A large group of men had profiles that were judged to be nondiscriminating because they displayed a moderate degree of response across age categories. Finally, two profile shapes show significant responding to children. In the child profile the archetypal pedophilic profile is found, with strong responsiveness to prepubescent children and little response to adolescents or adults. The child–adult profile had a bimodal shape with moderate or strong responsiveness to children and adults and less response to adolescents. The large majority of nonoffenders had adult profiles, with smaller numbers displaying the teen–adult and nondiscriminating profiles. Incest offenders were almost equally divided between the adult and nondiscriminating profile groups. Nonfamilial child molesters were a heterogeneous group, with 35% showing a child profile and the remainder approximately equally distributed among the other profile groups.

Men who showed child or child–adult profiles were of lower IQ and lower socioeconomic status than were the other offenders. Those who revealed a child profile had used more force in the commission of their previous offenses and had a greater number of previous victims. In addition, men in the child profile group did not exhibit any inhibition in their arousal when presented with stimuli containing cues of force and coercion, whereas men in the other groups were inhibited by these cues (Barbaree & Marshall, 1989).

The phallometric assessment of known or convicted child molesters assists in the evaluation of their treatment needs. It assists also in making an assessment of their risk for future reoffending against a child (Malcolm et al., 1993; Rice, Quinsey, & Harris, 1991). However, Barbaree and Peacock (1995) argued strongly against the use of phallometric assessment in the investigation of allegations of child sexual abuse or in assessing sexual interest in men who are accused of child sexual abuse. Phallometric assessment is unacceptable as a "screening" test because of its level of sensitivity (Freund & Blanchard, 1989; Freund & Watson, 1991). Some men who appear to be nondeviant in their responding have actually committed a sexual assault against a child.

TREATMENT

Treatment programs, whether they make this explicit or not, are predicated on certain assumptions regarding the factors that should be changed to reduce future offending. A distinction can therefore be made between "within-treatment" and "long-term outcome" goals (Seto, Barbaree, & Maric, 1996). In a program evaluation, the clinician needs to provide reports of an appropriate assessment of the within-treatment goal to demonstrate that the intervention has produced the anticipated benefits. Subsequent follow-up data would then allow the researcher to determine if, indeed, a within-treatment change is functionally related to the cessation of the offensive behaviors. Unfortunately, within-treatment goals are rarely identified, much less measured. If treatment seems to have been successful, we are simply left with changes in the offensive behavior with little basis for inferring what mediated these changes.

Clinical assessments are routine components of the intake process for many treatment programs. Ideally, these assessments should focus on the organic, behavioral, and cognitive excesses and deficits which are thought to characterize the offender and which are understood to have led to the offensive behavior. Unfortunately, clinical assessments are frequently unrelated to the goals of treatment or to the theoretical basis of the particular therapy used. The treatment approaches we describe below apply to all child molesters, not only pedophiles. Nonetheless, deviant sexual fantasies, urges, and arousal play an important role in all these approaches.

General Psychotherapy

General psychotherapy approaches typically focus on understanding the dynamics of sexual offending, increasing the offender's acceptance of responsibility, increasing victim empathy, reducing cognitive distortions, improving social functioning, stress management, and sex education. Many of these approaches are atheoretical in that they are not informed by a comprehensive model of sexual offending, or are not specifically developed for sex offenders.

A number of examples of these treatment programs are described in the literature. Castell and Yalom (1972) described a treatment program which used a one-on-one approach based on a psychodynamic model of psychopathology. Peters, Pedigo, Steg, and McKenna (1968) described an analytically oriented group therapy program located within a hospital setting. There have been many reports of psychodynamic group therapy programs in prisons or correctional settings (Brancale, Vnocolo, & Prendergast, 1972; Cabeen & Coleman, 1961; Groth, 1983; Pacht, Halleck, & Ehrmann, 1962). Most of these programs have included mixed groups of sex offenders and they have not reported separate results for child molesters. However, Cabeen and Coleman (1961) included only child molesters in their program. Outcome studies from these kinds of general treatment programs suggest that they are ineffective in reducing recidivism among treated offenders (see Furby, Weinrott, & Blackshaw, 1989).

Organic Treatments

The aim of the organic treatments is to suppress sexual urges and behavior so that deviant sexuality is reduced or eliminated (see Bradford, 1985). This suppression can be achieved by (1) inhibiting the gonadotropic pituitary function by administering medroxyprogesterone acetate (MPA); (2) blocking androgenic action at the target organs using an antiandrogen such as cyproterone acetate (CPA); (3) removing the main testosterone production centers, the testicles, by surgical castration; or (4) damaging the brain areas thought to influence sexual behavior. Neurosurgery is no longer used, and castrations are very uncommon (see Gijs & Gooren, 1996), so we will not review them here. We refer the reader to reviews by Bradford (1985) and Wille and Beier (1989).

The objectives of pharmacotherapy are straightforward: reductions in libido, deviant sexual arousal, deviant sexual fantasy, and the frequency of deviant sexual behavior (see Gijs & Gooren, 1996, for a review). Bradford (1985) made the additional claim that the hormonal treatment of sex offenders "is a pharmacological method of reducing sexual drive, as well as the direction of the drive" (p. 360). Bradford and Pawlak (1987, 1993) have presented data suggesting that CPA selectively reduces deviant sexual arousal. However, the majority of findings do not support this claim. Laschet (1973) concluded that "antiandrogens cannot alter the direction of sexual deviation; they can only reduce or inhibit the sexual reaction" (p. 317). Bancroft, Tennent, Loucas, and Cass (1974) evaluated hormonal interventions using penile response measures, and their results indicated that drug interventions do not alter deviant sexual interests. They found that both CPA and ethinyl estradiol reduced sexual interest and activity, as well as subjective deviant urges, but neither had any effect on phallometric indices of deviant sexual interests. Their patients continued to display preferences for deviant sexual acts or partners even after treatment had reduced their overall sexual urges to low levels. Similarly, Cooper, Sandhu, Losztyn, and Cernovsky (1992) found that CPA did not have a selective effect on deviant arousal.

A number of studies have evaluated the effects of pharmacotherapy on recidivism in sex offenders, particularly diagnosed pedophiles. Reviews of the effectiveness of CPA by Bradford (1985) and Ortmann (1980) were optimistic about the benefits of CPA in treating sex offenders. However, these reviewers were not critical of study methodologies, particularly the means for estimating recidivism, and did not take account of treatment withdrawal in reoffense rates. Overall, the results were mixed, with some studies showing reductions in recidivism while others did not. Hall's (1995) review found that hormonal treatment significantly reduced recidivism in a set of four studies published since 1989, but it did not differ from cognitive-behavioral treatment in its effectiveness.

MPA was first reported as a treatment for sex offenders by Money (1970). Since then a number of reports have become available. For example, Berlin and Meinecke (1981) followed 20 patients treated with MPA and found that three had repeated their offenses while still taking their medication, and that cessation of treatment led to rapid relapse into deviant behaviors. Gagne (1981) claimed that MPA reduced sexual fantasies and deviant urges but did not report reoffense rates. Cooper et al. (1992) found that MPA and CPA were equally effective in reducing self-reported sexual thoughts, fantasies, and masturbation. Their effects on penile response to sexual stimuli were more variable.

A major problem with pharmacotherapy is compliance. For example, in the largest double-blind, randomly controlled study, only 11 subjects completed the protocol out of an initial sample of 48 child molesters (Hucker, Langevin, & Bain, 1988). Langevin et al. (1979) found that administering MPA alone produced such high dropout rates that a proper evaluation of its effect was not possible and, indeed, this seems to be a common problem with hormonal intervention. Dropout rates in the hormonal treatment of sex offenders have varied from 30% (Meyer, Walker, Emory, & Smith, 1985) to 100% (Langevin et al., 1979). However, supplementing MPA with training in assertiveness increased the number of patients in Langevin et al.'s (1979) study who remained for the full course of treatment. Side effects may be a critical issue if offenders are treated with drugs for long periods of time. This would be necessary to maintain treatment gains, unless psychological procedures are also utilized. In a careful review of the literature, Lomis and Baker (1981) concluded that "little is known about the psychological effects or the long-term physical effects [of MPA] in human males" (p. 19). Meyer, Walker, Emory, and Smith (1985) reported the most extensive study of side effects associated with MPA. Patients received MPA for an average of 18 months. The side effects included: weight gain, smaller testes, increased blood pressure, increased gallbladder complaints, mild hyperinsulinism, and greater risk for diabetes.

With its problematic side effects and high dropout rates, pharmacotherapy is not a panacea. The drugs CPA and MPA, even if they are effective in reducing sexual behavior and recidivism, are unlikely to produce desirable changes in cognitive distortions and deviant sexual interests on their own. Moreover, much of the published research has been uncontrolled, with small sample sizes and no follow-ups. Nonetheless, Gijs and Gooren (1996) suggest that pharmacotherapy using MPA or CPA may be a useful component of a comprehensive treatment program. It has recently been suggested, however, that serotonergic agents can specifically reduce deviant sexual arousal without affecting normative sexual arousal (for a review see Gijs & Gooren, 1996). Compliance with this form of pharmacotherapy may therefore be higher. Note that this suggestion is based on uncontrolled case studies and only one double-blind trial (Kreusi, Fine, Valladares, Phillips, & Rapoport, 1992). The effectiveness of pharmacotherapy requires further evaluation.

Behavioral Therapies

Behavioral therapies have tended to focus on changing sexual response patterns and reorienting the pedophile toward a sexual preference for adults. Although there is a good deal of evidence for positive effects on sexual arousal patterns, there is no reason to believe that sexual preferences can be altered (see review by Barbaree, Bogaert, & Seto, 1995). Behavioral approaches have targeted deviant sexual arousal. Most authors assume that deviant sexual arousal results from a process of learning or conditioning (see Laws & Marshall, 1990, for a review; for different perspectives, see Freund, Seto, & Kuban, Chapter 6, this volume; and Quinsey & Lalumière, 1995).

Behavioral approaches to the treatment of pedophiles have been directed toward the modification of patterns of stimulus control of sexual arousal by decreasing deviant arousal and increasing appropriate arousal. Quinsey and Marshall (1983) critically reviewed a broad range of studies covering various offensive and eccentric sexual behaviors. They concluded that although some of the procedures appeared to offer some hope, there was little in the way of clear, convincing evidence of their efficacy. Kelly (1982) reviewed the literature on the behavioral treatment of child molesters and identified four controlled group studies and 10 controlled case studies that showed positive effects of behavioral procedures including aversion, covert sensitization, satiation, and masturbatory reconditioning procedures. Aversive procedures take various forms but basically they involve pairing the presently desired sexual stimulus (e.g., a child or coercive sex) with some aversive event. In overt aversive procedures, this aversive event has been one of a variety of physical stimuli such as a mild electric shock (Quinsey, Chaplin, & Carrigan, 1980) or a strong aversive odor (Laws, Meyer, & Holmen, 1978). In covert sensitization (covert aversion) the aversive event has been a negative imaginal event generated by the offender under instructions from the clinician. These negative imaginal cues have included physically aversive images such as thoughts about feces or vomit or psychologically aversive images such as being discovered during the commission of deviant acts by a spouse, relatives, or friends (Levin, Barry, Gambaro, Wolfinsohn, & Smith, 1977).

Perhaps the most helpful series of studies on aversion therapy in the treatment of pedophiles has been reported by Quinsey and his associates. Using a between-groups, crossover design, Quinsey et al. (1980) compared biofeedback with an electrical aversion procedure in the reduction of pedophilic arousal. Most heterosexual child molesters studied showed improvement in their arousal patterns. This study constitutes the only controlled treatment study which shows convincingly the effectiveness of electrical aversion with child molesters. This study is interesting as well because it is the only study of electrical aversion which involves a long-term follow-up of the study participants. Rice et al. (1991) studied the recidivism of 136 extrafamilial child molesters who had received phallometric assessment in a maximum security psychiatric institution from 1972 to 1983, with an average follow-up of 6 years. Fifty of these men participated in behavioral treatment to alter inappropriate sexual age preferences using the aversion procedure described above. In the follow-up study, 31% of the men were convicted of a new sex offense, 43% committed a violent or sexual offense, and 58% were arrested for some offense or returned to the institution. Compared with the men who succeeded in the community, men convicted of a new sex offense had previously committed more sex offenses, had been admitted to correctional institutions more frequently, were more likely to have been diagnosed as personality disordered, were more likely to have never married, and had shown more inappropriate sexual preferences in initial phallometric assessment. Unfortunately, participating in the aversion treatment was not related to recidivism.

Laws and Marshall (1991) reviewed the evidence for a second category of behavioral treatment for child molesters known as masturbation reconditioning. This procedure has advantages over other methods because it is a nonaversive and rewarding activity and can be done in "homework" (i.e., nonlaboratory) assignments. They reviewed four forms. The first was "thematic shift" (sometimes called "orgasmic reconditioning"), during which a man alters his deviant sexual fantasy during masturbation at the point of orgasm to a more appropriate stimulus (e.g., heterosexual relations). They reviewed seven studies. Although some studies reported effectiveness, it is difficult to isolate improvements to this procedure directly because of confounding additional treatments, and the most well-controlled study (Conrad & Winzce, 1976) failed to find positive effects using objective (i.e., phallometric) data. The second was "fantasy alternation," wherein a male changes or alters the content of his fantasies on a daily or weekly basis (but not within a masturbatory episode itself). Laws and Marshall (1991) reviewed five studies and some of these data were supportive, but one study actually found an increase in deviant arousal. The authors concluded that this method probably is not an appropriate reconditioning method because any pairing of orgasm with deviant stimuli should be avoided. The third was "directed masturbation," wherein a man masturbates exclusively to appropriate stimuli (e.g., heterosexual adult relations). They reviewed five studies. The authors concluded that this method is simple and straightforward and can be effective. The fourth method is "satiation therapy," wherein a man masturbates and fantasizes (out loud) to deviant stimuli for a long period of time, typically after ejaculation (i.e., during the refractory period) to produce boredom with the deviant fantasy. Laws and Marshall (1991) reviewed seven studies of satiation. There was some support offered for this procedure, particularly if combined with directed masturbation. In conclusion, the authors suggested that, although some promising results were reported in the literature, there is little evidence yet available that these techniques work in the long term.

In summary, three methods are in frequent use in attempts to reduce deviant sexual arousal, namely aversion therapy, covert sensitization, and satiation. However, the studies which attest to the effectiveness of these procedures are limited in number, although not in methodological rigor. These studies have indicated that the procedures used were responsible for the reductions seen in deviant arousal and they have shown that these reductions in deviant arousal persist over several weeks or months. However, there are no data yet published that indicate that reduced deviant sexual arousal leads in the end to reduced recidivism among child molesters.

We have found that men respond idiosyncratically to treatment procedures and that someone who fails to respond to one procedure may show beneficial effects from another. Accordingly, we tend to use several procedures in combination. It may be that different procedures influence different aspects of the attraction to deviant acts. For example, aversive therapy might reduce the valence of visual images (e.g., images of children in advertising or television) that might otherwise elicit arousal in these men, while satiation may alter masturbatory fantasy content which would otherwise maintain deviant interests.

It is important to point out that behavioral therapy is not exclusively "behavioral" because an important contribution to the eventual change in sexual responding is the offender's growing understanding of the factors which lead to his offending. While the treatment focuses on the reduction of deviant arousal, discussions with each man focus on his sexual fantasies and urges and the behavioral sequence which leads from urge or fantasy to offense. During homework assignments, the man learns what factors trigger or encourage deviant fantasies. For example, he may find that deviant fantasies are more likely to occur when he is distressed, or when he is feeling lonely or bored.

Relapse Prevention

The relapse prevention approach to treating sex offenders was adapted from research on addictive behavior. Marlatt and Gordon (1980, 1985) outlined a strategy for assisting individuals who have completed treatment to prevent the recurrence of drug-taking behavior. The strategy involves (1) identifying situations in which the individual is at high risk for relapse; (2) teaching the individual to identify these high-risk situations and to avoid them; (3) identifying lapses as behaviors which do not constitute full-fledged relapses but which constitute approximations to the drug-taking behavior and which may be a precursor to a relapse (e.g., spending time in bars as a precursor to drinking alcohol); (4) teaching the individual to identify a lapse; and (5) teaching the individual various coping strategies which might be used in response to both high-risk situations and lapses to minimize the chances of a relapse. Pithers, Marques, Gibat, and Marlatt (1983) extended the relapse prevention strategy for use with sex offenders. The principles involved are similar to those used with addicts. First, high-risk situations are identified for each offender and he learns to identify their occurrence (MacDonald & Pithers, 1989; Pithers, Beal, Armstrong, & Petty, 1989). Second, he learns to identify lapses or decisions he makes which lead him closer to a relapse (Jenkins-Hall & Marlatt, 1989). Finally, he learns to cope with high-risk situations and lapses to prevent the occurrence of a relapse (Carey & McGrath, 1989; Steenman, Nelson, & Viesti, 1989).

Authors who espouse a relapse prevention approach to the treatment of the sex offender refer to cognitive-behavioral chains (e.g., Pithers, 1990). It is widely recognized that sexual offenses are not isolated events independent of other aspects of the offender's current life. Instead, offenses are the final event in a long sequence of thoughts and actions (Nelson & Jackson, 1989). Pithers et al. (1983) were the first to describe the concept of an offense chain. They described the chain as involving four stages. First, the offender has certain lifestyle, personality, and circumstantial factors which serve as a background to his offense behavior. Second, the offender becomes dysphoric as a result of feelings of deprivation or loss, or in response to conflict or stress. As a result of this dysphoria, the offender allows himself to enter a high-risk situation which may include a potential and vulnerable victim. In the third stage, the offender "lapses," meaning they engage in behavior which approximates a sexual assault, such as fantasizing about children. In the fourth stage, a relapse occurs in which the offender assaults a child. Pithers et al. (1983) introduced three cognitive–emotional mechanisms which could be seen to operate in the transitions from stage to stage of the chain. First, seemingly irrelevant decisions are choices the offender had made which could be described superficially as innocent and not directed toward sexual assault, but which had the effect of allowing for increased opportunity for contact with a potential victim. Second, offenders respond to the immediate, powerful reinforcement or gratification of sexual assault without responding to the longer-term negative effects of the assault. Third, these authors describe an abstinence violation effect as a negative emotional reaction to a lapse or relapse. These convince the offender that he is unable to control his own urges, leading to increases in the dysphoria which initially began the chain.

Ward, Louden, Hudson, and Marshall (1995) elaborated on the concept of the offense chain further by providing a descriptive model of the offense chain for child molesters based on an empirical study of 26 incarcerated child molesters before their involvement in treatment. The study indicated that there are no fewer than eight or nine distinct stages in the offense cycle. In their study, Ward et al. described the offense as followed by a stage in which the offender evaluates his relationship and behavior with the child. If there was a positive evaluation, then the offender would express the expectation that he would likely commit such offenses in the future. If there was a negative evaluation, then the offender would make a renewed commitment to resist future urges to child sexual assault.

To properly plan relapse prevention for the individual offender, the therapist must first develop a detailed account of the chain of events leading to the offender's previous offenses. Cognitive-behavioral targets for treatment are then specified on the basis of the chain. For example, a child molester's previous offenses may demonstrate a pattern wherein stressors such as unemployment or social isolation lead to his seeking young children for social interactions, which in turn lead to fantasies about sex with children, masturbation to these fantasies, and eventually offending. Treatment targets might therefore include vocational counseling, stress management, social skills training, sex education, and behavioral interventions to reduce deviant sexual arousal.

In a sense it is inaccurate to call some of these interventions "treatment," because we do not construe our patients as having a disorder which can be cured. We view child molesters as individuals who have exhibited unacceptable behaviors to obtain rewards and satisfactions that may have been more difficult to obtain by more acceptable means. We view pedophilic child molesters as having a sexual preference that they must learn to control and, where possible, redirect toward a more appropriate outlet, that is, consensual sex with adults. Because sexual interactions with children have produced strong immediate rewards in the past and because thoughts of deviant acts frequently have been associated with strong sexual arousal and gratification through masturbation, we expect deviant tendencies to retain some degree of strength even after the best available treatment program. Pithers (1990) made the important distinction between two critical aspects of relapse prevention. First, in teaching the offender ways of coping with high-risk situations, we are enhancing his capacity for self-management. A second critical aspect of relapse prevention is providing an environment that supports the offender's attempts at relapse prevention. Posttreatment management and supervision is therefore essential.

EXTANT AND COMPREHENSIVE TREATMENT PROGRAMS

Most extant treatment programs have been implemented for clinical or program purposes, rather than for the purposes of treatment outcome research. These programs have tended to borrow from what is perceived by the program staff as the best or essential aspects of each of the treatment approaches described above. Most current programs for child molesters now involve some work on denial and minimization, victim empathy, modification of deviant arousal, and relapse prevention. Depending on the professional backgrounds of the treatment providers or consultants connected to the program, some participants may be offered medication to reduce their sex drive. While most extant programs offer some mix of these elements, there is wide variability in terms of the emphasis placed on each. Program descriptions should more adequately describe the mix of treatment targets and the relative emphasis of the program.

Marshall and his associates (e.g., Marshall & Barbaree, 1990) used the term "comprehensive" to refer to these more eclectic programs. The rationale for a comprehensive program is straightforward. Child molesters are a heterogeneous group (Knight & Prentky, 1990) with various and numerous treatment needs. A comprehensive approach will more likely meet the needs of a larger proportion of the participants. A recent meta-analysis of treatment outcome studies published in the last 15 years indicated that cognitive-behavioral and organic treatment approaches produce an overall reduction in recidivism of approximately 30% (Hall, 1995). Programs which have been described as comprehensive and have been evaluated by a nonexperimental treatment outcome methodology have shown promising results (Marshall & Barbaree, 1988).

TREATMENT EVALUATION

The majority of treatment programs described in the literature have not been formally evaluated. This is not surprising, because treatment outcome research with sex offenders is very difficult to conduct in applied settings. There currently is a great deal of controversy regarding treatment outcome for sex offenders (cf. Furby et al., 1989; Marshall, Jones, Ward, Johnston, & Barbaree, 1991; Quinsey, Rice, Harris, & Lalumière, 1993). We will consider a number of the more salient methodological difficulties in evaluating treatment efficacy in this area.

Because the primary objective in treating sex offenders is preventing further offending, the most important criterion measure of treatment success is a reduction in the rate of reoffending. However, reoffense rate can be an elusive measure. It is well known that the official rate of reoffense taken from police records of charges and convictions is an underestimate of the actual rate of reoffense (Furby et al., 1989; Quinsey, 1983). Arrests and convictions are a product of factors such as the offender's luck or skill at avoiding being caught, the quality of prosecution efforts, and the inclinations of victims to report the matter. It is possible to get information concerning additional reoffenses which have not been recorded by the police. Estimates of recidivism based on these unofficial sources have been up to 2.5 times higher than those derived from the official records (Marshall & Barbaree, 1988). Obtaining unofficial reports of reoffense will increase the base rate and may make the detection of a real treatment effect more likely.

The accuracy of outcome measures is another important methodological issue. Some studies (e.g., Abel, Barlow, Blanchard, & Guild, 1977) relied on the self-reports of their patients as to whether or not they have reoffended. However, in other studies, attempts to secure self-reports of reoffenses from former patients were not successful (e.g., Marshall & Barbaree, 1988). The majority of offenders did not respond to written and oral requests for information and the self-reports received were inaccurate. Therefore, outcome data must be based on some verifiable measure of reoffense. Although Abel and his associates relied on self-report, their special procedures for guaranteeing confidentiality appeared to increase the likelihood that such reports would be more accurate (Kaplan, Abel, Cunningham-Rathner, & Mittelman, 1990).

Variables other than treatment can influence outcome results. In their review of the recidivism literature on sex offenders, Furby et al. (1989) found rates of reoffense among untreated offenders to be remarkably different across studies, with rates of 10% to 29% among nonfamilial child molesters who offended against girls, and rates of 13% to 40% among men who molested boys. Some of the variability between studies can be attributed to differing lengths of the follow-up period. Longer follow-up periods are associated with greater numbers of reoffenses (Gibbens, Soothill, & Way, 1981; Hanson et al., 1993). Marshall and Barbaree (1988) reported reoffense rates of 12.5%, 38.5%, and 64.3% for groups of men who had been in the community for periods of 0 to 2 years, 2 to 4 years, and from 4 to 10 years, respectively. Sturup (1972) showed that recidivism rates for sex offenders vary considerably depending on whether the patient is a first-time offender or a repeat offender. Meyer and Romero (1980), for example, showed that sex offenders with a low prior rate of arrests for sex crimes (0 to 0.3 per year) had a far lower subsequent recidivism rate than did offenders whose prior arrest rate was high (0.31 to 1.39 per year), 7.9% compared with 26.2%. Barbaree and Marshall (1989) demonstrated that two features of child molesters are related to reoffense. First, offenders who showed deviant sexual arousal, committed more severe prior offenses, had a large number of victims, and had intercourse with victims were more likely to reoffend. Second, offenders who had a low IQ and were of low socioeconomic status had a larger number of reoffenses. Rice et al. (1991) reported that child molesters who reoffended were more likely to have deviant sexual arousal, higher psychopathy scores, committed previous sex offenses, been admitted to correctional facilities, been diagnosed as personality disordered, and never been married.

Most published treatment outcome studies have not compared treated subjects with a suitable comparison group. Instead, the rate of failure among the treated men usually was compared with a hypothetical failure rate for sex offenders in general. Given the large number of variables which can influence outcome, this method of treatment evaluation clearly is inadequate. To complete an adequate treatment evaluation it is essential to compare reoffenses among treated offenders with the reoffenses among a group of untreated offenders who are equivalent to the treated group in all important respects except treatment involvement.

Of course, the ideal design for a treatment outcome study would include a comparison between a treated and an untreated group using random subject assignment. We know of only two such studies in the literature (see Marques, Day, Nelson, & West, 1994; Meyer & Romero, 1980). Marques et al. avoided ethical difficulties because they drew their treatment sample from a large pool of treatment volunteers in a jurisdiction in which other treatment programs were not available. Meyer and Romero were able to compare sex offenders released on probation who were randomly assigned to either treatment- or probation-only groups. These studies have not demonstrated a treatment effect.

Because sexual offenses are so abhorrent, some people have argued that a treatment outcome study using random assignment to treatment or no-treatment conditions is ethically unacceptable in most settings. There are certainly practical and political obstacles to clinical investigators' proposing such a study. For example, denying treatment to a high-risk offender willing to participate in treatment could be difficult to justify to politically active individuals concerned about public safety. Also, participating in treatment can influence correctional decision making. Offenders might be very unlikely to participate in a controlled study if being assigned to the control condition would mean a lower chance of being conditionally released or being transferred to a lower level of security. If such a study were to be conducted in a community setting, referral sources would presumably send their clients to other settings where they would be assured of treatment involvement. Finally, parties involved in a randomly controlled treatment outcome study, such as a research group, funding agency, and sponsoring institution might be held civilly liable if a high-risk offender assigned to the no-treatment condition eventually committed another serious sexual offense. Nonetheless, these practical and political obstacles should not prevent investigators from pursuing treatment outcome research that is methodologically rigorous and meets accepted scientific standards.

Most treatment outcome studies published to date have involved compromises to the standards for internal validity typically required of treatment outcome research. It is clear that a comparison group is required to assess the effectiveness of treatment, but studies have varied as to how the comparison group has been formed. If the comparison group cannot be a randomly assigned control group, the next-best option would be an untreated group who would accept treatment, but for whom treatment is unavailable for one reason or another, such as the distance to travel to the clinic (Marshall & Barbaree, 1988). Reports of treatment programs often fail to specify demographic, offense history, and other characteristics of their samples. To adequately evaluate treatment outcome research in this area, it is essential to be able to characterize the treated and untreated samples and to be able to show that the samples do not differ prior to treatment on an important demographic or offense history variable associated with recidivism.

One approach is to compare the relative efficacy of different treatment models instead of comparing only treated and untreated groups. A comprehensive, sex offender-specific treatment model such as relapse prevention could be compared with an established psychotherapeutic approach, for example, based on Ellis's rational–emotive therapy using a randomized, experimental design; these two treatment groups could then be compared with a group of men who refused treatment. Demonstrating that either of the treatment programs is superior to the other—and to the untreated control group—would demonstrate that a difference between treated and untreated groups is not explainable entirely by self-selection of participants.

Foa and Emmelkamp (1983) described a variety of indices of treatment success or failure. They noted that the real value of a program is revealed not only by the success of those who complete treatment, but also by the number of patients who refuse to enter the program or who drop out once they have commenced therapy. Obviously there is not much value in a program that has a high success rate with those who complete treatment but is rejected by most of its potential clients. The most frequent reason for a child molester to refuse treatment is that he denies committing the offense.

Many studies report a highly selective intake process, accepting only men who are deemed to be well suited for the program. For example, in a treatment program described by Brancale et al. (1972), only 30% of incarcerated offenders were recommended as treatment candidates, and only two thirds of these were finally accepted. Only 25% of the final sample were repeat offenders, unlike the proportions typically found in incarcerated samples of child molesters. Selection of patients can also occur at the time of release. As an example, Cabeen and Coleman (1961) reported that in their program, only patients who were judged to "no longer be a menace" were released from the program. In the treatment program described by Brancale et al. (1972), only 46% of the treated men were finally judged to be fit for release. This filtering process is fatal to program evaluation or to a proper estimate of treatment effectiveness, especially when comparisons of recidivism are made between those selected for treatment and an unselected, untreated group. Unfortunately for program evaluation, judgments regarding suitability for treatment usually are synonymous with estimates of likely success upon release. Selection processes are likely to distort comparisons between treated and untreated groups and estimates of treatment.

Another variable which we must consider in evaluating these treatment programs is the dropout rate. Many treatment outcome studies have reported outcome only for men who have completed the program. Men who drop out may be more likely to fail than those who have completed treatment; these dropouts have to be taken into consideration in program evaluations. In other areas, such as alcoholism treatment (Nathan & Lansky, 1978), and in many areas of behavior therapy (Foa & Emmelkamp, 1983), dropouts are considered to be treatment failures. Abel et al. (1988) reported a very high dropout rate from their treatment program. Almost 35 percent of the patients entering their program withdrew. Of these, 13 percent were terminated by the therapists because their behavior in treatment was too disruptive, they became psychotic, or their alcoholism was too problematic. Of the remaining patients, 10% were jailed before treatment was completed, 51% refused to continue but did not say why, and 24% did not return and could not be contacted. As part of the voluntary consent procedure, the patients in Abel et al.'s program were repeatedly told that they could withdraw from treatment at any time and at no cost to them.

One last issue is not methodological, but still is important in evaluating the effectiveness of treatment for sex offending. The length of treatment varies considerably across programs, with some offering 2 years or more of treatment. Most treatment programs depend on a long period of intense involvement between offender and treatment staff. Such long-term therapy not only is very expensive, it also markedly limits the number of patients who can be treated in any one period. This in turn encourages careful selection of those patients most likely to benefit. This operates against the treatment of the most dangerous offenders. If society's response to sexual assault is to be based on an empirically driven model, programs have to be developed which offer access to a large number of offenders at a reasonable cost.

SUMMARY AND CONCLUSIONS

Applying standard scientific criteria to existing outcome studies, it is clear that the effectiveness of treatment is uncertain at this time. We nonetheless suggest a number of guidelines regarding treatment. First, treatment that seeks to modify a single problem or pathology is not likely to succeed. A good example of a treatment approach focusing on a single problem is conditioning to reduce deviant sexual arousal. A review of the literature failed to find evidence that such an approach reduces the likelihood of reoffending. Second, programs which fail to define clearly the nature of the problems that need to be addressed in sex offenders are not likely to succeed. Good examples of programs which fail to define carefully the within-treatment goals are the nonbehavioral psychotherapies that have been used. Sexual offenses are the final result of a complex interaction of physiological, cognitive, and situational variables. Accordingly, a comprehensive treatment program which targets deficits and excesses considered to be important is our best hope for preventing reoffending. Last, comprehensive programs need to effectively integrate the criminal justice and mental health systems; treatment and corrections can and should be mutually reinforcing.

Society's emerging and evolving response to the problem of sexual offending involves many components. Prevention programs educate victims and potential victims, as well as potential offenders. Increasing public awareness makes it more difficult for offenders to escape detection, apprehension, and intervention. Continued political and social pressure may change attitudes and behaviors which have caused or condoned sexual assaults. Changes and improvements in the legal system will bring more offenders to prosecution. However, prevention, education, and political and legal action are not sufficient to solve the problem of the sex offender. Once sentenced and incarcerated, offenders will someday be released. Their treatment and continued management is a crucial part of any intelligent response to the problem of sexual assault.

REFERENCES

Abel, G. G., Becker, J. V., Mittelman, M., Cunningham-Rathner, J. , Rouleau, J. L., & Murphy, W. D. (1987). Self-reported sex crimes of nonincarcerated paraphiliacs. *Journal of Interpersonal Violence, 2,* 3–25.

Abel, G. G., Barlow, D. H., Blanchard, E. B., & Guild, D. (1977). The components of rapists' sexual arousal. *Archives of General Psychiatry, 34,* 895–903.

Abel, G. G., Becker, J. V., Cunningham-Rathner, J., & Mittelman, M. (1988). Multiple paraphilic diagnoses among sex offenders. *Bulletin of the American Academy of Psychiatry and the Law, 16,* 153–168.

Abel, G. G., Gore, D. K., Holland, C. L., Camp, N., Becker, J. V., & Rathner, J. (1989). The assessment of the cognitive distortions of child molesters. *Annals of Sex Research, 2,* 135–153.

American Psychiatric Association. (1994). *Diagnostic and statistical manual of mental disorders* (4th ed.). Washington, DC: Author.

Barbaree, H. E., Bogaert, A. F., & Seto, M. C. (1995). Sexual reorientation therapy: Practices and controversies. In L. Diamant & R. D. McAnulty (Eds.), *The psychology of sexual orientation, behavior, and identity: A handbook* (pp. 357–383). Westport, CT: Greenwood.

Barbaree, H. E., & Cortoni, F. A. (1993). Treatment of the juvenile sex offender within the criminal justice and mental health systems. In H. E. Barbaree, W. L. Marshall, & S. M. Hudson (Eds.), *The juvenile sex offender* (pp. 243–263). New York: Guilford Press.

Barbaree, H. E., & Marshall, W. L. (1988). Deviant sexual arousal, offense history, and demographic variables as predictors of reoffense among child molesters. *Behavioral Sciences and the Law, 6,* 267–280.

Barbaree, H. E., & Marshall, W. L. (1989). Erectile responses among heterosexual child molesters, father–daughter incest offenders, and matched non-offenders: Five distinct age preference profiles. *Canadian Journal of Behavioural Science, 21,* 70–82.

Barbaree, H. E., & Peacock, E. J. (1995). Assessment of sexual preferences in cases of alleged child sexual abuse. In T. Ney (Ed.), *True and false allegations in child sexual abuse.* New York: Brunner/Mazel.

Beitchman, J. H., Zucker, K. J., Hood, J. E., DaCosta, G. A., Akman, D., & Cassavia, E. (1992). A review of the long-term effects of child sexual abuse. *Child Abuse and Neglect, 16,* 101 118.

Berlin, F. S., & Meinecke, C. F. (1981). Treatment of sex offenders with antiandrogenic medication: Conceptualization, review of treatment modalities and preliminary findings. *American Journal of Psychiatry, 138,* 601–608.

Bradford, J. M. W. (1985). Organic treatments for the male sexual offender. *Behavioral Sciences and the Law, 3,* 355–375.

Bradford, J. M. W., & Pawlak, A. (1987). Sadistic homosexual pedophilia: treatment with cyproterone acetate: a single case study. *Canadian Journal of Psychiatry, 32,* 22–30.

Bradford, J. M. W., & Pawlak, A. (1993). Effects of cyproterone acetate on sexual arousal patterns of pedophiles. *Archives of Sexual Behavior, 22,* 629–641.

Brancale, R., Vnocolo, A., & Prendergast, W. E. (1972). The New Jersey Program for sex offenders. In H. L. P. Resnick & M. F. Wolfgang (Eds.), *Sexual behaviors: Social, clinical, and legal aspects* (pp. 331–350). Boston: Little, Brown.

Cabeen, C. W., & Coleman, J. C. (1961). Group therapy with sex offenders: Description and evaluation of a group therapy program in an institutional setting. *Journal of Clinical Psychology, 17,* 122–129.

Carey, C. H., & McGrath, R. J. (1989). Coping with urges and craving. In D. R. Laws (Ed.), *Relapse prevention with sex offenders* (pp. 188–196). New York: Guilford Press.

Castell, R., & Yalom, I. (1972). Institutional group therapy. In H. L. P. Resnick & M. F. Wolfgang (Eds.), *Sexual behaviors: Social, clinical, and legal aspects* (pp. 305–330). Boston: Little, Brown.

Conrad, S. R., & Winnze, J. P. (1976). Orgasmic reconditioning: A controlled study of its effects upon sexual arousal and behavior of adult homosexuals. *Behavior Therapy, 7,* 155–166.

Conte, J. R. (1988). The effects of sexual abuse on children: Results of a research project. In R. A. Prentky & V. L. Quinsey (Eds.), *Human sexual aggression: Current perspectives* (pp. 310–326). New York: New York Academy of Sciences.

Cooper, A. J., Sandhu, S., Losztyn, S., & Cernovsky, Z. (1992). A double-blind placebo controlled trial of medroxyprogesterone acetate and cyproterone acetate with seven pedophiles. *Canadian Journal of Psychiatry, 37,* 687–693.

Earls, C. M., & Marshall, W. L. (1983). The current state of technology in the laboratory assessment of sexual arousal patterns. In J. G. Greer & I. R. Stuart (Eds.), *The sexual aggressor: Current perspectives on treatment* (pp. 336–362). New York: Van Nostrand Reinhold.

Federoff, J. P. (1993). Serotonergic drug treatment of deviant sexual interests. *Annals of Sex Research, 6,* 105–121.

Finkelhor, D. (1994). The international epidemiology of child sexual abuse. *Child Abuse and Neglect, 18,* 409–417.

Finkelhor, D. , Hotaling, G. , Lewis, I. A., & Smith, C. (1990). Sexual abuse in a national sample of adult men and women: Prevalence, characteristics, and risk factors. *Child Abuse and Neglect, 14,* 19–28.

Foa, E. B., & Emmelkamp, P. M. G. (1983). *Failures in behavior therapy.* New York: Wiley.

Freund, K. (1967). Erotic preference in pedophilia. *Behaviour Research and Therapy, 5,* 339–348.

Freund, K. (1981). Assessment of pedophilia. In M. Cook & K. Howells (Eds.), *Adult sexual interest in children* (pp. 139–179). London: Academic Press.

Freund, K. (1991). Reflections on the development of the phallometric method of assessing erotic preferences. *Annals of Sex Research, 4,* 221–228.

Freund, K., & Blanchard, R. (1989). Phallometric diagnosis of pedophilia. *Journal of Consulting and Clinical Psychology, 57,* 100–105.

Freund, K., McKnight, C. K., Langevin, R., & Cibiri, S. (1972). The female child as a surrogate object. *Archives of Sexual Behavior, 2,* 119–133.

Freund, K., & Watson, R. J. (1991). Assessment of the sensitivity and specificity of a phallometric test: An update of phallometric diagnosis of pedophilia. *Psychological Assessment, 3,* 254–260.

Freund, K., Watson, R., & Dickey, R. (1991). Sex offenses against female children perpetrated by men who are not pedophiles. *Journal of Sex Research, 28,* 409–423.

Furby, L., Weinrott, M. R., & Blackshaw, L. (1989). Sex offender recidivism: A review. *Psychological Bulletin, 105,* 3–30.

Gagne, P. (1981). Treatment of sex offenders with medroxyprogesterone acetate. *American Journal of Psychiatry, 138,* 644–646.

Gibbens, T. C. N., Soothill, K. L., & Way, C. K. (1981). Sex offenses against young girls: A long-term record study. *Psychological Medicine, 11,* 351–357.

Gijs, L., & Gooren, L. (1996). Hormonal and psychopharmacological interventions in the treatment of paraphilias: An update. *Journal of Sex Research, 33,* 273–290.

Griffiths, D., Hindsburger, D., & Christian, R. (1985). Treating developmentally handicapped sexual offenders: The York Behaviour Management Services treatment program. *Psychiatric Aspects of Mental Retardation Reviews, 4,* 49–52.

Groth, A. N. (1983). Treatment of the sexual offender in a correctional institution. In J. Greer & I. Stuart (Eds.), *The sexual aggressor: Current perspectives on treatment* (pp. 160–176). New York: Von Nostrand Reinhold.

Hall, G. C. N. (1995). Sexual offender recidivism revisited: A meta-analysis of recent treatment studies. *Journal of Consulting and Clinical Psychology, 63,* 802–809.

Hanson, R. K., Cox, B. J., & Woszcyzyna, C. (1991). Assessing treatment outcome for sexual offenders. *Annals of Sex Research, 3,* 177–208.

Hanson, R. K., Steffy, R. A., & Gauthier, R. (1993). Long-term recidivism of child molesters. *Journal of Consulting and Clinical Psychology, 61,* 646–652.

Hucker, S. J., Langevin, R. , & Bain, J. (1988). A double-blind trial of sex drive reducing medication in pedophiles. *Annals of Sex Research, 1,* 227–242.

Jenkins-Hall, K. D., & Marlatt, G. A. (1989). Apparently irrelevant decisions in the relapse process. In D. R. Laws (Ed.), *Relapse prevention with sex offenders* (pp. 47–55). New York: Guilford Press.

Kaplan, M. S., Abel, G. G., Cunningham-Rathner, J., & Mittelman, M. S. (1990). The impact of parolees' perception of confidentiality of their self-reported sex crimes. *Annals of Sex Research, 3,* 293–303.

Kelly, J. R. (1982). Behavioral reorientation of pedophiliacs: Can it be done? *Clinical Psychology Review, 2,* 387–408.

Knight, R. A., & Prentky, R. A. (1990). Classifying sexual offenders: The development and corroboration of taxonomic models. In W. L. Marshall, D. R. Laws, & H. E. Barbaree (Eds.), *Handbook of sexual assault: Issues, theories, and treatment of the offender* (pp. 23–52). New York: Plenum Press.

Kreusi, M. P. J., Fine, S., Valladares, L. Phillips, R. A., & Rapoport, J. (1992). Paraphilias: A double blind cross-over comparison of clomipramine versus desipramine. *Archives of Sexual Behavior, 21,* 587–593.

Lalumière, M. L., & Earls, C. M. (1992). Voluntary control of penile responses as a function of stimulus duration and instructions. *Behavioral Assessment, 14,* 121–132.

Langevin, R., Paitich, D., Hucker, S. J., Newman, S., Ramsay, G., Pope, S., Geller, G., & Anderson, C. (1979). The effect of assertiveness training, Provera, and sex of therapist in the treatment of genital exhibitionism. *Journal of Behavior Therapy and Experimental Psychiatry, 10,* 275–282.

Laschet, U. (1973). Anti-androgen in the treatment of sex offenders: Mode of action and therapeutic outcome. In J. Zubin & J. Money (Eds.), *Contemporary sexual behavior: Critical issues in the 1970s* (pp. 311–319). Baltimore, MD: Johns Hopkins University Press.

Laws, D. R., & Marshall, W. L. (1990). A conditioning theory of the etiology and maintenance of deviant sexual preference and behavior. In W. L. Marshall, D. R. Laws, & H. E. Barbaree (Eds.), *Handbook of sexual assault: Issues, theories, and treatment of the offender* (pp. 209–229). New York: Plenum Press.

Laws, D. R., & Marshall, W. L. (1991). Masturbatory reconditioning with sexual deviates: An evaluative review. *Advances in Behavior Research and Therapy, 13,* 13–25.

Laws, D. R., Meyer, J., & Holmen, M. L. (1978). Reduction of sadistic sexual arousal by olfactory aversion: A case study. *Behaviour Research and Therapy, 16,* 281–285.

Laws, D. R., & Rubin, H. B. (1969). Instructional control of an automatic response. *Journal of Applied Behavior Analysis, 2,* 93–99.

Levin, S. M., Barry, S. M., Gambaro, S., Wolfinsohn, L., & Smith, A. (1977). Variations of covert sensitization in the treatment of pedophilic behavior: A case study. *Journal of Consulting and Clinical Psychology, 45,* 896–907.

Lomis, M. J. & Baker, L. L. (1981, March). *Medroxyprogesterone acetate in the treatment of sex offenders: A literature review.* Paper presented at the Third National Conference on the Evaluation and Treatment of Sexual Aggressives, Avila Beach, CA.

Longo, R. E., & Groth, A. N. (1983). Juvenile sexual offenses in the histories of adult rapists and child molesters. *International Journal of Offender Therapy and Comparative Criminology, 27,* 150–155.

MacDonald, R. K., & Pithers, W. D. (1989). Self-monitoring to identify high-risk situations. In D. R. Laws (Ed.), *Relapse prevention with sex offenders* (pp. 96–104). New York: Guilford Press.

Malcolm, P. B., Andrews, D. A., & Quinsey, V. L. (1993). Discriminant and predictive validity of phallometrically measured sexual age and gender preference. *Journal of Interpersonal Violence, 8,* 486–501.

Marlatt, G. A., & Gordon, J. R. (1980). Determinants of relapse: Implications for the maintenance of behavior change. In P. O. Davidson & S. M. Davidson (Eds.), *Behavioral medicine: Changing health lifestyles* (pp. 410–452). New York: Brunner/Mazel.

Marlatt, G. A., & Gordon, J. R. (1985). *Relapse prevention: Maintenance strategies in the treatment of the addictive behaviors.* New York: Guilford Press.

Marques, J. K., Day, D. M., Nelson, C. , & West, M. A. (1994). Effects of cognitive-behavioral treatment on sex offender recidivism: Preliminary results of a longitudinal study. *Criminal Justice and Behavior, 21,* 28–54.

Marshall, W. L., & Barbaree, H. E. (1988). The long-term evaluation of a behavioral treatment program for child molesters. *Behaviour Research and Therapy, 26,* 499–511.

Marshall, W. L., & Barbaree, H. E. (1990). Outcome of comprehensive cognitive-behavioral treatment programs. In W. L. Marshall, D. R., Laws, & H. E. Barbaree (Eds.), *Handbook of sexual assault: Issues, theories, and treatment of the offender* (pp. 363–385). New York: Plenum Press.

Marshall, W. L., Barbaree, H. E., & Butt, J. (1988). Sexual offenders against male children: Sexual preferences for gender, age of victim, and type of behavior. *Behaviour Research and Therapy, 26,* 383–391.

Marshall, W. L., Jones, R., Ward, T., Johnston, P., & Barbaree, H. E. (1991). Treatment outcome with sex offenders. *Clinical Psychology Review, 11,* 465–485.

Meyer, L., & Romero, J. (1980). *A ten-year follow-up of sex offender recidivism.* Philadelphia: Joseph J. Peters Institute.

Meyer, W. J., III, Walker, P. A., Emory, L. E., & Smith, E. R. (1985). Physical, metabolic, and hormonal effects on men of long-term therapy with medroxyprogesterone acetate. *Fertility and Sterility, 43,* 102–109.

Money, J. (1970). Use of androgen-depleting hormone in the treatment of male sexual offenders. *Journal of Sex Research, 6,* 165–172.

Murphy, W. D., & Barbaree, H. E. (1994). *Assessments of sex offenders by measures of erectile response: Psychometric properties and decision making.* Brandon, VT: Safer Society Press.

Murphy, W. D., Haynes, M. R., Stalgaitis, S. J., & Flanagan, B. (1986). Differential sexual responding among four groups of sexual offenders against children. *Journal of Psychopathology and Behavioral Assessment, 8,* 339–353.

Nathan, P. E., & Lansky, D. (1978). Common methodological problems in research on the addictions. *Journal of Consulting and Clinical Psychology, 46,* 713–726.

Nelson, C., & Jackson, P. (1989). High-risk recognition: The cognitive-behavioral chain. In D. R. Laws (Ed.), *Relapse prevention with sex offenders* (pp. 167–177). New York: Guilford Press.

Nichols, H. R., & Molinder, I. (1984). *Multiphasic Sex Inventory manual.* (Available from the authors, 437 Bowes Drive, Tacoma, WA, 98466.)

O'Donohue, W. T., & Letourneau, E. (1992). The psychometric properties of the penile tumescence assessment of child molesters. *Journal of Psychopathology and Behavioral Assessment, 14,* 123–174.

Ortmann, J. (1980). The treatment of sexual offenders: Castration and antihormone therapy. *International Journal of Law and Psychiatry, 3,* 443–451.

Pacht, A. R., Halleck, S. L., & Ehrmann, J. C. (1962). Diagnosis and treatment of the sexual offender: A nine year study. *American Journal of Psychiatry, 118,* 802–808.

Paitich, D., Langevin, R., Freeman, R., Mann, K., & Handy, L. (1977). The Clarke SHQ: A clinical sex history questionnaire for males. *Archives of Sexual Behavior, 6,* 421–436.

Peters, J. J., Pedigo, J. M., Steg, V., & McKenna, J. J. (1968). Group psychotherapy of the sex offender. *Federal Probation, 32,* 41–46.

Pithers, W. D. (1990). Relapse prevention with sexual aggressors: A method for maintaining therapeutic gain and enhancing external supervision. In W. L. Marshall, D. R. Laws, & H. E. Barbaree (Eds.), *Handbook of sexual assault: Issues, theories, and treatment of the offender* (pp. 343–361). New York: Plenum Press.

Pithers, W. D., Beal, L. S., Armstrong, J., & Petty, J. (1989). Identification of risk factors through clinical interviews and analysis of records. In D. R. Laws (Ed.), *Relapse prevention with sex offenders* (pp. 77–87). New York: Guilford Press.

Pithers, W. D., Marques, J. K., Gibat, C. C., & Marlatt, G. A. (1983). Relapse prevention with sexual aggressives: A self-control model of treatment and maintenance of change. In J. G. Greer & I. R. Stuart (Eds.), *The sexual aggressor: Current perspectives on treatment* (pp. 214–239). New York: Von Nostrand Reinhold.

Quinsey, V. L. (1983). Prediction of recidivism and the evaluation of treatment programs for sex offenders. In S. Simon-James & A. A. Keltner (Eds.), *Sexual aggression and the law* (pp. 27–37). Burnaby, BC: Criminology Research Centre.

Quinsey, V. L., & Chaplin, T. C. (1988). Preventing faking in phallometric assessment of sexual preference. In R. A. Prentky & V. L. Quinsey (Eds.), *Human sexual aggression: Current perspectives* (pp. 49–58). New York: New York Academy of Sciences.

Quinsey, V. L., Chaplin, T. C., & Carrigan, W. F. (1979). Sexual preferences among incestuous and nonincestuous child molesters. *Behavior Therapy, 10,* 562–565.

Quinsey, V. L., Chaplin, T. C., & Carrigan, W. F. (1980). Biofeedback and signaled punishment in the modification of inappropriate sexual age preferences. *Behavior Therapy, 11,* 567–576.

Quinsey, V. L., & Lalumière, M. L. (1995). Evolutionary perspectives on sexual offending. *Sexual Abuse, 7,* 301–315.

Quinsey, V. L., & Marshall, W. L. (1983). Procedures for reducing inappropriate sexual arousal: An evaluative review. In J. G. Greer & I. R. Stuart (Eds.), *The sexual aggressor: Current perspectives on treatment* (pp. 267–289). New York: Van Nostrand Reinhold.

Quinsey, V. L., Rice, M. E., Harris, G. T., & Lalumière, M. L. (1993). Assessing treatment efficacy in outcome studies of sex offenders. *Journal of Interpersonal Violence, 8,* 512–523.

Quinsey, V. L., Steinman, C. M., Bergersen, S. G., & Holmes, T. F. (1975). Penile circumference, skin conductance, and ranking responses of child molesters and "normals" to sexual and nonsexual visual stimuli. *Behavior Therapy, 6,* 213–219.

Rice, M. E., Quinsey, V. L., & Harris, G. T. (1991). Sexual recidivism among child molesters released from a maximum security psychiatric institution. *Journal of Consulting and Clinical Psychology, 59,* 381–386.

Ryan, G., Lane, S., Davis, J., & Isaac, C. (1987). Juvenile sex offenders: Development and correction. *Child Abuse and Neglect, 11,* 385–395.

Saunders, E. B., & Awad, G. A. (1988). Assessment, management, and treatment planning for male adolescent sexual offenders. *American Journal of Orthopsychiatry, 58,* 571–579.

Seto, M. C., Barbaree, H. E., & Maric, A. (1996, November). Sex offender behaviour in treatment as a predictor of proximate treatment outcomes. In H. E. Barbaree (Chair), *Treatment readiness in sex offenders*. Symposium conducted at the 15th Annual Research and Treatment Conference of the Association for Treatment of Sexual Abusers, Chicago, IL.

Seto, M. C., Lalumière, M. L., & Kuban, M. (1997). *The sexual age preferences of incestuous and nonincestuous child molesters*. Manuscript submitted for publication.

Steenman, H. , Nelson, C. , & Viesti, C. J. (1989). Developing coping strategies for high risk situations. In D. R. Laws (Ed.), *Relapse prevention with sex offenders* (pp. 178–187). New York: Guilford Press.

Sturup, G. K. (1972). Castration: The total treatment. In H. L. P. Resnick & M. F. Wolfgang (Eds.), *Sexual behaviors: Social, clinical, and legal aspects* (pp. 361–382). Boston: Little, Brown.

Ward, T., Louden, K., Hudson, S.M., & Marshall, W.L. (1995). A descriptive model of the offense chain for child molesters. *Journal of Interpersonal Violence, 10,* 452–472.

Welham, C. V. J. (1990). Incest: An evolutionary model. *Ethology and Sociobiology, 11,* 97–111.

Wille, R., & Beier, K. M. (1989). Castration in Germany. *Annals of Sex Research, 2,* 103–133.

10

SEXUAL SADISM

Psychopathology and Theory

Stephen J. Hucker

The term "sadism" was originally used in the French medical literature of the early 19th century in connection with the writings of the Marquis de Sade, whose novels depicted scenes of torture, cruelty, and killing for erotic purposes. Later, it was taken up by Krafft-Ebing (1886/1965), whose *Psychopathia Sexualis* remains a classic source of case material on sexual sadism and other sexual anomalies. For Krafft-Ebing sadism centered on

> the experience of sexual, pleasurable sensations (including orgasm) produced by acts of cruelty, bodily punishment afflicted on one's person or when witnessed in others, be they animals or human beings. It may also consist of an innate desire to humiliate, hurt, wound or even destroy others in order, thereby, to create sexual pleasure in ones self. (p. 109)

Other writers emphasized the infliction of pain as the main feature of sadism. Thus, Schrenck-Notzing (1895/1956) coined the term "algolagnia" (pain craving) and divided the category into active (sadism) and passive (masochism) forms, conceptualizing them as two poles of the same disorder. Eulenberg (1911) expanded this definition to include psychic (i.e., humiliation) as well as physical pain. Karpman (1954, p. 10) indicated that in the sadist "the will to power is sexually accentuated" and "he revels in the fear, anger and the humiliation of the victim." Hence, pain is important not in itself but because it symbolizes power and control. Fromm (1977) proposed that the "core of sadism . . . is the passion to have absolute and unrestricted control over living beings . . . whether an animal, child, a man or a woman. To force someone to endure pain or humiliation without being able to defend himself is one of the manifestations of absolute control, but it is by no means the only one. The person who has complete control over another living being makes this being into his thing, his property, while he becomes the other being's god" (pp. 383–384). This passage is highly reminiscent of the personal account written by the sadist reported by Dietz, Hazelwood, and Warren (1990, p. 165). The central importance of the eroticized feelings of power and control are also emphasized by Brittain (1970) and by MacCulloch, Snowden, Wood, and Mills (1983).

More recent official classifications retain a broad conceptualization. Thus, ICD-10 (World Health Organization, 1992) defines sadism as "preference for sexual activity that involves bondage or infliction of pain or humiliation." DSM-IV (American Psychiatric Association, 1994, p. 530) requires the following criteria:

A. Over a period of at least 6 months, recurrent, intense sexually arousing fantasies, sexual urges, or behaviors involving acts (real, not simulated) in which the psychological or physical suffering (including humiliation) of the victim is sexually exciting to the person.

B. The fantasies, sexual urges, or behaviors cause clinically significant stress or impairment in social, occupational, or other important areas of functioning.

One study using DSM-III-R (American Psychiatric Association, 1987) criteria for sexual sadism (Hucker et al., 1988) found high diagnostic agreement between experienced forensic practitioners in their cases. However, Knight, Prentky, and Cerce (1994), in developing their Multidimensional Assessment of Sex and Aggression (MASA), found great difficulty in operationalizing sexual sadism. Their group had previously experienced problems in achieving reliability and differentiating sadism from other types of violent sexual aggression (Knight & Prentky, 1990; Prentky & Knight, 1991).

PREVALENCE

There is little certain knowledge of the prevalence of sexual sadism in the community. Kinsey, Pomeroy, Martin, and Gebhard (1953) found that 3% to 12% of women and 10% to 20% of men admitted to responding sexually to sadomasochistic narratives. Crepault and Couture (1980) found that among their sample of men in the general population, there was a 14.9% incidence of fantasies of humiliating a woman and 10.7% of beating up a woman. Arndt, Foehl, and Good (1985) found that about one third of women and about 50% of men had sexual fantasies of tying up their partner. However, it is not clear whether these represent sustained, *preferred* activities or, as seems more likely, part of a repertoire of activities that may be carried out from time to time. Also of note is that 10% to 20% of pornographic magazines feature bondage and discipline themes (Dietz & Evans, 1982). Finally, Hunt (1974) found that 5% of men and 2% of women reported they obtained sexual gratification from inflicting pain. Krafft-Ebing (1886/1965) stated that sadistic acts were more common in men and argued that subjugation of women was the natural inclination of males. It is, therefore, paradoxical that in advertisements in magazines, as well as in sadomasochistic pornography, there is a predominance of female dominatrices (Weinberg, 1987), though it is likely that these women are prostitutes specializing in this clientele (Breslow, Evans, & Langley, 1985; Scott, 1983).

ASSOCIATED FEATURES

Even allowing for definitional problems, research has found that sadism is commonly found in association with other paraphilias. Many authors consider sadism and masochism to be complementary anomalies (e.g., Karpman, 1954). The finding that individuals with masochistic fantasies often have sadistic fantasies as well (Arndt et al., 1985) supports this notion. Spengler (1977), in a survey of self-identified West German sadomasochists, found that 29% alternated between dominant and submissive roles. Hucker and Blanchard (1992) also noted

an association between asphyxiophilia (extreme masochism) and sadistic murder (Smith &
Braun, 1978).

Abel et al.'s work on the overlap of paraphilic diagnoses, derived from subjects whose
confidentiality could be guaranteed (Abel, Mittelman, & Becker, 1985), therefore is
especially enlightening. These authors found that, on average, paraphiliacs with one
diagnosis have two or three others as well, often not initially admitted or recognized (see
also Freund et al., Chapter 6, this volume). Thus, 18% of sadists were also masochistic and
46% had also engaged in rape, 21% in exhibitionism, 25% each in voyeurism and frottage,
and about a third in pedophilia (Abel, Becker, Cunningham-Rathner, Mittelman, & Rouleau,
1988). Other authors have noted an overlap between sadism, masochism, fetishism, and
transvestism (Gosselin & Wilson, 1980) in samples of self-identified sadomasochists. Among
much more serious sadistic offenders, transvestism and fetishism are strongly represented
(Dietz et al., 1990; Prentky, Cohen, & Seghorn, 1985).

It is well recognized that not all those who engage in cruelty, torture, and so forth are
sexually aroused while engaging in such behavior (Dietz et al., 1990; Hazelwood, Dietz, &
Warren, 1992). Interest has developed in the possibility of including a sadistic personality
disorder in the *Diagnostic and Statistical Manual of Mental Disorders* (Fiester, 1991; Simons,
1987). Several previous authors, mainly psychoanalysts, documented the essential features
of a sadistic personality disorder (Fenichel, 1945; Kernberg, 1970; Schad-Somers, 1982).
The criteria suggested in DSM-III-R included "a pervasive pattern of cruel, demeaning, and
aggressive behavior directed toward other people, beginning by early adulthood" (p. 371).
There was considerable overlap with personality disorders, in particular, antisocial and
narcissistic subtypes (Spitzer, Fiester, Gay, & Pfohl, 1991). However, there appeared to be
insufficient evidence to support the inclusion of sadistic personality disorder as a separate
diagnostic category in DSM-IV.

TYPES OF SADISTIC BEHAVIOR

Krafft-Ebing (1886/1965) subclassified sexual sadism into several categories including:

1. Lust–murder. Here he included cases in which there was a connection between sexual
    arousal and killing which may extend to anthrophagy or cannibalism (eating body
    parts of the victim). Among examples he included "Jack the Ripper" and similar
    types of homicide.
2. Mutilation of corpses or necrophilia.
3. Injury to females (stabbing, flagellation, etc.).
4. Defilement of women.
5. Other kinds of assaults on women—symbolic sadism in which, for example, the
    perpetrator cuts the hair of his victims rather than harming them directly.
6. Ideal sadism or sadistic fantasies alone without acts.
7. Sadism with other objects, for example, whipping boys.
8. Sadistic acts with animals.

Hirschfeld (1956) more simply distinguished "major" and "minor" categories. The former
includes such acts as stabbing, lust–murder, and necrophilia. The rest of Krafft-Ebing's
subcategories he relegated to his "minor" category. These include the sadistic fantasies that
are not acted on as well as actual humiliation of a consenting partner by means of bondage,
mild flagellation, or submission to degrading acts.

Those who participate in giving or receiving acts of minor sadism in a consenting relationship often refer to the activity as "bondage and discipline," "dominance and submission," or "sadomasochism" (Gosselin, 1987; Weinberg, Williams, & Moser, 1984). In these activities, the dominant partner places the submissive one in a position of helplessness and then applies some form of discipline or punishment, usually accompanied by verbal degradation. Administration of pain, humiliation, or bondage is effected through such acts as whipping or fisting (inserting a fist into the anus or vagina; see Spengler, 1977). Use of the roles of master–slave, governess–pupil, and so forth, ensures a tone of humiliation, as does cross-dressing the submissive, treating him or her like an animal, and sometimes urinating or defecating on his or her body. The submissive may be further humiliated by being forced to wear a diaper or to lick the dominant's boots. Flagellation or flogging is almost exclusively applied to the buttocks. Bondage, including the use of gags and blindfolds to render the submissive helpless and immobile, are also common elements. The breasts of a female submissive may be bound tightly and clothespins or clamps may be attached to the nipples of either sex or to the penis, in the case of a male submissive. In "water sports" the submissive partner is urinated upon or forced to drink the dominant's urine. Enemas may be administered to deprive the submissive of control of his or her bodily functions and he or she may be forced to retain the enema for uncomfortably long periods. Sadomasochistic partnerships are a specialized subculture in the homosexual community and in large cities networks exist for those who have this interest.

Early identification of "dangerous" or "predatory" sadism is often difficult. Some rapists may begin their careers with apparently nonsexual crimes such as burglaries during which they rape their victims (Revitch, 1978; Ressler, Burgess, & Douglas, 1983), but later they manifest clear-cut predatory sadism. Some predatory cases may be preceded initially by patterns of mildly sadistic behavior (see Freund et al., Chapter 6, this volume) or the predatory pattern may have been present from the outset but not disclosed by the subject.

Major, dangerous, or predatory sadism includes piqueurism, in which the assailant stabs a female victim, usually in the breast or buttocks, and then escapes (de River, 1958; Eulenberg, 1911). Vampirism, a rare anomaly, involves sexual arousal from drawing, and sometimes drinking, blood by cutting or biting (Jaffe & DiCataldo, 1994). In some cases, the individual will draw blood from him or herself for this purpose (McCully, 1964; Prins, 1985; Vanden Bergh & Kelly, 1964). Closely related to vampirism are the phenomena of necrophilia, the erotic attraction to corpses, and lust–murder.

Necrophilia

As with sexual sadism, at first sight this term appears to identify a fairly clear-cut aberration of sexual behavior. The concept has been employed in a variety of ways and extended to behavior that does not involve physical contact with corpses at all. Similarly, some authors have described "neurotic equivalents" of necrophilia (Calef & Weinshel, 1972; Reider, 1976) which include nebulous descriptions derived from conscious and unconscious fantasy material produced during psychoanalytic sessions. Krafft-Ebing (1886/1965) regarded necrophilia as a manifestation of sadism, although Moll (1912) and Ellis (1936) noted that infliction of pain is not necessarily a feature. However, Krafft-Ebing (1886/1965, p. 129) seemed aware of this and noted that in some cases

> there is undoubtedly some direct preference for a corpse to a living woman. When no other act of cruelty—cutting into pieces etc.,—is practised on the cadaver, it is probable that the lifeless condition itself, forms the stimulus for the perverse individual. It is possible that the corpse—a

human form absolutely without will—satisfies an abnormal desire, in that the object of desire is seen to be capable of absolute subjugation, without possibility of resistance.

These cases show a strong fetishistic component (Ellis, 1936). Like Krafft-Ebing, Hirschfeld (1956) agreed that necrophiliacs could be divided into those who violate an individual who already is dead and those who sexually abuse the corpse of a victim that they, themselves, have murdered, the act deriving from a "frenzied intensification of the aggressive and destructive impulse. The murderer is not satisfied by merely killing his victim; he also wants to possess her and destroy her beyond death" (p. 425).

Wulffen (1910) divided necrophilia into three types: lust–murder or "necrosadism," in which the murder precedes the sexual act with the corpse; "necrostuprum," in which the necrophiliac steals the corpse; and "necrophagy," in which the necrophiliac mutilates and eats part of the corpse. In the nineteenth century the term "vampire" was applied to individuals engaging in this kind of behavior; two of the classic cases of necrophilia in the literature (Bertrand, the Vampire of Paris, and Ardisson, the Vampire of Muy, cited by Krafft-Ebing [1885/1965] from French authors) are examples of this.

Rosman and Resnick (1989), in a review of reported and unreported cases of necrophilia, discriminated "genuine" necrophilia, in which the subjects fulfilled DSM-III-R criteria, from pseudonecrophilia. The former included the presence, over a period of at least 6 months, of recurrent and intense urges and sexually arousing fantasies involving corpses which are either acted upon or have been markedly distressing. "Pseudonecrophilia," on the other hand, included "incidental" cases in which the subject had sexual relations with cadavers without preexisting fantasies of so doing, "necrophilic homicide," in which the subject committed a murder to obtain the body with which to engage in sexual activity, and "necrophilic fantasy" of activity with corpses without actually carrying out the fantasy.

The behavior that those categorized as necrophiles engage in may be quite varied. Some appear content with being in the presence of a corpse, but some may kiss, fondle, or perform sexual intercourse or cunnilingus to the corpse (Hucker, 1990). Others engage in even more grotesque behavior, such as mutilating the corpse (Krafft-Ebing, 1886/1965) or drinking the corpse's blood or urine (de River, 1958). Rosman and Resnick (1989) found that pseudone-crophiles engaged in mutilation and, less commonly, necrophagia more frequently than did genuine necrophiles. Especially alarming are those who murder to obtain a body for subsequent sexual violation or for whom the act of killing itself appears to generate sexual frenzy (Brittain, 1970; Podolsky, 1965; Ressler, Burgess, Hartman, Douglas, & McCormack, 1986). Among Rosman and Resnick's (1989) total sample of necrophiles, 42% committed homicide. Smith and Braun's (1978) subject needed to have complete control over his sexual partners, by them either simulating death or unconsciousness or by strangling them himself to achieve the same result. However, it appears that sadism is not an intrinsic characteristic of true necrophilia (Rosman & Resnick, 1989).

Sadistic and Lust Murders

Lust murders are those in which the killer derives sexual arousal from killing (Arndt, 1991; Krafft-Ebing, 1886/1965; Bartholemew, Milte, & Galbally, 1975) and sexual sadism is the usual underlying paraphilia (Brittain, 1970; Dietz et al., 1990; Ressler, Burgess, & Douglas, 1988). In some cases there may be no actual sexual contact with the victim, as the killing replaces the sexual act completely (Podolsky, 1965). Other authors have referred to Brittain's (1970) composite profile of the sadistic murderer, and some of his observations have been supported (e.g., Bartholemew et al., 1975) and others not (Langevin, Ben-Aron, Wright, Marchese, & Handy, 1988). Brittain's (1970) description was of an overcontrolled, introverted, timid, and socially aloof individual who is typically prudish and sanctimonious. He is sexually inexperienced though profoundly deviant, as indicated by a vivid and violent sadistic fantasy life. Vain and egocentric, he has, nevertheless, a low estimate of himself and his crimes give him a feeling of superiority and power that he cannot otherwise achieve. MacCulloch et al. (1983) emphasized the importance of fantasy as a precursor to such offenses. Similarly, Burgess, Hartman, Ressler, Douglas, and McCormack (1986), Ressler et al. (1986), and Prentky et al. (1985) found that relevant sadistic fantasies usually preceded the crimes. Some such offenders reveal these fantasies directly upon questioning whereas others reveal it in their collections of fantasy material, drawings, videotapes, and so on. Often the kinds of pornography that appeal to sadists are not seen as obviously pornographic to others. Detective magazines, *Soldier of Fortune,* and the like may be preferred (Dietz, Harry, & Hazelwood, 1986).

The most detailed studies to date of the extreme types of sexual sadists have been derived from material collected by the FBI (Dietz et al., 1990). All 30 cases were of males, the majority were white, and almost half were married at the time of the offense. Forty-three percent had a history of homosexual experience, 20% cross-dressed, and 20% had a history of other sexually anomalous behavior. Almost half experienced parental infidelity or divorce. Twenty-three percent reported that they had been physically abused, and 20% sexually abused, as children. More than half had no previous criminal record and a number had a reputation in their community as "solid citizens." Fifty percent tended to drive excessively with no clear goal and 30% were "police buffs," collecting police related paraphernalia or modifying their cars to resemble police vehicles. Nearly all had carefully planned their offenses. Abducting their victim and holding them captive for more than 24 hours was common, as was binding, blindfolding, or gagging the victim. Preferred sexual activities were sexual bondage, anal rape, and forced fellatio, though vaginal intercourse and insertion of foreign objects were also common. By definition for inclusion in the study all the subjects had tortured their victims. Seventy-three percent of the victims were murdered. Subjects recorded more than half of their crimes in diaries, audio- and videotapes, photographs, and drawings and 40% kept a memento belonging to the victim. Dietz et al. (1990) made the point that all of the sadistic offenders had profoundly narcissistic personality traits. Other authors have also drawn attention to their self-aggrandizement and media hunger (Brittain, 1970). In Dietz et al.'s (1990) study 50% had a history of drug abuse other than alcohol, and in Langevin et al.'s (1988) research 75% abused nonmedical drugs and 50% were heavy drinkers. Poor socialization and disturbed parent–child relationships were common (Dietz et al., 1990; Langevin et al., 1988) and 40% had antisocial personalities with a strongly narcissistic element (Brittain, 1970). Brittain (1970) noted that many sadistic murders have an "effeminate tinge" and Langevin et al. (1988) also noted a strong tendency for sadists to engage in cross-dressing or to experience gender dysphoria.

A partner assisted more than a third of Dietz et al.'s (1990) subjects in their crimes. Such accomplices are interesting and they illustrate the dominance of one partner over the other (see Wilson & Seaman, 1992, chaps. 4 and 6). Hazelwood, Warren, and Dietz (1993) reported on seven women who became involved with criminal sexual sadists and eight similar cases have been studied subsequently (R. Hazelwood, personal communication, April 15, 1995). Typically, these women are themselves subjected to a subtle process of seduction and transformation involving psychological, physical, and sexual abuse and they gradually become "compliant appendages" of the sexually sadistic man. Some cases involve an extraordinary measure of compliance over long periods of time (see, for example, McGuire & Norton, 1988). On the other hand, the extent of their apparent willingness to be involved in acts of extreme depravity often tests the credibility of testimony they may provide against their former sadistic partners (e.g., Hill, 1995).

Gratzer and Bradford (1995) compared data from Dietz et al.'s (1990) paper with 29 sadistic and 28 nonsadistic sex offenders from their own facility. They found a number of differences between their sadists and those reported by Dietz et al., suggesting that the FBI-identified cases may not be representative of sexual sadists from other sources. Grubin (1994a, 1994b) noted that we know little about men who kill in a sexual context. He presented data on 21 men who killed during the course of a sexual attack, comparing them with 121 rapists who did not kill their victims. There was little to suggest that Brittain's (1970) classic sadistic characteristics distinguished the two groups. However, lifelong difficulties with hetero-sexual relationships and social isolation were very typical of the sexual killers.

There is some evidence to suggest a link between lust murders and autoerotic asphyxia. Two men who practiced autoerotic asphyxia had also committed lust murders or had fantasized committing a murder (Brittain, 1970; Hucker & Blanchard, 1992).

Sadistic Rape

Rape is a complex, multidetermined behavior (Hucker & Stermac, 1992; Marshall & Barbaree, 1984, 1990) and rapists are clearly not a homogeneous group (Prentky & Knight, 1991). Most probably are not paraphilic at all (see Freund et al., Chapter 6, this volume). The degree of deviant arousal as measured by phallometry appears to be associated with the frequency and degree of violence in sexual assault (Abel, Barlow, Blanchard, & Guild, 1977; Becker, Blanchard, & Djenderedjian, 1978), suggesting that deviant arousal charac-terizes the most violent and habitual rapists. Further, some such men show a strong preference for sexually aggressive stimuli, leading to the proposal that some men show a preference for this type of sexual interaction. This has been referred to as the "preferential rape pattern" (Freund, Scher, & Hucker, 1983, 1984), "paraphilic coercive disorder" (Abel, 1989; American Psychiatric Association, 1987), or "biastophilia" (Money, 1990). Such men are sexually aroused by fantasies and urges of forcing themselves sexually on their victims. The sexual sadist is aroused by the use of gratuitous violence, whereas the preferential rapist is thought not to use greater force than is necessary for victim compliance (Abel, 1989), though the offender's estimate may be highly inaccurate. Preferential-rape proneness may involve coercing the victim into fellating the perpetrator or to submitting to anal intercourse, behaviors typical of sexual sadism (Dietz et al., 1990). Similarly, preferential rapists characteristically target strangers, as do sexual sadists (Dietz et al., 1990). Because focusing on unknown victims is a reliable indicator of a disorder of courtship phasing, we may conceptualize predatory sadism as an overlap of a courtship disorder (Freund et al., 1983, 1984) and sexual sadism (see Freund et al., Chapter 6, this volume). Supportive of this notion is that 9 of a sample of 17 serial sexual murderers showed an interest in voyeurism, telephone scatologia, or exhibitionism (Warren, Hazelwood & Dietz, 1992). However, obscene telephone calls by sexual sadists are atypical, as they often involve threats. Similarly, "voyeurism" by sexual sadists may be the result of prowling by night in search of a victim to assault (see Freund et al., Chapter 6, this volume). The sadistic rapist is also distinguished in phallometric assessment by a higher level of arousal to descriptions of physical, but nonsexual, assault on female victims (Abel, 1989). However, the simple dichotomy between sadistic and nonsadist rape has not been supported by the work of Knight and Prentky (1990, 1994). It may be that a range of force is used by rapists and the degree of force is a continuous rather than a categorical variable (McConaghy, 1993).

Most researchers (Abel et al., 1988; Freund et al., 1983, 1984; Groth, 1979) have reported that only 5% to 10% of rapists fulfill DSM-III-R (American Psychiatric Associa-tion, 1987) criteria for sexual sadism, although a number of authors have reported prevalence estimates as high as 45% (Fedora et al., 1992; Hucker et al., 1988). Such disparate estimates may reflect the fact that subjects studied are from very different populations, namely, mental health patients versus correctional inmates, although it is also likely that different researchers have used varying conceptualizations of sexual sadism.

K. Freund (personal communication, May 30, 1995) suggested that the term "dangerous" or "predatory" sadism should be restricted to mean the "erotic drive to cause bodily harm or physical suffering to another organism," whereas the broader concept, involving the desire to humiliate and dominate a partner, could be referred to as "erotic hyperdominance." When one reviews the definition of sexual sadism in DSM-IV (American Psychiatric Association, 1994), it is clear that Freund's categories are subsumed under the one term. DSM-IV suggests that some rapists are sexually aroused by forcing their victims to engage in intercourse, but their arousal is neither increased nor inhibited by their victims' suffering. Rapists as a group do respond with greater arousal to nonsexual violence than do nonrapists (Barbaree, Marshall, & Lanthier, 1979; Quinsey, Lalumière, & Seto, 1994), and violent rapists tend to respond more strongly to depictions of sexual violence than do comparatively less violent rapists (Quinsey et al., 1994). The absolute magnitude of these responses is, however, quite small. Furthermore, rapists do not respond with significant arousal to nonsexual violence perpetrated by men against men. Relative arousal to descriptions of nonsexual violence between men and women appears to occur because of the implied sexual elements in the act, rather than as a pure response to aggression (Quinsey, Chaplin, & Upfold, 1984).

Further complicating discussion of the conceptualization of sexual sadism among rapists is the finding that many "normal," nonoffender males acknowledge sexual arousal to the idea of raping or hurting a woman. Of men who indicate a likelihood that they could rape, 16% to 20% indicate that they experience a great arousal to descriptions of sadomasochistic scenes (Malamuth, Haber, & Feshbach, 1980) and to descriptions in which the victim experiences pain (Malamuth & Check, 1983) than do those who do not admit to this proclivity. Similarly, most young men appear to be more aroused by pictures of women bound and in distress than by pictures of women who are smiling and cooperative (Heilbrun & Leif, 1988), and about half report a willingness to engage in bondage and a third in whipping and spanking (Malamuth, 1988). Among the general male population, 30% report fantasies of tying up and raping a woman (Crepault & Couture, 1980), though whether occasionally or persistently and preferentially is not clear.

Male college students, in another study, estimated that approximately 45% of men would commit a rape if certain that they would not be caught and 32% of women would enjoy being raped if no one were to know (Malamuth, Heim, & Feshbach, 1980). When asked about their own potential, 51% of these men reported some likelihood that they would commit a rape if assured that they would not be caught, whereas only 2% of women reported believing that they would enjoy being raped. On average, about 35% of college-aged males admitted that they might commit a rape under certain circumstances (Malamuth, 1981), although in another sample as many as 60% of males admitted such desires (Briere & Malamuth, 1983). What appears to be sexually arousing to such males is the fantasy of engaging in aggressive sexual activity with a complete stranger, overcoming her initial resistance, and stimulating her to the point that she eventually enjoys the experience. These elements are also present in the fantasies of some sadists, though victim enjoyment of aggression and rape are less salient than the perpetrator's pleasure or gratification. Self-reported likelihood of raping is correlated with the acceptance of rape myths, fantasies about forced sex, and sexual arousal to rape depictions (Malamuth, 1981).

Although these studies may have questionable ecological validity, at least one quarter of males acknowledge using coercion to achieve sexual relations with an unwilling partner (Koss, Gidycz, & Wisniewski, 1987) and 10% to 15% of women report initially being coerced into, then enjoying, sexual activity (McConaghy, 1993). It appears that some degree of coercion in sexual relationships can lead to arousal and enjoyment for both men and women and plays a part in traditional heterosexual courtship behaviors (Ellis, 1936). Common though aggressive themes may be in fantasy or courtship, however, such studies do not provide information regarding the frequency with which truly sadistic fantasies are acted upon, or, more importantly, regarding whether these themes relate to a preferred method of sexual arousal.

ETIOLOGICAL HYPOTHESES

As with other sexual anomalies, up to 75% of males became aware of their sadomasochistic inclination before they left their teens (Breslow et al., 1985; Spengler, 1977). Similarly, although some sadomasochistic men were able to trace back the association between excitement and punishment to some incident in childhood, for the majority the propensity developed without any encouragement from pornography or from other individuals (Breslow et al., 1985). For sadistic females, who reported taking longer to discover their sadomasochistic tendencies than did men, most were drawn into the behavior by men who wanted to be dominated and on so doing discovered that they are able to be excited by it (Scott, 1983).

Psychodynamic Theories

As in other matters, Sigmund Freud's views on sadism and masochism changed over the course of his long professional life, thereby making it difficult to trace the evolution of his thought. He initially conceptualized the association of aggressiveness with sexuality as a combination of "mental impulses" (Freud, 1961). Later, he suggested that a possible explanation was the child's witnessing the "primal scene," coming to view his parents having intercourse as an act of ill treatment or subjugation (Freud, 1961, p. 198).

In *Beyond the Pleasure Principle*, Freud (1920/1961) questioned his earlier view of the connection between libido and aggression and suggested that, rather than deriving from the pleasure principle, sadism derived from the "death instinct." However, this does not explain why some develop sadism whereas others do not, or why, in some, the aggression is directed outward, as in sadism, and in others, inward, as in masochism. As a result of Freud's apparent uncertainty, much theorizing followed. Sadger (1926) thought that children developed a tendency toward sadism when their caretakers both bring sexual pleasure and deny it when initiating toilet training or preventing masturbation. Alternatively, Friedenberg (1956) suggested that teething is the root of sadism. As Siomopoulos and Goldstein (1976) indicated, "a tendency to generalize is apparent in all these theories. To assume that the same psychologic forces operate in the person who enjoys verbally humiliating others and the pathetic man who engages in ritualistic spanking before sexual intercourse as well as the psychotic patient who molests and mutilates or kills his victim would be, we think, a gross violation of common sense" (p. 632). Psychodynamic explanations have tended to be based on case studies or small samples and overgeneralized, and their authors usually do not clearly define their terms (Breslow, 1989).

Behavioral Views

Typically the behavioral literature has been more concerned with treatment than with etiological issues; sadistic and masochistic behavior have not usually been discussed as individual entities. Raymond (1956) suggested that an individual develops a rapid association, rather like imprinting, during some early sexual experience. In this way, he explained the development of a fetish for female stockings when the individual saw his mother's stockings hanging in the bathroom while he was masturbating. As most people do not develop fetishes so quickly, he suggested some have a predisposition to rapid pairings. Others suggested a slower process of pairing in which the individual has some experience in which he is sexually excited and then incorporates it into masturbation fantasies which are later modified and reinforced (McGuire, Carlisle, & Young, 1965). However, as with sexual behavior generally, sadism is a complex behavior which is difficult to modify using behavioral treatments (Mees, 1966).

Endocrine Abnormalities

Among a group of 20 sadists (Bain, Langevin, Dickey, & Ben-Aron, 1987) there were no differences, when compared with controls, on nine different hormones, including sex hormones. On the other hand, some individuals had undoubted chromosome or endocrine abnormalities such as Klinefelter's syndrome (see also Money, 1990; Money & Lamacz, 1989). Although few in number, these suggest subtle abnormalities, and investigation of brain levels of sex hormones or use of luteinizing hormone releasing hormone may be worth pursuing in further studies of sadists.

Brain Abnormalities

Money (1990) stated categorically that "like other paraphilias, sexual sadism is a brain disease" (p. 27). Evidence for such a claim, however, is not conclusive, as most paraphiliacs do not show evidence of brain damage or disorder. Sporadic reports of brain abnormalities in those with sexual anomalies (especially fetishism) have been reported from time to time (e.g., Kolarsky, Freund, Machek, & Polak, 1967; Langevin, 1990). In studies by Graber, Hartmann, Coffman, Huey, and Golden (1982), Langevin et al. (1988), and Hucker et al. (1988) using computed tomographic scanning and neuropsychological assessments, there have been statistically significant associations between sadism and right temporal horn damage, although the individuals with abnormalities on different measures did not overlap completely. More recently, Gratzer and Bradford (1995) indicated that 55% of their sadists showed neurological abnormalities, primarily in the temporal lobe. A small study using positron emission tomography scanning in three individuals, including a sadist, did not show any abnormality (Garnett, Nahmias, Wortzman, Langevin, & Dickey, 1988). However, further research using magnetic resonance imaging, which has better resolution, may be helpful (Raine, 1993).

FORENSIC ISSUES

When a particularly sensational murder takes place it is common for the prosecution and defense to select mental health expert witnesses to assist them by providing reports on their examinations and court testimony on the issues of fitness to stand trial and criminal responsibility. Such testimony is fraught with difficulties for the professional and it is not unusual for it to be criticized. Storr commented interestingly on the problem in his postscript to an excellent journalistic account of the trial of the British necrophilic serial killer, Dennis Nielsen (Masters, 1985). The philosophical and legal difficulties are also well discussed in *Mad or Bad?* (Bavidge, 1989) and in *Evil or Ill?* (Resnek, 1997).

Brittain (1970) noted that the emotional flattening and introversion common in sadistic murderers (Dietz et al., 1990; Hazelwood et al., 1992) leads some psychiatric examiners to conclude that the individual is schizophrenic. In his view, most were not grossly psychotic, they know the nature and quality of their acts, and they know that they are wrong (i.e. they do not fulfill the requirements of the McNaughton Rule; Hucker, Ben-Aron, & Webster, 1981). Further, they would not murder if a police officer were standing near or if they thought there was any real possibility of being apprehended. On the other hand, Revitch (1965a, 1965b, 1980) stated that, in his review of the literature available at the time, "one gains an impression that the majority of the reported sadistic acts were perpetrated by either overt or latent psychotics with poor control and explosive breaks with reality." He cites Krafft-Ebing's (1886/1965) report of Vacher the Ripper who, though found "sane," had a history of admissions to an asylum for "persecution mania." In Revitch's own case material (Revitch, 1965a, 1965b), 19 out of 43 murderers were "considered schizoid or dynamically schizophrenic and 9 cases overtly." However, given the known overdiagnosis of schizophrenia in the United States at the time of his report, it is likely that his cases would not meet current criteria under the DSM-IV.

Although it seems clear that none of the murderers described by Dietz et al. (1990) and Warren et al. (1996) were considered psychotic, reports from other jurisdictions suggest that in practice an insanity plea may succeed. Thus, Bartholomew et al. (1975) noted that in their six cases, three pleaded insanity and two were successful. They noted, however, that evidence of planning in many of the cases precluded an insanity verdict. Similarly, Langevin et al. (1988) reported cases from Canada, where a modified McNaughton Rule is the test for criminal responsibility; 8% of sex killers were considered psychotic compared with 11% of other sexual aggressors and 15% of non-sex killers. On the other hand, 64% of these sex killers were acquitted by reason of insanity, compared with none of the sexual aggressors and 23% of the non-sex killers. Further, 23% of the sex killers were found unfit to stand trial. These authors suggested that in some cases the examining professional took the bizarre nature of the sadistic acts as *prima facie* evidence of mental illness.

Money (1990) provided an interesting case report with some novel suggestions for a "forensic sexological" defense. The offender, a sexual sadist, was described as having "a history of paraphilic attacks which resemble psychomotor seizures," even though there was no frank evidence of temporal lobe epilepsy. While there has been some evidence of structural and functional damage to the right temporal lobes of some sadistic rapists (Hucker et al., 1988), it seems purely speculative to argue for a "paraphilic fugue state" (Money, 1990, pp. 32–33) in which there is an "altered state of consciousness."

Palermo and Knudten (1994) provided an account of the recent sensational U.S. trial of Jeffrey Dahmer, a homosexual, necrophilic serial murderer who attempted a defense of insanity. A number of prominent experts testified in support of the defense, others contradicted it successfully. Certainly, court cases involving brutal but bizarre sadistic crimes are like a modern-day morality play in which concepts of sickness, evil, and criminal responsibility are explored and debated and current social values are decided and upheld.

FUTURE DIRECTIONS

It is apparent from the foregoing that definitions of sexual sadism have expanded and contracted in the hands of different writers and there has been difficulty in demonstrating reliability of the diagnosis. Extreme cases, such as those reported by Dietz et al. (1990), appear to be a homogeneous group for whom the desire for total control of the victim seems to be crucial. However, noncriminal, self-identified sadomasochists (e.g., Gosselin, 1987) seem to constitute a rather different group among whom sexual partners are considered precious and every effort is made to ensure that no harm is really suffered. There is clearly a need to explore whether these types of behavior, as well as other varieties of "minor" sadism, are qualitatively or quantitatively different from major, dangerous or predatory sadism. It is also not clear whether one evolves over time into the other or whether they can coexist in the same individual at the same time.

Although, following Krafft-Ebing (1886/1965) and others, lust–murders tend to be viewed as "sadistic," not all appear to be preceded by violent sexual fantasies or to lead to serial crimes. Thus, it is important to know whether these crimes are simply different varieties of the same sadistic species or different types of acts altogether, as suggested by Schlesinger and Revitch (1983). There have been few empirical studies correlating crime scene characteristics with psychopathological features of the perpetrator; these may provide further clues to more helpful classification of these sexual crimes with a view toward more accurate assessments of future risks and treatment possibilities.

Although phallometric testing of sexual arousal has become an established component in the assessment of sex offenders (Murphy & Barbaree, 1994), it has been the area of identifying those who are rape prone or sadistic that has given rise to the most conflicting results. Most studies of rapists who have been examined phallometrically included only small numbers of sadistic individuals. Some authors (e.g., Fedora et al., 1992) have been able to differentiate sadistic from nonsadistic offenders, and more recently Seto and Kuban (1996), examined the discriminant validity of a phallometric test for rape proneness and sadism. Those who fantasized sadistic acts, rapists and admitted sadists, had higher relative responses to sadistic rape and nonsexual violence and tended to be more responsive to rape depictions than was a comparison group, but the first three groups were not distinguishable from each other. The usefulness of phallometric testing in identifying different paraphilic arousal patterns is now well established and the development of a test which can accurately differentiate sadists from other types of sexual assaulters is much needed.

As noted earlier, the most complete studies of serious sadistic offenders to date (e.g., Dietz et al., 1990) did not employ controls, though there has been a recent replication using comparative groups (Gratzer & Bradford, 1995). These studies raise interesting and important questions about possible relationships between sadistic offending and adverse early childhood experiences such as family breakdown and physical and sexual abuse. There are also other characteristics of severely sadistic offenders, such as bisexuality and gender dysphoria, evidence of multiple paraphilias, use of pornography, and relevance of preexisting fantasies, that require further exploration. Finally, few studies explore further the possible links between sadistic behavior and cerebral damage, subtle hormone abnormalities, and alcohol and drug use despite suggestive results from earlier research (Langevin, 1990).

Sexual sadists, at the extreme, comprise a group of the most intelligent, resourceful, and malignant types of criminals and as such they deserve extensive documentation and study.

REFERENCES

Abel, G. G. (1989). Paraphilias. In H. I. Kaplan & B. J. Sadock (Eds.), *Comprehensive textbook of psychiatry* (Vol. 1, 5th ed., pp. 1069–1085). Baltimore: Williams & Wilkins.

Abel, G. G., Barlow, D. H., Blanchard, E. B., & Guild, D. (1977). The components of rapists' sexual arousal. *Archives of General Psychiatry, 34,* 895–903.

Abel, G. G., Becker, J. V., Blanchard, E. B., & Djenderedjian, A. (1978). Differentiating sexual aggressives with penile measures. *Criminal Justice and Behavior, 5,* 315–322.

Abel, G. G., Becker, J. V., Cunningham-Rathner, J., Mittelman, M. S., & Rouleau, J. L. (1988). Multiple paraphilic diagnoses among sex offenders. *Bulletin of the American Academy of Psychiatry and the Law, 16,* 153–168.

Abel, G., Mittelman, M., & Becker, J. (1985). Sexual offenders: Results of assessment and recommendations for treatment. In M. Ben-Aron, S. J. Hucker, & C. D. Webster (Eds.), *Clinical criminology* (pp. 191–205). Toronto: M&M Graphics.

American Psychiatric Association. (1987). *Diagnostic and statistical manual of mental disorders* (3rd ed., rev.). Washington, DC: Author.

American Psychiatric Association. (1994). *Diagnostic and statistical manual of mental disorders* (4th ed.). Washington, DC: Author.

Arndt, W. B. (1991). *Gender disorders and the paraphilias.* Madison, CT: International Universities Press.

Arndt, W., Foehl, J., & Good, F. (1985). Specific sexual fantasy themes: A multidimensional study. *Journal of Personality and Social Psychology, 48,* 472–480.

Bain, J. , Langevin, R., Dickey, R., & Ben-Aron, M. (1987). Sex hormones in murders and assaulters. *Behavioral Science and the Law, 5,* 95–101.

Barbaree, H. E., Marshall, W. L., & Lanthier, R. D. (1979). Deviant sexual arousal in rapists. *Behaviour Research and Therapy, 17,* 215–222.

Bartholemew, A., Milte, K., & Galbally, A. (1975). Sexual murder: Psychopathology and psychiatric jurisprudential considerations. *Australia and New Zealand Journal of Criminology, 8,* 163–152.

Bavidge, M. (1989). *Mad or bad?* Bristol, England: Bristol Classical Press.

Breslow, N. (1989). Sources of confusion in the study and treatment of sadomasochism. *Journal of Social Behavior and Personality, 4*(3), 263–274.

Breslow, N., Evans N., & Langley, J. (1985). On the prevalence and roles of females in sadomasochistic sub-culture: Report of an empirical study. *Archives of Sexual Medicine, 14,* 303–317.

Briere, J., & Malamuth, N. M. (1983). Self-reported likelihood of sexually aggressive behavior: Attitudinal versus sexual explanations. *Journal of Research in Personality, 17,* 315–323.

Brittain, R. (1970). The sadistic murderer. *Medicine, Science and the Law, 10,* 198–207.

Burgess, A. W., Hartman, C. R., Ressler, R. K., Douglas, J. E., & McCormack, A. (1986). Sexual homicide: A motivational model. *Journal of Interpersonal Violence, 1,* 251–272.

Calef, V., & Weinshel, E. M. (1972). On certain neurotic equivalents of necrophilia. *International Journal of Psychoanalysis, 53,* 67–75.

Crepault, E., & Couture, M. (1980). Men's erotic fantasies. *Archives of Sexual Behavior, 9,* 565–581.

de River, P. (1958). *Crime and the criminal psychopath.* Springfield, IL: Charles C Thomas.

Dietz, P., Harry, B., & Hazelwood, R. (1986). Detective magazines: Pornography for the sexual sadist? *Journal of Forensic Science, 31,* 197–211.

Dietz, P., & Evans, B. (1982). Pornographic imagery and prevalence of paraphilia. *American Journal of Psychiatry, 139,* 1493–1495.

Dietz, P. E., Hazelwood, R. R., & Warren J. (1990). The sexually sadistic criminal and his offenses. *Bulletin of the American Academy of Psychiatry and the Law, 18,* 163–178.

Ellis, H. (1936). *Studies in the psychology of sex, Vol. II.* New York: Random House.

Fedora, O., Reddon, J. R., Morrison, J. W., Fedora, S. K., Pascoe, H., & Yeudall, L. T. (1992). Sadism and other paraphilias in normal controls and aggressive and non-aggressive sex offenders. *Archives of Sexual Behavior, 21,* 1–15.

Fenichel, O. (1945). *The psychoanalytic theory of the neuroses.* New York: Norton.

Fiester, S. (1991). Sadistic personality disorder: A review of data and recommendations for DSM-IV. *Journal of Personality Disorders, 5*(4), 376–85.

Freud, S. (1961). Beyond the pleasure principle. In J. Strachey (Ed.), *The standard edition of the complete psychological works of Sigmund Freud* (Vol. 18). London: Hogarth Press. (Original work published 1920)

Freud, S. (1961). *On sexuality.* Markham, Ontario: Penguin.

Freund, K., Scher, H., & Hucker, S. (1983). The courtship disorders. *Archives of Sexual Medicine, 12,* 369–379.

Freund, K., Scher, H., & Hucker, S. (1984). The courtship disorders: A further investigation. *Archives of Sexual Behavior, 13,* 133–139.

Friedenberg, F. S. (1956). A contribution to the problem of sadomasochism. *Psychoanalytic Review, 43,* 91–96.

Fromm, E. (1977). *The anatomy of human destructiveness.* Markham, Ontario: Penguin.

Garnett, E. S., Nahmias, C., Wortzman, G., Langevin, R., & Dickey, R. (1988). Positron emission tomography and sexual arousal in a sadist and two controls. *Annals of Sex Research, 1,* 387–399.

Gosselin, C. C. (1987). The sadomasochistic contract. In G. D. Wilson (Ed.), *Variant sexuality: Research and theory* (pp. 229–257). Baltimore: John Hopkins University Press.

Gosselin, C. C., & Wilson G. D. (1980). *Sexual variations.* London: Faber & Faber.

Graber, B., Hartmann, K., Coffman, J., Huey, C., & Golden, C. (1982). Brain damage among mentally disordered sex offenders. *Journal of Forensic Science, 27,* 127–134.

Gratzer, T., & Bradford, J. (1995). Offender and offense characteristics of sexual sadists: A comparative study. *Journal of Forensic Sciences, 40*(3), 450–455.

Groth, A. N. (1979). *Men who rape: The psychology of the offender.* New York: Plenum Press.

Grubin, D. (1994a). Editorial: Sexual sadism. *Criminal Behavior and Mental Health, 4,* 3–9.

Grubin, D. (1994b). Sexual murder. *British Journal of Psychiatry, 165,* 624–629.

Hazelwood, R. R., Dietz, P. E., & Warren, J. (1992). The criminal sexual sadist. *FBI Law Enforcement Bulletin, 61,* 12–20.

Hazelwood, R., Warren, J., & Dietz, P. E. (1993). Compliant victims of the sexual sadist. *Australian Family Physician, 22*(4), 43–48.

Heilbrun, A., & Leif, D. (1988). Autoerotic value of female distress in sexually explicit photographs. *Journal of Sex Research, 24,* 47–57.

Hill, B. (1995). *Double jeopardy.* New York: William Morrow.

Hirschfeld, M. (1956). *Sexual anomalies.* New York: Ermerson.

Hucker, S. J. (1990). Necrophilia and other unusual philias. In R. Bluglass & P. Bowden (Eds.), *Principles and practice of forensic psychiatry* (pp. 723–728). London: Churchill Livingstone.

Hucker, S. J., Ben-Aron, M., & Webster, C. J. (1981). *Mental disorder and criminal responsibility.* Toronto, Ontario: Butterworks.

Hucker, S. J., & Blanchard, R. (1992). Death scene characteristics in 118 fatal cases of autoerotic asphyxia compared with suicidal asphyxia. *Behavioral Sciences and the Law, 10,* 509–523.

Hucker, S. J., Langevin, R., Wortzman, G., Dickey, R., Bain, J., Handy, L., Chambers, J., & Wright, P. (1988). Cerebral damage and dysfunction in sexually aggressive men. *Annals of Sex Research, 1,* 33–47.

Hucker, S. J., & Stermac, L. (1992). The evaluation and treatment of sexual violence, necrophilia, and asphyxiophilia. *Psychiatric Clinics of North America, 15,* 703–719.

Hunt, M. (1974). *Sexual behavior in the 1970's.* New York: Playboy Press.

Jaffe, P. D., & DiCataldo, F. (1994). Clinical vampirism: Blending myth and reality. *Bulletin of American Academy of Psychiatry and the Law, 22*(4), 533–544.

Karpman, B. (1954). *The sexual offender and his offenses: Etiology, pathology, psychodynamics and treatment.* New York: Julian Press.

Kernberg, O. F. (1970). A psychoanalytic classification of character pathology. *Journal of American Psychoanalytic Association, 18,* 800–822.

Kinsey, A. C., Pomeroy, W. B., Maratin, C. E., & Gebhard, P. H. (1953). *Sexual behavior in the human female.* Philadelphia: Saunders.

Kolarsky, A., Freund, K., Machek, J., & Polak, O. (1967). Male sexual deviation: Association with early temporal lobe damage. *Archives of General Psychiatry , 17,* 735–743.

Knight, R. A., & Prentky, R. A. (1990). Classifying sexual offenders: The development and corroboration of taxonomic models. In W. L. Marshall, D. R. Laws, & H. E. Barbaree (Eds.), *Handbook of sexual assault: Issues, theories, and treatment of the offender* (pp. 23–52). New York: Plenum Press.

Knight, R., Prentky, R., & Cerce, D. (1994). The development, reliability, and validity of an inventory for the multidimensional assessment of sex and aggression. *Criminal Justice and Behavior, 21*(1), 72–94.

Koss, M. P., Gidycz, C., & Wisniewski, N. (1987). The scope of rape: Incidence and prevalence of sexual aggression in a national sample of higher education students. *Journal of Consulting and Clinical Psychology, 55,* 162–170.

Krafft-Ebing, R. von. (1965). *Psychopathia sexualis*. New York: Stein & Day. (Original work published 1886)

Langevin, R. (1990). Sexual anomalies and the brain. In W. L. Marshall, D. R. Laws, & H. E. Barbaree (Eds.), *Handbook of sexual assault: Issues, theories, and treatment of the offender* (pp. 103–113). New York: Plenum Press.

Langevin, R., Ben-Aron, M., Wright, P., Marchese, V., & Handy, L. (1988). The sex killer. *Annals of Sex Research, 1*, 263–301.

MacCulloch, M., Snowden, P., Wood, P., & Mills, H. (1983). Sadistic fantasy, sadistic behavior, and offending. *British Journal of Psychiatry, 143*, 20–29.

Malamuth, N. M. (1981). Rape proclivity among males. *Journal of Social Issues, 37*, 138–157.

Malamuth, N. M. (1988). A multidimensional approach to sexual aggression: Combining measures of past behavior and present likelihood. In R. A. Prentky & V. L. Quinsey (Eds.), *Human sexual aggression: Current perspectives* (pp. 123–132). New York: Academy of Sciences.

Malamuth, N. M., & Check J. V. P. (1983). Sexual arousal to rape depictions: Individual differences. *Journal of Abnormal Psychology, 92*, 55–67.

Malamuth, N. M. Haber, S., & Feshbach, S. (1980). Testing hypotheses regarding rape: Exposure to sexual violence, sex differences and the normality of rapists. *Journal of Research in Personality, 14*, 121–137.

Malamuth, N. M., Heim, M., & Feshbach, S. (1980). Sexual responsiveness of college students to rape depictions: Inhibitory and disinhibitory effects. *Journal of Personality and Social Psychology, 38*, 399–408.

Marshall, W. L., & Barbaree, H. E. (1984). A behavioral view of rape. *International Journal of Law and Psychiatry, 7*, 51–77.

Marshall, W. L., & Barbaree, H. E. (1990). An integrated theory of the etiology of sexual offending. In W. L. Marshall, D. R. Laws, & H. E. Barbaree (Eds.), *Handbook of sexual assault. Issues, theories, and treatments of the offender* (pp. 257–275). New York: Plenum.

Masters, B. (1985). *Killing for company*. London: Coronet.

McConaghy, N. (1993). *Sexual behavior: Problems and management*. New York: Plenum Press.

McCully, R. S. (1964). Vampirism: Historical perspective and underlying process in relation to a case of auto-vampirism. *Journal of Nervous and Mental Disease, 139*, 440–451.

McGuire, R. J., Carlisle, J. M., & Young, B. G. (1965). Sexual deviation as a conditioned behavior: A hypothesis. *Behavior Research and Therapy, 2*, 185–190.

McGuire, C., & Norton, C. (1988). *Perfect victim*. New York: Dell.

Mees, H. L. (1966). Case histories and short communications: Sadistic fantasies modified by aversive conditioning and substitution: A case study. *Behaviour Research and Therapy, 4*(4), 317–320.

Moll, A. (1912). *Handbuch de sexual wissenshaften*. Vogel: Leipzig.

Money, J. (1990). Forensic sexology: Paraphilic serial rape (Biastrophilia) and lust murder (Erotophonophilia). *American Journal of Psychotherapy, 44*(1), 26–36.

Money, J., & Lamacz, M. (1989). *Vandalized lovemaps*. Buffalo, NY: Prometheus.

Murphy, W. D., & Barbaree, H. (1994). *Assessments of sex offenders by measures of erectile response*. Brandon, VT: Safer Society Press.

Palermo, G. B., & Knudten, R. D. (1994). The insanity plea in the case of a serial killer. *International Journal of Offender Therapy and Comparative Criminology, 38*(1), 3–16.

Podolsky, E. (1965). The lust murderer. *Medico-Legal Journal, 33*, 174–178.

Prentky, R. A., Cohen, M. L., & Seghorn, T. K. (1985). Development of a rational taxonomy for the classification of sex offenders: Rapists. *Bulletin of the American Academy of Psychiatry and the Law, 13*, 39–70.

Prentky, R., & Knight, R. (1991). Identifying critical dimensions for discriminating amongst rapists. *Journal of Consulting and Clinical Psychology, 59*, 643–661.

Prins, H. (1985). Vampirism: A clinical condition. *British Journal of Psychiatry, 146*, 666–668.

Quinsey, V. L., Chaplin, T. C., & Upfold, D. (1984). Sexual arousal to nonsexual violence and sadomasochistic themes among rapists and non-sex offenders. *Journal of Consulting and Clinical Psychology, 52*, 651–657.

Quinsey, V., Lalumière, M., & Seto, M. (1994). The current status of phallometric assessment. *Violence Update, 4*, 1–2, 4.

Raine, A. (1993). *The psychopathology of crime.* San Diego, CA: Academic Press.

Raymond, M. J. (1956). Case of fetishism treated by aversion therapy. *British Medical Journal, 2,* 854–857.

Reider, N. (1976). On a particular neurotic equivalent of necrophilia. *Psychoanalytic Quarterly, 45,* 288–289.

Resnek, L. (1997). *Evil or ill? Justifying the insanity defense.* London: Routledge.

Ressler, R., Burgess, A. W., & Douglas, J. (1983). Rape and rape–murder: One offender and twelve victims. *American Journal of Psychiatry, 140,* 36–40.

Ressler, R., Burgess, A. W., & Douglas, J. (1988). *Sexual homocide: Patterns and motives.* Toronto: D.C. Heath & Co.

Ressler, R., Burgess, A. W., Hartman, C. R., Douglas, J., & McCormack, A. (1986). Murderers who rape and mutilate. *Journal of Interpersonal Violence, 1,* 273–287.

Revitch, E. (1965a). Extreme manifestation of sexual aggression. *The Welfare Reporter, xvi*(i), 10–16.

Revitch, E. (1965b). Sex murder and the potential sex murderer. *Disorders of the Nervous System, 26,* 640–648.

Revitch, E. (1978). Sexually motivated burglaries. *Bulletin of the American Academy of Psychiatry and the Law, 6,* 277–283.

Revitch, E. (1980). Gynocide and unprovoked attacks on women. *Corrective and Social Psychiatry and Journal of Behavior Technology, Methods and Therapy, 26*(1), 6–11.

Rosman, J., & Resnick, P. (1989). Necrophilia: An analysis of 122 cases involving necrophilic acts and fantasies. *Bulletin of the American Academy of Psychiatry and the Law, 17*(2), 153–163.

Sagder, J. (1926). A contribution to the understanding of sadomasochism. *International Journal of Psycho-Analysis, 7,* 484–491.

Schad-Somers, S. P. (1982). *Sadomasochism: Etiology and treatment.* New York: Human Sciences Press.

Schlesinger, L. B., & Revitch, E. (1983). *Sexual dynamics of anti-social behavior.* Springfield, IL: Charles C Thomas.

Scott, G. G. (1983). *Dominant women, submissive men.* New York: Praeger.

Seto, M., & Kuban, M. (1996). Criterion related validity of a phallometric test for paraphilic rape and sadism. *Behavior Research and Therapy, 34,* 175–183.

Simons, R. (1987). Self-defeating and sadistic personality disorders: Needed additions to the diagnostic nomenclature. *Journal of Personality Disorders, 1*(2), 161–167.

Siomopoulos, V., & Goldsmith, J. (1976). Sadism revisited. *American Journal of Psychotherapy, 30,* 631–640.

Smith, S., & Braun, C. (1978). Necrophilia and lust murder: Report of a rare occurrence. *Bulletin of the American Academy of Psychiatry and the Law, 6,* 259–268.

Spengler, A. (1977). Manifest sadomasochism of males: Results of an empirical study. *Archives of Sexual Behavior, 6,* 441–456.

Spitzer, R., Fiester, S., Gay, M., & Pfohl, B. (1991). Is sadistic personality disorder a valid diagnosis? The results of a survey of forensic psychiatrists. *American Journal of Psychiatry, 148,* 586–590.

Vanden Bergh, R. L., & Kelly, J. F. (1964). Vampirism: A review with new observations. *Archives of General Psychiatry, 11,* 543–547.

von Eulenberg, A. (1911). *Sadism and masochism.* New York: Bell.

von Schrenck-Notzing, A. (1956). *The use of hypnosis in psychopathia sexualis.* New York: Julian Press. (Original work published 1895)

Warren, J., Hazelwood, R., & Dietz, P. (1996). The sexually sadistic serial killer. *Journal of Forensic Sciences, 41*(6), 970–974.

Weinberg, T. S., Williams, C. J., & Moser, C. (1984). The social constituents of sadomasochism. *Social Problems, 31,* 379–389.

Weinberg, T. S. (1987). Sadomasochism in the United States: A review of recent sociological literature. *Journal of Sex Research, 23,* 50–69.

Wilson, C., & Seaman, D. (1992). *The serial killers.* London: Virgin.

World Health Organization. (1992). *The ICD-10 classification of mental and behavioral disorders.* Geneva: World Health Organization.

Wulffen, E. (1910). *Enzyklopadie de modernen Kriminalistik.* Berlin: Langenscheidt.

11

SEXUAL SADISM

Assessment and Treatment

Clive R. Hollin

"When Sexual Sadism is severe, and especially if it is associated with Antisocial Personality Disorder, individuals with Sexual Sadism may seriously injure or kill their victims" (DSM-IV, American Psychiatric Association, 1994, p. 530).

Regretfully, there are many high-profile cases of sexually motivated murder. These cases typically involve the very extremes of human behavior, involving acts such as torture of victims, mutilation, necrophilia, and cannibalism. Holmes and Holmes (1994) noted examples of the cases in America of John Wayne Gacy, Ted Bundy, and Jeffery Dahmer, whereas in the United Kingdom similar cases would include Dennis Neilsen and Peter Sutcliffe. In a paper not recommended for those with a weak constitution, Simonsen (1989) gave details (with accompanying photographs) from a forensic pathology report from the scene of an apparent homicide of a 37-year-old woman.

> The breasts had been cut off, exposing the ribs and sternum. The abdominal cavity had been cut wide open and several organs had obviously been removed with a sharp instrument, possibly a knife. An empty beer bottle, one of the breasts, a large carrot, large amounts of toilet paper, and scalp hair were found in the abdominal cavity, and the handle of a spatula was found in the vagina. There were cuts at both sides of the mouth, and a piece of lemon and an abundant amount of scalp hair had been placed in the oral cavity. The right eye was enucleated. There were cuts in the genital region, and the labia majora and labia minora had been removed and were found together with the tongue on the bed. The small and large intestines as well as the left kidney had been placed in a plastic bag beside the bed. (pp. 159–160)

Now, it is tempting to come to the conclusion that this class of human behavior is a rarity. Though this might be true at the extreme level described above, there is evidence for a more widespread occurrence of sadistic acts. For example, Young, Sachs, Braun, and Watkins (1991) discussed the accounts of victims of ritual sadistic abuse by satanic cults. Young (1993) described a syndrome called sadistic ritual abuse, reported primarily by adult psychiatric patients typically with a dissociative disorder, and by young children. However, as Young et al. noted, the issue of ritual abuse is controversial given the unresolved issues of the reliability of the victim accounts.

This, of course, is not to say that all claims about sadistic abuse are open to question. Prentky et al. (1991) examined the differences between abducting and nonabducting child molesters. Their findings indicted a higher prevalence of sadism, defined as "evidence that the offender was sexually aroused or otherwise derived pleasure from placing the victim in pain or fear" (p. 217), among molesters who abducted their victims. Hazelwood, Warren, and Dietz (1993) gave an account of the experiences of a sample of women subjected to physical, sexual, and psychological abuse by sadists with whom they formed relationships. It is likely that, to a greater or lesser degree, these experiences are a part of the lives of a substantial number of women who are battered and sexually victimized by men (Frude, 1994; Pollard, 1994).

On another level, there are "willing victims" of sexual sadism, often called *sexual masochists*. The defining qualities of sexual masochism involve the infliction of physical pain and humiliation with a partner, or autoerotic acts such as hypoxyphilia (Hucker, 1990; Baumeister & Butler, Chapter 12, this volume).

DIAGNOSTIC ASSESSMENT

Whereas it is possible to witness the distressing and often devastating effects of sexual sadism, the pressing issue for investigative personnel, clinicians, and researchers is how to know that a given individual is a sexual sadist. It is evident that some agreed diagnostic criteria need to be defined. In their analysis of the accounts given by sexual murderers, Holmes and Holmes (1994) extracted several elements of sexual homicide that clearly inform the debate.

The first of these elements is *fantasy*, the imagining and cognitive rehearsal of acts that one might like to experience. Of course, everyone has sexual fantasies, but those of the sexual murderers involved visions of bondage, torture, and mutilation. Holmes and Holmes noted that: "We have also found that in every case the killers attempted to carry their fantasies out on their victims" (1994, p. 157).

The second element described by Holmes and Holmes is *symbolism*: this is composed of two types, fetishes and partialisms. The first is a sexual attachment to an inanimate object, such as shoes or other items of clothing. The second is an undue sexual need, detached from the person, for a part of the body such as feet, breasts, or buttocks. *Ritualism* is the third element defined by Holmes and Holmes. Like other people, sexual sadists have rituals (including sexual rituals) that they find rewarding and continue to repeat, with the possibility that the ritual changes and develops over time. Unlike the rituals of other members of society, the rituals of the sexual sadists are focused on the suffering of their victims.

Finally, *compulsion* is the fourth element given by Holmes and Holmes (1994), and is "the sole common element in all the sexual murderers we have studied" (p. 160). The nature of the compulsion is clearly described by sexual sadists as a strong internal drive, with both psychological and physical components, to enact their fantasies and carry out the sadistic act.

Thus, by case study and observation, Holmes and Holmes (1994) provided forensic practitioners with the key elements of the phenomenon of sexual sadism. Based on a detailed review of the clinical literature, Grubin (1994) arrived at a remarkably similar list of prognostic indices of sexual sadism. However, the fourth edition of the *Diagnostic and Statistical Manual of Mental Disorders* (DSM-IV; American Psychiatric Association, 1994) takes this process a step further by offering the formal diagnostic criteria given below (p. 530).

A. Over a period of at least 6 months, recurrent, intense sexually arousing fantasies, sexual urges, or behaviors involving acts (real, not simulated) in which the psychological or physical suffering (including humiliation) of the victim is sexually exciting to the person.

B. The fantasies, sexual urges, or behaviors cause clinically significant distress or impairment in social, occupational, or other important areas of functioning.

Thus, there is a considerable overlap between the analyses based on case material discussed above and the formal diagnostic criteria given in DSM-IV. Thus, it is possible to formulate an answer to the question, "How do we know the client has the problem?" by devising assessment strategies based on the key indices from the above material. To focus the discussion, I have selected these key points for assessment: (1) sexually arousing fantasies that involve inflicting pain on a victim, (2) an urge or compulsion to enact these fantasies, (3) the nature of the act itself, and (4) the presence of clinical and social impairments other than sexual disorders. The next section of this chapter will consider the fine points of the assessment of sexual sadism.

ASSESSMENT FOR TREATMENT

Fantasies

How to assess private events such as thoughts and feelings is a problem as old as psychology itself. In essence there are two ways to approach the problem of assessment of fantasy. The first is to trust to the individual's self-report. The second is to try to create an analogue of the fantasy and then measure some behavioral correlate of the accompanying sexual arousal.

Self-Report Assessment

Person, Terestman, Myers, Goldberg, and Salvadori (1989) reported the findings of a study of sexual behaviors and fantasies in a college population. They used a typical self-report methodology in the form of a sexual inventory. Each individual completed this inventory, consisting of 67 experience and 55 fantasy items, by rating each item on a 4-point scale (*never, not in the last 3 months, less than 5 times in the last 3 months, more than 5 times in the past 3 months*). Some of the fantasy items included in this inventory—for example, "whipping/beating partner," "torturing sex partner"—are clearly relevant to sexual sadism. There are a variety of similar inventories that focus on sexual behavior and fantasies, including the Aggressive Sexual Behaviour Inventory (Mosher, 1988; Mosher & Anderson, 1986), the Coercive Sexual Fantasies Questionnaire (Greendlinger & Byrne, 1987), and the Sexual Arousability Inventory (Chambless & Lifshitz, 1984).

Another self-report approach is to use a standardized interview rather than an inventory or questionnaire. For example, Reich (1993) used the Personality Disorder Examination, version 2 to screen for sadistic personality disorder.

The main problem with self-report measures is one of veracity: How can assessors be sure that the individual is giving truthful replies? In an assessment conducted for forensic purposes the individual may have very strong reasons for withholding or distorting information.

Physiological Assessment

Another route to the assessment of the images that men find sexually arousing lies in the measurement of physiological responses to different types of stimuli. For some time direct measurement of penile tumescence has been considered the strongest indicator of male sexual arousal (Zuckerman, 1972). The technique of penile plethysmography (PPG) has become accepted in both the clinical and research literature for the assessment of sexual interest and arousability.

As explained by Murphy, Haynes, and Worley (1991), PPG assessment requires laboratory apparatus to measure changes in penis size and sexual stimuli to invoke sexual arousal. Three transducers are commonly used to measure penile changes. The mercury and rubber circumferential strain gauge (Bancroft, Jones, & Pullman, 1966), and the metal band circumferential strain gauge (Barlow, Becker, Leitenberg, & Agras, 1970) measure changes in penile circumference; the volumetric device (Freund, Sedlack, & Knob, 1965) measures change in penile volume. Similarly, there are three types of stimulus material in common use: videotapes, slides, and audiotaped accounts.

The procedure of PPG assessment involves the person attaching the recording device in privacy, and then watching, hearing, or imagining the stimulus material. The data from the assessment is typically recorded as a polygraph or continuous chart.

PPG methodology can be used to assess both normal and deviant sexual arousal and a substantial research literature has evolved (e.g., Freund & Blanchard, 1989; Hall, 1989; Hall, Proctor, & Nelson, 1988; Lalumière & Quinsey, 1993, 1994). However, from their review of the literature Harris, Rice, Quinsey, Chaplin, and Earls (1992) made several recommendations to maximize the validity of phallometric assessment. Of particular concern with respect to sexual sadism is their view that stimuli depicting brutal sexual coercion will produce the most distinctive pattern of responding. This view was supported by the finding of Fedora et al. (1992) that phallometric assessment did identify a group of sexual aggressors who responded most to "sadism slides." These slides showed acts of nonsexual violence against fully clothed females. Thornton (1993) suggested that the evidence regarding PPG assessment now shows a clear picture.

> Three distinct offence-related forms of deviant sexual interest can now be reliability identified through plethysmography: arousal to children; arousal to physical violence against women; and arousal to the domination and humiliation of women. Arousal to each of these deviant themes seems to be related to distinct forms of offending. Thus, for example, Proulx et al. found that rapists who showed an arousal to humiliation themes in PPG assessment tended to have done things like urinating on their victim during the offence, whereas those who showed arousal to violent themes were more likely to have used force in excess of that required to obtain the victim's compliance. (pp. 186–787)

Thus, through PPG assessment it is possible to begin to determine the types of images that individuals find sexually arousing. It is a logical inference that similar images will play a part in the individual's sexual fantasies. It seems likely that PPG assessment will become ever more widely used and will play an important role in assessment of deviant sexual arousal, including sexual sadism. However, PPG assessment is not suitable for the next part of the formal assessment of sexual sadism, the urge or compulsion to enact sexual fantasies.

Compulsion to Enact Fantasies

To know if an individual has a compulsion to enact their fantasies means that there must be knowledge of the content of those fantasies. In terms of the sequence of assessment, it follows that assessment of fantasies must precede the assessment of compulsion. There are three sources of detail regarding compulsion to enact fantasies. The first is the individual's self-report, most likely in the context of an interview. The second source of information is those who have close relations with the individual. Those who know the individual well, even intimately, can provide descriptions of the individual's behavior that can be set against the individual's own descriptions of their fantasies. It should be noted, however, that some individuals may not wish to reveal a compulsion, while partners and peers may have a vested interest in withholding evidence or may be unaware of the actions of the individual.

The third source of information is the forensic evidence, including crime scene analysis and witness and victim statements. If the individual has enacted specific fantasies, then it would be expected that the forensic evidence would match the elements of the fantasy. The type of forensic detail in the case described earlier (Simonsen, 1989) would provide several factors to be cross-checked against an individual's account of their actions driven by their fantasies.

Nature of the Act

Assessment here overlaps considerably with the previous section. The essential elements of the act—the psychological or physical suffering and humiliation of the victim—will be evident from crime scene analysis and witness and victim statements.

Other Clinical Distress or Impairment

Alongside the specific assessments relating to fantasy, it is also necessary to assess whether the experience of these fantasies and their associated sexual urges is related to clinically significant distress or other impairment in sexual, social, and occupational functioning. In other words, a full clinical assessment should accompany the specific focus on sadistic factors. Such an assessment will, of course, be a matter of routine to clinical practitioners. However, specifically regarding a full assessment of sex offenders, Hanson, Cox, and Woszcznya (1991) offered a helpful review of assessment measures.

ASSESSMENT: TOWARD A CONSENSUS?

It is evident from the above that the assessment of sexual sadism demands a multimodal approach, requiring assessment of the complex interplay between thoughts, feelings, physiological activity, and behaviors. Those practitioners conducting a forensic assessment have available the specific measures discussed above, along with other global and indirect measures of psychopathology such as projective and personality tests. Note that several commentators do not recommend undue reliance on indirect methods of assessment with sex offenders (Hall, Graham, & Shepherd, 1991; Quinsey, 1986). One practical difficulty is that a diversity of assessment methods will produce a piecemeal assessment, with the possibility of different practitioners reaching different conclusions. Although there is a certain air of inevitability about this state of affairs, progress toward a multidimensional assessment procedure has been made by a team of researchers at the Massachusetts Treatment Center.

Knight, Prentky, and Cerce (1994) reported on the development of an inventory called the Multidimensional Assessment of Sex and Aggression (MASA). The MASA seeks to incorporate a wide range of information, based on clinical and criminal files and self-report, giving assessment information on social competence, juvenile antisocial behavior, adult antisocial behavior, pervasive anger, sexualization, sexual aggression, and offense planning. The MASA was shown to have high levels of test–retest reliability, along with acceptable levels of concurrent validity.

With a specific focus on sexual sadism, analysis of the MASA responses of known sex offenders revealed three components within the sadism scale: *bondage, synergism between sexual arousal and aggression,* and *sadistic fantasy.* Unfortunately, the psychometric properties of these subscales were rather poor, with low test–retest reliability. Knight et al. (1994) suggested that the scale items may need further refinement, or that parallel items may need to be created. In addition, further work is needed to develop scales to identify defensiveness and faking in responding. Nonetheless, the MASA represents a significant step in the assessment of sex and aggression which, perhaps when combined with PPG assessment, offers forensic practitioners a means by which to conduct a comprehensive assessment.

THEORIES OF THERAPY

It is axiomatic that theories of therapy are closely related, if not dependent upon, the theory used to understand the phenomenon at hand. It follows, therefore, that the identification of theories of sexual aggression will, in turn, identify theories of therapy. (I assume that sexual sadism is a type of sexual aggression, and that theories and therapies applied to sexual aggression will, to a greater or lesser extent, also be applicable to sexual sadism.)

A trawl through the literature reveals a broad range of theories of sexual aggression, a review of which clearly is beyond the scope of this chapter (see Hucker, Chapter 10, this volume; Hudson & Ward, Chapter 25, this volume). However, it is illuminating just to consider the range of approaches applied in an attempt to understand sexual aggression. The catalog of such approaches includes a feminist perspective (Herman, 1990), psychodynamic theories (Groth, Hobson, & Gary, 1982), courtship disorder (Freund, 1990), learning theory (Laws & Marshall, 1990), biological approaches (Langevin, 1992; Money, 1990), biosocial theory (Ellis, 1993), views drawn from social psychology (Stermac, Segal, & Gillis, 1990) and from cognitive psychology (Segal & Stermac, 1990), and complex multidimensional theories and models (Malamuth, Heavey, & Linz, 1993; Marshall & Barbaree, 1984, 1990). Each of these approaches translates into its own recommendations and methods for the amelioration of sexual aggression, not all of which would be readily classified as "therapy." There is a wide debate about the relative strengths and weakness of these and other analyses and their implications for therapy (Hollin & Howells, 1991).

Another approach, rather more utilitarian than intellectual, is to adopt an empirical stance and ask the following question: "From a therapy viewpoint, what do we know to be the most effective means to reduce sexual aggression?" Armed with this knowledge, we will be in a position to consider the special case of sexual sadism. Knowledge of the effective therapies comes from clinical outcome studies. With a focus on the more serious acts, I give a brief overview of this literature below.

Therapy Outcome with Sex Offenders

As detailed by Hanson, Cox, and Woszcznya (1991), there are many technical and methodological difficulties in assessing treatment outcome for sex offenders. I begin with a note of caution regarding what we know about the effectiveness of therapy for sex offenders in general.

The research literature on sexual offending provides no tidy or conclusive findings that can easily direct the design of correctional treatments. Despite a substantial and steadily growing level of knowledge in the field, there remains considerable speculation about what motivates these individuals to commit their offences, and considerable uncertainty about how best to treat or manage those who seem to pose the greatest risk. (Solicitor General Canada, 1990, p. 9)

The sentiments expressed by the Canadian Working Group are almost as valid in 1995 as they were when they appeared in print. However, the word "almost" is important: Since 1990 there have been several important publications that lead to some qualification of the views expressed in the above quotation (Marshall, 1993; Marshall, Jones, Ward, Johnson, & Barbaree, 1991; Marshall & Pithers, 1994; Pithers, 1993; Quinsey et al., 1993). The extent to which knowledge about the effectiveness of treatment of sex offenders generally can be generalized to sexual sadists specifically will be addressed after a discussion of the key publications.

What Is Effective?

In the field of offender rehabilitation the issue of treatment outcome is of wide concern. Simply, there are two classes of measures that we need to hold conceptually distinct. The first of these can be thought of as "process measures": that is, those targets for change specifically addressed by treatment programs, such as sexual arousal, attitudes toward women, and social skills. The second type of measure is an "outcome measure": that is, the effect of the treatment on sexual offending, typically measured using recidivism. Whereas the former are necessary and important, both in terms of fine-tuning treatment programs and enhancing our understanding of outcome findings, recidivism rates are the acid test of treatment effectiveness.

Treatment and Recidivism

In a comprehensive review of the evidence Furby et al. (1989) drew similar conclusions to those expressed by the Canadian Working Group cited earlier. Acknowledging the methodological shortcomings in some of the published evidence, Furby et al. found little support in the outcome literature for the position that treatment can consistently and effectively reduce sex offending. It is important to say that Furby et al. did not dismiss the possibility of effective treatment; indeed, they expressed the hope that effective treatment programs will be forthcoming.

From their review of the literature, with a clear focus on recidivism as an outcome measure, Marshall et al. (1991) drew a more optimistic message with regard to treatment effectiveness. They reviewed a range of outcome studies from several different treatment philosophies, beginning with the effectiveness of physical treatments. They identified three types of physical treatment used with sex offenders: *psychosurgery, castration,* and administration of *pharmacological agents.* They concluded that there is little supportive evidence for the first two, but the third holds promise. Specifically, Marshall et al. suggested that the combination of the hormonal analogue cyproterone acetate and psychological treatment is of potential value in reducing sex offending.

Moving to nonbehavioral treatments, Marshall et al. (1991) discussed the outcomes of several studies that employed a variety of approaches such as emotional release therapy, psychoanalytic treatment, and humanistic self-help programs. They found little in the way of supportive evidence for the effectiveness of these approaches in reducing sex offending.

Finally, Marshall et al. (1991) considered outcome studies wherein the treatment, in both institutional and outpatient settings, was behavioral and cognitive-behavioral in orientation. They reached the view that

> Evaluations of outpatient cognitive/behavioral programs, then, are definitely encouraging. While there is not an extensive body of outcome literature, what there is suggests that at least child molesters and exhibitionists can be effectively treated by these comprehensive programs. However, as with the institutionally based programs, outpatient programs are not uniformly effective and none of them as yet have demonstrated effectiveness with rapists. (p. 480)

Quinsey et al. (1993) took issue with Marshall et al.'s (1991) conclusion on the grounds that "the approach taken in Marshall et al.'s review is unable to provide satisfactory answers to questions concerning treatment efficacy" (p. 513). Specifically, Quinsey et al. were dissatisfied with Marshall et al.'s (1991) stance on methodological issues. Quinsey et al. argued that (1) control groups are both desirable and necessary in treatment outcome studies, (2) to ignore those who refuse or drop out of treatment potentially overestimates treatment effectiveness, and (3) recidivism data aggregated across different legislator and police jurisdictions are fatally flawed as an outcome measure. Quinsey et al. then moved to a discussion of the outcome evidence, focusing specifically on the evidence for cognitive-behavioral programs. Applying strict methodological criteria along the lines noted above, Quinsey et al. concluded that "the effectiveness of treatment in reducing sexual recidivism remains moot" (p. 519).

In defense of his position, Marshall (1993) highlighted the basic issues in the field. Marshall argued that expectations of levels of high methodological rigor are unrealistic in a newly developing field. On the issue of dropouts from treatment, Marshall argued that treatment effectiveness can be judged realistically only when offenders have completed the program. Further, given the lack of strong data (i.e., from random allocation comparison group designs), aggregated data does offer a valid, if not perfect, comparison. Indeed, Marshall made the point that random allocation designs have the potential to pose both political and ethical problems when treatment is withheld from those who might benefit from participating.

Pithers (1993) and Marshall and Pithers (1994) rehearsed essentially the same arguments, albeit with the benefit of more published studies than in the Marshall et al. (1991) review. Both publications again reached the conclusion that treatment can be effective in reducing sex offending.

The basic issue in this debate is the level of satisfactory proof that one is willing to accept regarding treatment outcome. Marshall embodies a belief held by one camp of practitioners that treatment can be effective and, at this stage in the development of the field, we should be content to build on that foundation. On the other hand, Quinsey and his colleagues take a more rigorous scientific stance, demanding high-quality empirical evidence before making a commitment to treatment effectiveness. Quinsey et al. (1993) made the point that the field is in desperate need of a meta-analysis, an approach that has had profound effects in other areas of treatment work with offenders (e.g., Lipsey, 1992).

Hall (1995) reported just such a meta-analysis and reached the conclusion that sexual offenders who complete treatment show a modest but significantly lower rate of reoffending than untreated sex offenders. With regard to type of treatment, Hall concluded that treatment is most effective when conducted "with outpatient participants and when it consists of hormonal or cognitive-behavioral treatments" (p. 808). As with general offending, the force of the literature appears to suggest that effective work with sex offenders to reduce recidivism is possible.

Finally, with regard to sexual sadism, the picture is even more uncertain. There is very little in the way of strong outcome evidence by which to recommend tried and tested treatment strategies. In recommending treatment strategies, it is necessary, remembering the debate discussed above, to look to what are generally seen as advantageous ways to change sexual preferences.

RECOMMENDED TREATMENT STRATEGIES

There are two strands to thinking about treatment strategies: the first is the treatment techniques themselves, and the second is the overall system within which treatment is delivered.

Treatment Techniques

As Pithers (1993) made clear, there are several potential targets for treatment with men who are sexually aggressive. These targets for change include patterns of sexual arousal, empathic responsivity, cognitive distortions, and interpersonal competence. In addition, programs may include treatment for drug and alcohol problems and work on the offender's own (possible) victimization. There is considerable overlap between these targets and the diagnostic criteria for sexual sadism.

Changing Sexual Arousal Patterns

If there is a relationship between fantasy, sexual arousal, and preferred sexual acts, then there are grounds to believe that this must be at the very heart of an effective treatment program. Certainly the diagnostic criteria for sexual sadism stress the interplay between these factors, strongly suggesting that this must be a target for change.

As noted above, there is some evidence that antiandrogen medication can be effective in treating deviant sexual impulses. However, Cooper (1986) suggested that this approach is most likely to be successful with individuals who are volunteers and are not diagnosed as psychopathic or personality-disordered hypersexuals. Bradford (1990) also stressed the need for careful selection of which individuals would most benefit from antiandrogen treatment. Whereas pharmacological advances may provide more effective drug regimes in the future, psychological therapy currently offers the most likely alternative means of behavior change.

Pithers (1993) noted four commonly used methods to modify sexual interest: *covert sensitization, olfactory/gustatory aversion, masturbatory satiation,* and *orgasmic* (or *masturbatory*) *reconditioning.* The first three aim to reinforce decreased arousal to sexually aggressive fantasies, whereas the latter seeks to reinforce arousal to nondeviant fantasies. The evidence for the effectiveness of these methods is, as Quinsey and Earls (1990) pointed out, limited in both depth and significance. Laws and Marshall (1991) concluded their review of masturbatory reconditioning with cautious optimism.

> There are insufficient data meeting empirical standards to permit us to conclude that masturbatory reconditioning, in any of the forms reviewed here, is a clearly effective treatment for sexual deviations of any kind. Although the data from a small number of controlled studies are promising, the case remains to be made that any of these treatments are effective over the long term. (p. 24)

Increasing Victim Empathy

Although clearly not the only cognitive factor contributing to sexual violence (Rice, Chaplin, Harris, & Coutts, 1994), there is a substantial body of evidence to support the position that sexual aggressors have low empathy for their victims. It follows that empathy (or perspective) skills training has become part of many treatment programs. However, the force of the contribution to program effectiveness made by such training remains uncertain.

Changing Cognitive Distortions

As with victim empathy, there is ample evidence to suggest that sexual aggressors report cognitive distortions such as victim enjoyment of the assault, blaming the victim, and a general belief in rape myths (Murphy, 1990). In treatment, these distortions are met with a range of cognitive change techniques, including educational input on the real effects of victimization and peer challenging of distortions. The relative impact of this component of treatment programs is yet to be established.

Other Targets for Change

On a case-by-case basis, individuals have different treatment needs such as improved in social skills and dealing with alcohol and drug misuse. The treatment techniques for these targets are well established in mainstream clinical practice.

Treatment Systems

It is self-evident that any treatment program needs a system of delivery both to ensure efficient use of resources and to maximize their effectiveness. In the main, treatment systems need to consider recruitment into treatment, assessment, treatment process, follow-up, and outcome evaluation. In a typical example, Marshall, Eccles, and Barbaree (1993) discussed a three-tiered approach to the rehabilitating incarcerated sex offenders.

In the Marshall et al. (1993) program, sex offenders are first assessed for their degree of risk of reoffending and treatment need. Those offenders designated as moderate to high risk are placed in an extensive treatment program, Tier 1, in conditions of medium or high security. Sex offenders judged to be of low risk are placed in a less extensive program, Tier 2, in low security conditions. Those who complete Tier 1 can progress to Tier 2 to develop a relapse prevention plan before their release into the community. Tier 3 of the system is the community component that puts into action the relapse prevention plan. At this stage there is reassessment of the risk and treatment needs of the offender, with support to help the offender enact treatment gains and overcome setbacks. Marshall et al. are optimistic that this approach produces benefits in terms of reduced recidivism and substantial financial savings (see also Prentky & Burgess, 1991).

The concept of relapse prevention has been established as an essential ingredient in treatment systems (Laws, 1989; Pithers, 1990). Initially developed in the field of addiction, relapse prevention refers to equipping the offender with the self-management skills and strategies to cope effectively with high-risk situations which are likely to lead to a relapse into reoffending. Indeed, the Sex Offender Treatment and Evaluation Project (SOTEP) in California took the principles of relapse prevention as the guiding orientation for the entire program (Marques, Day, Nelson, & West, 1993).

Although the fine details might differ from program to program, it is the case that developing treatment programs (e.g., Grubin & Thornton, 1994) follow a path similar to that described by Marshall et al. (1993).

There is, however, a grave lack of relevant outcome data to guide the design of effective treatment strategies. In such a case, as Pithers (1993) noted, there is ample opportunity for the exercise of clinical creativity. Thus, matching assessment criteria to successful treatment strategies on the basis of the evidence discussed above suggests that a treatment program for sexual sadism should include several components.

The first component would be modifying sexual fantasies and preferences. As noted, the use of antiandrogens and masturbatory reconditioning have been tried, but with equivocal outcomes. The second component would address the need for cognitive change, most probably with a focus on increasing victim empathy. Finally, a relapse prevention component would seek to help the individual recognize high-risk situations and increase their self-control over the compulsion to offend. This is, however, speculative and based on extrapolation from an outcome literature that obviously is relevant with respect to sexual violence, but which does not have *sadism* as its direct concern. In practice, clinicians will have to use all their powers of creativity in designing treatment programs for sexual sadism.

FORENSIC ISSUES

There are two forensic issues that need to be emphasized with respect to sexual sadism. The first is the problem of assessment. The central elements of sexual sadism, fantasies and the compulsion to enact those fantasies, are difficult to assess. Self-report assessments are problematic when an individual is motivated to withhold information; whereas PPG assessment can be informative, clearly it is not without limitations. It is my view that a focus on the act itself, along with information from crime scene analysis, provides the most defensible forensic evidence. It seems likely, therefore, that forensic assessment must be both expansive in its methods and cautious in its conclusions.

The second issue is with regard to therapy. Given the current debate about the effectiveness of sex offender treatment generally, it would be premature to draw any conclusions regarding treatment of sexual sadism. It is my view that there are grounds for optimism and that the outline of a treatment program for at least some sexual sadists can be constructed. However, given the current state of knowledge, my overall position is one of extreme caution. The depth of forensic knowledge about sexual sadism is not great, and one should express extreme prudence in formulating one's opinions about both diagnosis and suitability for therapy.

FUTURE DIRECTIONS

As always, there clearly is a need for more empirical research. Although the literature contains case studies and informed opinions from experienced practitioners, there is a marked lack of rigorous data. We need a greater understanding of all aspects of sexual sadism—from etiology to maintenance, through detection and assessment, to therapy and behavior change—before we can express any confidence in managing this aspect of human sexual behavior. The work of Hanson and Bussière (1996), reporting a meta-analysis of the literature predicting sexual offender recidivism, offers a model for future research in this area. Hanson and Bussière showed that sexual offense recidivism was best predicted by both measures of sexual deviance such as deviant sexual preferences and, less so, by more general criminological factors, such as the total number of prior offenses. However, Hanson and Bussière noted that a great deal more remains to be understood with respect to changeable, dynamic risk factors. Clearly, a great deal more basic research is needed before we can begin to feel confident in our ability to successfully assess and treat sexual deviance. If it is the case that our society is becoming increasingly violent, then the need for such research will become ever more pressing.

REFERENCES

American Psychiatric Association. (1994). *Diagnostic and statistical manual of mental disorders* (4th ed.). Washington, DC: Author.

Bancroft, J., Jones, H. C., & Pullman, B. P. (1966). A simple transducer for measuring penile erections with comments on its use in the treatment of sexual disorders. *Behaviour Research and Therapy, 4,* 239–241.

Barlow, D. H., Becker, R., Leitenberg, H., & Agras, W. S. (1970). A mechanical strain gauge for recording penile circumference change. *Journal of Applied Behavior Analysis, 3,* 73–76.

Bradford, J. M. W. (1990). The antiandrogen and hormonal treatments of sex offenders. In W. L. Marshall, D. R. Laws, & H. E. Barbaree (Eds.), *Handbook of sexual assault: Issues, theories, and treatment of the offender* (pp. 343–361). New York: Plenum Press.

Chambless, D., & Lifshitz, J. L. (1984). Self-reported sexual anxiety and arousal: The expanded sexual arousability inventory. *Journal of Sex Research, 20,* 241–254.

Cooper, A. J. (1986). Progestogen in the treatment of male sex offenders: A review. *Canadian Journal of Psychiatry, 31,* 73–79.

Ellis, L. (1993). Rape as a biosocial phenomenon. In G. C. N. Hall, R. Hirschman, J. R. Graham, & M. S. Zaragoza (Eds.), *Sexual aggression: Issues in etiology, assessment, and treatment* (pp. 17–41). Washington, DC: Taylor & Francis.

Fedora, O., Reddon, J. R., Morrison, J. W., Fedora, S. K., Pascoe, H., & Yeudall, L. T. (1992). Sadism and other paraphilias in normal controls and aggressive and nonaggressive sex offenders. *Archives of Sexual Behavior, 21,* 1–15.

Freund, K. (1990). Courtship disorder. In W. L. Marshall, D. R. Laws, & H. E. Barbaree (Eds.), *Handbook of sexual assault: Issues, theories, and treatment of the offender* (pp. 343–361). New York: Plenum Press.

Freund, K., & Blanchard, R. (1989). Phallometric diagnosis of pedophilia. *Journal of Consulting and Clinical Psychology, 57,* 100–105.

Freund, K., Sedlack, J., & Knob, K. (1965). A simple transducer for mechanical plethysmography of the male genital. *Journal of the Experimental Analysis of Behavior, 8,* 169–170.

Frude, N. (1994). Marital violence: An interactional perspective. In J. Archer (Ed.), *Male violence* (pp. 153–169). London: Routledge.

Furby, L., Weinrott, M. R., & Blackshaw, L. (1989). Sex offender recidivism: A review. *Psychological Bulletin, 105,* 3–30.

Greendlinger, V., & Byrne, D. (1987). Coercive sexual fantasies of college men as predictors of self-reported likelihood to rape and overt sexual aggression. *Journal of Sex Research, 23,* 1–11.

Groth, A. N., Hobson, W. F., & Gary, T. S. (1982). The child molester: Clinical observations. In J. Conte & D. A. Shore (Eds.), *Social work and child sexual abuse* (pp. 129–144). New York: Haworth Press.

Grubin, D. (1994). Editorial: Sexual sadism. *Criminal Behaviour and Mental Health, 4,* 3–9.

Grubin, D., & Thornton, D. (1994). A national program for the assessment and treatment of sex offenders in the English prison system. *Criminal Justice and Behavior, 21,* 55–71.

Hanson, R. K., Cox, B., & Woszcznya, C. (1991). Assessing treatment outcome for sexual offenders. *Annals of Sex Research, 4,* 177–208.

Hall, G. C. N. (1989). Sexual arousal and arousability in a sexual offender population. *Journal of Abnormal Psychology, 98,* 145–149.

Hall, G. C. N. (1995). Sexual offender recidivism revisited: A meta-analysis of recent treatment studies. *Journal of Consulting and Clinical Psychology, 63,* 802–809.

Hall, G. C. N., Graham, J. R., & Shepherd, J. B. (1991). Three methods of developing MMPI taxonomies of sexual offenders. *Journal of Personality and Assessment, 56,* 2–13.

Hall, G. C. N., Proctor, W. C., & Nelson, G. M. (1988). Validity of physiological measures of pedophilic sexual arousal in a sexual offender population. *Journal of Consulting and Clinical Psychology, 56,* 118–122.

Hanson, R. K., & Bussière, M. T. (1996). *Predictors of sexual recidivism: A meta-analysis.* (User Report No. 1996-04). Ottawa: Department of the Solicitor General of Canada.

Hanson, R. K., Cox, B., & Woszcznya, C. (1991). Assessing treatment outcome for sexual offenders. *Annals of Sex Research, 4,* 177–208.

Harris, G. T., Rice, M. E., Quinsey, V. L., Chaplin, T. C., & Earls, C. (1992). Maximizing the discriminant validity of phallometric assessment data. *Psychological Assessment, 4,* 502–511.

Hazelwood, R., Warren, J., & Dietz, P. (1993). Compliant victims of the sexual sadist. *Australian Family Physician, 22,* 474–479.

Herman, J. L. (1990). Sex offenders: A feminist perspective. In W. L. Marshall, D. R. Laws, & H. E. Barbaree (Eds.), *Handbook of sexual assault: Issues, theories, and treatment of the offender* (pp. 343–361). New York: Plenum Press.

Hollin, C. R., & Howells, K. (Eds.). (1991). *Clinical approaches to sex offenders and their victims.* Chichester: Wiley.

Holmes, R. M., & Holmes, S. T. (1994). *Murder in America.* Thousand Oaks, CA: Sage.

Hucker, S. (1990). Sexual asphyxia. In R. Bluglass & P. Bowden (Eds.), *Principles and practice of forensic psychiatry* (pp. 717–721). Edinburgh: Churchill Livingstone.

Knight, R. A., Prentky, R. A., & Cerce, D. D. (1994). The development, reliability, and validity of an inventory for the multidimensional assessment of sex and aggression. *Criminal Justice and Behavior, 21,* 72–94.

Lalumière, M. L., & Quinsey, V. L. (1993). The sensitivity of phallometric measures with rapists. *Annals of Sex Research, 6,* 123–138.

Lalumière, M. L., & Quinsey, V. L. (1994). The discriminability of rapists from non-sex offenders using phallometric measures: A meta-analysis. *Criminal Justice and Behavior, 21,* 150–175.

Langevin, R. (1992). Biological factors contributing to paraphilic behavior. *Psychiatric Annals, 22,* 307–314.

Laws, D. R. (Ed.). (1989). *Relapse prevention with sex offenders.* New York: Guilford Press.

Laws, D. R., & Marshall, W. L. (1990). A conditioning theory of the etiology and maintenance of deviant sexual preference and behavior. In W. L. Marshall, D. R. Laws, & H. E. Barbaree (Eds.), *Handbook of sexual assault: Issues, theories, and treatment of the offender* (pp. 209–229). New York: Plenum Press.

Laws, D. R., & Marshall, W. L. (1991). Masturbatory reconditioning with sexual deviates: An evaluative review. *Advances in Behavior Research and Therapy, 13,* 13–25.

Lipsey, M. W. (1992). Juvenile delinquency treatment: A meta-analytic inquiry into the variability of effects. In T. D. Cook, H. Cooper, D. S. Cordray, H. Hartmann, L. V. Hedges, R. J. Light, T. A. Louis, & F. Mosteller (Eds.), *Meta-analysis for explanation: A casebook* (pp. 83–127). New York: Russell Sage.

Malamuth, N. M., Heavy, C., & Linz, D. (1993). Predicting men's antisocial behavior against women: The interaction model of sexual aggression. In G. C. N. Hall, R. Hirschman, J. R. Graham, & M. S. Zaragoza (Eds.), *Sexual aggression: Issues in etiology, assessment, and treatment* (pp. 63–97). Washington, DC: Taylor & Francis.

Marques, J. K., Day, D. M., Nelson, C., & West, M. A. (1993). Findings and recommendations from California's experimental treatment program. In G. C. N. Hall, R. Hirschman, J. R. Graham, & M. S. Zaragoza (Eds.), *Sexual aggression: Issues in etiology, assessment and treatment* (pp. 197–214). Washington, DC: Taylor & Francis.

Marshall, W. L. (1993). The treatment of sex offenders. What does the outcome data tell us? A reply to Quinsey, Harris, Rice, and Lalumière. *Journal of Interpersonal Violence, 8,* 524–530.

Marshall, W. L., & Barbaree, H. E. (1984). *The Kingston Penitentiary treatment program for protective custody of sex offenders*. Report to Correctional Services of Canada, Ottawa.

Marshall, W. L., & Barbaree, H. E. (1990). An integrated theory of the etiology of sexual offending. In W. L. Marshall, D. R. Laws, & H. E. Barbaree (Eds.), *Handbook of sexual assault: Issues, theories, and treatment of the offender* (pp. 343–361). New York: Plenum Press.

Marshall, W. L., Eccles, A., & Barbaree, H. E. (1993). A three–tiered approach to the rehabilitation of incarcerated sex offenders. *Behavioral Sciences and the Law, 11,* 441–455.

Marshall, W. L., Jones, R., Ward, T., Johnston, P., & Barbaree, H. E. (1991). Treatment outcome with sex offenders. *Clinical Psychology Review, 11,* 465–485.

Marshall, W. L., & Pithers, W. D. (1994). A reconsideration of treatment outcome with sex offenders. *Criminal Justice and Behavior, 21,* 10–27.

Money, J. (1990). Forensic sexology: Paraphilic serial rape (Biastophilia) and lust murder (Erotophonohilia). *American Journal of Psychotherapy, 44,* 26–36.

Mosher, D. L. (1988). Aggressive Sexual Behavior Inventory. In C. M. Davis, W. L. Yarber, & S. L. Davis (Ed.), *Sexuality related measures: A compendium* (pp. 9–10). Lake Mills, IA: Graphic.

Mosher, D. L., & Anderson, R. D. (1986). Macho personality, sexual aggression, and reactions to guided imagery of realistic rape. *Journal of Research in Personality, 20,* 77–94.

Murphy, W. D. (1990). Assessment and modification of cognitive distortions in sex offenders. In W. L. Marshall, D. R. Laws, & H. E. Barbaree (Eds.), *Handbook of sexual assault: Issues, theories, and treatment of the offender* (pp. 343–361). New York: Plenum Press.

Murphy, W. D., Haynes, M. R., & Worley, P. J. (1991). Assessment of adult sexual interest. In C. R. Hollin & K. Howells (Eds.), *Clinical approaches to sex offenders and their victims* (pp. 77–92). Chichester: Wiley.

Person, E. S., Terestman, N., Myers, W. A., Goldberg, E. L., & Salvadori, C. (1989). Gender differences in sexual behaviors and fantasies in a college population. *Journal of Sex and Marital Therapy, 15,* 187–198.

Pithers, W. D. (1993). Considerations in the treatment of rapists. In G. C. N. Hall, R. Hirschman, J. R. Graham, & M. S. Zaragoza (Eds.), *Sexual aggression: Issues in etiology, assessment and treatment* (pp. 167–196). Washington, DC: Taylor & Francis.

Pithers, W. D. (1990). Relapse prevention with sexual aggressors: A method for maintaining therapeutic gain and enhancing external supervision. In W. L. Marshall, D. R. Laws, & H. E. Barbaree (Eds.), *Handbook of sexual assault: Issues, theories, and treatment of the offender* (pp. 343–361). New York: Plenum Press.

Pollard, P. (1994). Sexual violence against women: Characteristics of typical perpetrators. In J. Archer (Ed.), *Male violence* (pp. 170–194). London: Routledge.

Prentky, R., & Burgess, A. W. (1991). Rehabilitation of child molesters: A cost–benefit analysis. *American Journal of Orthopsychiatry, 60,* 108–117.

Prentky, R. A., Knight, R. A., Burgess, A. W., Resler, R., Campbell, J., & Lanning, K. V. (1991). Child molesters who abduct. *Violence and Victims, 6,* 213–224.

Quinsey, V. L. (1986). Men who have sex with children. In D. N. Weisstub (Ed.), *Law and mental health: International perspectives* (Vol. 2, pp. 140–172). New York: Pergamon Press.

Quinsey, V. L., & Earls, C. M. (1990). The modification of sexual preferences. In W. L. Marshall, D. R. Laws, & H. E. Barbaree (Eds.), *Handbook of sexual assault: Issues, theories, and treatment of the offender* (pp. 343–361). New York: Plenum Press.

Quinsey, V. L., Harris, G. T., Rice, M. E., & Lalumière, M. L. (1993). Assessing treatment efficacy in outcome studies of sex offenders. *Journal of Interpersonal Violence, 8,* 512–523.

Reich, J. (1993). Prevalence and characteristics of sadistic personality disorder in an outpatient veterans population. *Psychiatry Research, 48,* 267–276.

Rice, M. E., Chaplin, T. C., Harris, G. T., & Coutts, J. (1994). Empathy for the victim and sexual arousal among rapists and nonrapists. *Journal of Interpersonal Violence, 9,* 435–449.

Segal, Z. V., & Stermac, L. E. (1990). The role of cognition in sexual assault. In W. L. Marshall, D. R. Laws, & H. E. Barbaree (Eds.), *Handbook of sexual assault: Issues, theories, and treatment of the offender* (pp. 343–361). New York: Plenum Press.

Simonsen, J. (1989). A sadistic homicide. *American Journal of Forensic Medicine and Pathology, 10,* 159–163.

Solicitor General Canada. (1990). *The management and treatment of sex offenders* (Report of the Working Group Sex Offender Treatment Review). Ottawa: Department of the Solicitor General of Canada.

Stermac, L. E., Segal, Z. V., & Gillis, R. (1990). Social and cultural factors in sexual assault. In W. L. Marshall, D. R. Laws, & H. E. Barbaree (Eds.), *Handbook of sexual assault: Issues, theories, and treatment of the offender* (pp. 343–361). New York: Plenum Press.

Thornton, D. (1993). Sexual deviancy. *Current Opinion in Psychiatry, 6,* 786–789.

Young, W. C. (1993). Sadistic ritual abuse: An overview in detection and management. *Primary Care, 20,* 447–458.

Young, W. C., Sachs, R. G., Braun, B. G., & Watkins, R. T. (1991). Patients reporting ritual abuse in childhood: A clinical syndrome. Report of 37 cases. *Child Abuse and Neglect, 15,* 181–189.

Zuckerman, M. (1972). Physiological measures of sexual arousal in the human. In N. S. Greenfield & R. A. Sternback (Eds.), *Handbook of psychophysiology* (pp. 709–740). New York: Holt, Rinehart & Winston.

12

SEXUAL MASOCHISM
Deviance without Pathology

Roy F. Baumeister
Jennifer L. Butler

Among the various sexual deviations, masochism is of special interest for several reasons. Foremost among these is the paradoxical core of it: How can the experience of pain, humiliation, and loss of control enhance any sort of pleasure, sexual or otherwise? Why would anyone seek out experiences that seem to defy the essential principle of the rational pursuit of self-interest?

Masochism is of interest also because in the contemporary United States it lies right on the borderline of sexual deviance. Many practices such as oral sex or masturbation that were once condemned have now become relatively common and accepted. Meanwhile, others, such as fetishism and bestiality, remain taboo and are widely perceived as perverse. In between these extremes of acceptance and condemnation lies masochism. It remains the province of a small minority of the population, yet it has acquired a certain chic from its frequent appearance in movies, television shows, and comedy routines, which imply a degree of acceptance. For many sexually adventurous people it is the most extreme thing that they will do; masochism rests at the borderline of convention.

For professional psychologists, interest in masochism is enhanced by the substantial theoretical baggage the phenomenon has accumulated over the decades. Early theorists were intrigued by seeming parallels between masochistic sex and nonsexual self-defeating behavior, and some concluded that the pursuit of pain and failure was a deeply rooted aspect of human nature that explained both phenomena. Broad assertions that women are typically masochistic have generated controversy (and hence more interest), as has the hypothesis that women who remain with abusive husbands must derive some masochistic satisfaction from being beaten (e.g., Young & Gerson, 1991).

Mindful of the problems of generalizing from sexual masochism to nonsexual behavior, recent clinical theorists have begun to differentiate between "psychic" or "moral" masochism and sexual masochism. Moral masochism is the use of self-destructive behavior to resolve inner problems, such as punishing the self for bad behavior (Maleson, 1984) or avoiding aggression toward others by directing it toward the self (MacGregor, 1991). Some have proposed that moral masochism is linked to depression (Cartwright & Wood, 1993; Friedman, 1991). The term "moral masochism" is used to define the intent of the behavior: In moral masochism, the goal allegedly is to prevent or punish immoral, unethical behavior, whereas the main goal of sexual masochism is sexual arousal leading to sexual satisfaction.

At present it appears that there are important and fundamental differences between moral and sexual masochism, even beyond the fact that one is a form of sex play and the other embodies a destructive approach to life in general. Sexual masochism, which seeks pain or humiliation as a means to sexual gratification, nearly always involves a relationship (either real or fantasized), whereas moral masochism tends to be solitary and focused mainly on the self (e.g., Kernberg, 1991). Whereas sexual masochism transforms or removes the self (as we will explain shortly), some theorists have proposed that moral masochism idealizes the self, partly because the person proves that he or she can tolerate suffering and partly because the person seems to gain extra credit for triumphing over the obstacles, even if they are somewhat self-imposed (Warren, 1985). Zerbe (1992) proposed that eating disorders often are a form of moral masochism, and Young and Gerson (1991) drew the same conclusion about people who remain in abusive relationships.

At present the evidence suggests that there is little or no overlap between sexual masochism and nonsexual forms of self-defeating behavior such as moral masochism (Baumeister, 1989, 1991; Baumeister & Scher, 1988; Berglas & Baumeister, 1993; Friedman, 1991; Grossman, 1986). The resemblance is largely superficial, and where there is resemblance it appears to be commonly misunderstood. To refer to a nonsexual behavior pattern as masochistic is to invoke an analogy to a pattern of sexual behavior, and until that sexual pattern is well understood, it is impossible to say whether the analogies are apt or misinformed.

Our own interest in masochism stems from an appreciation of the paradoxical nature of the phenomena (seeking out pain, humiliation, and so forth). It began with a recognition that the theories of the 1920s and 1930s found very little support in the data of the 1970s and 1980s. Although we shall briefly cover the early theories below for historical reasons, they have mostly been rendered untenable by the accumulation of evidence. New theories are slowly emerging to make sense of masochism, but the problem remains an attractive one for budding theorists looking to tackle a fascinating, elusive paradox.

PATHOLOGY

Before proceeding to an examination of the core features of masochism, it is necessary to consider briefly the issue of pathology. Most people do not incorporate whips and chains into their lovemaking routines, and they would probably have doubts or second thoughts if a prospective sex partner suggested a spanking. Popular spokespersons for conventional wisdom have tended to condemn masochism: "sick, sick, sick," in the summary judgment of advice columnist Ann Landers (see Cowan, 1982). Greene and Greene (1974) reviewed considerable evidence and concluded that the prevailing opinions of many influential people oppose masochism. In the two decades since those opinions were published, there has been some movement toward tolerance, but conventional wisdom changes only slowly at best. On the other hand, conventional wisdom has been wrong before, and it would be a form of prejudice and intolerance to condemn a practice without clear evidence that it is dangerous or harmful. It therefore is instructive to examine the evidence about masochism and pathology.

Perhaps surprisingly, sexual masochism emerges from recent empirical evidence as a fairly innocuous activity that is entirely compatible with an otherwise healthy, normal, successful approach to life. Studies of practicing masochists have repeatedly found them to be reasonably well-adjusted, successful individuals (Moser & Levitt, 1987; Scott, 1983; Spengler, 1977). Some have characterized them as above average on several indices of adjustment and mental health (e.g., Cowan, 1982). They tend to be reliable and to have high standards for themselves and others (Kernberg, 1988). Moreover, the practice of masochism itself is generally conducted with an eye toward safety, so that no lasting harm is done (Scott, 1983; Weinberg & Kamel, 1983).

If masochism is fairly safe and harmless, and masochists are not mentally ill, what justifies the opinion of some experts that masochism is a form of mental illness? Three patterns of potential pathology are noteworthy and deserve consideration. First, it seems quite plausible that masochism might appeal to mentally ill individuals for pathological reasons. Although early studies indeed characterized masochists as mentally healthy and well-adjusted, it is plausible that some are mentally ill. In such cases, the masochism is not the problem, but merely a sign or symptom of the problem. If the underlying pathology could be resolved, the masochistic feelings may also vanish, although there would be no particular reason to eliminate them too.

The second potential pathology in masochism is that some people may become dependent on it. One common definition of perversion refers to any activity (other than intercourse or orgasm) becoming indispensable to a person's sexual pleasure, and we concur with that view. Thus, an occasional masochistic fantasy or episode may be quite innocuous, but if someone is unable to enjoy sex without pain or bondage then it may be appropriate to regard the person's dependence as pathological (see Coen, 1988). Once again, though, there is no need to aim therapeutic efforts toward removing the masochistic feelings; the crucial thing would be to reopen the other, more standard avenues of sexual response.

Last, some people may engage in dangerous or injurious behavior during their masochistic episodes. These behaviors may reflect some deeper pathology or may simply reflect bad judgment. In certain extreme types of autoerotic stimulation, for example, people seek severe or even life-threatening pain and danger, often as a prelude to masturbation. The term "autoerotic" refers to a broad range of behaviors including electrical stimulation, hanging or asphyxiation, nonasphyxual sexual bondage, or taking poisons. The element of danger to the self is much greater in these patterns than in sexual masochism. Most cases are discovered when the participant is seriously injured or killed, although such suicidal outcomes are largely unintentional (O'Halloran & Deitz, 1993). In any case, though, such reckless or destructive behavior is cause for concern. Proponents of masochism generally emphasize the importance of safety, and unsafe practices should be noted and stopped.

Apart from these marginal, extreme cases, however, masochism does not usually cause harm to the individual and is popular among many people who seem fully normal and well adjusted in other domains. There does not, therefore, seem to be any valid scientific basis for regarding masochism as pathological. To be sure, science is hardly the only source of sexual morality, and there may be religious or other bases for condemning masochism, but the social scientist must give it a fairly clean bill of health.

There are several important implications of this recognition. First, if masochism is not a disease, then there is no need to "cure" it. People should not be encouraged to enter into therapy simply because they have masochistic desires or fantasies (or activities). If someone who desired masochistic sex could be transformed through therapy techniques into someone who would not derive any enjoyment or pleasure from masochism, this should not be regarded as a positive mental health outcome.

The second implication has to do with the masochists themselves. The evidence about the relative innocence of masochism is rather new and runs contrary to conventional wisdom. As a result, many people may fear that their masochistic desires or fantasies indicate some serious mental illness. Those who go to the library to read early psychological theories about masochism will find themselves compared to mass murderers, necrophiliacs, neurotics, and other disturbed individuals. Even the most self-confident individual would likely experience some distress and worry about seeing oneself characterized in that fashion.

As a result, many people may request psychotherapy because of their own masochistic feelings (Cowan, 1982). They may want to be cured, by which they would presumably mean that the therapist would make them stop desiring masochistic experiences. They may also be consumed with worry about what deeper problem in their psyche may lie at the root of their masochistic wishes.

The ethics of professional response to such a request for treatment invoke broad issues that we cannot debate here. Still, it is clear that a therapist should not simply acquiesce in the client's panic by embarking on an attempt to change the person's pattern of sexual response. Ethical concern and simple human decency presumably require that the therapist at least make an attempt to educate the client to the effect that masochism is not inherently pathological nor incompatible with a healthy, well-adjusted life.

EPIDEMIOLOGY

Multiple difficulties attend any effort to estimate the prevalence of masochism. Many people are reluctant to admit to themselves, let alone to survey researchers, that they have masochistic fantasies. Many who engage in masochistic activities are reluctant to let anyone know this. Moreover, there may be wide gaps between the frequency of fantasies and actual experiences, because many would-be masochists are unable to find a partner with whom to share such activities. Even if someone had no qualms about masochism and were eager to try it, he or she might happen to be involved with a romantic partner who is completely unwilling.

After reviewing several studies on the prevalence of masochism, Baumeister (1989) estimated that 5% to 10% of the population has engaged in some masochistic sex play, including blindfolding or slapping (but not including biting and scratching, which seem to belong to a separate pattern). Perhaps twice as many have occasionally enjoyed masochistic fantasies, although probably fewer than 1% have engaged in masochistic sex on any regular basis. More precise estimates cannot be gleaned from existing data for many reasons, particularly including the reluctance of people to admit such fantasies and activities to interviewers. Indeed, surveys of sexual behavior routinely suffer from nonsystematic samples and low rates of compliance. People who are willing to respond to sex surveys are often more sexually active and uninhibited than those who are unwilling to talk, so that the data furnish a misleading picture. People might be more willing to admit masochistic desires or experiences on an anonymous questionnaire than in a face-to-face interview, but anonymous surveys typically have low return rates. Moreover, the highly praised survey of sexual behavior by Michael, Gagnon, Laumann, and Kolata (1994) unfortunately neglected to ask anything about masochism.

The weight of the evidence suggests that somewhat more males than females engage in masochistic activities (e.g., Moser & Levitt, 1987; Scott, 1983; see Baumeister, 1989, for review). Some have used this to suggest that males are more masochistic than females, contrary to certain assertions, but in our view this conclusion is unwarranted. Males exceed females in most forms of unusual sexual activity, so the higher rate of male masochism may be simply a reflection of the broader sexual adventure seeking of males. In any case, it is clear that masochists are a small minority of the population and it is misleading to assert that masochism is characteristic or typical of either sex.

Of potentially greater interest is the socioeconomic distribution of masochism. All evidence suggests that masochism is positively correlated with socioeconomic status. The poor, disadvantaged, and oppressed rarely turn to masochism, whereas among the rich and powerful masochism is much more common. Although the data behind this correlation are far from rigorous, there is convergence from multiple sources. Membership in S&M clubs tends to involve upper-middle-class, well-educated individuals (e.g., Moser & Levitt, 1987; Scott, 1983; Spengler, 1977). Prostitutes and call girls who cater to the upper classes get many more requests for sexual domination than do the prostitutes and call girls who cater to the lower classes (Diana, 1985; Janus, Bess, & Saltus, 1977; Smith & Cox, 1983). There also are indications that masochism is more popular among white than black people (Moser & Levitt, 1987), although this may simply mirror the socioeconomic distribution.

The cultural and historical distribution of masochism also is important. A review of multiple sources of historical and cross-cultural evidence by Baumeister (1988a, 1989) concluded that masochism is distributed quite differently than most sexual variations. Evidence of the majority of sexual practices can be found in ancient times and across most cultural boundaries, but masochism appears to be fairly specific to modern, Western cultures. It was conspicuous by its absence before about 1500, when the first clear references to it appear. The trickle of initial mentions were soon followed by a minor flood of evidence indicating that by the 18th century it was widespread in Europe and the United States. Clubs, pornography, professional dominatrices, and more have all catered to the new and growing taste for masochism since about 1700.

A last point which holds considerable theoretical interest is that masochism appears to be far more common than its complement, sadism. A broad range of evidence is quite uniform on this. Baumeister (1988a, 1989) tallied fantasy and self-report letters in sex magazines and found a substantial preponderance of submissive over dominant experiences. Friday (1980) solicited sexual fantasies of all sorts and found that submissive ones outnumbered dominant or sadistic ones by a 4:1 margin. Scott (1983) reported the same 4:1 margin with reference to membership in S&M clubs. Prostitutes tend to report even higher ratios in the requests they receive (e.g., Janus et al., 1977). Moreover, it appears that the majority of people who do enjoy the dominant or sadistic role started out as masochists themselves and changed only after a period of time (Baumeister, 1988a, 1989; Scott, 1983).

To summarize, masochists are a small minority of males and females, but it is difficult to say how small. It is possible that as much as a third of the population has occasionally enjoyed a masochistic fantasy or desire, whereas the number of people who regularly engage in masochistic sexual practices probably is 1% or less. Masochism is more common among the middle and upper classes than the lower ones, and it appears to be found mainly in modern Western cultures. Given the rising socioeconomic situation and gradual Westernization of many non-Western lands, it seems reasonable to expect that masochism will gradually spread throughout the world. Sadism is not directly comparable to masochism and indeed it is far less common.

WHAT MASOCHISTS WANT AND DO

We turn now to consider the core features of masochism. Three main features of masochism can be identified: pain, loss of control, and embarrassment or humiliation. Let us consider each of these in turn.

Pain is central to the stereotype of masochism, although there are in fact many masochists who use little or no pain. Nonetheless, pain remains a vital and prominent feature of the majority of masochistic experiences. The means by which pain is administered do not vary greatly. Spanking on the bare buttocks probably is the favorite technique. Some people like to be paddled, whipped, or caned, which presumably causes more severe pain than does a hand spanking. Studies consistently find that over half of masochists enjoy spanking or whipping (Baumeister, 1989; Moser & Levitt, 1987). In contrast, only a small minority of masochists use other sources of pain, such as dripping the wax from a burning candle onto the bare skin, piercing the skin with needles, rubbing the skin with ice, or pinching sensitive skin with clamps or clothespins.

There are several features of masochistic pain that carry considerable theoretical importance. First, masochists appear to desire their pain to be kept within well-defined limits. People desire to be spanked up to a certain point and then no more. Second, the pain does appear to be unpleasant, although not terrible. Sexual arousal may make the pain more tolerable. It is likely that part of the appeal of the standard bare-bottom spanking is that the nudity and skin contact enhance sexual arousal, making the spanking less aversive. Pain does not become magically transform into pleasure, however (e.g., Reik, 1941/1957). Third, pain is divorced from its biological function of warning of injury. Masochists desire pain but not injury, and indeed most of them are extremely careful to avoid any risk of harm (e.g., Lee, 1983; Scott, 1983). Fourth, masochists' desire for pain seems to be restricted mainly to their sexual activities and games. Several sources have reported that masochists do not enjoy going to the dentist or having their hand smashed in the car door any more than other people do (e.g., Scott, 1983; Weinberg, Williams, & Moser, 1984).

Loss of control is an even more pervasive feature of masochism than is pain, and indeed some people may enjoy the pain or spanking because it symbolizes their loss of control over the situation. The best known and most direct form of control deprivation in masochism is bondage. For many people, bondage is the centerpiece of the masochistic episode, whereas for others it is merely one feature of the situation. Many masochists enjoy being tied up, blindfolded, and/or handcuffed. Some like to be suspended from ceilings or tied in various positions. The emphasis on this feature of masochism is seen in the subgenre of bondage pornography, which produces photos or films of attractive people (usually young women) tied up and struggling against their bonds—often without any story, dialogue, or other activity.

The masochistic deprivation of control takes a variety of forms other than bondage. Submitting to rules and commands is an important one. Many masochists seem to enjoy being ordered to perform various duties for their partner, ranging from housecleaning to manicure to oral sex. Arbitrary rules may be imposed, sometimes apparently for the mere purpose of furnishing a pretext for punishing the individual who breaks them.

An important feature of the loss of control is that it is at least partly illusory. Contrary to appearances, S&M scenes are typically enacted at the behest and for the satisfaction of the masochist. Masochists often work out elaborate scripts of what they want to happen, thereby reducing the dominant partner to a role player, and when the partners are not well acquainted the scripts tend to be even more thorough and elaborate. Dominant partners who acquire the reputation of not staying within the bounds of the script are seen as undesirable partners (e.g., Lee, 1983), and masochists tend to be less satisfied with such experiences. Some masochists use prearranged signals or code words to indicate just how much pain they should receive (e.g., Scott, 1983).

Despite these broad tendencies, one should not conclude that masochism is a means of controlling the partner; indeed, if one wanted to exert control over others, inducing them to tie one up and spank one would be a most peculiar way of going about this. The appearance of helplessness and being under another person's power is central to masochism and represents what the masochist often most earnestly seeks. The degree of control exerted by the masochist is often a means to ensure that he or she will be able to experience the precise degree of apparent loss of control that is most stimulating and arousing to him or her.

The third feature of masochism is humiliation and/or embarrassment. A broad variety of experiences fit into this category, which consists essentially of actions and experiences that seem designed to produce shame-related emotions by being incompatible with the person's normal identity. Gender differences (to which we shall return shortly) are most pronounced with respect to this feature of masochism, although there are some practices, such as being designated as a slave or submitting to anal penetration, that seem common to masochists of both sexes (Baumeister, 1988b, 1989).

Some masochists seem to favor experiences which demean or degrade them. Thus, loss of status seems to be an important feature of the humiliation desired by these individuals. Some like to be converted symbolically into a dog (e.g., put on a leash and required to walk about on all fours) or an infant (e.g., put in diapers). Many seem to desire symbolic feminization, such as being forced to wear women's underwear or to perform traditionally female sex-role actions such as housework. Others wish to be subjected to verbal insults. Physical acts of submission are also popular, such as being required to kneel or to kiss the partner's feet or anus.

Other masochists seek experiences of sexual shame and embarrassment. Foremost among these is being put on display naked. Being required to strip in front of an audience is one form of this, as is masturbating while others watch. Another is to be naked in the presence of the fully clothed partner and possibly others, such as while carrying out a servant's duties (e.g., bringing drinks).

A handful of more extreme and presumably more rare experiences reflects similar themes of embarrassment and humiliation. Being ordered to perform sex acts that had previously been off limits, such as homosexual acts, is occasionally reported, as is being lent out by the dominant partner to perform sexual (or occasionally other) services for other people. Being cuckolded is a form of humiliation, especially if one is required to be present or even to assist in the partner's infidelity. This pattern figured prominently in the writings and even in the personal life of Leopold von Sacher-Masoch, in whose honor the term *masochism* was coined (Cleugh, 1951). Being required to masturbate while the dominant partner and possibly others watch seems like an extension of being displayed naked. Being urinated on, which Scott (1983) described as "the ultimate insult," is another powerful symbolic degradation.

We must acknowledge that some masochistic practices combine elements of more than one of these three features. A spanking, for example, is a means of administering pain, but it is probably also a humiliating and embarrassing experience, and it may also contain some element of being under the control of someone else.

THEORIES OF MASOCHISM

The paradoxical nature of masochism has long posed a significant challenge to psychological theory. The seeming wish to experience pain while losing control and status runs contrary to most general assumptions and observations about human nature.

For decades the most influential theorizing about masochism came from the psychoanalytic tradition. Several psychodynamic theories about masochism have been proposed. Freud's (1938, 1924/1961) own writings proposed that masochism is derived from sadism:

More precisely, the person wishes to dominate and hurt others, but this desire gives rise to guilt, so the person defensively converts it into its opposite, namely a desire to submit to domination by others (see also Reik, 1941/1957). The view that masochism is derived from sadism is difficult to assert in light of recent evidence. As already noted, masochism appears to be far more common than sadism, and among people who show both patterns, masochism appears earlier than sadism (Baumeister, 1988a, 1989; Lee, 1983; Scott, 1983). It is illogical to argue that masochism is the derivative form if it appears earlier and is more common than sadism.

Another problem with the original psychodynamic theory of masochism is even more relevant to the recent, revised theories which place greater emphasis on guilt. Thus, masochism is sometimes regarded as a wish for punishment arising from an inner sense of guilt, or as an effort to expiate one's sex guilt in advance to prevent sex guilt from impairing one's enjoyment of sex (e.g., Bader, 1993). These theories, like the defense mechanism theory, were plausible but are difficult to reconcile with recent evidence. Several aspects of recent evidence argue against basing a theory of masochism on guilt. First, research on guilt does not show that guilt makes people desire punishment; indeed, although guilt does motivate a variety of responses aimed at alleviating guilt, seeking punishment does not seem to be one of them (see Baumeister, Stillwell, & Heatherton, 1994, for review).

Second, research on masochism has failed to turn up much evidence that masochists suffer from a great deal of inner guilt (see Baumeister, 1989, pp. 93–100). Some do, and others do not, just as in the population at large. Moreover (and third), masochists who do suffer from guilt in connection with sex generally seem to have the greatest amount of guilt in connection with their masochistic feelings and activities per se (e.g., Cowan, 1982). They may request therapy in the hope of being restored to desiring only conventional forms of sex. Thus, masochism is the problem, not the solution, for those masochists who suffer from sexual guilt. Most people who engage in sadomasochistic activities appear to be relatively uninhibited and sexually adventurous, and it would be misleading to try to explain their activities on the basis of sex guilt (Scott, 1983).

Stolorow and Lachmann (1980) proposed a recent and quite different psychodynamic theory of masochism. They characterized masochists as narcissistic individuals who have suffered some trauma or damage and seek masochistic experiences as a way of building up their senses of self. They proposed that to be slapped or hurt is to be noticed, which is better than being ignored. Masochists can supposedly interpret pain as proof of selfhood or as proof of attention received from the abusive partner, which can supposedly affirm the masochist's identity and self-worth (see also Gordon, 1987; Mollinger, 1982). Kernberg (1988) speculated that masochists take pride in the amount of pain and humiliation they can withstand, indicating that they can tolerate more than other people could. Still, all these arguments seem weak, and narcissism seems much better suited to describing sadism than masochism, because sadism does build up a strong sense of self through giving commands and administering pain. The observation that masochists desire to relinquish control is especially problematic for the narcissism theory of masochism, because relinquishing control seems contrary to any effort to build up a sense of self. Meanwhile, of course, the sadist gains control over another human being, so once again it is more plausible to explain sadism than masochism by the narcissism theory.

The opposite view, that masochism is a technique for getting rid of one's sense of self, has been argued by Baumeister (1988a, 1989, 1991). According to this theory, self-awareness can be unpleasant, stressful, and burdensome under various circumstances, and therefore people sometimes become motivated to escape it. The mechanism relies on a process of cognitive deconstruction or mental narrowing, which consists of stripping away the elaborately defined, meaningful aspects of personal identity, thereby reducing the self to a minimal but intense here-and-now awareness of physical sensation and movement. The features of masochism can all be understood as techniques of accomplishing this subjective transformation. Pain captures attention and focuses it narrowly on immediate physical sensation, thereby preventing abstract or meaningful thought (Scarry, 1985). Loss of control removes one of the core functions of the self, namely as active decision maker. Humiliation consists of performing acts that are incompatible with the person's normal identity as well as thwarting another pervasive function of the self, namely the pursuit and maintenance of esteem.

The theory that masochism involves escape from self has the advantage over the previous theories in that it was constructed on the basis of the empirical evidence about masochism that has accumulated in recent decades (e.g., Scott, 1983; Weinberg & Kamel, 1983). It is therefore reasonably consistent with what we know about masochism. Its historical and cultural distribution is particularly relevant: The modern West, which has placed the highest emphasis on autonomous individuality (and therefore presumably created the heaviest burden of selfhood) has been the almost exclusive preserve of sexual masochism. Theories that attempt to explain masochism on more general psychological patterns and principles, such as the psychodynamic theories invoking defense mechanisms, guilt, or narcissism, have considerable difficulty accounting for this severe cross-cultural and cross-historical variation.

Probably the most important critique of the escape theory is that it does not provide a satisfactory explanation of the intense craving for submissive experiences that some masochists report. It offers a plausible explanation of what masochism achieves and why some people may find it appealing, but why do some people become obsessed with thoughts of sexual masochism? Baumeister (1991) has sought to place masochism in a broader context by describing other activities that can accomplish similar escapes from self-aware-ness, and it is noteworthy that many of them—binge eating, suicidal actions, alcohol and drug abuse, spiritual strivings, and meditation—also seem able to create strong cravings and nearly obsessional fascinations. However, the theory does not explain why some people fall into these pseudoaddictive patterns while others merely dabble casually in the same pastimes.

In addition, like most theories about masochism, the escape theory has not been subjected to laboratory experimentation or to other rigorous empirical tests. The patterns of escape from self-awareness have been well documented in other contexts (see Baumeister, 1989, for review), and laboratory tests of similar predictions have been conducted with parallel patterns such as binge eating (e.g., Heatherton, Polivy, Herman, & Baumeister, 1993), but the empirical support for the escape theory rests on autobiographical narratives (which feature transformations of selfhood), interviews, and cross-cultural and cross-historical accounts.

Several other theoretical efforts deserve mention. Some authors, notably Cowan (1982), have proposed that masochism is a therapeutic process. Cowan (1982) contended that masochism promotes insight and self-knowledge, thereby allowing the person to grow and change for the better. Stolorow, Atwood, and Brandschaft (1988) suggested that masochism sheds the societal image that the person must live up to, thereby allowing the true self to emerge. Money (1987) noted that some masochists claim that masochism is a good way to strengthen their willpower and self-control. Masochists periodically assert that their experiences leave them feeling refreshed and cured of various problems (such as stress), and many are likely to be fond of the view that masochism is good for them.

The view of masochism as therapy, however, must be regarded as quite dubious. It is difficult to envision how being tied up and spanked can make someone into a better person—or, indeed, how doing so on multiple occasions can continue to provide valuable or useful advances in self-knowledge. Although other authors such as Cowan (1982) characterized masochists as above average on mental health and adjustment in many respects, it is doubtful that their sex games brought about this positive adjustment or cured their psychological problems. Rather, it seems more likely that whatever advantages they enjoyed are independent of (or even precursors to) their involvement in masochism. There is nothing to indicate that masochistic experiences produce therapeutic effects. The self-reports of feeling better afterward may be common to a broad range of sexual satisfactions, or they may be self-serving attempts to justify a deviant enjoyment, or indeed they could reflect the stress-releasing benefits of escaping from self-awareness.

Indeed, both the escape theory and the therapy theory contend that masochism offers psychological benefits. The difference is in the nature and time frame of these benefits. If masochism is therapy, its benefits should presumably be permanent (such as improved self-knowledge and the resulting pragmatic changes in one's life). In contrast, if it is escape from self-awareness, its benefits will be temporary, along the lines of feeling better in the wake of a successful escape from stresses and worries. Until evidence can be provided that engaging in this unusual form of sex play produces lasting positive changes in the individual, the latter seems far more plausible.

A last source of contribution to theory about masochism is learning theory. Many writers, including some masochists themselves, assume that the roots of masochism lie in some conditioning or early experiences that form strong associative links between sexual pleasure and the receipt of pain (e.g., Cooper, 1993; Fraiberg, 1982). For example, a child might receive bare-bottom spankings as punishment and find the nakedness or skin contact somewhat exciting, thus forming a link which could emerge as masochistic desire later in life. This theory is plausible but does not correspond closely to what scant evidence is available, which suggests that many masochists do not have such childhood experiences and that many who do have them fail to develop a taste for masochism (Scott, 1983). Moreover, the theory easily degenerates into a circular argument: The reason some children might form such a positive association between sexual arousal and spanking whereas others do not is that the former were already inclined toward masochism. The cross-cultural and cross-historical variation in masochism is difficult to reconcile with a simple association theory, because the opportunities to associate pain with arousal are certainly not limited to the modern West.

A more intriguing contribution from learning theory is the opponent-process theory proposed by Solomon and Corbit (1974). This theory proposes that the body's homeostasis is based on processes that offset any departure from it. Intensely positive, euphoric experiences such as drug or alcohol intoxication are followed by depressed or hangover experiences that counteract the initial euphoria, persist longer than it does, and eventually result in the return to the baseline state (Solomon, 1980). Masochism in this view might become appealing because its painful or embarrassing experiences set off an opponent process of pleasure. One might therefore classify masochism alongside other experiences that induce fear or discomfort to evoke the opposing euphoria, such as bungee jumping or skydiving.

It is difficult to evaluate the relevance of opponent-process theory to masochism because there is little evidence that bears directly on it and it is particularly hard to see how the theory could be falsified. Still, it does fit the common observation by masochists that the sexual pleasure following the seemingly unpleasant submission experience is often especially euphoric. The opponent-process account seems compatible with most of the other theories about masochism, so it is possible to reserve judgment on it while still reaching conclusions about the other theories.

GENDER DIFFERENCES IN MASOCHISM

Decades of theoretical debate about the hypothesized masochism of women has made it important to consider what recent evidence indicates about gender differences in masochism. As already noted, masochism is slightly more common among men than among women (e.g., Moser & Levitt, 1987), and this may reflect nothing more than the different baseline frequency among sexual variations in general. Hence, it is probably a serious mistake to characterize either gender as masochistic. Masochism is practiced by a small, atypical minority of both genders. In this sense, masochism is not linked to gender.

On the other hand, there is some evidence that men and women tend to differ as to how they practice masochism. As we have indicated, there is a broad range of masochistic practices, and most masochists do not engage in all of them to the same degree. Based on a statistical compilation of self-reports and fantasies published in a popular magazine that regularly devoted a section to such accounts, one of us (Baumeister, 1988b, 1989) concluded that males and females tend to follow somewhat different scripts in their most common approaches to masochism. What follows is a summary of those results.

Both male and female masochists use pain, although pain seems to be slightly more central to female masochism. Male fantasies tend to emphasize severe pain, whereas female ones tend to prefer milder forms of pain (e.g., a hand spanking instead of a whipping). Female masochists are more likely to describe an ongoing relationship context for pain than are male masochists (Baumeister, 1988b). For example, a male masochistic fantasy might describe a spanking delivered for no reason except the whim of the dominant partner, whereas the corresponding female fantasy would involve being spanked every time she failed at some household chore. These results suggest that male masochists focus on the intense sensation of substantial pain, whereas for females the pain is part of a relationship context in which it carries some symbolic meaning.

The category of humiliation and embarrassment yielded many sex differences, possibly because male and female egos differ somewhat in the basis for dignity and esteem. For males, the loss of status is central, hence many male masochists seek out experiences in which they are symbolically reduced to something "less than a man," such as a dog or a baby. Oral humiliations (i.e., being forced to do something embarrassing with one's mouth, such as kissing feet) were far more common among male than female masochists (Baumeister, 1988b, 1989). The implication may be that the enjoyment of high status is an important part of the male ego, so explicitly undermining that status is central to masochistic enjoyment in many cases.

Transvestism is also quite relevant to that argument. If masochism is escape from self, then becoming symbolically converted into the opposite gender could in principle be a powerful, appealing technique for both men and women. Yet Baumeister's (1988b, 1989) sample contained no accounts at all in which female masochists were symbolically masculinized (and likewise no accounts by male dominants who masculinized their submissive female partners). In contrast, 39% of the male masochists in that same sample described some form of gender switching, usually involving dressing in female clothes. This striking difference in rates of transvestism may reflect the notion that male status is traditionally higher than female, so for a female masochist to become masculinized would be an incongruous gain in status. Whatever the explanation, it is apparent that transvestism is far more common among male than female masochists.

For females, on the other hand, the overwhelming favorite among all humiliating and embarrassing activities was simply to be displayed naked (Baumeister, 1988b, 1989). Female masochists described being tied up with their legs spread for the partner (and occasionally others) to look at them, or being required to walk around in the nude while others remained dressed. Some elaborate fantasies revolved around this kind of display, such as that of a woman who described being posed naked and open on a table full of hors d'oeuvres during a cocktail party. Nearly half of the reports by female masochists involved some sort of exhibitionistic display.

Partner infidelity has been regarded as a form of humiliation in many contexts for centuries, and some masochists have adapted it as well. This too seems to be far more common among male than female masochists (Baumeister, 1988b, 1989). A minority of male masochists reported having their partners engage in sex with someone else; almost no female masochists reported this. This difference suggests again that the relationship context is quite important and compelling to the female masochist, to the extent that she does not want her partner to show sexual interest in anyone else. The male masochist, however, may enjoy the humiliation of being cuckolded.

The explicit sexual activities masochists engage in also show gender differences. Baumeister (1988b) found that genital intercourse was far more commonly practiced by female than male masochists, whereas oral sex was slightly more commonly performed by male than by female masochists, and anal sex was reported by both with equal frequency. For male masochists with female partners, this was accomplished by her using a dildo or vibrator, rather than by having the masochist's penis enter the anus of the partner. Thus, with both oral and anal sex, it was overwhelmingly the mouth or anus of the masochist that was used. It may symbolize submission to have one's mouth or anus penetrated (or otherwise used) by the dominant partner. Such a symbolic message may help explain the vast difference in rates of genital intercourse: For a female masochist to be vaginally penetrated by her dominant partner would be in keeping with her submissive attitude, whereas the submission of a male masochist might be symbolically contradicted if he were to penetrate his dominant partner.

A last sex difference involves the presence of other people. A small minority of both male and female masochists reported the presence of someone other than the dominant partner during their submissive scenes. Although the rate of third party presence was about equal, the function of the third party differed significantly. Female masochists usually described other people as being merely an audience, whereas male masochists usually described the other people joining in the activities (such as by helping to whip the masochist or receiving oral sex from him). This pattern seems to parallel several others noted already, such as the emphasis on being displayed as the center of attention as opposed to being subjected to complex, intense sensations.

FUTURE DIRECTIONS

Considerable room remains for research on masochism. Nearly all the findings covered in this chapter stand in need of replication, verification, and extension by additional studies. Meanwhile, there are other issues and questions for which evidence is almost entirely lacking.

As we suggested, one feature of masochism that is hardly explained by any theory is the intense, recurrent craving for such experiences that some individuals report. The individual differences in this craving are also worth considering, because there is some evidence that some people are casual and almost indifferent about engaging in masochism while others think about it frequently and become acutely unhappy when unable to engage in it (see Scott, 1983).

How people first become sexually interested in masochism is yet another important question that remains unanswered. A couple of studies have asked small samples of masochists how they got started, and the results usually show almost no uniform pattern (e.g., some masochists can cite interest going back to childhood, whereas others never even considered it until adulthood; see Moser & Levitt, 1984; Spengler, 1977). A more aggressive and systematic search for predisposing factors and focal experiences would make a valuable contribution.

CONCLUSION

Although sexual masochism remains understudied and inadequately understood, recent studies have begun to construct an empirical basis for ruling out some theories and drawing some conclusions about it. Sexual masochism does not appear to be itself pathological or a symptom of deeper problems, nor does it generally involve wish for injury, punishment for sexual guilt, or self-destructive impulses. It appeals to a small minority of both males and females and is typical of neither sex. Males and females do seem to differ somewhat in their preferred scripts and practices for masochistic scenes, however.

The essence of sexual masochism is the use of pain, bondage (or other deprivation of control and initiative), and humiliation or embarrassment to enhance sexual arousal. Nearly all researchers have noted that masochists report that sadomasochistic activities enhance sexual pleasure (Baumeister, 1989; Moser & Levitt, 1987; Scott, 1983), although objective verification of this enhancement is lacking. It is also important to note that the use of pain, bondage, and humiliation are often embedded into a game or scene that lasts much longer than ordinary sexual intercourse and that often lends context and meaning (however artificial) to the activities.

A broad variety of theories has been put forward to explain sexual masochism, but many of them have become obsolete in light of recent data. Theories of opponent process and escape from self seem best able to handle recent findings, but even these leave certain questions only partly answered. Meanwhile, most of the information about masochism comes from a mere handful of empirical studies. It is thus clear that there is still ample room for future researchers to make substantial contributions to the understanding of masochism, both by collecting data and by building theory.

ACKNOWLEDGMENTS

Preparation of this chapter was facilitated by a grant from the National Institutes of Health (MH 51482) to Roy F. Baumeister.

REFERENCES

Bader, M. J. (1993). Adaptive sadomasochism and psychological growth. *Psychoanalytic Dialogues, 3*, 279–300.

Baumeister, R. F. (1988a). Masochism as escape from self. *Journal of Sex Research, 25*, 28–59.

Baumeister, R. F. (1988b). Gender differences in masochistic scripts. *Journal of Sex Research, 25*, 478–499.

Baumeister, R. F. (1989). *Masochism and the self.* Hillsdale, NJ: Erlbaum.

Baumeister, R. F. (1991). *Escaping the self: Alcoholism, spirituality, masochism, and other flights from the burden of selfhood.* New York: Basic Books.

Baumeister, R. F., & Scher, S. J. (1988). Self-defeating behavior patterns among normal individuals: Review and analysis of common self-destructive tendencies. *Psychological Bulletin, 104*, 3–22.

Baumeister, R. F., Stillwell, A. M., & Heatherton, T. F. (1994). Guilt: An interpersonal approach. *Psychological Bulletin, 115,* 243–267.

Berglas, S. C., & Baumeister, R. F. (1993). *Your own worst enemy: Understanding the paradox of self-defeating behavior.* New York: Basic Books.

Cartwright, R. D., & Wood, E. (1993). The contribution of dream masochism to the sex ratio difference in major depression. *Psychiatry Research, 46*(2), 165–173.

Cleugh, J. (1951). *The Marquis and the Chevalier.* London: Melrose.

Cooper, A. M. (1993). Psychotherapeutic approaches to masochism. *Journal of Psychotherapy Practice and Research, 2*(1), 51–63.

Coen, S. J. (1988). Sadomasochistic excitement: Character disorder and perversion. In R. A. Glick & D. I. Myers (Eds.), *Masochism: Current psychoanalytic perspectives* (pp. 43–60). Hillsdale, NJ: Analytic Press.

Cowan, L. (1982). *Masochism: A Jungian view.* Dallas, TX: Spring.

Diana, L. (1985). *The prostitute and her clients.* Springfield, IL: Charles C Thomas.

Fraiberg, S. (1982). Pathological defenses in infancy. *Psychoanalytic Quarterly, 51,* 612–633.

Freud, S. (1938). Sadism and masochism. In *Basic writings of Sigmund Freud* (A. A. Brill, Trans.). New York: Modern Library. (Reprinted in T. Weinberg & G. Kamel (Eds.), *S and M: Studies in sadomasochism* (pp. 30–32). Buffalo, NY: Prometheus.)

Freud, S. (1961). The economic problem of masochism. In J. Strachey (Ed. and Trans.), *The standard edition of the complete psychological works of Sigmund Freud* (Vol. 19, pp. 159–170). London: Hogarth Press. (Original work published 1924)

Friday, N. (1980). *Men in love.* New York: Dell.

Friedman, R. C. (1991). The depressed masochistic patient: Diagnostic and management considerations. *Journal of the American Academy of Psychoanalysis, 19*(1), 9—30.

Gordon, R. (1987). Masochism: The shadow side of the archetypal need to venerate and worship. *Journal of Analytical Psychology, 32,* 227–240.

Greene, G., & Greene, C. (1974). *S–M: The last taboo.* New York: Grove Press.

Grossman, W. I. (1986). Notes on masochism: A discussion of the history and development of a psychoanalytic concept. *Psychoanalytic Quarterly, 55,* 379–413.

Heatherton, T. F., Polivy, J., Herman, C. P., & Baumeister, R. F. (1993). Self-awareness, task failure, and disinhibition: How attentional focus affects eating. *Journal of Personality, 61,* 49–61.

Janus, S., Bess, B., & Saltus, C. (1977). *A sexual profile of men in power.* Englewood Cliffs, NJ: Prentice-Hall.

Kernberg, O. F. (1988). Clinical dimensions of masochism. In R.A. Glick & D. I. Meyers (Eds.), *Masochism: Current psychoanalytic perspectives* (pp. 61–79). Hillsdale, NJ: Analytic Press.

Kernberg, O. F. (1991). Sadomasochism, sexual excitement, and perversion. *Journal of the American Psychoanalytic Association, 39*(2), 333–362.

Lee, J. A. (1983). The social organization of sexual risk. In T. Weinberg & G. Kamel (Eds.), *S and M: Studies in sadomasochism* (pp. 175–193). Buffalo, NY: Prometheus.

MacGregor, J. (1991). Identification with the victim. *Psychoanalytic Quarterly, 60*(1), 53–68.

Maleson, F. G. (1984). The multiple meanings of masochism in psychoanalytic discourse. *Journal of the American Psychoanalytic Association, 32*(2), 325–356.

Michael, R. T., Gagnon, J. H., Laumann, E. O., & Kolata, G. (1994). *Sex in America: A definitive survey.* Boston: Little, Brown.

Mollinger, R. N. (1982). Sadomasochism and developmental stages. *Psychoanalytic Review, 69*(3), 379–389.

Money, J. (1987). Masochism: On the childhood origin of paraphilia, opponent-process theory, and anti-androgen therapy. *Journal of Sex research, 23*(2), 273–275.

Moser, C., & Levitt, E. E. (1987). An exploratory-descriptive study of a sadomasochistically oriented sample. *Journal of Sex Research, 23*(3), 322–337.

O'Halloran, R. L., & Deitz, P. E. (1993). Autoerotic fatalities with power hydraulics. *Journal of Forensic Sciences, 38*(2), 359–364.

Reik, T. (1957). *Masochism in modern man* (M. H. Beigel & G. M. Kurth, Trans.). New York: Grove Press. (Original work published 1941)

Scarry E. (1985). *The body in pain: The making and unmaking of the world.* New York: Oxford University Press.

Scott, G. G. (1983). *Erotic power: An exploration of dominance and submission.* Secaucus, NJ: Citadel Press.

Smith, H., & Cox, C. (1983). Dialogue with a dominatrix. In T. Weinberg & G. Kamel (Eds.), *S and M: Studies in sadomasochism* (pp. 80–86). Buffalo, NY: Prometheus.

Solomon, R. L. (1980). The opponent process theory of acquired motivation: The costs of pleasure and the benefits of pain. *American Psychologist, 35,* 691–712.

Solomon, R. L., & Corbit, J. D. (1974). An opponent-process theory of motivation: I. Temporal dynamics of affect. *Psychological Review, 81,* 119–145.

Spengler, A. (1977). Manifest sadomasochism of males: Results of an empirical study. *Archives of Sexual Behavior, 6,* 441–456.

Stolorow, R. D., Atwood, G. E., & Brandschaft, B. (1988). Masochism and its treatment. *Bulletin of the Menninger Clinic, 52*(6), 504–509.

Stolorow, R. D., & Lachmann, F. M. (1980). *Psychoanalysis of developmental arrests.* New York: International Universities Press.

Warren, V. L. (1985). Explaining masochism. *Journal for the Theory of Social Behavior, 15*(2), 103–130.

Weinberg, M. S., Williams, C. J., & Moser, C. (1984). The social constituents of sadomasochism. *Social Problems, 31,* 379–389.

Weinberg, T., & Kamel, W. L. (Eds.). (1983). *S and M: Studies in sadomasochism.* Buffalo, NY: Prometheus.

Young, G. H., & Gerson, S. (1991). New psychoanalytic perspectives on masochism and spouse abuse. *Psychotherapy, 28*(1), 30–38.

Zerbe, K. J. (1992). Eating disorders in the 1990s: Clinical challenges and treatment implications. *Bulletin of the Menninger Clinic, 56*(2), 167–187.

13

SEXUAL MASOCHISM
Assessment and Treatment

David Thornton
Ruth Mann

Some sexual deviations clearly are antisocial. Some may cause real distress or damage to those who practice them. Others may be harmless expressions of human diversity. Where the borderline between these categories lies is invariably a matter of controversy. The subject is made more difficult because both the distress and the antisocial quality of a deviation may be products of a condemnatory societal reaction. It is therefore all too easy for those who in good faith provide "treatment" for sexual deviants to find at a later date that they have, in effect, been colluding with societal oppression.

Sexual masochism—obtaining sexual pleasure from pain, humiliation, or loss of control—is precisely the kind of sexual deviation where these difficulties are most acute, and some would therefore argue that it is inappropriate even to consider the possibility of offering treatment to someone presenting with sexual masochism. It is unusual, however, for sexual masochism to be the presenting problem. More commonly it will come to light in the course of working with someone who has come to attention for some other reason. The therapist will then be faced with either ignoring this facet of the person's sexuality or incorporating it into the treatment agenda. This chapter looks at sexual masochism occurring in the context of male sexual offending. It considers the potential links between the two and discusses some of the treatment strategies which may be adopted if it is decided that the person's masochistic sexual interests must be dealt with in treatment.

POTENTIAL LINKS BETWEEN MASOCHISM
AND SEXUAL OFFENDING

There are a number of ways in which an offender's masochism may be linked to the factors sustaining offending. In this section, we analyze some potential links; evidence to support our assertions is discussed in the following section.

Effects of Masochism on Values and Sensitivities

Expression of sexual masochism through either fantasy or behavior may undermine the values and sensitivities which normally serve as a barrier to sexual offending. This may happen in three ways: First, masochists may draw analogies from their own experience when trying to understand others' reactions to different kinds of sexual approach. Thus, if they (under some circumstances) are attracted by sexual experiences involving pain, loss of control, and humiliation then they may suppose that other people will likewise be attracted by these things (but perhaps pretend they are not because it is not "respectable" to have these interests).

Second, like any paraphilia, sexual masochism is likely to mean that the person's expression of sex becomes more a relationship between themselves and their sexual interest, and less a relationship with another person. This impersonal approach to sexual behavior might contrast with the norms, sensitivities, and values which represent sex not just as a sensual experience, but as an expression of a loving relationship. Most people's actual sexual lives are some compromise between what might be called the hedonistic and the relational view of sex. The more someone's sex life becomes dominated by the fantasy or practice of impersonal sex, the more their sexual value system will adapt to support this until their ideology of sex becomes simply that everyone is entitled to satisfy their "sexual needs."

Finally, some loss of ordinary valuing and moral reasoning around sexuality is, perhaps, intrinsic to the way in which sexual masochism works. At least one of the mechanisms through which sexual masochism is supposed to gain its appeal has a striking resemblance to a mechanism which supposedly underlies the development of the cognitive distortions involved in sexual offending. Baumeister (1989, 1991; see also Baumeister & Butler, Chapter 12, this volume) has developed the concept of cognitive deconstruction. In developing his concept of "escape from the self," Baumeister argues that people attempt to avoid the negative implications of self-awareness to escape from the effects of traumatic or particularly stressful experiences, and that this strategy may become entrenched as a way of dealing with ongoing stress. He proposes that there are multiple, hierarchically structured levels of meaning associated with human action, ranging from the more concrete to the more abstract. By narrowing the focus of attention to more concrete levels of meaning the person can avoid having to engage in self-evaluation and may, for example, diminish awareness that they are transgressing self-standards.

Baumeister (1989, 1991) argued that one of the primary appeals of sexual masochism is that it allows just this kind of escape from the self. Similar analyses have been made of alcoholism, binge eating, and self-injury. More recently, Ward, Hudson, and Marshall (1995) argued that this same process of cognitive deconstruction—a retreat to concrete levels of processing meaning—plays a critical role in the development of sexual offending. More specifically, they proposed that both the distorted thinking and the affective deficits which are commonly observed as a prelude to sexual offending arise through just this process of cognitive deconstruction. Thus, sexual masochism involves both practicing the same dynamic cognitive–affective process that leads to sexual offending and more specifically, it involves deliberately suspending normal self-standards when behaving sexually.

Effects of Masochism on Sexual Interests

The forbidden quality of a socially disapproved behavior, the genuine risks that may sometimes be involved, and the escape from the mundane "self" of everyday life may add to the intensity of the masochistic sexual experience, giving it a special excitement. More ordinary sexual behavior may seem dull in comparison. With repetition, though, masochistic sexuality may pall, at least temporarily. Attuned to exploratory, hedonistic sex, the individual may explore other paraphilias, returning to masochism when it has reacquired some novelty. As this pattern develops masochism will become part of a repertoire of paraphilic interests, not a phenomenon which occurs in isolation (and of course it may not have been the first interest to develop). Paraphilic interests are, by definition, generally considered to be socially unacceptable, and their expression often constitutes a sexual offense.

A paraphilic interest which is particularly likely to develop from masochism is sadism. At first this might seem odd; the infliction of pain, humiliation, or the loss of control on someone else apparently is quite different from the receiving of these things. However, the expression of masochism normally involves an interaction with another who takes the sadistic role. Such encounters, "scenes," may be highly scripted. As these scenes are repeatedly experienced, the scene itself rather than a particular role in it may become eroticized. Enacting the scene from the dominant role rather than the submissive one may be a natural step if the scene itself has become eroticized. Indeed, the novelty involved may refresh its sexual interest. And of course, some sexual activities may then allow both masochistic and sadistic elements to be combined.

Effects of Masochism on Emotional Intimacy

Masochism may lead to reduced emotional intimacy. Sexual relationships are normally a source of emotional intimacy and support as well as sexual satisfaction. In turning to an impersonal source of sexual gratification, masochists are largely removing this source of emotional intimacy and making themselves more and more dependent on nonsexual friendships or on parental relationships. Modern Western culture is, however, not very well organized for heterosexual men to obtain emotional intimacy through these routes. Even where some potential source of emotional intimacy is preserved, its value is likely to be undermined by the felt need to keep one emotionally important area of life (sexual life) disguised. If masochism is linked to reduced emotional intimacy, then there may be increased potential for sexual offending, as there is persuasive evidence that sexual offenders are deficient in emotional intimacy and suffer from significant emotional loneliness (e.g., Ward, McCormack, & Hudson, 1997; Seidman, Marshall, Hudson, & Robertson, 1994).

CONTRASTING PICTURES OF SEXUAL MASOCHISM

The picture of sexual masochism conjured up by the preceding analysis contrasts quite strongly with Baumeister and Butler's (Chapter 12, this volume) depiction of masochism as "psychologically healthy" and at the very least, harmless. There are a number of predictions which stem from our analysis and which, if substantiated, are hard to reconcile with Baumeister and Butler's view.

Specifically we predict that sexual masochism is correlated with (1) sexual offending; (2) cognitive distortions of the kind that can be used to justify sexual offending; (3) a wide range of other unusual sexual interests (including especially sadism); (4) sensation seeking; and (5) emotional loneliness. We examine evidence relevant to these predictions below. Because the published literature on sexual masochism is comparatively slight, we rely heavily on reanalyses of data collected by us in the course of other studies, notably from Thornton, Todd, and Thornton's (1996) study of the correlates of fantasy and cognitive distortions in a student population, Thornton, Mann, Bowers, Sheriff, and White's (1996) study of convicted sexual offenders in a therapeutic community, and our ongoing research into the operation of an intensive residential treatment program for less violent child molesters.

Correlation with Sexual Offending

McCollaum and Lester (1994), in an anonymous survey of students, reported a significant positive correlation of $r - .58$ between masochistic sexual interests and admissions of sexual aggression. This correlation was of the same magnitude as the correlations of other sexual fantasy measures (sadism, etc.) with self-reported sexual aggression. Re-analysis of data from Thornton et al. (1996) found that some interest in sexual masochism was relatively common among convicted sexual offenders; the strength of these interests as measured by Laws' Sexual Deviance Card Sort task (Laws, 1986) was associated with having been repeatedly convicted for sexual offenses ($r = .34$).

Correlation with Cognitive Distortions

Thornton and colleagues (1996) reported a study of factors affecting students' abilities to distinguish appropriate from inappropriate sexual approaches. Their subjects also completed the Wilson Sexual Fantasy Inventory (Wilson, 1978). A 4-item masochism scale (with a reliability of .83) correlated negatively with Hanson and Scott's (1995) Empathy for Women measure ($r = -.21$; $p = .05$). Therefore, those men with masochistic sexual interests were on average less able to distinguish the kind of sexual approaches which women find distressing.

In the therapeutic community sex offender sample, degree of interest in sexual masochism was correlated with acceptance of rape myths ($r = .31$), with believing that one is entitled to satisfy one's sexual needs ($r = .29$), with seeing children as sexual ($r = .59$), and with accepting justifications for adults having sex with children ($r = .45$).

Correlation with Sexual Interests

Table 13.1 shows the correlation between masochistic sexual interests and various sexual interest factors identified through factor analysis of responses to the Wilson Sexual Fantasy Inventory (Wilson, 1978) using the data from Thornton et al. (1996). All scales had reliabilities of at least .8.

Masochistic interests were closely associated with sadistic interests. Strong associations were also apparent for an interest in indiscriminate sex with multiple unknown partners (orgy) and with interests in bestiality, flashing, and sex with people of a very different age (deviant). On the other hand, interest in masochism showed only a much smaller relationship with interest in fantasies of sex with a loved partner in a romantic or intimate setting. Thus, masochistic interests are not simply a matter of a generalized interest in sex. Rather, they

TABLE 13.1. Correlation of Other Fantasy Themes with Masochistic Interests

Fantasy variables	Correlations with masochistic interests
Sadism	.76
Orgy	.53
Deviant	.53
Intimacy	.19

TABLE 13.2. Correlation of Fantasy Themes with Loneliness and Sensation Seeking

Fantasy variables	Emotional loneliness	Sensation seeking
Sadism	+.18	+.20
Orgy	−.03	+.42
Deviant	+.06	+.03
Intimacy	−.09	+.32

involve a tilting of the balance of someone's sexual interests in favor of impersonal, or indeed antisocial, sexual themes.

Correlation with Sensation Seeking and Emotional Loneliness

Table 13.2 shows the correlations from the same study of the various sexual interests factors with sensation seeking (measured by the Eysenck I7 Questionnaire's Venturesomeness scale; Eysenck, Pearson, Easting, & Allsop, 1985) and emotional loneliness (measured by the Revised UCLA Emotional Loneliness Scale; Russell, Peplau, & Cutrona, 1980). Most types of sexual interest appear to be associated with sensation seeking; masochistic interests show this association but are not unusual in this respect. Emotional loneliness, on the other hand, was distinctively associated with masochistic interests (none of the other correlations with emotional loneliness were statistically significant).

Overall Picture of the Sexual Masochist

The results of these studies are largely consistent with our theoretical analysis of factors which may link masochism to sexual offending. Not only is masochism positively correlated with sexual offending, but it is also related to having generalized impersonal sexual interests, to various cognitive distortions of the kinds which can be used to rationalize sexual offending, and to difficulties forming emotionally intimate relationships. On the other hand, except for the correlation with other impersonal sexual interests, associations with the other factors are sufficiently weak to suggest that it must be perfectly possible to develop and express masochistic interests without necessarily developing these other problems.

ASSESSMENT OF SEXUAL OFFENDERS WITH MASOCHISTIC INTERESTS

Assessment of sexual offenders' masochistic interests should have three goals: determining which offenders have masochistic interests, investigating the functional significance of these interests, and preparing the ground for relevant interventions. It is important that masochistic interests are placed in the context of the person's other sexual interests, so that the starting point is to screen for the range of interests commonly found among sexual offenders.

Identifying Masochistic Interests

Except in particularly extreme cases, subjects will identify masochistic interests only if the matter is directly investigated. In our experience it is seldom productive to attempt this until the clinician has built up considerable rapport and has substantially undermined the facade of denial and minimization through which offenders initially present themselves and their offending (O'Donohue & Letourneau, 1993). Another critical issue is the appearance and demeanor of the interviewer—seeming inexperienced, shockable, or vulnerable can make for particular difficulties. Interviewed by a fresh-faced graduate, a middle-aged and some-what prudish child abuser is likely to find it hard to disclose any unusual sexual interests. Some rapists, on the other hand, will respond to the same situation by taking particular relish in producing fantasies in a way which they hope will embarrass the interviewer. This kind of behavior can easily get out of hand—one colleague believed that she was successfully eliciting the details of a previously undisclosed sadistic fantasy until she realized that the offender was actually elaborating a fantasy about her.

After establishing rapport and overcoming denial and minimization surrounding the offending itself, it is possible to use a combination of questionnaire and interview techniques to elicit meaningful information. A useful approach is to use questionnaires to survey a broad range of potential interests and then to follow this up with an interview.

A number of questionnaires are potentially useful here. Laws (1986) has developed a Sexual Deviance Card Sort task with groups of items which cover the paraphilias more commonly found among sex offenders. A particular feature of this card set is that many of the items have a floridly deviant quality. The advantage to this method is that it is clinically significant when offenders admit any kind of interest in the cards. The disadvantage is that some offenders will be affronted or upset by them. Assuming that cooperation can be maintained, this is something which can sometimes be turned to therapeutic advantage, but it can nevertheless present problems and it does mean that the procedure is practical only in rather limited contexts. One advantage of the technique is that it can be focused on specific periods of the offender's life (e.g., "as you feel now," "as you felt in the month before you committed this offense"). In our experience, focusing on more than one time period with this task produces more useful information—offenders are more likely to admit to having had deviant interests if they can deny that they presently have them.

At the other extreme there is the Wilson Sexual Fantasy Questionnaire (Wilson, 1978). The items are quite bland, easily accepted by most subjects, and consequently of a kind which can more readily be used with untreated sex offenders or with more general populations. The questionnaire has the merit of investigating interest in a variety of less pathological themes, but needs additional items if it is to properly cover the range of paraphilias common in sex offenders. It does, however, assess masochistic interest fairly well (see, for example, Gosselin, Wilson, & Barrett, 1991).

Another scale designed to measure sexual fantasy has been developed by O'Donohue, Letourneau, and Dowling (1997). This measure has a Masochism subscale. Probably the most established questionnaire for obtaining a general picture of the range of paraphilic interests common in sex offenders is the Clarke Sexual History Inventory (Langevin, 1991). There are wide-ranging normative data for this questionnaire. Whichever questionnaires the clinician uses, it is essential to explore and clarify questionnaire responses through inter-views.

Investigating the Functional Significance of Masochistic Interests

The clinician should then conduct a sexual history interview which clarifies the meaning of interests apparently indicated by questionnaire to trace the development of these interests from early childhood. Minimally, this should seek to cover the development of the fantasy themes corresponding to particular interests and their behavioral expression. Behavioral outlets need to be placed in the kinds of relationships within which they are expressed, and the clinician must explore the individual's feelings about and during various sexual expressions and the way the subject now rationalizes this sexual activity (and how it was rationalized at the time). This kind of analysis may have to be fairly sketchy in relation to early sexual development, because memories of early experiences can be incomplete and unreliable. We do not think that there is any merit in trying to "recover" early memories of being sexually abused if these are not already something the offender can easily recall. Those experiences of unwanted or age-inappropriate sex which are easily recalled should be explored with a particular emphasis on identifying methods of coping used at the time and the sense that the offender now makes of the experience.

More detailed and careful analyses are warranted of recent sexual experiences, covering the major sexual outlets in the 5 years preceding the index offense. Here we suggest that the clinician undertake a proper functional analysis for each kind of outlet that is employed with any frequency. This involves identifying recent typical examples of these outlets and then distinguishing four phases in relation to each outlet: (1) an *antecedent phase* covering the normal precursors to the outlet; (2) an *activity phase*— while the sexual activity concerned is actually taking place; (3) an *immediate aftermath phase* covering the rest of that day; and (4) a *reflection phase* covering any effects on lifestyle. For each phase, a systematic investigation should be undertaken, covering the following areas:

1. The sequence of situations and behaviors occurring in that phase.
2. General attitudes that played a role in leading to those behaviors in these particular situations.
3. Significant relationships pertinent at the time.
4. The different kinds and intensities of affect felt during that phase.
5. Typical physical state (notably, effects of drugs, alcohol and fatigue).
6. Specific thoughts which provoke or justify the behavior occurring in that phase.
7. The particular sexual interests which found expression during the phase.

The assessor should examine the raw material gained from such a functional analysis to explore the links between masochism and sexual offending. As indicated above, we see three areas in which there may be "toxic links" between masochism and sexual offending: effects on values and sensitivities, on sexual interests, and on emotional intimacy. The following sections suggest ways in which to use the interview material to test for the presence of any of these links.

Links to Values and Sensitivities

We have identified three possible links here: analogies from experience, orientation to impersonal sex, and cognitive deconstruction. Each possibility should be tested, remembering that the issue is not so much what the functional significance of masochism was during the individual's developmental history, but rather what significance it might have in the future.

Drawing Analogies from the Offender's Own Experience

Test questions here are as follows: is the offender's representation of his victim's reactions similar to his representation of his own reactions during masochistic fantasy/experience, or similar to his representation of other people's reactions during masochistic sex? Does he think that his victim will develop sexual fantasies about being abused/raped?

Impersonal Approach to Sexual Behavior

Test questions here are as follows: Does the offender understand sex as basically hedonistic rather than relational? Perhaps the offender has distinct models for these two kinds of sexual interaction; if so, do they see relational sex as a possibility for them, and what do they see as the pros and cons of each form of sexual expression? Are the justifications developed for hedonistic sex similar to the justifications employed in relation to their sexual offending? A common justification here is a sense of sexual entitlement—"I have a right to satisfy my sexual needs."

Cognitive Deconstruction

Test questions here are as follows: Does the offender enter a "deconstructed state" both before sexual offending and before engaging in masochistic sex? If so, are there state-specific types of cognitive distortions (for example, disregarding his normal self-image) which play a part in both? How crucial are these distortions to allowing offending to occur?

Links to Sexual Interests

There are two main issues which the clinician needs to test for. First, is the interest in sexual masochism part of a more general exploration of different paraphilias? If so, how are they linked? Is masochism central or peripheral to this process? One common pattern is for interests to be explored in turn with switches between interests arising when the current interest has become boring. Another pattern is for multiple interests to be explored simultaneously in an opportunistic way.

Second, has this exploration of different sexual possibilities rendered more conventional relational sex dull by comparison? Does conventional relational sex satisfy the emotional needs addressed by this wider range of sexual activities?

Links to Emotional Intimacy

Has the expression of masochistic interests, or linked paraphilias, made it difficult to develop appropriate emotionally intimate relationships? This may have arisen either through the need to conceal masochistic practices from partners or through an obsessional involvement with impersonal sex. What effect would masochistic interests/practices have on plausible sources of emotional intimacy in the offender's future environment?

TREATING SEXUAL OFFENDERS WITH MASOCHISTIC INTERESTS

Setting the Treatment Agenda

If assessment has highlighted links between an offender's sexual offending and their masochistic interests, then the therapist must judge whether it is worth trying to address these links in treatment. One possibility is to disregard the offender's masochistic interests and to concentrate instead on factors which are more directly related to his offending. We can raise several arguments in favor of this stance: The techniques for modifying masochistic interests may have a limited, perhaps temporary effect; it may be hard to motivate an offender to modify these interests; and masochistic interests may be the least concern of a range of paraphilic interests in the offender's repertoire. In addition, the clinician may feel that it is just simpler to tackle factors which are more directly linked to sexual offending.

However, although there certainly is something to be said for this view, there is a range of complications which the clinician needs to consider even if he or she decides not to try to modify the offender's masochistic interests. Simply treating factors more directly linked to sexual offending runs the risk that these factors may diminish during treatment but subsequently return as the offender continues to act out masochistic interests. There also is the danger that some conventional procedures may produce unexpected results. For example, phallometric assessment of interest in rape may spuriously indicate a rape preference when the subject actually is a gay man with masochistic interests. Equally, some methods of trying to induce victim empathy can be counterproductive with masochistic offenders. In one example from our clinical work, a serial rapist went on, following victim empathy work, to develop a fantasy identification with rape victims—but because he found these fantasies sexually exciting, he supposed that his victims would have done so also.

Minimally then, there needs to be a careful evaluation of the likelihood and seriousness of complications of this kind, as standard sex offender assessment and treatment procedures may need to be modified for offenders with masochistic interests.

Motivating Offenders to Modify Masochistic Interests

The offender's masochism must be addressed in treatment, then one obvious approach is to try to reduce the attraction of this interest. A major concern here will be engaging the offender's motivation. We recommend a motivational interviewing approach as described by Miller and Rollnick (1991). This approach is defined importantly by its treatment *style,* which is nonjudgmental and facilitates clients to think things through for themselves, and its *goal,* which is that the client (not the therapist) should express concerns about behavior and reasons for change.

There are a range of motivational interviewing strategies for facilitating problem recognition in clients who are not yet ready to change. One particular strategy that we recommend for motivating offenders to modify their masochistic interests is known as "Good Things, Less Good Things" (Rollnick, Heather, & Bell, 1992). In this strategy, the therapist asks the offender to list all the "good things" that exist for them about masochism. It is important that the therapist draws out the client to give a full explanation of each "good thing." The therapist needs to fully explore the contingencies surrounding and maintaining the behavior, and must demonstrate a genuine desire to understand the offender's perceptions of his behavior. Once the offender has exhausted his ability to describe positive outcomes of masochism, the therapist should move gently on to asking about "less good things" regarding the behavior. If the offender is resistant to offering any "less good things," then the therapist should gently prompt around the following areas:

Risk to Physical Safety of Self

Some masochistic practices are physically unsafe and could place the masochist at risk of injury or death. Autoerotic practices such as autoerotic asphyxiation are particularly unsafe and several deaths from such practices are reported in the literature (e.g., O'Halloran & Dietz, 1993).

Link to Sexual Offending

The assessment of links between the individual's sexual offending and their masochistic interests should have uncovered material which can be used to raise this issue directly with the offender. If the offender can develop an enhanced awareness of links between his masochism and his offending, then he may reevaluate the harmlessness of his masochistic interests.

Dependence

Many people who hold an interest in sexual masochism report a diminished enjoyment in nonmasochistic sexual practices and a developing obsession with masochistic practices. For some, this sense of dependence on a sexual practice, of their lives therefore being out of control, is something they dislike.

Reduction in Emotional Intimacy

For the reasons indicated earlier, masochistic interests can undermine the person's ability to develop emotionally intimate relationships. As most sex offenders feel a real need for emotional intimacy, this may be a powerful source of motivation.

Methods of Modifying Masochistic Interests

We advocate four strategies here. First, clinicians can use standard behavior therapy techniques to decrease interest in preferred masochistic scenarios. Verbal satiation (Laws, 1995) is probably the technique of choice here. Satiation is one of the limited number of procedures for which there is some evidence of effectiveness in modifying sexual interests. It is easier to monitor treatment compliance with verbal satiation than with many behavioral techniques, the procedure requires little in the way of technical equipment (a tape recorder), and boredom is a more effective antidote to masochism than are aversive smells or shocks (which the masochist may even be able to incorporate into his fantasies).

Second, behavior therapy techniques can strengthen interest in other sexual outlets if fantasies with an appropriate relational theme can be developed. Directed masturbation (Maletzky, 1985) is an appropriate procedure.

Third, relapse prevention strategies (Laws, 1989) can enable control over or avoidance of factors which make masochistic interests more compelling (the functional analyses carried out as part of the assessment process should provide the raw material for identifying relevant risk factors). The relapse prevention strategies developed should provide alternative satisfactions for some of the emotional needs which once were satisfied through the masochistic outlet (as identified by the functional analysis).

Fourth, some pharmacological interventions may be helpful. The usual range of antiandrogen drugs (see Bradford, Chapter 23, this volume) may be pertinent, but fluoxetine hydrochloride is also worth considering (Kafka, 1991; Masand, 1993).

Breaking the Links

A more subtle approach is not to try to modify masochistic interests, but rather to seek to break or at least weaken its links to sexual offending. This approach is not always practical, but when it is, it may be preferable to either of the other two possibilities. We give three examples of instances when it may be practical here. Note that a confrontational approach will not facilitate the process of weakening links, nor do we consider a didactic approach to be particularly effective. We strongly suggest that clinicians facilitate exploration of the issues by the client by thought experiments and Socratic questioning techniques (Overholser, 1993a, 1993b) of the kind commonly employed in motivational interviewing.

Analogies from Masochistic Experience

Suppose that an offender draws analogies between their own masochistic fantasies and the experience which they suppose their victims have, essentially supposing that their victims may find being raped sexually exciting because they themselves enjoy fantasies of humiliation and loss of control. Here the task is to get the offender to elaborate their understanding of both the victim's experience and of their own sexual experiences until the analogy dissolves. One line of attack is to encourage an elaboration of the idea that different people have different tastes. It should be easy to identify examples in which the offender has tastes different from other members in the treatment group (say, in music) and to explore how he would feel about having someone else's musical preferences imposed on him.

Another approach is to explore the subtle nature of "loss of control" in masochism. In practice, even people with masochistic sexual interests usually wish to lose control only in a controlled way—fantasizing about being kidnapped and gang-raped by a leather-clad motorcycle gang is one thing, but most masochists recognize that the reality would be dangerous. The therapist can then encourage the offender to define from their own experiences the parameters of control which they require over their behavior, and then apply these parameters to the potential experiences of other people, drawing conclusions about appropriate ways of treating others.

Impersonal Approach to Sex

If the offender plans to continue his interest in masochistic sex, there is clearly no point in seeking to encourage the view that only relational sex is appropriate, but two goals can be identified: one is disentangling impersonal sex from a sense of sexual entitlement; the other is articulating the values which can be achieved via relational sex.

The first task can be approached by focusing on how S/M sexuality can be expressed in safe and consenting interactions. This approach is consistent with the official norms of most S/M clubs, so some subcultural support is available. One feature of some masochistic offenders is that they express their masochistic interests in an abusive way, seeking, for example, to impose them on sexual partners who find this kind of sexuality distressing. It is therefore important that the offender realizes that moral restraint still can apply to S/M activity. By seeking to develop a socialized expression of S/M the therapist may both break the links to other kinds of sexual offending and avoid the masochism developing into abusive behavior.

The second task may be accomplished through the "Good Things, Less Good Things" approach described above; this process can provide a basis for articulating what is missing in impersonal S/M interactions, thus contributing to the development of the offender's concept of relational sex.

Cognitive Deconstruction

Suppose that cognitive deconstruction has been established as a way of coping with stress, with both sexual offending and masochistic behavior performed in a deconstructed state. A possible strategy is to develop other ways of coping with stress, including lifestyle adjustments which remove some of the sources of stress and cognitive therapy designed to modify some of the dysfunctional beliefs which underlie stress.

CONCLUDING REFLECTIONS

The preceding discussion may give the impression that we think the treatment issues raised by links between masochistic interests and sexual offending are easy to address. We are well aware that in practice the whole matter can be complicated and difficult, especially when masochistic interests are combined with, for example, borderline personality disorder. All we contend is that it does not help to disregard the matter. Masochistic interests in sexual offenders often are interwoven with the factors sustaining their sexual offending, and we ignore these links at our peril.

We must add that no good outcome data exist on the treatment of sexual masochism. The recommendations made in this chapter are based on our clinical and research experience, and research, even single-subject designs, is most desperately needed to advance understanding in this area. Because of this, we must caution that to make representations (e.g., to a court) on the probable effectiveness of treatment of sexual masochism is a position that would be difficult for any therapist to substantiate.

REFERENCES

Baumeister, R. F. (1989). *Masochism and the self.* Hillsdale, NJ: Erlbaum.

Baumeister, R. F. (1991). *Escaping the self: Alcoholism, spirituality, masochism, and other flights from the burden of selfhood.* New York: Basic Books.

Eysenck, S. G. B., Pearson, P. R., Easting, G., & Allsop, J. (1985). Age norms for impulsiveness, venturesomeness and empathy in adults. *Personality and Individual Differences, 6,* 613–620.

Gosselin, C. C., Wilson, G. D., & Barrett, P. T. (1991). The personality and sexual preferences of sadomasochistic women. *Personality and Individual Differences 12*(1), 11–15.

Hanson, R. K., & Scott, H. (1995). Assessing perspective-taking among sexual offenders, non-sexual criminals, and non offenders. *Sexual Abuse, 7*(4), 259–277.

Kafka, M. P. (1991). Successful anti-depressant treatment of non-paraphiliac sexual addictions and paraphilias in men. *Journal of Clinical Psychiatry, 52,* 60–65.

Laws, D. R. (1986). *The Sexual Deviance Card Sort.* Unpublished manuscript.

Laws, D. R. (Ed.). (1989). *Relapse prevention with sex offenders.* New York: Guilford Press.

Laws, D. R. (1995). Verbal satiation: Notes on procedure with speculations on its mechanism of effect. *Sexual Abuse, 7*(2), 155–166.

Langevin, R. (1991). *Clarke Sexual History Questionnaire for Males: Manual.* Etobicoke, Canada: Juniper Press.

Maletzky, B. M. (1985). Orgasmic reconditioning. In A. S. Bellack & M. Hersen (Eds.), *Dictionary of behavior therapy techniques.* New York: Pergamon Press.

Masand, P. S. (1993). Successful treatment of sexual masochism and transvestic fetishism associated with depression with fluoxetine hydrochloride. *Depression, 1,* 50–52.

McCollaum, B., Lester, D. (1994). Violent sexual fantasies and sexual behavior. *Psychological Reports, 75*(2), 742.

Miller, W. R., & Rollnick, S. (1991). *Motivational interviewing: Preparing people to change addictive behavior.* New York: Guilford Press.

O'Donohue, W., & Letourneau, E. (1993). A brief group treatment for the modification of denial in child sexual abusers. *Child Abuse and Neglect, 17,* 299–304.

O'Donohue, W., Letourneau, E., & Dowling, H. (1997). Development and preliminary validation of a paraphiliac sexual fantasy questionnaire. *Sexual Abuse: A Journal of Research and Treatment, 9,* 167–178.

O'Halloran, R. L., & Dietz, P. E. (1993). Autoerotic fatalities with power hydraulics. *Journal of Forensic Sciences, 38*(2), 359–364.

Overholser, J. C. (1993a). Elements of the Socratic method: I. Systematic questioning. *Psychotherapy,* *30,* 67–74.

Overholser, J. C. (1993b). Elements of the Socratic method: II. Inductive reasoning. *Psychotherapy,* *30,* 75–85.

Rollnick, S., Heather, N., & Bell, A. (1992). Negotiating behavior change in medical settings: The development of brief motivational interviewing. *Journal of Mental Health, 1,* 25–37.

Russell, D., Peplau, L. A., & Cutrona, C. E. (1980). The Revised UCLA Loneliness Scale. *Journal of Personality and Social Psychology, 39,* 472–480.

Seidman, B., Marshall, W. L., Hudson, S. M., & Robertson, P. J. (1994). An examination of intimacy and loneliness in sex offenders. *Journal of Interpersonal Violence, 9,* 518–534.

Thornton, D., Mann, R., Bowers, L., Sheriff, N., & White, T. (1996). *Sex offenders in a therapeutic community.* Unpublished Internal Prison Service Research Report.

Thornton, S., Todd, B., & Thornton, D. (1996). Empathy and the recognition of abuse. *Legal and Criminological Psychology, 1,* 147–153.

Ward, T., Hudson, S. M., & Marshall, W. L. (1995). Cognitive and affective deficits in sexual aggression: A cognitive deconstructionist analysis. *Sexual Abuse: A Journal of Research and Treatment, 7,* 67–83.

Ward, T., McCormack, J., & Hudson, S. M. (1997). Sexual offenders' perceptions of their intimate relationships. *Sexual Abuse: A Journal of Research and Treatment, 9*(1), 57–74.

Wilson, G. D. (1978). *The secrets of sexual fantasy.* London: J. M. Dent.

14

TRANSVESTIC FETISHISM
Psychopathology and Theory

Kenneth J. Zucker
Ray Blanchard

DESCRIPTIVE TERMINOLOGY

The literal meaning of the word "transvestism" is to wear the clothing of the opposite sex (Hirschfeld, 1910). In contemporary clinical sexology and, more specifically, in the fourth edition of the *Diagnostic and Statistical Manual of Mental Disorders* (American Psychiatric Association, 1994), the use of the term "transvestism" is delimited to describing biological males who cross-dress in women's clothing which is accompanied, at least at times, by sexual arousal (e.g., Blanchard, Racansky, & Steiner, 1986; Ovesey & Person, 1973; Stoller, 1971), and that is how the term, or its variant, transvestic fetishism (TF), will be used in this chapter.

At the outset, we need to emphasize that TF has been observed by several generations of clinicians and researchers to occur virtually exclusively in biological males. Although Stoller (1982) reported on three cases of women who showed some features of sexual arousal associated with cross-dressing, the clinical and research literature remains silent on whether there is a truly analogous form of TF in biological females. A recent feminist–psychoanalytic perspective has discussed the concept of fetishism in women (Gamman & Makinen, 1994; see also Findlay, 1992; Grosz, 1991), but in a manner that goes beyond the more restrictive definitional scope that serves as the boundary for the material considered in this chapter. We will also not address Freud's possibly sarcastic remark, made in 1909 at a meeting of the Vienna Psychoanalytic Society, that all women are "clothes fetishists" (see Rose, 1988).

In the older clinical literature, the term "transvestism" was used in diverse ways (e.g., Housden, 1965; Lukianowicz, 1959, 1962; Northrup, 1959; Randell, 1959; Taylor & McLachlan, 1962), so without studying the actual case material, one could never be certain whether the patient was, by "modern" terminology, a transvestite (as defined above), a transsexual (a person who experiences him- or herself as a member of the opposite sex, who wishes to be perceived that way by others, and who seeks out, when it is available, hormonal and surgical sex reassignment), or a homosexual cross-dresser or "drag queen" (Person & Ovesey, 1984; Pettiway, 1996). (Among homosexuals who cross-dress, sexual arousal never accompanies this activity.) The term "transvestism" has also been used to characterize the behavior of young children who show patterns of marked cross-gender behavior that signal a strong identification with the opposite sex, including the desire to change sex, even though the cross-dressing itself is not accompanied by sexual arousal (Bakwin, 1960). Thus, any clinician or researcher who studies the extant literature must be very careful to recognize that the term "transvestism" has been used in diverse and, at times, confusing ways (for a most thorough bibliography on TF, see Demeyere, 1992).

Although TF (or, perhaps, its immature precursors) has been observed in prepubertal children (see below, Case 3), patients most commonly come to the attention of clinicians during their adolescence or adulthood. The following two vignettes illustrate the core phenomenology during these phases of the life cycle:

CASE 1

Bill, age 14 (Verbal IQ = 92; Performance IQ = 100), was referred by his mother. He had a younger sibling, age 9. Bill's parents were lower-middle class. His parents separated when he was 8 years old, following years of marital discord characterized by intense verbal abuse on the part of both parents and physical abuse by the father to the mother. In terms of his phenotypic appearance, Bill was conventionally masculine in terms of hairstyle and choice of clothing.

Around age 12, Bill began to wear his mother's undergarments on a regular basis. When Bill's mother would find him cross-dressed, he would tell her that he hated her. In an effort to curtail access to her clothing, his mother put a lock on her bedroom door. When initially confronted about his behavior, Bill denied that he took the clothes, but then cried and said, "Mommy, I put them on because I feel good, then I rip them off because I'm angry." Bill's mother also noted lipstick stains on his pillowcase and that he would take anything of hers that was black, such as her boots. Bill's mother could detect semen stains on her underwear and, at one point, threatened that if he continued to take them that she would "get even" and "teach him a lesson" by urinating on his clothes.

Apart from the transvestic fetishism, Bill had also engaged in minor thievery, such as taking cassette tapes from a relative. Bill's defense was that the family was poor. Bill's mother felt that he coped with sadness by withdrawing (e.g., going to sleep early). For reasons noted below, Bill's mother had been involved in social causes over the past year and, as a result, he was left in charge of looking after his younger sibling, which he resented because he felt it interfered with his own interests and activities. Bill's mother indicated that they had a lot of conflicts pertaining to his desire to become more independent: "I guess you have to draw a line as a parent regarding who runs the show."

Prior to the onset of the cross-dressing, the family situation had been extremely stressful. There was a great deal of quarreling about the father's visitation rights and, in the context of one argument, Bill's mother apparently threatened to have the father killed, and she was subsequently arrested and charged with uttering a death threat. She was found guilty and fined. Bill's mother found this experience to be extremely traumatic and humiliating. She was preoccupied with the event, as one might observe in a person suffering from posttraumatic stress disorder. She alleged that the police, the courts, and her own lawyer—"the best feminist lawyer in the city"—had engaged in systematic racism toward her, which, on the basis of a variety of clinical evidence, had a paranoid flavor. As a result of the experience, Bill's mother became an activist in a group concerned with police racism, and spent long hours away from home in the evening involved in the cause. During the joint interview with his mother, as his mother spoke at length and with great force about these events, Bill fell asleep. Bill's mother acknowledged that she had been consumed with anger and rage over the past 2 years and that this had strongly colored her relationship with Bill. Bill's mother commented that when she was angry she would scream, throw shoes, and felt like she was losing control. During the clinical interview, the mother's felt experience of rage and anger was extremely palpable. As a result of these life events, Bill had had no contact with his father over the past 2 years. Despite the family turmoil, Bill was a good student at school, commensurate with his intellectual ability. DSM-III-R diagnoses were transvestic fetishism and parent–child problem.

CASE 2

Mario was the third of five children born to immigrant parents. He initially looked forward to starting school but soon rebelled against the regimented activities. In childhood, Mario was obese and clumsy. He was therefore unskilled at sports, although he tried hard to excel at them. He was teased by other children because of his weight problem and became a loner with few close friends of either sex. In prepubescence, he was, by his own description, "somewhat antisocial," and he got into a number of fights. This aggressiveness persisted to some extent into later life, and he was arrested three times in adulthood for getting into fights after drinking. By age 12, Mario's teachers were sufficiently disturbed by his difficulties in getting along with other children that they referred him to the school psychologist, with no particular outcome.

At the age of 11 or 12, Mario began dressing in his sister's clothes when no one was home. This initially was lingerie but later came to include dresses and makeup on occasion. Mario was sexually naive at this point and did not understand the arousal he felt when he put on women's clothes. He continued to cross-dress for the next 2 or 3 years with no masturbation or spontaneous ejaculation.

Mario's first ejaculation occurred at age 14. He was lying face down on his bed wearing a brassiere and panty hose and examining the lingerie pages of a department store catalog. While studying the photograph of a model with panty hose like those he had on, he began unconsciously to thrust against his mattress, with resulting ejaculation. In later life, he continued to find women in lingerie more attractive than nude women and to be more aroused by lingerie advertisements than by pornography. The young Mario realized that there was something unusual about his sexual behavior and wondered for a time if he were homosexual.

In later adolescence and adulthood, Mario's transvestic and masturbatory activities were accompanied by fantasies of sexual interaction with women. In one favorite fantasy, Mario cross-dressed with a woman's permission (sometimes at her insistence) and then had sex with her in a quasi-lesbian interaction. In a variant of this, he was a lesbian, and, in the aggressive role, made love to another woman. In a different fantasy vein, he "worshiped" a woman, putting her, figuratively speaking, on a pedestal, dressed her completely from underwear outward, and styled her hair. Mario was also sexually aroused by the sight of himself cross-dressed in the mirror. Although he felt like a woman when cross-dressed, he never developed any desire for hormonal or surgical feminization, and his only fantasies of sex change were of some temporary metamorphosis with a prompt return to the male role.

Mario's cross-dressing remained, by and large, a private activity. In later years he did, however, occasionally indulge in the thrill of driving around in his car at night dressed as a woman.

Mario experienced his first heterosexual intercourse at age 18. Over the next several years, he had a number of heterosexual relationships of short duration until he met his wife. He never fantasized sex with a man, even when cross-dressed, and he never had any homosexual experiences, even though he was propositioned on several occasions when hitch-hiking in his youth.

At the age of 28 he met Maria, a woman 4 years younger than himself and from the same ethnic background. They married 3 years later. The couple had a very active sexual life, with intercourse occurring up to 20 times per week. Mario, however, tended to indulge in private fantasies during coitus, including the fantasy that he and Maria were two women engaged in a lesbian interaction. Maria was completely ignorant of Mario's transvestic behavior.

Mario first consulted a psychiatrist at the age of 32, complaining of headaches and dizzy spells which appeared to be related to problems at the family business he ran with his father. He initially denied any marital problems but finally admitted his cross-dressing after several months in treatment. Mario subsequently decided that, if he could bring up the subject with a psychiatrist, he could bring it up with his wife.

Maria reacted very negatively to this information, which did not fit with her expectations of her husband. She initially feared that Mario's cross-dressing had something to do with homosexuality but later came to realize that this was not the case. On the few occasions when Maria saw Mario in women's attire, she became highly distressed, and she grudgingly tolerated his cross-dressing only in her absence. She told Mario that she believed he was afflicted by the "evil eye," and she wanted his cross-dressing to stop, certainly before they began having children.

Mario had, in fact, throughout his life, repeatedly tried to overcome his transvestism, quite apart from any pressure from Maria. Overwhelmed by guilt and shame, he had, on numerous occasions, thrown away his entire feminine wardrobe, with the resolution never to cross-dress again. Prolonged abstinence, however, made him very nervous, and he always returned to cross-dressing when the tension became unbearable.

This was the condition under which Mario asked his psychiatrist for a referral to the Adult Gender Identity Clinic at our Institute. He presented as a masculine-looking

TABLE 14.1. Diagnostic Criteria for Transvestic Fetishism in DSM-III, DSM-III-R, and DSM-IV

DSM-III criteria for transvestism
A. Recurrent and persistent cross-dressing by a heterosexual male.
B. Use of cross-dressing for the purpose of sexual excitement, at least initially in the course of the disorder.
C. Intense frustration when the cross-dressing is interfered with.
D. Does not meet the criteria for Transsexualism.
DSM-III-R diagnostic criteria for transvestic fetishism
A. Over a period of at least six months, in a heterosexual male, recurrent intense sexual urges and sexually arousing fantasies involving cross-dressing.
B. The person has acted on these urges, or is markedly distressed by them.
C. Does not meet the criteria for Gender Identity Disorder of Adolescence or Adulthood, Nontranssexual Type, or Transsexualism.
DSM-IV diagnostic criteria for transvestic fetishism
A. Over a period of at least 6 months, in a heterosexual male, recurrent, intense sexually arousing fantasies, sexual urges, or behaviors involving cross-dressing.
B. The fantasies, sexual urges, or behaviors cause clinically significant distress or impairment in social,occupational, or other important areas of functioning.
Specify if:
With Gender Dysphoria: if the person has persistent discomfort with gender role or identity.

Note. From American Psychiatric Association (1980, p. 270; 1987, p. 289; 1994, p. 531). Copyright 1980, 1987, 1994 by the American Psychiatric Association. Reprinted by permission.

and acting individual, appearing his stated age. His presenting complaint reflected his ongoing conflict: preferably to cure him of his transvestism, but otherwise to help him and his wife learn to live with it.

DIAGNOSTIC ISSUES

In terms of formal nosological systems, such as the DSM, TF has had a long history. It was included in the original DSM (American Psychiatric Association, 1952) and in all subsequent editions (American Psychiatric Association, 1968, 1980, 1987, 1994). This contrasts with other sexological diagnoses, such as the gender identity disorders, which appeared for the first time on the nosological scene only in the third edition of the DSM (American Psychiatric Association, 1980). Table 14.1 shows the diagnostic criteria for TF in DSM-III, DSM-III-R, and DSM-IV.

Placement in the Nomenclature

In the three recent editions of the DSM, TF has been included in the section of the manual as one of the paraphilias. In DSM-IV, this placement is in the section entitled "Sexual and Gender Identity Disorders."

Changes in the Diagnostic Criteria for Transvestic Fetishism between DSM-III and DSM-IV

From Table 14.1, it can be seen that there have been several changes in the diagnostic criteria for TF. These changes appear to have been made on the basis of expert clinical consensus, that is, by the subcommittees responsible for the TF diagnosis, as there has been little in the way of formal empirical research, such as field trials, regarding the reliability and validity of the TF diagnostic criteria.

In DSM-III-R, Criterion A combined in a more efficient manner Criteria A and B from the DSM-III. At the same time, there appears, at least to us, a somewhat odd change. In DSM-III-R, "actual" cross-dressing was eliminated from Criterion A and shifted to Criterion B.

Criterion C in DSM-III appears to index one of the core clinical observations regarding TF, namely, the felt anxiety or irritability that occurs when, for various reasons, cross-dressing needs to be restricted or halted, such as due to the social demands to dress and appear in the masculine social role (Person & Ovesey, 1978) or to the protests of a spouse (Woodhouse, 1989). It also reflects, albeit in a somewhat indirect way, the core concept of *distress* that guided the more general definition of mental disorder in DSM-III (Spitzer & Endicott, 1978).

Criterion C in DSM-III seems to have been replaced by a rewording of Criterion B in DSM-III-R. Criterion B is met if there is actual cross-dressing *or* if the fantasy of cross-dressing is accompanied by distress. Criterion B in DSM-IV also emphasizes distress *or* impairment associated with cross-dressing.

In our view, the wording of Criterion B in both DSM-III-R and DSM-IV raises substantial conceptual issues. In DSM-III-R, one could be given the diagnosis of TF *in the absence of distress* because Criterion B could be met if the person had simply "acted" on the urge to cross-dress. But in DSM-IV, Criterion B is *not* met if there is an absence of distress or impairment in "social, occupational, or other important areas of functioning."

Gert (1992) criticized Criterion B in DSM-III-R on the grounds that the diagnosis of TF could be made in the absence of distress and argued that it should be made only if there was associated distress. The changes in DSM-IV appear to reflect this criticism.

In our view, there are complex problems with the DSM-IV criteria for TF because of the wording of Criterion B. We have a population of males who engage in the behaviors and fantasies that define TF, but a diagnosis of TF can be made only for those males within this population who are distressed or impaired by such behaviors and/or the fantasies. From a practical point of view, this is likely of little import, as individuals with TF who consult mental health professionals are presumably, in some respect, distressed or impaired by their condition. However, from a conceptual and philosophical standpoint, the matter seems confused and muddled. (Note that Criterion B (distress or impairment) has been applied to all of the paraphilias in DSM-IV. Thus, for example, one cannot give the diagnosis of pedophilia to an individual who is not distressed by the condition or if it does not cause impairment in social, occupational, or other important areas of functioning.) We consider the implications of this matter more fully below.

Relation between Transvestic Fetishism and Gender Identity Disorder (Transsexualism)

For decades, clinicians have observed that a subgroup of men with TF also experience *gender dysphoria,* which can be defined as discontent with one's biological sex, the desire to possess the body of the opposite sex, and the desire to be regarded by others as a member of the opposite sex (e.g., Benjamin, 1966; Blanchard, 1985, 1988, 1989a, 1989b, 1990, 1991, 1992, 1993a, 1993b, 1993c, 1994; Blanchard, Clemmensen, & Steiner, 1987; Bonfilio, 1980; Buhrich and McConaghy, 1977a, 1977b, 1978a, 1979; Docter, 1985, 1988; Freund, Steiner, & Chan, 1982; Hirschfeld, 1910, 1918; Levine, 1993; Lothstein, 1979; Newman & Stoller, 1973; Person & Ovesey, 1974a, 1974b; Ovesey & Person, 1976; Schaefer & Wheeler, 1995; Stoller, 1968; van Kammen & Money, 1977; Wise & Meyer, 1980). In its extreme form, gender dysphoria can be indexed by the diagnosis of transsexualism in DSM-III and DSM-III-R or of gender identity disorder in DSM-IV.

Despite the observation that TF can co-occur with gender dysphoria, the presence of transsexualism was deemed an exclusion criterion for the diagnosis of TF in both DSM-III and DSM-III-R (see Tables 14.1). A formal empirical study (Blanchard & Clemmensen, 1988) showed that this was incorrect. In DSM-IV, the presence of gender dysphoria is no longer an exclusion criterion for the diagnosis of TF (see Table 14.1).

Autogynephilia: Expanding the Boundaries of Transvestic Fetishism

Although not part of any formal nosological system, there appear to be a wide range of cross-gender behaviors and fantasies that are sexually arousing to subgroups of men who also cross-dress. Blanchard (1989b) coined the term "autogynephilia" to refer to the full gamut of erotically arousing cross-gender behaviors and fantasies, which was intended to subsume TF as well as erotic ideas or situations in which women's garments per se play a small role or none at all. The term "autogynephilia" was constructed from the Greek roots meaning "love of oneself as a woman" and was formally defined as a male's propensity to be sexually aroused by the thought or image of himself as a female.

Blanchard (1991; see also Blanchard, 1992) identified at least four major subtypes of "autogynephilia," which tend to occur in combination rather than alone:

1. "Physiologic autogynephilia": Hirschfeld (1918) characterized this type as consisting of "pregnancy transvestites," in which masturbation was accompanied by the fantasy of being pregnant or of giving birth. Along similar lines, masturbation may be accompanied

by the fantasy of lactation or breast-feeding (Hirschfeld, 1910), which are enhanced by the use of appropriate props.

2. "Behavioral autogynephilia": This involves the thought of performance of activities that symbolize femininity. For example, Blanchard (1990) described one patient who reported that his early masturbation fantasies included the thought that he was helping the maid clean the house or that he was sitting in a girls' class at school. Another patient reported that his current masturbation fantasies were knitting in the company of other (*sic*) women and being at the hairdresser's with other (*sic*) women. The most common behavioral fantasies appear to involve the thought of oneself as a woman engaging in sexual intercourse or other erotic activities. Some patients report inserting dildos or similar objects into their rectum while masturbating and this behavior is accompanied by the fantasy that their anus is a vagina. The same fantasy may be inferred in other male populations. For example, Blanchard and Hucker (1991) found a significant correlation in 117 fatal cases of *autoerotic asphyxia* between the presence of dildos at the death scene and feminine attire on the corpse, suggesting that anal self-stimulation had a symbolic cross-gender meaning within that group of men as well. Along similar lines, Denko (1976) reported the presence of autogynephilic fantasies in a man with an erotic preference for enemas, termed "klismaphilia."

3. "Anatomic autogynephilia": This is represented, in its purest form, by rather static fantasies or images consisting of little more than the idea of having a woman's body. These may focus on female anatomic structures such as the breasts or the vulva or on typical but acquired characteristics such as hairless legs.

4. "Transvestic autogynephilia": This refers to the fact that in TF sexual excitement often results from the behavioral or fantasized act of making oneself, in some sense, more like a woman, regardless of the co-occurring conscious thoughts. In fact, most men with TF fantasize themselves as females when they are cross-dressing and may also act this out in their behavior. Other patients, who have no explicit thoughts of femininity, spend considerable amounts of time admiring their appearance in the mirror and are sexually aroused by the image of themselves as women (Buhrich and McConaghy, 1977a; Gutheil, 1954; Ovesey & Person, 1976). Several psychoanalytic writers have, in fact, emphasized that it is this creation of "illusion," that is, the woman-with-a-penis, that elicits sexual excitement (Bak, 1968; Chasseguet-Smirgel, 1981; Greenacre, 1970; Person & Ovesey, 1978; Stoller, 1968).

Is Transvestic Fetishism Really a Mental Disorder?

So far in this section, we have considered diagnostic issues within the relatively narrow confines of conventional nosological matters and phenomenology. We would be remiss, however, not to comment on the more controversial issues that have surrounded, at least in some quarters, the diagnosis of TF.

Critics of psychiatric diagnosis have long mused about how behavioral phenomena come to be viewed as "disorders." Szasz's (1961) seminal critique of the concept of "mental illness" probably represents the most well-known intellectual springboard for discourse on this matter. Interestingly, the debate in the 1970s regarding the pathological status of homosexuality, and the subsequent delisting of homosexuality from the DSM, played a major role in the DSM framers' conceptualization of the boundaries of mental disorder (see, e.g., Bayer, 1981; Bayer & Spitzer, 1982; Spitzer, 1981).

Over the past few years, there has been some debate from outside the disciplines of clinical psychiatry and psychology, mainly from the social constructionist school and from activists within the "transvestite subculture" or community, as to whether TF should be considered a mental disorder (see King, 1993; Woodhouse, 1989). Even Ann Landers, that sage of social wisdom and advice, has entered the fray: "I don't care what kind of underwear people wear" (Landers, 1990).

What is the basis, then, for considering TF a disorder? In addressing this question, one must acknowledge the absence of intellectual consensus regarding the definition of "mental disorder" (see, e.g., Scott, 1958; Spitzer & Endicott, 1978). For example, statistical deviation from the norm has been used as one definition (Scott, 1958). In this regard, TF would clearly qualify as a mental disorder, but it is well known that such a definition is problematic. Given this state of affairs, we will comment on whether TF is consistent with the DSM's definition of disorder—in other words, with the "rules of the game."

Spitzer and Endicott (1978) argued that *distress, disability,* and *disadvantage* should be present for a behavioral syndrome to qualify as a disorder. Spitzer and Endicott contended that the concept of disorder presupposes "negative consequences of the condition, an inferred or identified organismic dysfunction, and an implicit call for action" (1978, p. 17). They defined distress as a subjective complaint or a complaint that could be inferred from manifest behavior (e.g., the anxiety experienced during panic attacks) they defined disability as functional impairment across a wide range of activities (e.g., inability to concentrate when depressed) and they defined disadvantage as the negative sequelae occurring when the individual interacts with aspects of the physical or social environment (e.g., anorgasmia).

Recently, Wakefield (1992a, 1992b) offered some penetrating critiques of the DSM conceptualizations of disorder. Some DSM disorders (e.g., premature ejaculation) do not necessarily result in impairment in a *wide* range of activities, but may be delimited to single areas of functioning. Wakefield (1992a) argued that the concept of disorder needs to incorporate better the notion of "harmful dysfunction," defined as the "failure of a mechanism in the person to perform a natural function for which the mechanism was designed by natural selection" (p. 236). Wakefield's postulate is reminiscent of King's (1945) simple definition of "normal"—"that which functions in accordance with its design" (p. 494).

Do Men with Transvestic Fetishism Manifest Distress?

Spitzer and Endicott (1978) spent little time elaborating on the concept of distress, perhaps because the subjective complaints of adults are what usually bring them to the attention of clinicians. Moreover, most psychiatric disorders in adults consist of complaints that are, in Wakefield's (1992a) terms, "in the person."

Yet, the concept of distress is surely more complicated than this. Several psychiatric disorders common in adults may cause subjective distress only in reaction to specific conflict with the external world (e.g., antisocial personality). In these cases, it is questionable whether distress is simply "in the person." The assessment of distress may also not be as straightforward as one might think. For example, a patient, for whatever reason, might simply lie about the felt experience of distress. Clinicians comfortable with the notion of defense mechanisms might also argue that patients employ *denial* as a coping maneuver. In fact, in classical psychoanalytic theory, the dictum that "neuroses are the negative of perversions" (the paraphilias) was intended to reflect this idea, in the sense that the pleasure derived from the "perverse act" was a defense against conflict and distress; in contrast, neurotic symptomatology was always experienced as distressing (see Fenichel, 1945; Freud, 1953; Goldberg, 1975).

Regarding men with TF, we need to ask two interrelated questions: Are they distressed by their condition, and if so, what are the reasons for the distress? On the first question, the mere inclusion of Criterion B in DSM-IV diagnostic criteria, by implication, suggests that the answer to this question is: "not always." The second question thus needs to address the reasons for such variability. There appear to be two broad views on this matter. The first view is that men with TF become distressed about their condition only after it creates social difficulties. For example, a wife may discover her husband cross-dressing and threaten divorce or forbid access to children if the behavior does not cease. On this view, the distress is induced by social circumstances alone—if society or significant others were only more tolerant of the cross-dressing, the individual would not experience psychological distress.

The second view is that the distress is inherent to the condition and the behavioral or fantasied acts of cross-dressing function to alleviate anxiety. As alluded to earlier, this view has been advanced primarily by psychoanalytic clinicians (e.g., Bak, 1953; Berman, 1953; Greenacre, 1955, 1968; Jucovy, 1976; Lewis, 1963; Ovesey & Person, 1976; Person & Ovesey, 1978; Segal, 1965). For those who uphold this view, the compulsive, obligatory, and rigid patterns of cross-dressing are viewed as symptoms of an underlying disordered psychological state.

Do Men with Transvestic Fetishism Manifest Disability?

Spitzer and Endicott (1978) stated that disability must be shown in "more than one area of functioning" to avoid *a priori* decisions as to what areas of human activity are basic or essential. There is little need to quibble about the concept of disability when we consider DSM diagnoses such as major depression, in which social and occupational functioning are grossly impaired. Surely, however, the concept of disability becomes fuzzier when we consider other kinds of DSM diagnoses. For example, as noted earlier, several sexological DSM diagnoses do not necessarily result in generalized impairment (Wakefield, 1992a).

Although systematic empirical studies have been scant, considerable clinical evidence suggests that TF impairs the ability to form intimate pair bonds with other persons in the sense that relationships tend to break down because the individual with TF often has more interest in the nonhuman aspects of the partner (e.g., her clothing) or because the source of erotic excitement is directed more to the self than to a significant other (Blanchard, 1991). In a gregarious species such as our own, such difficulties surely qualify as disability. Nevertheless, it remains an open question as to whether sequelae such as relationship breakdown are inevitable.

Conclusion

A conceptual analysis of TF as disorder leads, of course, to other questions. For example, sociobiologists routinely ask, both with respect to proximate and ultimate causes, why there might be such a "thing" as transvestic fetishism. Bowlby's (1969) exegesis of infantile attachment is the best-known example of this line of inquiry in developmental psychiatry and psychology. Phylogenetically, the function of attachment in man's "environment of evolutionary adaptedness" was protection; ontogenetically, that function has been claimed to provide the infant with a sense of felt security that encourages exploration of the social and physical environment and promotes autonomous functioning.

Can similar analyses prove profitable in understanding TF? Unfortunately, little attention has been given to this question. At present, it appears that an understanding of the development of TF as an erotic anomaly or sexual deviation would best profit from an understanding of typical heterosexual development, an observation that Freud (1953) also made with regard to understanding homosexuality. This is for two reasons: (1) TF occurs exclusively in men with a heterosexual sexual orientation (as noted earlier, TF does not occur in men with a homosexual sexual orientation, including those homosexual men who cross-dress as adults, e.g., drag queens)[1]; (2) TF functions as a kind of competition with the erotic attraction to women that is experienced by "ordinary" heterosexual men. Regarding the latter, it can be argued that there are fetishistic elements to all sexual interactions; for example, a man may experience a woman as more sexually exciting if she is wearing a short skirt and a low-cut blouse as opposed to wearing a dirty sweatshirt and baggy pants. Along this line, the first author was once informed by a female colleague that she found her male partner more sexually exciting when he removed one of his false teeth (this example, of course, is more along the lines of simple fetishism); however, in these instances, the partner's clothing or physical appearance plays a minor role in fueling excitement. In TF, the situation is inverted: clothing becomes the "figure," rather than the "ground."

Regarding homosexuality, Bowlby (1969, pp. 130–131) argued that there is an "error" (phylogenetically speaking) in the stimulus that activated a sexual behavior sequence (i.e., the "object" was a same-sex person instead of an opposite-sex person). Thus, in TF, one could argue that the error is that the stimulus that activates sexual arousal is primarily the associated nonhuman features of a woman (e.g., her clothing), not the person herself or, in the case of autogynephilia, the individual is aroused by the appearance of an attractively clad woman, but he locates this image on himself rather than on another person.

This line of reasoning returns us to Wakefield's (1992a, 1992b) notion of "harmful dysfunction"—the "failure of a mechanism in the person to perform a natural function for which the mechanism was designed by natural selection" (p. 236) and King's (1945) simple definition of "normal"—"that which functions in accordance with its design" (p. 494). If the phylogenetic function of sexuality or eroticism is reproduction, and if its ontogenetic function is to enhance pair-bond formation and intimacy, then TF clearly is problematic at both levels of analysis.

Nevertheless, we posit that this argument does not entirely resolve the question of whether or not it is best to characterize TF as a mental disorder. In many respects, a nosological system such as the DSM has many built-in problems. A system that can characterize schizophrenia and childhood enuresis as mental disorders with equality is, perhaps, inherently doomed. We suspect that the question of characterizing the paraphilias in general as mental disorders will continue to be debated. But even if one abandons equating the paraphilias with mental disorder, this need not imply that they are of no concern to the individual or to the culture in which he or she lives. And, of course, from an intellectual standpoint, it remains an interesting and challenging question of how erotic anomalies, such as TF, develop. An answer to this question will not only be of clinical utility but will also provide clues to the origins of normative erotic development.

DEVELOPMENTAL COURSE

Men with TF are not effeminate in childhood (e.g., Buhrich & McConaghy, 1985; Doorn, Poortinga, & Verschoor, 1994), as are many men with a homosexual sexual orientation (Bailey & Zucker, 1995). Similarly, prepubertal boys or adolescent males who manifest precursor behaviors to mature TF do not manifest cross-gender behaviors, as do boys who meet the diagnostic criteria for gender identity disorder (Zucker & Bradley, 1995). Men with TF were not markedly prone to play with girls or to play girlish games, and they are not "mother's helpers." It is unclear whether they cherish secret fantasies of being a female or the inchoate form of such ideas, or whether this is true in some cases but not in others. Transvestic boys, at any rate, do not communicate cross-gender feelings to other persons.

Men with TF are also unremarkably masculine in their adult hobbies and in their career choices. They are frequently found in traditionally male-dominated occupations, from truck driver to business executive, and almost never in jobs commonly held by male homosexuals

(Chung & Harmon, 1994; Whitam & Mathy, 1986). Some are highly successful in their careers (Person & Ovesey, 1978; for a recent example reported in the popular press, see Berendt, 1995). In occasional cases, however, extreme preoccupation with cross-dressing interferes with work and lowers the individual's level of achievement.

Transvestite boys begin secret cross-dressing in childhood or puberty, rarely later than midadolescence (Zucker & Bradley, 1995). The first act of cross-dressing is sometimes preceded by a period of fascination with women's garments. The boy borrows articles of clothing—often, but not always, underwear—without permission from a mother, sister, or other female in the household.

Prior to puberty, cross-dressing produces generalized feelings of pleasurable excitement or a type of self-soothing. With the arrival of puberty, dressing in women's clothes begins to elicit penile erection, and, in some cases, leads directly to the boy's first ejaculation. However, reports of associated penile erection have also been observed in boys in the years well before puberty. The following case vignette provides such an example.

CASE 3

Dan, age 3 (Verbal IQ = 98; Performance IQ = 115), was referred at the suggestion of a social worker, who was treating Dan's mother. He had two older sisters. Dan's parents were middle-class in socioeconomic status. His parents had separated about 9 months before the assessment, ending a 25-year relationship. After the separation, the children lived with the mother; however, Dan's father participated fully in the evaluation. Interestingly, Dan had the same given name as his father. Over a 17-year period, Dan represented one of only four prepubertal boys (age range, 3–5 years) referred for transvestic behaviors to the Child and Adolescent Gender Identity Clinic at our Institute.

About a year before the assessment, Dan's mother began to observe his interest in cross-dressing. He wore her underwear "a lot" or tried on his sisters' lingerie, slips, and nighties; at times, Dan spent a lot of time in his mother's underwear observing himself in a mirror. He also tried on sanitary napkins several times. On occasion, Dan tried to wear his sister's underwear under his own clothing to nursery school. The cross-dressing was episodic, not continuous; when it recently recurred, the referral was made. Dan's mother also noticed that he got erections when looking at women's clothing in magazine advertisements and would instruct her to buy the items that he was viewing. On occasion, his mother also noticed erections when he wore her clothing or his sisters' clothing. When his mother tried to talk to him about his behavior, Dan yelled at her to "go away." Dan had a long history of sleep difficulties; since the parental separation, his mother found it necessary to go to bed at the same time as Dan; otherwise, he would refuse to go to sleep. As a result, Dan often slept with his mother; at times, Dan's mother stated that he rubbed her pubic hair and buttocks and tried to take off her underwear. Dan's mother provided the interviewer with her personal notations of this episode: "I started reading a book of my own, hoping that Dan would settle down to sleep. When he didn't, I turned out the lights and told him to lie down and get under the covers. He then started touching me in the pubic area, stroking with his hands. I asked him to stop and told him that isn't a nice thing to do. He continued, putting his hands down my underwear. I rolled onto my stomach, so he put his hands on my buttocks and tried to pull my underwear off. I became very annoyed and told him that he must not touch me like that." Regarding the last remark, it was of interest that during the mother's individual interview she wondered about whether or not she had overreacted to Dan's "aggressive sexual come-on. . . . I guess if it's been a long time since someone's been attracted to you, it feels nice."

Apart from the fetishistic cross-dressing, there was no clear evidence that Dan was conflicted about being a boy or that his sex-typed activities and preferences were feminine. However, Dan did appear to have several other difficulties, including a mild articulation problem, delayed expressive language development, and traits of separation anxiety.

Before the onset of Dan's cross-dressing, the family situation had become increasingly tense. The marriage was failing and both parents were extremely unhappy. Dan's mother had an affair, which was concealed from his father. Dan's mother was clinically depressed and was taking Prozac. She was extremely angry at her husband, which was also a feeling she held for men in general, including her father and male doctors whom she had seen over the years. She recalled with intense bitterness and anger the way that she was treated by her doctor during her very difficult delivery with Dan, noting that after he was born "I didn't look up (at him), didn't care." In addition to the depression and the marital discord, Dan's mother also was quite preoccupied with her business, which was in financial jeopardy. Dan's father was also depressed, which he seemed to cope with by withdrawal. He felt very angry toward his ex-wife, and complained with some intensity that she did not allow him as much contact with the children as he would have liked.

After a joint parental interview, Dan's father asked to be seen alone. He stated with little affect that he had "a fetish for ladies' lingerie." Further exploration indicated an adolescent onset, an episodic course, and no evidence of co-occurring gender dysphoria. He had told his ex-wife about his "fetish" early in their relationship. Early in the marriage, they would occasionally make love with both of them clad in pantyhose. However, he stated that the clothing was "always a poor substitute" for lovemaking. He acknowledged dressing up on occasion completely in women's clothing and also masturbating while cross-dressed. Dan's father indicated that he had recently begun dating a woman, which his ex-wife did not know about. He stated that his ex-wife, who had been his first and only sexual partner, had always seen sex as "being dirty," which was not the case with his current partner. He stated that his transvestic feelings disappeared since he began dating his new partner, commenting "I had never had a woman who wears lingerie, now I have a woman who wears it, I feel the problem has been solved." There was no indication that Dan had ever observed his father cross-dressing, although the father commented that Dan had observed him rubbing his wife's back and wondered whether or not he was imitating this.

The DSM-III-R diagnosis was gender identity disorder not otherwise specified (a residual diagnostic category for fetishistic cross-dressing in prepubertal boys), and separation anxiety disorder and articulation disorder were queried as possible diagnoses.

Adolescents with TF vary in the degree to which they cross-dress. They also vary in the extent to which they acknowledge associated sexual arousal. Some adolescents report that they only hold women's underclothing (e.g., underpants, nylons, stockings) because they like its texture. The claim that they are not aroused sexually by the cross-dressing may be true, but they may also be lying. Other adolescents report that they wear women's undergarments, are aroused by them, and subsequently masturbate. Some adolescents wear the clothing episodically; others wear the clothing compulsively under their own masculine apparel. In extreme cases, the adolescent will engage in "full" cross-dressing, attempting to emulate the phenotype of a woman. Unlike adults with TF, who attempt to pass publicly as women, this is very rare during adolescence. In addition to masturbation, some adolescents mutilate the female apparel (e.g., cutting it to pieces with a scissors) or defecate or urinate on it.

In adolescents and adults with TF, episodes of cross- dressing are accompanied by fantasies of being female. The same thought or image is likely to arise at moments of sexual excitement even when the transvestite is not cross-dressed. The idea of being a woman may form the nucleus of sexual fantasies or activities in which garments per se play a small role or none at all. Some transvestites are fond of imagining themselves, as females, engaging in lesbian interactions with other women. As noted earlier, there are occasional cases, called "pregnancy transvestites" by Hirschfeld (1918), who masturbate with the fantasy of being a pregnant woman or of giving birth. There are also transvestites—who may mislead the inexperienced clinician into a diagnosis of homosexuality—who most often fantasize that they are women engaging in sexual intercourse with men. The male partner represented in these fantasies is usually a vague, anonymous figure rather than a real person and probably has little excitatory function beyond that of completing the transvestite's fantasy of vaginal intercourse in the female role. In adulthood and middle age, the relation between the simple act of cross-dressing and sexual arousal becomes rather more complicated. In many cases, cross-dressing elicits less and less sexual excitement as the transvestite grows older; eventually, it may produce no discernible penile response at all. The desire to cross-dress, at the same time, remains the same or grows even stronger. In such cases, it is reported that the sexual excitement of cross-dressing has been replaced by feelings of comfort or well-being. A different example of dissociation between sexual arousal and the desire to cross-dress comes from those transvestites who report that they do continue to be sexually aroused by women's attire, but that they regard such arousal as a nuisance which interferes with their activities (Blanchard & Clemmensen, 1988; Buhrich, 1978). Perhaps this dissociation between cross-dressing and sexual arousal has some analogue in the permanent love bond that may remain between two people after their initial strong sexual attraction has largely disappeared (Blanchard, 1991).

As mentioned previously, older transvestites frequently describe the subjective experience of cross-dressing as one of comfort, relaxation, or well-being. Some subjects make the complementary statement that a lack of opportunities to cross-dress results in a severely dysthymic mood and marked irritability. Whether from positive or negative incentives, many transvestites make a daily habit of wearing women's undergarments beneath their normal male attire.

Transvestism generally competes and interferes with heterosexual attraction to some degree; however, a majority of transvestites marry and father children. It is quite common for transvestites to stop cross-dressing spontaneously when they first fall in love with a woman and begin a relationship. This reduction in interest may last for a few years, but the cross-dressing almost inevitably reappears.

In some transvestites, cross-dressing and intercourse with women appear to be equal and relatively independent erotic interests. Such persons achieve erection and ejaculation in coitus without recourse to cross-gender fantasies. Many others, however, are able to maintain potency with their wives only by means of private fantasies during intercourse. Some imagine that they are cross-dressing; others, whose wives will permit this, actually wear some article of feminine attire, such as a nightgown. In a similar vein, many transvestites prefer to have intercourse with their wives in the female superior position. The transvestite then fantasizes that his wife—imagined as a man—is penetrating him—a woman. Still other transvestites fantasize during heterosexual intercourse that they and their partners are two women having lesbian relations.

Individual transvestites react differently to the fact of having a sexual deviation. In two regards, their individual reactions parallel those of homosexuals: self-acceptance versus self-abhorrence, and socialization with similarly inclined men versus isolation from them. There are some transvestites (corresponding to socialized gays) who join clubs and organizations for heterosexual cross-dressers, and others (corresponding to "closet case" homosexuals) who cross-dress secretly and in private their entire lives. Similarly, there are ego-syntonic transvestites (corresponding to ego-syntonic homosexuals), who accept their cross-dressing as a pleasurable pastime and their feminine feelings as a valued part of their personality, and ego-dystonic transvestites (corresponding to ego-dystonic homosexuals) who feel guilt and shame over their deviation and wish to be otherwise.

Ego-dystonic transvestites, throughout their lives, make repeated and usually vain efforts to overcome their anomaly. Vowing to renounce cross-dressing, they periodically destroy all their feminine clothes, only to begin the process of acquiring new ones a few months later. This cycle of wardrobe purge and acquisition is also seen in many young transvestites who later come to accept their deviation.

Transvestism probably has a greater than chance association with certain other erotic anomalies, in particular, masochism and autoerotic asphyxia. Many clinical observers have noted the frequent co-occurrence of masochism and transvestism (Chivers & Blanchard, 1996; Gutheil, 1954; Ovesey & Person, 1973; Thorne, 1967). This association has also been confirmed for nonpatient subjects, by investigators who studied members of transvestic and sadomasochistic clubs (Wilson & Gosselin, 1980).

Masochistic transvestic fantasy takes different forms. One common fantasy of transvestic men is that they are forced to cross-dress or to put on makeup by a dominant woman. This is often described frankly as a masturbation fantasy by transvestic patients, but the same fantasy frequently occurs in ostensibly nonerotic contexts. Transvestite magazines often publish short works of fiction, in which the protagonist first dresses as a woman because he is forced to do so by circumstances or by a group of hostile female tormentors (Beigel & Feldman, 1963; Buhrich & McConaghy, 1976). He inevitably turns out to make a beautiful and alluring female on the first trial. Once introduced to cross-dressing in this manner, the fictional hero discovers his pleasure in it and makes it part of his future life. Other masochistic transvestic fantasies are of bondage or whipping at the hands of a dominant woman, serving as the maid of a severe and demanding mistress, and coercion to perform cunnilingus or anilingus on a controlling and sadistic female. It must be emphasized, however, that strong masochistic trends are found in only a minority of cases.

A much rarer sexual deviation associated with transvestism is autoerotic asphyxia. This is the practice of inducing cerebral anoxia, usually by means of self-devised ligatures, while the individual masturbates to orgasm. Death sometimes results from this practice when the individual's escape mechanism fails or he loses consciousness before he can employ it. About one quarter or one fifth of autoerotic fatalities are found cross-dressed (Hazelwood, Dietz, & Burgess, 1983; see also Shankel & Carr, 1956).

EPIDEMIOLOGY

Prevalence

No formal epidemiological study has ever been conducted to assess the prevalence of TF. As noted earlier, however, TF is a disorder that appears to be unique to biological males. Without any formal documentation, Bullough and Bullough (1993) stated that the prevalence "figure of 1 percent of the adult male population is often mentioned, and it conforms with our own tentative conclusions; we will use it until better statistics are available" (p. 315). In our view, this claim is based on sheer conjecture and should in no way be taken as the result of any serious epidemiological effort.

Incidence

No formal epidemiological study has ever been conducted to assess the incidence of TF. Chasseguet-Smirgel (1981), a psychoanalyst, speculated that "perversions" in general, which would include TF, were becoming more frequent, but provided no systematic documentation. The increased visibility of men with TF appears to be, in part, the result of the development of what Bullough and Bullough (1993) characterized as "organized transvestism," that is, educational, social, and support groups that have emerged over the past few decades. As well, any casual observer of popular culture cannot escape notice of the amount of attention given to transvestism in the press, on television talk shows, and in films.

ETIOLOGY

Biological Research

Over the past few years, there has been a kind of renaissance in biological research with regard to the development of "typical" sexual orientation (homosexuality and heterosexuality), that is, sexual orientations that are not complicated by an age-atypical preference, as in pedophilia, or by co-occurring fetishism. Domains of research include behavior genetics, molecular genetics, prenatal sex hormones, prenatal maternal stress, neuropsychology, neuroanatomy, and familial demographic variables. Much of this research was summarized by Zucker and Bradley (1995).

If one takes as a starting point the assumption that TF is related more strongly to ordinary heterosexuality than to homosexuality, then one would expect men with TF to show biological traits (or corresponding behavioral markers) more similar to that of heterosexual men than to homosexual men (or, for that matter, to heterosexual women). For example, let us suppose that certain childhood sex-typed behaviors, such as toy preferences and involvement in rough-and-tumble play, are partly influenced by biological factors (see, e.g., Collaer & Hines, 1995). Given that these behaviors clearly distinguish preheterosexual boys from prehomosexual boys (Bailey & Zucker, 1995; Green, 1987), one would predict that pretransvestitic boys would be more similar to preheterosexual boys. As noted earlier, this is exactly what has been observed in retrospective studies of adolescent and adult males with TF. Unfortunately, unlike the recent increase in biological research on ordinary homosexuality and heterosexuality, very little work of this type has been conducted on men with TF. In this section, we will summarize the available material.

Familiality

Although case reports have documented the co-occurrence of TF between probands and fathers or male siblings (Buhrich, 1977; Edelstein, 1960; Kasantikul & Roback, 1978; Krueger, 1978; Liakos, 1967) or in monozygotic twin pairs (Cryan, Butcher, & Webb, 1992), there is very little systematic research regarding familial patterns. Croughan, Saghir, Cohen, and Robins (1981) studied 70 men with TF and concluded that it was not familial; however, this judgment might be premature, given that evidence for familiality hinges on knowledge of base rates. Croughan et al. reported that 1% of fathers and 2% of brothers of their probands apparently cross-dressed. Given that we really know nothing about the prevalence of TF, it is difficult to know if these rates are, in fact, elevated.

Neurological Impairment

Although brain mechanisms responsible for sexual arousal have not been definitively identified, there is a general consensus that limbic and temporal lobe structures are important for both sexual interest or arousal and for inhibition of sexual behaviors (Blumer

& Walker, 1975). Generally, temporal lobe epilepsy (TLE) produces a state of hyposexuality. However, case reports of hypersexuality, and of fetishistic and transvestic behaviors associated with TLE, led Epstein (1960, 1961, 1969, 1973) to hypothesize that some forms of fetishism arise as a result of inhibition or release of limbic regions with seizure activity (see also Kolarsky, Freund, Machek, & Polak, 1967). Other reports have linked TF and other types of fetishism with head injury (e.g., Miller, Cummings, McIntyre, Ebers, & Grode, 1986; Pandita-Gunawardena, 1990). This theory is supported by the fact that in several cited cases transvestic and fetishistic impulses were reduced or eliminated through either surgical removal of the irritating focus or medication to control the seizures (e.g., Davies & Morgenstern, 1960; Hunter, Logue, & McMenemy, 1963; Mitchell, Falconer, & Hill, 1954; Walinder, 1965). The idea that abnormalities in limbic structures may facilitate transvestic behavior is illustrated by a case report in which such behavior, previously extinguished by behavioral treatment, returned with the development of a seizure-provoking mass and then diminished with treatment of the seizures (Ball, 1968; for additional reports, see Blumer, 1970; Malitz, 1966; Thomas & DeAlwis, 1995; Tuchman & Lachman, 1964; Walinder, 1965). Hoenig (1985) has also summarized the literature on the relationship between electroencephalographic (EEG) abnormalities and transsexualism (in whom some patients had a history of TF).

In the first author's (KJZ's) Child and Adolescent Gender Identity Clinic at our Institute, referral for neurological assessment to rule out a temporal lobe focus revealed only one significant abnormality by history and EEG testing (total N = 79). However, three other adolescents had a documented history of epilepsy or EEG abnormality before the onset of TF, and a fourth had Tourette's syndrome. In one of the adolescents with an established seizure disorder, the frequency of transvestic behaviors escalated and a diaper fetish also began as seizure control diminished. Several other youngsters had severe head injuries as toddlers and several had been exposed to very severe environmental deprivation, both of which are suggestive of cerebral insult. Lastly, it is of interest that Bowler and Collacott (1993) reported verbal learning disabilities in cross-dressing men, which dovetails nicely with our own finding that adolescent males with TF showed deficits in Verbal IQ compared with Performance IQ (Zucker & Bradley, 1995).

Sibling Sex Ratio and Birth Order

Sibling sex ratio is the ratio of brothers to sisters collectively reported by a given group of probands. In white populations, the ratio of male live births to female live births is close to 106:100 (Chahnazarian, 1988). Birth order can be calculated with Slater's (1958) index—a proband's number of older siblings divided by the total number of siblings—which expresses birth order as a quantity between 0 (first born) and 1 (last born). Observed birth orders can be compared between groups or with the theoretical mean of .50 for samples drawn at random from the general population.

Sibling Sex Ratio

The relation between sibling sex ratio and sexual orientation, particularly in males, was first studied by several investigators between the 1930s and the early 1960s. Blanchard and Sheridan (1992) recently reviewed this literature and noted that homosexual men came from sibships with an excess of brothers to sisters. Money (1970) had also identified this pattern, but interest in the phenomenon waned, perhaps because the initial attention given to it had been guided by the inaccurate hypothesis that homosexual men were genetic females.

Over the last few years, however, several studies from our Institute have taken another look at this somewhat forgotten biodemographic variable. For example, we have examined sibling sex ratio in homosexual men (unselected for gender dysphoria), and in homosexual and heterosexual men with gender dysphoria (transsexualism). Among the heterosexual men with gender dysphoria, almost all of had a history of TF.

In our five studies on homosexual men, the sibling sex ratio did not differ significantly from the known proportion of male live births in the general population (Blanchard & Bogaert, 1996a; 1996b; Blanchard & Zucker, 1994; Blanchard, Zucker, Siegelman, Dickey, & Klassen, in press; Zucker & Blanchard, 1994). In contrast, in our two studies of homosexual men with gender dysphoria, the sibling sex ratio indicated a significant excess of brothers, but this was not apparent among the heterosexual men with gender dysphoria (Blanchard & Sheridan, 1992; Blanchard, Zucker, Cohen-Kettenis, Gooren, & Bailey, 1996). Unfortunately, there are no adequate studies of sibling sex ratio in men with TF and without gender dysphoria. In the KJZ's sample of adolescent males with TF, the sibling sex ratio did not show a significant excess of brothers (Zucker, 1997).

Birth Order

In our five studies of homosexual men (Blanchard & Bogaert, 1996a, 1996b; Blanchard et al., in press; Blanchard & Zucker, 1994; Zucker & Blanchard, 1994) and in the two samples of gender-dysphoric homosexual men (Blanchard & Sheridan, 1992; Blanchard et al., 1994), were all shown to be later born. In contrast, in the two samples of gender-dysphoric heterosexual men, they were not later born. Again, there are no adequate studies of birth order in non-gender-dysphoric men with TF. In the first author's (KJZ's) sample of adolescent males with TF, their birth order was not significantly different from the expected population value of .50 (Zucker, 1997).

Thus, our studies of sibling sex ratio and birth order suggest that males with TF are more similar to ordinary heterosexual men than to ordinary homosexual men. Thus, if there are biological mechanisms to explain the observed effects, men with TF should be more similar to heterosexual men than to homosexual men (for a summary of possible mechanisms, see Blanchard, in press; Blanchard & Klassen, 1997; Blanchard & Sheridan, 1992; Blanchard et al., 1996; Zucker & Bradley, 1995).

Height and Weight

Several studies have found that homosexual men are lighter, or lighter in proportion to their height, than are heterosexual men (see Blanchard & Bogaert, 1996a). Fewer studies have compared the mean heights of heterosexual and homosexual males; in contrast to the studies of weight, these have found no differences (see Blanchard & Bogaert, 1996a).

Blanchard, Dickey, and Jones (1995) found that homosexual, gender-dysphoric men were shorter, lighter, and lighter in proportion to their height compared with heterosexual, gender-dysphoric men. The homosexual, gender-dysphoric men were also shorter than men in the general population, whereas the heterosexual, gender-dysphoric men were not. Unfortunately, there are no adequate studies of height and weight in men with TF and without gender dysphoria.

The height and weight differences indicate that homosexual, gender-dysphoric men are shifted toward the female-typical pattern (i.e., shorter and lighter), but the heterosexual, gender-dysphoric men are not. The differences might be explained by divergent patterns of pubertal growth. Several studies have shown that homosexual men in general reach puberty earlier than do heterosexual men, which is of interest in light of the fact that women reach puberty earlier than do men (see Blanchard & Bogaert, 1996a; Bogaert & Blanchard, 1996). Other things being equal, an earlier pubertal age results in a shorter adult stature. Obviously, the somewhat accelerated pubertal age of ordinary homosexual men is not sufficient to produce an observable reduction in their adult height, or at least one demonstrable in less than very large samples. It is possible, however, that the pubertal age of gender-dysphoric, homosexual men is even earlier than that of ordinary homosexuals and does result in a detectable lowering of adult stature.

Psychosocial Research

There is very little methodologically adequate psychosocial research on the origin of TF. Much of the available work is primarily retrospective in nature and subject to many problems (e.g., demand characteristics, absence of validity checks, etc.). It appears that much of the research has been guided by general theoretical notions about the psychosocial determinants of ordinary heterosexuality and homosexuality. Unfortunately, these ideas are confusing because TF has been more closely linked with homosexual development (or to the development of those transsexuals with a homosexual sexual orientation) than to heterosexual development, which we believe is inaccurate.

Mechanisms of Reinforcement

Some clinicians have suggested that TF results from forced cross-dressing during childhood, particularly by mothers or other female figures, as a form of punishment or humiliation—the so-called "petticoat punishment." Stoller (1968) provided such an example:

> For the first three years of [this man's] life, his masculinity was more or less that of other boys his age. Then it was his bad fortune, because of a prolonged and eventually fatal illness of his mother, to fall into the hands of his aunt and her daughter. These women hated males. For the first time, both of them were provided with a defenseless male on whom they could expend their rage and envy. . . . They let his hair grow long, and they designed, cut, and sewed for him new and effeminate clothes. They kept him this way for three years. One day, shortly before she died, his mother came home on a visit from the hospital. The two women had a clever idea: They dressed this by-now feminized little boy as a little girl, introduced the little "girl" to the visiting mother, who never learned the child was her son, and a snapshot was taken to commemorate the occasion of the vicious joke. . . . At age 6 appears his first memory: he has been "bad" because he dripped wax on his stepmother's sister's stockings. With the uncanny sense of destruction that some women have when in the exciting presence of little boys, she chose what she felt was the perfect punishment, and forced him to put on stockings. He dates his transvestism from this point, and for him transvestism means *pleasure* in cross-dressing. (p. 182, emphasis in original)

Stoller's (1968) explanation of why the transvestism persists is that

> the passively endured experience of being a living puppet . . . was transformed into an active experience colored by sexual excitement. Now what had been traumatic was mastered, becoming his greatest pleasure. In this way the victim has his own sort of triumph. (p. 182)

Other clinicians have not shared this view, claiming that forced cross-dressing is rare. For example, Person and Ovesey (1978) stated:

Most often it is the child himself who initiates the cross-dressing. In the predominant pattern, the child spontaneously cross-dresses, the activity most often remains surreptitious, and it is not reinforced by the mother or a mother-surrogate. (p. 306)

Person and Ovesey's view is similar to views advanced by various behaviorists, who often see the origin of TF as resulting from accidental exposure to women's clothing (e.g., Strzyzewsky & Zierhoffer, 1967)—a sort of "close encounter of the wrong kind!" Unfortunately, there has never been a controlled study comparing men with TF with ordinary heterosexual men regarding possible learning experiences of this kind. In the first author's (KJZ's) experience assessing adolescent males with TF, his clinical impressions concur more with Person and Ovesey's (1978) than with Stoller's (1968), in that I have never encountered a case in which forced cross-dressing was reported, either by the patient himself or by the parents.

Even if the cross-dressing is not externally induced or reinforced, there are other ways to conceptualize the role of reinforcement processes. As noted earlier, cross-dressing is often reported to be soothing when it first occurs and, when it is accompanied by sexual excitement, masturbation, and orgasm, there is an added reinforcing property (see, e.g., Crawford, Holloway, & Domjan, 1993; Laws & Marshall, 1991). As Freud (1959) once noted, "hardly anything is harder for a man than to give up a pleasure which he has once experienced" (p. 145). Thus, cross-dressing may be self-perpetuating because of the pleasure associated with it. Of course, the notion of some type of reinforcing property was the basis for the early efforts to treat TF by behavior therapy techniques, such as aversive conditioning (Bancroft, 1974).

In some of the formulations of TF by psychoanalytic theorists, cross-dressing has been viewed as a way of handling various forms of anxiety—separation anxiety, castration anxiety, and so on. In these accounts, cross-dressing can be viewed as a source of reinforcement because it reduces anxiety (Person & Ovesey, 1974b, 1978). To date, this explanation has been based exclusively on inferences from clinical data, not controlled empirical studies. Theorists such as Person and Ovesey (1974b, 1978) have argued that the personality organization of men with TF is largely pre-oedipal, which also explains why there is a concomitantly high rate of Axis II personality disorders. An aspect of their account that remains unexplained is why most men with pre-oedipal personality pathology do not manifest TF. In other words, there is a lack of specificity to the model—something else beside pre-oedipal pathology is needed to explain the development of TF in its own right. Also, there are conflicting data on the patterns of associated psychopathology in men with TF and what, if any, causal relation such psychopathology has on the development of TF (e.g., Beatrice, 1985; Brown, 1995; Buhrich, 1981; Croughan et al., 1981; Fagan, Wise, Derogatis, & Schmidt, 1988; Fagan et al., 1991; Wise, Fagan, Schmidt, Ponticas, & Costa, 1991).

Parental Relationships

The role of parents in the development of TF has been studied exclusively by retrospective self-report, never by a systematic study of the parents themselves. In itself, this is a clear methodological weakness.

Various hypotheses have been proposed and, at times, they have been contradictory to one another. In one study, Newcomb (1985) found that men with TF were more likely than ordinary heterosexual men to characterize their parents as "less sex-typed or more sex-reversed in terms of dependence and affiliation" (p. 160), which was judged as support for a "pattern of parent sex role reversal" (p. 160). In contrast, Newcomb found no differences in parental attributes when homosexual men were compared with heterosexual men. To some extent, these results are surprising because it is homosexual men, not TF men, who are feminine during childhood. Thus, if parental sex-typed characteristics are in some way causally related to the child's sex-typed characteristics, one would expect to find atypical personality constellations in the parents of homosexual men, not in those of men with TF.

Another line of exploration has examined the quality of the parent–child relationship in TF, in which variables such as closeness and hedonic tone have been rated (Buhrich & McConaghy, 1978b). Schott (1995), for example, found that men with TF recalled better relationships with their mothers than with their fathers, but so did a control sample (which, incidentally, was very poorly matched to the probands).

If one examines carefully the writings of certain psychoanalytic authors who have been most interested in parental influences, it becomes apparent that the central maternal influence in TF has been judged to be hostility and anger toward males. This contrasts rather sharply with the observations made by psychoanalysts regarding maternal influences on homosexuality, such as smothering overcloseness and intrusiveness, which have also been implicated in an even more extreme manner with regard to transsexualism of the homosexual type (Stoller, 1968).

In the first author's clinical experience with adolescent males with TF, the presence of severe mother–son conflict, characterized by anger, hostility, and rejection, has been common. These clinical observations were complemented by the objective finding that many of these youngsters had, at some point prior to the onset of the TF, a long-term or permanent separation from their mothers. Of 79 adolescents, 36 were not living with their biological mothers at the time of assessment; another 4 adolescents had experienced a separation from their mothers, but were living with them again at the time of the assessment. Thus, the rate of maternal separation was 50.6%, which was considerably higher than the rates of maternal separation among our comparison samples of gender-dysphoric and homosexual adolescents (Zucker & Bradley, 1995).

The clinical evidence of maternal–son distance and the co-occurring hostility has been used to explain the function of the transvestism, which is to maintain some kind of representational connection, in part analogous to other, more ordinary types of transitional objects, such as security blankets (Sullivan, Bradley, & Zucker, 1995). However, other behaviors that at times accompany the cross-dressing, such as defecation in the mother's underwear or shredding it, point to the associated feelings of anger and unresolved conflict.

Along these lines, LaTorre (1980) conducted an interesting experiment with male university students. Men who were informed that they had been rejected for a potential date by an attractive unknown female subsequently reported less sexual attraction and other positive feelings to pictures of attractive women than did men who had been accepted for a potential date; moreover, the rejected men reported more sexual attraction and other positive feelings for pictures of women's panties than to the pictures of attractive women.

Elsewhere, Blanchard (1991, 1992; see also Freund & Blanchard, 1993; Pinkava, 1987) advanced the notion that TF and autogynephilia are conditions that interfere or compete with ordinary heterosexual attraction. Although Blanchard (1991) speculated that some biological mechanism accounts for this interference, LaTorre's (1980) data and the clinical observations reported by Zucker and Bradley (1995) suggest that psychosocial factors, such as devaluation or hostility in relationships with female figures, may also explain the phenomenon. Obviously, the matter is far from settled and requires a good deal more systematic empirical research.

FUTURE DIRECTIONS

Over the past several years, a clearer understanding of the diagnostic and phenomenological issues involved in TF has emerged. The concept of "autogynephilia" has expanded our understanding of the phenomenological net and the relation of TF to gender dysphoria has been extensively studied. What is sorely lacking is sound etiological research in both the biological and psychosocial arenas. This is where contemporary sexologists should focus their energies in the years to come.

NOTE

1. It is, of course, well known that both heterosexual and homosexual men can have co-occuring simple fetishism, such as erotic arousal to feet or to shoes. But is there an analogous form of TF in homosexual men? A recent survey effort by Bullough and Bullough (1997) to answer this question was, unfortunately, methodologically inadequate. They sent a questionnaire to members of Tri Ess, a national cross-dressing organization (presumably for men with TF); to members of the American Educational Gender Information Service, a national organization of gender-dysphoric or "transgendered" individuals (some of whom might have TF); and to other miscellaneous sources of subjects. Of the 368 respondents (all males), 9 (2.4%) self-reported their sexual orientation as homosexual. From this, Bullough and Bullough (1997) concluded that homosexuality and trans-vestism co-occur, and they criticized DSM-IV for its restriction of TF to heterosexual males. Apart from rather simple validity issues (e.g., reliance on anonymous subjects' self-reporting of their sexual orientation), Bullough and Bullough failed to document that, among their cross-dressers classified as homosexual, there was a sexual arousal component to the transvestism. Without such documentation, their conclusions are severely suspect and, from a sexological perspective, astonishingly naive.

   Zavitzianos (1972, 1977) described one man with a homosexual sexual orientation who was sexually aroused when wearing masculine clothing, such as a jockstrap or underwear similar to the kind worn by his father and brother, which he labeled "homeovestism." From the clinical material presented, however, it did not appear that the erotic arousal activated by the clothing was preferred by the patient to actual partners, as is the case in TF. Thus, in our view, it remains unclear if homeovestism in homosexual men is truly an analogous form of TF that is observed in heterosexual men. As an aside, Zavitzianos's (1972) case example is muddled by the comment that his patient had been a "transvestite before resorting to homeovestism" (p. 474). The patient did not have TF, as defined in this chapter, but rather showed elements of childhood cross-gender behavior which, as noted earlier, has been labeled as "transvestism" in the older clinical literature.

REFERENCES

American Psychiatric Association. (1952). *Diagnostic and statistical manual: Mental disorders*. Washington, DC: Author.

American Psychiatric Association. (1968). *Diagnostic and statistical manual of mental disorders* (2nd ed.). Washington, DC: Author.

American Psychiatric Association. (1980). *Diagnostic and statistical manual of mental disorders* (3rd ed.). Washington, DC: Author.

American Psychiatric Association. (1987). *Diagnostic and statistical manual of mental disorders* (3rd ed., rev.). Washington, DC: Author.

American Psychiatric Association. (1994). *Diagnostic and statistical manual of mental disorders* (4th ed.). Washington, DC: Author.

Bailey, J. M., & Zucker, K. J. (1995). Childhood sex-typed behavior and sexual orientation: A conceptual analysis and quantitative review. *Developmental Psychology, 31,* 43–55.

Bak, R. C. (1953). Fetishism. *Journal of the American Psychoanalytic Association, 1,* 285–298.

Bak, R. C. (1968). The phallic woman: The ubiquitous fantasy in perversion. *Psychoanalytic Study of the Child, 23,* 15–36.

Bakwin, H. (1960). Transvestism in children. *Journal of Pediatrics, 56,* 294–298.

Ball, J. R. B. (1968). A case of hair fetishism, transvestism, and organic cerebral disorder. *Acta Psychiatrica Scandinavica, 44,* 249–254.

Bancroft, J. (1974). *Deviant sexual behavior: Modification and assessment.* Oxford: Oxford University Press.

Bayer, R. (1981). *Homosexuality and American psychiatry: The politics of diagnosis.* New York: Basic Books.

Bayer, R., & Spitzer, R. L. (1982). Edited correspondence on the status of homosexuality in DSM-III. *Journal of the History of the Behavioral Sciences, 18,* 32–52.

Beatrice, J. (1985). A psychological comparison of heterosexuals, transvestites, preoperative transsexuals, and postoperative transsexuals. *Journal of Nervous and Mental Disease, 173,* 358–365.

Beigel, H. G., & Feldman, R. (1963). The male transvestite's motivation in fiction, research, and reality. In H. G. Beigel (Ed.), *Advances in sex research* (pp. 198–210). New York: Harper & Row.

Benjamin, H. (1966). *The transsexual phenomenon.* New York: Julian Press.

Berendt, J. (1995, January 16). High-heel Neil. *The New Yorker,* pp. 38–45.

Berman, L. (1953). Perception and object relations in a patient with transvestite tendencies. *International Journal of Psycho-Analysis, 34,* 25–34.

Blanchard, R. (1985). Typology of male-to-female transsexualism. *Archives of Sexual Behavior, 14,* 247–261.

Blanchard, R. (1988). Nonhomosexual gender dysphorias. *Journal of Sex Research, 24,* 188–193.

Blanchard, R. (1989a). The classification and labeling of nonhomosexual gender dysphoria. *Archives of Sexual Behavior, 18,* 315–334.

Blanchard, R. (1989b). The concept of autogynephilia and the typology of male gender dysphoria. *Journal of Nervous and Mental Disease, 177,* 616–623.

Blanchard, R. (1990). Gender identity disorders in adult men. In R. Blanchard & B. W. Steiner (Eds.), *Clinical management of gender identity disorders in children and adults* (pp. 47–76). Washington, DC: American Psychiatric Press.

Blanchard, R. (1991). Clinical observations and systematic studies of autogynephilia. *Journal of Sex and Marital Therapy, 17,* 235–251.

Blanchard, R. (1992). Nonmonotonic relation of autogynephilia and heterosexual attraction. *Journal of Abnormal Psychology, 101,* 271–276.

Blanchard, R. (1993a). Varieties of autogynephilia and their relationship to gender dysphoria. *Archives of Sexual Behavior, 22,* 241–251.

Blanchard, R. (1993b). The she-male phenomenon and the concept of partial autogynephilia. *Journal of Sex and Marital Therapy, 19,* 69–76.

Blanchard, R. (1993c). Partial versus complete autogynephilia and gender dysphoria. *Journal of Sex and Marital Therapy, 19,* 301–307.

Blanchard, R. (1994). A structural equation model for age at clinical presentation in nonhomosexual male gender dysphorics. *Archives of Sexual Behavior, 23,* 311–320.

Blanchard, R. (in press). Birth order and sibling sex ratio in homosexual versus heterosexual men and women. *Annual Review of Sex Research.*

Blanchard, R., & Bogaert, A. F. (1996a). Biodemographic comparisons of homosexual and heterosexual men in the Kinsey interview data. *Archives of Sexual Behavior, 25,* 545–573.

Blanchard, R., & Bogaert, A. F. (1996b). Male homosexuality and number of older brothers. *American Journal of Psychiatry, 153,* 27–31.

Blanchard, R., & Clemmensen, L. H. (1988). A test of the DSM-III-R's implicit assumption that fetishistic arousal and gender dysphoria are mutually exclusive. *Journal of Sex Research, 25,* 426–432.

Blanchard, R., Clemmensen, L. H., & Steiner, B. W. (1987). Heterosexual and homosexual gender dysphoria. *Archives of Sexual Behavior, 16,* 139–152.

Blanchard, R., Dickey, R., & Jones, C. L. (1995). Comparison of height and weight in homosexual versus nonhomosexual male gender dysphorics. *Archives of Sexual Behavior, 24,* 543–554.

Blanchard, R., & Hucker, S. J. (1991). Age, transvestism, bondage, and concurrent paraphilic activities in 117 fatal cases of autoerotic asphyxia. *British Journal of Psychiatry, 159,* 371–377.

Blanchard, R., & Klassen, P. (1997). H-Y antigen and homosexuality in men. *Journal of Theoretical Biology, 185,* 373-378.

Blanchard, R., Racansky, I. G., & Steiner, B. W. (1986). Phallometric detection of fetishistic arousal in heterosexual male cross-dressers. *Journal of Sex Research, 22,* 452–462.

Blanchard, R., & Sheridan, P. M. (1992). Sibship size, sibling sex ratio, birth order, and parental age in homosexual and nonhomosexual gender dysphorics. *Journal of Nervous and Mental Disease, 180,* 40–47.

Blanchard, R., & Zucker, K. J. (1994). Reanalysis of Bell, Weinberg, and Hammersmith's data on birth order, sibling sex ratio, and parental age in homosexual men. *American Journal of Psychiatry, 151,* 1375–1376.

Blanchard, R., Zucker, K. J., Cohen-Kettenis, P. T., Gooren, L. J. G., & Bailey, J. M. (1996). Birth order and sibling sex ratio in two samples of Dutch gender-dysphoric homosexual males. *Archives of Sexual Behavior, 25,* 495–514.

Blanchard, R., Zucker, K. J., Siegelman, M., Dickey, R., & Klassen, P. (in press). The relation of birth order to sexual orientation in men and women. *Journal of Biosocial Science.*

Blumer, D. (1970). Changes of sexual behavior related to temporal lobe disorders in man. *Journal of Sex Research, 6,* 173–180.

Blumer, D., & Walker, A. E. (1975). The neural basis of sexual behavior. In D. F. Benson & D. Blumer (Eds.), *Psychiatric aspects of neurologic disease* (pp. 199–217). New York: Grune & Stratton.

Bogaert, A. F., & Blanchard, R. (1996). Physical development and sexual orientation in men: Height, weight and age of puberty differences. *Personality and Individual Differences, 21,* 77–84.

Bonfilio, V. P. (1980). *Gender dysphoria: Examining a typology.* Unpublished doctoral dissertation, California School of Professional Psychology, Berkeley.

Bowlby, J. (1969). *Attachment and loss: Vol. 1. Attachment.* New York: Basic Books.

Bowler, C., & Collacott, R. A. (1993). Cross-dressing in men with learning disabilities. *British Journal of Psychiatry, 162,* 556–558.

Brown, G. R. (1995). Transvestism. In G. O. Gabbard (Ed.), *Treatments of psychiatric disorders* (Vol. 2, 2nd ed., pp. 1977–1999). Washington, DC: American Psychiatric Press.

Buhrich, N. (1977). A case of familial heterosexual transvestism. *Acta Psychiatrica Scandinavica, 55,* 199–201.

Buhrich, N. (1978). Motivation for cross-dressing in heterosexual transvestism. *Acta Psychiatrica Scandinavica, 57,* 145–152.

Buhrich, N. (1981). Psychological adjustment in transvestism and transsexualism. *Behaviour Research and Therapy, 19,* 407–411.

Buhrich, N., & McConaghy, N. (1976). Transvestic fiction. *Journal of Nervous and Mental Disease, 163,* 420–427.

Buhrich, N., & McConaghy, N. (1977a). The clinical syndromes of femmiphilic transvestism. *Archives of Sexual Behavior, 6,* 397–412.

Buhrich, N., & McConaghy, N. (1977b). The discrete syndromes of transvestism and transsexualism. *Archives of Sexual Behavior, 6,* 483–495.

Buhrich, N., & McConaghy, N. (1978a). Two clinically discrete syndromes of transsexualism. *British Journal of Psychiatry, 133,* 73–76.

Buhrich, N., & McConaghy, N. (1978b). Parental relationships during childhood in homosexuality, transvestism and transsexualism. *Australian and New Zealand Journal of Psychiatry, 12,* 103–108.

Buhrich, N., & McConaghy, N. (1979). Three clinically discrete categories of fetishistic transvestism. *Archives of Sexual Behavior, 8,* 151–157.

Buhrich, N., & McConaghy, N. (1985). Preadult feminine behaviors of male transvestites. *Archives of Sexual Behavior, 14,* 413–419.

Bullough, B., & Bullough, V. (1997). Are transvestites necessarily heterosexual? *Archives of Sexual Behavior, 26,* 1–12.

Bullough, V. L., & Bullough, B. (1993). *Cross dressing, sex, and gender.* Philadelphia: University of Pennsylvania Press.

Chahnazarian, A. (1988). Determinants of the sex ratio at birth: Review of recent literature. *Social Biology, 35,* 214–235.

Chasseguet-Smirgel, J. (1981). Loss of reality in the perversions—with special reference to fetishism. *Journal of the American Psychoanalytic Association, 29,* 511–534.

Chivers, M., & Blanchard, R. (1996). Prostitution advertisements suggest association of transvestism and masochism. *Journal of Sex and Marital Therapy, 22,* 97–102.

Chung, Y. B., & Harmon, L. W. (1994). The career interests and aspirations of gay men: How sex-role orientation is related. *Journal of Vocational Behavior, 45,* 223–239.

Collaer, M. L., & Hines, M. (1995). Human behavioral sex differences: A role for gonadal hormones during early development? *Psychological Bulletin, 118,* 55–107.

Crawford, L. L., Holloway, K. S., & Domjan, M. (1993). The nature of sexual reinforcement. *Journal of the Experimental Analysis of Behavior, 60,* 55–66.

Croughan, J. L., Saghir, M., Cohen, R., & Robins, E. (1981). A comparison of treated and untreated male cross-dressers. *Archives of Sexual Behavior, 10,* 515–528.

Cryan, E. M. J., Butcher, G. J., & Webb, M. G. T. (1992). Obsessive–compulsive disorder and paraphilia in a monozygotic twin pair. *British Journal of Psychiatry, 161,* 694–698.

Davies, B. M., & Morgenstern, F. S. (1960). A case of cysticercosis, temporal lobe epilepsy, and transvestism. *Journal of Neurology, Neurosurgery, and Psychiatry, 23,* 247–249.

Demeyere, G. (1992). *Transvestism and its wide context: A working bibliography.* (Available from G. Demeyere, Turnhoutsebaan 588, B 2110 Wignegem, Belgium)

Denko, J. D. (1976). Klismaphilia: Amplification of the erotic enema deviance. *American Journal of Psychotherapy, 30,* 236–255.

Docter, R. F. (1985). Transsexual at 74: A case report. *Archives of Sexual Behavior, 14,* 271–277.

Docter, R. F. (1988). *Transvestites and transsexuals: Toward a theory of cross-gender behavior.* New York: Plenum Press.

Doorn, C. D., Poortinga, J., & Verschoor, A. M. (1994). Cross-gender identity in transvestites and male transsexuals. *Archives of Sexual Behavior, 23,* 185–201.

Edelstein, E. L. (1960). Psychodynamics of a transvestite. *American Journal of Psychotherapy, 14,* 121–131.

Epstein, A. W. (1960). Fetishism: A study of its psychopathology with particular reference to a proposed disorder in brain mechanisms as an etiological factor. *Journal of Nervous and Mental Disease, 130,* 107–119.

Epstein, A. W. (1961). Relationship of fetishism and transvestism to brain and particularly to temporal lobe dysfunction. *Journal of Nervous and Mental Disease, 133,* 247–253.

Epstein, A. W. (1969). Fetishism: A comprehensive view. In J. H. Masserman (Ed.), *Science and psychoanalysis: Vol. XV. Dynamics of deviant sexuality* (pp. 81–87). New York: Grune & Stratton.

Epstein, A. W. (1973). The relationship of altered brain states to sexual psychopathology. In J. Zubin & J. Money (Eds.), *Contemporary sexual behavior: Critical issues in the 1970s* (pp. 297–310). Baltimore: Johns Hopkins University Press.

Fagan, P. J., Wise, T. N., Derogatis, L. R., & Schmidt, C. W. (1988). Distressed transvestites: Psychometric characteristics. *Journal of Nervous and Mental Disease, 176,* 626–632.

Fagan, P. J., Wise, T. N., Schmidt, C. W., Ponticas, Y., Marshall, R. D., & Costa, P. T. (1991). A comparison of five-factor personality dimensions in males with sexual dysfunction and males with paraphilia. *Journal of Personality Assessment, 57,* 434–448.

Fenichel, O. (1945). *The psychoanalytic theory of neurosis.* New York: Norton.

Findlay, H. (1992). Freud's "fetishism" and the lesbian dildo debates. *Feminist Studies, 18,* 563–579.

Freud, S. (1953). Three essays on the theory of sexuality. In J. Strachey (Ed. and Trans.), *The standard edition of the complete psychological works of Sigmund Freud* (Vol. 7, pp. 123–243). London: Hogarth Press. (Original work published 1905)

Freud, S. (1959). Creative writers and day-dreaming. In J. Strachey (Ed. and Trans.), *The standard edition of the complete psychological works of Sigmund Freud* (Vol. 9, pp. 141–153). London: Hogarth Press. (Original work published 1908)

Freund, K., & Blanchard, R. (1993). Erotic target location errors in male gender dysphorics, paedophiles, and fetishists. *British Journal of Psychiatry, 162,* 558–563.

Freund, K., Steiner, B. W., & Chan, S. (1982). Two types of cross-gender identity. *Archives of Sexual Behavior, 11,* 49–63.

Gamman, L., & Makinen, M. (1994). *Female fetishism.* New York: New York University Press.

Gert, B. (1992). A sex caused inconsistency in DSM-III-R: The definition of mental disorder and the definition of paraphilias. *Journal of Medicine and Philosophy, 17,* 155–171.

Goldberg, A. (1975). A fresh look at perverse behaviour. *International Journal of Psycho-Analysis, 56,* 335–342.

Green, R. (1987). *The "sissy boy syndrome" and the development of homosexuality.* New Haven, CT: Yale University Press.

Greenacre, P. (1955). Further considerations regarding fetishism. *Psychoanalytic Study of the Child, 10,* 187–194.

Greenacre, P. (1968). Perversions: General considerations regarding their genetic and dynamic background. *Psychoanalytic Study of the Child, 23,* 47–62.

Greenacre, P. (1970). The transitional object and the fetish, with special reference to the role of illusion. *International Journal of Psycho-Analysis, 51,* 447–456.

Grosz, E. A. (1991). Lesbian fetishism? *differences: A Journal of Feminist Cultural Studies, 3,* 39–55.

Gutheil, E. A. (1954). The psychologic background of transsexualism and transvestism. *American Journal of Psychotherapy, 8,* 231–239.

Hazelwood, R. R., Dietz, P. E., & Burgess, A. W. (1983). *Auto-erotic fatalities.* Lexington, MA: Lexington Books.

Hirschfeld, M. (1910). *Die Transvestiten: Eine Untersuchung uber den erotischen Verkleidungstrieb.* Berlin: Pulvermacher.

Hirschfeld, M. (1918). *Sexualpathologie [Sexual pathology]* (Vol. 2). Bonn: Marcus & Weber.

Hoenig, J. (1985). Etiology of transsexualism. In B. W. Steiner (Ed.), *Gender dysphoria: Development, research, management* (pp. 33–73). New York: Plenum Press.

Housden, J. (1965). An examination of the biological etiology of transvestism. *International Journal of Social Psychiatry, 11,* 301–305.

Hunter, R., Logue, V., & McMenemy, W. H. (1963). Temporal lobe epilepsy supervening on longstanding transvestism and fetishism. *Epilepsia, 4,* 60–65.

Jucovy, M. E. (1976). Initiation fantasies and transvestism. *Journal of the American Psychoanalytic Association, 24,* 525–546.

Kasantikul, D., & Roback, H. (1978). Sex role identification [Letter to the editor]. *American Journal of Psychiatry, 135,* 1426.

King, C. D. (1945). The meaning of normal. *Yale Journal of Biology and Medicine, 18,* 493–501.

King, D. (1993). *The transvestite and the transsexual: Public categories and private identities.* Aldershot, England: Avebury.

Kolarsky, A., Freund, K., Machek, J., & Polak, O. (1967). Male sexual deviation: Association with early temporal lobe damage. *Archives of General Psychiatry, 17,* 735–743.

Krueger, D. W. (1978). Symptom passing in a transvestite father and three sons. *American Journal of Psychiatry, 135,* 739–742.

Landers, A. (1990, July 18). Cross-dresser speaks for others. *The Valley News,* p. 29.

LaTorre, R. A. (1980). Devaluation of the human love object: Heterosexual rejection as a possible antecedent to fetishism. *Journal of Abnormal Psychology, 89,* 295–298.

Laws, D. R., & Marshall, W. L. (1991). Masturbatory reconditioning with sexual deviates: An evaluative review. *Advances in Behaviour Research and Therapy, 13,* 13–25.

Levine, S. B. (1993). Gender-disturbed males. *Journal of Sex and Marital Therapy, 19,* 131–141.

Lewis, M. D. (1963). A case of transvestism with multiple body-phallus identification. *International Journal of Psycho-Analysis, 44,* 345–351.

Liakos, A. (1967). Familial transvestism. *British Journal of Psychiatry, 113,* 49–51.

Lothstein, L. M. (1979). The aging gender dysphoria (transsexual) patient. *Archives of Sexual Behavior, 8*, 431–443.

Lukianowicz, N. (1959). Survey of various aspects of transvestism in the light of our present knowledge. *Journal of Nervous and Mental Disease, 128*, 36–64.

Lukianowicz, N. (1962). A rudimentary form of transvestism. *American Journal of Psychotherapy, 16*, 665–675.

Malitz, S. (1966). Another report on the wearing of diapers and rubber pants by an adult male. *American Journal of Psychiatry, 122*, 1435–1437.

Miller, B. L., Cummings, J. L., McIntyre, H., Ebers, G., & Grode, M. (1986). Hypersexuality or altered sexual preference following brain injury. *Journal of Neurology, Neurosurgery, and Psychiatry, 49*, 867–873.

Mitchell, W., Falconer, M. A., & Hill, D. (1954). Epilepsy with fetishism relieved by temporal lobectomy. *Lancet, 2*, 626–630.

Money, J. (1970). Sexual dimorphism and homosexual gender identity. *Psychological Bulletin, 74*, 425–440.

Newcomb, M. D. (1985). The role of perceived relative parent personality in the development of heterosexuals, homosexuals, and transvestites. *Archives of Sexual Behavior, 14*, 147–164.

Newman, L. E., & Stoller, R. J. (1973). Nontranssexual men who seek sex reassignment. *American Journal of Psychiatry, 131*, 437–441.

Northrup, G. (1959). Transsexualism: Report of a case. *Archives of General Psychiatry, 1*, 332–337.

Ovesey, L., & Person, E. (1973). Gender identity and sexual psychopathology in men: A psychodynamic analysis of homosexuality, transsexualism, and transvestism. *Journal of the American Academy of Psychoanalysis, 1*, 53–72.

Ovesey, L., & Person, E. (1976). Transvestism: A disorder of the sense of self. *International Journal of Psychoanalytic Psychotherapy, 5*, 219–236.

Pandita-Gunawardena, R. (1990). Paraphilic infantilism: A rare case of fetishistic behaviour. *British Journal of Psychiatry, 157*, 767–770.

Person, E., & Ovesey, L. (1974a). The transsexual syndrome in males. I: Primary transsexualism. *American Journal of Psychotherapy, 28*, 4–20.

Person, E., & Ovesey, L. (1974b). The transsexual syndrome in males. II. Secondary transsexualism. *American Journal of Psychotherapy, 28*, 174–193.

Person, E., & Ovesey, L. (1978). Transvestism: New perspectives. *Journal of the American Academy of Psychoanalysis, 6*, 301–323.

Person, E. S., & Ovesey, L. (1984). Homosexual cross-dressers. *Journal of the American Academy of Psychoanalysis, 12*, 167–186.

Pettiway, L. E. (1996). *Honey, honey, Miss Thang: Being black, gay, and on the streets*. Philadelphia: Temple University Press.

Pinkava, V. (1987). Logical models of variant sexuality. In G. D. Wilson (Ed.), *Variant sexuality: Research and theory* (pp. 116–141). London: Croom Helm.

Randell, J. B. (1959). Transvestitism and trans-sexualism: A study of 50 cases. *British Medical Journal, 2*, 1448–1452.

Rose, L. (Ed. and Trans.). (1988). Freud and fetishism: Previously unpublished minutes of the Vienna Psychoanalytic Society. *Psychoanalytic Quarterly, 57*, 147–166.

Schaefer, L. C., & Wheeler, C. C. (1995). Harry Benjamin's first ten cases (1938–1953): A clinical historical note. *Archives of Sexual Behavior, 24*, 73–93.

Schott, R. L. (1995). The childhood and family dynamics of transvestites. *Archives of Sexual Behavior, 24*, 309–327.

Scott, W. A. (1958). Research definitions of mental health and mental illness. *Psychological Bulletin, 55*, 29–45.

Segal, M. M. (1965). Transvestism as an impulse and a defense. *International Journal of Psycho-Analysis, 46*, 209–217.

Shankel, L. W., & Carr, A. C. (1956). Transvestism and hanging episodes in a male adolescent. *Psychiatric Quarterly, 30*, 478–493.

Slater, E. (1958). The sibs and children of homosexuals. In D. R. Smith & W. M. Davidson (Eds.), *Symposium on nuclear sex* (pp. 79–83). London: Heinemann Medical Books.

Spitzer, R. L. (1981). The diagnostic status of homosexuality in DSM-III: A reformulation of the issues. *American Journal of Psychiatry, 138,* 210–215.

Spitzer, R. L., & Endicott, J. (1978). Medical and mental disorder: Proposed definition and criteria. In R. L. Spitzer & D. F. Klein (Eds.), *Critical issues in psychiatric diagnosis* (pp. 15–39). New York: Raven Press.

Stoller, R. J. (1968). *Sex and gender: Vol. I. The development of masculinity and femininity.* New York: Jason Aronson.

Stoller, R. J. (1971). The term "transvestism." *Archives of General Psychiatry, 24,* 230–237.

Stoller, R. J. (1982). Transvestism in women. *Archives of Sexual Behavior, 11,* 99–115.

Strzyzewsky, J., & Zierhoffer, M. (1967). Aversion therapy in a case of fetishism with transvestistic component. *Journal of Sex Research, 3,* 163–167.

Sullivan, C. B. L., Bradley, S. J., & Zucker, K. J. (1995). Gender identity disorder (transsexualism) and transvestic fetishism. In V. B. Van Hasselt & M. Hersen (Eds.), *Handbook of adolescent psychopathology: A guide to diagnosis and treatment* (pp. 525–558). New York: Lexington Books.

Szasz, T. S. (1961). *The myth of mental illness.* New York: Hoeber-Harper.

Taylor, A. J. W., & McLachlan, D. G. (1962). Clinical and psychological observations on transvestism. *New Zealand Medical Journal, 61,* 496–506.

Thomas, P. R., & DeAlwis, K. (1995). Transvestism in a person with learning disabilities presenting with behavioural problems. *Journal of Intellectual Disability Research, 39,* 454–456.

Thorne, M. Q. (1967). Marital and LSD therapy with a transvestite and his wife. *Journal of Sex Research, 3,* 169–177.

Tuchman, W. W., & Lachman, J. H. (1964). An unusual perversion: The wearing of diapers and rubber pants in a 29-year-old male. *American Journal of Psychiatry, 120,* 1198–1199.

van Kammen, D. P., & Money, J. (1977). Erotic imagery and self-castration in transvestism/transsexualism: A case report. *Journal of Homosexuality, 2,* 359–366.

Wakefield, J. C. (1992a). Disorder as harmful dysfunction: A conceptual critique of DSM-III-R's definition of mental disorder. *Psychological Review, 99,* 232–247.

Wakefield, J. C. (1992b). The concept of mental disorder: On the boundary between biological facts and social values. *American Psychologist, 47,* 373–388.

Walinder, J. (1965). Transvestism: Definition and evidence in favor of occasional derivation from cerebral dysfunction. *International Journal of Neuropsychiatry, 1,* 567–573.

Whitam, F. L., & Mathy, R. M. (1986). *Male homosexuality in four societies: Brazil, Guatemala, the Philippines, and the United States.* New York: Praeger.

Wilson, G. D., & Gosselin, C. (1980). Personality characteristics of fetishists, transvestites and sadomasochists. *Personality and Individual Differences, 1,* 289–295.

Wise, T. N., Fagan, P. J., Schmidt, C. W., Ponticas, Y., & Costa, P. T. (1991). Personality and sexual functioning of transvestitic fetishists and other paraphilics. *Journal of Nervous and Mental Disease, 179,* 694–698.

Wise, T. N., & Meyer, J. K. (1980). The border area between transvestism and gender dysphoria: Transvestitic applicants for sex reassignment. *Archives of Sexual Behavior, 9,* 327–342.

Woodhouse, A. (1989). *Fantastic women: Sex, gender and transvestism.* New Brunswick, NJ: Rutgers University Press.

Zavitzianos, G. (1972). Homeovestism: Perverse form of behaviour involving wearing clothes of the same sex. *International Journal of Psycho-Analysis, 53,* 471–477.

Zavitzianos, G. (1977). The object in fetishism, homeovestism and transvestism. *International Journal of Psycho-Analysis, 58,* 487–495.

Zucker, K. J. (1997). [Birth order and sibling sex ratio in clinic-referred adolescents with transvestic fetishism.] Unpublished raw data.

Zucker, K. J., & Blanchard, R. (1994). Re-analysis of Bieber et al.'s 1962 data on sibling sex ratio and birth order in male homosexuals. *Journal of Nervous and Mental Disease, 182,* 528–530.

Zucker, K. J., & Bradley, S. J. (1995). *Gender identity disorder and psychosexual problems in children and adolescents.* New York: Guilford Press.

15

TRANSVESTIC FETISHISM
Assessment and Treatment

Gwen Adshead

Although the subject of much study over the last 30 years, transvestic fetishism remains something of a mystery. Discussion of etiology and psychopathology have tended to be psychodynamic in approach, whereas the principal treatment approaches are behavioral.

Transvestism as a behavior has a long history (Ackroyd, 1979). The extent to which this behavior reflects serious psychopathology is still unknown. Many different cultures tolerate or encourage transvestic behavior, at least in men, and social and political constructions of gender are likely to profoundly influence its meaning (Brierley, 1979; Christie Brown, 1983).

It is important to distinguish between transvestic behavior and transvestic fetishism. Males (and to a lesser extent females) may exhibit transvestic behavior in a variety of nonerotic settings, and it may not be associated with sexual arousal. Such men are satisfied with their cross-dressing behavior (Bentler & Prince, 1970) and rarely seek psychiatric help (Prince & Bentler, 1972). Both Buhrich (1978) and Gosselin and Eysenck (1980) described samples of cross-dressing men who felt more comfortable and relaxed when cross-dressed. Such behavior may be part of the normal heterosexual repertoire for some couples. Clinically, in terms of DSM-IV (American Psychiatric Association [APA], 1994) simple transvestite behaviors are categorized as a form of gender identity disorder (GID).

In contrast, transvestic fetishism describes a paraphilia in which the subject (usually a man) becomes sexually aroused to the look and feel of clothes conventionally associated with the opposite sex. Although this behavior may be confined to just looking and touching for sexual arousal, increased arousal and orgasm usually requires the subject to wear the clothes. This behavior may occur in the context of heterosexual or homosexual intercourse. Like other fetishistic behavior, it may come to replace regular intercourse or it may be associated with dysfunction in other forms of sex. The current definition in DSM-IV restricts transvestic fetishism to heterosexual men only, despite ample evidence that fetishism may occur in both homosexual and heterosexual cross-dresser populations (Blanchard & Collins, 1993). The behavior of "drag queens" as a form of cross-dressing was specifically excluded from transvestic fetishism. In contrast, studies of men with clinically diagnosable transvestic fetishism have revealed that 48% have had one or more homosexual experience (Brown et al., 1996). Very little is known about transvestic fetishism in homosexual men, not least because homosexual men are excluded from the diagnosis. However, Brown's study certainly suggests that there is a population of men who are transvestic fetishists and are at least bisexual.

This chapter will focus on the assessment and treatment of male transvestic fetishism. This task is complicated by three factors. First, assessment is hampered by the lack of information about the etiology and psychopathology of this disorder. Second, early studies of treatment often did not differentiate between transvestic behavior and transvestic fetishism, or it treated such men under the general rubric of "sexual deviant," making it difficult to draw conclusions about specificity of treatment for this condition. Finally, in common with much sexual behavior perceived by contemporary mores as "abnormal," it is likely that clinical descriptions have focused only on those individuals with more severe and complex psychopathology.

DIAGNOSTIC ASSESSMENT

Mason (Chapter 4, this volume) and Zucker and Blanchard (Chapter 14, this volume) offer detailed accounts of the assessment and psychopathology of fetishism in general, and transvestic fetishism in particular. A further review would therefore be redundant, but I will briefly describe some specific aspects of psychopathology relevant to treatment.

In formulating the fourth version of the *Diagnostic and Statistical Manual of Mental Disorders* (APA, 1994), the extent to which transvestic fetishism could be distinguished from GID was debated (Bradley et al., 1991). It is now clear that fetishistic arousal and gender dysphoria can and do co-exist, although their relationship is uncertain. For example, between 20% and 50% of men seeking sex reassignment surgery (SRS) demonstrate fetishistic behavior (Langevin, 1983). The relationship between erotic arousal and cross-dressing appears to vary over time, so that as the urge to cross-dress becomes more established, the fetishistic component wanes (Buhrich & Beaumont, 1981; Buhrich & McConaghy, 1977; Wise & Meyer, 1980).

Fetishistic arousal should not be an exclusion criteria for gender identity disorder, as it seems likely that a proportion of transvestic fetishists progress to full-blown GID and transsexualism. Most clinical samples include men with varying degrees of gender dysphoria and fetishistic behavior. Buhrich and Beaumont (1979) described three different groups of transvestites: a "nuclear" group, who seem content to cross-dress, a "transsexual" group who seek or have had SRS, and a third group of transvestic fetishists who want to be feminized, described as "marginal."

Although traditionally transvestic fetishists were said to be predominantly heterosexual, and transsexuals homosexual (Freund, Steiner, & Chan, 1982), it is clear that there is a marked diversity of erotic object choice and activity among transvestite men (Blanchard, 1989). Blanchard and Collins (1993) described three groups of men seeking homosexual activity with others for whom feminine appearance was important ("gynandromorphophilia"). In addition to cross-dressing men who sought similar partners, there were a group of apparently "straight," non-cross-dressing men who liked feminized men. There was also a group of cross-dressing men who sought these apparently "straight" partners.

Blanchard (1991) suggested that for all paraphilias, there is a developmental error in locating heterosexual targets. In an earlier paper, he suggested that transvestite men are aroused by thoughts of themselves as female, so-called "autogynephilia" (Blanchard, 1989). For some groups of homosexual men, there may also be confusion about the selection of erotic "target." It is noteworthy in this respect that heterosexual transvestites and homo-sexual are almost indistinguishable on the Masculinity–Femininity (Mf) scale of the MMPI (Langevin, Wright, & Handy, 1990). This suggests that identification with female behaviors and attitudes alone does not determine erotic object choice.

Several studies have suggested that transvestic fetishism often co-exists with other paraphilias, especially in clinical samples. In samples of sexual offenders, the presence of one paraphilia increases the likelihood of others (Abel, Becker, Cunningham-Rathner, Mittelman, & Rouleau, 1988). In a sample of 443 males charged with various offenses, Bradford, Boulet, and Pawlak (1992) found that 11% had engaged in transvestic behavior. Increased fetishistic behavior in transvestites was associated with a younger age group who were generally more likely to be involved with crime (Buhrich & Beaumont, 1981; Wise, 1979). There appears to be considerable overlap between sadomasochistic behavior, general fetishism, and transvestic fetishism (Gosselin & Wilson, 1984). This may be understandable in terms of social and cultural constructions of femininity and masculinity, which are stereotypically presented as opposite poles of passivity and aggression, respectively. Sexuali-zation of these stereotypes exists in heterosexual sadomasochistic pornography, which varies from fairly mild power imbalances to vicious and degrading material, sometimes involving the real torture of photographed subjects. This type of behavior reflects an interest in power and control which may go beyond notions of feminine "passivity." In their study of men seeking transvestite male partners, Blanchard and Collins (1993) found that their masculine, "straight" subjects associated themselves with dominance, whereas their "feminine," cross-dressing subjects identified themselves with submission, a quality suggesting more than just passivity.

Docter and Fleming (1992) described four factors relating to cross-genderism: identity, feminization, social–sexual role, and sexual arousal. Disorders of all four factors could produce very different clinical pictures, with very different psychopathology. Uncertainty about normal human sexual development complicates the matter. For example, it is not clear to what extent these factors are related to, or independent of, one another. For heterosexual erotic orientation to take place, there must be a very early understanding of the social construct "feminine," presumably linked to early experiences of both "masculine" and "feminine" behaviors. To the extent that "feminine" as a construct is associated with relationships and intimacy (see Gilligan, 1982), some degree of psychological feminization must be necessary for males to form intimate relationships. Nor is it clear to what extent the construct "feminine" and sexual arousal are normally mutually exclusive in the developing male.

ASSESSMENT FOR TREATMENT

There is currently no agreed-upon diagnostic method for the identification and assessment of transvestic fetishism. A review of the literature makes it clear that even within the DSM system, not all writers mean the same thing by "transvestic fetishism." Different practitioners are likely to see different populations; those in private practice who see self-referrals may be less likely to see more deviant or criminal populations. An essential first step in the assessment process are answers to the following questions: Why is the patient coming now? Is there an outstanding court report or charge? Is there pressure from a partner for change?

The patient's motivation and expectations may be separate from the etiology (Money, 1973), but will be crucial in all treatment modalities. A patient who presents for treatment to make the court case go away or because his wife wants him "cured" may differ in motivation from the patient whose sexual behavior is becoming increasingly ego-dystonic to him. Some patients want to give up their behavior altogether; others want help to make their behavior more manageable, in terms of both their home life and the criminal law.

Assessment of any paraphilic behavior needs to be multimodal and multidimensional, taking into account all aspects of the patient's life which are likely to be affected by the paraphilic behavior and its removal. The specific aspects of the assessment that need to be addressed, which I will deal with in turn, are the following:

1. Sexual history and assessment of sexual behavior.
2. Past or present mental disorder.
3. Social supports, employment, and family life.
4. Level of intelligence.
5. Biochemical assessment.
6. Dangerousness and forensic issues.

Sexual History and Assessment of Sexual Behavior

Initial assessment of a patient presenting with transvestic fetishism involves those measures applicable to the assessment of any paraphilia. These may include a measure of fantasy life, measures of sexual appetite, and psychological measures of anxiety and self-esteem. No standard approach to the assessment of transvestic fetishism exists in the literature. Many standard instruments used in the assessment of paraphilias have not been widely used in transvestic samples.

Assessment of sexual behavior and function in transvestic fetishists may be broken down into (1) self-reported sexual history, (2) gender role and identity, (3) sexual fantasy, and (4) deviant arousal.

Self-Reported Sexual History

Assessment should begin with a clinical interview to gain the patient's understanding of his problems. This may require several interviews. Particular aspects of the sexual history which need investigation are comfort with gender role, gender identity, and erotic orientation. Ask for details of the earliest feelings of erotic arousal, the earliest object of erotic arousal, and the earliest childhood sexual activity. Elicit a detailed account of all preferred sexual behavior, masturbatory history and preferred sexual fantasies. Seek out third party reports as well, such as notes from the general practitioner, details of any criminal convictions, and accounts from friends or partners.

Various self-report questionnaires and inventories may be of particular use in the assessment of transvestic fetishism. The Multiphasic Sex Inventory (Nichols & Molinder, 1984) is a 300-item inventory consisting of statements about sexual activities, problems, and experiences, including items about transvestic behaviors. The Clarke Sexual History Questionnaire (Paitich, Langevin, Freeman, Mann, & Hardy, 1977) allows subjects to identify those sexual behaviors they find desirable and report the frequency of such behaviors. This is important because of the likely presence of other paraphilias in clinical samples.

Gender Identity

Gender identity and the identification with feminine role are important areas for assessment. The Gender Identity Scale (Freund, Langevin, Sakterberg, & Steiner, 1977) is an instrument which differentiates between different groups of transvestite men (Langevin et al., 1990). Clinicians may also assess gender identity using the Mf scale of the MMPI (Langevin et al., 1990). This scale gives a measure of gender role and gender identity; high scores for males suggest greater interest in traditionally feminine activities and attributes. In Langevin et al.'s (1990) study of transvestites, transsexuals, and normal controls, 28% of the subjects had abnormal Mf scores. Feminine interests and femininity did discriminate between controls and subjects. The Mf scale discriminated well between sexually deviant men and community controls, and correlated moderately with feminine gender identity (Langevin et al., 1990), suggesting that the Mf scale may be useful in the assessment of the transvestite patient.

Another tool for the assessment of gender identity is the Bem Sex Role Inventory (Bem, 1974), which has been used widely in the study of androgyny and gender roles. There is little information about its use with transvestite subjects, however. The relationship between this inventory and the MMPI Mf scale is inconsistent (Bain, Langevin, & Sanders, 1985), and further information is needed to elicit what aspects of gender role are addressed by each instrument. The Bem Sex Role Inventory has the advantage of being widely used in research and validated in a number of clinical settings.

Fantasy Life

Fantasy life appears to be important for transvestic fetishists. The Wilson Sex Fantasy Questionnaire is a standard assessment tool for assessing sexual fantasies in paraphilic men (Wilson, 1978). There is little specific data available on transvestite fetishists; clinical assessment suggests that their fantasy life is rich and polymorphous (Gosselin & Wilson, 1984). This may be of special relevance in forensic settings (Prentky et al., 1989).

Deviant Arousal

Quinsey and Earls (1990) described the difficulties of assessing deviant sexual arousal in paraphilic men in general. There is little specific information about the use of the penile plethysmograph (PPG) with transvestic fetishists, but in principle, there appears to be no reason not to use it, for both assessment and treatment of this group, as with other paraphiliacs (Barker & Howells, 1992; Launay, 1994). Laws and Osborn (1983) described how to operate a phallometric assessment laboratory. In relation to transvestic fetishism, PPG may offer a chance to assess in detail those stimuli which cause sexual arousal in individual transvestites and to look for evidence of other paraphilias. As is common in PPG work, there is little information available about specific training or quality of information which is relevant in the assessment of transvestic fetishism.

Other Issues

We do not yet know how relevant the sex of the patient is in relation to treatment and prognosis. Stoller (1982) described a similar condition in women but there is very little information available as to how similar the conditions are and what the treatment implications might be. Similarly, we do not yet know how relevant the erotic orientation of the patient is in terms of treatment and prognosis; further work is needed in this area.

Past or Present Mental Disorder

Like other patients who seek psychiatric or psychological help, men with transvestic fetishism may suffer from mental disorders. Paraphilias in general may co-exist with both mental illnesses and personality disorders, and the management and treatment may be compounded by both Axis I and Axis II disorders.

In relation to transvestic fetishists, it appears that psychological distress is common in clinical samples. In one study of transvestites (not necessarily fetishists), subjects showed significantly more distress on the Brief Symptom Inventory (Derogatis, Rickells, & Rock, 1976) than did a comparison group of heterosexual males. (Fagan, Wise, & Derogatis, 1988). Mood disorders should be assessed using a standard instrument such as the Beck Depression Inventory (BDI; Beck, 1967). More general psychiatric symptomatology may be assessed using standard tools such as the SCL-90 (Derogatis, 1983), which include measures of symptomatic distress. Any concurrent psychiatric illness requires treatment, especially if behavioral treatments are planned, as many Axis I conditions affect learning.

Concurrent Axis II disorders should be assessed, when possible, using instruments that are consistent with DSM-IV categories of personality disorder. The Personality Disorder Questionnaire—Revised (PDQ-R; Hyler, Reider, Spitzer, & Williams, 1987) uses DSM-III-R (APA, 1987) criteria, but may still be meaningful. It is a 162-item, self-report measure which applies diagnostic criteria for the 11 categories of personality disorder described in DSM-III-R. It also contains an "impairment distress scale" measuring disturbance in social, psychological, and occupational functioning. It may be problematic in that it generated more than one diagnostic category (Dolan, Evans, and Norton, 1995).

We know little about the prevalence of personality disorders in transvestic fetishists. Transvestite men are often classically described as "narcissistic," but there are no studies using standardized instruments confirming this. Studies of nonclinical populations suggest that the majority do not have personality disorders (Bentler & Prince, 1970). However, this probably is less likely in clinical samples. The presence of a personality disorder, particularly of the DSM-IV Cluster B category (the dramatic or flamboyant group) may have implications for engagement in treatment and the patient's ability to remain in treatment.

As with other clinical populations, a history of substance abuse is relevant to therapeutic prognosis. Extensive drug and alcohol usage of long duration may suggest a high degree of anxiety in an individual and a reduced capacity to tolerate stress. Given that any treatment strategy may be stressful and all treatments require active cooperation and learning, a significant substance abuse problem may need treatment before any other treatment can begin. There is little evidence that transvestic fetishism is particularly associated with substance abuse any more than any other paraphilia. Substance abuse may facilitate the commission of criminal acts associated with the fetishism, and thus increase dangerousness.

Social Supports, Employment, and Family Life

Assessment of this area of patient functioning is of particular relevance for treatment and rehabilitation, especially for those patients who wish to maintain a transvestite lifestyle and who may need an appropriate peer group for support and containment. Employment history may also give a clue about stability of personality and ability to interact with others. In nonclinical samples, the majority of transvestic fetishists are employed in professional or managerial roles (Brierley, 1979).

Assessment of the patient's ability to make and maintain relationships is crucial. Over 50% of transvestite men in nonclinical samples are married (Brierley, 1979) and the problems of the spouses of transvestites have been described in a number of studies. Marital difficulty seems to be common and may prompt referral, often when the transvestite behavior is first discovered by the wife. Wives often have negative feelings toward their husbands' behaviors, even when they knew early on in the relationship about the transvestic behavior (Bullough & Weinberg, 1988). Most women do not abandon their husbands when they find out about the fetishism (Woodhouse, 1985). They may develop significant psychological distress themselves. In one study, self-esteem in wives of transvestite fetishists was related to how they had adjusted to their husbands' behavior, and it was also correlated with other aspects of the women's lives such as occupation and a sense of control over their own lives (Weinberg & Bullough, 1988).

Some authors have suggested that the wives of transvestic fetishists may need treatment themselves. Wise (Wise, Dupkin, & Meyer, 1981; Wise, 1985) described transvestites wives as "moral masochists," with histories of multiple losses and poor parenting. However, other studies of partners of transvestites dispute this notion. In Brown and Collier's (1989) study, none of the wives were "traumatized" by discovering their husbands' behavior. They themselves had formed a support group in conjunction with a transvestite social organization. The only finding of note was obesity in 50% of the subjects. Different findings may reflect the difference between clinical and nonclinical transvestite populations.

The relevance of these studies is in their impact on treatment. The quality of the relationship is likely to have a substantial influence on the success of treatment (De Silva, 1993). If the presenting patient has a partner, interview her separately if possible and assess her attitude toward the problem and her expectations of treatment.

Level of Intelligence

Level of intelligence is relevant to the capacity to learn and to comply with behavioral regimes. It may be difficult to help a handicapped individual toward more appropriate heterosexual behavior if there is little realistic prospect of this being tolerated within the disabled person's living environment. Problems of this sort emphasize the importance of multidisciplinary and multidimensional assessment of paraphilic behavior. Bowler and Collacott (1993) described some of the particular difficulties associated with transvestic behavior in the learning disabled patient. Assess IQ using a standardized assessment tool such as the WAIS (Wechsler, 1958).

Biochemical Assessment

There are no studies which have confirmed endocrine disorder in transvestic fetishists. There appears to be little indication for biochemical testing based on what we currently know about etiology. The exception to this is when gender identity disorder is suspected to be associated with endocrine or chromosomal abnormality.

Dangerousness and Other Forensic Issues

Traditionally, transvestic fetishism has not been considered a potentially dangerous paraphilia. The common perception of a transvestic fetishist is that of an older man who enjoys dressing up on weekends and whose behavior is generally harmless to others. Although it is likely that this is true of the majority of nonclinical subjects, transvestic fetishism may be associated with dangerous behavior in some groups.

Within clinical samples, the danger may present in different forms. Nonforensic clinicians are likely to see cases wherein the principal danger is to self, through autoerotic asphyxia. In this practice, sexual arousal is increased by hypoxia, and death may occur accidentally in the subjects's pursuit of this (see Hucker, 1985, for a detailed description). In their 1983 study, Hazelwood, Dietz, and Burgess found that 13.3% of autoerotic fatalities were known to be either transvestites or fetishists. However, at death, 20.5% of their sample were cross-dressed (Hazelwood et al., 1983).

Blanchard and Hucker (1991) found that older practitioners of autoerotic asphyxia were more likely to engage in transvestic fetishism or sadomasochistic practices such as bondage. In their 1992 study, the same authors compared suicides by asphyxia and deaths by autoerotic asphyxia. They found that nudity, exposure of genitals, or signs of transvestic fetishism were present in half of the autoerotic deaths, but in only one of the suicides ($n = 118$ in both cases; Hucker & Blanchard, 1992).

Forensic clinicians are likely to see those men whose transvestic fetishism is part of a wider paraphilic disturbance which may well involve practices that are dangerous to others. An association of transvestic fetishism and sadomasochism has been described previously (Gosselin & Wilson, 1984; Wilson & Gosselin, 1980). Buhrich and Beaumont (1981) reported that over a third of their sample described fantasies of bondage. Croughan, Soghir, Cohen, and Robins (1981) found that 4% of their sample had actually engaged in sadomasochistic practices, with many more reporting such fantasies. Steiner, Sanders, and Langevin (1985) compared heterosexual transvestites with homosexual transsexuals in terms of erotic preferences and aggression. Transsexuals showed a range of erotic preferences, but 88% of transvestic fetishists described an interest in cross-dressing and sadomasochistic practices. Given that sadomasochistic practices can range from fairly mild physical touching to fairly brutal assaults, the sexualization of aggression may be an important factor for some transvestic fetishists, and clinicians should look for it during assessment. Transvestic fetishism has been reported in association with other types of sexual offenses. Langevin and Lang (1987) described an association with exhibitionism. In an earlier study, Langevin, Paitich, and Russon (1985) described an association with rape. They compared rapists with nonviolent sex offenders, non sexual violent offenders, and normal controls in terms of sexual histories and erotic preferences. Rapists and sexual offenders were most alike, but 25% of the rapists described transvestic fetishism behavior, more than did the nonviolent sex offenders (20%). In terms of body image, many rapists said that they felt less masculine than other males. It is well known that rape is an offense frequently associated with issues of power and control (Groth & Birnbaum, 1979; Prentky, Knight, & Rosenberg, 1988). The relevance of this for assessment may be a connection between a comparative lack of a masculine gender identity and fantasies of dominance and submission. Langevin's work suggested that for some rapists, a violent repudiation of their feminine gender identity may be relevant to their offending behavior.

Assessment of dangerousness, and especially the presence of other dangerous paraphilias, also is justified by the small number of case reports of sadistic sexual murder which involve transvestic fetishism (Bartholomew, Miltak, & Galbally, 1975; Brittain, 1970). In Ressler's study of murderers who rape and mutilate, 72% were found to be fetishists (Ressler, Burgess, Hartman, Douglas, & McCormack, 1986). Prentky and others (1989) compared the fantasy life of single and serial sexual murderers and found a significantly higher proportion of both fetishistic and transvestic fantasy in the serial group. A study by Wise (Wise, Fagan, Schmidt, Ponticas, & Costa, 1991) found high levels of hostility in both transvestic fetishists and other paraphiliacs.

These findings suggest that assessment of any transvestic fetishist should include questions about sadomasochistic practices, autoerotic asphyxiation practices, and rape fantasies. Clearly, clinicians must do this sensitively, and it raises issues of confidentiality in the nonoffender subject. Suspicion should be heightened if the patient is young, exhibits other paraphilias, or has a record of violence to others, even if nonsexual. Such variations are more likely to be found in more disordered individuals (such as those with personality disorders or substance abuse), or those who exhibit other risk factors for criminal behavior, such as previous criminal convictions.

TREATMENT STRATEGIES

As with other paraphilias, treatment approaches tend to be behavioral in orientation, emphasizing the reduction of the abnormal behavior and reinforcement of normal behaviors. A lack of a well-defined behavioral theory of transvestic fetishism complicates this approach. Bancroft (1974) offered a description in terms of classical conditioning, but questioned how it is that the arousing stimuli (women's clothing) becomes separated from the conditioning stimulus (the original female image). Other accounts couched in classical behavioral terms of exposure and modeling offer, as evidence, case reports of transvestite sons recollecting watching transvestite fathers (Buhrich, 1977; Krueger, 1978). Interestingly, an early psychoanalytic case study makes a similar observation (Scharfman, 1976).

As suggested earlier, it can be extremely difficult to review and compare accounts of treatment of paraphilias (Gudjonsson, 1986). Brierley (1979) reviewed early treatments. Over 17 years ago, he highlighted the problem of the lack of definition of transvestite behavior and the importance of case selection, and these issues remain relevant to any new review of treatment. Many early clinical reports combined transvestite and transsexual subjects, and the degree of fetishism and/or gender dysphoria often was unclear. Even if these behaviors represent a continuum, this does not imply that treatment is equivalent across behaviors.

Where possible in this review, I will describe the definition of transvestite behavior offered in each study reviewed. However, few early treatment studies defined their samples closely, and not all studies quoted are of transvestic fetishism as currently defined in DSM-IV. Assessment of each individual as an individual is therefore essential. I can offer no definitive prescription for treatment, based on the current state of research. Treatment approaches need to develop in parallel with improved descriptions of psychopathology and better epidemiological research, which may indicate which types of this behavior are egodystonic and require treatment, and which are not.

Cognitive-Behavioral Treatment

The bulk of treatment regimes described which have involved transvestite subjects are cognitive-behavioral in orientation. It is not always possible to determine whether patient populations are comparable, even in studies utilizing similar treatment packages. However, very few of the behavioral approaches used in the treatment of other paraphilias have been described in any detail for use with transvestic fetishism. Very few clinical accounts of treatment describe treatment failures or offer follow-up data or accounts of how gains were maintained. None of the behavioral techniques described below have been used or evaluated in large homogeneous samples of transvestic fetishists.

For 20 years, behavioral treatment approaches have focused on extinction of the deviant behavior (in this case, cross-dressing behavior or sexual arousal to being cross-dressed) and positive reinforcement of the wanted behavior (usually heterosexual arousal when not cross-dressed; Bancroft, 1974). Early treatment approaches attempted to reduce deviant behavior either by punishing arousal to deviant fantasies or by punishing the cross-dressing behavior. Different types of aversion therapy utilized punishment for both.

Bancroft (1974) described two types of aversion therapy: electrical and chemical. The aim of aversion therapy is for the subject to associate a noxious stimulus with the transvestite response. Chemical aversion therapy requires subjects to take emetics before cross-dressing and to continue to cross-dress while vomiting (Bancroft, 1974). Morgenstern and others (Morgenstern, Pearse, & Linford Rees, 1965) described the use of chemical aversion in 13 transvestite subjects and claimed that by the end of treatment 7 had stopped. However, follow-up time was short, and there is no record of whether or how gains were maintained.

Electrical aversion therapy consists of giving electric shocks to a cross-dressed man (Bancroft, 1974). The frequency of shocks decreased with the speed of removal of the deviant clothing. Marks, Gelder, & Bancroft (1970) also described electrical aversion therapy. Of their sample of 12 transvestites, 67% improved with the treatment but 33% remained unchanged. These results were unchanged at 2-year follow-up. The original sample contained seven other subjects who were actually transsexual, none of whom "improved" with aversion therapy. This study is unusual in having a group of untreated controls, 25% of whom made some improvement in the 2-year follow-up period, suggesting that transvestic behavior may not be a rigid behavioral maladaptation, but it may instead reflect an individual's response to current stressors or difficulties.

One final type of aversion therapy used in the treatment of transvestite behavior is shame aversion therapy (Serber, 1970). The patient is exposed to ridicule by therapist aides while cross-dressed. Such an approach has only been described in individual cases, and has not been evaluated.

Although it is clear that aversion therapy had its proponents and its successes in some studies, such therapies have fallen into disfavor. The chief concerns have been ethical ones about the morality of inflicting suffering, even for some good purpose (Meyer & Chesser, 1970). Other concerns relate to the long-term efficacy of punishment of deviant behaviors as a means of eliminating them. Given the known association of transvestite behavior with sadomasochistic fantasy and behavior, there also is concern that the infliction of submission, pain, or discomfort could be therapeutically counterproductive.

More recently, behavior therapists treating paraphiliacs have advocated the modification or management of deviant behavior and the positive reinforcement of nondeviant behaviors, rather than an approach which emphasizes complete suppression of the deviant response (Hawton, 1983). The importance of the visual erotic imagery has been noted in all types of paraphilias (Wilson, 1978). One aspect of erotic imagery is the fantasy (or fantasies) used in masturbation. Masturbatory reconditioning and modification of fantasy are an important part of the treatment of many paraphilias (Marshall, 1973). The theoretical basis for this technique states that the content of masturbatory fantasies guides overt expression of sexual behavior.

Modification of deviant sexual fantasy has been used in transvestite populations. Two principal methods are described for the modification of sexual fantasy. Cautela (1967) first described covert sensitization. This involves the subject relaxing and visualizing the deviant image. The clinician then coaches him to imagine a noxious image, such as nausea or vomiting. Bancroft (1974) cited studies which suggested that covert sensitization is more effective than punishment in the treatment of transvestites, but offered no detailed figures. The other type of fantasy modification involves orgasmic reconditioning. The clinician encourages the subjects to masturbate to orgasm using the deviant fantasy, and then asks him to switch to a "normal" fantasy just before orgasm. Lambley (1974) described this technique with a group of transvestite men, with some success. Laws and Marshall (1991) reviewed the use of masturbatory reconditioning in sexual deviation. Some of the studies reviewed include transvestite subjects for whom this technique can be used with good results.

Psychodynamic Treatment

There are many case reports of the efficacy of psychodynamic therapy in the treatment of transvestic men. Most of these studies have involved the subject receiving daily psychoanalysis for many years. Few studies provide any follow-up data or offer controls for comparison. It is likely that subjects who have been treated psychoanalytically may have greater similarity to nonclinical subjects and conversely that few of the more deviant subjects have been exposed to this type of treatment. Practically, the analytic treatment of transvestic fetishism is difficult (Wise, 1985). The analytic process or the analyst may be incorporated into the fetish, corrupting the transference (Renick, 1992). Individual therapy which relies solely on patient self-report for assessment of efficacy may be particularly problematic in those with sexual deviation because of the frequency of denial and minimization of offending in this group (Laws, 1984; Salter, 1988). Group therapies may be of more use in the psychodynamic treatment of sexual deviation in general, and may be combined with cognitive-behavioral approaches (Beckett, Beech, Fisher, & Fardham, 1994).

Pharmacological Treatment

As with other treatments, little specific information exists about the use of pharmacological agents in the treatment of transvestic fetishism. The main pharmacological treatments used may be divided into those which involve the use of antiandrogenic drugs and those which involve the use of psychotropic medications. Treatment with antiandrogens can reduce the amount of circulating sex hormones with the aim of reducing sexual interest and thus the transvestite behavior. Psychotropic medication aims to reduce the symptoms associated with transvestic behavior and its maintenance.

Antiandrogenic Medication

Antiandrogenic drugs (usually medroxyprogesterone acetate in the United States and cyproterone acetate in the United Kingdom) are generally indicated for the reduction of sexual drive. They are most frequently prescribed in conjunction with other forms of treatment. Brantley and Wise (1985) described the successful use of antiandrogens in the treatment of a transvestic fetishist as a means of decreasing interest in the deviant behavior. Another method of reducing circulating sex hormones is by surgical castration. There appears to be only one report of the successful use of surgical castration in a transvestic fetishist, in a man whose fetishistic behavior was combined with life-threatening autoerotic strangulation practices (Hucker, 1983, cited in Steiner et al., 1995). A further form of biological treatment for transvestic fetishism affecting hormone production involves the surgical destruction of the ventromedial hypothalamic nucleus (Christie Brown, 1983). Generally psychosurgery is of uncertain benefit in such conditions, and the ethical justification is doubtful.

Psychotropic Medication

Antidepressants have been used with some success in the treatment of transvestic fetishism. Federoff (1988, 1992) described the use of buspirone hydrochloride to treat two persons with atypical paraphilia and transvestic fetishism. Treatment outcome was assessed using self-report and retrospective examination of patients' private notes. Buspirone appeared to be effective in reducing the degree of fantasy life. Other authors have disputed these findings (e.g., Fishbain, 1989), arguing that the anxiolytic effect of the deviant behavior may confound the possible therapeutic effect of buspirone.

The resemblance between transvestic fetishism symptoms and obsessional symptoms has been noted, and the possible success of antidepressants adds further support to the importance of monoamine disorder in the genesis of fetishistic behavior (Kafka, 1994). In particular, serotonergic mechanisms have been hypothesized as important in disorders of compulsion. Three case reports described the use of fluoxetine and clomipramine (both serotonergic agents) in the treatment of transvestic fetishism (Clayton, 1993; Masand, 1993; Lorefice, 1991). The authors described reduction of fantasies and intrusive thoughts leading to masturbation within 5 months of starting medication. However, in a recent comparison of clomipramine (which has a strong serotonergic effect) with desipramine (which does not) in the treatment of a group of transvestic fetishists, both drugs were equally effective in reducing symptoms and were more effective than placebo (Kruesi, Fine, Valladies, Phillips, & Rapoport, 1992). The numbers in this study, however, were very small.

EFFICACY OF TREATMENT

One of the main difficulties in the treatment of transvestic fetishism lies in reliably evaluating therapeutic success and maintaining treatment gains. Means of assessing therapeutic efficacy have not been tested on a large scale, and the need for close assessment during treatment is emphasized by those clinical accounts of patients who appeared to be doing well but were actually noncompliant with treatment (Laws, 1989).

Kilmann (1982) reviewed the efficacy of treatment of paraphilias. His study contained only a small number of transvestic fetishists and he did not clarify how he defined them. Kilmann suggested that generally the results of treatment are good, but that booster treatment may be needed when there is a chronic problem. His paper also suggests that best results happen when the aims of treatment combine reduction of deviant behavior with increases in nondeviant behavior. The unreliability of patient feedback alone in the treatment of transvestite fetishism is demonstrated in a paper by Rosen and Kopel (1977). They used biofeedback procedures combined with penile plethysmographic evaluation. The patient was 42-year-old cross-dressing married man who was treated in hospital. An apparently successful outcome was established after 12 sessions. At 2-year follow up, during which time the patient appeared to be working well with therapists, his wife reported that he had restarted cross-dressing and had deceived the therapists during the follow-up period. In a later paper (Rosen & Kopel, 1978) the authors suggested that they might have used the penile plethysmograph more powerfully to show the ineffectiveness of treatment. Such papers which describe both follow-up and poor outcome are helpful and they demonstrate the importance of establishing a therapeutic engagement with the patient.

CONCLUSION

Assessment and treatment of transvestic fetishism can only improve with a concurrent improvement in our understanding of its etiology and psychopathology. An understanding of the social construction of femininity and individual gender roles is crucial. For the majority of transvestic men, their fetishism is crucially associated with their fantasies of what it is to be female. This usually involves classically stereotypical views of females which bear little resemblance to the lives of real women (Brierley, 1979). Transvestic fetishists show apparently little interest in being working women or seeking female company. The vision of femininity pursued is almost a pastiche of a very particular type of woman, the "pretty girl," or the "raving beauty" whose relationships with others are based solely on appearance.

This type of stereotyping is almost identical to that which is presented in most heterosexual pornography. It may be hard to alter male transvestic sexual fantasies, wherein passivity, submission, and "girlish" sensuality are highly sexualized, when such images are portrayed daily in newspapers, magazines, and billboards. Further information is needed about what femininity means to these men, and this information should be gathered from both clinical and nonclinical samples.

It may be that these men identify with a concept of submission and vulnerability which reflects some uncertainty about themselves and their defined gender role as men. Being "female" may be less important than being able to be vulnerable, passive, and submissive without fear of losing total self-identity and self-esteem. It would be of interest to assess self-esteem in a large number of both clinical and nonclinical transvestic men. Self-esteem and agency are crucially related to mood, and the repeated associations of transvestic fetishism with depression suggest that mood disorder may be not only a possible effect of fetishism, but also an etiological factor. The relationship between fantasies of violence and hostility is also relevant to fantasies of submission and vulnerability. We need further work to elucidate the relationship between fantasies of femininity and sadomasochistic fantasy and practice.

Specifically in relation to treatment strategies, these will only become more effective when more detail of psychopathology is available. In the meantime, treatment research needs to occur with subjects whose transvestic problem is closely defined. The severity of the problem and the occurrence of co-existing problems such as other paraphilias or psychiatric disorders needs to made clear in any treatment protocol, as there is repeated evidence that some transvestite subjects are much less disordered and deviant than others. It may be of little use to compare the treatment of an older, married transvestite who is depressed but has no other pathology with the treatment of a young man with multiple paraphilias (of which transvestism is only one) and substance abuse.

PPG could be used with larger samples, both at assessment and during treatment, generating more information about which aspects of which type of femininity are seen as arousing; this might act as a method of checking treatment efficacy. Longer follow-up times, combined with more details of how the patients cope without their symptoms, would be helpful. It appears that the rate of relapse of treatment is quite high, suggesting that more information is needed from patients about their experiences of therapy. Finally, accounts of treatment failures can be just as illuminating for researchers and clinicians as those accounts which claim quick therapeutic success.

REFERENCES

Abel, G., Becker, J. V., Cunningham-Rathner, J., Mittelman, M. S., & Rouleau, J. L. (1988). Multiple paraphilic diagnoses among sex offenders. *Bulletin of the American Academy of Psychiatry and Law, 16,* 153–168.

Ackroyd, P. (1979). *Dressing up: Transvestism and drag: The history of an obsession.* London: Thames & Hudson.

American Psychiatric Association. (1987). *Diagnostic and statistical manual of mental disorders* (3rd ed., rev.). Washington, DC: Author.

American Psychiatric Association. (1994). *Diagnostic and statistical manual of mental disorders* (4th ed.). Washington, DC: Author.

Bain, J., Langevin, R., & Sanders, R. M. (1985). Appendix D. In R. Langevin (Ed.), *Erotic preference, gender identity and aggression in men* (p. 357). Hillsdale, NJ: Erlbaum.

Bancroft, J. (1974). *Deviant sexual behavior: Modification and assessment.* Oxford: Clarendon.

Barker, J. G., & Howells, R. J. (1992). The plethysmograph: A review of recent literature. *Bulletin of the American Academy of Psychiatry and Law, 20,* 13–25.

Bartholomew, R., Miltak, L., & Galbally, F. (1975). Sexual murder: Psychopathology and psychiatric jurisprudential consideration. *Australia and New Zealand Journal of Criminology, 8,* 143–152.

Beck, A. T. (1967). *Depression: Causes and treatment.* Philadelphia: University of Pennsylvania Press.

Beckett, R., Beech, A., Fisher, D., & Fardham, A. S. (1994). *Community based treatment for sex offenders: An evaluation of seven treatment programmes.* London: Home Office.

Bem, S. (1974). The measurement of psychological androgyny. *Journal of Consulting and Clinical Psychology, 42,* 155–162.

Bentler, P. M., & Prince, C. (1970). Personality characteristics of male transvestites. *Journal of Clinical Psychology, 26,* 287–291.

Blanchard, R. (1989). The concept of autogynephilia and the typology of male gender dysphoria. *Journal of Nervous and Mental Disease, 177,* 616–623.

Blanchard, R. (1991). Clinical observations and systematic studies of autogynephilia. *Journal of Sex and Marital Therapy, 17,* 235–251.

Blanchard, R., & Collins, P. (1993). Men with sexual interest in transvestites, transsexuals and she-males. *Journal of Nervous and Mental Disease, 181,* 570–575.

Blanchard, R., & Hucker, S. (1991). Age, transvestism, bondage and concurrent paraphilic activity in 117 cases of auto-erotic asphyxia. *British Journal of Psychiatry, 159,* 371–377.

Bowler, C., & Collacott, R. (1993). Cross dressing in men with learning difficulties. *British Journal of Psychiatry, 162,* 556–558.

Bradford, J., Boulet, J., & Pawlak, A. (1992). The paraphilias: A multiplicity of deviant behaviors. *Canadian Journal of Psychiatry, 37,* 104–108.

Bradley, S., Blanchard, R., Coates, S., Green, R., Levine, S., Meyer-Bahlburg, H., Pauly, I., & Zucker, K. (1991). Interim report of the DSM-IV sub-committee on gender identity disorders. *Archives of Sexual Behavior, 20,* 333–343.

Brantley, J., & Wise, T. (1985). Anti-androgenic treatment of a gender-dysphoric transvestite. *Journal of Sex and Marital Therapy, 11,* 109–112.

Brierley, H. (1979). *Transvestism: A handbook with case studies for psychologists, psychiatrists and counsellors.* Oxford: Pergamon Press.

Brittain, R. (1970). The sadistic murderer. *Medicine, Science, and the Law, 10,* 198–207.

Brown, G., & Collier, L. (1989). Transvestites' women revisited: A non-patient sample. *Archives of Sexual Behavior, 18,* 73–83.

Brown, G. R., Wise, T. N., Costa, P. T., Herbst, J. H., Fagan, P. J., & Schmidt, C. (1996). Personality characteristics and sexual functioning of 188 cross-dressing men. *Journal of Nervous and Mental Disease, 184,* 265–273.

Buhrich, N. (1977). A case of familial heterosexual transvestism. *Acta Psychiatrica Scandinavica, 55,* 199–201.

Buhrich, N. (1978). Motivation for cross-dressing in heterosexual transvestism. *Acta Psychiatrica Scandinavica, 57,* 142–152.

Buhrich, N., & Beaumont, N. (1979). Three clinically discrete categories of fetishistic behavior. *Archives of Sexual Behavior, 8,* 151–157.

Buhrich, N., & Beaumont, N. (1981). Comparison of transvestism in Australia and America. *Archives of Sexual Behavior, 10,* 269–279.

Buhrich, N., & McConaghy, N. (1977). Clinical comparison of transvestism and transsexualism. *Australia and New Zealand Journal of Psychiatry, 11,* 83–86.

Bullough, V., & Weinberg, T. (1988). Women married to transvestites: Problems and adjustments. *Journal of Psychology and Human Sexuality, 1,* 83–104.

Cautela, J. (1967). Covert sensitization. *Psychological Reports, 20,* 459–468.

Christie Brown, J. (1983). Paraphilias: Sadomasochism, fetishism, transvestism and transsexuality. *British Journal of Psychiatry, 143,* 227–231.

Clayton, A. (1993). Treatment of a transvestite fetishist with clomipramine [Letter]. *American Journal of Psychiatry, 150,* 673–674.

Croughan, J. L., Soghir, M., Cohen, R., & Robins, E. (1981). A comparison of treated and untreated cross dressers. *Archives of Sexual Behavior, 10,* 515–528.

De Silva, P. (1993). Fetishism and sexual dysfunction: Clinical presentation and management. *Journal of Sexual and Marital Therapy, 8*, 147–156.

Derogatis, L. R. (1983). *SCL-90R: Administration, scoring and procedures manual* (2nd ed.). New York: Clinical Psychometric Research.

Derogatis, L. R., Rickells, K., & Rock, A. F. (1976). SCL-90 and the MMPI: A step in the validation of a new self-report scale. *British Journal of Psychiatry, 128*, 280–289.

Docter, R., & Fleming, J. (1992). Dimensions of transvestism and transsexualism: The validation and factorial structure of the Cross-Gender Questionnaire [Special Issue: Gender Dysphoria]. *Journal of Psychology and Human Sexuality, 5*, 15–37.

Dolan, B., Evans, C., & Norton, K. (1995). Multiple Axis-II diagnoses of personality disorder. *British Journal of Psychiatry, 166*, 107–112.

Fagan, P., Wise, T., & Derogatis, L. (1988). Distressed transvestites: Psychometric characteristics. *Journal of Nervous and Mental Disease, 176*, 626–632.

Federoff, P. (1988). Buspirone hydrochloride in the treatment of transvestic fetishism. *Journal of Clinical Psychiatry, 49*, 408–409.

Federoff, P. (1992). Buspirone hydrochloride in the treatment of an atypical paraphilia. *Archives of Sexual Behavior, 21*, 401–406.

Fishbain, D. (1989). Buspirone and transvestic fetishism [Letter]. *Journal of Clinical Psychiatry, 50*, 436–437.

Freund, K., Langevin, R., Salterberg, J., & Steiner, B. (1977). Extension of the gender identity scale for males. *Archives of Sexual Behavior, 6*, 507–519.

Freund, K., Steiner, B., & Chan, S. (1982). Two types of cross gender identity. *Archives of Sexual Behavior, 11*, 49–63.

Gilligan, C. (1982). *In a different voice*. Cambridge, MA: Harvard University Press.

Gosselin, C., & Eysenck, S. (1980). The transvestite double image: A preliminary report. *Personality and Individual Differences, 1*, 172–173.

Gosselin, C., & Wilson, G. (1984). Fetishism and sadomasochism. In K. Howells (Ed.), *The psychology of sexual diversity* (pp. 83–85). Oxford: Basil Blackwell.

Groth, N., & Birnbaum, H. (1979). *Men who rape*. New York: Plenum Press.

Gudjonsson, G. (1986). Sexual variations: Assessment and treatment in clinical practice. *Sexual and Marital Therapy, 1*, 191–214.

Hawton, K. (1983). Behavioural approaches to the management of sexual deviations. *British Journal of Psychiatry, 143*, 248–255.

Hazelwood, R. R., Dietz, P. E., & Burgess, A. W. (1983). *Autoerotic fatalities*. Lexington, MA: D.C. Heath.

Hucker, S. (1985). Sexual asphyxia. In P. Bowden & R. Bluglass (Eds.), *Principles and practice of forensic psychiatry* (pp. 717–721). Edinburgh: Churchill Livingstone.

Hucker, S., & Blanchard, R. (1992). Death scene characteristics in 118 fatal cases of autoerotic asphyxia compared with suicidal asphyxia. *Behavioral Sciences and the Law, 10*, 509–523.

Hyler, S., Reider, R., Spitzer, R. L., & Williams, J. (1987). *Personality Diagnostic Questionnaire*. New York: New York State Psychiatric Institute.

Kafka, M. P. (1994). Sertraline pharmacotherapy for paraphilias and paraphilia related disorders: An open trial. *Annals of Clinical Psychiatry, 6*, 189–194.

Kilmann, P. (1982). The treatment of sexual paraphilias: A review of the outcome research. *Journal of Sex Research, 18*, 193–252.

Krueger, D. (1978). Symptom passing in a transvestite father and three sons. *American Journal of Psychiatry, 135*, 739–742.

Kruesi, M., Fine, S., Valladares, L., Phillips, R., & Rapoport, J. (1992). Paraphilias: A double blind cross-over comparison of clomipramine and desipramine. *Archives of Sexual Behavior, 21*, 587–593.

Lambley, P. (1974). Treatment of transvestism and subsequent coital problems. *Journal of Behavior Therapy and Experimental Psychiatry, 5*, 101–102.

Langevin, R. (1983). *Sexual strands: Understanding and treating sexual anomalies in men*. Hillsdale, NJ: Erlbaum.

Langevin, R., & Lang, R. A. (1987). The courtship disorders. In G. D. Wilson (Ed.), *Variant sexuality: Research and theory* (pp. 222–228). London: Croom Helm.

Langevin, R., Paitich, D., & Russon, A. (1985). Are rapists sexually anomalous, aggressive or both? In R. Langevin (Ed.), *Erotic preference, gender identity and aggression in men* (p. 17). Hillsdale, NJ: Erlbaum.

Langevin, R., Wright, P., & Handy, L. (1990). Use of the MMPI and its derived scales with sex offenders. *Annals of Sex Research, 3,* 245–291.

Launay, G. (1994). The phallometric assessment of sex offenders: Some professional and research issues. *Criminal Behaviour and Mental Health, 4,* 48–70.

Laws, R. (1984). The assessment of dangerous sexual behavior in males. *Medicine and the Law, 3,* 127–140.

Laws, R. (1989). Direct monitoring by penile plethysmography. In D. R. Laws (Ed.), *Relapse prevention with sex offenders* (pp. 105–114). New York: Guilford Press.

Laws, R., & Marshall, W. (1991). Masturbatory conditioning with sexual deviates: An evaluative review. *Advances in Behavioral Research and Therapy, 13,* 13–25.

Laws, D. R., & Osborn, C. A. (1983). How to build and operate a behavioural laboratory to evaluate and treat sexual deviance. In J. G. Greer & I. R. Stuart (Eds.), *The sexual aggressor: Current perspectives on treatment* (pp. 293–335). Toronto: Van Nostrand Reinhold.

Lorefice, L. (1991). Fluoxetine treatment of a fetish [Letter]. *Journal of Clinical Psychiatry. 52,* 41.

Marks, I., Gelder, M., & Bancroft, J. (1970). Sexual deviants two years after electric aversion therapy. *British Journal of Psychiatry, 117,* 173–185.

Marshall, W. (1973). Modification of sexual fantasies: A combined treatment approach to the reduction of deviant sexual behaviour. *Behaviour Research and Therapy, 11,* 557–564.

Masand, P. S. (1993). Successful treatment of sexual masochism and transvestic fetishism associated with depression with fluoxetine hydrochloride. *Depression, 1,* 50–52.

Meyer, V., & Chesser, E. S. (1970). *Behavior therapy in clinical psychiatry.* Harmondsworth, England: Penguin.

Money, J. (1973). Prenatal hormones and post-natal socialization in gender identity differentiation. *Nebraska Symposium on Motivation, 21,* 221–295.

Morgenstern, F. S., Pearse, J. P., & Linford Rees, W. (1965). Predicting the outcome of behaviour therapy by psychological tests. *Behaviour Research and Therapy, 3,* 253–258.

Nichols, H. R., & Molinder, I. (1984). *The Multiphasic Sex Inventory manual.* Tacoma, WA: Author.

Paitich, D., Langevin, R., Freeman, R., Mann, K., & Handy, L. (1977). The Clarke Sexual History Questionnaire: A clinical sex history questionnaire for males. *Archives of Sexual Behavior, 6,* 421–435.

Prentky, R. A., Knight, R. A., & Rosenberg, R. (1988). Development of a rational taxonomy for the classification of rapists: The Massachusetts Treatment Centre System. *Bulletin of the American Academy of Psychiatry and Law, 13,* 39–70.

Prentky, R. A., Burgess, A. W., Rokous, F., Lee, A., Hartman, C., Ressler, R., & Douglas, J. (1989). The presumptive role of fantasy in serial sexual homicide. *American Journal of Psychiatry, 146,* 887–891.

Prince, V., & Bentler, P. M. (1972). Survey of 504 cases of transvestism. *Psychological Reports, 31,* 903–917.

Quinsey, V., & Earls, C. (1990). Modification of sexual preferences. In W. L. Marshall, D. R. Laws, & H. Barbaree (Eds.), *Handbook of sexual assault* (pp. 279–295). New York: Plenum Press.

Renick, 0. (1992). Use of the analyst as a fetish. *Psychoanalytic Quarterly, 61,* 542–563.

Ressler, R., Burgess, A. W., Hartman, C., Douglas, J., & McCormack, A. (1986). Murderers who rape and mutilate. *Journal of Interpersonal Violence, 1,* 273–287.

Rosen, R. C., & Kopel, S. A. (1977). PPG and biofeedback in the treatment of a transvestite exhibitionist. *Journal of Consulting and Clinical Psychology, 45,* 908–916.

Rosen, R. C., & Kopel, S. A. (1978). Role of penile tumescence measurement in the behavioral treatment of sexual deviation: Issues and validity. *Journal of Consulting and Clinical Psychology, 46,* 1519–1521.

Rubenstein, E. B., & Engle, N. L. (1996). Successful treatment of transvestic fetishism with sertraline and lithium. *Journal of Clinical Psychiatry, 15,* 92–96.

Salter, A. C. (1988). *Treating child sex offenders and their victims: A practical guide.* Beverly Hills, CA: Sage.

Scharfman, M. (1976). Perverse development in a young man. *Journal of the American Psychoanalytic Association, 24,* 499–524.

Serber, M. (1970). Shame aversion therapy. *Journal of Behavior Therapy and Experimental Psychiatry, 1,* 217–226.

Spitzer, R. C., & Williams, E. (1983). *Structured Clinical Interview for DSM-III Disorders (SCID).* New York: Biometric Research Department, New York State Psychiatric Institute.

Steiner, B., Sanders, M., & Langevin, R. (1985). Cross dressing, erotic preference and aggression: A comparison of male transvestites and transsexuals. In R. Langevin (Ed.), *Erotic preference, gender identity and aggression in men* (p. 261). Hillsdale, NJ: Erlbaum.

Stoller, R. (1982). Transvestism in women. *Archives of Sexual Behavior, 11,* 99–115.

Wechsler, D. (1958). *The measurement and appraisal of adult intelligence* (4th ed.). Baltimore: Williams & Wilkins.

Weinberg, T., & Bullough, V. (1988). Alienation, self-image and the importance of support groups for the wives of transvestites. *Journal of Sex Research, 24,* 262–268.

Wilson, G. (1978). *The secrets of sexual fantasy.* London: Dent.

Wilson, G., & Gosselin, C. (1980). Personality characteristics of fetishists, transvestites and sadomasochists. *Personality and Individual Difference 1,* 289–295.

Wise, T. (1979). The psychotherapy of an aging transvestite. *Journal of Sex and Marital Therapy, 5,* 368–373.

Wise, T. (1985). Fetishism: Etiology and treatment—a review from multiple perspectives. *Comprehensive Psychiatry, 26,* 249–256.

Wise, T., Dupkin, C., & Meyer, J. (1981). Partners of distressed transvestites. *American Journal of Psychiatry, 138,* 1221–1224.

Wise, T., Fagan, P., Schmidt, C., Ponticas, Y., & Costa, P. (1991). Personality and sexual functioning of transvestic fetishists and other paraphilics. *Journal of Nervous and Mental Disease, 179,* 694–698.

Wise, T., & Meyer, J. (1980). The border area between transvestism and gender dysphoria: Transvestites applying for sex reassignment. *Archives of Sexual Behavior, 9,* 327–342.

Woodhouse, A. (1985). Forgotten women: Transvestism and marriage. *Women's Studies: An International Forum, 8,* 583–592.

16

VOYEURISM

Psychopathology and Theory

Meg S. Kaplan
Richard B. Krueger

DESCRIPTION OF THE DISORDER

"Voyeurism" is viewing some form of nudity or sexual activity, accompanied by sexual arousal. To be classified as a sexual disorder, or a paraphilia, voyeurism must be characterized by observing unsuspecting individuals, usually strangers, who are naked or engaging in sexual activity, for the purpose of seeking sexual excitement (American Psychiatric Association, 1994). Usually, the voyeur seeks no contact with the observed individual or individuals. "Orgasm, usually produced by masturbation, may occur during the activity or later in response to the memory of what the person has witnessed. Often these individuals have the fantasy of having a sexual experience with the observed person, but in reality this rarely occurs" (American Psychiatric Association, 1994, p. 532).

According to the fourth edition of the *Diagnostic and Statistical Manual of Mental Disorders* (DSM-IV; American Psychiatric Association, 1994, p. 532), the diagnostic criteria for voyeurism are "A. Recurrent, intense sexual arousing fantasies, sexual urges or behaviors involving voyeuristic activity," and "B. The fantasies, sexual urges, or behaviors cause clinically significant distress or impairment in social, occupational, or other important areas of functioning."

For some individuals, voyeurism is the exclusive form of sexual activity. For others, these fantasies are preferred but not obligatory for sexual arousal. In a third group of individuals these fantasies and urges become more intense only during periods of stress, and they are episodic. Many individuals include voyeuristic fantasy or behavior in a repertoire of sexual fantasies (American Psychiatric Association, 1994, p. 532). It is only when these fantasies become a focus for an extended period of time (6 months or more) and cause distress or impairment in one's life that this would be diagnosable as a paraphilia.

John Money (1996, p. 273) defined voyeurism as "a paraphilia of the solicitational allurative type in which sexualerotic arousal and facilitation or attainment of orgasm are responsive to, and dependent upon, the risk of being discovered while covertly watching a stranger disrobing or engaging in sexual activity." Other clinicians have used terms other than voyeurism. For example, "peepers" (Gebhard, Gagnon, Pomeroy, & Christianson, 1965), "inspectionalism" (Coleman, 1964) and "mixoscopia" (Money, 1996) have all been used. In addition, there are related terms and/or sexual disorders which include voyeurism, or wherein gratification may be received from looking instead of participating. These include the following:

1. Scoptolagnia: Sexuoerotic gratification produced by watching people engaging in sexual activity (Money, 1996, p. 270).
2. Scopophilia: The sexual need to watch others undress.
3. Scoptophilia: Excessive interest in looking at genitals or sex acts as a sexual stimulus (Karpman, 1954), and, according to Money (1996) sexual gratification which depends upon watching others engaging in sexual activity.
4. Troilism (or triolism): A paraphilia wherein there is a dependence on "observing one's partner on hire or loan to a third person while engaging in sexual activities, including intercourse, with that person. A threesome or group sex does not, per se, constitute a paraphilia" (Money, 1996, p. 272). Troilism differs from voyeurism in that the person being observed is not a stranger.
5. Pictophilia: Dependence upon viewing obscene or pornographic pictures or video tapes (Money, 1996, p. 268).

Money (1996), in discussing scoptophilia and pictophilia, speaks of both as pertaining to being turned on by "being an invited guest at someone else's erotic performance, either in pictures, on film, or live, which is far more likely to be an occasional pastime than a paraphilia. Observing qualifies as scoptophilia or pictophilia only if it is an imperative on which one's own arousal and orgasm depend. Unlike voyeurism, scoptophilia is with the consent of the participant" (pp. 82–83).

AGE OF ONSET AND COURSE

According to DSM-IV (American Psychiatric Association, 1994), the onset of voyeuristic behavior is usually before age 15. The course tends to be chronic and lasts a lifetime.

Abel and Rouleau (1990) conducted an 8-year longitudinal study of 561 male sexual assaulters who sought voluntary assessment and/or treatment for their paraphilic disorders at the University of Tennessee Center for the Health Sciences in Memphis, and at the New York State Psychiatric Institute in New York City. At the former site, all categories of paraphiliacs were included, whereas at the latter site, because of preselection, only subjects whose inappropriate sexual behavior involved children were evaluated. In their study, 50% of voyeurs had interest in that deviant behavior prior to age 15.

EPIDEMIOLOGY

The extent to which voyeurism exists in the general population is unknown because most individuals who have this problem are secretive and fearful of arrest, so they are unlikely to report it even if specifically asked. The legal system collects arrest and conviction data; however, these data are not representative because many voyeurs are not arrested and many acts are committed against an unknowing victim.

Of those who are arrested, the charges are usually nonsexual, such as loitering or disorderly conduct. Data from victim sources may not be representative and do not single out noncontact offenses such as voyeurism apart from other noncontact offenses such as exhibitionism. According to Meyer (1995) as many as 20% of women may have been the target of exhibitionism and voyeurism. Another source of information regarding the incidence of voyeurism is clinics that treat paraphiliacs. These data do not reflect all individuals with voyeurism, as most paraphiliacs are not motivated to seek treatment and they do so only when apprehended.

Of those paraphiliacs who sought outpatient treatment in a clinic in Atlanta, 13.9% of the adolescents were voyeurs and 12.9% of the adults were voyeurs. The median number of reported voyeuristic acts per patient for voyeurs was 17 (Abel, 1989).

GENDER ISSUES

The exact incidence of sexual crimes committed by women is unknown. However, the reported incidence is low compared with reports of male sexual offenders. According to Finkelhor (1986) 90% of reported cases are male. The cases of female offenders least frequently reported are those where there is no physical contact involved, such as voyeurism. In the few studies available, female sexual offenders have been described as having severe psychiatric impairment (McCarty, 1986; Mayer, 1983; O'Conner, 1987) and prior sexual victimization (McCarty, 1986; Mathews, Mathews, & Speltz, 1989; Travin, Cullen, & Protter, 1990). None of these studies included voyeurism per se.

In a recent study by Kaplan and Green (1995), 11 incarcerated female sexual offenders against children were matched with a comparison group of 11 female offenders incarcerated for nonsexual crimes as to their own prior sexual and physical victimization experiences and sexual histories. Both groups of offenders were given a self-report sexual interest card sort in which they rated various sexual scenes on a 3-point scale with the following responses: "I don't like this" (1), "neutral" (2), and "I like this" (3). Three of the female sexual offenders against children endorsed sexual scenes of voyeurism, whereas only one of the comparison offenders endorsed such scenes.

According to Meyer (1995), perversion in females is expressed in a more subtle form. He states, "The old saw that 'if a man stops by a window to watch a woman undress, he is arrested for peeping, and if a woman stops by a window to watch a man undress, he is arrested for exposure' reflects both the subtlety of and the cultural tolerance for what in some women is the female equivalent of paraphilic activities" (p. 1346). Due to the fact that female sex offenders are an understudied group, and that there is a paucity of data on voyeurism per se among female sex offenders, future studies will need to include larger samples comparing contact and noncontact sexual offenses among female sex offenders.

ASSOCIATED FEATURES

Paraphiliacs tend to have multiple paraphilias as well as a high frequency of deviant acts per individual (Bradford, Boulet, & Pawlak, 1992). In a study by Abel, Mittelman, and Becker (1985), 411 paraphiliacs admitted to committing 218,900 sex offenses against 138,137 victims. In this group, 13% (62 men) were diagnosed with voyeurism, and they self-reported 52,669 voyeuristic acts against 55,887 victims (Abel & Rouleau, 1990). In this study, the men diagnosed as voyeurs all revealed histories of additional paraphilic behaviors in addition to voyeurism. Thirty-seven percent had been involved in rape, 52% in female, nonincestuous pedophilia, 63% in exhibitionism, and 11% in sadism. The results of this study suggest that paraphiliacs, including voyeurs, frequently participate in a variety of different paraphilias, some overtly aggressive.

Abel, Mittelman, and Becker (1985) reported on initial paraphilic behavior of adult child molesters and rapists. The first paraphilic behavior was voyeurism for 9% of the voyeurs and 3% of the child molesters. In addition, of the child molesters, 14% were involved in voyeurism. Of the rapists, 20% were involved in voyeurism. In another study, Bradford et al. (1992) studied multiple paraphilias in a group of 274 paraphiliacs in a forensic setting. They found that 115 voyeurs had committed 1,160 incidents of voyeurism (mean = 10). They also found that voyeurism was commonplace among those who had committed rape. These results emphasize the diverse nature of the paraphilias, voyeurism included.

Few studies have researched characteristics of voyeurs exclusively. Symptoms of depression are common in adults with paraphilias (Grossman & Cavanaugh, 1990; Kafka & Prentky, 1994), as well as juvenile sexual offenders (Becker, Kaplan, Tenke, & Tartaglini, 1991). A history of maltreatment during childhood, including physical and/or sexual abuse, is common in the backgrounds of both adult and adolescent sexual offenders (Becker, Cunningham-Rathner, & Kaplan, 1986; Rogers & Terry, 1984). Other characteristics common among voyeurs are social skills and assertiveness skills deficits, deficits of sexual knowledge, sexual dysfunction (Abel, Rouleau, & Cunningham-Rathner, 1986; Marshall & Eccles, 1991), hypothesized deficits in empathy (Finkelhor, 1984), and problems with intimacy (Marshall, 1989).

Offenders often justify their behavior with rationalizations or cognitive distortions (Abel et al., 1984; Hunter, Becker, Kaplan, & Goodwin, 1991). These distortions, or thinking errors, allow the voyeur to continue his behavior without feeling guilty or shameful. Examples of distortions that adult voyeurs use are: "Many people leave their shades up because they want to be seen undressing or having sex," "There is nothing wrong with looking in the girl's locker room while they are changing clothes or showering," "Lots of women walk around their house naked hoping someone will look in," or "Watching a woman through a window while she takes a shower will not cause her any harm."

Gebhard and his colleagues (1965) studied characteristics of sex offenders and divided the voyeurs, or "peepers," into a separate category. According to their findings, peepers almost never watch females who are known to them. Forty-five percent of the peepers were married; they had a lower percentage of extramarital coitus than did other sex offenders. Twenty-nine percent had juvenile court convictions, but only 11% of these were sex offenses. Other offenses were minor, only 20% involving any force. These findings cannot be generalized, as these offenders were incarcerated and had been convicted.

Although some voyeurs do not commit more serious paraphilic acts, there are some suggestions in the literature that serial rapists and murderers began with histories of voyeurism (Rosenfeld, 1985). For example, Holmes (1991) noted that Ted Bundy, a serial killer and serial rapist, self-reported that he started his sex crimes as a voyeur at age 9. Other authors (Freund, 1990; Freund & Blanchard, 1986; Freund, Scher, & Hucker, 1984) hypothesized that voyeurism, exhibitionism, toucheurism–frotteurism, and preferential rape patterns are all part of the same syndrome, namely courtship disorder (see Freund, Seto, & Kuban, Chapter 6, this volume). Freund and Watson (1990) demonstrated that the preferential rape pattern co-occurred with voyeurism, exhibitionism, and toucheurism–frotteurism to a higher degree than other paraphilic patterns did.

ASSOCIATED JUVENILE ISSUES

Although the exact incidence of sexual offenses committed by adolescents is unknown, the problem is serious. A number of studies identified the onset of sexual misconduct in adolescence (Awad, Saunders, & Levene, 1979; Becker, Cunningham-Rathner, et al., 1986). Abel, Osborn, and Twigg (1993) documented the age of onset of paraphilic interest in a group of adult men with paraphilias. The average age of onset for 133 adult male voyeurs was 18. The percentage of voyeurs who demonstrated paraphilic interests by age 17 was 65%.

Adolescents commit a wide variety of paraphilic acts (Deisher et al., 1982; Fehrenbach, Smith, Monastersky, & Deisher, 1986). "Hands off" offenses, such as voyeurism, are common in the histories of adolescent rapists and child molesters (Becker, Cunningham-Rathner, & Kaplan, 1986; Fehrenbach et al., 1986). Several researchers have also found that juveniles commit many more offenses than they are arrested for (Fehrenbach et al., 1986; Becker, Kaplan, et al., 1986).

Becker, Cunningham-Rathner, and Kaplan (1986) conducted a study to provide data regarding the characteristics of adolescents who had been identified as sexual offenders and had been permitted to remain in the community under supervision rather than being incarcerated. Participating in the study were 67 adolescent males between the ages of 13 and 19 (mean, 15.47 years), the majority of whom had been charged with or convicted of a sexual crime. Of the subjects, 10% reported never having been arrested for a sexual crime, 79% reported being arrested once, 8% twice, and 3% three times or more. Those juvenile offenders who looked at other people (usually through windows) for the express purpose of obtaining sexual excitement were labeled as voyeurs. (These were also subdivided by age and sex of the victim). Two of these adolescents self-reported that they had engaged in voyeurism. One boy had completed 20 acts of voyeurism against five adult women and the other boy had completed 30 acts of voyeurism against five teenaged girls. In another study by Becker, Kaplan, Cunningham-Rathner, and Kavoussi (1986), of 22 adolescent incest perpetrators between the ages of 13 and 18, 41% had also engaged in nonincest paraphilic behaviors unknown to the referral sources. Of these, two boys reported that they committed 50 acts of voyeurism against 10 victims. One boy, who had 30 adolescent female victims, began this activity when he was 10; the other, who targeted adult females, started when he was 16.

To date, there is not an empirically validated model to explain the development of a paraphilia in adolescents. Becker and Kaplan (1989) proposed a model for the development of atypical sexual behavior in adolescents. This model incorporates individual characteristics, family variables, and social environmental variables as possible precursors to the commission of the adolescents' first inappropriate sexual act. Following the first sexual offense, they believe that there are three main paths an adolescent might follow:

1. The *dead end path,* in which an adolescent never commits any further deviant sexual behavior. These adolescents are likely to be the ones who suffer the most negative consequences for their behavior, for whom the behavior may have been exploratory, lacking in violence, related to the lack of a peer partner, or as modeling.
2. The *delinquency path,* in which an adolescent commits deviant sexual acts as part of a general antisocial personality pattern.
3. The *sexual interest pattern path,* in which an adolescent commits further sexual crimes and develops a paraphilic arousal pattern. These adolescents are likely to be those who (a) found the behavior to be very pleasurable, (b) experienced minimal

or no consequences in relation to commission of the sexual crime, (c) experienced reinforcement of the deviant sexual behavior through masturbation activity and fantasies, and (d) are deficient in their ability to relate to age-appropriate peers.

It is important for the clinician to distinguish between sexually exploratory behavior, innocent sex play, and an atypical sexual interest pattern. For example, teenage boys may "peep" into the girls' locker room at school and be caught. A clinician assessing such an adolescent should determine if a boy is at risk to develop a paraphilic pattern. Guidelines would be sexual arousal associated with the act, frequency, recurrent voyeuristic fantasy and urges, and impairment in functioning (i.e., cutting classes to peep).

In working with adolescents, it is also imperative that information, when available, be obtained from outside sources such as parents, school, victim reports, court reports, and referral sources, so that other risk factors of an environmental or familial nature can be evaluated. Family risk factors may include intrafamily violence, poor parental management techniques, and criminal behavior by family members. Social environmental risk factors may include bonding with delinquent peers and inappropriate role models.

THEORIES OF ETIOLOGY

Psychoanalytic Theory

The psychoanalytic theory views perversion as symptomatic of underlying psychopathology which originates in unresolved conflicts during psychosexual development (Freud, 1969). Freud emphasized that perversion may be a regression to an earlier level of development and that perversions can themselves be extensive formations to prevent more threatening impulses from entering consciousness (cited in Smith, 1976, p. 594).

According to Meyer (1995), later observations by Freud reemphasized the complexity of the perverse formations in terms of the conscious and unconscious components, the role of guilt and conscience, the contributions of both aggression and libidinal interests, the symbolic representation of developmental missteps, and the adaptive functions. "The preferential object is selected because of attributes which facilitate her substitution for mother in reenacting the struggle over separation and castration. The voyeur watches a woman to note the true nature of her genitals and identifies with her. However, he reassures himself through masturbation that his penis is intact and that he is superior" (Meyer, 1995, p. 1342).

In a critique of psychodynamic theory as etiology of paraphilias, Abel and Rouleau (1990) posited that if specific emotional conflicts produced specific sexual offenses, why then would paraphiliacs perpetrate such varied sex crimes? Instead of assuming that many sex offenders have multiple, specific emotional conflicts, one could assume more parsimoniously that a general deficit of control over deviant behavior is at fault in many sex offenders.

Stoller (1991) wrote extensively on the perversions and their psychodynamic origins. He defines perversion as "a habitual, preferred aberration necessary for one's full satisfaction, primarily motivated by hostility. The hostility in perversion takes form in a fantasy of revenge hidden in the actions that make up the perversion and serves to convert childhood trauma to adult triumph. To create the greatest excitement, the perversion must also portray itself as an act of risk taking" (Stoller 1975, 1985, 1991, p. 37). According to Stoller, the excitement comes from an awareness—conscious or unconscious—that one is harming and that the harm done is an act of humiliation in revenge for one's having been humiliated.

Stoller suggests that one of the dynamics that energizes erotic pleasure is "symbiosis anxiety" or "merging anxiety." By this he means:

> Little boys must perform an act of separation from their mothers not required of little girls; they must establish within themselves a barrier against the earliest stage of wanting to stay as one with their mothers, of not being individuals separate from their mothers, and therefore of not being sure they are fully male: fear of becoming female. Much of masculinity in all cultures is made up of manifestations of this conflict: emphasis on the phallus, fear of intimacy with women, fear of being humiliated by women, need to humiliate women (such as insulting, locker-room vocabulary), fetishizing women. (Stoller, 1991, p. 47)

He posited that voyeurism in males is due to their needing to preserve a distance between their bodies/selves and their mothers. They would then close this distance by the less intimate technique of looking.

Social Learning Theory

Ford and Beach (1951) stated that human sexuality is affected by experience in two ways. First, the kinds of stimulation and the types of situations that become capable of evoking sexual excitement are determined in a large measure by learning. Second, the overt behavior through which this excitement is expressed depends largely upon the individual's previous experience. Kinsey and colleagues also concluded that "the sexual capacities which an individual inherits at birth appear to be nothing more than the necessary anatomy and the physiologic capacity to respond to a sufficient physical or psychological stimulus. . . . but apart from these few inherent capacities, most other aspects of human sexual behavior appear to be the product of learning and conditioning" (Kinsey, Pomeroy, Martin, & Gebhard, 1953, p. 644).

Numerous other researchers also cite social learning approaches as important contributing factors to the development and maintenance of paraphilias. Laws and Marshall's (1990) model suggested that deviant sexual behaviors are learned in the same manner by which other persons learn sexual behavior and expression. Laws and Marshall hypothesized that sexual arousal patterns are acquired and established through Pavlovian and operant conditioning, learned from observation and modeling, and shaped through differential reinforcement. Masturbatory fantasy and orgasm increases higher-order conditioning and reinforces the behavior so that it becomes more powerful and refined.

Sociobiological Theory

Symons (1979) and other authors (Ford & Beach, 1951) bring an evolutionary perspective to sexual arousal and interest in visual stimuli in relation to the selection process. Symons (1979) stated that "anthropological discussions of sex differences in dress and posture emphasize the likelihood of male sexual arousal at the sight of the female genitals" (p. 177). Ford and Beach (1951) wrote: "There are no peoples in our sample who generally allow women to expose their genitals under any but the most restricted circumstances. The wearing of clothing by women appears to have as one important function the prevention of accidental exposure under conditions that might provoke sexual advances by men."

Symons went on to state that "The male's desire to look at female genitals, especially genitals he has not seen before, and to seek out opportunities to do so, is part of the motivational process that maximizes male reproductive opportunities" (p. 181). He explains this in terms of ultimate causation; natural selection favors male abilities to assess reproductive value largely through visual cues. "Because a male can potentially impregnate a female at almost no cost to himself in terms of time and energy, selection favored the basic male tendency to become sexually aroused by the sight of females" (p. 180).

Other Theories

John Money (1996) stated:

> A paraphilia is a mental template or "love map" that, in response to the neglect, suppression or traumatization of its normophilic (in conformity with the legal or social standard) formation, has developed with distortions, namely, omissions, displacements, and inclusions that would otherwise have no place in it. A paraphilia permits sexuoerotic arousal, genital performance, and orgasm to take place, but only under the aegis, in fantasy or live performance, of the special substitute imagery of the paraphilia. (p. 39)

According to Money (1984), voyeurism is a displacement paraphilia, one that "involves a segment of the preparatory phase of an erotic and sexual activity before genital intercourse begins" (p. 174). Thus, he hypothesized that a displacement paraphilia is a "love map that goes awry . . . by the displacement of original elements" (p. 178).

According to Money, voyeurism is one of the showing and looking "allurative" paraphilias. He has coined the term "phylism," which refers to an aspect of behavior or unit of response which is shared by all members of the human race. He theorized the following: "In the genesis of a paraphilia, a phylism that is not ordinarily programmed into sexuoerotic functioning becomes disengaged from its regular context to become enlisted in the service of sexual eroticism, and enchained to it" (1996, p. 86). He then went on to speak about voyeurism:

> In the solicitational and allurative paraphilias, the phylisms that become attached to sexuoeroti-cism are actually reattached, but out of sequence. They belong originally in the preparatory or proceptive phase of the sexuoerotic sequence. Their reattachment is to the acceptive phase, the phase that leads to the climax of orgasm. There are three subgroups of solicitational and allurative paraphilias. They relate, respectively, to showing, touching, and narrating, and conversely, to looking, being touched, and listening to or reading. (p. 98)

Freund and Blanchard (1986) described four phases of erotic interaction: (1) location and first appraisal of a suitable partner, (2) pretactile interaction (looking, smiling, talking) to a prospective partner, (3) tactile interaction, and (4) effecting genital union. According to Freund (1990), voyeurism would be an exaggeration and distortion of the first phase of normal sexual interaction. Freund chose the term "courtship disorder" for this disturbance (Freund, Scher, & Hucker, 1983). The courtship disorder hypothesizes that a particular class of erotic anomalies are distorted counterparts of the four normal phases, with voyeurism involving the first phase (location of the partner); exhibitionism and obscene phone calling, the second phase (pretactile interaction); frotteurism, the third phase (tactile interaction); and a preferential rape pattern, the fourth phase (effecting genital union).

Biological Factors

Recently, biological factors have been postulated as playing a role in the development of paraphilias. Several researchers have investigated the role of androgens, principally testosterone, the hormone most responsible for male sexual behavior (Bancroft, Tennet, Loveas, & Cass, 1974; Bradford & McLean, 1984). Other researchers used medroxyprogesterone acetate (MPA) to study the male sexual drive (Money, 1970) and antiandrogenic medication in the treatment of sex offenders (Berlin & Meinecke, 1981). Schiavi and his colleagues (Schiavi, Theilgaard, Owen, & White, 1984) investigated sex chromosome anomalies in sex offenders. No consistent conclusions can yet be drawn from any of the above studies. Flor-Henry (1987) postulated that neuropsychological deficits may account for the development of a paraphilia. Although the studies on possible biological factors as etiological in the paraphilias are minimal, further research should be conducted in this area. Several promising studies have investigated the selective serotonin reuptake inhibitors in the treatment of paraphilias, including voyeurism (Bradford et al., 1992)

TREATMENT AND TREATMENT RECOMMENDATIONS

The literature on treatment specifically for voyeurism is sparse. There are several early case reports of successful treatment using behavior modification techniques (cited in Smith, 1976, p. 603). More recently, there have been case reports of favorable response to fluoxetine, which is reported to be effective for the treatment of obsessive–compulsive disorder (Emmanuel, Lydiard, & Ballenger, 1991). Treatment recommendations, therefore, have been developed from research with a heterogeneous group of paraphiliacs, many of whom have multiple paraphilias, including voyeurism. Major current treatment strategies are based on various theoretical orientations. Traditionally, psychoanalysis was used in the treatment of the paraphilias; in general, this has yielded disappointing results (Cook & Howells, 1981).

Cognitive-behavioral therapy is well established in the treatment of the paraphilias and involves at the outset a thorough assessment to obtain a psychiatric diagnosis, identify sexual arousal patterns, and determine specific treatment needs (Becker & Kaplan, 1990; Laws & Osborn, 1983). Cognitive-behavioral therapy's focus is on helping individuals control their sexual impulses. This treatment is well described in several reviews (Abel, Osborn, Anthony, & Gardos, 1992; Abel et al., 1986). Abel and his colleagues (1984) described a multicomponent treatment for sex offenders. This program included (1) *satiation,* in which the offender learned how to use his deviant fantasies postorgasm in a repetitive manner to the point of satiating himself with the very stimuli used to become aroused; (2) *covert sensitization,* a technique utilized to improve awareness of the antecedents to the offender actually coming into contact with a victim; (3) *cognitive restructuring,* which confronted the sex offender's distorted belief system about the appropriateness of his behaviors, (4) *social and assertiveness skills training,* in which offenders learned to relate to peers in a socially appropriate manner; and (5) *sexual knowledge and treatment of sexual dysfunction* to ensure that offenders had adequate sexual knowledge to relate to peers and that they obtained treatment for any sexual dysfunctions that may have been present (Abel et al., 1984). Marshall, Jones, Ward, Johnston, and Barbaree (1991) also published a review, as did Laws and Marshall (1991).

Adherents to a biological treatments have utilized medications to block or decrease the level of circulatory androgens. In Europe, castration was used with incarcerated sex offenders (Heim, 1981). There are several reviews of antiandrogen therapy (Berlin & Meinecke, 1981; Bradford, 1985; Cooper, 1986). These have focused on the use of Depo- or oral provera, which lowers testosterone, in the United States, and cyproterone acetate, which acts through competitive inhibition of androgen receptors, blocking the action of testosterone and dihydrotestosterone, in Canada. Selective serotonin reuptake inhibitors have also been tried successfully (Kafka, 1991). Perilstein, Lipper, and Friedman (1991) reported on the apparently successful treatment of three individuals, including one with voyeurism/frotteurism, with fluoxetine.

Relapse prevention strategies have been described and employed recently with paraphiliacs (Freeman-Longo & Pithers, 1992; Laws, 1989). This therapeutic modality emphasizes helping individuals to identify the chain of antecedent thoughts, situations, and behaviors that lead to a relapse and offers strategies to an individual to avoid lapses.

Because paraphiliacs are a heterogeneous group with multiple problems, and often with multiple paraphilias existing in the same individual, treatment must be comprehensive as well as individualized. Dwyer (1988) listed 16 goals to conducting effective treatment with paraphiliacs, including voyeurs. Smith (1976, p. 605) stated regarding treatment of voyeurism that "the therapist should not lose sight of the fact that sexual enjoyment from looking is a natural instinct and a normal part of sexual behavior." He emphasized treatment that controls voyeuristic impulses and attempts to satisfy those impulses through socially acceptable means.

FORENSIC ISSUES

In our culture, voyeurism is considered to be a nuisance crime rather than a crime against society (Holmes 1991; Smith, 1976). These nuisance acts are sexual acts that cause no obvious physical harm to the victim. Voyeurism is one such act, in that there are usually infrequent consequences for engaging in this behavior.

Voyeurism is often committed against a victim who is unaware of what is happening and, as a result, does not lead to apprehension. Voyeurs as a rule cruise specific areas and look for opportunities to peep where they may not be seen. When an individual is caught for peeping, punishment depends on whether the victim files a complaint. According to Smith (1976), voyeurism is not a criminal act in and of itself, as looking is not a crime; however, most voyeurs break the law by trespassing or illegal entry. Other common charges from a sampling of prosecutors reveals that voyeurism is generally considered a minor crime. In New York and New Jersey, for example, voyeurism is not in the penal code as a sex offense. Historically it has not been a municipal ordinance violation under the term itself, in that the actual criminal charges are other nonsexual offenses such as loitering, vagrancy, or disorderly conduct.

Because individuals with paraphilias are usually not motivated to enter treatment without a mandate to do so from the criminal justice system, and sentences are usually short, this poses a problem for long-term treatment once a client has been evaluated.

Every state has sex abuse reporting laws. Therefore, it is important that clients be informed before any interview being conducted that if the specifics of past sexual offenses which involved minors are disclosed, then the therapist is obliged to report this information. However, to treat the voyeur, therapists must have truthful information from the client as to the extent of paraphilic behavior. Protection of confidentiality is of the utmost importance in obtaining valid self-reports from clients (Kaplan, Abel, Rathner, & Mittelman, 1990).

A thorough evaluation is important to determine risk assessment and to make treatment recommendations. We recommend that all patients sign informed consents before assessment and/or treatment and release of information to the criminal justice system or to the individual who is supervising the case.

FUTURE DIRECTIONS

Although there is a large body of literature on the paraphilias in general, there is little that concentrates on voyeurism. Throughout the literature it is emphasized that "looking" for sexual pleasure is normative. It is only when the looking is nonconsensual and preferred that it is considered a paraphilia. Voyeurism, like any form of sexual behavior, is culturally determined to be acceptable or not acceptable. In several reviews of cross-cultural sexual attitudes and behavior, voyeurism was not mentioned (Broude & Greene, 1976; Grubin, 1992). Because voyeurism in and of itself is not a criminal act, punishment is generally mild, and consequently, without a mandate for treatment. Therefore, even when individuals start treatment, many do not remain. However harmless it is considered to be, voyeurism does have victims, in that it is not a consensual act and can range from being a nuisance to a coercive harassing behavior, which can have great psychological consequences for the victim.

There needs to be early intervention to assess the needs of adolescents who engage in voyeurism and other paraphilic acts to prevent further victimization and to help individuals who have this problem satisfy their impulses though socially acceptable means, such as viewing legally sanctioned pornography.

Future research should look at samples from different populations including the general population to get a better understanding of voyeurism, how it develops, and its prevalence. A study of voyeurs needs to be undertaken to determine which voyeurs are at risk to develop other more coercive paraphilias, and to develop risk assessments for this population. Case histories and reports of drug or other behavioral interventions would be most useful to clinicians in the field.

REFERENCES

Abel, G. G. (1989). Paraphilias. In H. I. Kaplan & B. J. Sadock (Eds.), *Comprehensive textbook of psychiatry* (pp. 1069–1085). Baltimore: Williams & Wilkins.

Abel, G. G., Becker, J. B., Cunningham-Rathner, J., Rouleau, J. L., Kaplan, M., & Reich, J. (1984). *Treatment manual: The treatment of child molesters*. Atlanta, GA: Authors.

Abel, G., Mittelman, M., & Becker, J. (1985). Sexual offenders: results of assessment and recommendations for treatment. In M. M. Ben-Aaron, S. I. Huckers, & C. D. Webster (Eds.), *Clinical criminology: Current concepts* (pp. 191–205). Toronto: M & M Graphics.

Abel, G. G., Osborn, C. A., Anthony, D., & Gardos, P. (1992). Current treatments of paraphiliacs. *Annual Review of Sex Research, 3,* 255–290.

Abel, G., Osborn, C., & Twigg, D. (1993). Sexual assault through the life span: Adult offenders with juvenile histories. In H. E. Barbaree, W. Marshall, & S. M. Hudson (Eds.), *The juvenile sex offender* (pp. 104–117). New York: Guilford Press.

Abel, G. G., & Rouleau, J. L. (1990). The nature and extent of sexual assault. In W. L. Marshall, D. R. Laws, & H. E. Barbaree (Eds.), *Handbook of sexual assault: Issues, theories and treatment of the offender* (pp. 9–21). New York: Plenum Press.

Abel, G. G., Rouleau, J. L., & Cunningham-Rathner, J. (1986). Sexually aggressive behavior. In W. J. Curran, A. L. McGarry, & S. Shah (Eds.), *Forensic psychiatry and psychology* (pp. 289–313). Philadelphia: F.A. Davis.

American Psychiatric Association. (1994). *Diagnostic and statistical manual of mental disorders* (4th ed.). Washington, DC: Author.

Awad, G. A., Saunders, E., & Levene, J. (1979). A clinical study of male adolescent sex offenders. *International Journal of Offender Therapy and Comparative Criminology, 28,* 105–116.

Bancroft, J. A., Tennet, G., Loveas, G., & Cass, J. (1974). The control of deviant sexual behavior by drugs: Behavioral changes following estrogens and antiandrogens. *British Journal of Psychiatry, 25,* 310–315.

Becker, J. V., Cunningham-Rathner, J., & Kaplan, M. S. (1986). Adolescent sexual offenders: Demographics, criminal and sexual histories and recommendations for reducing future offenses. *Journal of Interpersonal Violence, 1*(4), 431–445.

Becker, J. V., & Kaplan, M. S. (1988). The assessment of adolescent sexual offenders. In R. Prinz (Ed.), *Advances in behavioral assessment of children and families* (Vol. 4, pp. 97–118). Greenwich, CT: JAI Press.

Becker, J. V., & Kaplan, M. S. (1990). Assessment of the adult sex offender. In P. Reynolds, J. Rosen, & G. Chelune (Eds.), *Advances in psychological assessment* (pp. 261–283). New York: Plenum Press.

Becker, J. V., Kaplan, M. S., Cunningham-Rathner, J., & Kavoussi, R. J. (1986). Characteristics of adolescent incest sexual perpetrators: Preliminary findings. *Journal of Family Violence, 1*(1), 85–97.

Becker, J. V., Kaplan, M. S., Tenke, C. E., & Tartaglini, A. (1991). The incidence of depressive symptomatology in juvenile sex offenders with a history of abuse. *Child Abuse and Neglect: The International Journal, 15*(3), 531–536.

Berlin, F. S., & Meinecke, C. F. (1981). Treatment of sex offenders with antiandrogenic medication: Conceptualization, review of treatment modalities, and preliminary findings. *American Journal of Psychiatry, 138*(5), 601–607.

Bradford, J. M. (1985). Organic treatments for the male sexual offender. *Behavioral Sciences and the Law, 3*(4), 355–375.

Bradford, J. B., Boulet, J., & Pawlak, A. (1992). The paraphilias: A multiplicity of deviant behaviors. *Canadian Journal of Psychiatry, 37*(3), 104–108.

Bradford, J. B., & McLean, D. (1984). Sexual offenders, violence and testosterone: A clinical study. *Canadian Journal of Psychiatry, 29,* 335–343.

Broude, G. J., & Greene, S. J. (1976). Crosscultural codes on 20 sexual attitudes. *Ethnology, 15,* 409–430.

Coleman, J. (1964). *Abnormal psychology and modern life* (3rd ed.). Glenview, IL: Scott Foresman.

Cook, M., & Howells, E. (Eds). (1981). *Adult sexual interest in children.* New York: New York Academic Press.

Cooper, A. J. (1986). Progestogens in the treatment of male sex offenders: A review. *Canadian Journal of Psychiatry, 31,* 73–79.

Deisher, R. W., Wenet, G. A., Paperny, D. M., Clark, T. F., & Fehrenbach, P. A. (1982). Adolescent sexual offense behavior: The role of the physician. *Journal of Adolescent Health Care, 2,* 279–286.

Dwyer, M. (1988). Exhibitionism/voyeurism. *Journal of Social Work and Human Sexuality, 7*(1), 101–112.

Emmanuel, N., Lydiard, R., & Ballenger, J. (1991). Fluoxetine treatment of voyeurism. *American Journal of Psychiatry, 148*(7), 950.

Fehrenbach, P. A., Smith, W., Monastersky, C., & Deisher, R. W. (1986). Adolescent sexual offenders: Offenders and offense characteristics. *American Journal of Orthopsychiatry, 56,* 225–233.

Finkelhor, D. (1984). *Child sexual abuse: New theory and research.* New York: Free Press.

Finkelhor, D. (1986). *Sourcebook on child sexual abuse.* Beverly Hills, CA: Sage.

Flor-Henry, P. (1987). Cerebral aspects of deviation. In G. D. Wilson (Ed.), *Variant sexuality research and theory* (pp. 49–83). Baltimore, MD: Johns Hopkins University Press.

Ford, C., & Beach, F. (1951). *Patterns of sexual behavior.* New York: Harper & Row.

Freeman-Longo, R., & Pithers, W. D. (1992). *Client's manual: A structured approach to preventing relapse: A guide for sex offenders.* Brandon, VT: Safer Society Press.

Freud, S. (1969). *Collected works: Vol. 5.* New York: Basic Books.

Freund, K. (1990). Courtship disorder. In W. L. Marshall, D. R. Laws, & H. E. Barbaree (Eds.), *Handbook of sexual assault: Issues, theories and treatment of the offender* (pp. 195–207). New York: Plenum Press.

Freund, K., & Blanchard, R. (1986). The concept of courtship disorder. *Journal of Sex and Marital Therapy, 12*(2), 79–92.

Freund, K., Scher, H., & Hucker, S. (1983). The courtship disorders. *Archives of Sexual Behavior, 12*(5), 369–379.

Freund, K., Scher, H., & Hucker, S. (1984). The courtship disorders: A further investigation. *Archives of Sexual Behavior, 12*(2), 133–139.

Freund, K., & Watson, R. (1990). Mapping the boundaries of courtship disorder. *Journal of Sex Research, 27*(4), 589–606.

Gebhard, P. H., Gagnon, J. H., Pomeroy, W. B., & Christenson, C. V. (1965). *Sex offenders*. New York: Harper & Row.

Grossman, L. S., & Cavanaugh, J. L. (1990). Psychopathology and denial in alleged sex offenders. *Journal of Nervous and Mental Diseases, 178,* 739–744.

Grubin, D. (1992). *Annual Review of Sex Research: Vol. III. Sexual offending: A cross-cultural comparison.* Mount Vernon, IA: Society for the Scientific Study of Sex.

Heim, N. (1981). Sexual behavior of castrated sex offenders. *Archives of Sexual Behavior, 10,* 11–19.

Holmes, R. M. (1991). *Sex crimes*. Newbury Park, CA: Sage.

Hunter, J. A., Becker, J. V., Kaplan, M. S., & Goodwin, D. W. (1991). The reliability and discriminative utility of the adolescent cognitions scale for juvenile offenders. *Annals of Sex Research, 4,* 281–286.

Kafka, M. P. (1991). Successful antidepressant treatment of nonparaphilic sexual addictions and paraphilias in men. *Journal of Clinical Psychiatry, 52*(2), 60–65.

Kafka, M. P., & Prentky, R. A. (1994). Preliminary observations of DSM-III-R Axis I comorbidity in men with paraphilias and paraphilia-related disorders. *Journal of Clinical Psychiatry, 55*(11), 481–487.

Kaplan, M. S., Abel, G. G., Rathner, J., & Mittelman, M. (1990). The impact of parolees' perceptions of confidentiality on self-reported sex crimes. *Annals of Sex Research, 3*(3), 293–305.

Kaplan, M., & Green, A. (1995). Eleven incarcerated female sexual offenders: A comparison of sexual histories with non-offenders. *Sexual Abuse: A Journal of Research and Treatment, 7*(4), 287–299.

Karpman, B. (1954). *The sexual offender and his offenses*. New York: Julian Press.

Kinsey, A., Pomeroy, W., Martin, C., & Gebhard, G. (1953). *Sexual behavior in the human female*. Philadelphia: W. B. Saunders.

Laws, D. R. (Ed.). (1989). *Relapse prevention with sex offenders*. New York: Guilford Press.

Laws, D. R., & Marshall, W. L. (1990). A conditioning theory of the etiology and maintenance of deviant sexual preference and behavior. In W. L. Marshall, D. R. Laws, & H. E. Barbaree (Eds.), *Handbook of sexual assault: Issues, theories, and treatment of the offender* (pp. 209–227). New York: Plenum Press.

Laws, D. R., & Marshall, W. L. (1991). Masturbatory reconditioning with sexual deviates: An evaluative review. *Advances in Behaviour Research and Therapy, 13,* 13–25.

Laws, D. R., & Osborne, C. (1983). How to build and operate a behavioral laboratory to evaluate and treat sexual deviance. In J. Greer & I. Stuart (Eds.), *The sexual aggressor: Current perspectives on treatment* (pp. 293–336). New York: Van Nostrand Reinhold.

Marshall, W. L. (1989). Intimacy, loneliness and sexual offenders. *Behaviour Research and Therapy, 27,* 491–503.

Marshall, W. L., & Eccles, A. (1991). Issues in clinical practice with sex offenders. *Journal of Interpersonal Violence, 6*(1), 68–93.

Marshall, W. L., Jones, R., Ward, T., Johnston, P., & Barbaree, H. E. (1991). Treatment outcome with sex offenders. *Clinical Psychology Review, 11,* 465–485.

Mathews, R., Mathews, J. K., & Speltz, K. (1989). *Female sexual offenders; An exploratory study.* Brandon, VT: Safer Society Press.

Mayer, A. (1983). *Incest: A treatment manual for therapy with victims, spouses, and offenders.* Holmes Beach, FL: Florida Learning Publications.

McCarty, L. (1986). Mother–child incest: Characteristics of the offender. *Child Welfare, 65,* 447–458.

Meyer, J. K. (1995). Paraphilias. In H. I. Kaplan & B. J. Sadock (Eds.), *Comprehensive textbook of psychiatry VI* (Vol. 1, 6th ed., pp. 1334–1347). Baltimore: Williams & Wilkins.

Money, J. (1970). *Paraphilias: Phyletic origins*. Unpublished manuscript, Johns Hopkins University, Baltimore, MD.

Money, J. (1984). Paraphilias: Phenomenology and classification. *American Journal of Psychotherapy, 37*(2), 164–179.

Money, J. (1996). *Lovemaps: Clinical concepts of sexual/erotic health and pathology, paraphilia and gender transposition in childhood, adolescence, and maturity.* New York: Irvington.

O'Connor, A. (1987). Female sex offenders. *British Journal of Psychiatry, 150,* 615–620.

Perilstein, R. D., Lipper, S., & Friedman, L. J. (1991). Three cases of paraphilias responsive to fluoxetine treatment. *Journal of Clinical Psychiatry, 52*(4), 169–170.

Rogers, C. M., & Terry, T. (1984). Clinical interventions with boy victims of sexual abuse. In I. Stuart & J. Greer (Eds.), *Victims of sexual aggression* (pp. 91–104). New York: Van Nostrand Reinhold.

Rosenfield, A. (1985, April). Sex offenders: Men who molest: Treating the deviant. *Psychology Today,* pp. 8–10.

Schiavi, R. C., Theilgaard, A., Owen, D. R., & White, D. (1984). Sex chromosome anomalies, hormones and aggressivity. *Archives of General Psychiatry, 41,* 93–99.

Smith, S. R. (1976). Voyeurism: A review of the literature. *Archives of Sexual Behavior, 5*(6), 585–608.

Stoller, R. (1975). *Perversion: The erotic form of hatred.* New York: Pantheon Books.

Stoller, R. (1985). *Observing the erotic imagination.* New Haven, CT: Yale University Press.

Stoller, R. (1991). The term perversion. In G. Fogel, & W. Myers (Eds.), *Perversions and near perversions in clinical practice.* New Haven, CT: Yale University Press.

Symons, D. (1979). *The evolution of human sexuality.* New York: Oxford University Press.

Travin, S., Cullen, K., & Protter, B. (1990). Female sex offenders, severe victims and victimizers. *Journal of Forensic Sciences, 35,* 140–150.

17

VOYEURISM

Assessment and Treatment

R. Karl Hanson
Andrew J. R. Harris

VOYEUR

Voyeuristic SWM, 38, seeks exhibitionist type
female for mutually stimulating great times.
25–35, slim to medium build. Lets get together
and see what develops. # 5830

As demonstrated in the above personal advertisement, voyeurism is not always defined as
a pathology. Some of the most general definitions of voyeurism refer simply to the
association of sexual arousal with viewing sexually desirable objects (Agnew, 1965; Forsyth,
1996; Gebhard, Gagnon, Pomeroy, & Christenson, 1965; Kutchinsky, 1976). In itself, sexual
interest in viewing naked women or men should not be considered deviant, as it is an
important component of normative sexual response. Crepault and Couture (1980), for
example, found that over 50% of their sample of community men (51 of 94) reported having
had a sexual fantasy of a "scene where you witness the sexual performance of other persons"
(p. 570). In a survey of 60 normal college-aged males, Templeman and Stinnett (1991) found
that 32 (53%) stated that they had some interest in voyeurism and 25 (42%) had actually
engaged in some voyeuristic activity. Further, using Farrenkopf's (1986) card sort, Templeman and Stinnett (1991) found that the males in their study expressed most interest in
descriptions of voyeurism and frottage of all the "deviant" sexual stimuli.

Although some voyeuristic interest is normative, sexual interest in viewing can be
considered deviant when it is overemphasized in the repertoire of sexual activities. Freud
(1962), for example, considered normal voyeurism to become a perversion when "instead
of being preparatory to the normal sexual aims, it supplants it" (p. 62). Many definitions
of voyeurism further restrict the meaning to cases in which there is an exaggerated interest
in viewing unsuspecting persons in sexual contexts (Freund, Watson, & Rienzo, 1988;
Yalom, 1960).

Defining voyeurism in terms of a disproportionate interest requires some comparison with "normal" sexual interests. In contrast, voyeurism involving an unsuspecting person does not require a normative standard to be considered problematic. Observing unsuspecting victims is a clear violation of social ethics, as the observed sexual object is unable to consent. In the classic legend of Lady Godiva, Tom peeped through a knothole despite community agreement not to watch the naked, benevolent princess on her famous ride (Hartland, 1890). Observing unsuspecting persons also raises the possibility of atypical sexual interests. Yalom (1960), for example, considered the forbiddenness of the activity to be an essential component of the voyeur's sexual interest. Other researchers, however, have questioned whether voyeurs are sexually interested because of, or despite, the forbiddenness of the activity (Kutchinsky, 1976; Langevin, Paitich, & Russon, 1985). Kutchinsky (1976), in arguing against the forbiddenness hypothesis, reported that when sexually explicit material became widely available in Copenhagen, the annual police reports of peeping decreased from 76 to 2.

The DSM-IV definition of voyeurism is close to that of many other definitions in that it requires an exaggerated interest in observing an unsuspecting person in a sexual context (American Psychiatric Association, 1994). The DSM-IV definition, however, does not necessarily consider such interest or activities to be pathological. To meet DSM-IV criteria for voyeurism, the clients' voyeuristic tendencies must also be personally distressing or must interfere with social or occupational functioning. Specifically, the criteria are as follows:

A. Over a period of at least 6 months, recurrent, intense sexually arousing fantasies, sexual urges, or behaviors involving the act of observing an unsuspecting person who is naked, in the process of disrobing, or engaging in sexual activity.
B. The fantasies, sexual urges, or behaviors cause clinically significant distress or impairment in social, occupational, or other important areas of functioning. (p. 532)

By requiring personal distress or social impairment, the DSM-IV definition avoids the problems of defining voyeurism as a deviation from normal sexuality and avoids defining psychopathology on ethical grounds (i.e., lack of consent). This avoidance of the ethical/normative issues is understandable, but clinicians will, nevertheless, have to address these issues in their assessment and treatment of voyeurs.

Hans Strupp once commented that there were three perspectives against which to judge the outcome of psychotherapy: that of the client, the community, and the therapist (Strupp & Hadley, 1977). Clients typically define success in terms of subjective well-being or the attainment of personally valued goals. The community defines success according to the capacity to fulfill valued roles (e.g., worker, parent, friend). Therapists, in contrast, judge success against some theoretical model of optimal psychological functioning. In practice, therapists treating voyeurs need some model of healthy sexuality to identify where and how to intervene.

THE COURTSHIP DISORDER MODEL

Our discussion of voyeurism is guided by the assumption that normative sexuality serves two important functions: it promotes pair bonding and intimacy and, for heterosexual interactions at least, it allows for the possibility of procreation. Voyeurism is pathology, as it fulfills neither of these functions. Our approach to voyeurism is consistent with Freund's (1988, 1990; see also Freund, Scher, & Hucker, 1983) concept of courtship disorder. According to Freund, typical sexual interactions progress through four stages, beginning with visual selection, followed by nonphysical interaction, physical touching, and then intercourse. Courtship disorders such as voyeurism, exhibitionism, frottage, toucheurism, and rape are those that fail to follow the normal sequence by omitting stages or by overemphasizing a particular stage. In this model, voyeurism is a preoccupation or fixation with the first stage, the visual selection of potential partners.

The theory that voyeurism is part of the spectrum of courtship disorders is supported by the high likelihood that voyeurs engage in other paraphilias. As shown by the studies summarized in Table 17.1, pure cases of voyeurism are rare. Most voyeurs have engaged in at least one other sexually deviant behavior, most typically exhibitionism or frot-

TABLE 17.1. Voyeurism: Comorbidity with Other Paraphilias

Study	Findings
Day (1994)	Of 47 mentally handicapped sex offenders, voyeurism was the principal concern in only two.
Freund (1990)	Of 94 men who admitted to voyeuristic activity (not a "pure" voyeur group), 77 (82%) had also engaged in exhibitionism, 36 (38%) had also engaged in toucheurism or frottage, and 18 (19%) had engaged in rape. Of the 94 men, 85 (90%) had engaged in at least one other sexual anomaly.
Freund & Watson (1990)	Of 125 voyeurs, 50 were also exhibitionists, 52 were toucheurs, and 73 (58%) had related paraphilias (including rape).
Abel & Rouleau (1988)	Of 62 voyeurs, only 1 was a "pure" voyeur, 6 had one additional paraphilia, 17 had two additional paraphilias, 9 had three additional paraphilias, and the remaining 29 (46.8%) had four or more additional paraphilias.
Lang, Langevin, Checkley, & Pugh (1987)	Of 34 exhibitionists, 22 (71%) had also peeped at solitary females disrobing, 14 (41%) had peeped at intercourse, 9 (26%) were involved with toucherism, 11 (32%) with obscene phone calls, and 6 (18%) with rape.
Freund & Blanchard (1986)	Of 7 voyeurs, 2 had engaged in exhibitionistic behavior and of 86 exhibitionists, 22 were also voyeurs (also reported in Freund, Scher, & Hucker, 1983). The sexual anomaly comorbidities for 950 undifferentiated sex offenders whose primary diagnosis with other than voyeurism or exhibitionism are as follows: 28% of those who admitted to voyeurism were also exhibitionistic; 74% of those who admitted to exhibitionistic behavior had also engaged in voyeurism, and 87% of those who admitted to voyeurism had at least one other sexual anomaly.
Langevin, Paitich, & Russon (1985)	In the first study, from a data base containing 422 sexually anomalous men, there were no "pure" voyeurs. Of the 45 who admitted to voyeuristic behavior, 33 had engaged in outdoor masturbation, 25 had exhibited, 22 engaged in frottage, and 20 in toucheurism. In a second study, of 31 men who had admitted to voyeuristic activity, voyeurism was the most frequent or dominant sexual outlet for only 7, and an additional 24 had engaged in outdoor masturbation and 23 in exhibitionism.
Gebhard, Gagnon, Pomeroy, & Christenson (1965)	Of 56 voyeurs, 34 of their criminal convictions were for sex offenses and of these, 25 (45%) had been convicted solely of sex offenses; 24 had been convicted of exhibitionism and 11 had been convicted of offenses involving coercion.
Yalom (1960)	Of 8 voyeurs, only 1 had also engaged in exhibitionism; 6 of these patients had serious charges involving various forms of assault.

tage/toucheurism (Freund & Watson, 1990; Gebhard et al., 1965; Langevin et al., 1985). Approximately 20% of voyeurs have committed sexual assault or rape (Freund & Watson, 1990; Gebhard et al., 1965; Lang, Langevin, Checkley, & Pugh, 1987).

The high co-occurrence of the various courtship disorders has several implications for the assessment and treatment of voyeurism. First, voyeurs require a comprehensive psychosexual assessment addressing a wide range of related paraphilias. There is a strong probability that the results of the assessment will suggest that interventions should initially focus on other, more serious paraphilias, rather than on the presenting problem of peeping. Another implication is that clinicians should look for common factors underlying the various paraphilias. The high co-occurrence of voyeurism, exhibitionism, and toucheurism/frottage suggest that these paraphilias may be initiated and maintained by similar processes. Some suggestions concerning potentially common factors are discussed in the later sections of this chapter.

ASSESSMENT

Most clinicians will encounter voyeurism when conducting thorough assessments of other paraphilias, such as exhibitionism. Whenever clients present with any paraphilia, clinicians need to consider whether voyeurism is a problem. A thorough assessment should also collect information that could be used to plan treatment.

Diagnosis

The diagnosis of voyeurism requires consideration of several different factors. The initial factor is the extent of the client's interest in voyeuristic activities. As previously mentioned, some sexual interest in viewing is normal and desirable. Consequently, general questions about surreptitiously viewing other persons naked have little diagnostic utility (e.g., "How much would you like to watch an unsuspecting woman undressing?"). More useful questions would be those that assess the relative importance of voyeurism in comparison with other sexual behaviors. For example, clinicians can ask clients whether they ever have preferred to watch another person naked rather than have sex with that person. Another important consideration is the relative preference for viewing unsuspecting persons versus viewing consenting partners (of equal physical attractiveness). Most people show some interest in viewing an attractive, unsuspecting person disrobe, but would show an even greater interest, should that person intentionally disrobe in the context of sexual courting. A preference for unsuspecting persons suggests problems with sexual intimacy rather than a simple failure to respect privacy codes.

Another consideration in assessing voyeuristic interest is whether the voyeur wants to observe the same person or different persons. Gebhard et al. (1965) argued that the desire for novelty is one of the important motivating factors for voyeurs. In support of their position, they found that most of the voyeurs in their study targeted strangers and reported little or no interest in peeping on known persons (Gebhard et al., 1965). In general, those voyeurs who choose only one victim appear to have an intense, often compulsive attraction to a particular person (erotomania) rather than being classically voyeuristic. Day (1994), for example, reported on several cases of intellectually challenged men who secretly spied on neighbors/helpers for whom they had developed unrequited romantic interest. Voyeurism and erotomania can be distinguished by the degree of desired relationship with the victim. Frustrated lovers may seek opportunities to secretly observe the objects of their desire, but they would have a clear preference for increased intimacy, should the possibility arise. In contrast, the classical voyeur neither attempts nor desires a close relationship with his or her victims (American Psychiatric Association, 1980; Gebhard et al., 1965).

Although some voyeuristic interest is normative, such interest can become problematic when it is intense and recurrent. Clinicians can ask clients directly about the intensity of their interest. Perhaps a more useful approach, however, would be to monitor the frequency of voyeuristic activities, as well as the frequency of associated thoughts and fantasies. A useful starting point for assessment is the amount of time the client devotes to the pursuit of voyeuristic opportunities. Some voyeurs report spending many hours each week searching for, or waiting in, good locations (Kutchinsky, 1976; Yalom, 1960). Other voyeurs may deny prowling with voyeuristic intent, but may, nevertheless, "incidentally" arrange their lifestyles to allow for voyeuristic opportunities (e.g., job as window washer, night walks with dog). The frequency with which clients actually observe unsuspecting persons needs to be assessed separately from the amount of time and effort clients devote to their pursuit.

Another important factor to assess is the role of voyeurism in the client's masturbation fantasies. Some voyeurs masturbate while observing their victims, but voyeurs more commonly masturbate later, while remembering the events (Gebhard et al., 1965; Kutchinsky, 1976). Clinicians should ask voyeurs specifically when and how often they masturbate to voyeuristic images and fantasies. Any instances of masturbation to orgasm while peeping are significant, as such behavior is rare, except for those with well-established voyeuristic inclinations (Langevin et al., 1985). Clinicians need to make some judgment as to the extent to which voyeurism permeates the client's sex life. Given the high co-occurrence of voyeurism and other paraphilias, exclusively voyeuristic activities are not to be expected. There are cases, however, in which voyeurism appears to be the almost exclusive sexual outlet (Hurlbert, 1992; Kutchinsky, 1976). Similarly, Gaupp, Stern, and Ratcliff (1971) reported a case in which a client used voyeuristic fantasies to sustain heterosexual intercourse.

Problems Caused by Voyeurism

Even though the client may think and act like a voyeur, such behaviors are insufficient for DSM-IV diagnostic criteria (American Psychiatric Association, 1994). Most clinicians and diagnostic systems (including DSM-III-R) would consider a recurrent pattern of observing unsuspecting persons naked to be problematic and worthy of intervention. The DSM-IV criteria, however, further requires that these voyeuristic impulses or activities are personally distressing or cause social/occupation impairment. The "impairment" requirement, however, has little real influence in applied settings, as voyeurs do not present for assessment/treatment unless somebody (if not the client) perceives their behavior to be problematic. Nevertheless, the impairment criteria is clinically useful, because a thorough evaluation of the negative impact of voyeurism can aid in setting treatment goals and in motivating clients for treatment.

Clients are most likely to self-identify problems with voyeurism in terms of loss of control. As with many sexual behaviors, clients may feel compelled toward voyeurism even though they disapprove of their own behavior. Typically, however, the switch from ego-syntonic to ego-dystonic voyeurism is precipitated by external factors, such as detection or interference with other valued goals (e.g., job security). Useful questions for the assessment of personal problems with voyeurism include the following: "Have you ever wanted to stop peeping, but were unable to?"; "If you had not gotten into trouble, would you have wanted to stop?"; and "Leaving aside what other people think, how much do you think that peeping is a problem for you?"

Clients should also be asked about specific ways in which voyeurism has interfered with their lives. One potential problem is conflict with the law. Although voyeurism violates social ethics, it is not necessarily illegal. Voyeurs, nonetheless, can engage in a range of criminal activities while in pursuit of voyeuristic opportunities, for example, trespassing, loitering, property damage (to fences, walls). Voyeurs who masturbate at the scene may also be apprehended for indecency or exhibitionism. In general, however, the chances that a voyeur will come into contact with the law are relatively small.

In contrast, there is a strong possibility that voyeurism could interfere with normative psychosexual development. Time spent fantasizing or acting on voyeuristic activities is time not spent on the development of the skills needed for appropriate sexuality. As well, voyeurs may correctly anticipate rejection, should their activities become known to their current or potential love interests.

Voyeurism may also interfere with men's nonsexual relationships with women, particularly when the voyeuristic interests become generalized to inappropriate contexts. The prototypic voyeur remains hidden, but some voyeurs extend their activity to public settings (e.g., beaches), or to nonsexual relationships. Leering at coworkers does little to enhance one's profile in the business environment.

Voyeurism may impair occupational adjustment in several ways. The stigma associated with voyeurism, should it become obvious, limits career opportunities and could be grounds for dismissal from certain positions (e.g., minister, police chief, politician). As well, voyeurs may deliberately forego career advancement to maximize their opportunities for voyeurism. A voyeur, for example, may remain as a roving security guard despite repeated requests to take a management position. The dedicated voyeur also devotes a considerable amount of time to his sexual deviance, time which could otherwise be devoted to more constructive ends.

In summary, clinicians need to consider four general factors when diagnosing voyeurism: (1) the extent of voyeuristic interest and impulses; (2) the extent of voyeuristic activities; (3) personal distress caused by voyeurism; and (4) impairment in social and occupational functioning. Even if a client meets the diagnostic criteria for voyeurism, voyeuristic behaviors may not be the immediate focus of treatment. Voyeurs will often engage in other, more serious, sexual deviations that justify immediate clinical attention (e.g., rape, child molestation, exhibitionism). Treatment should first be directed to those behaviors that have the greatest probability of victim harm, and those that have the most serious social consequences. However, even when the focus of treatment is on other disorders, voyeuristic behaviors may justify immediate attention if voyeurism forms the target acquisition phase of a more serious offense pattern (e.g., a pedophile watching kids at a wading pool).

Voyeurism becomes a clinically significant treatment target in its own right when it results in significant subjective distress or significant social impairment. Intervention targeting voyeurism is appropriate in most cases when an individual self-identifies the need for treatment. Such need will probably be associated with feelings of loss of control and compulsion to peep despite known risks. Clients whose only voyeuristic behavior involves masturbating in complete privacy to publicly available images (e.g., beach scenes) typically would not require specialized voyeurism treatment, even if the clients were concerned about their own behavior. Such ego-dystonic voyeurs may benefit, instead, from more general counseling concerning their feelings and values concerning masturbation and human sexuality. Treatment would be justified, however, should the behavior of the ego-dystonic voyeur violate accepted social norms (e.g., violation of privacy, intrusive staring, trespassing). Even for unmotivated clients, treatment is justified, should the voyeur risk serious, negative consequences. Such negative consequences would most likely concern imminent threats to employment, marriage, or family life. For these unmotivated clients, the first task of intervention would be to help them realize the potential benefits of treatment.

Assessment for Treatment

A valid diagnosis is only one goal of the assessment process. The other major goal of clinical assessment is to acquire information that could be useful for treatment. When establishing the goals of treatment, it is desirable to conduct a functional analysis of the factors that motivate, maintain, and reinforce the behavior. It is also useful to compile a detailed inventory of the problems caused by voyeurism. As a general approach to treatment, we propose that the goal should be to minimize the problems while continuing to fulfill as many of the needs as possible. The establishment of treatment goals requires considering the perspectives of both the client and the therapist and coming to some mutually acceptable agreement. In some cases, the goal may be the development of long-term relationships characterized by intimacy, cooperation and trust. For other cases, the goal may be simply to eliminate illegal activities (e.g., "Don't trespass and masturbate only in private").

Although voyeurism is socially deviant, it is not without certain benefits. Each case has unique features, but there are several common motivating factors that clinicians should consider. One of the primary functions of voyeurism is to find sexualized images for masturbation. As previously mentioned, almost everybody has some interest in viewing attractive sexual partners. Voyeurs are stealing sexual images, but some voyeurs would be as interested in obtaining the same images through other means. Langevin et al. (1985) found that, contrary to their expectations, voyeurs were as interested in pornography as were other groups in their study. Similarly, Kutchinsky (1976) reported a dramatic drop in the incidence of voyeurism once pornography was legalized in Copenhagen. When assessing individual voyeurs, it is therefore important to determine the extent to which they would be satisfied with other forms of sexualized images (e.g., adult movies, magazines, exotic shows).

Voyeurs may prefer peeping to pornography because peeping involves a relationship with a real person. The voyeur–victim relationship is so distant, however, that it almost seems inappropriate to call it a relationship. The victim, in most cases, is completely unaware of being observed. Why would the voyeur choose this extreme level of distance? One possibility is that the voyeur may lack the skills or opportunities to develop more intimate relationships. There are, however, certain advantages to distant sexual relationships. Close relationships require commitments and emotional risks. Distant, impersonal sexual relationships provide an opportunity to fulfill sexual needs without exposure to the usual emotional vulnerability. Voyeurism can be seen as an extreme expression of impersonal sex. Because the victim is unaware of being observed, the voyeur may feel in complete control over the relationship and feel no risk of rejection. The preference for unsuspecting versus consenting targets may be based on the anonymity provided when observing unsuspecting victims. It is interesting to note that the interpersonal relationships of the female voyeur described by Hurlbert (1992) were so distant as to justify the diagnosis of schizoid personality disorder.

In comparison to engaging a prostitute, voyeurism is inexpensive, with low risk for sexually transmitted diseases and relatively low risk for involvement with the law. Even though the prostitute–client relationship requires little emotional involvement, the voyeur–victim relationship requires even less.

An underlying desire to maintain emotional distance may help explain the high comorbidity of voyeurism, exhibitionism, and frottage. These paraphilias are all characterized by a minimum level of connection with the victim. The offender typically aims to remain anonymous. Voyeurism, however, is not only a distant relationship; it also is an intrusive relationship. Voyeurism, exhibitionism, frottage, and rape are each increasingly interactive forms of intrusive sexuality. Although voyeurs do not necessarily escalate to rape, there is some data indicating that the interest in voyeurism develops earlier than does an interest in exhibitionism/frottage, which, in turn, develops earlier than an interest in rape (Abel & Rouleau, 1990). Consequently, when assessing the voyeur–victim relationship, it is important to identify the extent to which the voyeur is motivated by thoughts of coercive sexual behavior.

For some cases, voyeurism provides adventure and excitement in otherwise tedious lives. The lifestyles of many voyeurs provide limited opportunities for occupational and social stimulation (see case studies summarized in Table 17.2). For these clients, voyeurism was the one area of their lives in which they displayed commitment, skill, and daring. For many voyeurs, peeping resembles other types of sports (e.g. hunting, fishing, birdwatching) where the goal is achieved infrequently and with considerable effort. Such intermittent reinforcement schedules make voyeuristic activity highly resistant to extinction.

Though normal processes may motivate the development of voyeurism, voyeurs typically present for treatment after their behavior has become compulsive. Some voyeurs may believe that they are engaging in a deliberate, intentional activity, but voyeurs often feel compelled to peep despite obvious negative personal and social consequences. As with any compulsion, voyeurism may become a restricted, overlearned response to deal with a variety of personal and emotional needs. There are, however, a variety of specific factors that could contribute to voyeurism. Knowledge of these risk factors can guide the selection of treatment targets as well as aiding in the prediction of recidivism.

Although systematic studies have not been conducted, it is likely that voyeurs hold specific beliefs and attitudes that support their voyeuristic activities. Voyeurs, for example, may state that the victim was deliberately exposing, that voyeurism is not morally wrong, or that everybody does it so it is normal. Like other sex offenders, voyeurs may also minimize or deny their sexual deviance by making excuses, such as they were looking for their cat, or even that they were planning a burglary (Gebhard et al., 1965; Smith, 1976; Yalom, 1960).

Most voyeurs prowl alone, but voyeuristic groups are not uncommon, particularly among adolescents (Gebhard et al., 1965). Forsyth (1996), for example, reported on groups of maintenance staff in high-rise buildings who routinely use telescopes for voyeuristic activities during work breaks. Even the solitary, adult voyeur may have some direct social support for their activity. Kutchinsky (1976) described how some voyeurs meet in parks and other public places were there are opportunities for viewing erotic scenes. These voyeurs may exchange information about particular places or people to watch (Kutchinsky, 1976).

Assessments should also consider lifestyle and environmental factors that may reinforce voyeurism. Some jobs, such as window washer, provide exceptional opportunities to pursue voyeuristic interests. Other lifestyle factors to consider include solitary evening walks, and certain high-risk hobbies (e.g., bird watching, astronomy).

An important voyeurism risk factor is the inability to establish close, cooperative sexual relationships. For some voyeurs, peeping appears to be a relatively transient, secondary interest for individuals who have well-established intimate relationships (e.g., Konopacki & Oei, 1988). For other voyeurs, peeping is part of a general personality style that avoids all opportunities for intimacy (Hurlbert, 1992; Yalom, 1960). Such voyeurs would likely have few close friends, be single or in unsatisfactory marriages, and be difficult to treat successfully. Consequently, the assessment of voyeurs benefits from general assessments of the voyeur's capacity for intimacy, empathy, and caring.

Measures

As there are few established measures for assessing voyeurism, clinical assessments need to rely on guided interviews. These interviews should address the major diagnostic indicators as well as the factors useful for treatment. There are, however, a number of questionnaire measures that might be useful as screening instruments.

The Erotic Preferences Examination Scheme (EPES) developed by Freund and others contains six items addressing voyeurism (Freund et al., 1988). The first question considers whether the respondent has ever been more interested in secretly viewing other people than in sexual contact. The next three questions concern masturbation while secretly watching intercourse, watching a girl or woman, or while remembering other people's sexual activity. Respondents then answer whether they have ever spent a substantial amount of time in pursuit of voyeuristic opportunities. The final question is whether they have ever identified with people whom they secretly observed making love.

Freund et al. (1988) used the EPES to compare 60 voyeurs with 221 nonvoyeur sex offenders, 69 student controls, and 35 nonstudent controls. The voyeurs were identified as men referred for assessment after being accused of, convicted for, or admitting to voyeurism. Each question significantly differentiated the voyeurs from each of the control groups. The strongest discriminations were for the question concerning excessive time spent peeping and the question concerning masturbating while observing unsuspecting women undressing. Eighty-five percent of the voyeurs endorsed each of these items, whereas they were endorsed by only 20% of the comparison groups. The internal consistency (alpha) of the total scale was .83.

The EPES appears to be a clinically useful questionnaire for assessing voyeurism. It appears to have good psychometric properties, and the constructs it addresses are clinically relevant. However, because there are many aspects of voyeurism not addressed by the EPES Voyeurism scale (e.g., compulsion, social impairment), clinicians should consider the EPES as a screening instrument in the context of a full psychosexual assessment.

The Multiphasic Sex Inventory (MSI) contains nine items related to voyeurism (Nichols & Molinder, 1984). These items cover a range of voyeuristic activities as well as two items addressing voyeuristic compulsions (e.g., "I have not been able to stop myself from looking at others in a sexual way"). The MSI manual provides no reliability or validity information; however, a subsequent study found that the MSI Voyeurism scale had a moderate level of internal consistency (alpha = .70) in a sample of 144 rapists (Kalichman, Henderson, Shealy, & Dwyer, 1992). The MSI items have face validity, but their ability to distinguish voyeurs from other groups has yet to be tested.

The Clarke Sex History Questionnaire contains a six-item Peeping scale (Langevin, Paitich, Russon, Handy, & Langevin, 1990). The questionnaire asks respondents how frequently they have secretly observed intercourse, openly observed intercourse (with the lovers' knowledge), and secretly observed women undressing. Each item is followed by an additional item inquiring whether the respondent has ever masturbated or climaxed while observing the activity.

The manual reports acceptable internal consistencies for the total scale based on a diverse sample of paraphiliacs (alphas of .76 and .84). To our knowledge, the Clarke voyeurism scale has not been used to compare known groups of voyeurs with other paraphiliacs. There is some indirect validity evidence for the scale, however, in that exhibitionists scored substantially higher than did control groups of sexual aggressives, pedophiles, nonsexual criminals, and community controls (Langevin et al., 1990). As previously mentioned, there is an extremely high comorbidity between voyeurism and exhibitionism.

The Sexual Behavior Inventory (SBI) contains a number of items addressing consensual looking (Robinson & Annon, 1975). These items address looking at one's own sexual parts or those of one's partner (e.g., "I have looked closely at my pubic hair"; "I have looked closely at my partner's pubic hair"). The SBI comes in separate versions for males and females. For the female version, there are 11 items concerning looking at oneself and eight items concerning looking at one's partner. For the male version, there are nine self items and 10 partner items. The 60 items of the SBI were intended to assess the range of normal sexual activity, not sexual deviance. The SBI, however, may have some usefulness in monitoring the treatment of certain exclusive voyeurs, particularly when one of the goals of treatment is to expand the range of acceptable sexual behavior.

Three different sexual interest card sort measures include items related to voyeurism. The Abel–Becker Card Sort (Salter, 1988) contains 5 (out of 75) items targeting voyeurism. For each item, the respondent rates its sexual attractiveness on a 7-point scale from "extremely sexually repulsive" to "extremely sexually arousing." The Abel–Becker items address peeping on adult or sexually mature females (e.g., "I go by the girl's gym at college and look though the dressing room window. I can see several girls there, all partly undressed"). Laws's revision of the Abel–Becker card sort included five items concerning peeping on young boys and five items concerning peeping on young girls (Laws, Greenbaum, Murrin, & Osbourn, 1994). The Laws version does not contain items concerning peeping at adults. To our knowledge, the psychometric properties of the Abel–Becker and Laws voyeurism scales have not been investigated.

Farrenkopf's (1988) further revision of the Abel–Becker–Laws card sort contains three voyeurism items, two concerning adult women and one item concerning peeping on a couple. The card sort was designed to be used as part of a comprehensive sexual interest assessment that also contains an "arousal portfolio" (Farrenkopf, n.d.). This portfolio contains a variety of photographs depicting various sexual targets (children, adult males, etc.) and activities (e.g., rape, exposure). One of the portfolio pictures depicts a naked man secretly observing a naked woman. For each of the card sort and portfolio items, respondents rate their sexual interest from 0% (no interest) to 100% (high arousal). Templeman and Stinnett (1991) found Farrenkopf's four voyeurism items (three cards, one picture) to have high internal consistency (alpha of .84). In their sample of "normal" males, however, the Farrenkopf (1988) card sort items correlated only .22 with self-reported voyeuristic activity (Templeman & Stinnett, 1991) as measured by the Clarke Sexual History Questionnaire (Langevin et al., 1990).

Phallometrics

Although phallometric procedures have been developed for the assessment of voyeuristic interests, these procedures have not, to our knowledge, been used to compare voyeurs with other groups. There appears to be some indirect evidence for the validity of these phallometric procedures, however, based on their ability to detect unusual levels of voyeuristic interest in those with other courtship disorders.

Freund, Scher, Racansky, Campbell, and Heasman (1986) compared the responses of 11 rape-prone males and 11 paid community controls to six audiotaped voyeuristic scenarios. They found that rapists responded significantly more to the voyeuristic scenarios than did the normal controls. Freund et al. (1983) found that a mixed group of 17 paraphiliacs showed greater penile responses to audiotaped descriptions of voyeurism than did 20 paid volunteers. Interestingly, the sexually anomalous group responded as highly to voyeuristic scenarios as to descriptions of sexual intercourse. The Freund et al. (1983) paper is disappointing, however, in that it did not report phallometric results for their seven voyeuristic patients.

Fedora et al. (1992) used slides of "single fully clothed adult females in public settings viewed from a distance" (p. 5) to assess interest in "courtship disorders." They found that the responses of the 60 sexually aggressive offenders (mainly rapists) were greater than were the responses of the 60 paid normal volunteers. The responses of the 167 nonaggressive sexual offenders (mainly child molesters) were intermediate between that of the other two groups. Phallometrics have also been used to control contingent electric shock in a process of aversion therapy and to assess the presence or absence of arousal to voyeuristic stimuli in a case study (Tollison & Adams, 1979).

Overall, the results of these initial phallometric studies suggest that it is possible to develop stimuli for the assessment of voyeurs. Such stimuli, however, have yet to be evaluated. It is likely that phallometric procedures will be useful for assessing voyeuristic interests, as phallometric measures have differentiated rapists from nonrapists (Hall, Shondrick, & Hirschman, 1993; Murphy & Barbaree, 1988) and have proved useful for the assessment of other sexual deviations (Freund, Watson, & Dickey, 1991; Hanson & Bussière, 1996; Murphy & Barbaree, 1988).

TREATMENT

The treatment of voyeurism has received little attention in the research literature. In 1976, Smith stated that "the most startling thing about the literature on voyeurism is the relative lack of material in print" (p. 585). The same conclusion would be drawn today. Apart from descriptions of programs that include voyeurs in generic sexual offender groups (Dwyer & Myers, 1990), the literature consists entirely of single case studies (see Table 17.2). Most of these studies have employed some form of behavior therapy, but there is insufficient consistency in the literature to support any particular treatment approach. Consequently, all treatment for voyeurism should be considered experimental. A review of the case studies can, nevertheless, provide some guidance for clinicians developing their own methods for treating voyeurs.

Jackson (1969) reported on an unmarried, 20-year-old male who referred himself to a mental health clinic due to anxiety, depression, and irritability. The patient complained of a directionless life, having left school in grade 8 and worked at menial jobs well below his capabilities. The patient stated that he had peeped in windows an average of five times per week for the last 5 years. His preferred targets were young, nude females. The treatment method chosen was orgasmic reconditioning: the therapist instructed the patient to masturbate to orgasm to "Playboy"-type pictures whenever he had the urge to peep. The patient attended for eight sessions, after which he reported an increase in heterosexual relations and a marked decrease in the urge to peep. When contacted 9 months later, he stated that his urge to peep had dissipated.

Gaupp et al. (1971) treated a single male client, a married graduate student, aged 24 years, with electrical aversion procedures (Barker, 1965). The patient reported the onset of peeping behavior at the age of 10. He attended for treatment in an attempt to avoid adjudication after being apprehended for peeping. The "aversion-relief" treatment consisted of 11 slides containing words and phrases related to peeping ("peeping, wasting time while peeping, spying on strange girl's sexual privacy"; p. 586). These phrases were temporally paired with an electric shock delivered to the right ankle 7 seconds after visual stimulus onset. The relief stimuli consisted of 11 slides with words or phrases relating to sexual behaviors with the patient's wife. At 8-month follow-up the patient reported no peeping behavior, an improvement in sexual behavior with his wife, and that he no longer felt "inferior" to women.

Stoudenmire (1973) treated a 44-year-old, African American, married father of 12, who had been peeping since the age of 13. The patient began peeping at neighbors and his sisters and had progressed to other neighbors and his teenaged daughters. This patient requested help before and had been hospitalized at one point at his own request to get help with this problem. This patient was described as having a WAIS Full Scale IQ of 77. The treatment involved recommendations for increased normative heterosexual contact with his wife and masturbation when intercourse was not an option. Nine sessions were held with the client and his wife over a period of 9 months. Therapy was directive and focused on the here and now. There were concerns of symptom substitution in this case when the client started

TABLE 17.2. Characteristics of Single-Case Treatment Studies

Study	Gender of subject	Marital status	IQ or level of achievement	Age at presentation	Age at onset	Length of peeping behavior
Jackson (1969)	Male	Single	Grade 8, menial jobs	20	15	5 years
Gaupp, Stern, & Ratcliff (1977	Male	Married	Graduate student	24	10	14 years
Stoudenmire (1973)	Male	Married, father of 12	FS WAIS = 77	44	13	31 years
Fensterheim (1974)	Male	Married, father of 3	Window washer and motel night-manager	38	30	8 years
Tollison & Adams (1979)	Male	Married	Businessman	35	15	20 years
Rangaswamy (1987)	Male	Single	Failing grade 9	15	13+	18 months
Konopacki & Oei (1988)	Male	Married	Clerical officer	49	47	2 years
Emmanuel, Lydiard, & Ballenger (1991)	Male	No data	"Employed"	30	14	16 years
Malkin (1991)	Male	Single	Left school at 15; IQ reported as above average	27	13	14 years
Hurlbert (1992)	Female	Annulled (never consum-mated)	IQ reported as 145	26	Elementary school age	14 years +

drinking heavily and became excessively jealous over his wife's ex-husband. According to the authors, these concerns were dealt with effectively by refocusing the patient on the here and now. Voyeuristic behavior decreased from 15 times per month in the first session to less than once per month by the seventh session. A 6-month follow-up recorded an improvement in marital satisfaction and family life, and maintenance of the low rate of voyeuristic activity.

Fensterheim (1974) reported on the behavioral treatment of a 38-year-old man with repeated arrests for voyeurism. The patient's peeping followed confrontations with authority figures. At times, he would use various ruses to set up voyeuristic opportunities. He would, for example, pretend to be a plumber, inform the occupant of an apartment that the water would be turned off, and suggest that she use her facilities now. This patient would then

Frequency of peeping behavior	Treatment modality	Number of sessions	Follow-up period	Success reported
Peeping five times per week	Orgasmic reconditioning to photos	8	9 months	Self-reported urge to peep "dissipated."
Peeping behavior at baseline estimated as twice per week	"Aversion relief" with electric shock	12	8 months	No peeping and an increase in heterosexual behavior.
Estimated as 15 times per month	Increase heterosexual relations	9	6 months	Less than one peeping incident per month at 6 month follow-up.
Sufficient for him to have "repeated arrests for voyeurism"	(1) Desensitization to confrontation; (2) covert sensitization	12	None	By session 10 the patient reported handling confrontation without relapse.
Masturbates to peeping fantasies twice per day, was apprehended	Aversion (electric shock) controlled by penile arousal	24	6 months	No penile arousal to voyeuristic stimuli; improvement in marital relations.
Sufficient to interfere with sleep and scholastic behavior	(1) Aversion (electric shock); (2) covert sensitization	10	1 year	Patient and his mother report him as "problem free."
Peeping behavior at baseline = 13/week	"Response facilitation" (satiation)	20	4 years	Patient reports urges under control and peeping behavior "near zero levels."
Behavior reported as "compulsive"	Fluoxetine (drug therapy)	No data	None	Self-report of "success."
Part of a larger pattern of sexually anomalous behaviors	Humanistic/transpersonal; hypnosis and several associated therapies	19	5 years	Patient had not returned to the prison system.
Sufficient to be apprehended twice by police	Talk therapy (school not stated)	3	None	Patient left therapy after three sessions, never to return; found therapy "humiliating."

masturbate while attempting to observe the tenant, sometimes even entering the apartment to improve his view. The intrusiveness of his ploys raised some concern that he might escalate to rape. This subject reported the onset of voyeuristic activity at age 30. The patient had been sentenced to 30-day terms on several occasions and had several suspended sentences on his record. He had dropped out of previous, traditional psychotherapies. The present therapy proceeded by attempting, with little success, to desensitize the subject to confrontations with authority. Next, treatment involved covert sensitization with the aversive image of vomiting, paired with an image of starting to peep through an apartment peephole.

In this rather unusual case report, it appears that no attempt was made to change the patient's daytime occupation as a window washer and his night time job as a motel manager where, according to the patient, couples were often not careful about drawing the drapes. The therapist in this case, for reasons not stated, found it necessary to "attempt to desensitize him to having an extramarital sexual experience" (p. 27). The patient appears to have accepted this therapeutic suggestion and promptly had two extramarital sexual experiences. The patient was seen for 12 appointments and during the last two sessions the patient reported that he had handled a confrontation with an authority figure with no resulting voyeurism. No follow-up data was offered.

Tollison and Adams (1979) reported on a 35-year-old businessman with a 20-year history of voyeurism. Referred by his minister under threat of divorce by his wife, this patient presented with a high frequency of masturbation to peeping fantasies, averaging twice a day. In assessment the patient "read explicit literature and viewed . . . slides and pictures depicting voyeuristic behaviours" (p. 257) while connected to a phallometer. The phallometric results confirmed a sexual arousal pattern to peeping and a lack of arousal to sexual intercourse with his wife or other females. Electrical aversion was administered to the patient's left forearm "contingent upon physiologically measured penile arousal" (p. 257). After being shocked the patient looked at pictures of his wife (ranging from fully dressed to nude) in an attempt to pair "aversion relief" with his wife. Concurrently the patient was encouraged to masturbate to pornographic pictures whenever he had an urge to peep. Over a 2-month period the pornography was faded out and the pictures of his wife were faded in as masturbatory stimuli. Assertiveness training, counseling for his wife, a variant of sensate focus, and resumption of marital coitus were also included in the treatment program. At 6-month follow-up the couple was reported to be living happily together, the patient reporting no voyeuristic episodes. Phallometrics confirmed no sexual arousal to voyeuristic stimuli.

Rangaswamy (1987) presented the behavioral treatment of a 15-year-old boy who had a history of voyeuristic behavior during the previous 18 months. The boy started with watching his mother and sister in the bath and then graduated to peeping on extended family members and neighbors. The patient reported that he masturbated after peeping. The voyeuristic behavior was reported as sufficiently intrusive to be responsible for failing grade 9 and the adoption of a peer group "who were not having good character as per parents" (p. 73). As well, the boy "some days used to stay at home without any reason" (p. 73). During electrical aversion therapy, the patient formed a clear mental picture of a peeping scenario and was then immediately given a painful electric shock and "asked to shout 'no' loudly so as to suppress the urge" (p. 74). After three sessions the patient, not surprisingly, lost the ability to form clear mental images of a peeping scenario, and treatment continued for a further seven sessions following standard, if somewhat vivid, covert sensitization procedures. At 1-year follow-up the patient and his mother reported a rebound in his school marks and no return of the voyeuristic behavior.

Konopacki and Oei (1988) reported on the treatment, by "response facilitation," of a 49-year-old, married, clerical officer who reported experiencing irresistible urges to peep on an attractive next-door neighbor. Because this patient was generally law abiding and his peeping consisted of looking from his own property to that of the attractive neighbor, the treatment used "response facilitation" with an ABAB design. The patient monitored his urges and peeping behavior during an initial 3-week baseline period. During this period, the patient actively resisted the urges and reported five urges for each incidence of actual peeping. After baseline, the treatment was initiated and the client instructed to submit to the urges as often as possible. This process continued for 7 weeks, at which time there was a significant decrease in urges and actual peeping behavior. A return-to-baseline condition (i.e., inhibiting the peeping behavior) started at 10 weeks and this resulted in a significant increase in urges to peep. The treatment condition was reinstated at week 13 and urges to peep and actual peeping behavior declined greatly until week 20, when treatment terminated. At both 2- and 4-year follow-ups the patient reported having his urges to peep under complete control.

Emmanuel, Lydiard, and Ballenger (1991) reported on the successful pharmacological treatment of a 30-year-old, white male with a 16-year history of voyeurism. Because the patient's behavior seemed particularly compulsive, fluoxetine was prescribed due to reports of its effectiveness for other compulsive disorders. The dosages of fluoxetine were increased over a 60 day period from 20 mg per day to 60 mg per day, which was the therapeutic dosage in this case. Success in this case was judged by self-report.

Malkin (1991) presented the case study of a 27-year-old male prisoner with above-average intelligence, an extensive criminal history, and a long-time problem with voyeuristic impulses. Malkin utilized an eclectic, predominantly humanistic approach with techniques drawn from "Jungian and Gestalt dreamwork, hypnosis, meditation, cognitive, and behavioral [rubber band snapping] methods" (p. 117). The primary goal of therapy appeared to have been an increase in the patient's self-esteem through an integration of the various aspects of the personality. The patient appeared to become highly involved in the treatment and participated in related therapeutic activities, such as a weekly meditation group. Therapy ended with the patient's release from prison and success was judged by no further convictions in the subsequent 5 years.

Hurlbert (1992) reported on a single case of an attractive, 26-year-old female who was arrested on two occasions for voyeuristic activity. The interesting features of this case included an early exposure to pornographic materials, being able to overhear the sexual activity of her parents as a child, a restricted social development, a 2-year lesbian relationship, no sexual contact with males in spite of having been briefly married, and an IQ score of 145. In general, her social relationships were sufficiently distant to justify the diagnosis of schizoid personality. The subject reported sexual contacts with people to be "humiliating" and "not enjoyable." The subject reported masturbating while engaged in voyeurism and that when masturbating privately she had "vivid cognitive images in which she was always the unknown observer or listener and never the participant" (p. 20). This patient also found therapy "humiliating" and never returned after her third session.

With the exception of Hurlbert (1992), all case studies reported positive treatment outcomes. Such positive treatment gains are noteworthy, as most of the patients had long histories of voyeurism. It is difficult to generalize from the case studies because a diverse set of methods were used, and the mechanisms responsible for treatment change are hard to identify. As with all case study research, there may be a large number of unreported cases in which the same treatment methods were ineffective.

In the absence of empirical evidence, clinicians will, nevertheless, have to make decisions on how best to intervene in particular cases. One potential source of direction is the research on the treatment of other sexual offenders, particularly exhibitionists and rapists. The most common approach to treating sexual offenders is some variation of cognitive-behavioral therapy, such as relapse prevention (Freeman-Longo, Bird, Stevenson, & Fiske, 1994; Wormith & Hanson, 1992). Structured, cognitive-behavioral approaches have been the most effective with general criminal populations (Andrews et al., 1990); consequently, it is likely that such approaches should also be effective with sexual offenders, even though there is insufficient research evidence to make strong conclusions (see reviews by Hall, 1995; Marshall & Pithers, 1994; Quinsey, Harris, Rice, & Lalumière, 1993).

The application of relapse prevention therapy (Marlatt & Gordon, 1985) to sexual offenders has been criticized because of the difficulty in defining lapses versus relapses (Hanson, 1996; Ward, Hudson, & Marshall, 1994; Ward, Hudson, & Siegert, 1995). Single instances of child molestation or rape are considered signs of treatment failure (i.e., relapse), which requires that the definition of "lapse" be moved to an earlier point in the offense cycle. In contrast, single instances of peeping could be considered an undesirable, although tolerable, violation of abstinence (i.e., a lapse). Consequently, many of the concepts and methods of relapse prevention theory may be more appropriate for voyeurs than for other sexual offenders.

Our general recommendation is that the treatment of voyeurs should have two broad concerns: (1) setting up blocks or obstacles to continued voyeuristic behavior; and (2) finding alternate, socially acceptable means of meeting the needs/desires the voyeur has been attempting to fulfill through peeping. When considering blocks, therapists should pay particular attention to environmental factors that facilitate voyeurism, such as occupation, residence, and associates. Relapse prevention therapy includes numerous specific methods for setting up blocks to deviant sexual behavior (e.g., Laws, 1989). The appeal of the images associated with voyeurism can also be reduced through various forms of cognitive-behavioral therapy, such as covert sensitization or aversive conditioning.

Therapy is likely to be successful if alternate means can be found to fulfill the voyeurs' desired goals. Careful assessments are required because the desired goals of voyeurs can be quite different. In some cases, simply substituting legally available pornography in place of unsuspecting victims may be sufficient to end the voyeuristic activity (Jackson, 1969; Kutchinsky, 1976). In other cases, considerable intervention may be needed to prepare the voyeur for engaging in intimate relationships with appropriate partners. Voyeurs are likely to have skills deficits, attitudes, and expectations (e.g., fears of rejection) that inhibit their capacity for empathy and intimacy. Such deficits could be addressed by guided practice and social skills training. Some voyeurs use peeping as a method of coping with subjective distress; these clients may benefit from a clear interpretation of their offense cycle followed by stress management and relaxation training.

Although interventions are most likely to be effective when they are tailored to individual cases, the next section provides some general recommendations for the treatment of voyeurs. A model treatment program would last approximately 10 to 12 months and involve a combination of individual and group treatment. In the first two individual sessions, the therapist screens for diverse paraphilias and examines the role that voyeurism plays in the client's psychosexual functioning. Should treatment for voyeurism be deemed appropriate, part of the initial sessions would then be devoted to motivating and engaging the client in the treatment process (e.g., helping the client to imagine a positive new lifestyle, inspiring confidence in the treatment/therapist).

The next two individual sessions address specific lifestyle changes that the client could immediately initiate to reduce the risk of voyeuristic activities. For example, if a client was tempted to peep while walking the dog at night, the client could begin walking the dog during the day or have someone else walk the dog. Other examples of environmental reorganization include leaving high-risk occupations (maintenance worker, security guard), avoiding high-risk areas and situations (e.g, night walks), and getting rid of aids such as telescopes and binoculars. If possible, it would also be useful to engage significant others in monitoring the client's high-risk behaviors. Any contact outside of treatment with individuals who support or participate in voyeuristic activities should be avoided.

The next couple of individual treatment sessions examine ways of replacing voyeuristic behavior with more appropriate sexual outlets. At this stage, the clinician needs to assess whether the client has the realistic possibility of developing a satisfactory sexual relationship in the near future. For clients with marked social handicaps and little or no prior appropriate sexual experience, the immediate goal may be to replace voyeurism with legal methods of obtaining images for masturbation (e.g., adult magazines, peep shows). Such replacement can probably be accomplished through explicit direction and monitoring. For voyeurs with a history of some level of sexual competence, the goal is to restore or improve their social–sexual functioning. The treatment of sexual competence could be conducted through referrals to specialized marriage, sex, or relationship/dating counseling.

After the initial environmental changes and alternate outlets are initiated, the next stage of treatment is a generic relapse prevention group for sexual offenders (e.g., Laws, 1989; Pithers, Marques, Gibat, & Marlatt, 1983). In these groups, the offenders learn the language and techniques of relapse prevention and learn to apply these skills to their particular offense cycles. Such groups typically require 30 to 35 sessions spaced over a 6- to 8-month period. The initial group sessions could be scheduled twice per week, with the sessions gradually spaced to weekly or monthly by the end of the group. Materials to help guide relapse prevention groups, such as offender workbooks, are widely available (Bays & Freeman-Longo, 1989; Bays, Freeman-Longo, & Hildebran, 1990; Freeman-Longo & Bays, 1988).

After the completion of the relapse prevention group, clinicians can reevaluate the client's progress in individual sessions. Signs of treatment progress would include decreased incidents of peeping, decreased urges to peep, a reduction of the use of voyeuristic imagery during masturbatory fantasies, and client reports of satisfaction with the changes accomplished. Although the frequency of voyeuristic behaviors can be drastically reduced, it is unrealistic to expect all voyeuristic impulses to stop completely. Successful clients will internalize the principles of relapse prevention and demonstrate their ability to self-regulate their behavior. Specifically, successful clients will recognize their continued risk for relapse, be willing to make sacrifices to avoid high-risk situations, and have repeatedly managed difficult situations without recourse to peeping. Clients who make sufficient progress can then attend at a diminishing frequency to monitor their ongoing adjustment.

Although aversive conditioning procedures have been used successfully with voyeurs, we do not believe that such procedures are the treatment of choice for most cases. Instead, we recommend organizing changes in the client's life that could block voyeuristic activities and promote appropriate sexuality. When voyeuristic activity appears particularly compulsive, the use of medications (such as the selective serotonin reuptake inhibitors) may be a useful adjunct to treatment.

FORENSIC ISSUES

For those voyeurs assessed as a consequence of criminal activity, the most important question is the risk of recidivism: How likely is the client to stop peeping, to continue peeping, or to escalate to more serious sexual deviance? Given the high comorbidity of the courtship disorders, another important question is whether the voyeur is already engaging in other, more serious, sexual deviancies (e.g., exhibitionism, frottage, or rape). To our knowledge, there have been no studies that have specifically examined the recidivism rates of voyeurs; consequently, estimates of their recidivism risk need to be inferred from recidivism studies of other sexual offenders. Hanson and Bussière (1996) completed a meta-analytic review of recidivism risk factors for sexual offenders. Their review covered 61 follow-up studies conducted between 1943 and 1995. The majority of the offenders were child molesters or rapists, although small samples of voyeurs were included in some samples. Overall, the major predictors of sexual offense recidivism were measures of sexual deviancy, and, to a lesser extent, general criminological factors (age, antisocial personality, total prior offenses). Included in the measures of sexual deviance were prior sexual offenses, phallometric assessment of interest in children, early onset of sexual offending, and diverse sexual crimes (Hanson & Bussière, 1996). Other factors related to sexual recidivism were low motivation for treatment and a history of victimizing strangers. In general, the predictors of nonsexual violent recidivism (e.g., robbery) among sexual offenders were similar to the factors identified for nonsexual criminals (e.g., age, prior violent offenses, juvenile delinquency). Given the high co-occurrence of voyeurism with other paraphilias, it is likely that the same factors that predict recidivism among general groups of sexual offenders should also apply to voyeurs.

Because dropping out of treatment is a recidivism risk factor for sexual offenders, forensic assessments need to address the likelihood that a voyeur will successfully complete treatment. Again, there is no specific evidence concerning voyeurs, but, in general, those who drop out of treatment tend to have unstable lifestyles (e.g., young, low education, antisocial personality) and to be unable to appreciate how therapy will address their problems (Baekeland & Lundwall, 1975; Wierzbicki & Pekarik, 1993).

Issues of mental competence are rare in the forensic assessment of voyeurs, as few suffer from major mental disorders (Gebhard et al., 1965). There are, however, some cases in which voyeuristic activity is present in individuals with low levels of intellectual functioning (Day, 1994). In general, however, when voyeurs have other mental disorders, these disorders are most likely to be related to sexual deviance.

CONCLUSION

Although rarely seen, pure voyeuristic behavior is generally viewed as a nuisance offense by the law, as a pathetic attempt to steal sexual pleasure by members of the public, and as a curious, but not particularly important sexual deviance by the psychological/psychiatric community. Against widespread, intense, public concern over child sexual abuse and rape, the overall clinical priority afforded the voyeur remains low. The clinical needs of voyeurs, however, should not be underestimated. Voyeuristic behavior deserves immediate clinical attention when it represents the target acquisition phase of other, more serious, disorders. As well, voyeuristic behavior can represent a serious threat to the psychological and social adjustment of the client. Whenever voyeuristic behavior presents a threat to society or to the well-being of the client, the voyeuristic offender deserves the clinician's full skill and attention.

REFERENCES

Abel, G. G., & Rouleau, J. L. (1990). The nature and extent of sexual assault. In W. L. Marshall, D. R. Laws, & H. E. Barbaree (Eds.), *Handbook of sexual assault: Issues, theories, and treatment of the offender* (pp. 9–21). New York: Plenum Press.

Agnew, L. R. C. (1965). *Dorland's illustrated medical dictionary* (24th ed.). Philadelphia: W. B. Saunders.

American Psychiatric Association. (1980). *Diagnostic and statistical manual of mental disorders* (3rd ed.). Washington, DC: Author.

American Psychiatric Association. (1994). *Diagnostic and statistical manual of mental disorders* (4th ed.). Washington, DC: Author.

Andrews, D. A., Zinger, I., Hoge, R. D., Bonta, J., Gendreau, P., & Cullen, F. T. (1990). Does correctional treatment work? A clinically relevant and psychologically informed meta-analysis. *Criminology, 28,* 369–404.

Baekeland, F., & Lundwall, L. (1975). Dropping out of treatment: A critical review. *Psychological Bulletin, 82,* 738–783.

Barker, J. C. (1965). Behavior therapy for transvestism: A comparison of pharmacological and electrical aversion techniques. *British Journal of Psychiatry, 111,* 268–276.

Bays, L., & Freeman-Longo, R. (1989). *Why did I do it again?* Shoreham, VT: Safer Society Press.

Bays, L., Freeman-Longo, R., & Hildebran, D. (1990). *How can I stop?* Shoreham, VT: Safer Society Press.

Crepault, C., & Couture, M. (1980). Men's erotic fantasies. *Archives of Sexual Behavior, 9,* 565–581.

Day, K. (1994). Male mentally handicapped sex offenders. *British Journal of Psychiatry, 165,* 630–639.

Dwyer, M. S., & Myers, S. (1990). Sex offender treatment: A six-month to ten-year follow-up study. *Annals of Sex Research, 3*(3), 305–318.

Emmanuel, N. P., Lydiard, R. B., & Ballenger, J. C. (1991). Fluoxetine treatment of voyeurism. *American Journal of Psychiatry, 148*(7), 950.

Farrenkopf, T. (1986). Comprehensive arousal pattern assessment. In S. Satterfield (Ed.), *Treating the juvenile sexual abuse perpetrator: Proceedings on a national training conference, April 27–30, 1986.* Bloomington, MN: Program in Human Sexuality, University of Minnesota.

Farrenkopf, T. (1988, May). *Sexual arousal measures in a non-offender sample.* Paper presented at the Oregon Psychological Association Convention, Rippling River Resort, OR.

Farrenkopf, T. (n.d.). *Arousal portfolio.* (Available from the author at 2256 N. W. Pettygrove, Portland, OR 97210.)

Fedora, O., Reddon, J. R., Morrison, J. W., Fedora, S. K., Pascoe, H., & Yeudall, L. T. (1992). Sadism and other paraphilias in normal controls and aggressive and non-aggressive sex offenders. *Archives of Sexual Behavior, 21*(1), 1–15.

Fensterheim, H. (1974). Behavior therapy of the sexual variations. *Journal of Sex and Marital Therapy, 1,* 16–28.

Forsyth, C. J. (1996). The structuring of vicarious sex. *Deviant Behavior, 17,* 279–295.

Freeman-Longo, R., & Bays, L. (1988). *Who am I and why am I in treatment?* Shoreham, VT: Safer Society Press.

Freeman-Longo, R. E., Bird, S. L., Stevenson, W. F., & Fiske, J. A. (1994). *1994 nation-wide survey of juvenile and adult sex offender treatment programs and models.* Brandon, VT: Safer Society Press.

Freud, S. (1962). *Three essays on the theory of sexuality* (J. Strachey, Trans.). London: Hogarth. (Original work published 1905)

Freund, K. (1988). Courtship disorder: Is this hypothesis valid? In R. A. Prentky & V. L. Quinsey (Eds.), *Human sexual aggression: Current perspectives* (pp. 172–182). New York: New York Academy of Sciences.

Freund, K. (1990). Courtship disorder. In W. L. Marshall, D. R. Laws, & H. E. Barbaree (Eds.), *Handbook of sexual assault* (pp. 195–207). New York: Plenum Press.

Freund, K., & Blanchard, R. (1986). The concept of courtship disorder. *Journal of Sex and Marital Therapy, 12,* 79–92.

Freund, K., Scher, H., & Hucker, S. (1983). The courtship disorders. *Archives of Sexual Behavior, 12*(5), 369–379.

Freund, K., Scher, H., Racansky, I. G., Campbell, K., & Heasman, G. (1986). Males disposed to commit rape. *Archives of Sexual Behavior, 2,* 23–35.

Freund, K., & Watson, R. (1990). Mapping the boundaries of courtship disorder. *Journal of Sex Research, 27*(4), 589–606.

Freund, K., Watson, R. J., & Dickey, R. (1991). Sex offenses against female children perpetrated by men who are not pedophiles. *Journal of Sex Research, 28,* 409–423.

Freund, K., Watson, R., & Rienzo, D. (1988). The value of self-reports in the study of voyeurism and exhibitionism. *Annals of Sex Research, 1*(2), 243–262.

Gaupp, L. A., Stern, R. M., & Ratcliff, R. G. (1971). The use of aversion-relief procedures in the treatment of a case of voyeurism. *Behavior Therapy, 2,* 585–588.

Gebhard, P. H., Gagnon, J. H., Pomeroy, W. B., & Christenson, C. V. (1965). *Sex offenders.* New York: Harper & Row.

Hall, G. C. N. (1995). Sexual offender recidivism revisited: A meta-analysis of recent treatment studies. *Journal of Consulting and Clinical Psychology, 63*(5), 802–809.

Hall, G. C. N., Shondrick, D. D., & Hirschman, R. (1993). The role of sexual arousal in sexually aggressive behavior: A meta-analysis. *Journal of Consulting and Clinical Psychology, 61,* 1091–1095.

Hanson, R. K. (1996). Evaluating the contribution of relapse prevention theory to the treatment of sexual offenders. *Sexual Abuse: A Journal of Research and Treatment, 8,* 201–208.

Hanson, R. K., & Bussière, M. T. (1996). *Predictors of sexual offender recidivism: A meta-analysis* (User Report No. 1996-04). Ottawa: Solicitor General Canada.

Hartland, E. S. (1890). Peeping Tom and Lady Godiva. *Folklore, 1,* 207–226.

Hurlbert, D. F. (1992). Voyeurism in an adult female with schizoid personality: A case report. *Journal of Sex Education and Therapy, 18*(1), 17–21.

Jackson, B. T. (1969). A case of voyeurism treated by counter conditioning. *Behaviour Research and Therapy, 7,* 133–134.

Kalichman, S. C., Henderson, M. C., Shealy, L. S., & Dwyer, M. (1992). Psychometric properties of the Multiphasic Sex Inventory in assessing sex offenders. *Criminal Justice and Behavior, 19,* 384–396.

Konopacki, W. P., & Oei, T. P. S. (1988). Interruption in the maintenance of compulsive sexual disorder: Two case studies. *Archives of Sexual Behavior, 17,* 411–419.

Kutchinsky, B. (1976). Deviance and criminality: The case of a voyeur in a peeper's paradise. *Diseases of the Nervous System, 37*(3), 145–151.

Lang, R. A., Langevin, R., Checkley, K. L., & Pugh, G. (1987). Genital exhibitionism: Narcissism or courtship disorder? *Canadian Journal of Behavioural Science, 19*(2), 216–232.

Langevin, R., Paitich, D., & Russon, A. E. (1985). Voyeurism: Does it predict sexual aggression or violence in general. In R. Langevin (Ed.), *Erotic preference, gender identity, and aggression in men* (pp. 77–98). Hillsdale, NJ: Erlbaum.

Langevin, R., Paitich, D., Russon, A. E., Handy, L., & Langevin, R. (1990). *The Clarke Sex History Questionnaire for Males: Manual.* Toronto: Juniper Press.

Laws, D. R. (Ed.). (1989). *Relapse prevention with sex offenders.* New York: Guilford Press.

Laws, D. R., Greenbaum, P. E., Murrin, M. R., & Osbourn, C. A. (1994). *Classification of pedophiles by plethysmographic assessment of sexual arousal and a self-report measure of sexual preference.* Unpublished manuscript.

Malkin, D. (1991). Individuation in a voyeur recidivist. *Australian Journal of Clinical and Experimental Hypnosis, 19*(2), 117–131.

Marlatt, G. A., & Gordon, J. R. (Eds.). (1985). *Relapse prevention: Maintenance strategies in the treatment of addictive behaviors.* New York: Guilford Press.

Marshall, W. L., & Pithers, W. D. (1994). A reconsideration of treatment outcome with sex offenders. *Criminal Justice and Behavior, 21,* 10–27.

Murphy, W. D., & Barbaree, H. E. (1988). *Assessments of sex offenders by measures of erectile response: Psychometric properties and decision making.* Brandon, VT: Safer Society Press.

Nichols, H., & Molinder, I. (1984). *Manual for the Multiphasic Sex Inventory.* (Available from the authors at 437 Bowes Drive, Tacoma, WA 98466.)

Pithers, W. D., Marques, J. K., Gibat, C. C., & Marlatt, G. A. (1983). Relapse prevention: A self-control model of treatment and maintenance of change for sexual aggressives. In J. Greer & I. R. Stuart (Eds.), *The sexual aggressor: Current perspective on treatment* (pp. 214–239). New York: Van Nostrand Reinhold.

Quinsey, V. L., Harris, G. T., Rice, M. E., & Lalumière, M. L. (1993). Assessing treatment efficacy in outcome studies of sex offenders. *Journal of Interpersonal Violence, 8,* 512–523.

Rangaswamy, K. (1987). Treatment of voyeurism by behavior therapy. *Child Psychiatry Quarterly, 20,* 73–76.

Robinson, C. H., & Annon, J. S. (1975). *The Heterosexual Behavior Inventory (male form and female form)*. Honolulu, HI: Enabling Systems.

Salter, A. C. (1988). *Treating child sex offenders and victims: A practical guide*. New Delhi: Sage.

Smith, R. S. (1976). Voyeurism: A review of the literature. *Archives of Sexual Behavior, 5*(6), 585–608.

Stoudenmire, J. (1973). Behavioral treatment of voyeurism and possible symptom substitution. *Psychotherapy: Theory, Research, and Practice, 10*, 328–330.

Strupp, H. H., & Hadley, S. W. (1977). A tripartite model of mental health and therapeutic outcomes: With special reference to the negative effects in psychotherapy. *American Psychologist, 32*(3), 187–196.

Templeman, T. L., & Stinnett, R. D. (1991). Patterns of sexual arousal and history in a "normal" sample of young men. *Archives of Sexual Behavior, 20*(2), 137–150.

Tollison, C. D., & Adams, H. E. (1979). *Sexual disorders: Theory, treatment, and research*. New York: Gardner Press.

Ward, T., Hudson, S. M., & Marshall, W. L. (1994). The abstinence violation effect in child molesters. *Behaviour Research and Therapy, 32*, 431–437.

Ward, T., Hudson, S. M., & Siegert, R. J. (1995). A critical comment on Pithers' relapse prevention model. *Sexual Abuse: A Journal of Research and Treatment, 7*, 167–175.

Wierzbicki, M., & Pekarik, G. (1993). A meta-analysis of psychotherapy dropout. *Professional Psychology: Research and Practice, 24*, 190–195.

Wormith, J. S., & Hanson, R. K. (1992). The treatment of sexual offenders in Canada: An update. *Canadian Psychology/Psychologie Canadienne, 33*, 180–198.

Yalom, I. D. (1960). Aggression and forbiddenness in voyeurism. *Archives of General Psychiatry, 3*(2), 305–319.

18

RAPE

Psychopathology and Theory

Stephen M. Hudson
Tony Ward

One of the most obvious aspects of sexual aggression is the heterogeneity involved. This is particularly so for rapists and it has caused a variety of conceptual and nosological problems. The heterogeneity is evident in two major ways. Sexually assaultive behavior toward adult women ranges from relatively minor instances of unwanted gestures and verbal behavior to quite the opposite extreme, when a savage sexual assault leads to mutilation and death. Second, the men who perpetrate rape vary from those who are indiscriminable from nonoffenders to those thankfully few men with sadistic fantasies and marked delusions. Not surprisingly, this heterogeneity has generated confusion concerning a number of issues, for example, the prevalence and incidence of rape and factors associated with it, and has lead to multiple attempts at classification and the establishment of subtypes. It has also led to a number of explanatory models, theories, and explanatory frameworks.

A further complication unique to sexual assault are the social factors that very substantially reduce the probability of reporting of a rape to the authorities and the subsequent prosecution compared with both other types of sexual assault and other crimes. The end result of these processes is that, with the exception of the work by Koss and Malamuth and their associates (see for example, Koss, 1985, 1989, 1992; Koss, Gidycz, & Wisniewski, 1987; Malamuth, 1981, 1983, 1986; Malamuth, Heavey, & Linz, 1993) with college-aged males, much of what we do know comes from the small minority of men convicted and incarcerated for this crime.

In this overview we review some of the conceptual difficulties, prevalence and incidence, classificatory devices, models, and theoretical frameworks that have been put forward to help us understand rape and thus to inform treatment, and then we conclude with some thoughts and suggestions regarding the research agenda over the next decade. We focus exclusively on sexual crimes against women and do not address the issue of homosexual rape. This reflects the fact that most rape is directed against women by men, and that there has been relatively little research on homosexual sexual assaults.

DESCRIPTION OF THE PROBLEM

The usual starting place for a review such as this is the relevant nosological system; however, rape is not included as a paraphilia in DSM-IV (American Psychiatric Association [APA], 1994). Here a paraphilia is defined as characterized by recurrent, intense sexual urges, fantasies, or behaviors that involve unusual objects, activities, or situations. Second, this pattern of behavior needs to generate significant distress for the individual or impairment in functioning. It is doubtful whether many of the men presenting for treatment for their sexually abusive behavior fit these criteria regardless of what type of paraphilia they exhibit. For example, frotteurism involves a nonconsenting person, and is described as rarely involving self-referral (APA, 1994). The same is generally true for child molestation. The implication is that neither personal distress nor impaired functioning is necessarily a feature. This is probably also true for rape; therefore, its absence from the list of paraphilias is puzzling. Interestingly though, rape is mentioned as one of the behaviors that a sexual sadist might do to his victim, along with a catalogue of other physically abusive possibilities.

Typically rape is defined both by the nature of the sexual assault itself and by the age of the victim. The latter criterion is most commonly set by legal statute at 16 years of age. Offenders, not surprisingly, do not always recognize this distinction and in situations where it is not easily applied, the age discrepancy between the victim and offender and types of sexual acts are usually examined (e.g., Seghorn, Prentky, & Boucher, 1987).

From a legal perspective rape is usually taken to mean "carnal knowledge of a female forcibly and against her will" (Koss, 1992, p. 61), wherein carnal knowledge refers quite specifically to penile–vaginal penetration. This is the definition that the Federal Bureau of Investigation (FBI) use in their collection of crime statistics. However, as Muehlenhard, Powch, Phelps, and Giusti (1992) suggested, the definition of sexual assault varies along several dimensions, including the sexual behaviors specified, the criteria for establishing nonconsent, the individuals specified, and who gets to decide whether a sexual assault has occurred. For example, Koss (1992) referred to the Bureau of Justice Statistics that include homosexual rape (i.e., male victims raped by other men) but noted that the authors did not change the penile–vaginal requirement! Similarly, Searles and Berger (1987) described the "reform-statutes rape," which uses the broader term "sexual penetration," referring to behaviors including penile–vaginal intercourse as well as cunnilingus, fellation, anal intercourse, and other bodily intrusions.

RAPISTS AND THEIR CLASSIFICATION

Classification is the fundamental problem which handicaps our understanding of sexual assaults (Grubin & Kennedy, 1991). Good theory construction requires that phenomena are ordered or grouped in a coherent and valid manner (Millon, 1991). The major difficulty in the area of psychopathology is that there is no "natural" way in which to carve up the world. Any classificatory system needs to be reliable and valid; only then may it assist with designing and evaluating treatment, predicting especially the assessment of future risk, and clarifying etiologic factors.

At a general level it has often been suggested that rapists and child molesters are fundamentally different groups (e.g., Grubin & Kennedy, 1991). Research has revealed a number of significant differences between these groups on a variety of developmental indices (see the "Rapists and Their Characteristics" section for details). However, in view of the fact that the distinction is based on an arbitrary age rather than on a developmentally meaningful event, for example, puberty (e.g., what are the essential differences between a 15-year-old versus a 16-year-old victim?), the research findings may not hold for all types of rapists or child molesters.

Other efforts to develop classificatory devices or taxonomies for rapists have typically resulted in the identification of four major components (Prentky & Knight, 1991). The most robust dimension has been the amount of aggression involved in the offense, with the usual distinction made between instrumental violence, wherein only sufficient force was used to commit the crime, and expressive violence, which essentially covers the range involving gratuitous aggression. Although this distinction is intuitively appealing and continues to be a major feature for a number of classification systems, determining the intent of the perpetrator with respect to violence, particularly at the level of physical injury, is problematic (see for example, Rosenberg, Knight, Prentky, & Lee, 1988).

Where the level of aggression is relatively low a further distinction is typically made between those offenses that appear primarily sexual in nature, in the sense of having strong paraphilic aspects, and those committed by men high on traditional psychopathy and/or antisocial personality features such as impulsivity and low emotional reactivity. When aggression is high, that is, at expressive levels of violence, a further distinction is typically made between those assaults that appear sadistic, in that the harm inflicted is clearly part of the sexual gratification, and more indiscriminate violence (Prentky & Knight, 1991). Examples of these dimensions are evident in the psychodynamic-oriented and rationally derived classification systems of Groth, Burgess, and Holmstrom (1977), who differentiated between power assertive, power reassurance types on the one hand and anger retaliation and anger excitation on the other, and Seghorn and Cohen's (1980) sexual, aggressive, impulsive, and sexual diffusion types.

Hall and Hirschman (1991) developed an alternative rationally derived system in the context of their quadripartite theory of etiology. Their four factors (sexual arousal, cognitive processes, affective dyscontrol, and personality problems) each define a subtype by virtue of the motivational primacy of that factor. The most interesting of these is the cognitive process subtype, characterized by distorted attitudes and beliefs concerning sex roles and appropriate female behavior. This type of offender is arguably most conspicuous at the date- or acquaintance-rape end of the sexual aggression continuum and may be the most common of all (Koss, 1985; Koss et al., 1987). Cognitive processes such as interpreting the victim's responses as indicating enjoyment or a desire for sexual contact may reduce the perceived deviance of the sexual assault and therefore the subjective probability of apprehension. Indeed, Craig (1990) suggested that some men selectively attend to aspects of the dating situation that encourage sexual advances while minimizing features that would limit sexual activity.

Knight and Prentky (1990) and Prentky and Knight (1991) developed a set of empirically driven classificatory taxonomy based on earlier work by Cohen, Seghorn, and Calmas (1969). Knight, Rosenberg, and Schneider (1985) developed the Massachusetts Treatment Center: Rape 1 (MTC:R1) on the basis of what they saw as the four most common rape dimensions: compensatory, impulsivity, displaced aggression, and sex–aggression diffusion. Knight and Prentky (1990) modified this original taxonomy primarily by adding a set of second-tier decisions concerning lifestyle impulsivity and in addition by modifying the first-tier labels to "compensatory," "exploitive," "displaced anger," and "sadistic" to better represent the constructs involved. Although several validity studies suggested that lifestyle impulsivity tapped a valid construct (Prentky & Knight, 1991) and that salient developmental antecedents, such as antisocial behavior, showed predictable linkages in path-analytic studies (Rosenberg & Knight, 1988; Rosenberg, Knight, Prentky, & Lee, 1988), reliability and applicability problems (especially among the less serious offenders) resulted in a further revision.

The latest revision, the MTC:R3, broadened the construct of lifestyle impulsivity to the more general issue of social competence (Knight & Prentky, 1990). This resulted in 9 types: "opportunistic" (with high or low social competence), "pervasively angry," "sadistic" (overt or muted), "sexual nonsadistic" (also with high or low social competence), and "vindictive" (again with high or low social competence). Of the hypothetically discriminating dimensions identified by this research group, irrational cognitions and disinhibitors remains to be included in the taxonomic system. This system is currently being evaluated with respect to reliability and validity. An assessment of its applicability to broader samples of rapists, a significant difficulty in the early versions, will then be needed.

RAPISTS AND THEIR CHARACTERISTICS

At a general level rapists, at least those who are incarcerated, are much like the rest of the prison population in that they are generally of low socioeconomic status, tend to have dropped out of high school, show an unstable employment history in unskilled jobs (Bard et al., 1987), and show similar psychiatric treatment rates (Christie, Marshall, & Lanthier, 1979) and levels of general social competence, with the exception of assertiveness (Stermac & Quinsey, 1986).

However, there are fundamental differences between rapists and child molesters, with respect both to adult characteristics and to antecedent developmental events. In this sense child molesters are dissimilar to the remainder of the prison population. Rapists, in comparison with child molesters, tend to be younger, more likely to have gone to high school, more likely to be overassertive (aggressive) than underassertive (passive), more likely to have been married or lived with a woman for at least a year (Christie et al., 1979), and less likely to show mental retardation or an organic brain syndrome (Henn, Herjanic, & Vanderpearl, 1976; Swanson, 1968). Developmentally, rapists are more likely than child molesters to have their parents' marriage intact, less likely to have natural siblings with psychiatric histories, half as likely to have been sexually abused, less likely to have had physical health problems, and were more likely to have shown cruelty to animals and other behavior problems in school (Bard et al., 1987). Interestingly, if the rapist was sexually abused, it was three times more likely than for child molesters to have been perpetrated by the victim's father within a dysfunctional family context of psychiatric, drug/alcohol, or criminal difficulties (Seghorn et al., 1987).

In an effort to provide some structure with respect to salient developmental events, Prentky et al. (1989) used factor analysis to generate four developmentally significant constructs: caregiver inconsistency, institutional history, physical abuse and neglect, and sexual abuse. They then related these four constructs to both sexual aggression and nonsexual aggression in adulthood. Caregiver inconsistency and sexual deviation in the family were related to severity of sexual aggression, with the other two factors (institutional history and physical abuse) predicting the severity of nonsexual aggression. Their conclusion, that a male child's experience of sexual abuse and the quality of early interpersonal relationships are likely to be of importance in understanding sexual violence, is both unsurprising and consistent with some recent explanatory models (Marshall, 1989a; Ward, Hudson, Marshall, & Siegert, 1995).

The use of pornography by sex offenders has been of interest both as a developmental antecedent (as it condones sexual aggression) and because it has the potential to be used in a manner that provokes a sexual assault. Again, there are differences between rapists and child molesters, at least in adulthood, with most studies finding that rapists report less pornography use overall and a lower likelihood of use prior to offending than do child molesters (Carter, Prentky, Knight, Vanderveer, & Boucher, 1987; Cook, Fosen, & Pacht, 1971; Goldstein, Kant, Judd, Rice, & Green, 1971). It is likely that these differences reflect different types of pornography, and that more child molesters use relevant material for their masturbatory fantasies between offenses (Marshall, 1989b).

From a different perspective, phallometric differentiation of rapists from nonrapists has in recent years suffered a significant reversal. In the late 1970s and early 1980s the literature clearly stated that sexual arousal patterns of rapists were different than those of nonrapists (Abel, Barlow, Blanchard, & Guild, 1977; Barbaree, Marshall, & Lanthier, 1979; Carter et al., 1987; Quinsey, Chaplin, & Upfold, 1984), usually with the observation that rapists also respond similarly to nonsexual violence involving women, suggesting that violence cues may be the mediating link. However, more recent studies show rapists' and nonrapists' phallometric profiles to be similar in that both groups exhibit lower levels of sexual arousal to coercive (both rape and nonsexual violence) stimuli than to stimuli depicting consenting sexual intercourse (Baxter, Barbaree, & Marshall, 1986; Baxter, Marshall, Barbaree, Davidson, & Malcolm, 1984; Blader & Marshall, 1989; Murphy, Coleman, & Haynes, 1986; Murphy, Haynes, Coleman, & Flanagan, 1985). The probable reason for these discrepant findings is that participants in the early studies were typically drawn from the more deviant and extreme end of the offender continuum.

A substantive set of reasons for further caution with respect to phallometric assessments are the practical, conceptual, and ethical problems inherent in measuring penile tumescence. There is increasing awareness of the ethical difficulties surrounding the abusive origins of the stimulus material. Although these may be surmountable using nonabusive, computer-generated materials (for example, Konopasky, 1993) there is also increasing resistance to undergoing phallometric assessment from offenders on the basis that even when carried out in the most professional manner, it still constitutes a humiliating and degrading procedure. Finally, and most critically, there is increasing awareness that what the penis is doing is probably not the *sine qua non* of sexual motivations (see, for example, Marshall, 1996). Thus, one of the significant challenges for the area over the next few years is to develop conceptualizations, and appropriate assessment methods, capable of dealing with a more broadly defined construct of sexual preference.

Finally, from the perspective of the natural history of the problem, the major issue concerns reoffense rates. Reoffense rates for sexual assaults are generally difficult to determine, to the extent that some authors have suggested that there is so much variation between studies that untreated recidivism rates are impossible to infer (Furby, Weinrott, & Blackshaw, 1989). These issues have been argued at length (see Marshall, 1993; Marshall, Jones, Ward, Johnston, & Barbaree, 1991; and Quinsey, Harris, Rice, & Lalumière, 1993 for a full discussion of these) and the difficulty probably reflects the heterogeneity of offenders as much as the inherent methodological problems.

Notwithstanding these issues, untreated rapists are typically seen as having a low recidivism rate relative to other sex offenders, with the notable exception of those men who commit incest. Official rates are said to vary from 6% to 35% (Marshall & Barbaree, 1990b) with most clustering around 10%, at least where there is a sufficiently long period of time at risk for reoffense (i.e., approximately 4 years; Hudson & Bakker, 1997). A recent meta-analysis of 61 studies reported an 18.9% reoffense rate for the 1,839 rapists involved (Hanson & Bussière, 1996), suggesting that the rate may be higher than previously thought. Marshall and Barbaree's (1988) follow-up study of those men they treated at the Kingston Sexual Behavior Clinic remains one of the few that used other than official records. Their suggestion that the true rate of reoffending in child molesters is probably 2.4 times the official rate and 2.8 time for exhibitionists is a salutary warning. If one takes the multiplier suggested by Koss (1992) of at least 4 times, perhaps as high as 10 times, then the reoffense rates for rapists are likely to be similar to other types of incarcerated sex offenders, if not higher when we consider the broad spectrum of sexual assaults against adults.

In summary, rapists seem distinctly different, at least on average, from those men who molest children, but they are remarkably similar to the rest of the general prison population. Bear in mind that this is likely to be a limited perspective and an inevitable reflection of the incarcerated group being most available to study; date rapists, arguably the most numerous, are significantly underrepresented. In terms of the rates at which rapists reoffend, it is likely that they are not dissimilar to the majority of other sex offenders.

EPIDEMIOLOGY

We must also approach prevalence and incidence rates with caution. Koss (1992) noted several features of the methodologies used by both researchers and statutory authorities that serve to heighten underdisclosure, for example, the use of broad screening questions that may not be correctly interpreted and the presence of family members during any interview of the victim. Even the FBI believes that their own data on rape reflects the greatest underreporting of all the crimes they measure (Federal Bureau of Investigation, 1982).

Russell's (1984) large random sample of San Francisco women is the most in-depth community study that we know of measuring the prevalence of experiencing unwelcome sexual experiences. The 24% figure found for rape in this study compares well with Koss et al.'s (1987) 27.5% of a national sample of American university women reporting having experienced rape or attempted rape since age 14 years. Gavey's (1991) New Zealand study, also using Koss's self-report Sexual Experiences Survey (Koss & Gidycz, 1985; Koss & Oros, 1982), found a very similar rate (25.3%) of rape and attempted rape reported by women in the sample.

Russell's (1984) study focused on women's self-reported experiences of sexual victimization. An alternate approach is to review the incidence (or number of complaints, prosecutions, and convictions) over some unit of time, typically 1 year. However, clearly this still depends on victims volunteering information and as such, constitutes fragile data (Koss, 1992). For example, Curtis (1976) in a reverse records check found that only 54% of rape complainants would confirm that they had indeed made a complaint to the Police.

The two American federal sources of incidence data are the FBI's Uniform Crime Reports (UCR), which abstracts complaints to local authorities, and the Bureau of Justice Statistics' household victimization survey, the National Crime Survey (NCS). Koss (1992) reported that the UCR recorded 102,555 rapes in 1990, which accounted for 6% of all violent crime reported. The NCS data for the similar period totalled 135, 410 rapes, but only 51% of those who experienced them claimed to have reported them to the police. This is a substantially lower rate than was actually reported, again reinforcing the fragility of the data.

Koss (1992) reviewed independent survey studies (e.g., Kilpatrick & Best, 1990; Koss, Woodruff, & Koss, 1991, Russell, 1984) and suggested that the true rate is likely to be 6 to 10 times the current NCS estimates. Koss further noted that a woman is four times as likely to be raped by someone she knows than by a stranger. This accords well with Gavey's (1991) data, which suggested that nearly two thirds of the unwanted sexual incidences reported by the women in her sample were perpetrated in the context of a heterosexual relationship (i.e., by boyfriends, husbands, de facto partners, dates, and lovers), with this figure rising to 82.5% with the inclusion of acquaintances, ex-husbands, ex-boyfriends, and ex-lovers.

From the alternate perspective, that is, the prevalence of males who admit to perpetrating sexual aggression, we are again dependent on Koss et al.'s (1987) study of college students and Gavey's (1991) replication with a similar age group. Koss et al. found that 25% of their sample admitted to sexual aggression, with Gavey's New Zealand data suggesting a prevalence of approximately half of that (13.6%). It is unclear what factors are responsible for this difference.

ASSOCIATED FEATURES

From a comorbidity perspective there are really two questions: Do rapists typically show the presence of major psychiatric diagnoses, and do rapists typically commit other sorts of criminal activity?

The presence of major psychiatric diagnoses is not uncommon in rapists. Substance and alcohol abuse or dependence have been diagnosed in up to 70% of rapists, with depressive disorder diagnosed in approximately one third (Hillbrand, Foster, & Hirt, 1990). A random sample of 94 men in a New Zealand prison found 58% of the 12 rapists selected met criteria for a DSM-III-R (APA, 1987) Axis I diagnosis (not including drug and alcohol issues) (Hudson & Murrow, 1997). Seghorn et al. (1987) reported lower rates of psychiatric disorder for men in their treatment center, with 7% diagnosed as schizophrenic, 2% as schizoaffective, 3% as having a major depression, and 6% as showing some organic syndrome. However, it is very unlikely that these rates are higher than base rates for the general prison population (see, for example, Hudson & Murrow, 1997).

With respect to Axis II disorders, Seghorn et al. (1987) suggested that around one third of their sample exhibited a personality disorder. Again, much higher prevalence rates (up to 90%) have been found by others (Berner, Berger, Gutierez, Jordan, & Berger, 1992; Serin, Malcolm, Khanna, & Barbaree, 1994; Stermac & Quinsey, 1986). Again, this likely reflects sampling issues. It is also possible that these rates are not dissimilar to those in the general prison population.

The associated question is, "Do rapists just rape?" If not, do they exhibit other sexually anomalous activities (as Freund [1990] suggested is likely), and/or other criminal activities? Exhibitionism has commonly been linked to rape (Paitich, Langevin, Freeman, Mann, & Handy, 1977; Rooth, 1973; Yalom, 1960); Gebhard, Gagnon, Pomeroy, and Christensen (1965) suggested that one in 10 exhibitionists has attempted or seriously contemplated rape. Additionally, Stermac and Hall's (1989) study suggested that those offenders who had escalated their offending were more likely to have committed a previous "hands off" offense such as exhibitionism. Finally, Abel, Becker, Cunningham-Rathner, Mittleman, and Rouleau's (1988) confidential self-report study with respect to other paraphilias suggested that of the 126 rapists in the study, 44% had also molested nonfamilial female children, with 14% molesting nonfamilial male children as well.

The more general issue of offense specificity is more problematic. The overall consensus against a specialization position needs to be modified according to offense type (Blumstein, Cohen, Das, & Moitra, 1988; see Cornish & Clarke, 1989, for discussion regarding specialization). It is likely, at least for incarcerated rapists, given their similarity to the general prison population, that most have convictions for other offenses. This seems to be true for adolescent rapists (e.g., Epps, 1991). Similarly, Stermac and Quinsey (1986) found that half of their sample of rapists had other convictions for offenses against persons, a figure similar to that found by Weinrott and Saylor (1991) in their self-report study. These authors noted that all of their subjects had at least one nonsex offense. Whether these findings apply to the wider rapist population, particularly to date rapists, has not yet been determined.

ETIOLOGY

The major task of a good etiological theory is to account for the onset, development, and maintenance of the phenomenon. Theories can be evaluated on a number of dimensions, including their ability to account for the facts or data, the degree of internal and external coherence, simplicity, explanatory depth, and heuristic value. In our view one of the problems in the sexual aggression area has been the failure to distinguish between theories, theoretical frameworks, and models. A theory aims to specify the causal mechanisms that generate data (Hooker, 1987), for example, the presence of deviant sexual fantasies or empathy deficits in rapists. The various causal factors are clearly described and their relationships with each other are spelled out. The major function of a theoretical framework is to help organize research by providing a loose set of constructs with which to approach empirical problems. There is no attempt to describe in detail the relationships between the different causal factors or processes. A model is the application of an idea or mechanism to a phenomenon (e.g., sexual aggression) from another domain of inquiry, and it fleshes out theories in their early stages of development. For example, the model of the heart as a pump was developed to attempt to understand and explain the functions of the heart and blood. As a model is tested and evaluated it hopefully leads to explanatory theories of more depth (Hooker, 1987). It is our contention that although there has been a gradual shift over the last 30 years in the complexity of the theories proposed to explain sexual aggression, none are really adequate as theories in the sense described above. The major positions (e.g., Ellis, 1991; Hall & Hirschman, 1991; Malamuth, 1986; Marshall & Barbaree, 1990a) are really still theoretical frameworks. It is important to stress that theoretical frameworks provide an invaluable focus for both empirical and conceptual research. However, for a field to make substantial progress it is necessary to construct good theories and models.

There are a number of ways to classify etiological theories. In this section we have divided theories into the following categories: psychodynamic, behavioral, feminist, sociobiological, social–cognitive, and comprehensive (multivariate) theories. In view of space constraints it is not been possible to cover all the various theories of rape. We have focused on what we see as exemplars within each category, taking into account the current status of each theory. We present Ellis's sociobiological theory in some detail because of its contentiousness. We discuss the comprehensive models in some detail, as it is our belief that an adequate theory (or theories) of rape need to be multivariate and comprehensive.

Psychodynamic Theories

The earliest coherent explanatory attempts belong to the psychodynamic perspective. At a general level Freud (1905/1953) saw deviant sexual behavior as a direct reflection of a form of character disorder, with infantile sexual desires that have continued into adulthood as the origin; as such, the possibility of change was seen as remote. Lanyon (1991) described subsequent psychoanalytic writers as having expanded and elaborated Freud's position (e.g., Fenichel, 1945; Hammer, 1957; Rada, 1978) with these explanations typically involving both castration anxieties and Oedipus conflicts.

The specific applications of psychodynamic theorizing to rape owes much to two theoretically driven typologies described above, those developed by Cohen, Garofolo, Boucher, and Seghorn (1971) and Groth et al. (1977). The essence of these typologies holds that a variety of feelings of anxiety and inadequacy, both sexual and interpersonal, together with the probability of unacknowledged homosexual tendencies, interact with aggression, thought to be directed at the victim as a substitute object for the mother, to produce a sexual assault. In extreme cases aggression is so sexualized that when aggression is triggered it overwhelms the ego and control mechanisms fail. Lanyon (1991) noted that whereas the psychodynamic perspective has been very influential with respect to discourse on sexual offending, it has not significantly informed either treatment or prevention and it lacks empirical support.

Behavioral Theories

The first influential etiological model of sexual aggression based on contemporary behavioral principles argued that sexual arousal in the presence of rape cues is the critical motivation for sexual assaults (Amir, 1971; Abel et al., 1977; Freund & Blanchard, 1981; Quinsey et al., 1984). However, conceptual critiques, particularly from a feminist perspective (e.g., Brownmiller, 1975; Burt, 1980; Darke, 1990; Herman, 1990) concerning the centrality of aggressive rather than sexual motivations, together with the failure of phallometric studies to continue to find differences between rapists and nonrapists once a broad range of offenders were included (e.g., Blader & Marshall, 1989), led to significantly more complex frameworks. These frameworks attempt both to integrate the duality of sexual and aggressive motives and to provide a developmental and situational context for sexual assaults.

Whereas the current frameworks for understanding sexual assault are multifaceted, all continue to include deviant arousal as one factor (e.g., Hall & Hirschman, 1991; Malamuth, 1986, Marshall & Barbaree, 1990a). We will discuss these more comprehensive theories later in this section, but within this context Barbaree and Marshall (1991) provided by far the most detailed account of how deviant sexual arousal might operate.

They proposed six models which could account for sexual arousal during rape. The first of these, the "sexual preference model," suggests that strongest sexual arousal is associated with maximum gratification, and further, that if this gratification is in response to deviant images or acts, then these constitute sexual preferences, are likely to be most reinforcing, and are a relatively stable trait. Most of the evidence for this hypothesis comes from phallometric studies which, as noted previously, produced equivocal results. The second model, "trait inhibition of rape arousal," suggests that nonconsent together with displays of pain, fear, and discomfort on the part of the woman serve to inhibit sexual arousal in most men. This is potentially mediated by an empathy response (Malamuth & Check, 1983). Empirical support for this hypothesis comes from phallometric studies suggesting that the ratio of arousal to rape versus consenting sexual interactions is higher in rapists and is related to number of victims and amount of violence (Abel et al., 1977; Abel, Blanchard, Becker, & Djenderedjian, 1978). The work of Malamuth and his colleagues (Malamuth, 1981, 1983, 1986; Malamuth & Check, 1983), that suggested a continuum of "likelihood of raping" that is directly related to inhibition of sexual arousal in response to rape cues (Malamuth & Check, 1983), provides additional evidence in support of the "trait inhibition of rape arousal" model.

The third model presented by Barbaree and Marshall (1991) is "state disinhibition of arousal." Ordinarily occurring inhibition of arousal to rape cues disappears for some reason. The reasons or circumstances under which this might occur are anything which decreases a man's motivation to behave in a prosocial fashion (e.g., when a potential victim has behaved in a manner judged by the rapist to be responsible for an assault, such as "provocative" clothing or being in a remote area [Sundberg, Barbaree, & Marshall, 1991]) and circumstances which generate anger toward a potential victim (e.g., a female confederate making a disparaging remark concerning the male subject's performance [Yates, Barbaree, & Marshall, 1984]). The fourth model, "emotional state augmentation," suggests that nonsexual emotional states act synergistically with sexual arousal to determine the strength of the sexual response. This is a possible mechanism in both positive (love) and negative (hate or hostility) sexual interactions.

The final two models examine response control and suggest on the one hand that rapists are characterized by their relative inability to voluntarily suppress sexual arousal (Hall, 1989) or alternatively by their capacity to be both aggressive and sexually aroused at the same time, that is, "response compatibility" (Blader & Marshall, 1989). "Response control" is a general term covering the inability to voluntarily suppress sexual arousal (Model 5) and the capacity to be both aggressive and sexually aroused (Model 6).

Feminist Theories

Feminist theories view rape as a pseudosexual act which is primarily motivated by male sociopolitical dominance. During the 1970s rape become a major issue for the feminist movement, at least in part because feminists saw this form of violence against women as a means of enforcing precisely the gender roles that women were changing (Donat & D'Emilio, 1992). Not only rape, but the fear of rape, serves as a mechanism of social control (Brownmiller, 1975; Riger & Gordon, 1981). This view has had a very significant impact not only on etiological theories by challenging the uncontrollable sex urge notion, but also on the way sexual assault is defined, the way rape victims are perceived and treated, and in identifying rape-supportive aspects of the culture. For example, Burt's (1980) feminist theory of rape described how culturally derived attitudes might facilitate sexual aggression. She suggested that sex role stereotypical beliefs, adversarial sexual beliefs, and acceptance of interpersonal violence are critical factors in mediating the link between culture and sexual aggression.

The most obvious consequence of the reconceptualization of rape is the burgeoning literature on date rape and sexual harassment. Koss et al.'s (1987) prevalence data of over 50% for some form of unwelcome sexual contact and/or sexually assaultive behavior reinforces both the change in definition and the notion that sexual aggression is almost a normative experience for the majority of women. This has led a number of authors to suggest that rape is supported culturally, particularly by media portrayals of women (Jozsa & Jozsa, 1980; Read, 1989). Most pernicious in this regard are pornographic descriptions depicting a woman's initial protest giving away to overwhelming sexual desire. Groth and Birnbaum (1979) described pornography as the media equivalent of rape.

The racial aspects of rape, at least in the United States, also support the view that rape is about power. The myth of the black man as sexually uncontrollable serves to oppress both black men and white women (Donat & D'Emilio, 1992). Not infrequently, white males convicted of rape were sent to state hospitals, whereas black men were sent to jail, where execution or castration were not uncommon (D'Emilio & Freedman, 1988). Black offenders still receive more severe sentencing penalties (Hall, 1983).

Similarly, perceptions of the rape victim reflect power issues, particularly her "responsibility" for being raped, reportedly having developed during the middle part of the 20th century as a function the female nature "becoming" sexualized (Freedman, 1989). This responsibility issue had direct effects on court processes. Juries are frequently instructed to be suspicious of the victim's evidence to a far greater degree than is the case in other criminal cases (Berger, 1977), leading to remarkably low conviction rates, often as low as 1% (Deckard, 1983). Recent and ongoing legal reforms focus on the perpetrator's behavior, particularly the use of or threat of force, rather than on the behavior of the victim. This applies both to her behavior during the assault, for example, in the degree of resistance exhibited, and in terms of sexual history. There is still a long way to go; only six states in the United States prohibit admitting details of the victim's sexual history in court cases (Searles & Berger, 1987).

Social–Cognitive Theories

An exciting theoretical development has been the application of social cognition methods and theories to rape (Johnston & Ward, 1996). As Sherman, Judd, and Park (1989) stated, "social cognition represents not a domain of inquiry within social psychology but an approach or set of assumptions guiding research in a variety of traditional substantive domains" (p. 281). In essence, social cognition concerns the study of social knowledge (its structure and content) and cognitive processes (including acquisition, representation, and retrieval of information) in an attempt to understand social behavior and its mediating factors. Three fundamental questions underlie the study of social cognition: (1) What type of information is stored and how is it organized in memory?; (2) How does social information stored in memory affect subsequent information processing, decision making, and behavior?; and (3) How and when is stored information altered, both by new information and by cognitive processes? (Sherman et al., 1989).

Biased information processing has frequently been described by clinicians (e.g., Marshall & Barbaree, 1989), and to a lesser extent by the sex offender research literature at all stages of the offense chain. Offenders' expectancies or beliefs about their sexual behaviors and victims bias the processing of sex-relevant information (Stermac & Segal, 1989; Ward, Hudson, Marshall, & Siegert, 1995). Rapists see the way their victims dress as a "come-on," and tend to have difficulty viewing the situation from their victims' perspectives (Scully, 1988). Similarly, during the actual offense the rapist sees the passivity or frightened compliance of the women as a desire for, and enjoyment of, the rape. The more ambiguous the behavior or situation, the easier it is for the rapist to interpret it incorrectly.

We will briefly review some recent studies utilizing this approach to the study of sexual aggression. Check and Malamuth (1983), in their research on the impact of nonoffending males' stereotypes on reactions to rape depictions, found that these men tended to interpret the acquaintance-rape victim as responding more favorably to the assault, despite the depictions being no different in content from stranger rape (i.e., same responses as stranger-rape victim). Lipton, McDonel, and McFall (1987) examined social information processing in rapists and found that they exhibited deficits in processing specific interpersonal cues from women. More precisely, rapists experienced problems accurately identifying cues in first-date situations, particularly negative mood states.

In a recent study Malamuth and Brown (1994) tested three explanations of findings concerning sexually aggressive men's perceptions of women's interpersonal behavior. These were the overperception of hostility/seductiveness (i.e., aggressive men have difficulty distinguishing between friendliness and seductiveness, and between assertiveness and hostility), negative blindness (i.e., sexually aggressive men are unable to accurately read women's negative cues), and suspicious schema hypotheses (i.e., sexually aggressive men believe that women's communications about sexual interest/intimate relationships are not trustworthy). Their results supported the suspiciousness schema model and suggested that rapists tend to process women's sexual communications in a distorted manner. Such biased information processing creates greater levels of mistrust and hostility toward women, and ultimately, sexual aggression.

In a related area, Pryor and Stoller (1994) showed that men high in likelihood to sexually harass (LSH) tended to perceive a stronger link between sexuality and social dominance than did men low in LSH. This sexuality/dominance link biased the processing of social information so as to create an illusory correlation between dominance and sexuality terms in a frequency estimation task for high-LSH men. Such results are consistent with the finding that men high in LSH hold adversarial sexual beliefs and they believe that women accept, and even enjoy, male domination even when it means physical coercion (Pryor, 1987). Such a belief structure can also bias social information processing to provide a memory base which supports these beliefs. Similarly, finding oneself in a position of power (e.g., the boss) may prime thoughts of sexual liaison for men high in LSH. Inferences about the appropriate choice of action could be influenced by the cognitive link between these two constructs. Sexual harassment appears to be the result of a combination of personal (high LSH) and situational (approving social norms) factors (Pryor, LaVite, & Stoller, 1993).

The possession of inappropriate sex-related cognitions is likely to predispose the individual to sex offenses, given a combination of other situational and circumstantial factors. It is important, therefore, to establish the nature of offenders' beliefs about sexual targets: women and children. One problem in current social–cognitive theories is that they tend to undervalue the importance of motivational and affective processes. However, recent work has started to address this problem (Fiske & Taylor, 1991), and we believe that the cognitive paradigm has much to offer in understanding rape.

Sociobiological Theories

There have been a number of different sociobiological models developed in recent years to account for the existence of sexual aggression. In this section we focus on Ellis's sociobiological theory (Ellis, 1989, 1991), as it is arguably currently the most influential. In the sociobiological model espoused by Ellis, biological variables have evolutionary significance. Ellis's evolutionary thesis suggests that unlike women, men may maximize their reproductive potential by copulating with numerous sex partners. Thus, men who are at least "pushy" in sexual matters, if not outrightly tolerant of forced copulation, may have been favored in the evolutionary stakes (Ellis, 1991). He has extended this position, combining it with aspects of both feminist and social learning theories, and presented it in terms of four propositions. First, that there exists two largely unlearned drives, sex and a desire to possess and control, that motivate sexual behavior, including rape. The notion that a drive for possession and control forms part of sexual behavior originates with Maslow's (1940) concept of dominance and rests primarily upon nonhuman literature which suggests that behaviors such as territorial defensiveness and proximity seeking reflect possessiveness and need for control. The implication is that males experience this drive more strongly than do females, but as Ellis himself notes, both men and women are often possessive toward each other in terms of mutual control over sexual behavior. Some authors have suggested that the animal literature is seriously flawed in that both what is observed and the interpretations made are paradigmatically driven and therefore have typically reflected a male-centered view.

These difficulties aside, Ellis's position clearly proposes a relatively pure sexual motivation for rape. This is at variance with the feminist (Brownmiller, 1975) and broader social learning positions (e.g., Marshall & Barbaree, 1990a; Pithers, 1990). Ellis suggested that nonsexual aspects, that is, the aggressive and dominating behavior exhibited by rapists, are best seen as tactics rather than as goals. The evidence presented in support of this revolves largely around date rape by male college students wherein deceit, pressure, ignoring protests, and getting their dates intoxicated may well be tactics in service of sex; however, this ignores the broader range of rapists and particularly the notion of expressive aggression (Knight & Prentky, 1990).

Additionally, he ascribed a central role to testosterone. However, whereas elevated testosterone levels have been found in very violent sexual offenders, this is likely an artifact. What relationship there is is likely to be with violence generally rather than specifically with sexual violence (Berlin, 1983; Bradford & McLean, 1984), and additionally it is improbable that a single neurotransmitter is associated exclusively with sexual aggression (Prentky, 1985).

Ellis's second proposition suggested that natural selection has favored men with stronger sex drives and greater tolerances of forced copulation. Ellis cites as evidence for this position studies suggesting that men typically masturbate more, desire higher frequencies of sexual intercourse, are more likely to initiate sexual contact, report finding sex more reinforcing, have more sexual dreams and thoughts, and are less likely to report nonsexual reasons for sexual intercourse than do women. As he himself noted, all of these findings are explicable by cultural factors, and none in and of themselves directly support the notion of acceptance of forced copulation.

Third, Ellis suggested that as males have a higher sex drive, copulation is likely a more potent primary reinforcer for them than for women. This, if true, has two implications. First, direct experience rather than modeling or instructional/attitudinal modalities are likely to be most powerful in affecting behavior. This seems remarkably similar to Bandura's social learning position with respect to the most efficacious ways of changing behavior quite independently of the nature of reinforcement (Bandura, 1986). Second, this lower intensity of the sex drive for women, in combination with differing evolutionary pressures, allows a social exchange mechanism to develop wherein it is in the women's interest to restrict access to copulation to maximize bonding commitment. This, according to Ellis, introduces ambiguity into the sexual courtship process. This ambiguity, he posited, allows the possibility of increasing levels of coercion on the part of the male. Ellis suggested that this coercion may subsequently generalize to other relationships. The evidence provided for this notion of shaping is that some women fantasize about forced copulation (Ellis, 1989; Gold, 1991); also, within the context of date rape, victims of completed rapes were more likely to stay in a relationship with their assailants than were victims of attempted rapes (Koss, 1989; Wilson & Durrenberger, 1982). These data, nonetheless, are somewhat tangential and again applicable only within the context of date rape.

Ellis's fourth proposition suggested that males' greater exposure to androgens (especially testosterone) affects not only the strength of the sex drive relative to women, but also their sensitivity to the threat of punishment and ability to be empathic with others' suffering. The evidence he presented is again rather tangential and primarily related to establishing that testosterone has a significant role in sexual motivation and behavior. An additional line of research he reported relates to sensitivity to environmental stimuli, specifically that exposure to androgens during fetal development causes desensitization later in life (Sar & Stumpf, 1977; Stumpf, Sar, Reisert, & Pilgrim, 1983; Teyler, Vardaris, Lewis, & Rawitch, 1980).

The major criticisms of the sociobiological position center around the relatively low levels of serious sexual aggression, such as rape, compared with the model's predictions (although of course this may reflect significant underreporting of rape), the problems extrapolating from animal behavior, the preoccupation with the environment as the source of behavior control, and finally, from a sociopolitical perspective the damage that the tacit victim-blaming stance causes (Hall & Hirschman, 1991).

Comprehensive Theories

The first of the more complex theoretical frameworks developed to explain the etiology of rape was originally developed by Malamuth (1986). Malamuth et al. (1993) described the most recent version of this interactive or confluence model of sexual aggression. There are four key features to this model, namely (1) that for sexual aggression to occur several factors must converge, (2) that these factors are quite domain specific, but (3) within that domain (i.e., social relationships and conflicts with women by men) some degree of generalization is expected; and finally, (4) that the social environment, defined quite broadly to include adverse developmental experiences, acts to increase or decrease the likelihood that a male will sexually coerce a female.

The three general categories of proximate causes identified by Malamuth and his colleagues are remarkably similar to the list of preconditions for child sexual abuse proposed by Finkelhor (1984), that is: (1) motivation to commit the aggressive act; (2) reductions in any inhibitions which serve to prevent aggression; and finally, (3) the opportunity. Malamuth and colleagues (1993) made the sensible comment that although it is useful to see these three categories as separable, especially at a theoretical level (Malamuth, 1986), this is not always the case.

The six predictor variables used by Malamuth and his colleagues (1993) are also familiar: tumescence to depictions of rape, the dominance motive, hostility toward women, attitudes which facilitate aggression against women such as acceptance of rape myths (Burt, 1980), antisocial personality characteristics, and sexual experience as a measure of opportunity to aggress. What is novel and indeed the core feature of their model is the dramatic evidence they present (Malamuth et al., 1993) for the synergistic interaction of the six factors, with a six fold increase in frequency of sexually aggressive acts where all six factors were deemed high.

Malamuth and his colleagues put these proximate causes into a developmental context. They noted, as have others (e.g., Marshall & Barbaree, 1990a) that adverse early developmental experiences, such as parental violence and physical and sexual abuse, lead to the development of other than prosocial views on male–female relationships (Huesmann, 1988). They also lead to deficits in other areas of social competence, especially intimacy skills and self-esteem (Marshall, 1989a). Malamuth, Sockloskie, Koss, and Tanaka (1991) proposed two interacting pathways that lead to sexual aggression: hostile masculinity and sexual promiscuity. The hostile masculinity pathway reflects the authors' belief that the hostile home environments mentioned above are frequently associated with a variety of antisocial behaviors (Patterson, DeBaryshe, & Ramsey, 1989), including a controlling and adversarial male orientation wherein aggressive courtship and sexual conquest reflects being a "real" man (Gilmore, 1990). They suggested that the first four of their predictors belong to this path. The second path, sexual promiscuity, reflects the overuse of sexuality as a source of self-esteem and potentially leads to increased opportunity to use coercive tactics in the pursuit of sexual conquest and increased likelihood that such tactics will be used. This is similar to the notions proposed by Marshall and Barbaree (1990a) and Marshall (1989a).

Marshall and Barbaree's (1990a) integrated theory placed greatest emphasis on the distal causal factors of sexual aggression, still acknowledging the importance of transient situational variables. They saw sexually aggressive behavior as multiply determined and they provided a detailed description of the critical adverse developmental antecedents and resulting vulnerabilities.

The evidence they presented suggests that adverse developmental experiences, for example, poor parenting, especially inconsistent, harsh physical discipline in the absence of warmth and accepting support, precede failure in socialization tasks such as the development of positive attitudes toward relationships (Ward, Hudson, Marshall, & Siegert, 1995). Further, these negative developmental experiences also fail to help the young male develop needed social controls with respect to sex and aggression. They may serve to fuse these two aspects of functioning. They therefore described a picture of a vulnerable adolescent passing through puberty with poor social skills, particularly with respect to intimacy (Marshall, 1989a; Ward, Hudson, Marshall, & Siegert, 1995), negative attitudes, and an impaired ability to distinguish between sexuality and aggression.

With respect to the biological factors in relation to sexual assaults, Marshall and Barbaree (1990a) made the point strongly that although sex and aggression are mediated by the same neural substrates that predominantly involve midbrain structures, and although the same sex steroids, particularly but not exclusively testosterone, mediate both, this does not mean that sexual aggression is unavoidable or excusable. Their position is that biology sets the developmental task, as it is likely that the physiological substrate supports the ready capacity to sexually aggress, and that between individuals, variations in hormonal functioning serve to potentiate this. The need for socially created inhibitors is therefore of critical importance. This is particularly so for males at puberty, when there is a marked increase in hormonal activity. As such, the primary developmental task for males at adolescence is the inhibition of aggression in a sexual context. It may well be that, as Ellis (1991) and others argued, our biological and evolutionary history makes this a difficult task; it does not, however, make it any less important or possible.

Marshall and Barbaree (1990a) suggested that the vulnerable adolescent male is likely to use a paternalistic cultural tradition that sees women and children as objects for the sexual satisfaction of males to boost his sense of masculinity and self-esteem. These vulnerability factors then interact with more transient situational elements such as intoxication, strong negative affect, a belief that he will not be caught, and the presence of a potential victim to determine the occurrence of a sexual assault. Indeed, anger, alcohol intoxication, and sexual arousal are commonly reported as present preceding rapes (Macdonald & Pithers, 1989; Pithers, Beal, Armstrong, & Petty, 1989).

This model is flexible and broad enough to cope with the heterogeneity involved in sexual assault as it covers both child molestation and the sexual assault of adults. However, this breadth leaves considerable room for expansion with respect to middle-level explanations, in particular how the various factors interact with each other and directly affect behavior in ways relevant to offending.

Hall and Hirschman's (1991) quadripartite model is one of the few models that specifically addresses rape. It describes four components that said to be motivational precursors that both increase the probability of sexual aggressive behavior and defines subtypes according to the relative prominence of each factor for any one individual. This view suggests that various combinations of physiological sexual arousal, cognitions that justify sexual aggression, affective dyscontrol, and personality problems will be more or less prominent depending on the typologies of the aggressor and the act (Hall & Hirschman, 1991).

Hall and Hirschman (1991) noted that despite the intuitively compelling nature of a sexual arousal hypothesis, the empirical evidence is lacking, for example, regarding the failure of phallometric differentiation of rapists and nonrapists (Blader & Marshall, 1989), and the general failure of posttreatment phallometry to predict recidivistic sexual aggression (Marshall, 1996; Marshall & Barbaree, 1988, 1990b; Quinsey, 1983). Through we agree with their position, we see the picture as necessarily being more complex. Prediction of reoffending using posttreatment phallometry is both logically and statistically flawed. The aim of most programs is control, not cure, such that posttreatment phallometry is not necessarily relevant. Also, many programs will not recommend release until deviant sexual arousal levels are eliminated, thereby removing any significant variance from the predictor variable. This is compatible with Hall and Hirschman's (1991) contention that in rape, as opposed to child molestation, the sexual arousal need not be deviant to be a part of the offense chain. Equally, it may, but this is likely to be the case for only a subset of rapists for whom sexually deviant fantasies are a critical aspect of motivation.

It is clear that for most rapists, it is not the sexual arousal per se that is critical; rather, it is the man's cognitive processes that are important, and these constitute the second factor of the model. Hall and Hirschman (1991) suggested that if the appraised benefits of sexual aggression (e.g., sexual gratification, expression of anger, victim will enjoy it) are greater than risks (e.g., of being punished, the sense of wrongness of it), then the man is more likely to sexually aggress. As they imply, this is compatible with a staged process model such as the information-processing analysis proposed by McFall (1990). What are lacking, however, are both an adequate conceptual model for these cognitions and a competent description of how they operate.

The third aspect of Hall and Hirschman's (1991) model addressed the affective component. Many authors have suggested that negative affective states typically occur early in the chain of events leading to sexual aggression (e.g., Pithers, 1990). Depressive states are typically seen as precipitating assaults against children, with hostility seen as facilitating sexual aggression against adults (Knight & Prentky, 1990; Pithers, 1990; Quinsey, 1984). Although this is likely an oversimplification (for example, early-onset pedophiles with male victims typically offend in a positive emotional context; Ward, Louden, Hudson, & Marshall, 1995), it is a position generally compatible with feminist views regarding the primacy of anger and violence (Brownmiller, 1975). Hall and Hirschman (1991) took essentially the same position as did Finkelhor (1984) in suggesting that there is a reciprocal relationship between these negative affect states and the normal inhibitions that prevent the expression of sexually aggressive behavior such as victim empathy, guilt, moral conviction, and anxiety regarding being prosecuted. This quite appropriately suggests a degree of temporal instability to such notions as cognitive and emotional processes, such as empathy deficits, and as such is in contrast with much of the literature which treats such phenomena as traitlike, almost entirely in the absence of any evidence (see Marshall, Hudson, Jones, & Fernandez, 1995). It also is compatible with the state disinhibition model proposed by Barbaree and Marshall (1991) and Baumeister's (1989) self-regulatory construct of cognitive deconstruction (Ward, Hudson, & Marshall, 1995).

The final component of Hall and Hirschman's (1991) model attends to what they described as more enduring, traitlike aspects of the man's functioning. In particular, they reported the negative types of early developmental experiences, such as parental divorce and physical/sexual abuse (Bard et al., 1987), that both increase the chances of negative and antisocial attitudes (Baxter et al., 1984; Hall & Proctor, 1987) and diminish the probability of adequate socialization (Lipton et al., 1987; Marshall & Barbaree, 1984; Overholser & Beck, 1986; Stermac & Quinsey, 1986). It is likely that most of the variance is contained within this last, least well-articulated factor. A problem with having such a general dispositional factor is that it is difficult to unpack it in a coherent way.

The final comprehensive approach to sexual aggression we will discuss is the relapse prevention model. This is arguably the most influential of the current comprehensive theoretical frameworks, at least as far as informing treatment is concerned. Relapse prevention (Marlatt & Gordon, 1985) was adapted by Pithers and his coworkers to clarify the processes determining relapse in sexual offenders in general (Laws, 1989; Pithers, 1990; Pithers, Marques, Gibat, & Marlatt, 1983). It is important to stress that it focuses primarily on the processes governing relapse in sexual offenders and is not really an etiological model. However, we have included it in the chapter because of its immense influence on current treatment and research, and because of its potential value in highlighting some of the key processes associated with rape.

The relapse prevention model focuses on factors proximal to offending, describing the process as an affective–cognitive–behavioral chain that culminates in the recurrence of sexually aggressive behavior. The typical description of this process (Pithers, 1990) suggests that it begins with some negative affect (e.g., loneliness or confusion), often arising as the result of interpersonal conflict (Pithers, Kashima, Cumming, & Beal, 1988). This negative affect leads to fantasies of performing sexually abusive acts which are seen as learned ways of reducing negative feelings. These fantasies are often associated with a stream of distorted cognitions which serve to rationalize deviant sexuality. As a result of these cognitive–affective processes, the offender begins to plan an assault which he finally acts out.

As an overarching framework that guides interventions, this model has considerable strengths. However, it has weaknesses on two fronts. First, the model does not aim to explain the initial offense, and therefore, not surprisingly, the framework does not articulate factors thought to be important in the early genesis of sexual aggression. This severely limits the model's comprehensiveness. Second, and more relevant in terms of the aims of the model, there is some confusion regarding the definitions of both lapse and relapse, and with respect to some of the mediating mechanisms thought to drive the transitions (Ward, Hudson, & Siegert, 1995). We recently developed a descriptive model of the relapse process for child molesters based upon this model (Ward, Louden, et al., 1995). The resulting model, though applying only to child molesters, has more elements or steps in the chain and a greater variety of choices or possibilities at most of these steps. It is therefore able to cope with the complexity and heterogeneity imposed by a variety of offense styles. We need to extend this with subtypes of rapists.

In summary, the various theories developed to explain the occurrence of rape vary in terms of their foci, comprehensiveness, and degrees of integration. It is likely that a problem as complex as rape is unlikely to be explained by single-factor theories. At this point in time there are a number of promising comprehensive theoretical frameworks suggesting important research foci and methods. All of them point to the importance of adverse developmental experiences and biological factors in creating substantial vulnerability in adolescent males. What remains unclear is how these experiences are encoded, and further, how they act to generate deficiencies in adult social performance.

FUTURE DIRECTIONS

In our view, beside further empirical research into the demographic (e.g., research extended to different populations of rapists), physiological, and psychological characteristics of rapists (and their social–cultural concomitants), there are two major conceptual tasks which urgently need attention: first, the development of a valid, reliable, practical, meaningful, and broadly applicable taxonomy for men who sexually assault women. Attempts to construct classification systems for rapists must be guided by theory (Millon, 1991). The work of Prentky, Knight, and their co-workers (e.g., Prentky & Knight, 1991; Knight & Prentky, 1990) is particularly promising and has the benefit of utilizing rigorous multivariate methodologies. Another interesting innovation is the use of qualitative methodologies to create theoretically rich categories and to build descriptive models. For example, in our own research we have used grounded theory (Strauss & Corbin, 1992) to construct a model of the offense chain in child molesters (Ward, Louden, et al., 1995). One of the interesting findings emerging from this work is that child molesters can be divided into two major groups based upon different pathways through the offending process. In another research program we have developed a model of intimacy deficits in sex offenders based on attachment style (Ward, Hudson, Marshall, & Siegert, 1995). The different attachment styles (secure, anxious/ambivalent, fearful, and dismissive) theoretically are related to different offending variables, and they provide an alternative means of classifying offenders. We currently are in the process of testing out the model, and early results are promising (Ward, Hudson, & Marshall, 1996).

The second major conceptual task is the development of theories in the strong sense of the word. This involves the development of models of underlying mechanisms and theories that attempt to specify the relationships between the various causal variables. A fruitful strategy would be to use theoretical developments from other related areas (e.g., social cognition and attachment research) to provide middle-level explanatory models (e.g., Ward, Hudson, & Marshall, 1995; Ward, Hudson, Marshall, & Siegert, 1995). By middle level we mean constructing models of the various factors identified in the more comprehensive frameworks, for example, intimacy deficits and cognitive processes. As we flesh out these micromodels, we can create bridging theories to integrate them into an overarching theory.

We suspect that an understanding of the cognitive processes underlying the initiation, maintenance, and justification of sexual offending is an especially vital prerequisite to the development of comprehensive explanatory theories (Johnston & Ward, 1996). Pertinent research in the social cognition domain includes social information processing, the development and employment of stereotypes, mental control, and the impact of affective and motivational factors on cognitive processes.

Sexual offenses against women constitute a pernicious and distressingly prevalent social problem. We believe that the ideas suggested in this section will lead to increased understanding of the onset, maintenance, and recurrence of sexual aggression. This knowledge, in turn, will provide more focused and effective treatments for men who commit sexual crimes. Ultimately, this will provide a greater degree of safety for women.

ACKNOWLEDGEMENTS

We would like to thank Julie McCormack and Dr. Brian Haig for their helpful comments on an earlier version of this chapter.

REFERENCES

American Psychiatric Association. (1987). *Diagnostic and statistical manual of mental disorders* (3rd ed., rev.). Washington, DC: Author.

American Psychiatric Association. (1994). *Diagnostic and statistical manual of mental disorders* (4th ed.). Washington, DC: Author.

Amir, M. (1971). *Patterns of forcible rape.* Chicago: University of Chicago Press.

Abel, G. G., Barlow, D. H., Blanchard, E. B., & Guild, D. (1977). The components of rapist's sexual arousal. *Archives of General Psychiatry, 34,* 895–903.

Abel, G. G., Becker, J. V., Cunningham-Rathner, J., Mittleman, M., & Rouleau, J. (1988). Multiple paraphilic diagnoses among sex offenders. *Bulletin of the American Academy of Psychiatry and the Law, 16,* 153–168.

Abel, G. G., Blanchard, E. B., Becker, J. V., & Djenderedjian, A. (1978). Differentiating sexual aggressives with penile measures. *Criminal Justice and Behavior, 5,* 315–332.

Bandura, A. (1986). *Social foundations of thought and action: A social cognitive theory.* Englewood Cliffs, NJ: Prentice-Hall.

Barbaree, H. E., & Marshall, W. L. (1991). The role of male sexual arousal in rape: Six models. *Journal of Consulting and Clinical Psychology, 59,* 621–630.

Barbaree, H. E., Marshall, W. L., & Lanthier, R. D. (1979). Deviant sexual arousal in rapists. *Behaviour Research and Therapy, 17,* 215–222.

Bard, L. A., Carter, D. L., Cerce, D. D., Knight, R. A., Rosenberg, R., & Schneider, B. (1987). A descriptive study of rapists and child molesters: Developmental, clinical, and criminal characteristics. *Behavioral Sciences and the Law, 5,* 203–220.

Baumeister, R. F. (1989). Masochism as escape from self. *Journal of Sex Research, 25,* 28–59.

Baxter, D. J., Barbaree, H. E., & Marshall, W. L. (1986). Sexual responses to consenting and forced sex in a large sample of rapists and nonrapists. *Behaviour Research and Therapy, 24,* 513–520.

Baxter, D. J., Marshall, W. L., Barbaree, H. E., Davidson, P. R., & Malcolm, P. B. (1984). Deviant sexual behavior: Differentiating sex offenders by criminal and personal history, psychometric measures, and sexual response. *Criminal Justice and Behavior, 11,* 477–501.

Berlin, F. (1983). Sex offenders: A biomedical perspective and a status report on biomedical treatment. In J. G. Greer & I. R. Stuart (Eds.), *The sexual aggressor: Current perspectives on treatment* (pp. 83–125). New York: Van Nostrand Reinhold.

Berger, V. (1977). Man's trail, women's tribulation: Rape cases in the courtroom. *Columbia Law Review, 77,* 1–101.

Berner, W., Berger, P., Gutierez, K., Jordan, B., & Berger, J. (1992). The role of personality disorder in the treatment of sexual offenders. *Journal of Offender Rehabilitation, 18,* 25–37.

Blader, J. C., & Marshall, W. L. (1989). Is assessment of sexual arousal in rapists worthwhile? A critique of current methods and the development of a response compatibility approach. *Clinical Psychology Review, 9,* 569–587.

Blumstein, A., Cohen, J., Das, S., & Moitra, S. D. (1988). Specialization and seriousness during adult criminal careers. *Journal of Quantitative Criminology, 4,* 303–345.

Bradford, J. M., & McLean, D. (1984). Sexual offenders, violence and testosterone. *Canadian Journal of Psychiatry, 29,* 335–343.

Brownmiller, S. (1975). *Against our will: Men, women and rape.* New York: Simon & Schuster.

Burt, M. R. (1980). Cultural myths and supports for rape. *Journal of Personality and Social Psychology, 38,* 217–130.

Carter, D. L., Prentky, R. A., Knight, R. A., Vanderveer, P. L., & Boucher, R. J. (1987). Use of pornography in the criminal and developmental histories of sexual offenders. *Journal of Interpersonal Violence, 2,* 196–211.

Check, J. V. P., & Malamuth, N. M. (1983). Sex role stereotyping and reactions to depictions of stranger versus acquaintance rape. *Journal of Personality and Social Psychology, 45,* 344–356.

Christie, M. M., Marshall, W. L., & Lanthier, R. D. (1979). *A descriptive study of incarcerated rapists and child molesters* (Report to the Solicitor General of Canada). Ottawa: Office of the Solicitor General.

Cook, R. F., Fosen, R. H., & Pacht, A. R. (1971). Pornography and the sex offender: Patterns of previous exposure and arousal effects of pornographic stimuli. *Journal of Applied Psychology, 55,* 503–511.

Cohen, M. L., Garofolo, R., Boucher, R., & Seghorn, T. (1971). The psychology of rapists. *Seminars in Psychiatry, 3,* 307–323.

Cohen, M. L., Seghorn, T. K., & Calmas, W. (1969). Sociometric study of sex offenders. *Journal of Abnormal Psychology, 74,* 249–255.

Cornish, D. B., & Clarke, R. V. (1989). Crime specialization, crime displacement and rational choice theory. In H. Wegener, F. Iosel, & J. Haisch (Eds.), *Criminal behavior and the justice system: A psychological perspective* (pp. 1030–117). New York: Springer-Verlag.

Craig, M. E. (1990). Coercive sexuality in dating relationships: A situational model. *Clinical Psychology Review, 10,* 395–423.

Curtis, L. A. (1976). Present and future measures of victimization in forcible rape. In M. J. Walker & S. L. Brodsky (Eds.), *Sexual assault* (pp. 61–68). Lexington, MA: Heath.

Darke, J. L. (1990). Sexual aggression: Achieving power through humiliation. In W. L. Marshall, D. R. Laws, & H. E. Barbaree (Eds.), *Handbook of sexual assault: Issues, theories, and treatment of the offender* (pp. 55–72). New York: Plenum Press.

Deckard, B. S. (1983). *The woman's movement: Political, socioeconomic, and psychological issues* (3rd ed.). New York: Harper & Row.

D'Emilio, J., & Freedman, E. B. (1988). *Intimate matters: A history of sexuality in America.* New York: Harper Row.

Donat, P. L. N., & D'Emilio, J. (1992). A feminist redefinition of rape and sexual assault: Historical foundations and change. *Journal of Social Issues, 48,* 9–22.

Ellis, L. (1989). *Theories of rape: Inquiries into the causes of sexual aggression.* New York: Hemisphere.

Ellis, L. (1991). A synthesized (biosocial) theory of rape. *Journal of Consulting and Clinical Psychology, 59,* 631–642.

Epps, K. (1991). The residential treatment of adolescent sex offenders. *Issues in Criminology and Legal Psychology, 1,* 58–67.

Federal Bureau of Investigation. (1982). *Uniform crime reports*. Washington, DC: U.S. Department of Justice.

Fenichel, O. (1945). *The psychoanalytic theory of neurosis*. New York: Horton.

Fiske, S. T., & Taylor, S. E. (1991). *Social cognition* (2nd ed.). New York: McGraw-Hill.

Finkelhor, D. (1984). *Child sexual abuse: New theory and research*. New York: Free Press.

Freedman, E. B. (1989). Uncontrolled desires: The response to the sexual psychopath, 1920–1960. In K. Peiss & C. Simmons (Eds.), *Passion and power: Sexuality in history* (pp. 199–225). Philadelphia: Temple University Press.

Freud, S. (1953). Three essays on the theory of sexual deviation. In *The complete psychological works of Sigmund Freud* (J. Strachey, Ed. & Trans.; Vol. 7). London: Hogarth Press. (Original work published 1905)

Freund, K. (1990). Courtship disorder. In W. L. Marshall, D. R. Laws, & H. E. Barbaree (Eds.), *Handbook of sexual assault: Issues, theories, and treatment of the offender* (pp. 195–207). New York: Plenum Press.

Freund, K., & Blanchard, R. (1981). Assessment of sexual dysfunction and deviance. In M. Hersen & A. S. Bellack (Eds.), *Behavioral assessment: A practical handbook* (pp. 427–455). New York: Pergamon Press.

Furby, L., Weinrott, M. R., & Blackshaw, L. (1989). Sex offender recidivism: A review. *Psychological Bulletin, 105*, 3–30.

Gavey, N. (1991). Sexual victimization prevalence among New Zealand university students. *Journal of Consulting and Clinical Psychology, 59*, 464–466.

Gebhard, P. H., Gagnon, J., Pomeroy, W. B., & Christensen, C. (1965). *Sex offenders: An analysis of types*. New York: Harper Row.

Gilmore, D. D. (1990). *Manhood in the making: Cultural concepts of masculinity*. New Haven, CT: Yale University Press.

Gold, S. R. (1991). History of child sexual abuse and adult sexual fantasies. *Violence and Victims, 6*, 75–82.

Goldstein, M., Kant, H., Judd, L., Rice, C., & Green, F. R. (1971). Experience with pornography: Rapists, pedophiles, homosexuals, transsexuals, and controls. *Archives of Sexual Behavior, 1*, 1–15.

Groth, A. N., & Birnbaum, A. H. (1979). *Men who rape: The psychology of the offender*. New York: Plenum Press.

Groth, A. N., Burgess, A. W., & Holmstrom, L. L. (1977). Rape: Power, anger, and sexuality. *American Journal of Psychiatry, 134*, 1239–1243.

Grubin, D. H., & Kennedy, H. G. (1991). The classification of sexual offenders. *Criminal Behaviour and Mental Health, 1*, 123–129.

Hall, G. C. N. (1989). Sexual arousal and arousability in a sex offender population. *Journal of Abnormal Psychology, 98*, 145–149.

Hall, G. C. N., & Hirschman, R. (1991). Toward a theory of sexual aggression: A quadripartite model. *Journal of Consulting and Clinical Psychology, 59*, 662–669.

Hall, G. C. N., & Proctor, W. C. (1987). Criminological predictors of recidivism in a sex offender population. *Journal of Consulting and Clinical Psychology, 55*, 111–112.

Hall, J. D. (1983). The mind that burns in each body: Women, rape, and racial violence. In A. Snitow, C. Stansell, & S. Thompson (Eds.), *Powers of desire: The politics of sexuality* (pp. 328–349). New York: Monthly Review Press.

Hammer, E. F. (1957). A psychoanalytic hypothesis concerning sex offenders. *Journal of Clinical and Experimental Psychopathology, 18*, 341–360.

Hanson, R. K., & Bussière, M. T. (1996). *Predictors of sexual offender recidivism: A meta-analysis* (Report No. 1996-04). Ottawa: Solicitor General of Canada.

Hillbrand, M., Foster, H., & Hirt, M. (1990). Rapists and child molesters: Psychometric comparisons. *Archives of Sexual Behavior, 19*, 65–71.

Henn, F. A., Herjanic, M., & Vanderpearl, R. H. (1976). Forensic psychiatry: Profiles of two types of sex offenders. *American Journal of Psychiatry, 133*, 694–696.

Herman, J. L. (1990). Sex offenders: A feminist perspective. In W. L. Marshall, D. R. Laws, & H. E. Barbaree (Eds.), *Handbook of sexual assault: Issues, theories, and treatment of the offender* (pp. 177–193). New York: Plenum Press.

Hooker, C. A. (1987). *A realistic theory of science.* Albany, NY: State University of New York.

Huesmann, L. R. (1988). An information processing model for the development of aggression. *Aggressive Behavior, 14,* 13–24.

Hudson, S. M., & Bakker, L. (1994). *Reoffending in rapists: A re-examination of the New Zealand data.* Manuscript in preparation.

Hudson, S. M., & Murrow, S. (1997). *Prevalence of mental disorder in a medium security prison.* Manuscript in preparation.

Johnston, L., & Ward, T. (1996). Social cognition and sexual offending: A theoretical framework. *Sexual Abuse: A Journal of Research and Treatment, 8,* 55–80.

Jozsa, B., & Jozsa, M. (1980). Dirty books, dirty films, and dirty data. In L. Lederer (Ed.), *Take back the night: Women on pornography* (pp. 204–217). New York: Morrow.

Kilpatrick, D. G., & Best, C. B. (1990, August). *Violence as a precursor of women's substance abuse: The rest of the drugs–violence story.* Paper presented at the annual meeting of the American Psychological Association, Boston.

Knight, R. A., & Prentky, R. A. (1990). Classifying sexual offenders: The development and corroboration of taxonomic models. In W. L. Marshall, D. R. Laws, & H. E. Barbaree (Eds.), *Handbook of sexual assault: Issues, theories, and treatment of the offender* (pp. 23–52). New York: Plenum Press.

Knight, R. A., Rosenberg, R., & Schneider, B. (1985). Classification of sexual offenders: Perspectives, methods and validation. In A. Burgess (Ed.), *Rape and sexual assault: A research handbook* (pp. 222–293). New York: Garland Press.

Konopasky, R. J. (1993, November). *Virtual control of stimulus slides in penile plethysmography: A computer-based method for "constructing" slides.* Presented at the 12th Annual Research and Treatment Conference of the Association for the Treatment of Sexual Aggressors, Boston.

Koss, M. P. (1985). The hidden rape victim: Personality, attitudes, and situational characteristics. *Psychology of Women Quarterly, 9,* 193–212.

Koss, M. P. (1989). Hidden rape: Sexual aggression and victimization in a national sample of students in higher education. In M. A. Pirog-Good & J. Stets (Eds.), *Violence in dating relationships* (pp. 145–168). New York: Praeger.

Koss, M. P. (1992). The underdetection of rape: Methodological choices influence incidence estimates. *Journal of Social Issues, 48,* 61–75.

Koss, M. P., & Gidycz, C. A. (1985). Sexual Experiences Survey: Reliability and validity. *Journal of Consulting and Clinical Psychology, 53,* 422–423.

Koss, M. P., & Oros, C. J. (1982). Sexual Experiences Survey: A research instrument investigating sexual aggression and victimization. *Journal of Consulting and Clinical Psychology, 50,* 455–457.

Koss, M. P., Gidycz, C. A., & Wisniewski, N. (1987). The scope of rape: Incidence and prevalence of sexual aggression and victimization in a national sample of higher education students. *Journal of Consulting and Clinical Psychology, 55,* 162–170.

Koss, M. P., Woodruff, W. J., & Koss, P. G. (1991). Criminal victimization among primary care medical patients: Incidence, prevalence, and physician usage. *Behavioral Sciences and the Law, 9,* 85–96.

Lanyon, R. I. (1991). Theories of sex offending. In C. R. Hollin & K. Howells (Eds.), *Clinical approaches to sex offenders and their victims* (pp. 35–54). Chichester: Wiley.

Laws, D. R. (Ed.). (1989). *Relapse prevention with sexual offenders.* New York: Guilford Press.

Lipton, D. N., McDonel, E. C., & McFall, R. M. (1987). Heterosocial perception in rapists. *Journal of Consulting and Clinical Psychology, 55,* 17–21.

Macdonald, R. K., & Pithers, W. D. (1989). Self-monitoring to identify high-risk situations. In D. R. Laws (Ed.), *Relapse prevention with sex offenders* (pp. 96–104). New York: Guilford Press.

Malamuth, N. M. (1981). Rape proclivity among males. *Journal of Social Issues, 37,* 138–156.

Malamuth, N. M. (1983). Factors associated with rape as predictors of laboratory aggression against women. *Journal of Personality and Social Psychology, 45,* 432–442.

Malamuth, N. M. (1986). Predictors of naturalistic sexual aggression. *Journal of Personality and Social Psychology, 50,* 953–962.

Malamuth, N. M., & Brown, L. M. (1994). Sexually aggressive men's perceptions of women's communications: Testing three explanations. *Journal of Personality and Social Psychology, 67,* 699–712.

Malamuth, N. M., & Check, J. V. P. (1983). Sexual arousal to rape depictions. *Journal of Abnormal Psychology, 92,* 330–340.

Malamuth, N. M., Heavey, C. L., & Linz, D. (1993). Predicting men's antisocial behavior against women: The interaction model of sexual aggression. In G. C. N. Hall, R. Hirschman, J. R. Graham, & M. S. Zaragoza (Eds.), *Sexual aggression: Issues in etiology, assessment and treatment* (pp. 63–97). Washington, DC: Taylor and Francis.

Malamuth, N. M., Sockloskie, R., Koss, M. P., & Tanaka, J. (1991). The characteristics of aggressors against women: Testing a model using a national sample of college students. *Journal of Consulting and Clinical Psychology, 59,* 670–681.

Marlatt, G. A., & Gordon, J. R. (1985). *Relapse prevention: Maintenance strategies in the treatment of addictive behaviors.* New York: Guilford Press.

Marshall, W. L. (1989a). Invited essay: Intimacy, loneliness and sexual offenders. *Behaviour Research and Therapy, 27,* 491–503.

Marshall, W. L. (1989b). Pornography and sex offenders. In D. Zillman & J. Bryant (Eds.), *Pornography: Research advances and policy considerations* (pp. 185–214). Hillsdale, NJ: Erlbaum.

Marshall, W. L. (1993). The treatment of sex offenders: What do the outcome data tell us? A reply to Quinsey, Harris, Rice, and Lalumière. *Journal of Interpersonal Violence, 8,* 524–530.

Marshall, W. L. (1996). Assessment, treatment, and theorizing about sex offenders: Developments over the past 20 years and future directions. *Criminal Justice and Behavior, 23,* 162–199.

Marshall, W. L., & Barbaree, H. E. (1984). A behavioral view of rape. *International Journal of Law and Psychiatry, 7,* 51–77.

Marshall, W. L., & Barbaree, H. E. (1988). The long-term evaluation of a behavioural treatment program for child molesters. *Behaviour Research and Therapy, 26,* 499–511.

Marshall, W. L., & Barbaree, H. E. (1989). Sexual violence. In K. Howells & C. R. Hollin (Eds.), *Clinical approaches to violence* (pp. 205–246). New York: Wiley.

Marshall, W. L., & Barbaree, H. E. (1990a). An integrated theory of the etiology of sexual offending. In W. L. Marshall, D. R. Laws, & H. E. Barbaree (Eds.), *Handbook of sexual assault: Issues, theories, and treatment of the offender* (pp. 257–275). New York: Plenum Press.

Marshall, W. L., & Barbaree, H. E. (1990b). Outcome of cognitive-behavioral treatment. In W. L. Marshall, D. R. Laws, & H. E. Barbaree (Eds.), *Handbook of sexual assault: Issues, theories, and treatment of the offender* (pp. 363–385). New York: Plenum Press.

Marshall, W. L., Hudson, S. M., Jones, R., Fernandez, Y. M. (1995). Empathy in sex offenders. *Clinical Psychology Review, 15,* 99–113.

Marshall, W. L., Jones, R. J., Ward, T., Johnston, P. W., & Barbaree, H. E. (1991). Treatment outcome with sex offenders. *Clinical Psychology Review, 11,* 465–485.

Maslow, A. H. (1940). Dominance-quality and social behavior in infra-human primates. *Journal of Social Psychology, 11,* 313–324.

McFall, R. M. (1990). The enhancement of social skills: An information-processing analysis. In W. L. Marshall, D. R. Laws, & H. E. Barbaree (Eds.), *Handbook of sexual assault: Issues, theories, and treatment of the offender* (pp. 311–330). New York: Plenum Press.

Millon, T. (1991). Classification in psychopathology: Rationale, alternatives, and standards. *Journal of Abnormal Psychology, 100,* 245–261.

Muehlenhard, C. L., Powch, I. G., Phelps, J. L., & Giusti, L. M. (1992). Definitions of rape: Scientific and political implications. *Journal of Social Issues, 48,* 23–44.

Murphy, W. D., Coleman, E. M., & Haynes, M. R. (1986). Factors related to coercive sexual behavior in a nonclinical sample of males. *Violence and Victims, 1,* 255–278.

Murphy, W. D., Haynes, M. R., Coleman, E. R., & Flanagan, B. (1985). Sexual responding of "nonrapists" to aggressive sexual themes: Normative data. *Journal of Psychopathology and Behavioral Assessment, 7,* 37–47

Overholser, J. C., & Beck, S. (1986). Multimethod assessment of rapists, child molesters, and three control groups on behavioral and psychological measures. *Journal of Consulting and Clinical Psychology, 54,* 682–687.

Paitich, D., Langevin, R., Freeman, R., Mann, K., & Handy, L. (1977). The Clarke SHQ: A clinical sex history questionnaire for males. *Archives of Sexual Behavior, 6,* 421–435.

Patterson, G. R., DeBaryshe, B. D., & Ramsey, E. (1989). A developmental perspective on antisocial behavior. *American Psychologist, 44,* 329–335.

Pithers, W. D. (1990). Relapse prevention with sexual aggressors: A method for maintaining therapeutic gains and enhancing external supervision. In W. L. Marshall, D. R. Laws, & H. E. Barbaree (Eds.), *Handbook of sexual assault: Issues, theories, and treatment of the offender* (pp. 343–362). New York: Plenum Press.

Pithers, W. D., Beal, L. S., Armstrong, J., & Petty, J. (1989). Identification of risk factors through clinical interviews and analysis of records. In D. R. Laws (Ed.), *Relapse prevention with sex offenders* (pp. 77–87). New York: Guilford Press.

Pithers, W. D., Kashima, K. M., Cumming, G. F., & Beal, L. S. (1988). Relapse prevention. A method of enhancing maintenance of change in sex offenders. In A. C. Salter (Ed.), *Treating child sex offenders and victims: A practical guide* (pp. 131–170). Newbury Park, CA: Sage.

Pithers, W. D., Marques, J. K., Gibat, C. C., & Marlatt, G. A. (1983). Relapse prevention with sexual aggressives: A self-control model of treatment and the maintenance of change. In J. G. Greer & I. R. Stuart (Eds.), *The sexual aggressor: Current perspectives on treatment* (pp. 214–239). New York: Van Nostrand Reinhold.

Prentky, R. A. (1985). The neurochemistry and neuroendocrinology of sexual aggression. In D. P. Farrington & J. Gunn (Eds.), *Aggression and dangerousness* (pp. 7–55). New York: Wiley.

Prentky, R. A., & Knight, R. A. (1991). Identifying critical dimensions for discriminating among rapists. *Journal of Consulting and Clinical Psychology, 59,* 643–661.

Prentky, R. A., Knight, R. A., Sims-Knight, J. E., Straus, H., Rokous, F., & Cerce, D. (1989). Developmental antecedents of sexual aggression. *Development and Psychopathology, 1,* 153–169.

Pryor, J. B. (1987). Sexual harassment proclivities in men. *Sex Roles, 17,* 269–290.

Pryor, J. B., LaVite, C. M., & Stoller, L. M. (1993). A social psychological analysis of sexual harassment: The person/situation interaction. *Journal of Vocational Behavior, 42,* 68–83.

Pryor, J. B., & Stoller, L. M. (1994). Sexual cognition processes in men high in likelihood to sexually harass. *Personality and Social Psychology Bulletin, 20,* 163–169.

Quinsey, V. L. (1983). Prediction of recidivism and the evaluation of treatment programs for sex offenders. In S. N. Verdun-Jones & A. A. Keltner (Eds.), *Sexual aggression and the law* (pp. 27–40). Burnaby, B.C.: Criminology Research Center.

Quinsey, V. L. (1984). Sexual aggression: Studies of offenders against women. In D. Weisstub (Ed.), *Law and mental health: International perspectives* (Vol. 1, pp. 84–121). New York: Pergamon Press.

Quinsey, V. L., Chaplin, T. C., & Upfold, D. (1984). Sexual arousal to nonsexual violence and sadomasochistic themes among rapists and non-sex-offenders. *Journal of Consulting and Clinical Psychology, 52,* 651–657.

Quinsey, V. L., Harris, G. T., Rice, M. E., & Lalumière, M. L. (1993). Assessing treatment efficacy in outcome studies of sex offenders. *Journal of Interpersonal Violence, 8,* 512–523.

Rada, R. T. (1978). *Clinical aspects of the rapist.* New York: Grune & Stratton.

Read, D. (1989). (De)constructing pornography: Feminism in conflict. In K. Peiss & C. Simmons (Eds.), *Passion and power: Sexuality in history* (pp. 277–292). Philadelphia: Temple University Press.

Riger, S., & Gordon, M. T. (1981). The fear of rape: A study in social control. *Journal of Social Issues, 37,* 71–92.

Rooth, G. (1973). Exhibitionism, sexual violence and paedophilia. *British Journal of Psychiatry, 122,* 705–710.

Rosenberg, R., & Knight, R. A. (1988). Determining male sexual offender subtypes using cluster analysis. *Journal of Quantitative Criminology, 4,* 383–410.

Rosenberg, R., Knight, R. A., Prentky, R. A., & Lee, A. (1988). Validating the components of a taxonomic system for rapists: A path analysis approach. *Bulletin of American Academy of Psychiatry and the Law, 16,* 169–185.

Russell, D. E. H. (1984). *Sexual exploitation: Rape, child sexual abuse, and workplace harassment.* Thousand Oaks, CA: Sage.

Sar, M., & Stumpf, W. E. (1977). Androgen concentration in motor neurons of cranial nerves and spinal chord. *Science, 197,* 77–78.

Scully, D. (1988). Convicted rapists' perceptions of self and victim: Role taking and emotions. *Gender and Society, 2,* 200–213.

Searles, P., & Berger, R. J. (1987). The current status of rape reform legislation: An examination of the state statutes. *Women's Rights Law Reporter, 10,* 25–43.

Seghorn, T. K., & Cohen, M. (1980). The psychology of the rape assailant. In W. J. Curran, A. L. McGary, & C. Petty (Eds.), *Modern legal medicine, psychiatry, and forensic science* (pp. 533–551). Philadelphia: F. A. Davis.

Seghorn, T. K., Prentky, R. A., & Boucher, R. J. (1987). Childhood sexual abuse in the lives of sexually aggressive offenders. *Journal of the American Academy of Child and Adolescent Psychiatry, 26,* 262–267.

Serin, R. C., Malcolm, P. B., Khanna, A., Barbaree, H. E. (1994). Psychopathy and deviant sexual arousal in incarcerated sexual offenders. *Journal of Interpersonal Violence, 9,* 3–11.

Sherman, S. J., Judd, C. M., & Park, B. (1989). Social cognition. *Annual Review of Psychology, 40,* 281–326.

Stermac, L. E., & Hall, K. (1989). Escalation in sexual offending: fact or fiction? *Annals of Sex Research, 2,* 153–162.

Stermac, L. E., & Quinsey, V. L. (1986). Social competence among rapists. *Behavioral Assessment, 8,* 171–185.

Stermac, L. E., & Segal, S. V. (1989). Adult sexual contact with children: An examination of cognitive factors. *Behavior Therapy, 20,* 573–584.

Strauss, A., & Corbin, J. (1990). *Basics of qualitative research: Grounded theory procedures and techniques.* Newbury Park, CA: Sage.

Stumpf, W. E., Sar, M., Reisert, I., & Pilgrim, C. (1983). Estrogen receptor sites in the developing central nervous system and their relationship to catecholamine systems. *Monographs in Neural Science, 9,* 205–212.

Sundberg, S. L., Barbaree, H. E., & Marshall, W. L. (1991). Victim blame and the disinhibition of sexual arousal to rape. *Violence and Victims, 6,* 103–120.

Swanson, D. W. (1968). Adult sexual abuse of children: The men and the circumstances. *Diseases of the Nervous System, 29,* 677–683.

Teyler, T. J., Vardaris, R. M., Lewis, D., & Rawitch, A. B. (1980). Gonadal steroids: Effects on excitability of hippocampal pyramidal cells. *Science, 209,* 1017–1019.

Ward, T., Hudson, S. M., & Marshall, W. L. (1995). Cognitive distortions and affective deficits in sex offenders: A cognitive deconstructionist interpretation. *Sexual Abuse: A Journal of Research and Treatment, 7,* 67–83.

Ward, T., Hudson, S. M., & Marshall, W. L. (1996). Attachment style in sex offenders: A preliminary study. *Journal of Sex Research, 33,* 17–26.

Ward, T., Hudson, S. M., Marshall, W. L., & Siegert, R. J. (1995). Attachment style and intimacy deficits in sexual offenders: A theoretical framework. *Sexual Abuse: A Journal of Research and Treatment, 7,* 315–335.

Ward, T., Hudson, S. M., & Siegert, R. J. (1995). A critical comment on Pithers' relapse prevention model. *Sexual Abuse: A Journal of Research and Treatment, 2,* 167–175.

Ward, T., Louden, K., Hudson, S. M., & Marshall, W. L. (1995). A descriptive model of the offense chain for child molesters. *Journal of Interpersonal Violence, 10,* 453–473.

Weinrott, M. R., & Saylor, M. (1991). Self-report of crimes committed by sex offenders. *Journal of Interpersonal Violence, 6,* 286–300.

Wilson, W., & Durrenberger, R. (1982). Comparison of rape and attempted rape victims. *Psychological Reports, 50,* 198–199.

Yalom, I. (1960). Aggression and forbiddenness in voyeurism. *Archives of General Psychiatry, 3,* 305–319.

Yates, E., Barbaree, H. E., & Marshall, W. L. (1984). Anger and deviant sexual arousal. *Behavior Therapy, 15,* 287–294.

19

RAPE

Assessment and Treatment

Tony Ward
Julie McCormack
Stephen M. Hudson
Devon Polaschek

The sexual assault of women remains a distressingly frequent and poorly researched crime. In the past few decades there has been a dramatic increase in the number of men accused and convicted of the crime of rape (Hanson, Cox, & Woszczyna, 1991). The increasing incidence of reported rape and the magnitude of the negative social and personal consequences associated with this offense (Becker, Skinner, & Abel, 1983) underline the need for adequate assessment and treatment of the men who engage in sexually aggressive behavior.

No current single theory is able to explain rape satisfactorily. However, they point collectively to the important etiological role of sociocultural, psychological, and biological processes (Hudson & Ward, Chapter 18, this volume). Factors such as negative attitudes toward women, deficits in the regulation of affective states, insecure attachment, fear of intimacy, and the endorsement of traditional sex roles, have all been suggested as crucial pieces of the etiological puzzle. The complexity of the phenomenon of rape is reflected in the heterogeneity of rapists. There is such enormous diversity in the histories, personalities, and offending behaviors of the men who commit rape that no simple classification system is able to adequately inform treatment needs. Accordingly, both assessment and treatment need to address a wide range of psychological vulnerabilities and offense characteristics to effectively modify the sexually deviant behavior of each offender.

In this chapter we address what we consider to be the important issues with respect to the assessment and treatment of rapists. This includes the relevant content areas to be covered in an assessment, interviewing style, the various methods available to provide information about such areas, and a review of treatment strategies. We conclude with some final thoughts on the future direction of assessment and treatment in this area.

ASSESSMENT

The assessment of sex offenders is a complex affair that requires a high level of skill, subtlety, and resourcefulness from clinicians (Groth & Birnbaum, 1979). Often rapists lie, deny, distort, or minimize their sexually deviant behavior and they can be resentful and angry about the involvement of mental health professionals. In addition, ethical issues can arise because assessment is frequently requested by criminal justice agencies rather than because the offender is distressed about his behavior and wishes to change. Together, these factors converge to guarantee that the assessment of the rapist is an uniquely challenging task.

There are a number of different reasons to assess a rapist, each with its own specific goals and strategies. Initially, assessment may take place subsequent to an arrest for an alleged rape. The goal of this type of assessment is the identification or diagnosis of the sexual offender (Laws, 1984). In view of the current, limited level of assessment sophistication, the legitimacy and ethics of this type of assessment are at best questionable (Marshall, 1996). However, once convicted the aim is to assess issues such as treatment amenability and motivation (Laws & Osborn, 1983; McGrath, 1991; Marshall & Barbaree, 1989). Additionally, a comprehensive assessment of an offender's specific strengths and deficits is an essential prelude to effective treatment planning and implementation (Dougher, 1988; Laws & Osborn, 1983). At the conclusion of treatment, any evaluation of the individual's therapeutic progress also relies upon an accurate and thorough assessment (Hanson et al., 1991). Relatedly, often at the end of treatment, assessing an individual's risk of reoffending typically becomes an important issue (McGrath, 1991; Marshall & Barbaree, 1989). Risk assessments have important implications for both the safety of the community and the future lifestyle of the offender and therefore they deserve careful consideration.

Whatever the purpose of assessment, the clinician should endeavor to examine a wide range of pertinent information. Comprehensive coverage of the important content areas, determined by the empirical literature and clinical experience, enables clinical decisions to be based on the most scientifically accurate information available. Treatment is the optimal outcome of assessment; therefore, content areas which inform therapeutic intervention are of particular importance to mental health professionals.

The treatment of any clinically significant problem requires an understanding of both why it first developed and what currently is maintaining it. The treatment of a sexual deviation such as rape is no exception. The parallels between the practice of science and psychological assessment become apparent here (Ward & Haig, 1997). Like science, the goal of assessment is to collect data systematically to build a conceptual model of the client's various problems and their interrelationships (Ward & Haig, 1997). Therefore, a comprehensive clinical formulation of sexually aggressive behavior considers an individual's background, psychological vulnerabilities, current stresses, and the problem behavior itself. We suggest that the offense chain model provides a sound framework for understanding sexual aggression and also provides an intuitively useful way to structure the assessment process (Ward, Louden, Hudson, & Marshall, 1995). Focusing directly on the offending process enables clinicians to consider the role of developmental, cognitive, affective, social/contextual, and behavioral factors associated with sexually deviant behavior, and critically, their interrelationships.

ASSESSMENT AREAS

Developmental Factors

Family History

The family provides the primary context for an individual's learning history. A number of family variables have been identified that play an important role in the development of later sexual aggression. Both interpersonal factors, such as negative and distant relationships with parents; inconsistent and unstable caregiving; the loss of caregiver relationships through death, divorce, or separation; and high rates of physical abuse, sexual deviation, and abuse characterize the early childhood experiences of many sex offenders (Fagen & Wexler, 1988; Prentky et al., 1989; Ryan & Lane, 1991; Seghorn, Prentky, & Boucher, 1987; Tingle, Barnard, Robbin, Newman, & Hutchinson, 1986).

It therefore is important to obtain relevant information about the nature of the offender's relationships with parents and siblings; parental loss in the form of death, abandonment, or divorce; the safety, stability, and consistency of the home environment, caregivers, and discipline; the use of humiliation or ridicule and other insults to self within the family; trauma, neglect, and abuse within the home; and the adequacy of parental role models. The offender's family background is an ideal point from which to begin the assessment process and can facilitate the development of rapport before discussing more sensitive issues while still providing valuable clinical information.

Educational History

Rapists tend to drop out of high school (Bard et al., 1987) although academic achievement may vary widely across individuals. A person's level of intellectual functioning and educational achievement have implications for treatment. Therefore, the assessment should include a broad educational history covering areas such as level of educational attainment, general intelligence level and the presence of learning deficits, and qualitative aspects of school performance. A person's approach to educative tasks and general classroom behavior provides valuable information about their psychological strengths and weaknesses. For example, difficulties attending, impulsivity, poor self-discipline and goal setting, low self-esteem, and low persistence may all be obvious in a person's educational history. These factors have obvious implications for implementing treatment and may also point to the need to provide some form of remedial education intervention.

Occupational History

The presence of a stable occupational history is thought to provide some protection against the development of criminal behavior (Bartol, 1991). Consistent with this, rapists tend to have an unstable employment history in unskilled jobs (Bard et al., 1987). Therefore, it is useful to assess the rapist's occupational history detailing, for example, the stability, persistence, and type of employment, along with the level of skill and responsibility demonstrated, general attitude and approach to work, and level of performance attained. These factors may relate to psychological attributes such as persistence, ability to tolerate frustration, interpersonal style, ability to plan ahead and set goals, and sources of reinforcement. Information on employment history may also point to the need for specific interventions designed to enhance future employment.

Social History

People who have disruptive attachments with their caregivers are also likely to have dysfunctional relationships in other areas (Hazan & Shaver, 1994). In view of the multitude of disturbances in the family relationships of rapists identified above, it is not surprising that rapists typically have problematic social histories. Blaske, Borduin, Henggeler, and Mann (1989) reported that sex offenders typically have lower levels of emotional bonding with peers. Similarly, Tingle et al. (1986) found that 86% of adult rapists had few or no friends when young. Given the importance of the individual's early experiences for later social competence, interpersonal style, and social anxiety, we suggest that assessment should take a broad perspective with respect to social history.

Minimally, the assessment should cover the quantity, stability, and duration of friendships, the nature and extent of social isolation, the rapist's interpersonal style and associated beliefs and strategies, problems and difficulties experienced in early relationships, and the typography of intimate relationships. The types of deficits revealed in a rapist's social history are critical for treatment planning and may demand distinct interventions. For example, pronounced social isolation may indicate the existence of severe psychopathology, for example, a personality disorder (Dougher, 1995).

Sexual History

If we accept that rape is at least in part a sexual crime, the offender's sexual history, both appropriate and deviant, automatically becomes salient. The literature has identified a number of common features in the sexual backgrounds of men who commit rape. For example, men who perpetrate severe sexual aggression typically have earlier and more frequent childhood sexual experiences of both forced and voluntary natures (Koss & Dinero, 1989). Alternatively, it is not uncommon for sex offenders to have limited sexual experience and knowledge, and/or rigid and puritanical attitudes about sexuality (Marshall, 1989). Furthermore, there is an ongoing debate concerning the incidence of paraphilia among rapists (Freund, 1990; Marshall, Barbaree, & Eccles, 1991), with some studies suggesting that sex offenders exhibit multiple paraphilias. This research indicates that careful assessment for possible sexual disorders is a sensible strategy. Assessing the use and nature of pornography is also necessary, given the prevalence of its use among rapists (Carter, Prentky, Knight, Vanderveer, & Boucher, 1987; Cook, Fosen, & Pacht, 1971; Goldstein, Kant, Judd, Rice, & Green, 1971). The clinician also needs to assess the persistence of sexual activity, its frequency, compulsive or driven qualities, and any evidence of a progression in the type or frequency of deviant sexual activity (Groth & Loredo, 1981).

It is generally accepted that a significant number of rapists have been sexually abused as children or have witnessed sexually deviant or exploitative acts (Burgess, Hazelwood, Rokous, Hartman, & Burgess, 1988; Dhawan & Marshall, 1996). However, not all people who were sexually abused as children become sexual abusers. This highlights the importance of additional characteristics that mediate the abuse-to-enactment transition. Finkelhor (1984) suggested intense humiliation associated with the abuse, a lack of social conscience, or lack of identification with others may aid this transition. Therefore, the assessment process should include the collection of information relevant to these issues.

A sexual history should follow naturally from other aspects of the offender's developmental history. It is best timed when rapport and trust are already established and may provide an appropriate transition from historical elements to the offending behavior. Assessment should begin with more general information about sexuality, discovering the offender's knowledge about biological gender differences and the mechanics of sexual intercourse, moving on to his understanding and experience of normal sexual activity including masturbation, the nature of his sexual fantasies and preferences, and the nature and frequency of sexually deviant acts. It is also important to assess issues of sexual orientation, any witnessing of sexual acts, exposure to pornography, experience of sexual trauma and victimization, and finally, any sexual dysfunction.

A thorough sexual history will identify relevant information gaps concerning sexuality, whether the person requires additional therapy to work through personal abuse issues, and to what extent behavioral interventions such as sexual reconditioning are warranted. Compulsive or ritualistic rapists with extensive and often sadistic fantasies may require quite different treatment strategies than would a first-time offender. In addition, an evaluation of past offenses allows the therapist to identify the offender's typical offending style or modus operandi and the associated psychological vulnerabilities of the offender. Finally, the best predictor of future offending is previous offenses; therefore, most estimates of future risk include a consideration of the frequency and severity of previous offenses.

Psychological Characteristics

Denial/Perception of Responsibility

Admitting responsibility for actions which harm others is difficult; it is not surprising that many rapists deny responsibility for crimes they have committed (Maletzky, 1996). Sex offenders frequently deny all aspects of the accusations against them, often despite overwhelming evidence to the contrary. Even when such offenders admit their offending, they typically claim they did not offend as extensively or as severely as their accuser claims. They may minimize the intrusiveness of the sexual acts, minimize their responsibility for them, minimize the frequency of the offenses, or minimize their coerciveness. They may also minimize the impact of the abuse on the victim, both in the long and short terms. Furthermore, almost all sex offenders attempt to shift blame away from themselves by, for example, attributing responsibility to such factors as the use of alcohol, marital problems, or stress. The denial of any real possibility of future offending also is common and is related to the other forms of cognitive distortions.

In addition to these issues of denial and minimization, rapists often exhibit self-serving, distorted perceptions of their victims' behavior which assist them in justifying their behavior. For example, they see the "provocative" dressing of their victim as a "come-on," and they tend to have difficulty seeing the situation from their victims' perspectives (Scully, 1988). Similarly, the rapist construes the passivity or frightened compliance of women as a desire for, and enjoyment of, the rape. All of these rationalizations and distortions reflect the refusal to take personal responsibility for the offense. The general characteristics of irresponsibility and a lack of social conscience are often associated with sexual coercion (Rapaport & Burkhart, 1984). Often, men who commit sexual assaults do not view their behavior as rape and they attribute equal responsibility to their partners (Koss, 1988). Similarly, Marolla and Scully (1986) found that rapists are more likely to believe that women are responsible for rape, and that accused rapists are more likely to be innocent.

Admitting responsibility is often seen as an admission of weakness, vulnerability, or personal fault (Maletzky, 1996). Similarly, there is strong social pressure to deny or minimize sexually deviant behavior (Taylor, 1972). Assessments are not anonymous and offenders can face serious consequences with respect to issues of, for example, sentencing and release as a result of information obtained (Hanson et al., 1991). Assessments are usually conducted at the request of some authority; therefore, the rapist is frequently motivated to present the most positive image of himself and his actions as possible. Therefore, given the circumstances in which rapists typically find themselves, denial is likely to be adaptive in the short term (Roger & Dickey, 1991). The challenge for the clinician is to develop assessment strategies for working with, rather than against, the inclination of the rapist to deny important aspects of their offending. In the section on interview strategies we discuss this issue in some detail and at this point will only make a few general observations.

A key issue is that acceptance of responsibility needs to be presented as a positive option for the rapist. The risks of disclosure of deviant sexual behavior are obvious, but the offender will usually be unaware of the any benefits of accepting responsibility. McGrath (1991) suggested that the offender may experience relief once he discloses and will also be more in a position to receive help. The perception that admitting to sexual aggression is a sign of weakness and vulnerability can be countered by the suggestion that it takes strength and courage to accept responsibility for such behavior.

The clinician will be better equipped to deal with denial if they have access to multiple sources of information. A particularly useful strategy is to contrast police and victim reports with the information offered by the rapist. It may also prove worthwhile to assess general tendencies toward denial or social desirability with psychological scales, or to estimate tendencies toward positive self-presentation based on judgments of interpersonal style. This information may help the clinician modify his or her intervention strategies accordingly. For example clinicians ought to confront gently and/or offer alternative interpretations of the rape in a nonthreatening manner to a sex offender who is reluctant to acknowledge any personal failings. The key issue is that such a general defensive style ought to be worked around rather than directly confronted (Ward, Hudson, & Marshall, 1995).

Cognitive Processes

Research on cognitive factors associated with sexual offending has typically concentrated on cognitive distortions, usually defined as offense-supportive attitudes or beliefs. A major problem with this emphasis is the failure to systematically investigate other cognitive variables thought to play a role in the sexual offending process. The focus has been on the content of offenders' beliefs and not on the information-processing strategies which accompany and support sexual offending. Research to date has also been too static, typically focusing on postoffense cognitive distortions, that is, the distinction between attitudes that emerge as a consequence of offending and those that predispose men to sexual offending has not been clearly made. The emphasis on postoffending rationalizations also neglects the dynamic nature of the sexual offending process. There may be important and diverse cognitive processes occurring at quite different points in the offense chain which may merit investigation (Johnston & Ward, 1995).

In terms of cognitive content, rapists have typically been found to possess a number of beliefs which facilitate their engaging in sexual aggression. For example, the following beliefs have all been found commonly in rapists: the tendency to agree with rape myths and other rape-supportive attitudes (Burt, 1980; Koss, Leonard, Beezley, & Oros, 1985; Malamuth & Check, 1983); the endorsement of traditional gender roles, often evidenced by high sex-role stereotyping and conservative and traditional attitudes toward women (Scott & Tetreault, 1987); hostility toward woman (Koss & Dinero, 1989); and the acceptance and justification of violence against women (Dewhurst, Moore, & Alfano, 1992). Moreover, the possession of such beliefs and attitudes is associated with higher sexual arousal to rape, a need for dominance over sexual partners, more tolerance of rape, less empathy for rape victims, higher self-reported likelihood to rape, and an increased likelihood of having been a perpetrator of sexual aggression (Briere & Malamuth, 1983; Check & Malamuth, 1983; Koss et al., 1985; Muehlenhard & Linton, 1987; Rapaport & Burkhart, 1984).

However, when assessing rapists mental health professionals need to be aware of the base rates of these rape myths and other rape-supportive attitudes in normal populations. According to feminist theories, Western society perpetuates and supports a number of attitudes and myths which are conducive to rape (Brownmiller, 1975). Indeed, the majority of men and women share the same "cognitive distortions" as do the rapists (e.g., Malamuth, 1981, 1984; Quackenbush, 1991; Stermac, Segal, & Gillis, 1990). Nevertheless, clinicians need to ask questions that elicit this information routinely.

Assessment of cognition in rapists needs to include an evaluation of the attitudes and beliefs that a rapist holds, including: what he thinks caused him to offend, beliefs about the impact of his crime, understanding about what the male sex role involves, general attitudes toward women (e.g., beliefs such as all woman are rejecting, domineering, and calculating), female sex roles, beliefs about male sexual entitlement, and views on interpersonal violence. In addition, the clinician should note the rapist's overall cognitive style, for example, whether he has a tendency to avoid discussing certain issues, or how he justifies his attitudes. Finally, an evaluation of what level of understanding the offender has about rape, and sexuality in general, may point to treatment needs in these areas.

Empathy

A lack of empathy for their victims and an inability or refusal to consider how the trauma of sexual abuse affects victims appears to be a common feature of sex offenders (Ward, Hudson, & Marshall, 1995). Rapists are often unaware of the traumatic effects of their crime on victims, are unable to acknowledge emotions in others, and tend to lack empathy for their victims (Abel, Mittelman, & Becker, 1985; Rice, Chaplin, Harris, & Coutts, 1994; Scully, 1988). Relatedly, in nonoffender groups there is a relationship between empathy for rape victims and less self-reported likelihood to rape (Deitz, Blackwell, Daley, & Bentley, 1982).

Low levels of empathy for victims of sexual assault is correlated with higher arousal to rape depictions, suggesting that greater empathy may function as an inhibitory factor (Rice et al., 1994). In addition, increased levels of violence and victim distress increase arousal for the rapist. These observations have led to the suggestion that sex offenders possess a general empathy deficit that makes it easier for them to harm others. We doubt that this is the case and consider it more likely that offenders' rationalizations allow them to be selectively unempathic toward their own victims, rather than toward victims in general (Marshall, Hudson, Jones, & Fernandez, 1995; Marshall, Jones, Hudson, & McDonald, 1993).

A comprehensive clinical assessment of empathy requires an understanding of what empathy entails. Whereas empathy almost certainly has both cognitive and affective components (Goldstein & Michaels, 1985), we argue that the most useful way of conceptualizing it is as a four-step, staged process (Marshall, Hudson, et al., 1995). The steps in this social process involve (1) emotional recognition skills, (2) perspective taking, (3) the experience of a vicarious emotional response, and finally, (4) an appropriate behavioral response, for example, rendering assistance. It is critical for the clinician to assess deficits across this chain. For example, the sadistic rapist is almost certainly going to be quite skilled at the first two steps in the process, but probably lacks the ability or skill to experience the vicarious emotional response needed at step three that is essential to the competent completion of the process. The failure to conceptualize empathy in this fashion leads to clinically inappropriate statements such as, "Sadistic offenders do not lack empathy." It also risks the conclusion that such men do not need empathy training. It is also crucial that the clinician clarifies the situational specificity of the empathy deficit, that is, does he have difficulty being empathic toward victims in general, or women in general, or does he have specific trouble empathizing only with his own victim?

Social Competence

Rape is an inherently interpersonal crime and clinicians increasingly view social competence as critical to development of sexually deviant behavior (Ward, McCormack, & Hudson, 1997). An early study using a heterosexual behavioral checklist found skill deficiencies in a mixed group of sex offenders (Segal & Marshall, 1985). Since then a number of studies have found that rapists lack important social competence skills. For example, deficits in the identification of primary affective cues (Lipton, McDonel, & McFall, 1987), high levels of physiological anxiety in assertive role-play scenes (Overholser & Beck, 1986), particular problems interacting with women (Clark & Lewis, 1977; Laws & Serber, 1975), and a lack of assertiveness in heterosexual situations (Stermac & Quinsey, 1986) are all common among rapists.

Furthermore, a number of researchers have consistently observed that sexual offenders are often socially isolated, lonely individuals who appear to have few intimate relationships (Fagan & Wexler, 1988; Marshall, 1989; Tingle et al., 1986). Those sex offenders who do have numerous social contacts paradoxically described these relationships as superficial and lacking intimacy (Marshall, 1989). These observations have led researchers to investigate intimacy in sex offenders by isolating variables believed to be critical to the formation and maintenance of close adult relationships.

Failure to attain intimacy leads to the experience of loneliness, which is a common experience for sex offenders, compared with other offending groups and controls (Awad, Saunders, & Levene, 1984; Fagen & Wexler, 1988; Saunders, Awad, & White, 1986; Seidman, Marshall, Hudson, & Robertson, 1994; Tingle et al., 1986). Although sex offenders may desire or need intimacy, this indeed is a general feature of human beings; the fear of rejection may prevent its attainment. Two recent studies provided some evidence for the association among loneliness, intimacy deficits, and sexual offending. Seidman et al. (1994) compared rapists, child molesters, nonsexual violent offenders, and a community control group on a number of measures of loneliness and intimacy and found that the sex offender groups were more deficient in intimacy and more lonely than the other groups. Bumby and Marshall (1994) reported similar results from their group of incarcerated sex offenders. However, there were some additional interesting findings in this study. Intrafamilial child molesters were more fearful of intimacy in relationships than were rapists or the non-sexual-offending control group. Rapists also reported less intimacy in their relationships with males and family members than did child molesters.

We recently suggested that attachment theory can provide a useful theoretical framework to approach the study of interpersonal deficits in sexual offenders (Hudson, & Ward, 1997; Marshall, 1989, 1993; Ward, Hudson, Marshall, & Siegert, 1995; Ward, McCormack, & Hudson, 1997). In a recent study we tested our model of attachment style and intimacy deficits in sexual offenders (Ward, Hudson, & Marshall, 1996). In brief, we investigated romantic attachment style in an incarcerated group of child molesters, rapists, violent nonsexual offenders and nonviolent, nonsexual offenders. The majority of the participants reported an insecure attachment style. This led us to conclude that insecure attachment was likely to be a general vulnerability factor for offending behavior, rather than being specific to sex offenders. As predicted by our model, child molesters were more likely to have a preoccupied or fearful attachment style than were rapists, and they were less likely to be dismissive. Rapists were indiscriminable from violent offenders in that both groups tended to be dismissive in style; finally, the nonviolent, nonsexual offenders were compara- tively the most frequently securely attached. These encouraging results suggested that romantic attachment style is associated with different offending patterns, and may underlie the interpersonal difficulties of sexual offenders.

The focus of a another recent research project was to see how characteristics of offenders, such as their style of dealing with anger, attitudes toward women and sexual assault, loneliness, and fear of intimacy, would relate both to the predominant type of criminal activity they had committed and to the attachment style they reported as most closely resembling theirs (Hudson & Ward, 1997). We argue that attachment style provides more utility than does offense type as a categorizing variable. Attachment style is better able to predict the individual's experience of interpersonal relationships and general interpersonal style, from which we believe offense style is determined (Hudson & Ward, 1997). This suggests that attachment style may be more clinically useful than the offense itself for determining an individual's motivations for offending and offending style, and therefore it may more directly inform any intervention designed to reduce the potential for recidivism.

In a third study (Ward, McCormack, & Hudson, 1997b) we obtained more information about sex offenders' perceptions of their intimate relationships. We interviewed the partici- pants and developed a set of categories from these data using a grounded theory analysis. In the second part of this study we used these categories to identify differences in the perceptions of adult romantic relationships between sex offenders and the comparison groups (violent and nonviolent offenders). Relationship commitment, evaluation of the partner, self-disclosure, trust, expression of affection, sexual satisfaction, the giving and receiving of support, empathy, conflict resolution, autonomy, and sensitivity to rejection all emerged as significant aspects of sex offenders' perceptions of their intimate relationships. Our findings also suggested that sex offenders have a number of intimacy deficits that create difficulties in their romantic relationships. These deficits were to a large extent shared by the violent offenders, and therefore they are not specific to sex offenders. As with attachment style, they represent a general vulnerability factor leading to the development of a variety of offenses and life problems.

This study also attempted to fill in some of the gaps in our knowledge about various aspects of the internal working models of self and others. In general we found that sex and violent offenders described relationships with greater impairments of features of intimacy than did nonviolent offenders. Neither rapists and child molesters were very self-disclosing; they were reluctant to express physical affection, not very supportive or empathic, and had poor conflict resolution skills. These features of intimacy correspond with the behavioral plans and strategies for negative internal working models.

With respect to the differences between the sex offender types, child molesters were more sensitive to rejection, more committed to their relationship and more positive about their partners, and less satisfied with their sexual relationship than were rapists. The greater sensitivity to rejection in child molesters arguably reflects their negative beliefs about themselves and contrasts with the tendency to view their partners more favorably. On the other hand, rapists and violent offenders perceived themselves as receiving less support from their partner and tended to evaluate their partners more negatively than did nonviolent offenders. These findings provide some evidence for the existence of more negative internal working models of others and close relationships in these offenders.

Future research needs to separate the loneliness, intimacy, and social skill domains of social competence. McFall (1982) proposed that to be socially competent a person must be able to skillfully interpret perceptual information, select behavioral responses, and execute those responses. Rapists may have deficits in one or more of these areas. Stermac and Quinsey (1986) suggested that future research should look at anxiety, assertiveness, and interpretation of social stimuli to examine the exact nature of the deficiencies. An exciting new development is the investigation of the relationship between social competence, developmental variables, and offense type. For example, Knight and Prentky (1987) noted that sadistic rapists have generally suffered more sexual abuse than other sexual offenders and have poor social competence, low levels of heterosexual pair bonding, and unstable interpersonal relationships. Alternatively, the compensatory rapists (a milder subtype) reported more benign developmental histories and were more socially competent (Knight, Rosenberg, & Schneider, 1985).

Thus, a comprehensive assessment of a sexually aggressive offender includes an analysis of his social competence. This assessment should be broad and include an evaluation of interpersonal style, conflict resolution skills, intimacy and attachment styles, marital adjustment, loneliness, social problem solving, social perception, self-esteem, assertiveness, conversation skills, insight into social performance, and social anxiety. Some evidence of the level of social competence will be obvious in the individual's presentation, whereas other aspects may be best explored during the social history. Role plays, other analogue tasks, and the routine use of relevant psychometric instruments can provide additional information. An analysis of the offense process, particularly if any pattern exists, also may assist the clinician in identifying social competence deficits.

Sexual Preference/Sexual Arousal

Interest in assessing sexual preference arose from early conditioning views of sexual deviation which argued that conditioned sexual preferences are the basis of all deviant sexual activity. Sexual preference is an inferred construct, typically regarded as a stable characteristic which emerges in childhood (Langevin, 1985) and is indicated by high sexual arousal to preferred stimuli. Sexual behavior is thought normally to follow sexual preference, except under unusual circumstances. The modification of deviant sexual preference is frequently an important treatment objective (Laws, 1984). Despite these convictions and some general agreement that deviant sexual arousal has a role to play in the crime of rape, the exact nature of this role is not well understood (Barbaree & Marshall, 1991). However, in essence the problem in rape is typically seen as a failure to inhibit sexual arousal to violence rather than a preference for violence per se.

Sexual arousal patterns have typically been measured by penile plethysmographic assessment (see below). Early research suggested that rapists responded more to both sexual and nonsexual violence against women than did nonrapists (e. g., Abel, Barlow, Blanchard, & Guild, 1977; Barbaree, Marshall, & Lanthier, 1979). However, more recent studies with broader and less deviant participants have found the arousal patterns of both rapists and nonrapists to be similar, with both groups displaying more arousal to stimuli depicting consenting sexual intercourse than coercive sex (e.g., Baxter, Barbaree, & Marshall, 1986; Blader & Marshall, 1989; Murphy, Haynes, Coleman, & Flanagan, 1985). It is therefore possible that the sexual preference hypothesis applies primarily to the more extreme type of rapist (sadistic rapists). Barbaree, Seto, Serin, Amos, and Preston's (1994) finding that sexual arousal to rape stimuli was higher on the sexual subtypes on the Massachusetts typology (Knight & Prentky, 1990) supports this position. Also supportive is the finding that sexual arousal to nonsexual, violent stimuli may be associated with violent recidivism in rapists (Rice, Harris, & Quinsey, 1990), suggesting that it might be worthwhile to target this factor specifically in assessment. From a different perspective, Proulx and his colleagues related personality traits to sexual preference (Proulx, McKibben, Aubut, Côté, & Fournier, 1997). They found a preference for humiliation, physical rape was associated with antisocial personality disorder, a preference for humiliation rape was linked to avoidance personality disorder, and a preference for mutually consenting sex was related to dependent personality disorder.

These research initiatives may clarify the role of sexual arousal in rape and provide some rationale for continued attempts to assess sexual preference. However, until an adequate conceptual model of deviant sexual arousal is developed and supported by empirical research, the assessment of sexual preference in rapists remains problematic.

Psychopathology

Mental disorders such as schizophrenia and depression are sometimes reported as frequently found in rapists. For example, one recent study reported that one third of the sample received a diagnosis of depression, and around 70% were classified as suffering from alcohol abuse or dependence (Hillbrand, Foster, & Hirt, 1990). Seghorn et al. (1987) reported more conservative rates, concluding that 7% of their sample of rapists were schizophrenic, 2% had a schizoaffective disorder, 3% had major depression, and 6% had some organic syndrome. In another study, Dewhurst et al. (1992) identified high levels of anxiety in a rapist population.

Although it is unlikely that these rates are higher than those in the general population, the presence of psychopathology in rapists has important implications for case formulation and treatment. Psychotic disorders may require the use of psychotropic medication, whereas the existence of a depressive disorder might adversely affect treatment. Additionally, the use of medication can result in psychological interventions being viewed as of secondary importance because of the assumption that the cause of sexual aggression is primarily biological. Clearly, this is an overly simplistic view and could result in a failure to deliver effective psychological interventions.

The focus in recent models of sexual aggression has been on antisocial personality traits with little attention to other personality traits (Hall & Hirschman, 1991; Marshall & Barbaree, 1990). Certainly, those with entrenched antisocial personalities rarely respond well to treatment and hostile personality traits can lead to sexual coerciveness and aggression (Malamuth, Sockloskie, Koss, & Tanaka, 1991). However, psychometric studies have reported a diversity of maladaptive personality traits in rapists and a high incidence of personality disorder (e.g., Berner, Berger, Gutierez, Jordan, & Berger, 1992). Importantly, these personality traits appear to be related to levels of violence enacted during rape (Proulx, Aubut, McKibben, & Côté, 1994).

Religious Beliefs

Dougher (1988) suggested that religious beliefs be evaluated thoroughly within this population, as a religious background may be accompanied by repressive sexual attitudes, fears of adult sexuality, and a lack of accurate sexual knowledge. Alternatively, religious beliefs may allow some individuals to avoid accepting responsibility for their sexual aggression because of the belief that they have been forgiven. Such offenders may dispute the need for treatment and argue that their religious beliefs will prevent them from engaging in further sexual crimes. These individuals may also maintain that religious beliefs preclude their involvement in some treatments, such as sexual reconditioning procedures.

Affective and Motivational Factors

Identifying the motives or goals that underlie an individual's proclivity to sexually assault women can provide the therapist with valuable clinical information. The importance of such factors resides in their relationship with behavioral strategies and emotional states (Johnston & Ward, 1996). The failure to achieve important goals is likely to lead to negative emotions and an attempt to either change the situation in a goal-consistent way or to reevaluate the relevant goals. For example, if a rapist who expects women to satisfy his every need is rebuffed, he may attempt to restore his sense of control by force and, ultimately, sexual aggression. Some motives or goals are chronically accessible in memory and are easily activated in the appropriate contexts. The need to dominate, to humiliate, and to exert power over women have been identified as salient motives or chronic goal states for rapists and are associated with their offending behavior (Groth, Burgess, & Holmstrom, 1977; Scully, 1990).

Motivation is intrinsically linked to affective states. Theorists have argued that anger can lead men to use sex as a means of retaliation against women and result in social inhibitions against sexual aggression being overwhelmed (Brownmiller, 1975). Clinical experience and some preliminary research evidence suggests that a substantial proportion of rapists appear to have problems with anger (Hudson & Ward, 1997), although there has been a lack of systematic research into this issue (Marshall, 1996). Recent studies found a small difference between outpatient rapists and nonoffender controls on generalized anger (Seidman et al., 1994), and found that rapists were more likely to have high trait anger than child molesters (Hudson & Ward, 1997).

The difficulty rapists have with anger may be part of a broader problem with the regulation of emotion. A useful framework for approaching the understanding and assessment of affective states is attachment theory (Bowlby, 1969, 1973, 1980) because of the way it explicitly links interpersonal goals and affective states. The key construct of this approach is that of the attachment system, which was originally developed as an explanatory system for aspects of emotional regulation in infants. The goal of this system is to regulate behaviors designed to obtain and maintain proximity to a preferred individual, the attachment figure, to ensure that the infant is protected (Alexander, 1992). Attachments are thought to lead to positive emotional states such as joy (when attachments are renewed) and security (when the attachment bond is maintained). Negative emotional states can occur when attachments are threatened (anxiety and/or anger) or lost (sorrow and grief). These styles of emotional regulation persist into adulthood, as do the internal working models of self and significant others.

Recent work with sex offenders has utilized attachment theory and found that the majority of such individuals are insecurely attached (Ward, Hudson, & Marshall, 1996). Fearfully attached individuals desire social contact and intimacy but experience pervasive interpersonal distrust and fear of rejection. Because they desire intimacy, such individuals seek to establish close relationships, but their fear of rejection leads them to keep their partners at a distance. Dismissingly attached (the typical style for rapists) individuals are skeptical of the value of close relationships and place a great deal of value on remaining independent and invulnerable to negative feelings. Their overriding goal is to maintain a sense of autonomy and independence, and they are therefore likely to seek relationships or social contacts that involve minimal levels of emotional or personal disclosure. Finally, sex offenders with a preoccupied attachment style have a sense of personal unworthiness, which in conjunction with a positive evaluation of other people leads them to constantly seek the approval of valued others. This style is unlikely to lead to satisfactory relationships and may leave both partners feeling unhappy or lead to high levels of loneliness. Such individuals are typically sexually preoccupied and attempt to meet their strong needs for security and affection through sexual interactions.

The key issue from an assessment perspective is that various attachment styles are associated with different interpersonal goals. This arguably results in the tendency for offenders to experience some emotions more frequently than others, and to avoid or suppress others. For example, dismissingly attached individuals strive to feel in control of their relationships and actively suppress feelings of insecurity or powerlessness. The tendency to avoid acknowledging such emotional states may result in problems regulating behavior in situations that reliably elicit these feelings, for example, during an intense argument with a romantic partner. Instead of using the experience of feeling insecure as a prompt to resolve the conflict, the rapist may become aggressive and either intimidate his partner or displace his anger onto other women.

Offense Variables

Offense Antecedents

Comprehensive theories of sexual deviation often point to the role of disinhibiting factors in the etiology of a sexual offense (Finkelhor, 1984). These may include the use of alcohol or drugs, a particular stress or emotional state, or the use of pornography and subsequent deviant sexual fantasies. Identification of these factors in the assessment process may help reveal an offender's psychological vulnerabilities and identify which features require special attention in treatment.

Alcohol use is very common preceding rape. A review of the research indicates that over half of incarcerated rapists were drinking at the time of their offense (Seto & Barbaree, 1995). Similarly, alcohol use constitutes a major risk factor in acquaintance rape and has frequently been associated with sexual aggression (e.g., Abbey, 1991; Richardson & Hammock, 1991). When either the man or the woman is intoxicated there is an increased likelihood that a rape will occur (Jones & Meuhlenhard, 1990). Alcohol use has been specifically noted to be more common in spontaneous rather than planned assaults, and it is related to the increased use of force (Johnson, Gibson, & Linden, 1978). Given that alcohol use is widespread and has implications for other elements of the offending behavior, it is important to assess its role in the actual offense process and also whether an individual has an ongoing major alcohol problem. For example, alcohol may function as an disinhibitor or may provide an excuse for sexually aggressive behavior.

Comprehensive theories of sexual offending typically emphasize the influence of negative affective states and stress in the precipitation of the sexual assault (e.g., Hall & Hirschman, 1991; Marshall & Barbaree, 1990). Our model of the offense chain for child molesters (Ward, Louden, et al., 1995) points to the possibility of either positive or negative affect preceding an offense, and suggests that affective states have important implications for offense style. For example, we found that offenders who experience negative affective states early in the offense chain tend to engage in covert planning and are more likely to evaluate themselves negatively after a sexual offense. Those whose affective responses are primarily positive are more likely to consciously plan their offenses and to view the whole event as a pleasurable and beneficial to the victim. Similarly, the strategies rapists use in response to either negative or positive emotional states, and their impact on the unfolding offense chain, can help the clinician to identify appropriate intervention targets.

Pornography has the potential to disinhibit sexual aggression (Hudson & Ward, Chapter 18, this volume). It may have its influence as a developmental antecedent (as it condones sexual aggression), it may provide relevant material for fantasy, or it may increase sexual arousal and function as a proximal disinhibitor. The clinician should not assess just the type and amount of pornography used by the offender, but also method and history of use.

Frequently related to the consumption of pornography is the issue of sexual fantasies (Marshall, 1988; Murrin & Laws, 1990). This can be a sensitive area for offenders and many men will initially insist that they rarely fantasize about sexual activities. It is important that the clinician attempt to normalize the use of fantasy and also utilize a broad definition that explicitly includes both thoughts and images as components of fantasy. In an assessment of sexual fantasies, the following information should be sought: relationship to masturbation, frequency, themes (sexual and interpersonal; Marshall, 1996), role in offending, sources of material for fantasy, duration, presence of deviant and appropriate fantasy, the ratio of these types, and the development of fantasy over time. Fantasy material often has strong links with sexual preference and offending style, and may provide valuable information about these factors.

Planning

Inquiry as to the presence or absence of planning ought to follow the exploration of offense antecedents. In our model of the offense chain in child molesters (Ward, Louden, et al., 1995) we distinguished between distal and proximal planning, a distinction intuitively applicable to rapists. Distal planning involves setting up of an offense opportunity initially, and can be either covert or openly acknowledged by the offender. Covert planning is similar to what has been termed "apparently irrelevant decisions" (Pithers, 1990), and usually takes the form of numerous, seemingly unrelated mini decisions that collectively set up the high-risk situation, that is, they create an opportunity to offend sexually. Offenders freely acknowledge overt planning; this typically involves a careful evaluation of the risks associated with a potential assault before the crime takes place. A third category of unplanned offending is also important to consider: Individuals sometimes report sexually assaulting a woman on impulse, often when committing some other kind of crime (Knight & Prentky, 1990).

The importance of identifying these different types of planning in assessment is that they are likely to be related to quite different offense patterns, and therefore diverse cognitive, affective, and behavioral variables. For example, an offender whose planning is covert is likely to experience some degree of conflict over his sexual deviance and therefore experience greater levels of guilt. Also, he might attempt to persuade himself that the victim enjoyed the experience and ultimately be more responsive to empathy retraining. The sense that what they did was wrong, however, is likely to be absent from offenders who openly acknowledge planning.

Victim Characteristics and the Nature of the Offense

A description of the victims' characteristics can help the clinician clarify the preferred targets of rapists. Assessment should focus on the major demographic characteristics such as age, sex, and any distinguishing physical qualities or vulnerabilities due to disadvantage or handicap. It may also be useful to verify the difference in age between the offender and victim and to determine the nature of their relationship. Offenders may differ in their focus of attention, whether this is on themselves, on the relationship between the victim and the rapist, or on the victim. For example, in date- or spouse-rape situations the offender may attempt to convince himself that because he has a relationship with the victim he is entitled to have sex when he wants. He may even believe that because he has a defined relationship with his partner she may really want sex or accept that he has the right to demand it. However, if the offender's attention is on his own need to dominate or humiliate, he is unlikely to be particularly concerned about the victim's perception of the situation or the issue of legitimate rights.

We suggest that these distinctions have important implications for understanding offense style in rapists and are likely to be associated with variables such as the type of victim sought, the degree of violence used, and the nature of the underlying models of intimate relationships. The assessment of offenders' categorizations of the victim (i.e., as partner, surrogate, or object to be exploited), interpretation of their responses and subsequent behavior, feelings toward the victim, and understanding of her thoughts, feelings, and reactions should provide valuable information about the underlying cognitive and empathetic processes.

The details of the sexual offense can be difficult to establish due to the offender's denial and minimization. Rapists often give an inadequate version of their sexual offense(s) and they rarely offer spontaneous descriptions. It is therefore the role of the clinician to circumvent this reluctance and to ask the appropriate questions to lead the rapist through the various aspects of their offending behavior. It is necessary to assess specific offense-related variables in addition to the offense antecedents, planning, and situational and victim characteristics, as already discussed.

Once access to the victim is achieved, rapists exhibit proximal planning. This involves the strategies the offender uses to subdue the victim and to engage in the actual rape. The kinds of cognitions and emotions offenders report at this time can provide useful information about the way they view the victim and the underlying attitudes about rape and women. The manner in which the rapist coerces his victim into sexual activity is important to establish (Groth & Loredo, 1981). The extent of persuasion, enticement, threat, or coercion involved is reflective of personality style and alcohol or substance intake, and therefore has implications for treatment planning and risk assessment. For example, the existence of excessive violence and sadism in sexual aggression tend to predict negative treatment outcome and recidivism (Hobson, Boland, & Jamieson, 1985).

It is of obvious value to assess what type of sexual activities the offense actually involved; for example, did it include touching, oral sex, penetration with a penis or object, excessive and sadistic violence, or humiliation or other types of degradation? Understanding the precise nature of the offense helps the clinician to identify the motives and goals of the rapist and ultimately to classify the man, using available typologies (Knight & Prentky, 1990). For example, it is important to establish whether the rape was a reflection of sexual preference, anger toward women, antisocial personality traits, disinhibition, or a gross lack of judgment. The presence of aggression to a greater degree than is necessary to obtain sexual activity suggests that motives other than sexual gratification were in operation.

Analysis of the rapist's reactions after the offense can also provide useful assessment information. Clinical evidence suggests that considerable variation exists between offenders in the kinds of thoughts, feelings, and behaviors they experience after a sexual assault. For example, a positive evaluation may result in a resolution to continue offending, whereas a negative one may lead to a future attempt to avoid further sexual aggression against women. Additional information may include the precautions the rapist took not to be discovered, what he did immediately after the offense, his perceptions of the victim at this time, his knowledge of how the was offense was discovered, and perceptions of the reactions of others once the offense was attributed to him.

ASSESSMENT METHODS

A variety of methods have been used to assess and evaluate sex offenders, including the clinical interview, psychological tests, and phallometry. Each of these methods will be discussed in this section. In addition, it is also useful to supplement information obtained by these means with that provided by medical and neuropsychological examination; for some men, medical or cognitive problems may result in sexually deviant behavior (Berlin, 1983).

The Clinical Interview

The clinical interview is the most common, and arguably the most important assessment device available to the clinician, regardless of the area being investigated. However, this form of self-report is unreliable at the best of times, especially so in men accused of sexual aggressive crimes. The obvious corollary of this is that collateral information is of considerable value, for example, police reports, any victim statements or reports concerning him or her, arrest records, previous psychological or medical reports, and any prior documentation from other interviews or treatment. This information is not only useful in corroborating or challenging the offender's description of events during interview, it is also invaluable in preparing for the interview in that information regarding the type of offense and offender is likely to be of benefit in formulating interview strategies, as well as predicting issues and the likely excuse syntax.

It is important that the information gathered is accurate as well as complete. Completeness at this stage in the process means that the disclosure, often termed taking physical responsibility, has taken place. This implies that full acceptance of responsibility, including insight into the damage inflicted on the victim (i.e., empathy) is not a requirement of an acceptable assessment interview. Indeed, one can argue that this is a therapy issue and ought not be dealt with at the initial interview stage.

What this does raise, however, is the delicate balance between accepting the often very distorted views regarding the harm done (and locus of responsibility) to generate a full description of events, and the risk of collusion. Accepting that there can be a two-stage process, and deliberately not using the usual acceptance cues in the face of distorted thinking, is a middle path. More contentious is the use of strategies such as normalizing (e.g., "anyone in that situation would have done what you did"), actively seeking to reduce the moral seriousness of the offense, or even exploiting the offender's willingness to blame others, including the victim, that is, processes designed to create a close and supportive bond between the interviewer and the offender. These strategies risk collusion but can enhance the first level of acceptance of responsibility. At the very least we need a good physical description of the offense and its precursors and that should avoid as much as possible the offender's own blaming process, which might lead him to minimize or outrightly deny his behavior. Finally, the issue of accuracy is also important because material fabricated out of confusion, fatigue, or a desire to please the interviewer or to avoid punishment is of even less value than are inadequate accounts (Gudjonsson, 1992).

Clinicians can divide process issues into those that set the stage for the interview and those designed to manage the inevitable issues that arise during the interview itself: Sex offenders frequently have never talked to anyone about what they have done and are likely to be understandably reluctant to discuss such issues with the clinician. Ethical guidelines require informed consent. This implies that the offender is knowledgeable about the purpose of the interview and the limits, as there will inevitably be, of confidentiality. Mandatory reporting, where applicable, places even greater limits on confidentiality, as do some employer requirements (see Cumming & Buell, 1996, for a discussion of these issues in the context of managing offenders in the community). Offender disclosure is in most cases enhanced by an honest and direct discussion of the benefits and risks of cooperation. Not to inform regarding purpose and confidentially is ethically indefensible.

What is ethically less clear is the status of techniques such as leading questions and the more subtle variant, the presentation of alternatives. In this later case the clinician presents two alternatives to the offender, one of which is thought to be close to what actually happened, and the other, considerably more extreme. For a defensive client the presentation of the more extreme possibility can serve to alter his perception of moral defensibility and, therefore, his willingness to admit to what he has done. There is also the attendant risk that a fatigued, unassertive person will agree for reasons other than veracity. In any event, the use of any style of leading question needs to be based in an accurate understanding of what might at least have happened.

Procedural issues during the body of the interview include the need for balance between an open-ended, disclosure-enhancing style, and the more focused, closed questioning approach designed to elicit detail and to diminish the inevitable ambiguity involved in the offender's description. The major problem in interviewing offenders is denial and the various ways in which minimization can occur. Aggressive confrontation is unlikely to be successful, as these men are skilled at maintaining their privacy and have been defending against intrusion for most of their lives.

The four main approaches to circumventing denial are all predicated on the interviewer's ability to demonstrate a genuine awareness and understanding of the offender's situation. The offender is unlikely to have often experienced individuals communicating understanding and knowledge about offending, and is likely to respond positively to the interviewer viewing him as a whole person rather than as the personification of the offense. Empathy lead-ins such as, "I do understand how come you . . . ", "It is quite possible that you did not mean to hurt . . . ", and the like serve to avoid the moral inhibitors to disclosure mentioned above.

Second, invitations to "unburden," with descriptions of the benefits of catharsis, can be of considerable value with clients showing some emotional distress. Construing disclosure not as "getting caught" but as a fresh beginning and an opportunity to live life in a more positive, honest, and satisfying way can also be helpful. Third, maximizing retrospective caring about the victim, as in, "You may not have thought much about her at the time but it would be great if you were to consider how you could help her now," may prove useful.

The final strategy, one we have dubbed "successive approximation," is based on three assumptions: first, that the principle of a "yes set" is desirable; second, that there is a need to avoid trapping offenders into corners from which they cannot retreat, and finally, that it is useful to place the burden of denial on the offender in the now-classic Kinsey style of "When did you last masturbate?" rather than, "Do you masturbate?" In this approach, rather than asking about the offense directly, as in, "Tell me about when you raped . . . ", the interviewer first asks about known facts that approximate the offense behavior, for example, confirming that the offender knew the victim. The next step might be to establish that the offender in fact spent some time with the victim alone, after which questions, and admissions, might move to touching, to sexualized touching, to accidentally touching her vulva, and so on until the complete details of the offense have been traversed. This process can happen in one sequence or be interspersed throughout the interview.

Psychometric Scales

There are a large number of scales available that purport to measure variables associated with sexual offending. However, because the majority of these are either primarily research measures or they are too recent for us to be certain about their clinical value, we do not discuss them in this section. Instead, we focus on providing brief descriptions of measures that are both widely used clinically and have reasonable psychometric properties.

Self-report scales provide clinicians with an additional method of obtaining pertinent information about relevant details about rapists' functioning in such areas as social competence, attitudes toward women and rape, empathy, and sexual knowledge. Their value, is however, offset by their reliance on offenders' honesty and the degree to which offenders are aware of the actual issues in question. The problem of response bias is the most serious obstacle confronting the mental health professional, and even the assurance of anonymity does not preclude social desirability effects in self-report measures (Hall, 1990). Information provided by psychometric scales needs to be supplemented by the use of the other methods described in this chapter.

Measurement of Sexual Behaviors

Multiphasic Sex Inventory (MSI; Nichols & Molinder, 1984)

The MSI is a self-report test developed specifically to assess a broad range of psychosexual characteristics. It consists of 300 items scored as true–false, and has 14 clinical and validity scales which reflect Nichols and Molinder's (1984) views concerning the motivation of sex offenders These include scales for sexually deviant acts (child molestation, rape, paraphilias), cognitive processes (distortions, justifications, obsessions), behavioral aspects of offenses (cruising, assault), and deceptive styles (dishonesty, denial).

These scales seem to be related to progress in sex offender treatment (Miner, Marques, Day, & Nelson, 1990; Simkins, Ward, Bowman, & Rinck, 1990) and there have been moderate to high levels of internal consistency reported for most scales, with alpha coefficients ranging from .50 to .90 (Kalichman, Henderson, Shealy, & Dwyer, 1992). Research on the MSI's construct validity has been encouraging and found that there was an expected negative relationship between victims' ages and Child Molest scores and appropriate correlations between it and other psychometric instruments in the expected directions (Kalichman et al., 1992). However, concerns about face validity and contamination by response biases have been raised (Kalichman et al., 1992), as has the small number of sex offenders in the normative sample (Hanson et al., 1991).

Sexual Experiences Survey (SES; Koss & Oros, 1982)

The SES was developed to assess unreported rape and sexual aggression in community samples. It consists of 12 yes–no questions which inquire about sexual intercourse associated with varying levels of coercion, threat, and force. This is a useful short, self-report measure of sexual behavior, rather than a psychological test, and it addresses a wide range of behaviors. Scores on the SES have been found to correlate highly with power, anger, and disinhibition (Koss, Leonard et al., 1985; Lisak & Roth, 1988).

Clarke Sexual History Questionnaire (SHQ; Langevin, Paitich, Russon, Handy, & Langevin, 1990)

The SHQ is designed to measure the frequency of sexual behaviors and attitudes toward this behavior, and is the most-researched instrument in the field. It consists of 189 questions about the frequency of a diverse range of deviant and normal sexual acts, and includes questions concerning rape. It is easy to administer and interpret and it appears to be internally consistent. It may be most useful in providing a checklist of behaviors the rapist is willing to admit engaging in and in identifying appropriate treatment targets. The SHQ covers a broad range of relevant topics and is easy to administer. Critically, as this feature is rare, the SHQ can differentiate sex offenders from nonoffenders and it also differentiates between different types of sex offenders (Langevin et al., 1990).

Multidimensional Assessment of Sex and Aggression (MASA; Knight, Prentky, & Cerce, 1994)

This comprehensive inventory was designed to assess sexual and aggressive thoughts, fantasies and behaviors. It evolved from Knight and Prentky's (1990) empirical taxonomic work on variables associated with sexual aggression, for example, fantasies and sexual preoccupation. It consists of 403 items covering areas thought to be relevant to sex and aggression, and consists of 33 scales covering 8 domains. The sexual material includes normal and deviant sex, sexual preoccupation, sexual inadequacy, paraphilias, sadism, childhood sexual experiences, offense-related factors (e.g., degree of planning), and expressive aggression. The internal consistency of the scales is acceptable, with alphas of all scales exceeding .60, and 89% greater than or equal to .80. Test–retest reliability is reasonably good, although two scales (Vandalism in Adulthood and Impulsivity in the Offense) have proved to have unacceptably low reliabilities. The MASA appears to be a promising sexual and aggression assessment scale, although it is still in the early stages of development.

Attraction to Sexual Aggression Scale (ASA; Malamuth, 1989)

This self-report scale was designed to measure attraction to sexual aggression; it measures a number of theoretically relevant attitudes, behaviors, and perceptions. There are a number of scales, including the 14-item (scored on a 5-point, Likert scale) Attraction to Sexual Aggression, primarily assessing attraction to rape and forced sex, and five additional scales: Attraction to Bondage (12 items), Attraction to Conventional Sex (18 items), Attraction to Homosexuality (5 items), Attraction to Unconventional sex (11 items), and Attraction to Deviant Sex such as pedophilia and transvestism (12 items). All scales have high internal consistency ranging from .78 to .92. The ASA has both short and long versions which correlate .93, and the test–retest reliabilities of both versions are acceptable. Because the ASA was designed to assess factors associated with the likelihood of raping rather than for the assessment of rapists, it is not clear how useful it is in applied settings.

Measurement of Cognitions

A general observation is that none of the scales measuring rape-supportive attitudes and beliefs have received sufficient research support to lead to their unqualified use in clinical settings. Whereas the basic assumption underpinning all such scales, that rapists have attitudes that predispose them to sexually offend, is reasonable, none of the measures has been adequately validated in applied settings. Most lack internal consistency and fail to differentiate rapists from controls (Hanson et al., 1991).

Burt Rape Myth Acceptance Scale (RMAS; Burt, 1980)

The RMAS is one of several scales developed by Burt to assess culturally derived beliefs supportive of sexual aggression (Burt, 1980). The best known of these comprise Sex Role Stereotyping, Adversarial Sexual Beliefs, Acceptance of Interpersonal Violence, and Rape Myth Acceptance. Not surprisingly, these scales have substantial intercorrelations (Hanson et al., 1991). The RMAS is a self-report questionnaire consisting of 19 possible beliefs concerning rape rated on 7-point scales, ranging from "strongly agree" to "strongly disagree." Of these beliefs, 11 are related to the justification of rape and victim blaming, whereas 8 are primarily concerned with false accusations and the respondent's likelihood to believe various individuals' claims of rape (e.g., best friend, compared with a black woman or a young child). The RMAS has good internal consistency, with an alpha coefficient of .88 (Burt, 1980), and has been able to distinguish sexually aggressive men from community controls and college students (Burt, 1980, 1984; Muehlenhard & Linton, 1987). Little is known about its ability to discriminate between different types of sex offenders or the impact of social desirability. Of concern is that about one third of its items measure distortions/myths about age, race, gender, and familiarity biases, rather than cognitive distortions concerning rape.

Hostility toward Women Scale (HTW; Check, 1985) and Attitudes toward Women Scale (AWS; Spence, Helmreich, & Stapp, 1973)

The HTW is a 30-item, true–false, self-report questionnaire consisting of a number of possible beliefs reflecting these themes. Higher scores reflect greater hostility toward women. The internal consistency is satisfactory (over .80), and some research has found that the scale not only was significantly correlated with aggression against women, but also predicted aggressive behavior against men (Check, 1985).

The AWS was designed to assess individuals' beliefs about the roles of woman, particularly focusing on differentiating conservative sexist attitudes from more liberal views about female sex roles. There are 15 items rated by individuals on a 4-point scale. Koss et al. (1985), using a 25-item version of the AWS found that sexually aggressive men were more conservative in their attitudes toward women, although generally the AWS has not proven effective in discriminating between sex offenders and other offenders (Marolla & Scully, 1986; Sattem, Savells, & Murray, 1984; Segal & Marshall, 1985; Segal & Stermac, 1984). Scott and Tetreault (1987) were the only investigators to find that rapists score more conservatively on this measure than do violent offenders and community controls. Marolla and Scully (1986), in reanalyzing their data, found that rapists were more conservative on items relating to the need for women to maintain high moral standards.

Multiphasic Sex Inventory (MSI; Nichols & Molinder, 1984)

Two of the scales of the MSI, Justifications and Cognitive Distortions and Immaturity, were developed explicitly to measure cognitive distortions in sex offenders. The Justifications scale has 17 items which assess the various excuses sex offenders use to account for their offenses, for example, stress, alcohol, the victim's behavior, and/or some other external factor. This subscale presumes an individual has committed an offense, so it cannot be used to compare offenders with nonoffenders. Its internal consistency is moderate (.71). The Cognitive Distortions and Immaturity scale (18 items) addresses the extent to which the offender adopts a victim stance and it covers such issues as identification with children, feeling generally misunderstood, feeling unloved by parents, and delayed development of sexual interest. It has good internal consistency, with an alpha of .82. One recent study found that this scale failed to distinguish between rapists, nonviolent nonsexual, and nonsexual violent offender groups (Gillis, 1991). Both scales have moderate stability over time.

Measurement of Denial

The existence of denial can be assessed by measures of desirability, for example, the Marlowe–Crowne Social Desirability Scale (Crowne & Marlowe, 1960), or scales explicitly designed to measure lying, for example, the MMPI Lie scale (Graham, 1987) The utility of this strategy is based on the notion that although sex offenders may admit to minor faults, they may fail to acknowledge their sexual aggression. The MSI also contains two scales designed to assess lying, denial, and minimization. The Social Sexual Desirability scale of the MSI evaluates denial and minimization of normal sexual interests, and the Rape Lie Scale of the MSI assesses offenders' willingness to admit sexual offenses and deviations. The latter scale requires that the clinician possess accurate offense information because without this information the results are uninterpretable.

Measurement of Empathy

Interpersonal Reactivity Index (IRI; Davis, 1983)

The IRI was developed to measure the four components that Davis believes comprise the empathic response, that is, perspective taking, fantasy, empathic concern, and personal distress. A strength of this scale is that it divides empathy into cognitive and emotional components. The difference between perspective taking and empathic concern may be particularly important for sex offenders, as they often show the ability to take a victim's perspective but they use this knowledge to control or manipulate them (Marshall & Hall, 1995). What seems to be lacking is empathy for the victim's experience of the abuse.

The IRI has 28 items and is scored by calculating agreement and disagreement for each subscale. Davis provided data testifying to the reliability of the IRI and demonstrated that its factor structure is stable across samples. The IRI also appears to have convergent validity and is strongly associated with other measures of empathy.

Rape Empathy Scale (RES; Dietz et al., 1982)

The major aim of the RES is to assess empathy toward rape victims and rapists. It consists of 19 items, utilizes a forced-choice format, and is scored on a 7-point, Likert scale. The more self-reported empathy shown for a rape victim, the less likely a self-reported propensity to rape (e.g., Linz, Donnerstein, & Penrod, 1988). Its internal consistency is satisfactory, with a coefficient alpha of .89. RES scores have been shown to be predictive of rating of defendants' guilt, their recommended sentences, and attributions of responsibility for crime. Scores also were predictive of social perceptions of the rape victims and defendants and negatively correlated with self-reported desire to rape a woman. In a recent study with a slightly revised version Gillis (1991) was able to differentiate rapists from property offenders, but not rapists from violent controls. Although the RES appears to be potentially useful, offenders have reported that it is difficult to use.

Both of these empathy measures assume that empathy is a trait that does not vary across situations. However, recent theoretical and empirical research questions this assumption, working instead with the view that rapists may possess victim-specific rather than -generalized empathy deficits (Marshall, Hudson, et al. , 1995; Marshall et al., 1993). Future measures may well embody this perspective and tailor assessment more to sex offenders' specific experiences and deficits.

Measurement of Intimacy

Fear of Intimacy Scale (FIS; Descutner & Thelen, 1991)

The FIS attempts to assesses individuals' anxiety about close dating relationships. The scale consists of 35 statements reflecting a variety of fears concerning intimate relationships, which the participant rates on a 5-point scale indicating how characteristic the statement is of them in a close relationship. Higher scores suggest greater fear of intimacy. The FIS has good internal consistency and test–retest reliability (Descutner & Thelen, 1991). Its construct validity has been established with significant correlations between the FIS and the Revised UCLA Loneliness Scale (Russell, Peplau, & Cutrona, 1980), the Social Intimacy Scale (Miller & Lefcourt, 1982), and the Self-Disclosure Questionnaire (Journard, 1964), as well as subject self-report and therapist ratings of their client's fear of intimacy (Descutner & Thelen, 1991).

Revised UCLA Loneliness Scale (UCLS-R; Russell et al., 1980)

This 20-item scale focuses on the respondent's feelings about himself in relation to others. It is answered using a 4-point rating scale from 1 ("never feel") to 4 ("often feel"), and has been shown to have high internal consistency (alpha of .94) and to correlate highly with other measures of loneliness (Solano, 1980). High scores reflect loneliness and are correlated with limited social activities and a lack of interpersonal relationships. It is widely used but has been criticized for being unidimensional. In a recent study Robertson (1992) found that sex offenders were more lonely than violent and nonviolent offenders, but it was not possible to discriminate between child molesters and rapists.

Waring Intimacy Questionnaire (WIQ; Waring & Reddon, 1983)

The WIQ is a 90-item, true–false scale developed to measure the quantity and quality of marital intimacy. It is composed of a number of subscales which assess specific dimensions of intimacy, including Conflict Resolution, Affection, Cohesion, Identity, Compatibility, Expressiveness, and Autonomy, plus a social desirability scale. A total intimacy score is derived by selecting the 40 items which best discriminate between high and low intimacy and then subtracting a social desirability score. Its validity has been established by its ability to successfully predict marital adjustment and its strong association with other intimacy measures (Schaefer & Olson, 1981). Its test–retest reliability is satisfactory and its internal consistency acceptable (Waring, 1984). One limitation is that the scale was designed to be used in the family court context and therefore it presupposes that the respondent is in a close relationship.

Measurement of Anger

State–Trait Anger Expression Inventory (STAXI; Spielberger, 1988)

The STAXI measures several aspects of anger and anger expression. It is a three-part measure consisting of 44 questions answered on a 4-point, Likert scale from 1 ("not at all/never") to 4 ("very much so/almost always"). The STAXI measures five aspects of anger, including State Anger, the degree to which the respondent feels angry at a particular point in time; Trait Anger, the degree to which an individual feels disposed to being angry; Anger In, the degree to which a person internalizes anger; Anger Out, the degree to which the person externalizes anger by expressing it toward other people or objects; Anger Control, the frequency with which anger is controlled; and Anger Expression, the general tendency to express anger regardless of the direction of that expression.

Both the state and trait scales have been shown to have high internal consistency (alphas = .93 and .86, respectively; Spielberger, 1988). The anger expression scales (i. e., Anger In, Anger Out, and Anger Expression) have also been shown to be valid with respect to both New Zealand (Knight, Chisholm, Paulin, & Waal-Manning, 1988) and American (Spielberger, 1988) samples. Good levels of convergent and divergent validity have been demonstrated for the anger expression scales (Spielberger, 1988). Initial investigation has demonstrated the validity of the more recently developed Anger Control subscale (Spielberger, 1988).

The STAXI is an ideal instrument for prison populations because of the distinction drawn between the different aspects of anger. For sex offenders this is especially relevant because, rather than varying in anger experience, they tend to differ with respect to their expression of anger, or lack of it (Marshall & Barbaree, 1989).

Measurement of Personality

Millon Clinical Multiaxial Inventory (MCMI; Millon, 1983)

The MCMI is a self-report test of psychopathology intended for the assessment of psychiatric patients, rather than sex offenders, and covers longstanding pathology such as the personality disorders as well as the more acute clinical syndromes. It has 20 clinical scales which fall into three major categories: personality patterns, pathological personality disorders, and clinical symptoms syndromes, as well as two correction scales. The MCMI consists of 175 brief, self-descriptive, true–false statements. It is designed for clinical patients over 17 years old with a reading age of greater than 12 years. It has been through a number of revisions, with the third of these being published in 1994. The internal consistency is high (mean of .88; Millon, 1983) and factor analyses have revealed strong factor stability across diverse populations. The most limiting feature of this instrument, other than being mental illness oriented, is the amount of item overlap between different scales.

The use of the MCMI to assess personality features can help the clinician avoid simplistic assumptions about the nature of such deficits in rapists. For example, in an instructive recent study Proulx et al. (1997) found that physically violent rapists were characterized by high scores on the Antisocial scale, whereas less physical violence was associated with elevations of Avoidant, Dependent, and Schizoid scales.

Minnesota Multiphasic Personality Inventory (MMPI; Hathaway & McKinley, 1943)

The MMPI is a multi-item, true–false, self-report questionnaire originally designed to assess an array of psychological assets and deficits within the mental health arena. Individuals completing the scale require a reading age of 12 and an IQ greater than 80. It is available in various forms, with Form R consisting of 566 items, 16 of which are repeated. Its test–retest reliability for 1 to 14 days is .7 to .85, and at 1 year, .35 to .45. The internal consistency of the MMPI varies with Hysteria, Masculinity–Femininity and Hypomania scales being the least internally consistent, and Hypochondriasis and Psychasthenia the most consistent.

The MMPI can provide an overview of the rapist's strengths and deficits and indicate the presence of a character disorder, clinical syndromes, impulsivity, sexual identity conflicts, or other psychological characteristics likely to impact treatment. It can also provide information about any test-taking set, that is, whether the offender is attempting to portray himself in an overly negative or positive manner.

Traditionally, the MMPI has been used for descriptive purposes and to differentiate rapists from other offenders, although this has been of limited use because of a failure to recognize the heterogeneity of the rapist population. In addition, there have been a number of attempts to identify a single MMPI rapist profile (McCreary, 1975), and attempts to identify scales which discriminate sex offenders from nonsexual offenders (Marsh, Hilliard, & Liechti, 1955), with little success (Marshall & Hall, 1995; Rader, 1977). A general comment on this research is that the MMPI has limited power to discriminate between types of sex offenders (Levin & Stava, 1987), although it may be useful in identifying subtypes of rapists (e.g., Kalichman, 1990). Rapists and forceful pedophiles may be similar according to Levin and Stava's (1987) review because they both show the social alienation, chronic hostility, and peculiarities of thought, typical of a 4–6/8–4 profile.

Psychopathy Checklist—Revised (PCL-R; Hare, 1980)

The PCL-R is a clinician-administered checklist or interview guide developed to measure psychopathy in criminal populations. In its original form it consisted of 22 items which were completed by the use of interview and file data. The 22 items were collapsed into five factors: impulsive, unstable lifestyle with no long-term goals; self-centeredness, callousness, and lack of empathy and concern for others; superficial relationships with others; early appearance of antisocial behavior; and impulsive or inadequately motivated criminal acts. The interrater reliability of the initial version was very good (.93).

In 1990 the scale was revised and reduced to 20 items which were associated with two factors: the selfish, callous and remorseless use of others, and chronically unstable, antisocial, and socially deviant behavior (Hare et al., 1990). These two factors reflect both the traditional view of psychopathy and the more recent antisocial personality disorder conceptualization. Interrater reliability ranges from .78 to .94 ($M = .86$) for a single rating, and from .87 to .97 ($M = .93$) for a double rating. The internal consistency of the scales is excellent and ranges from .85 to .89 ($M = .88$) using Cronbach's alpha. The correlation between the PCL and PCL-R is .88 and suggests that the two scales measure essentially the same thing.

Physiological Assessment

Tollison, Adams, and Tollison (1979) identified five physiological responses relevant to male sexuality. These included electrodermal, cardiovascular, and respiratory responses which have since been rejected as useful for assessment of sexual offenders. Pupillary response has also been the focus of attention, but research on the assessment value of this approach is largely in the developmental phase (Rosen & Beck, 1988). This is also the case for the slow negative-going shift in the resting electrical potential of the brain occurring when the individual anticipates a meaningful stimulus (i.e., contingent negative variation; Costell, Lunde, Kopell, & Wittner, 1972; Howard, Longmore, & Mason, 1992). This leaves phallometric assessment as the only physiological method which has received any significant theoretical and research attention. This reflects the reality that most of these physiological responses associated with sexual arousal may occur under other conditions of physiological arousal, whereas the erection of the penis is almost exclusively related to sexual arousal.

Penile arousal is measured by penile plethysmograph. Usually the man places a mercury-in-rubber strain gauge around his penis (a penile transducer) which detects changes in penile tumescence, ranging from no arousal (flaccidity) to complete arousal (full erection). The changes in resistance as the strain gauge is stretched are reflected in current flow, which is amplified and forms the output. This is transformed into mm change in circumference, and typically is transformed again into a percentage of full erection to enable across-subject or -session comparisons. The purpose of the procedure is to measure the erectile response while the man is exposed to a variety of sexually oriented visual and/or auditory stimuli which represent a range of sexual preferences. Typically, these stimuli are classified as either deviant (e.g., sexual aggression) or appropriate (e.g., mutually consenting sex between adults). The relative ratio of arousal to both these types of stimuli is calculated and forms the rape index. The data arising from this procedure allows quantifiable records of sexual arousal patterns (Rosen & Beck, 1988).

There is very limited standardization within phallometric assessment. Different stimuli are frequently used, different instructions are given, and several different ways of interpreting the data exist (Marshall, 1996). This makes the results from this type of assessment particularly questionable in terms of group comparisons. Test–retest reliability is not acceptable with less than 75% arousal (Barbaree, Baxter, & Marshall, 1989) which eliminates the usefulness of the procedure with approximately 75% of subjects, and arguably makes it unnecessary with the remainder.

In addition to reliability and validity issues, there are problems associated with the participants' ability to suppress arousal. There is general agreement that suppression of arousal to a preferred stimulus is easier than is the generation of arousal to a nonpreferred stimulus (Laws & Holmen, 1978; Alford, Wedding, & Jones, 1983). Arguably, rapists are just as motivated to suppress sexual arousal as they are to deny other aspects of their offending behavior; therefore, precautions need to be taken to minimize this occurrence. On the other hand, the likelihood of a false positive is extremely rare, and there are no instances reported in the literature.

Finally, there are serious concerns with respect to the ethics of phallometry. For example, the use of explicitly deviant stimuli can be seen as providing tacit approval for such material, and may encourage deviant behavior. This is of particular concern if phallometry is used with juveniles (Marshall, 1996). Additionally, the stimuli are inherently degrading to women and children and involve the producer, if not the user, in acts that are at best of a borderline ethical and legal stature.

TREATMENT

Treatment Approaches

Over recent years, growth in the number and variety of programs available for the treatment of sex offenders has been paralleled by the development of increasingly sophisticated multiple-component treatment approaches (e.g., Marshall, Eccles, & Barbaree, 1993). Early behavioral programs focused largely on deviant sexual arousal, but more recent developments have broadened this focus to include cognitive and social characteristics thought to have etiological relevance (e.g., Hall & Hirschman, 1991; Marshall & Barbaree, 1990; Pithers, 1990)

The evaluation of treatment outcome recently has received considerable attention, particularly since the Furby, Weinrott, and Blackshaw (1989) review of recidivism, which concluded that because of profound methodological inadequacies in existing data it was not possible to establish whether treatment reduced recidivism (e.g., Quinsey, Harris, Rice, & Lalumière, 1993). However, the most optimistic evaluators have concluded that despite numerous methodological problems inherent in the best of the existing research, there is evidence that comprehensive cognitive-behavioral programs, and those that combine antiandrogens with psychological treatment, are associated with ecologically significant reductions in recidivism for treated sex offenders (Marshall, Jones, Ward, Johnston, & Barbaree, 1991; Marshall & Pithers, 1994; Pithers, 1993).

Hall (1995) has conducted a meta-analysis of 12 treatment outcome studies published since the Furby et al. (1989) study, which meet relatively stringent research criteria (e.g., reported recidivism rates, using a comparison or control group). Overall, a small but robust treatment effect was obtained; cognitive-behavioral and hormonal treatments were associated with a larger effect than were behavioral programs, as were studies with higher recidivism base rates and outpatient treatment studies. Over an average 6.85 years of follow-up, 19% of treated offenders and 27% of comparison/control offenders reoffended.

Many outcome studies do not provide data separately for each subtype of sex offender, so it is not possible to examine whether some groups show better outcomes than others. This was generally the case for the studies reviewed by Furby et al. (1989). Of those that do, most report better outcomes for child sex offenders and exhibitionists than for rapists. For example, Maletzky (1991) reported outcome data collated over a 17-year period for 5,000 sex offenders referred for treatment of a variety of paraphilias. Because this is an outpatient program, those assessed as most dangerous were not included but instead were referred for residential treatment elsewhere. Follow-up lengths varied from 1 to 17 years, with 65% followed for more than 3 years. Only 2.9% of the sample were rapists. Whereas 1.3% of the 2865 heterosexual pedophiles in the sample were apprehended by police during the follow-up period, the corresponding figure for rapists was 13.8% (Maletzky, 1991). Examination of recidivism over a 6-year period after treatment in the Vermont Treatment Program for Sexual Aggressors suggested similar differences; 15% of rapists were reconvicted compared with 2 to 3% of child sex offenders (Hildebran & Pithers, 1992; Pithers & Cumming, 1989).

Results such as these led some to conclude that current psychological treatment approaches are not as effective with rapists. This may be true, but given the variability in base rates of reoffending across different populations, it may simply reflect differential offending risk in the subtypes treated. Factors associated with variability in recidivism estimates may be even more influential for rapists than for child sex offenders. Reporting rates may be lower and greater heterogeneity in rapists may contribute to greater variability in recidivism (Rice et al., 1990). Typically, rapist research samples are small and thus may be more prone to skew by a small number of high risk, highly deviant individuals.

The California Sex Offender Treatment and Evaluation Project was a scientifically rigorous attempt to examine issues of treatment effectiveness with rapists and child sex offenders (Marques, Day, Nelson, & West, 1993, 1994). Although the treatment component of the program has closed, aftercare and follow-up continues, so data reported are suggestive. Findings reported by Marques et al. (1994) were for an average follow-up period of just under 3 years and for 59 rapists, of whom 22 were considered to have been treated; the remainder are untreated controls. Subsequent recidivism comparisons appear particularly positive; rapists with further sexual offenses have been detected in 9.1% of treated offenders and 27.8% of controls who volunteered to participate in the program but were randomly allocated to the no-treatment control condition.

Although increased interest in the treatment of sexual offending has led to the development of more sophisticated approaches which include a broader range of offense-related intervention components, to date many programs continue to treat different types of sex offenders using essentially similar programs and components. Close scrutiny of those treatment reports which describe the sample in terms of offense subtype (i.e., offenses involving adult victims, child sex offenses, exhibitionism) reveals generally that the vast majority of offenders in the program are child sex offenders (e.g., Marques et al., 1994). The number of rapists invariably is small; for example, Maletzky's (1991) findings were based on 145 rapists, 2.9% of his sample. Hildebran's and Pithers's (1992) conclusions are based on 20 rapists and 247 pedophiles. Although difficult to establish exactly (G. C. N. Hall, personal communication, August 28th, 1995), Hall's (1995) meta-analysis appears to be based on about 75 rapists fewer than 6% of the offenders in the total study pool. Thus, we can argue that such programs have been developed primarily to meet the perceived criminogenic needs of child sex offenders (Marshall, 1993), and the specific treatment issues for rapists have been underresearched. As noted earlier, there are substantial differences between child molesters and rapists, and yet few programs cater exclusively to rapists or even modify their general approach when rapists are included.

Even if we assume that treatment is effective for those who complete it, its value also is questionable if few offenders agree to participate in and complete the program. Clinical experience suggests that engaging rapists in treatment is much more difficult (Marshall, 1993) and the Marques et al. (1994) data clearly support this. Of those eligible for the California Sex Offender Treatment and Evaluation Project, 24.3% of rapists and 44% of child molesters volunteered to take part. Of those randomly selected for treatment from this group, 34% of rapists and 67% of child sex offenders were deemed to have completed treatment. Such attrition may account in part for the small sample sizes reported earlier.

Treatment Guidelines

There exist substantial grounds for arguing that rapists require concerted research and clinical attention if the gains made with child sex offenders, and arguably with exhibitionists, are to be paralleled with these serious sexual assaulters of adults. Some of the issues that still require work include treatment intensity, the context in which rapists may be best treated, pretreatment motivational interventions, and finally, how interventions might differ from what have become standard for child molesters.

Treatment intensity should be determined by the degree of risk posed by the offender. This will be related to the extensiveness of their criminogenic needs. The heterogeneity of offender deficits implies that a careful assessment of these needs is required, as is the need to tailor treatment to them as much as possible. For example, one offender may need to learn heterosocial conversation skills, another conflict resolution, and another the control of pervasive rape fantasies.

Decisions about whether to treat rapists separately from other sex offenders are not straightforward. There are considerable advantages to doing so, particularly when the bulk of offenders do not show strong evidence of an offense cycle with discriminable planning (either explicit or implicit, distal or proximal) or rape fantasizing. Those offenders who experience their offending as a result of "failing to resist an urge to offend" may be more suitable for slotting into a child molester group based around relapse prevention principles than those offenders committed to a pedophile lifestyle. It is likely to be very important with rapists that the treatment-friendly culture is created in the wider milieu. Prison environments are more supportive of key offender features (e. g., hostile masculinity, hostility toward women) of rapists than of child molesters. Therefore, it is essential that the wider unit staff are models of noncoercive, firm but fair authority, noncoercive conflict resolution, and reasonable levels of interpersonal warmth. A cost to running groups of these men is that it may well be the case that the process is more aversive for the therapist, particularly with overtly hostile macho individuals. However, less heterogeneity evident in a group reduces the likelihood of participants perceiving a component to be irrelevant to their needs and so reducing their motivation.

Rapists generally are seen as being less willing than other offenders to acknowledge the problematic consequences of their own behavior and to participate in treatment (Marques et al., 1994; Marshall, 1993; Pithers, 1993), so they may require more motivational pretreatment interventions. Techniques derived from motivational interviewing utilized in the drug and alcohol field may be helpful in this phase (e.g., Miller & Rollnick, 1991). In addition, external contingencies may be useful in countering the high dropout rates of these men, even once in treatment. For example, Marshall (1993) suggested that external incentives such as early parole are essential, given the greater level of psychopathic disposition in these men. Additionally, it is important to include components that address things the offender wants to address, for example, emphasizing personally valued outcomes such as self-confidence, as well as those the therapist judges important.

With regard to actual treatment components, Marshall (1993) suggested that specific training in recognizing own and others' emotional states may be a valuable addition to existing empathy training procedures. He considered that interventions oriented to deviant sexual arousal should be of diminished importance, but existing procedures dealing with the cognitive restructuring of denial and minimization should be retained. Although Marshall recognized the importance of treatment reflecting the suggested etiological role of the "intertwined issues of power, anger, hostility, aggression, and attempts to humiliate victims" (1993, p. 152), he noted that procedures for doing so have yet to be developed. Marshall, Eccles, and Barbaree (1993) contained a preliminary report on the implementation of some of these changes, which included a greater emphasis on motivation for treatment; empathy and intimacy deficits; low self-esteem; inappropriate attitudes toward women and sex; issues of power, violence, and intent to humiliate; and substance abuse. They acknowledged that as a result, it may be necessary to separate rapists from child sex offenders in group treatment, despite the benefits that can accrue from treating them together.

Pithers's (1993) relapse prevention-oriented suggestions were based on a number of preliminary observations about differences between *some* rapists and child sex offenders. He suggested that the finding that rapists are more likely to be career criminals does not sufficiently explain apparent differences in treatment efficacy found for rapists and child molesters. He described his suggestions about alterations to existing treatment as a mixture of speculation and process evaluation. His recommendations covered modifications to existing procedures for modifying sexual arousal to abusive fantasies, increasing emotional awareness and affective modulation, reducing emotional constriction thought to result from personal victimization, altering cognitive distortions through attributional change, and enhancing victim empathy.

Despite these ideas, the issue of intervention content with rapists remains vague. Clearly, considerable creativity and adaptation from other sources are needed, for example, from programs that deal with these issues among men who physically assault their partners. Given that hostility is a cognitive construct (Epps & Kendall, 1995) or processing bias, it should be amenable to techniques developed for other cognitive distortions.

In our view, the domain of social competence is of particular relevance for treatment, both in terms of the process of therapy as well as the content. A prerequisite for the delivery of treatment is the establishment of a therapeutic relationship; therefore, pay careful to the rapist's specific interpersonal style. The clinician can then modify his or her treatment delivery style accordingly while adhering to essential guidelines concerning the utilization of specific techniques. Some individuals may attempt to maintain a sense of felt security by eliciting indicators of support and acceptance from their therapist, whereas others prefer to retain strict control over personal disclosure and present as hostile and challenging. Such men require different therapeutic styles to prevent premature exit from treatment.

In terms of specific content, consent issues are important. With child molesters the inability of children to consent reduces uncertainty, whereas for rapists the boundaries are more ambiguous. Many rapists appear also to be violent, nonsexual offenders with highly developed skills in interpersonal coercion. They are accustomed to coercing others and often fail to appreciate that consent is not a valid concept for the victim against a relationship backdrop of coercion and fear of violence. This means that in practice, these men need to learn to clearly obtain consent rather than simply failing to obtain nonconsent prior to sexual activity to avoid "inadvertent" reoffending.

Cognitive distortions or inappropriate attitudes also require modification. These include those that assist in minimizing, denying, and justifying rape, as well as those more broadly held attitudes toward women and sex, toward their own sexuality, toward adversarial relationships between men and women, and toward the use of interpersonal violence to attain desired goals. A good procedure for modifying inappropriate attitudes is outlined in the eight steps described by Marshall (1993). These steps involve identifying the dysfunctional attitudes or beliefs, identifying the role these play in offending, providing contradictory evidence and costs to him for holding them, and finally, role-playing the expression of these beliefs together with presenting prosocial alternatives and the advantages they confer, which then are incorporated into further role plays. If aggression and the desire to hurt another really does come from the ability to perceive them as different from oneself, then part of this aspect of treatment must aim to get rapists to reduce their tendencies to view women as another "species," with differing needs and expectations from themselves.

Rapists are often seen as being psychopathic. This implies the need for treatment that much more heavily emphasizes empathy training and not just empathy for victims, but for other people generally. These men need to be trained first in basic interpersonal tasks such as recognizing own and others' emotional states (Marshall, Hudson, et al., 1995). Psychopathy is best construed as a personality disorder, suggesting that in the long term there may be benefits to treatment approaches that are based on cognitive-behavioral programs for these longstanding problems. The hypothesized higher incidence of hostile masculinity can only be addressed by reconstruction of the rapist's sense of self. Marshall (1993) suggests that the way to do this is to bolster self-efficacy through skills training tailored to offender needs (e. g., conversational skills, budgeting, assertiveness, leisure skills). This, in turn enhances feelings of power and control derived from nonoffending sources.

Another important issue for social competence concerns the assessment and treatment of intimacy deficits. The clinician should identify the offender's romantic attachment style and its associated beliefs and interpersonal strategies. The intimacy problems faced by a man whose offending is characterized by fears of rejection and the attempt to cultivate "safe" relationships are very different from one who is dismissive of the value of emotional intimacy. Unless appropriate goals related to overcoming the problematic relationship style are clearly specified, relationship or social skill interventions may be less than optimally effective. Rapists appear more likely to have a dismissive attachment style, associated with devaluing and avoidance of intimacy. Such an attachment style likely is influential in the difficulties experienced in engaging such offenders in a therapeutic relationship. Marshall (1993) suggested examination of childhood experiences of rejection by parental figures as a starting point in undermining this commitment to remaining emotionally disengaged from others. Once there is an acknowledgement of emotional loneliness and a desire for intimacy, then skills training procedures can begin.

Pithers (1993) suggested that rapists are also more impulsive than child molesters in that their relapse precursors can occur more rapidly. This implies that more emphasis needs to be given to identifying the features that trigger the chain, rather than being so concerned with what goes on in the middle. It also suggests that community external management aspects of interventions may need to be more intensive for these men when compared with those who become at risk more gradually. On release, monitoring of social contacts may be more important; antisocial, pro-rape peers may undermine treatment gains, as may difficulties in relating to women and establishing or resuming sexual relationships. For those for whom the impulse to offend genuinely appears only to occur immediately after being denied consensual sex, relapse prevention may not make good sense as an overall intervention. There are approaches elsewhere in the offender rehabilitation field for treatment of impulsivity that may well be more relevant (e.g., Serin & Kuriychuk, 1994). Similarly, the broad cognitive skills packages which attempt to correct other thinking process deficits often found in career criminals should be added for those whose offending forms part of a generally criminal lifestyle (Porporino, Fabiano, & Robinson, 1991; Porporino & Robinson, 1995).

Finally, anger management, stress management, and a variety of other interpersonal skills are likely to be important, at least for some individuals (Ward, Hudson, et al., 1995).

Similarly, drug and alcohol interventions are likely to be useful (Marshall, 1996). Generally, sexual reconditioning and/or fantasy retraining procedures are considered less important, but again they may be vital for particular offenders who either experience their own sexual urges as difficult to control (because they will be motivated to use coercion to deal with these) or experience frequent, intrusive rape fantasies (Johnston, Hudson, & Marshall, 1992).

CONCLUSION

The assessment and treatment of sexual aggression presents many difficulties for clinicians. The tendency of offenders to minimize or deny their offending and their frequent distrust of mental health professionals require high levels of skill to circumvent. In addition, the multifactorial nature of rape means that assessment needs to cover a broad range of content areas with a number of different methods. In our view, etiology, assessment, and treatment are firmly interrelated. Current knowledge of a disorder and its association with other problems can help suggest additional and competing hypotheses. For example, the close relationship between sexual disorders and substance abuse problems provides clinicians with some areas for exploration. This relationship might lead to the consideration of difficulty in regulating negative affect, poor impulse control, and the presence of overlapping cravings for psychoactive substances. The cluster of problems associated with rape might also lead to an exploration of the client's developmental history, with particular emphasis on the nature of family dynamics and their impact on self-esteem and identity formulation.

In this chapter we suggested that a comprehensive assessment should inquire into the developmental history of rapists, social competence, attitudes and beliefs about women and sexual crimes, sexual knowledge, preferences and disorders, empathy, offense variables, psychiatric history, and substance abuse. This information should be collected in a number of ways. Clearly, the clinical interview remains the primary method of information acquisition, and it needs to be tailored to match the particular interpersonal style of rapists. The use of psychometric and physiological measures are also valuable sources of clinical data. In the future we suspect that social–cognitive measures such as a version of the Stroop Test (Johnston, Hudson, & Ward, in press; Stroop, 1935) may be increasingly valuable. They have the advantage of being relatively unobtrusive, firmly tied to experimental psychology, they aim to assess core schema, and they are arguably harder to fake.

Good psychological assessment is the result of hard thinking; there are no shortcuts. Although the systematic collection of clinical data is a crucial component of assessment, clinical reasoning remains at the heart of that process. The traditionally strong tendency to treat clinical psychology as a science has directed researchers and theorists to the possible application of scientific method as a means of improving the quality of assessment and therapeutic intervention. The scientist–practitioner model stipulates that ideally psychologists should function as scientists as well as therapists (Stricker & Trierweiler, 1995). Thus, the implementing this model requires the direct utilization of scientific thinking in clinical problem solving, along with the use of empirically validated therapeutic techniques. Being a local clinical scientist requires psychologists to think more systematically and critically about individual subjects in addition to integrating research with routine clinical work (Stricker & Trierweiler, 1995).

It is our hope that using a scientific framework and the assessment framework outlined in this chapter will lead to increased interest in and understanding of the onset, maintenance, and recurrence of sexual aggression against women. This knowledge in turn should provide more focused and ultimately more effective treatment for men who commit these crimes.

REFERENCES

Abbey, A. (1991). Acquaintance rape and alcohol consumption on college campuses: How are they linked? *Journal of American College Health, 39,* 165–169.

Abel, G. G., Barlow, D. H., Blanchard, E. B., & Guild, D. (1977). The components of rapists' sexual arousal. *Archives of General Psychiatry, 34,* 895–903.

Abel, G. G., Mittelman, M. S., & Becker, J. V. (1985). Sex offenders: Results of assessment and recommendations for treatment. In M. H. Ben-Aron, S. J. Hucker, & C. D. Webster (Eds.), *Clinical criminology: The assessment and treatment of criminal behavior* (pp. 191–205). Toronto: M & M Graphics.

Alexander, P. C. (1992). Applications of attachment theory to the study of sexual abuse. *Journal of Consulting and Clinical Psychology, 60,* 185–195.

Alford, D. S., Wedding, D., & Jones, S. (1983). Faking "turn ons" and "turn offs": The effect of competitory covert imagery on penile tumescence responses to diverse extrinsic sexual materials. *Behavior Modification, 7,* 112–125.

Awad, G., Saunders, E., & Levene, J. (1984). A clinical study of male sex offenders. *International Journal of Offender Therapy and Comparative Criminology, 28,* 105–115.

Barbaree, H. E., Baxter, D. J., & Marshal, W. L. (1989). The reliability of the rape index in a sample of rapists and nonrapists. *Violence and Victims, 4,* 299–306.

Barbaree, H. E., & Marshall, W. L. (1991). The role of male sexual arousal in rape: Six models. *Journal of Consulting and Clinical Psychology, 59,* 621–630.

Barbaree, H. E., Marshall, W. L., & Lanthier, R. D. (1979). Deviant sexual arousal in rapists. *Behaviour Research and Therapy, 17,* 215–222.

Barbaree, H. E., Seto, M. C., Serin, R. C., Amos, N. L., & Preston, D. L. (1994). Comparisons between sexual and nonsexual rapist subtypes. *Criminal Justice and Behavior, 21,* 95–114.

Bard, L. A., Carter, D. L., Cerce, D. D., Knight, R. A., Rosenberg, R., & Schneider, B. (1987). A descriptive study of rapists and child molesters: Developmental, clinical, and criminal characteristics. *Behavioral Sciences and the Law, 5,* 203–220.

Barlow, D. H., Abel, G. G., Blanchard, E. B., Bristow, A. R., & Young, D. L. (1977). A heterosexual skills behavior checklist for males. *Behavior Therapy, 8,* 229–239.

Bartol, C. (1991). *Criminal behavior: A psychosocial approach.* Englewood Cliffs, NJ: Prentice Hall.

Baxter, D. J., Barbaree, H. E., & Marshall, W. L. (1986). Sexual responses to consenting and forced sex in a large sample of rapists and nonrapists. *Behaviour Research and Therapy, 24,* 513–520.

Becker, J. V., Skinner, L. J., & Abel, G. G. (1983). Sequelae of sexual assault: The survivor's perspective. In J. G. Greer & I. R. Stuart (Eds.), *The sexual aggressor: Current perspectives on treatment* (pp. 240–266). New York: Van Nostrand Reinhold.

Berlin, E. S. (1983). Sex offenders: A biomedical perspective and a status report on biomedical treatment. In J. G. Greer & I. R. Stuart (Eds.), *The sexual aggressor: Current perspectives on treatment* (pp. 83–123). New York: Van Nostrand Reinhold.

Berner, W., Berger, P., Gutierez, K., Jordan, B., & Berger, J. (1992). The role of personality disorder in the treatment of sexual offenders. *Journal of Offender Rehabilitation, 18,* 25–37.

Blader, J. C., & Marshall, W. L. (1989). Is assessment of sexual arousal in rapists worthwhile? A critique of current methods and the development of a response compatibility approach. *Clinical Psychology Review, 9,* 569–587.

Blaske, D. M., Borduin, C. M., Henggeler, S. W., & Mann, B. J. (1989). Individual, family and peer characteristics of adolescent sex offenders and assaultive offenders. *Developmental Psychology, 25,* 846–855.

Bowlby, J. (1969). *Attachment and loss: Vol. 1. Attachment.* New York: Basic Books.

Bowlby, J. (1973). *Attachment and loss: Vol. 2. Separation.* New York: Basic Books.

Bowlby, J. (1980). *Attachment and loss: Vol. 3. Loss, sadness and depression.* New York: Basic Books.

Briere, J., & Malamuth, N. M. (1983). Self-reported likelihood of sexually aggressive behavior: Attitudinal versus sexual explanations. *Journal of Research in Personality, 17,* 315–323.

Brownmiller, S. (1975). *Against our will: Men, women, and rape.* New York: Simon & Schuster.

Bumby, K. M., & Marshall, W. L. (1994, October). *Loneliness and intimacy deficits among incarcerated rapists and child molesters.* Paper presented at the 13th annual research and treatment conference of the Association for the Treatment of Sexual Abusers, San Francisco.

Burgess, A. W., Hazelwood, R. R., Rokous, F. E., Hartman, C. R., & Burgess, A. (1988). Serial rapists and their victims: Reenactment and repetition. *Annals of the New York Academy of Sciences, 528,* 277–295.

Burt, M. R. (1980). Cultural myths and supports for rape. *Journal of Personality and Social Psychology, 38,* 217–130.

Burt, M. R. (1984). Justifying personal violence: A comparison of rapists and the general public. *Victimology: An International Journal, 8,* 217–230.

Carter, D. L., Prentky, R. A., Knight, R. A., Vanderveer, P. L., & Boucher, R. J. (1987). Use of pornography in the criminal and developmental histories of sexual offenders. *Journal of Interpersonal Violence, 2,* 196–211.

Check, J. V. P. (1985). *The Hostility Toward Women Scale.* Unpublished doctoral dissertation, University of Manitoba, Winnipeg, Canada.

Check, J. V. P., & Malamuth, N. M. (1983). Sex role stereotyping and reactions to depictions of stranger versus acquaintance rape. *Journal of Personality and Social Psychology, 45,* 344–356.

Check, J. V. P., Perlman, D., & Malamuth, N. M. (1985). Loneliness and aggressive behavior. *Journal of Social and Personal Relationships, 2,* 243–252.

Clark, L., & Lewis, D. (1977). *Rape: the price of coercive sexuality.* Toronto: Women's Press.

Cook, R. F., Fosen, R. H., & Pacht, A. R. (1971). Pornography and the sex offender: Patterns of previous exposure and arousal effects of pornographic stimuli. *Journal of Applied Psychology, 55,* 503–511.

Costell, R. M., Lunde, D. T., Kopell, B. S., & Wittner, W. K. (1972). Contingent negative variation as an indicator of sexual object preference. *Science, 177,* 718–720.

Crowne, D. P., & Marlowe, D. (1960). A new scale of social desirability independent of psychopathology. *Journal of Consulting Psychology, 24,* 349–354.

Cumming, G. F., & Buell, M. M. (1996). Relapse prevention as a supervision strategy for sex offenders. *Sexual Abuse: A Journal of Research and Treatment, 8,* 231–241.

Davis, M. H. (1983). Measuring individual differences in empathy: Evidence for a multidimensional approach. *Journal of Personality and Social Psychology, 44,* 113–126.

Deitz, S. R., Blackwell, K. T., Daley, P. C., & Bentley, B. J. (1982). Measurement of empathy toward rape victims and rapists. *Journal of Personality and Social Psychology, 43,* 372–384.

Descutner, C., & Thelen, M. H. (1991). Development and validation of the Fear of Intimacy Scale. *Psychological Assessment: A Journal of Consulting and Clinical Psychology, 3,* 218–225.

Dewhurst, A. M., Moore, R. J., & Alfano, D. P. (1992). Aggression against women by men: Sexual and spousal assault. *Journal of Offender Rehabilitation, 18*(3/4), 39–47.

Dhawan, S., & Marshall, W. L. (1996). Sexual abuse histories of sexual offenders. *Sexual Abuse: A Journal of Research and Treatment, 8,* 7–15.

Dougher, M. J. (1988). Clinical assessment of sex offenders. In B. K. Schwartz (Ed.), *A practical guide to treating the incarcerated male sex offender* (pp. 77–84). Washington, DC: U.S. Government Printing Office.

Dougher, M. J. (1995). Clinical assessment of sex offenders. In B. K. Schwartz & H. R. Cellini (Eds.), *The sex offender: Corrections, treatment and legal practice* (pp. 11.1–11.13). Kingston, NJ: Civic Research Institute.

Epps, J., & Kendall, P. C. (1995). Hostile attributional bias in adults. *Cognitive Therapy and Research, 19,* 159–178.

Fagen, J., & Wexler, S. (1988). Explanations of sexual assault among violent delinquents. *Journal of Adolescent Research, 3,* 363–385.

Finkelhor, D. (1984). *Child sexual abuse: New theory and research.* New York: Free Press.

Freund, K. (1990). Courtship disorder. In W. L. Marshall, D. R. Laws, & H. E. Barbaree (Eds.), *Handbook of sexual assault: Issues, theories, and treatment of the offender* (pp. 195–207). New York: Plenum Press.

Furby, L., Weinrott, M. R., & Blackshaw, L. (1989). Sex offenders' recidivism: A review. *Psychological Bulletin, 105,* 3–30.

Gillis, J. R. (1991). *The rapist as a sexually deviant offender.* Unpublished doctoral dissertation, Queens University, Kingston, Ontario.

Goldstein, A. P., & Michaels, G. Y. (1985). *Empathy: Development, training, and consequences.* Hillsdale, NJ: Erlbaum.

Goldstein, M., Kant, H., Judd, L., Rice, C., & Green, F. R. (1971). Experience with pornography: Rapists, pedophiles, homosexuals, transsexuals, and controls. *Archives of Sexual Behavior, 1,* 1–15.

Graham, J. R. (1987). *The MMPI: A practical guide* (2nd ed.). New York: Oxford University Press.

Groth, A. N., & Birnbaum, A. H. (1979). *Men who rape: The psychology of the offender.* New York: Plenum Press.

Groth, A. N., Burgess, A. W., & Holmstrom, L. L. (1977). Rape: Power, anger, and sexuality. *American Journal of Psychiatry, 134,* 1239–1243.

Groth, A. N., & Loredo, C. M. (1981). Juvenile sexual offenders: Guidelines for assessment. *International Journal of Offender Therapy and Comparative Criminology, 25,* 265–272.

Gudjonsson, G. (1992). *The psychology of interrogations, confessions, and testimony.* Chichester: Wiley.

Hall, G. C. N. (1990). Prediction of sexual aggression. *Clinical Psychology Review, 10,* 229–245.

Hall, G. C. N. (1995). Sexual offender recidivism revisited: A Meta-analysis of treatment studies. *Journal of Consulting and Clinical Psychology, 63,* 802–809.

Hall, G. C. N., & Hirschman, R. (1991). Toward a theory of sexual aggression: A quadripartite model. *Journal of Consulting and Clinical Psychology, 59,* 662–669.

Hanson, R. K., Cox, B. C., & Woszczyna, C. (1991). Assessing treatment outcome for sexual offenders. *Annals of Sex Research, 4,* 177–208.

Hare, R. D. (1980). A research scale for the assessment of psychopathy in criminal populations. *Personality and Individual Differences, 1,* 111–119.

Hare, R. D., Harpur, T. J., Hakstian, A. R., Forth, A. E., Hart, S. D., & Newman, J. P. (1990). The Revised Psychopathy Checklist: Reliability and factor structure. *Psychological Assessment: A Journal of Consulting and Clinical Psychology, 2,* 338–341.

Hathaway, S. R., & McKinley, J. C. (1943). A multiphasic personality schedule (Minnesota): III. The measurement of symptomatic depression. *Journal of Psychology, 14,* 73–84.

Hazan, C., & Shaver, P. (1994). Attachment as an organizational framework for research on close relationships. *Psychological Inquiry, 5,* 1–22.

Hildebran, D. D., & Pithers, W. D. (1992). Relapse prevention: Application and outcome. In W. O'Donohue & J. H. Geer (Eds.), *The sexual abuse of children: Vol. 2. Clinical issues* (pp. 365–393). Hillsdale, NJ: Erlbaum.

Hillbrand, M., Foster, H., & Hirt, M. (1990). Rapists and child molesters: Psychometric comparisons. *Archives of Sexual Behavior, 19,* 65–71.

Hobson, W. F., Boland, C., & Jamieson, D. (1985). Dangerous sexual offenders. *Medical Aspects of Human Sexuality, 19*(2), 104–123.

Howard, R., Longmore, F., & Mason, P. (1992). Contingent negative variation as an indicator of sexual object preference: Revisited. *International Journal of Psychophysiology, 13,* 185–188.

Hudson, S. M., & Ward, T. (1997). Attachment, anger, and intimacy in sexual offenders. *Journal of Interpersonal Violence, 12,* 323–339.

Johnson, S. D., Gibson, L., & Linden, R. (1978). Alcohol and rape in Winnipeg, 1966–1975. *Journal of Studies on Alcohol, 39,* 1887–1894.

Johnston, L., Hudson, S. M., & Ward, T. (in press). The suppression of sexual thoughts by child molesters: A preliminary investigation. *Sexual Abuse: A Journal of Research and Treatment.*

Johnston, L., & Ward, T. (1996). Social cognition and sexual offending: A theoretical framework. *Sexual Abuse: A Journal of Research and Treatment, 8,* 55–80.

Johnston, P., Hudson, S. M., & Marshall, W. L. (1992). The effects of masturbatory reconditioning with nonfamilial child molesters. *Behaviour Research and Therapy, 30,* 559–561.

Jones, J., & Muehlenhard, C. (1990, November). *Using education to prevent rape on college campuses.* Presented at the annual meeting of the Society for the Scientific Study of Sex, Minneapolis.

Journard, S. M. (1964). *The transparent self*. Princeton, NJ: Van Nostrand Reinhold.

Kalichman, S. C. (1990). Affective and personality characteristics of MMPI profile subgroups of incarcerated rapists. *Archives of Sexual Behavior, 19*(5), 443–459.

Kalichman, S. C., Henderson, M. C., Shealy, L. S., & Dwyer, M. (1992). Psychometric properties of the Multiphasic Sex Inventory in assessing sex offenders. *Criminal Justice and Behavior, 19*(4), 384–396.

Knight, R. G., Chisholm, B. J., Paulin, J. M., & Waal-Manning, H. J. (1988). The Spielberger Anger Expression Scale: Some psychometric data. *British Journal of Clinical Psychiatry, 152,* 80–90.

Knight, R. A., & Prentky, R. A. (1987). The developmental antecedents and adult adaptations of rapist subtypes. *Criminal Justice and Behavior, 14,* 403–426.

Knight, R. A., & Prentky, R. A. (1990). Classifying sexual offenders: The development and corroboration of taxonomic models. In W. L. Marshall, D. R. Laws, & H. E. Barbaree (Eds.), *Handbook of sexual assault: Issues, theories, and treatment of the offender* (pp. 23–52). New York: Plenum Press.

Knight, R. A., Prentky, R. A., & Cerce, D. D. (1994). The development, reliability and validity of an inventory for the multidimensional assessment of sex and aggression. *Criminal Justice and Behavior, 21*(1), 72–94.

Knight, R. A., Rosenberg, R., & Schneider, B. (1985). Classification of sexual offenders: Perspectives, methods and validation. In A. Burgess (Ed.), *Rape and sexual assault: A research handbook* (pp. 222–293). New York: Garland Press.

Koss, M. P. (1988). Hidden rape: Sexual aggression and victimization in a national sample of students in higher education. In A. Burgess (Ed.), *Rape and sexual assault: II* (pp. 3–25). New York: Garland Press.

Koss, M. P., & Dinero, T. E. (1989). Predictors of sexual aggression among a national sample of male college students. In R. A. Prentky & V. L. Quinsley (Eds.), *Human sexual aggression: Current perspectives* (pp. 133–146). New York: New York Academy of Sciences.

Koss, M. P., & Gidycz, C. A. (1985). Sexual Experiences Survey: Reliability and validity. *Journal of Consulting and Clinical Psychology, 53,* 422–423.

Koss, M. P., Leonard, K. E., Beezley, D. A., & Oros, C. J. (1985). Nonstranger sexual aggression: A discriminant analysis of the psychological characteristics of undetected offenders. *Sex Roles, 12,* 981–991.

Koss, M. P., & Oros, C. J. (1982). Sexual Experiences Survey: A research instrument investigating sexual aggression and victimization. *Journal of Consulting and Clinical Psychology, 50,* 455–457.

Langevin, R. (Ed.). (1985). *Erotic preference, gender identity and aggression in men*. Hillsdale, NJ: Erlbaum.

Langevin, R., Paitich, D., Russon, A., Handy, L., & Langevin, A. (1990). *Clarke Sex History Questionnaire for Males manual*. Etobicoke, Ontario: Juniper Press.

Laws, D. R. (1984). The assessment of diverse sexual behaviors. In K. Howells (Ed.), *The psychology of sexual diversity*. Oxford: Basil Blackwell.

Laws, D. R., & Holmen, M. L. (1978). Sexual response faking by pedophiles. *Criminal Justice and Behavior, 5,* 343–356.

Laws, D. R., & Osborn, C. A. (1983). Setting up shop: How to build and operate a laboratory to evaluate and treat sexual deviance. In J. G. Greer & I. R. Stuart (Eds.), *The sexual aggressor: Current perspectives on treatment* (pp. 293–335). New York: Van Nostrand Reinhold.

Laws, D. R., & Serber, M. (1975). Measurement and evaluation of assertiveness training with sexual offenders. In R. E. Hosford & C. S. Moss (Eds.), *The crumbling walls: Treatment and counseling in prisons*. Champaign, IL: University of Illinois Press.

Levin, S. M., & Stava, L. (1987). Personality characteristics of sex offenders: A review. *Archives of Sexual Behavior, 16*(1), 57–79.

Linz, D. G., Donnerstein, E., & Penrod, S. (1988). Effects of long-term exposure to violent and sexually degrading depictions of women. *Journal of Personality and Social Psychology, 55,* 758–768.

Lipton, D. N., McDonel, E. C., & McFall, R. M. (1987). Heterosocial perception in rapists. *Journal of Consulting and Clinical Psychology, 55,* 17–21.

Lisak, D., & Roth, S. (1988). Motivational factors in nonincarcerated sexually aggressive men. *Journal of Personality and Social Psychology, 55,* 795–802.

Malamuth, N. M. (1981). Rape proclivity among males. *Journal of Social Issues, 37,* 138–156.

Malamuth, N. M. (1984). Aggression against women: Cultural and individual causes. In N. M. Malamuth & E. Donnerstein (Eds.), *Pornography and sexual aggression* (pp. 19–52). Orlando, FL: Academic Press.

Malamuth, N. M. (1989). The attraction to sexual aggression: Part one. *Journal of Sex Research, 26,* 26–49.

Malamuth, N. M., & Check, J. V. P. (1983). Sexual arousal to rape depictions: Individual differences. *Journal of Abnormal Psychology, 92,* 55–67.

Malamuth, N. M., Sockloskie, R., Koss, M. P., & Tanaka, J. (1991). The characteristics of aggressors against women: Testing a model using a national sample of college students. *Journal of Consulting and Clinical Psychology, 59,* 670–671.

Maletzky, B. (1991). *Treating the sexual offender.* Newbury Park, CA: Sage.

Maletzky, B. (1996). Denial of treatment or treatment of denial? *Sexual Abuse: A Journal of Research and Treatment, 8*(1), 1–5.

Marolla, J., & Scully, D. (1986). Attitudes toward women, violence, and rape: A comparison of convicted rapists and other felons. *Deviant Behavior, 7,* 337–355.

Marques, J. K., Day, D. M., Nelson, C., & West, M. A. (1993). Findings and recommendations from California's experimental treatment program. In G. C. N. Hall, R. Hirschman, J. R. Graham, & M. S. Zaragoza (Eds.), *Sexual aggression: Issues in etiology, assessment, and treatment* (pp. 197–214). Washington, DC: Taylor & Francis.

Marques, J. K., Day, D. M., Nelson, C., & West, M. A. (1994). Effects of cognitive-behavioral treatment on sex offender recidivism: Preliminary results of a longitudinal study. *Criminal Justice and Behavior, 21,* 28–54.

Marsh, J. T., Hilliard, J., & Liechti, R. (1955). A sexual deviation scale for the MMPI. *Journal of Consulting Psychology, 19,* 55–59.

Marshall, W. L. (1988). The use of explicit sexual stimuli by rapists, child molesters and nonoffender males. *Journal of Sex Research, 25,* 267–288.

Marshall, W. L. (1989). Invited essay: Intimacy, loneliness and sexual offenders. *Behaviour Research and Therapy, 27,* 491–503.

Marshall, W. L. (1993). A revised approach to the treatment of men who sexually assault adult females. In G. C. N. Hall, R. Hirschman, J. R. Graham, & M. S. Zaragoza (Eds.), *Sexual aggression: Issues in etiology, assessment, and treatment* (pp. 143–165). Washington, DC: Taylor & Francis.

Marshall, W. L. (1994). Treatment effects on denial and minimization in incarcerated sex offenders. *Behaviour Research and Therapy, 32*(5), 559–564.

Marshall, W. L. (1996). Assessment, treatment, and theorizing about sex offenders. *Criminal Justice and Behavior, 23,* 162–199.

Marshall, W. L., & Barbaree, H. E. (1989). Sexual violence. In K. Howells & C. R. Hollin (Eds.), *Clinical approaches to violence* (pp. 205–246). New York: Wiley.

Marshall, W. L., & Barbaree, H. E. (1990). An integrated theory of the etiology of sexual offending. In W. L. Marshall, D. R. Laws, & H. E. Barbaree (Eds.), *Handbook of sexual assault: Issues, theories, and treatment of the offender* (pp. 257–275). New York: Plenum Press.

Marshall, W. L., Barbaree, H. E., & Eccles, A. (1991). Early onset and deviant sexuality in child molesters. *Journal of Interpersonal Violence, 6,* 323–336.

Marshall, W. L., Eccles, A., & Barbaree, H. E. (1993). A three-tiered approach to the rehabilitation of incarcerated sex offenders. *Behavioral Sciences and the Law, 11,* 441–455.

Marshall, W. L., & Hall, G. N. (1995). The value of the MMPI in deciding forensic issues in accused sexual offenders. *Sexual Abuse: A Journal of Research and Treatment, 7,* 205–219.

Marshall, W. L., Hudson, S. M., Jones, R., & Fernandez, Y. M. (1995). Empathy in sex offenders. *Clinical Psychology Review, 15,* 99–113.

Marshall, W. L., Jones, R., Hudson, S. M., & McDonald, E. (1993). Generalized empathy in child molesters. *Journal of Child Sexual Abuse, 2,* 61–68.

Marshall, W. L., Jones, R. J., Ward, T., Johnston, P. W., & Barbaree, H. E. (1991). Treatment outcome with sex offenders. *Clinical Psychology Review, 11,* 465–485.

Marshall, W. L., & Pithers, W. D. (1994). A reconsideration of treatment outcome with sex offenders. *Criminal Justice and Behavior, 21,* 10–27.

McCreary, C. P. (1975). Personality differences among child molesters. *Journal of Personality Assessment, 39,* 591–593.

McFall, R. M. (1982). A review and reformulation of the concept of social skills. *Behavioral Assessment, 4,* 1–33.

McGrath, R. J. (1991). Sex-offender risk assessment and disposition planning: A review of empirical and clinical findings. *The International Journal of Offender Therapy and Comparative Criminology, 35*(4), 328–350.

Miller, R. S., & Lefcourt, H. M. (1982). The assessment of social intimacy. *Journal of Personality Assessment, 46,* 514–515.

Miller, W. R., & Rollnick, S. (1991). *Motivational interviewing: Preparing people to change addictive behavior.* New York: Guilford Press.

Millon, T. (1983). *Millon Clinical Multiaxial Inventory manual* (3rd ed.). Minneapolis, MN: National Computer Systems.

Miner, M. H., Marques, J. K., Day, D. M., & Nelson, C. (1990). Impact of relapse prevention in treating sexual offenders: Preliminary findings. *Annals of Sex Research, 3,* 165–185.

Muehlenhard, C. L., & Linton, M. A. (1987). Date rape and sexual aggression in dating situations: Incidence and risk factors. *Journal of Counseling Psychology, 34,* 186–196.

Murphy, W. D., Haynes, M. R., Coleman, E. R., & Flanagan, B. (1985). Sexual responding of "nonrapists" to aggressive sexual themes: Normative data. *Journal of Psychopathology and Behavioral Assessment, 7,* 37–47.

Murrin, M. R., & Laws, D. R. (1990). The influence of pornography on sex crimes. In W. L. Marshall, D. R. Laws, & H. E. Barbaree (Eds.), *Handbook of sexual assault: Issues, theories, and treatment of the offender* (pp. 73–91). New York: Plenum Press.

Nichols, H. R., & Molinder, I. (1984). *Multiphasic Sex Inventory.* Tacoma, WA: Authors. (Available from Nichols & Molinder, 437 Bowes Drive, Tacoma, WA 98466)

Overholser, C., & Beck, S. (1986). Multimethod assessment of rapists, child molesters, and three control groups on behavioral and psychological measures. *Journal of Consulting and Clinical Psychology, 53,* 55–63.

Pithers, W. D. (1990). Relapse prevention with sexual aggressors: A method for maintaining therapeutic gains and enhancing external supervision. In W. L. Marshall, D. R. Laws, & H. E. Barbaree (Eds.), *Handbook of sexual assault: Issues, theories, and treatment of the offender* (pp. 343–362). New York: Plenum Press.

Pithers, W. D. (1993). Treatment of rapists: Reinterpretation of early outcome data and exploratory constructs to enhance therapeutic efficacy. In G. C. N. Hall, R. Hirschman, J. R. Graham, & M. S. Zaragoza (Eds.), *Sexual aggression: Issues in etiology, assessment, and treatment* (pp. 167–196). Washington, DC: Taylor & Francis.

Pithers, W. D., & Cumming, G. F. (1989). Can relapses be prevented? Initial outcome data from the Vermont Treatment Program for Sexual Aggressors. In D. R. Laws (Ed.), *Relapse prevention with sex offenders* (pp. 313–325). New York: Guilford Press.

Porporino, F., Fabiano, E., & Robinson, D. (1991). *Focusing on successful reintegration: Cognitive skills training for offenders.* Ottawa: Correctional Service of Canada.

Porporino, F., & Robinson, D. (1995). An evaluation of the reasoning and rehabilitation program with Canadian federal offenders. In R. R. Ross & R. D. Ross (Eds.), *Thinking straight.* Ottawa: AIR Publications.

Prentky, R. A., Knight, R. A., Sims-Knight, J. E., Straus, H., Rokous, F., & Cerce, D. (1989). Developmental antecedents of sexual aggression. *Development and Psychopathology, 1,* 153–169.

Proulx, J., McKibben, A., Aubut, J., Côté, G., & Fournier, L. (1997). *Relationship between rape indexes and personality disorders in incarcerated rapists.* Manuscript under review.

Proulx, J., Aubut, J., McKibben, A., & Côté, G. (1994). Penile responses of rapists and non-rapists to rape stimuli involving physical violence or humiliation. *Archives of Sexual Behavior, 23,* 295–310.

Quackenbush, R. (1991). Attitudes of college men toward women and rape. *Journal of College Student Development, 32,* 376–377.

Quinsey, V. L., Harris, G. T., Rice, M. E., & Lalumière, M. L. (1993). Assessing treatment efficacy in outcome studies of sex offenders. *Journal of Interpersonal Violence, 8,* 512–523.

Rader, C. M. (1977). MMPI profile types of exposers, rapists, and assaulters in a court services population. *Journal of Consulting and Clinical Psychology, 45,* 61–69.

Rapaport, K., & Burkhart, B. R. (1984). Personality and attitudinal characteristics of sexually coercive college males. *Journal of Abnormal Psychology, 93,* 216–221.

Rice, M. E., Chaplin, T. E., Harris, G. E., & Coutts, J. (1994). Empathy for the victim and sexual arousal among rapists and nonrapists. *Journal of Interpersonal Violence, 9*(4), 435–449.

Rice, M. E., Harris, G. T., & Quinsey, V. L. (1990). A follow-up of rapists assessed in a maximum-security psychiatric facility. *Journal of Interpersonal Violence, 5,* 435–448.

Richardson, D. R., & Hammock, G. S. (1991). Alcohol and acquaintance rape. In A. Parrot & L. Bechhofer (Eds.), *Acquaintance rape: The hidden crime* (pp. 83–95). New York: Wiley.

Robertson, P. J. (1992). *Intimacy, loneliness and anger in incarcerated male offenders.* Unpublished masters thesis, University of Canterbury, Christchurch, New Zealand.

Roger, R., & Dickey, R. (1991). Denial and minimization among sex offenders: A review of competing models of deception. *Annals of Sex Research, 4,* 49–63.

Rosen, R. C., & Beck, J. G. (1988). *Patterns of sexual arousal: Psychophysiological processes and clinical applications.* New York: Guilford Press.

Russell, D., Peplau, L. A., & Cutrona, C. E. (1980). The revised UCLA Loneliness Scale. *Journal of Personality and Social Psychology, 39,* 472–480.

Ryan, G., & Lane, S. (1991). *Juvenile sexual offending: Causes, consequences and correction.* Lexington, MA: Lexington Books.

Sattem. L., Savells, J., & Murray, E. (1984). Sex-role stereotypes and commitment of rape. *Sex Roles, 11,* 849–860.

Saunders, E., Awad, G. A., & White, G. (1986). Male adolescent sexual offenders: The offender and the offence. *Canadian Journal of Psychiatry, 31,* 542–549.

Schaefer, M. T., & Olson, D. H. (1981). Assessing intimacy: The PAIR Inventory. *Journal of Marital and Family Therapy, 7,* 47–60.

Scott, R. L., & Tetreault, L. A. (1987). Attitudes of rapists and other violent offenders toward women. *The Journal of Social Psychology, 127*(4), 375–380.

Scully, D. (1988). Convicted rapists' perceptions of self and victim: Role taking and emotions. *Gender and Society, 2,* 200–213.

Scully, D. (1990). *Understanding sexual violence: A study of convicted rapists.* Boston: Unwin Hyman.

Segal, Z. V., & Marshall, W. L. (1985). Heterosexual social skills in a population of rapists and child molesters. *Journal of Consulting and Clinical Psychology, 53,* 55–63.

Segal, Z. V., & Stermac, L. E. (1984). A measure of rapists' attitudes toward women. *International Journal of Law and Psychiatry, 7,* 437–440.

Seghorn, T. K., Prentky, R. A., & Boucher, R. J. (1987). Childhood sexual abuse in the lives of sexually aggressive offenders. *Journal of the American Academy of Child and Adolescent Psychiatry, 26,* 262–267.

Seidman, B., Marshall, W. L., Hudson, S. M., & Robertson, P. J. (1994). An examination of intimacy and loneliness in sex offenders. *Journal of Interpersonal Violence, 9,* 518–534.

Serin, R. C., & Kuriychuk, M. (1994). Social and cognitive processing deficits in violent offenders: Implications for treatment. *International Journal of Law and Psychiatry, 17,* 431–441.

Seto, M. C., & Barbaree, H. E. (1995). The role of alcohol in sexual aggression. *Clinical Psychology Review, 15*(6), 545–566.

Simkins, L., Ward, W., Bowman, S., & Rinck, C. M. (1990). The Multiphasic Sex Inventory: Diagnosis and prediction of treatment response in child sexual abusers. *Annals of Sex Research, 2,* 205–226.

Solano, C. H. (1980). Two measures of loneliness: A comparison. *Psychological Reports, 46,* 23–28.

Spence, J., Helmreich, R., & Stapp, J. (1973). A short version of the Attitudes Toward Women scale. *Bulletin of the Psychonomic Society, 2,* 219–220.

Spielberger, C. D. (1988). *State–Trait Anger Expression Inventory (STAXI) professional manual.* Odessa, FL: Psychological Assessment Resources.

Stermac, L. E., & Quinsey, V. L. (1986). Social competence among rapists. *Behavioral Assessment, 8,* 171–185.

Stermac, L. E., Segal, Z. V., & Gillis, R. (1990). Social and cultural factors in sexual assault. In W. L. Marshall, D. R. Laws, & H. E. Barbaree (Eds.), *Handbook of sexual assault: Issues, theories, and treatment of the offender* (pp. 143–159). New York: Plenum Press.

Stricker, G., & Trierweiler, S. T. (1995). The local clinical scientist: A bridge between science and practice. *American Psychologist, 50,* 995–1002.

Stroop, J. R. (1935). Studies of interference in serial verbal reactions. *Journal of Experimental Psychology, 18,* 643–662.

Taylor, L. (1972). The significance and interpretation of replies to motivational questions: The case of sex offenders. *Sociology, 6,* 23–39.

Tingle, D., Barnard, G. W., Robbin, L., Newman., G., & Hutchinson, D. (1986). Childhood and adolescent characteristics of pedophiles and rapists. *International Journal of Law and Psychiatry, 9,* 103–116.

Tollison, C. D., Adams, H. E., & Tollison, J. W. (1979). Physiological measurement of sexual arousal in homosexual, bisexual, and heterosexual males. *Journal of Behavioral Assessment, 2,* 53–59.

Ward, T., & Haig, B. D. (1997). Abductive and clinical assessment. *Australian Psychologist, 32,* 1–8.

Ward, T., Hudson, S. M., & Marshall, W. L. (1995). Cognitive and affective deficits in sex offenders. *Sexual Abuse: A Journal of Research and Treatment, 7,* 67–83.

Ward, T., Hudson, S. M., & Marshall, W. L. (1996). Attachment style in sex offenders: A preliminary study. *Journal of Sex Research, 33,* 17–26.

Ward, T., Hudson, S. M., Marshall, W. L., & Siegert, R. (1995). Attachment style and intimacy deficits in sex offenders: A theoretical framework. *Sexual Abuse: A Journal of Research and Treatment, 7,* 317–335.

Ward, T., Louden, K., Hudson, S. M., & Marshall, W. L. (1995). A descriptive model of the offense chain for child molesters. *Journal of Interpersonal Violence, 10,* 452–472.

Ward, T., McCormack, J., & Hudson, S. M. (1997a). Attachment style, intimacy deficits, and sexual offending. In H. Cellini & B. Schwartz (Eds.), *The sex offender: Corrections, treatment and legal practice* (pp. 1–14). Kingston, NJ: Civic Research Institute.

Ward, T., McCormack, J., & Hudson, S. M. (1997b). Sexual offenders' perceptions of their intimate relationships. *Sexual Abuse: A Journal of Research and Treatment, 9,* 57–74.

Waring, E. M., & Reddon, J. R. (1983). The measurement of intimacy in marriage. *Journal of Clinical Psychology, 39,* 53–57.

Waring, E. M. (1984). The measurement of marital intimacy. *Journal of Marital and Family Therapy, 10,* 185–192.

20

PARAPHILIA NOT OTHERWISE SPECIFIED

Psychopathology and Theory

Joel S. Milner
Cynthia A. Dopke

The term "paraphilia" was first used to specify a "subclass" of psychosexual disorders in the third edition of the *Diagnostic and Statistical Manual of Mental Disorders* (DSM-III; American Psychiatric Association, 1980). The category of paraphilia not otherwise specified (paraphilia NOS), the current term for residual paraphilias, initially appeared in DSM-III-R (American Psychiatric Association, 1987).

CLASSIFICATION HISTORY OF PARAPHILIA NOS

Prior to the publication of the first DSM (DSM-I; American Psychiatric Association, 1952), paraphilias, including paraphilia NOS, were classified as cases of "psychopathic personality with pathologic sexuality" (American Psychiatric Association, 1952, p. 39). Continuing this practice, DSM-I included sexual deviation as a subtype of sociopathic personality disturbance within the broad category of personality disorders. The only qualification was that the diagnosis of sexual deviation was "reserved for deviant sexuality which [was] not symptomatic of more extensive syndromes, such as schizophrenic and obsessional reactions" (American Psychiatric Association, 1952, p. 38). In the sexual deviation category, the specific sexual disorder was described using a "supplementary term" (American Psychiatric Association, 1952, p. 7). DSM-I provided examples of supplementary categories: homosexuality, transvestism, pedophilia, fetishism, and sexual sadism (including rape, sexual assault, and mutilation) (American Psychiatric Association, 1952). Thus, the current paraphilia NOS category of urophilia would have been listed as: sociopathic personality disturbance—sexual deviation: urophilia. Because in the DSM-I it was possible for any paraphilia to be specified using a supplementary term, no residual category such as paraphilia NOS was needed.

In DSM-II (American Psychiatric Association, 1968), the term "sexual deviations" continued to be used. Sexual deviations, however, were no longer described as a subtype of sociopathic personality disturbance. Sexual deviations appeared under a catch-all category called "personality disorders and certain other non psychotic mental disorders," but the sexual deviations were listed as a category separate from the personality disorders. The sexual deviations category described individuals whose sexual interests were "directed primarily toward objects other than people of the opposite sex, toward sexual acts not usually associated with coitus, or toward coitus performed under bizarre circumstances as in necrophilia, pedophilia, sexual sadism, and fetishism" (American Psychiatric Association, 1968, p. 44). The deviant sexual behavior was seen as primary in that the individual was not able to substitute normal sexual behavior for the deviant behavior. In DSM-II, the following types of sexual deviations were listed: sexual orientation disturbance (homosexuality), fetishism, pedophilia, transvestitism (*sic*), exhibitionism, voyeurism, sadism, masochism, and other sexual deviation. While no definition or examples of other sexual deviation were provided, it is apparent that the other sexual deviation category was the forerunner of the current paraphilia NOS category.

When the term "paraphilia" was introduced in DSM-III (American Psychiatric Association, 1980), it was included under the broad category of psychosexual disorders. In the DSM-III, the following types of paraphilias were listed: fetishism, transvestism, zoophilia, pedophilia, exhibitionism, voyeurism, sexual masochism, sexual sadism, and atypical paraphilia. Thus, in DSM-III, the term "other sexual deviation" was replaced with the term "atypical paraphilia." Atypical paraphilia was defined as a residual category for types of paraphilias that did not meet the criteria for any of the listed paraphilias.

In DSM-III-R (American Psychiatric Association, 1987), the paraphilias were included under the broad category of sexual disorders, which was essentially the psychosexual disorders category from DSM-III renamed, and the following types of paraphilias were listed: exhibitionism, fetishism, frotteurism, pedophilia, sexual masochism, sexual sadism, transvestic fetishism, voyeurism, and paraphilia NOS. In DSM-III-R, the term "atypical paraphilia" (which was used in DSM-III) was replaced with "paraphilia NOS." Note also that in DSM-III-R, frotteurism was added to the list of specific paraphilias and zoophilia was omitted, which meant that zoophilia was moved to the paraphilia NOS category. For the first time, examples of paraphilia NOS were provided. The seven examples, which were not meant to be exhaustive, were: telephone scatologia, necrophilia, partialism, zoophilia, coprophilia, klismaphilia, and urophilia.

In DSM-IV (American Psychiatric Association, 1994), the paraphilias were still considered sexual disorders but they were included under a broader category of disorders titled sexual and gender identity disorders. In DSM-IV, with only minor definitional changes, the same categories of paraphilias listed in DSM-III-R appeared again. Similarly, the same seven examples of Paraphilia NOS were provided.

DIAGNOSTIC CRITERIA FOR PARAPHILIA NOS CATEGORIES

DSM-IV (American Psychiatric Association, 1994) does not provide individual diagnostic criteria for any of the paraphilia NOS categories. Whereas DSM-IV indicates that the paraphilia NOS category is to be used when the client's behavior does not meet criteria for any of the listed paraphilias, the only definitional information regarding what can be diagnosed as a paraphilia NOS is found in the general guidelines used to define the essential features of any paraphilia.

In the American Psychiatric Association's efforts to conceptualize paraphilia, the definition was guided in part by three considerations: the focus (preferred stimulus) of the sexual activity, the role of covert and overt sexual behavior, and the primacy of the preferred stimulus for sexual arousal. To provide a conceptual framework for DSM-IV criteria for paraphilia NOS, first we describe the evolution of these three components.

Historically, to make a diagnosis of paraphilia, the individual's sexual focus had to involve stimuli other than adult individuals of the opposite gender, sexual behavior that was not typically associated with coitus, or coitus performed under bizarre circumstances (DSM-II; American Psychiatric Association, 1968). With the exception of the removal of homosexuality from DSM-III, this standard has been maintained throughout previous DSM editions and guides the definition of paraphilias in DSM-IV.

The DSM description of what constitutes paraphilic behavior has been expanded across the different DSM editions so that the DSM-IV definition now includes covert activities (i.e., "sexually arousing fantasies and sexual urges") in addition to overt behaviors. In DSM-IV, unlike the DSM-I and -II, for an individual to be diagnosed with a paraphilia the individual no longer has to have acted on the sexual fantasy or urge; the sexual fantasy or urge only has to be present (and causing distress or impairment of functioning).

Finally, the requirement related to the primacy of the paraphilic stimuli or imagery for arousal has been modified. Originally, in DSM-II, the preferred sexual stimuli or imagery were described as necessary for sexual excitement in individuals diagnosed with a paraphilia. The primacy of the preferred stimuli or imagery was demonstrated by the fact that the individual was not able to substitute normal sexual behavior for the preferred stimuli. In DSM-III-R and DSM-IV, however, the primacy of the stimuli (fantasies, urges, or behaviors) for arousal is no longer included as a necessary diagnostic criterion. Instead, clinically significant distress or impairment in functioning (resulting from the sexual fantasies, urges, or behaviors) define the presence of a paraphilia. Although the primacy of the stimuli is not required, if the stimuli are obligatory or result in sexual dysfunction, these types of problems meet the impairment criterion for defining paraphilia (American Psychiatric Association, 1994, p. 525).

As previously mentioned, in DSM-IV for an individual to be diagnosed as having a paraphilia NOS it is necessary that the individual meet the general requirements for a paraphilia, which are represented in specific DSM-IV criteria for paraphilia. These criteria require that the individual displays the following: "recurrent, intense sexually arousing fantasies, sexual urges, or behaviors generally involving 1) nonhuman objects, 2) the suffering or humiliation of oneself or one's partner, or 3) children or other nonconsenting persons, that occur over a period of at least 6 months (Criterion A)" (American Psychiatric Association, 1994, pp. 522–523). In addition, the "behavior, sexual urges, or fantasies cause clinically significant distress or impairment in social, occupational, or other important areas of functioning (Criterion B)" (American Psychiatric Association, 1994, p. 523).

CONTROVERSIES SURROUNDING THE CRITERIA
FOR PARAPHILIA NOS

Examination of extant literature yields several areas of concern regarding the current diagnostic criteria. Potential problems involve the validity of the expansion of Criterion A to incorporate covert behavior, the limited array of stimulus categories listed in Criterion A, the arbitrary nature of the time period selected to define chronicity, and nosological confusion between paraphilia NOS categories and the eight individual paraphilias.

As discussed above, a recent change in the definition of paraphilia is that Criterion A has been expanded so that overt paraphilic behavior does not have to be present for a paraphilia diagnosis to be made. The presence of covert behavior (sexual urges or fantasies) is adequate for a diagnosis of paraphilia, if the duration and impairment criteria are met. However, the rationale for this definitional change is not adequately discussed in the DSM. As a person's covert sexual behavior, particularly fantasies, typically represents a broader range of interests than are present in their overt behavior, this definitional change substantially increases the number of individuals qualifying for a diagnosis of paraphilia. This may be problematic because research indicates that the relationship between cognitions, such as fantasies, and behavior is often modest (Gold, Letourneau, & O'Donohue, 1995; Lee, 1992). Thus, many people who have fantasies never act on them, and these individuals may be substantially different from those who display the overt behavior. Further, given the wide range of sexual fantasies reported by individuals in the general population (e.g., Allgeier & Allgeier, 1995; O'Donohue, Letourneau, & Dowling, 1997), the extent to which the presence of sexual fantasies without associated behaviors should be considered a mental disorder is unclear.

Although Criterion A has been expanded to include covert behavior, a problem with the current definition of paraphilia is that Criterion A is not broad enough to capture all of the paraphilia NOS categories described in the literature. We present a comprehensive, albeit not exhaustive, list of paraphilia NOS categories mentioned in the literature in Table 20.1. Inspection of these examples reveals a number of categories which do not appear to meet any of the three parts of Criterion A (i.e., focus on nonhuman subjects, focus on the suffering or humiliation of oneself or one's partner, or focus on children or other nonconsenting persons). A substantial number of the paraphilia NOS categories appear to represent an atypical sexual focus involving human subjects (self and others).

For example, individuals whose sexual focus is on an elderly partner (gerontophilia) or on being observed (autagonistophilia) or on one or more body parts of a sexual partner (partialism, morphophilia) do not clearly meet any of the three parts of Criterion A. These examples of paraphilia NOS usually involve a consenting adult partner, which means that they do not meet part 1 (nonhuman focus) or part 3 (children or nonconsenting persons) of Criterion A. Further, given the nature of the sexual foci in these examples, the sexual arousal does not appear to be related primarily to the suffering or humiliation of oneself or one's partner (part 2 of Criterion A).

The limitations in Criterion A can be resolved in one of two ways. Criterion A could be expanded by adding a fourth part which would allow for an atypical sexual focus involving human subjects (self and other; see Table 20.1), or the paraphilia NOS categories which do not meet one of the three parts of Criterion A could be removed from the paraphilia NOS category. In the latter case, either a new sexual deviation category (such as the old category of sexual disorders not elsewhere specified used in DSM-III) would be necessary, or sexual behaviors that represent an atypical focus involving human subjects (self and others) could be omitted from DSM-IV nosology of sexual disorders.

In the general criteria for paraphilia (and the definitions of each of the eight listed paraphilias in DSM-IV), there is a requirement that the deviant sexual focus must have lasted for 6 months before a diagnosis of paraphilia can be made. Although the literature suggests that most paraphilic urges, fantasies, and behaviors are chronic in nature, we could not find any data indicating that a 6-month duration (or any other specific duration of time) in the sexual focus should be used as a criterion for defining paraphilia NOS.

Another definitional problem is that many of the paraphilia NOS categories described in Table 20.1 are described as subtypes of one of the eight major paraphilia categories listed in DSM-IV, which suggests that they should not be considered a paraphilia NOS. However,

TABLE 20.1. Paraphilia NOS Categories, Erotic Focus, and Possible Overlapping Paraphilia Categories

Paraphilia NOS categories	Erotic focus	Possible overlapping paraphilia categories
	Nonhuman objects	
Zoophilia (zooerasty, zooerastia, bestiality, bestiosexuality)	Animals	
Formicophilia	Small creatures	Zoophilia
Klismaphilia	Enemas	
Olfactophilia (osmolagnia)	Odors	
Mysophilia	Filth	
Urophilia (urolagnia, urophagia, ondinisme, renifleurism, undinism)	Urine	Fetishism, sexual masochism, sexual sadism
Coprophilia (coprolagnia)	Feces	
Vampirism	Blood	Sexual sadism
	Suffering or humiliation of oneself or one's partner	
Telephone scatophilia (telephone, scatologia, telephonicophilia)	Obscenities over phone	Exhibitionism
Narratophilia	Obscene language with partner	
Chrematistophilia	Being charged or forced to pay	
Saliromania	Soiling/damaging clothing or body	Sexual sadism
Vomerophilia (erotic vomiting)	Vomiting	
	Children or other nonconsenting persons	
Necrophilia	Corpses	
Somnophilia	Sleeping partner	
Symphorophilia	Stage-managed disaster	
	Atypical focus involving human objects (self and others)	
Hypoxyphilia (asphyxiophilia, sexual asphyxia, autoerotic asphyxia, kotzwarrism)	Reduced oxygen intake	Sexual masochism
Urethral manipulation	Insertion of objects	Fetishism, sexual masochism
Morphophilia	One or more body characteristics of partner	Partialism
Partialism	Focus on a body part	Morphophilia
Stigmatophilia	Partner tattooed, scarified, or pierced for wearing jewelry	
Abasiophilia	Lamed or crippled partner	Morphophilia, partialism
Acrotomophilia	Amputation in partner	Morphophilia, partialism
Apotemnophilia	Own amputation	Sexual masochism
Infantilism (autonepiophilia)	Impersonating or being treated as an infant	Sexual masochism
Adolescentism (juvenilism)	Impersonating or being treated as an adolescent	Sexual masochism
Gerontophilia	Elderly partner	
Andromimetophilia	Andromimetic partner	
Gynemimetophilia	Gynemimetic partner	
Autogynephilia	Image of self as woman	Transvestic fetishism
Gynandromorphophilia	Cross-dressed feminized male	
Scoptophilia (scopophilia, scoptolagnia)	Viewing sexual activity	Voyeurism
Mixoscopia	Viewing couple having intercourse	Voyeurism
Triolism (troilism)	Observing partner having sex	Voyeurism
Pictophilia	Pornographic pictures, movies or videos	Voyeurism
Autagonistophilia	Being observed/being on stage	
Hybristophilia	Partner must have committed an outrageous act or crime	
Kleptophilia (kleptolagnia)	Stealing	

the inclusion of many of the categories listed in Table 20.1 as manifestations of one of the major paraphilias is often not supported by the literature. For example, in DSM-IV, hypoxyphilia is included as an example of sexual masochism. However, as discussed in a later section, case data suggest that individuals with hypoxyphilia often do not meet the criteria for sexual masochism, which requires a focus on suffering, and in such cases it qualifies as a paraphilia NOS. We include discussion of the degree of independence and comorbidity of the individual paraphilia NOS categories in the following sections.

PARAPHILIA NOS CATEGORIES

In the remainder of this chapter, we define the examples of paraphilia NOS presented in Table 20.1. Despite overlap, the paraphilia NOS categories are organized using the three-part definitional structure for types of paraphilic focus provided in DSM-IV (i.e., nonhuman objects, suffering or humiliation of oneself or one's partner, and children or other nonconsenting persons) plus the previously proposed fourth component of atypical focus involving human subjects (self and others). The extent to which we discuss each paraphilia varies. In some cases we provide only a brief definition of the paraphilia because of the paucity of information available. Where more information exists, we provide discussion on issues related to definition, epidemiology, associated features, and etiological theories of the disorder.

Nonhuman Objects

Zoophilia

Zoophilia (from the Greek, *zoon*, animal; *philia*, love; Money, 1986), a term coined by Krafft-Ebing (Traub-Werner, 1986), is defined as sexual fantasies, urges, or behaviors involving nonhuman animals (DSM-IV; American Psychiatric Association, 1994). Other terms used to describe this paraphilia are: zooerasty, zooerastia, bestiality, and bestiosexuality. Zoophilic behaviors include fellatio, cunnilingus, coitus, masturbation of the animal (London & Caprio, 1950), and anal intercourse (Peretti & Rowan, 1983). In addition, a case of zoophilic exhibitionism has been described (McNally & Lukach, 1991). The animal selected is often one with which the individual was in close proximity during childhood, such as a farm animal or pet (American Psychiatric Association, 1980).

Historically, references to sexual contact between humans and other animals date back to early civilization. For example, cave paintings created 15,000 to 20,000 years ago depict such behavior (Peretti & Rowan, 1983) and mythological narratives of many cultures contain references to zoophilia. Although some civilizations have sanctioned certain forms of zoophilia (see Traub-Werner, 1986), religious prohibitions against this form of sexual behavior can be found in both the Old Testament and the Talmud. Currently, in the United States, legal prohibitions exist against sexual contact with animals.

In the past, a distinction between covert and overt zoophilic behavior was made. For example, Krafft-Ebing distinguished between zoophilia, or lascivious emotion while petting domesticated animals, and zooerasty, or sexual involvement with animals and concomitant lack of "normal" sexual activity (cited in Rappaport, 1968). However, a distinction between fantasy, urges, and behavior is not maintained in DSM-IV.

Although zoophilia is considered a rare paraphilia (e.g., Cerrone, 1991; American Psychiatric Association, 1994), few data are available to either support or refute this claim. Estimates are available, however, on the rates of sexual contact with animals. In the general population, Kinsey and associates (Kinsey, Pomeroy, & Martin, 1948; Kinsey, Pomeroy,

Martin, & Gebhard, 1953) reported prevalence rates of at least one sexual contact between humans and other animals: 8% for males, and 1.5% (preadolescence) and 3.6% (postadolescence) for females. They found higher frequencies in rural settings, with 40% to 50% of the rural population engaging in sexual activity with animals. Rates were also higher among those with lower educational status. In contrast, Nagaraja (1983) examined sexual contacts with animals among Native American adolescents and reported a 1% prevalence rate. In a study of male sexual fantasies, Crepault and Couture (1980) found that only 5.3% of their sample had fantasized about sexual activity with an animal.

The average age of onset of zoophilia has been estimated to be 17.4 years (Abel & Osborn, 1992). After the initial preference for animals has appeared, it has been suggested that this paraphilia follows a progressive and chronic course (American Psychiatric Association, 1980). Examination of the available data, however, reveals a skewed distribution for the behavior such that most individuals commit only a few acts, whereas a smaller number of individuals engage in a large number of acts. Abel et al. (1987) found the median number of zoophilic acts committed by their sample was 2.2, whereas the average number of acts (distorted by outliers) was 222.4.

Many zoophiliacs appear to have more than one paraphilia. In a survey of 561 nonincarcerated paraphiliacs seeking treatment, Abel, Becker, Cunningham-Rathner, Mittelman, and Rouleau (1988) found that 100% of the zoophilic respondents (n = 14) reported more than one paraphilia, and 50% had 5 or more paraphilias. The average number of paraphilias present in the zoophiliacs in their sample was 4.8, with comorbid diagnoses of pedophilia, exhibitionism, voyeurism, frotteurism, telephone scatophilia, transvestic fetishism, fetishism, sexual sadism, sexual masochism, urophilia, and/or coprophilia.

The American Psychiatric Association (1994) suggested that other mental disorders are frequently present in paraphilic individuals. Evidence that this may apply to cases of zoophilia has been provided by Alvarez and Freinhar (1991). They found the prevalence of zoophilia (contacts and fantasies) to be higher among psychiatric inpatients (55%) relative to comparison individuals (10–15%). Case reports also frequently mention that withdrawal and poor interpersonal skills are associated with zoophilia (e.g., Cerrone, 1991; Chee, 1974, Holden & Sherline, 1973). In a study of motivations for zoophilia, Peretti and Rowan (1983) found that individuals often cited the ease and flexibility of involvement (e.g., no negotiation required) as contributing to their behavior.

Various theories of zoophilia have been put forth. Krafft-Ebing initially distinguished lustful emotion for domesticated animals from the ability to function sexually solely when the behavior involves "unnatural acts" with animals. He considered only the latter pathological (cited in Rappaport, 1968). Another early view considered zoophilia to be initiated by "simpletons—sometimes even imbeciles" or merely as a matter of convenience (e.g., Balint, 1956).

Contrary to earlier speculations, Shenken (1964) argued that zoophilia is neither practiced solely by those of below average intelligence nor used solely as a substitute for normal relations. He believed that it was sometimes a form of psychopathology itself and that it was always related to a general clinical problem (i.e., a neurosis or psychosis). He also proposed that zoophilia need not be defined as an exclusive preference for animals (i.e., normal human sexual relations may also be present). He theorized that zoophiliacs are not able to express emotions appropriately toward humans, so instead they direct feelings toward an animal (which is usually a parent substitute).

In 1968, Rappaport suggested that animals incite envy in children due to their unrestrained exhibition of animal instincts. He suggested that children are interested and aroused by the behavior (including sexual behavior) of animals. He believed that most often, cases of zoophilia are a result of object substitution or convenience. However, he also speculated that sexual contact with animals might represent a repetition compulsion, with the animal abuse serving as a reenactment of earlier traumatic experiences and rage felt toward the parents displaced onto the animal.

Traub-Werner (1986) conceptualized the syndrome as an old form of perversion that has been repressed by civilization. Traub-Werner argued that zoophilia manifests itself under either repressive failure or cultural sanction. He also described zoophilia as an inability to differentiate aggressive from sexual drives, a breakdown in integration of the genital body image, and actions against parent symbols. Cerrone (1991) hypothesized that individual, family, and sociocultural factors contribute to the manifestation of zoophilia. He suggested that intercourse with animals permits a release of repressed anger and that dominance over animals affords a sense of control that is otherwise lacking. Other explanations for zoophilic behavior focus on the role of incestuous desires (London & Caprio, 1950; Schneck, 1974), the relationship with borderline personality disorder with attachment-separation dynamics (Meyer, 1980), and the role of heterosexual fearfulness and extreme self-doubt (Kolb & Brodie, 1982). Using a social learning perspective, Nagaraja (1983) proposed that individuals become aroused by observing animals copulating. In the absence of a consenting sexual partner, individuals will then satisfy sexual urges with animals.

Formicophilia

Dewaraja and Money (1986) defined formicophilia (from the Latin, *formica,* ant; *philia,* love; Dewaraja & Money, 1986) as a subtype of zoophilia wherein the focus is on small creatures, such as "snails, frogs, ants, or other insects creeping, crawling or nibbling on the body, especially the genitalia, perianal area or nipples" (p. 140). In their description of formicophilia, Dewaraja and Money suggest that formicophilia arises developmentally during childhood. Dewaraja and Money (1986; Dewaraja, 1987) considered formicophilia to be very rare.

Klismaphilia

In klismaphilia (from the Greek, *klusma,* enema; *philia,* love; Money, 1986), the paraphilic focus is on receiving an enema. Historically, erotic enemas were provided in "specialty brothels" and in "enema spas" (Denko, 1976). Klismaphilic behavior is common to both genders. In fact, Kinsey's (Kinsey et al., 1948; Kinsey et al., 1953) survey research mentions females' use of enemas as a masturbatory procedure but does not mention enema use in the description of male masturbatory practices.

Boglioli, Taff, Stephens, and Money (1991) indicated that many individuals use warm water to clean the lower rectum (anal douching), whereas others use coffee, yogurt, air, whiskey, wine, beer, and cocaine. de Boer, Moolenaar, de Leede, and Breimer (1982) reviewed the actions of drugs introduced rectally and found that aqueous and alcoholic solutions are absorbed very rapidly. Absorption may be so rapid that it has a "mainlining effect" similar to intravenous injection. The use of enemas for erotic stimulation is not without risk. Accidental rectal trauma and the lodging of foreign bodies in the gastrointestinal tract have been reported (e.g., Eckert & Katchis, 1989; Eisele & Reay, 1980; Herrerias, Muniain, Sanchez, & Garrido, 1983).

There is a lack of information on the factors associated with klismaphilia. Because of the paucity of research, Arndt (1991) placed advertisements in sex tabloids in an attempt to obtain data on the practices of erotic enema users. Twenty-two individuals (21 males and 1 female) responded to his ad. The median age of the respondents was 39 years (range, 25–54 years). Approximately 60% were married or had been married. Eighty percent were heterosexual; the remaining 20% were bisexual. Median years of enema use was 20 years (range, 1–43 years); the median frequency of enema use was twice per week (range, once a day to once a month). Approximately one half of the respondents reported that enemas were self-administered, with the other half reporting giving and/or receiving enemas with a partner. Many without partners indicated a desire to find an enema partner. Forty percent of the sample reported accompanying paraphilic interests including mild spanking and other punishments, suggesting sexual masochism.

Based on a study of 15 cases, Denko (1976) concluded that klismaphiliacs fall into three groups. In his study, six individuals formed a group labeled Type A. This group consisted of individuals who were unhappy with their klismaphilia and viewed it as abnormal. Individuals in this group usually self-administered enemas and dated their behavior to childhood. In the Type A group, one case also involved mild sexual masochism, one case involved coprophilia, and one case involved fetishism. Despite unhappiness about their behavior, Denko indicated that this group "keep their condition compartmentalized, and it had little effect on their work or social lives (including marriage)" (p. 250). In cases wherein there is social or occupational impairment, Type A individuals appeared to be those who were most likely to be diagnosed as klismaphiliacs under the DSM-IV criteria. Type B individuals were similar to Type A individuals, with the exception that they accepted their klismaphilia. These individuals also were more likely to have involved a partner. Type C individuals were viewed as different from Type A and B individuals in that they had integrated the klismaphilic activity into their lives and relationships. They tended to know others with similar interests and displayed a variety of paraphilias including transvestic fetishism and sexual masochism. Type B and C individuals were less likely to be diagnosed with klismaphilia, and Type C individuals were more likely to be diagnosed with another paraphilia.

Agnew (1982) indicated that the enema ritual consists of insertion, filling, and expulsion activities. The insertion of the enema nozzle is experienced as pleasurable due to the highly sensitive nature of the anal and perineal areas. The filling and distention of the lower rectum causes internal pressure that can impact the prostate and seminal vesicles in the male and the back of the vagina in the female. In both males and females, filling produces stimulation of the rectal stretch receptors. Expulsion stimulates the rectal and perineal areas as well as producing waves of peristalsis which stimulate adjacent genital structures. In attempting to explain klismaphilia, Agnew (1982) provided a detailed description of the physiological similarities between rectal stimulation and vaginal intercourse. Although there is little information on the etiology of klismaphilia, it is clear that the physiological sensations produced by enemas are similar to those experienced during masturbation and intercourse, and are therefore very reinforcing. In discussing the etiology of klismaphilia, Denko (1973) suggested the possibility of childhood conditioning of the enema experience.

Olfactophilia

In olfactophilia (from the Latin, *olfacere,* to smell; *philia,* love; Money, 1986), also referred to as osmolagnia, the sexual focus involves smells and odors. Frequently, the focus is on body odors of a sexual partner, including odors from the genital area.

Mysophilia

In mysophilia (from the Greek, *mysos,* uncleanness; *philia,* love; Money, 1986), the paraphilic focus is on filth. This focus may involve the "smelling, chewing or otherwise utilizing sweaty or soiled clothing or articles of menstrual hygiene" (Money, 1986, p. 265).

Karpman (1948, 1949) provided several psychodynamic speculations on the etiological factors associated with mysophilia. For example, one analytic interpretation was that mysophilic behavior involves a symbolic association of sex with something that is dirty (i.e., bad). The pairing of sex and filth is functional because any guilt associated with sexual behavior can be washed away.

Urophilia

Urophilia (from the Greek, *ouron*, urine; *philia*, love; Money, 1986), also called urolagnia, urophagia, ondinisme, renifleurism, and undinism (Undine, a water nymph, from the Latin, *unda*, wave, Money, 1986), refers to a focus on the act of urination or on the urine itself. "Water sports" and "golden showers" are vernacular terms for urophilia. Historically, the terms urophilia, urolagnia, urophagia, and undinism have been used to describe any erotic use of the urinary stream, which may or may not involve a partner.

In DSM-IV, urophilia is listed as an example of paraphilia NOS. Subtypes of urophilia have been described. Denson (1982) suggested that undinism refers to those cases of urolagnia (urophilia) wherein urine constitutes a fetish. Further, when the fetishism leads to oral incorporation of the urine, Denson indicated that the diagnosis should be undinism with urophagia. Denson (1982) also contended that urination may serve masochistic (being urinated on) or sadistic (urination on one's partner) purposes, in which cases it should be labeled uromasochism and urosadism. These latter erotic foci suggest that in some cases Urophilia would fit more appropriately under part 2 of Criterion A in DSM-IV, which refers to a focus on suffering and humiliation of oneself or one's partner. In these cases, the diagnosis would more appropriately be sexual masochism and sexual sadism, respectively.

Coprophilia

Coprophilia (from the Greek, *kropos*, dung; *philia*, love; Money, 1986), or coprolagnia, represents a specific focus on feces. Although some have defined coprophilia as the act of elimination (McCary, 1967), others have defined the focus as the act of consumption of excrement (Allen, 1969). To further complicate the definition, it appears that some individuals may have an interest in excreting on one's partner or in playing with the fecal matter. Smith (1976) indicated a common analytic interpretation is that the excrement symbolically represents the penis and the presence of the fecal matter serves as a defense against castration anxiety.

Vampirism

Vampirism refers to sexual arousal attained through blood extraction. Prins (1985) proposed four types of vampirism: complete vampirism (defined as necrosadism, ingestion of blood, and necrophilic activity), vampirism without ingestion of blood (called necrophilia by Prins), vampirism without death being involved, and autovampirism (ingestion of one's own blood). As evident in this taxonomy, the definition of vampirism overlaps with necrophilia. Nevertheless, some authors (e.g., Vanden Bergh & Kelly, 1964) have distinguished between vampirism and necrophilia, as vampirism is sometimes directed toward the living. In addition, Vanden Berg and Kelly (1964) and Prins (1985) distinguished vampirism from sexual sadism because vampirism is not always accompanied by pain and suffering.

Although not directly addressed in DSM-IV (American Psychiatric Association, 1994), it appears that vampirism should be diagnosed as sexual sadism if pain and suffering are involved, but as paraphilia NOS if pain and suffering are not involved and the behavior is separate from necrophilia. This is congruent with DSM-IV paraphilia NOS classifications involving other body fluids that also are listed as separate syndromes (e.g., urophilia, coprophilia).

Suffering or Humiliation of Oneself or One's Partner

Telephone Scatophilia

Telephone scatophilia (from the Greek, *skopein*, to view; *philia*, love; Money, 1986), also referred to as telephone scatologia and telephonicophilia, involves "deception and ruse in luring or threatening a telephone respondent, known or unknown, into listening to, and making personally explicit conversation" (Money, 1986, p. 271) of a sexual nature. The literature indicates that most obscene callers are male (e.g., Matek, 1988).

Despite a statement in DSM-IV that the individually listed paraphilias occur more frequently than do the paraphilia NOS categories (hence the reference to residual paraphilias), Matek (1988) indicated that the frequency of telephone scatologia is "of a different magnitude" (p. 113) than other paraphilia NOS examples. Supporting this perspective, Murray (1967) found that 26% of college females reported receiving obscene (sexual suggestions and propositions) telephone calls. In a replication of the Murray (1967) study, Murray and Beran (1968) found that about 28% of female and 11% of male undergraduates had received obscene calls wherein sexual suggestions or propositions were made. However, these data do not reflect incidence rates for telephone scatophilia because no information is available on how many calls one individual might make or how many of the obscene callers meet the criteria for paraphilia NOS.

In a preliminary attempt to develop a typology, Mead (1975) described three types of obscene callers. The first type is the caller who immediately uses profanity and/or makes obscene propositions. Mead indicated that most of these callers are in their preteens or teens. A second type is described as "the ingratiating seducer." These callers are more subtle in their approach, often providing a plausible story about prior introductions, admiration from afar, and/or mutual friends. This initial discussion, however, leads to offensive suggestions. A third type is labeled the "trickster." This individual uses some type of ruse (e.g., survey taker) in order to discuss personal matters. The discussion invariably leads to offensive suggestions. Matek (1988) discussed a fourth type of caller, which he suggests does not fit into Mead's typology. Matek (1988) indicated that this fourth type uses crisis lines where they request help (from a female volunteer), discuss sexual material, and masturbate. Matek (1988) indicated that this type of caller is so common that "it is likely that not a single crisis telephone program anywhere in the U. S. A. has been free from these telephone masturbators" (Matek, 1988, p. 114).

Some case studies reported an association between telephone scatophilia and exhibitionism (Kentsmith & Bastani, 1974; Matek, 1988; Nadler, 1968). Matek (1988) described areas of conceptual overlap. For example, Matek suggested that the methods associated with both telephone scatophilia and exhibitionism demonstrate attempts to express aggression, to exhibit power and control, and to gain recognition. Further, it has been suggested that both obscene callers and exhibitionists require that the victim respond with shock or disgust (Hobson, 1983; Mead, 1975).

Although there appears to be some conceptual overlap between telephone scatophilia and exhibitionism, a distinction is that some obscene callers want complete anonymity. Further, case studies have been reported wherein obscene phone calls were made without evidence of any other paraphilia, including exhibitionism (Dalby, 1988). Whereas some have described the telephone as a fetish (Richards, 1989), case data do not support the view that the erotic focus of the obscene caller is the phone rather than the sexually oriented conversation with the victim and/or the associated victim reactions. In an evaluation of case data, Matek (1988) indicated that the most common features of the obscene phone callers are low self-esteem and anger toward women. Matek indicated that retardation, brain damage, psychosis, and intoxication (alcohol or drugs) are infrequently associated with obscene calls.

Freund (Freund & Blanchard, 1986; Freund, Scher, & Hucker, 1984; Freund, Seto, & Kuban, Chapter 6, this volume) proposed a "courtship disorder" model which has been used to explain telephone scatophilia. The courtship model contains four stages. Stage one involves seeking and evaluation of a partner. Stage two involves "pretactile interaction." Stage three involves "tactile interaction." Stage four involves "genital union." Freund suggested that both telephone scatophilic and exhibitionistic individuals have not been able to move out of the pretactile interaction stage. Though stage two of Freund's model appears to describe many cases of telephone scatophilia and exhibitionism, some obscene callers have been assessed as displaying adequate courtship behavior (Dalby, 1988).

Narratophilia

Narratophilia (from the Latin, *narrare,* to narrate; *philia,* love; Money, 1986) involves a focus on the use of dirty and obscene words with a sexual partner. The activity includes telling obscene or pornographic stories to a partner. According to Money (1986), narratophilia is also used to describe the reciprocal condition where an individual's sexual focus is on hearing (or reading) dirty, obscene, or pornographic words or stories. When the criteria for narratophilia are met, the mode of communication can take any form, including telephone sex services and computer-based erotic bulletin boards.

Chrematistophilia

In chrematistophilia (from the Greek, *chremistes,* money dealer; *philia,* love; Money, 1986), the paraphilic focus involves being charged money for sexual activities. Also included in chrematistophilia are cases wherein the erotic focus is on being robbed by one's sexual partner. There is no name for the reciprocal condition wherein the individual charges or robs one's sexual partner (Money, 1986).

Saliromania

In saliromania, the focus in on soiling or damaging a partner's clothing or body (McCary & McCary, 1982). The behavior may involve symbolic acts directed toward clothing, pictures, and statues of women or the behavior may involve the direct assault on a woman. Whereas saliromania has been described as a category separate from sexual sadism (McCary & McCary, 1982), it appears that most cases of saliromania meet the criteria for sexual sadism, as described in DSM-IV. At present, it is unclear if cases exist in which the saliromanic behavior (e.g., the act of damaging clothing) exists separate from a focus on the suffering and humiliation of the sexual partner.

Vomerophilia

Erotic vomiting, named vomerophilia (from the Latin, *vomere,* vomit; *philia,* love) by us, involves a paraphilic focus on the process of regurgitating. Congruent with DSM-IV conceptualization of paraphilias, Stoller (1982) provided case data suggesting that vomerophilia may manifest in a variety of ways: real or imagined, self or others, and facilitative or obligatory. Vomerophilia has been reported in both males and females (Stoller, 1982).

Children or Other Nonconsenting Persons

Necrophilia

Necrophilia (from the Greek, *nekros*, dead; *philia*, love; Money, 1986) is defined in DSM-IV as sexual fantasies, urges, or behaviors involving human corpses. Dead bodies may be the target of vaginal intercourse; anal intercourse; kissing, sucking, or fondling of breasts; fellatio; and cunnilingus. Necrophiliacs most commonly gain access to dead bodies through work, homicide, and chance occurrences (Rosman & Resnick, 1989), although some individuals may seek out corpses at mortuaries, funerals, or graveyards (Lancaster, 1978; Rapoport, 1942; Torre & Varetto, 1987) or preserve the bodies of loved ones (Foraker, 1976).

The term "necrophilia" has been used to describe myriad behavioral patterns, which is reflected in the nosological debate regarding this paraphilia over the past 100 years. In 1886, Krafft-Ebbing (cited in Burg, 1982) distinguished between individuals who sought sexual contact with dead bodies and those who engaged in murder and mutilation in addition to having sexual experiences with corpses. An early tripartite categorization of sexual activity with corpses was promulgated by Wulffen in 1910 (cited in Bartholomew, Milte, & Galbally, 1978). He described necrosadism (lust murder, erotophonophilia), necrostuprum (stolen corpses), and necrophagy (mutilation and cannibalism) as different manifestations of necrophilia. Later, Jones (1931) distinguished between inhibited necrophilia (extension of love in mourning) and overt necrophilic acts (sexual contact or mutilation and ingestion). Hirschfeld (1948) also discussed two forms of necrophilia: cases that involve murder and those involving existing corpses.

Thus, within the category of necrophilia, a distinction has frequently been made between sexual contact with corpses preceded by murder and sexual contact with corpses not preceded by murder. This division is supported by a review of cases reported in the literature (Rosman & Resnick, 1989) which suggests that the two syndromes may overlap but do not exclusively co-occur. DSM-IV employs this differentiation by separating lust murder, described as a form of sexual sadism, from necrophilia. If an individual meets the criteria for both sexual sadism and necrophilia, then the individual would receive both diagnoses (DSM-IV; American Psychiatric Association, 1994). Similarly, although it appears that there may be overlap between vampirism (attaining sexual excitement via blood extraction) and necrophilia, some authors (e.g., Vanden Bergh & Kelly, 1964) have distinguished between the two based on the observation that vampirism is sometimes directed toward the living.

Necrophilia is often cited as a rare clinical condition (e.g., Baker, 1984; Smith & Braun, 1978; Torre & Varetto, 1987); however, prevalence and incidence rates as well as other epidemiological data for the general population are unknown. The only available information is that reported in case studies. Rosman and Resnick (1989) reviewed 122 cases of necrophilia and found the mean age at the time necrophilia was reported was 34 years (range, 17–59). Of the cases reviewed, 92% were male and 8% were female. Seventy percent were heterosexual, 15% were bisexual, and 15% were homosexual in orientation. The distribution of sexual orientation paralleled the gender choice of corpses obtained. Rosman and Resnick (1989) also found a 57% incidence rate of occupational access among necrophiliacs, with the most common occupations being hospital orderly, cemetery employee, and morgue attendant.

Necrophilia has been associated with sadism and alcohol abuse (Burg, 1982; Hirschfeld, 1948). In a review by Rosman and Resnick (1989), 78% of the necrophiliacs who murdered to obtain corpses had a history of sadistic behavior, whereas 30% of those who engaged in sexual contact only and 56% of those who only fantasized had a history of sadistic behavior. They also found that 60% of those necrophiliacs who murdered their victims consumed alcohol before the event, whereas only 25% of the necrophiliacs engaging in sexual contact only consumed alcohol prior to engaging in the paraphilic behavior.

In the description of associated features, some have suggested that necrophiliacs are incapable of securing a consenting partner (see Burg, 1982; Klaf & Brown, 1958). However, in a review of cases by Rosman and Resnick (1989), 86% of the individuals had had "normal" intercourse before engaging in necrophilic activities. Sixty percent of all individuals were single, 26% were married, and 14% were widowed or divorced. Ninety percent of the "fantasizers only" were single. Although there is evidence that many necrophiliacs engage in normal forms of sexual behavior, the extent to which these individuals are able to obtain consenting partners regularly is not clear from the available literature.

An early conceptualization of necrophilia was provided by Krafft-Ebing. In 1886, he suggested several possible factors contributing to the manifestation of necrophilia: immorality, heredity, and subjection of another. Krafft-Ebing described the general condition of necrophilia as "perverse" and considered it not necessarily pathological unless accompanied by either "neuropathic or psychopathic" conditions or murder or mutilation of the bodies (cited in Burg, 1982). Other early theorists attributed necrophilia to "mental weakness or a lack of moral sense" (see Burg, 1982; Klaf & Brown, 1958). However, a review of 122 case reports by Rosman and Resnick (1989) refuted at least two of these notions. Although 59% of the cases had diagnoses of personality disorders, they found that only 11% of the sample was psychotic and only 14% of the individuals had IQs below 100.

From the 1930s to the present, speculation about the causes of necrophilia have been dominated by psychoanalytic views. Jones (1931) hypothesized that the necrophilic desires the helpless, faithful, and tireless nature of the partner (corpse). In addition, he posited that murder and mutilation as part of necrophilic behavior is evidence of a return to primitive oral and anal sadism. Other psychoanalytical theorists attributed necrophilia to weak sexual constitution and mother fixation (e.g., Brill, 1941), object loss (e.g., Rapoport, 1942), and satisfaction of primitive oral and anal drives (e.g., Baker, 1984; Rapoport, 1942). Baker (1984) noted that the corpse offers no resistance or opposition, and therefore there is no chance of rejection or retaliation for the necrophilic individual. He proposed that the necrophiliac's sense of being alive is enhanced by projection of annihilation onto the dead body.

Calef and Weinshel (1972) proposed the "Sleeping Beauty" syndrome (somnophilia), or the desire to engage sexually with someone who is sleeping, as a neurotic equivalent of necrophilia. As discussed in the next section, Burg (1982) suggested the possibility of a theoretical continuum from the "Sleeping Beauty" fantasy through necrophilic acts involving murder.

The understanding of necrophilia is limited by the paucity of data available beyond case reports. However, some ideas have received preliminary empirical support. For example, Rosman and Resnick (1989) examined the motives stated or implied by necrophiliacs in 122 case reports. They reported that the following characteristics were the most common: possessing an unresisting and nonrejecting partner (68%), reunion with a partner (21%), attraction to corpses (15%), gaining comfort or overcoming isolation (15%), and power over a homicide victim (12%).

Somnophilia

Somnophilia (from the Latin, *somnus*, sleep; *philia*, love; Money, 1986) or the "Sleeping Beauty" syndrome, involves an erotic focus on having sex with a partner who is sleeping. While little is known about somnophilia, Burg (1982) noted the apparent theoretical continuum evident from the somnophilic fantasy through necrophilic acts, whereas Calef and Weinshel (1972) suggested that somnophilia is a neurotic equivalent of necrophilia. However, Calef and Weinshel (1972) concluded that although somnophilia may appear to have some characteristics in common with necrophilia, the two syndromes do not necessarily reflect the same underlying pathology. These authors speculated that the wish to return to the maternal body, oedipal conflict, pregenital fixations, and castration anxiety contribute to somnophilia.

Symphorophilia

In symphorophilia (from the Greek, *stigma*, mark; *philia*, love; Money, 1986), the sexual focus involves staged-managing a "disaster, such as a conflagration or traffic accident, and watching for it to happen" (Money, 1986; p. 271).

Atypical Focus Involving Human Subjects (Self and Others)

Hypoxyphilia

Hypoxyphilia (from the Greek, *hupo*, under; *oxus*, sharp-oxygen; *philia*, love) is also known as asphyxiophilia, sexual asphyxia, autoerotic asphyxia, and kotzwarrism (after the musician Kotzwarra, who died in 1791 when a prostitute agreed to hang him briefly as part of a sexual encounter [Hazelwood, Dietz, & Burgess, 1983; Resnik, 1972]). This paraphilia is defined as achievement or enhancement of sexual arousal due to decreased arterial blood flow, which produces oxygen deprivation and an increase in carbon dioxide. In addition to the United States, this method of sexual arousal has been reported in Africa, Europe, and Eastern Asia (Byard & Bramwell, 1988; Garza-Leal & Landron, 1991; Innala & Ernulf, 1989). It has been a topic of interest for several centuries in western literature. For example, Arndt (1991) pointed out that in Marquis de Sade's (1791/1966) novel, *Justine*, a man has himself hanged in an attempt to experience sexual ecstasy. Innala and Ernulf (1989) have reported that historically brothels (e.g., "Hanged Men's Club") in England provided sexual asphyxia through controlled hanging as a means to enhance sexual pleasure. In addition, there have been reports that men who have been executed by hanging experience orgasm just prior to death (see Resnik, 1972, for a review).

In hypoxyphilia, oxygen deprivation is achieved by a variety of methods including "chest compression, noose, ligature, plastic bag, mask, or chemical (often a volatile nitrite that produces a temporary decrease in brain oxygenation by peripheral vasodilation)" (DSM-IV; American Psychiatric Association, 1994, p. 529). The most frequent method of inducing asphyxia is the use of a ligature around the neck (Sinn, 1993). Some of the chemicals used to increase autoerotic pleasure include dichlorodifluoromethane, nitrous oxide, and isobutyl nitrite (Gowitt & Hanzlick, 1992). It is generally believed that the focus of attention is not on the technique used, but on the asphyxia produced by these methods (Hazelwood et al., 1983).

In DSM-IV hypoxyphilia is described as a form of sexual masochism (American Psychiatric Association, 1994, p. 529). However, for sexual masochism to be diagnosed, the individual must have "over a period of at least 6 months, recurrent, intense sexually arousing fantasies, sexual urges, or behaviors involving the act (real, not simulated) of being humiliated, beaten, bound, or otherwise made to suffer" (DSM-IV; American Psychiatric Association, 1994, p. 529). In many cases, individuals do not appear to be interested in suffering per se, but rather in the enhancement of sexual arousal that is produced by a manipulation that limits oxygen intake. Innala and Ernulf (1989) also noted that many cases of hypoxyphilia do not appear to meet the criteria for sexual masochism, and Diamond, Innala, and Ernulf (1990) suggested that the association between hypoxyphilia and sexual masochism may not exist. In fact, there is evidence that hypoxyphiliacs may actively seek to avoid pain and suffering. Case studies reveal that safety devices are often present, and, in cases of hanging, padding may be used to avoid injury (e.g., rope burns) and pain (e.g., Diamond et al., 1990).

Estimates of the prevalence and incidence rates for hypoxyphilia are not available. However, estimates of the annual rates of fatalities resulting from the practice of hypoxyphilia have been made, and these numbers have increased over the past two decades. For example, in 1972, Resnik estimated that there were 50 deaths annually in the United States, and, in 1979 Rosenblum and Faber estimated 250 deaths per year. In 1983, Hazelwood et al. suggested that between 500 and 1,000 deaths occurred annually (the majority of which were adolescents and young adults). DSM-IV (American Psychiatric Association, 1994) indicated that one or two cases of hypoxyphilia-related fatalities per million individuals are detected annually. Despite an increased awareness of this paraphilia, it appears that current estimates of hypoxyphilia-related fatalities are underestimates because careful assessment is required to differentiate cases in which death is due to suicide from those wherein death is an unintended consequence of paraphilic behavior.

It is interesting to note that Sheehan and Garfinkel (1988) found that when all adolescent hanging deaths in two counties (Hennepin and Ramsey Counties in Minnesota) during a 20-year period from 1965 to 1985 were reevaluated, 31% of the deaths were judged to be accidental deaths due to sexual asphyxia and not suicides. If these findings can be replicated, they have implications not only for understanding adolescent sexual behavior, but would indicate also that adolescent suicide rates by hanging need to be adjusted for accidental deaths due to hypoxyphilia.

Although in the early case descriptions of hypoxyphilia it was indicated that "women never engage in these practices" (Edmondson, 1972), subsequent case studies have reported hypoxyphilia in females (e.g., Burgess & Hazelwood, 1983; Byard & Bramwell, 1988; Byard, Hucker, & Hazelwood, 1993; Danto, 1980; Sass, 1975). Nevertheless, the available data suggest that this paraphilia is infrequent in females. Diamond et al. (1990) estimated that females account for only 4% of hypoxyphilia cases, a rate found in a study of 132 asphyxial deaths (Burgess & Hazelwood, 1983). Byard, Hucker, and Hazelwood (1990, 1993) have pointed out that one reason the phenomenon is rarely reported in women may be because it has a less obvious presentation. For example, in a review of the literature, Byard et al. (1990) found that a majority of women, unlike males, did not use clothing, props, or other devices to augment the sexual asphyxia.

As with prevalence and incidence rates, definitive conclusions about the associated features of hypoxyphilia in the general population cannot be made because almost all of the reported cases involve those ending in death (e.g., Burgess & Hazelwood, 1983; Byard & Bramwell, 1988; Diamond et al., 1990; Eriksson, Gezelius, & Bring, 1987; Hazelwood et al., 1983). Even though the data primarily represent cases wherein fatalities have occurred, investigators have reported that the majority of cases do not contain evidence of sexual masochism. Supporting the conceptualization that hypoxyphilia is a separate paraphilia from sexual masochism, Hazelwood et al. (1983) estimated a 12% rate of sexual masochism in cases of hypoxphilia. Indeed, some cases show "no special activities beyond masturbation and self-asphyxiation" (Blanchard & Hucker, 1991, p. 375).

Many case descriptions, however, provide evidence of a variety of paraphilic stimuli. The two most frequently mentioned associated sexual behaviors are cross-dressing and bondage (Blanchard & Hucker, 1991; Hazelwood et al., 1983). Whereas cross-dressing appears common (e.g., 20.5%, Hazelwood et al., 1983), Diamond et al. (1990) stated that it is unclear if this fetishistic feature indicates fetishism, transvestic fetishism, sexual masochism, or some other phenomena. Also, cases involving cross-dressing in males may be more easily identified as accidental deaths and therefore appear to have a higher incidence rate. Bondage is indicated by case descriptions which report that the hands, feet, and other body parts are often bound (Hazelwood et al., 1983). Hazelwood et al. (1983) reported a rate of 51% (males) for bondage. Of course, bondage may be more often associated with fatal cases of hypoxyphilia simply because escape is more difficult. Bondage may or may not be typical of nonfatal hypoxyphilic behavior.

Fatal hypoxyphilia appears to be a solo activity performed by young males (Innala & Ernulf, 1989). These males tend to be partially or totally nude (Diamond et al., 1990), with pornographic material and a mirror present. The use of a mirror is thought by some to be related to the presence of cross-dressing behavior (Boglioli et al., 1991; Blanchard & Hucker, 1991). Fatal cases typically show evidence of penile engorgement or ejaculation. In a study of adolescents, Sheehan and Garfinkel (1988) compared the characteristics of an accidental death sexual asphyxia group and a suicide group to identify features that differentiated between the two groups. Deaths in the sexual asphyxia group were more likely to have the following associated features: partial or complete nudity, cross-dressing, bondage, obscene or pornographic materials near the body, a mirror for self-observation, and penile engorgement or ejaculation. Other distinguishing features of the adolescent sexual asphyxia group were that they were more often white, had more intact parental marriages, had less depression, had fewer conduct disorders, and had fewer previous suicide attempts. In contrast to the notes frequently found in suicide cases, Sheehan and Garfinkel reported that there was an absence of suicide notes in the sexual asphyxia group.

Hazelwood, Burgess, and Groth (1981) and Walsh, Stahl, Unger, Lilienstern, and Stephens (1977) reported that only a few hypoxyphilic accidental deaths are associated with intoxication. For example, Walsh et al. (1977) studied 21 autoerotic asphyxial fatalities in which toxicological analyses had been conducted. These analyses produced only two significant blood-alcohol concentrations and one toxic level of barbiturates. Hazelwood et al. (1983) reported that in a series of 157 autoerotic fatalities, only 6.3% of the victims had evidence of homosexual orientation. This finding prompted the authors to conclude that autoerotic asphyxia is not associated with homosexuality above base rates.

A review of the reported cases of hypoxyphilia reveals that many fatalities appeared to occur due to errors in the construction of the strangulation device and/or escape mechanisms. In addition, a physiological reflex (carotid sinus reflex) can result from sudden compression or pressure surge associated with sexual asphyxia. This stimulation of the carotid sinus can result in a rapid drop in blood pressure with sudden cardiac arrest (Diamond et al., 1990; Reay & Eisele, 1982; Resnik, 1972). Diamond et al. (1990) pointed out that most individuals who have a focus on sexual asphyxia are probably not aware of this reflex.

Diamond et al. (1990) noted that the etiology of hypoxyphilia is unknown. Although there are no well-developed explanatory models of hypoxyphilia, extant paradigms have been used to explain data found in case studies. Psychoanalytic theorists have advanced several explanations which are usually from the perspective that hypoxyphilia represents a form of masochistic behavior (see Resnik, 1972, for a discussion), which is congruent with the DSM-IV definition. For example, it has been suggested that sexual and aggressive impulses toward incestuous objects become masochistic (directed against the self because of castration fears) as punishment for the incestuous desires. Other dynamic interpretations suggest that sexual asphyxia is driven by a desire to assume a passive role with the father. Hanging behavior, which involves being suspended by the neck (symbolic castration), is thought to reduce castration fears. It has also been suggested that individuals engaging in hypoxyphilia have eroticized feelings of weakness and helplessness which are overcome through survival of the asphyxia (Litman & Swearingen, 1972). In another analytic interpretation, it has been suggested that asphyxia is a punishment for masturbation, which reduces superego-derived anxiety (Resnik, 1972).

From a social learning perspective, it has been suggested that the experience of strict, punitive parenting is the basis for an association between punishment (e.g., choking) and sexuality. The literature, however, provides only modest support for the existence of punitive parents in the childhood histories of hypoxyphilic individuals. For example, Friedrich and Gerber (1994) reported that in a group of five male adolescents, there was evidence that each male had experienced a history of choking in conjunction with physical and sexual abuse. However, Rosenblum and Farber (1979) reported that only two of four cases of nonfatal hypoxyphilia had controlling and punishing mothers and nonsupportive fathers, and Sheehan and Garfinkel (1988), who studied nine cases of adolescent autoerotic death, reported only two cases had "strict" parents.

An alternate behavioral model proposed here is that the act of producing sexual asphyxia represents an acquired behavior which becomes part of a paraphilic masturbatory ritual because of the positive effects it produces. In addition to the pleasurable effects of oxygen debt, it is proposed that the act of producing asphyxia enhances orgasm through increased sympathetic arousal. Although the male erection is associated with parasympathetic arousal (with similar assumptions for the female vulva and vaginal engorgement), the male and female orgasm are believed to be under sympathetic control (McCary & McCary, 1982). Thus, the enhancement of orgasm in hypoxyphilic individuals may be due, in part, to increased sympathetic arousal that occurs during the process of achieving asphyxia. Indirect support for this hypothesis can be found in reports that a variety of techniques, other than asphyxia, have been used to increase sympathetic arousal immediately prior to orgasm (e.g., icepack applied to the scrotum as orgasm approaches) to enhance the orgasm experience. If this hypothesis is correct, the asphyxia should be timed to occur after initial sexual arousal has been achieved and as an adjunct to the precipitation of orgasm.

Of course, the question remains as to how the choice to engage in this paraphilic activity is initially made. In contrast to complex speculations, it is possible that the discovery is due largely to chance exposure to the technique. For example, it has been suggested that many participants learn about autoerotic asphyxia from word of mouth, by reading pornographic literature, from the news media, from viewing films, or simply by self-discovery (e.g., Byard et al., 1990; O'Halloran & Lovell, 1988).

Urethral Manipulation

In urethral manipulation the erotic focus is on stimulation of the urethra, generally by insertion of objects. Wise (1982) noted that this may be accomplished either actively as part of autoerotic activities, or passively via requested medical procedures. Objects used in active manipulation include fingers, pencils, pens, lipstick containers, sticks, straws, candles, pins, wires, cuticle knives, and razors. Dangers associated with this form of sexual behavior include urinary tract damage, urinary tract and bladder infections, lodged objects in the bladder, and blocked urinary tracts due to tissue adhesions formed during wound healing. Because of these secondary effects, these individuals may present more often for medical services than for mental health services (Mitchell, 1968). Urethral manipulation has been reported in both males and females (Mitchell, 1968).

Psychodynamic interpretations have suggested that individuals whose erotic focus is urethral manipulation have underlying problems of fixation or regression and castration anxiety (Mitchell, 1968; Wise, 1982). Wise (1982) proposed that urethral manipulation shares features with both fetishistic and sadomasochistic behavior. However, reviews of case reports (Mitchell, 1968; Wise, 1982) do not indicate a strong association between these behaviors. In urethral manipulation, data suggest that the focus of arousal is not on the objects employed. Individuals also frequently report a lack of pain during stimulation. At present, without additional data, the extent to which urethral manipulation does or does not share qualities with fetishism and sexual masochism remains unclear.

Morphophilia

Morphophilia (from the Greek, *morphe*, form; *philia*, love; Money, 1986) involves an erotic focus on one or more of the body characteristics of one's sexual partner. Morphophilia appears to include partialism, which is defined as a focus on a single body part. It is unclear from the literature whether these two categories are unique paraphilias or different names for the same paraphilia. Both morphophilia and partialism are differentiated from fetishism, which involves a focus on "nonliving objects" (DSM-IV; American Psychiatric Association, 1994).

Partialism

In partialism, the paraphilic focus is on some part of the partner's body, such as the hands, legs, feet, breasts, buttocks, or hair. Partialism appears to overlap with morphophilia, which is defined as a focus on one or more body characteristics of one's sexual partner. As previously mentioned, it is unclear whether these two categories are unique paraphilias or different names for the same paraphilia. Historically, some authors (e.g., Berest, 1971; Wise, 1985) have included partialism as part of the general definition of fetishism, which included both parts of bodies and nonliving objects (e.g., shoes, underwear, skirts, gloves). However, in DSM-IV, the criteria for fetishism indicate that the focus must involve the "use of nonliving objects," which eliminates body parts from meeting this criterion.

Stigmatophilia

In stigmatophilia (from the Greek, *stigma*, mark; *philia*, love; Money, 1986), the focus is on a sexual partner who is tattooed or scarred. The focus can include a partner who has had a body part pierced to wear jewelry. In some cases the jewelry is worn in the genital area. According to Money (1986), stigmatophilia also refers to the reciprocal condition wherein the focus is on one's self having tattoos, scars, or pierced areas with jewelry.

Abasiophilia

Abasiophilia (from the Greek, *a*, negating; *basis*, step; *philia*, love; Money, 1990) involves an erotic focus on a partner who is "lamed, crippled and unable to walk" (Money, 1990, p. 165). Although Money only recently coined the term "abasiophilia," case examples have been previously described under other names, such as orthopedic fetishism (Fleischl, 1960). Abasiophilia, however, does not appear to qualify as fetishism because fetishism requires a sexual focus on a nonhuman object (DSM-IV; American Psychiatric Association, 1994). The degree to which a distinction should be made between abasiophilia and other similar paraphilia NOS categories, such as morphophilia and partialism, is less clear. For example, abasiophilia may be a subtype of morphophilia rather than a separate paraphilia. Although reported predominantly in males, abasiophilia has also been reported in females (Money, 1990). When the focus is on one's own condition of being "lame, crippled, or unable to walk," the diagnosis is autoabasiophilia.

While the etiology of abasiophilia is unknown, psychodynamic interpretations suggest that for males the deformed limb of a woman partner represents a female penis (Fleischl, 1960). According to analytic theory, a man may be attracted to a crippled woman because his anxiety and hostility related to "the shock of threatened castration at the sight of the female genital" (Fleischl, 1960, p. 741) is reduced when the deformed limb (representing a penis) is present.

Autoabasiophilia

Autoabasiophilia (from the Greek, *autos,* self; *a,* negating; *basis,* step; *philia,* love; Money, 1990) involves a focus on one's own condition of being "lame, crippled, or unable to walk" (Money, 1990, p. 165). This disorder contrasts with abasiophilia, which involves a focus on a partner who is "lamed, crippled and unable to walk." Although the vast majority of cases appear to involve males, autoabasiophilia has been reported in a female (Money, 1990).

Acrotomophilia

In acrotomophilia (from the Greek, *akron,* extremity; *tome,* a cutting; and *philia,* love; Money & Simcoe, 1984–1986), the sexual focus is the stump of a partner, which has resulted from the amputation of a body part. Typically there is sexual attraction to a partner who already has a stump. There is anecdotal evidence, however, that some individuals have requested that a partner have a limb amputated to obtain a stump (Taylor, 1976). Whereas the stump of an amputated limb appears to be the most common paraphilic focus, some cases involve a focus on mutilated genitalia (Taylor, 1976). Although acrotomophilia is presented as a separate category, the extent to which a distinction should be made between acrotomophilia, morphophilia, and partialism is unclear. As in the case of abasiophilia, acrotomophilia may be a subtype of morphophilia rather than a separate category. While usually reported in males, acrotomophilia has been reported in females (Money, 1990).

Apotemnophilia

In apotemnophilia (from the Greek, *apo,* from; *temnein,* to cut; *philia,* love; Money, 1986), the sexual focus is the stump resulting from one's own amputation. There is case evidence that some individuals have requested amputation (Everaerd, 1983; Money, Jobaris, & Furth, 1977) or engaged in self-mutilation (Taylor, 1976) to obtain a stump. The stump of an amputated limb appears to be the most common paraphilic focus. While evidence indicates that this disorder typically occurs in males, it has been reported in females (Money, 1990). According to Money et al. (1977), apotemnophilia may be conceptually related to sexual masochism, but it is not the same disorder. This view is supported by case data in which pain is not part of the clinical presentation. Although Money et al. (1977) indicated that the etiology of the disorder is unknown, they have suggested that apotemnophilia in males serves to avert or reduce castration anxiety.

Infantilism

In infantilism, which is also referred to as autonepiophilia (from the Greek, *autos,* self; *nepon,* infant; *philia,* love; Money, 1986), the sexual pleasure is derived from acting and dressing like an infant or by being treated as an infant by one's sexual partner (Money, 1986). Though infantilism is classified as sexual masochism in DSM-IV (APA, 1994, p. 529), it is questionable if the criteria for sexual masochism are always met. For example, if the infantile role playing does not involve feelings of humiliation and suffering, then the diagnosis of sexual masochism would not be appropriate and a diagnosis of infantilism as a paraphilia NOS appears warranted.

Adolescentilism

In adolescentilism, or juvenilism, the sexual pleasure is derived from acting (e.g., sexual ineptness, dependence) and dressing like an adolescent or by being treated as an adolescent by one's sexual partner. While adolescentilism, like infantilism, might be classified as sexual masochism (DSM-IV; American Psychiatric Association, 1994, p. 529), it is questionable whether the criteria for sexual masochism are always met. As with infantilism, if the adolescent role playing does not involve feelings of humiliation and suffering, then the diagnosis of sexual masochism is unwarranted.

Gerontophilia

In gerontophilia (from the Greek, *geras,* old age; *philia,* love; Money, 1986), the erotic focus involves a sexual partner who is in the age range of an individual's parent or grandparent.

Andromimetophilia

Andromimetophilia (from the Greek, *andros,* man; *mimos,* mime; *philia,* love; Money, 1986) involves a person who has an erotic focus on a sexual "partner who is andromimetic or, in some instances, a sex-reassigned, female-to-male transsexual" (p. 258), where andromimesis refers to a homosexual female who engages in male impersonation without sex-reassignment. In males, the paraphilic equivalent is gynemimetophilia.

Gynemimetophilia

Gynemimetophilia (from the Greek, *gune,* woman; *mimos,* mime; *philia,* love; Money, 1986) involves a person who has an erotic focus on "a partner who is a gynemimetic or, in some instances, a sex-reassigned, male-to-female transsexual" (Money, 1986, p. 262), where gynemimesis refers to a homosexual male who engages in female impersonation without sex reassignment. In females, the paraphilic equivalent is *andromimetophilia.*

Autogynephilia

Autogynephilia (from the Greek, *autos,* self; *gune,* woman; *philia,* love), which was coined by Blanchard (1989), refers to a focus on sexually arousing cross-gender fantasies and behaviors in males. It has alternately been referred to as automonosexuality, eonism, and sexo-aesthetic inversion. Four types of autogynephilia with defining features have been proposed by Blanchard (1991): physiological autogynephilia (i.e., physiological functions such as pregnancy, lactation, breast-feeding, menstruation), behavioral autogynephilia (i.e., stereotypical behaviors, such as knitting with other women, imaging oneself as a woman in intercourse), anatomic autogynephilia (i.e., body parts such as breasts, vulva, hairless legs), and transvestic autogynephilia (i.e., transvestic fetishism). There is evidence that approximately 10% of autogynephiliacs do not exhibit transvestic fetishism (Blanchard, 1991). Blanchard (1991) contended that the broader notion of autogynephilia has been overshadowed by one type, transvestic fetishism, and that the superordinate category is of interest itself and might prove useful in understanding the syndromes of transvestic fetishism and gender dysphoria.

Cases of autogynephilia have been conceptually differentiated from other manifestations of cross-gender behavior including gynemimetics, she-males, and gynandromorphophilia. Blanchard (1993b) has distinguished between partial autogynephilia, a subtype of anatomic autogynephilia wherein the erotic focus is on a mixture of male and female body parts (usually enlarged breasts with male genitalia; Blanchard, 1993a; Kremer & den Daas, 1990), and gynemimetics (Money & Lamacz, 1984), which refers to homosexual men who live as women without sex reassignment. Gynemimetic individuals may obtain breast augmentation, but are not erotically aroused by viewing themselves as females. The term "she-male," which refers to a particular physical status (dressed as a woman with or without breast augmentation and with male genitalia), overlaps with both autogynephilia and gynemimesis depending upon whether or not the characteristics are sexually arousing. Gynandromorphophilia, the attraction to anatomically or cross-dressed, feminized men, is the reciprocal paraphilia of autogynephilia.

There is evidence that autogynephilia is associated with fetishism (beyond transvestic fetishism) and gender dysphoria. In one study, 55% of the autogynephiliacs reported some history of fetishism (Blanchard, 1991). It has also been found that autogynephiliacs who imagine themselves nude as females are more gender dysphoric than are those who imagine themselves dressed in female clothing or underwear (Blanchard, 1993a). Additionally, autogynephilia appears more in individuals with heterosexual, bisexual, or analloerotic (unattracted to male or female partners) interests than in those with exclusive homosexual interests (Blanchard, 1989).

Gynandromorphophilia

Gynandromorphophilia (from the Greek, *gune*, woman; *andros*, man; *morphe*, form; *philia*, love) is defined as sexual interest in anatomically or cross-dressed, feminized men, including "cross-dressers, transvestites, transsexuals, or she-males" (Blanchard & Collins, 1993). An examination of 119 personal advertisements involving cross-dressing supported the concept of gynandromorphophilia (Blanchard & Collins, 1993). The authors found two groups of individuals displaying an interest in cross-dressers: gynandromorphophiliacs (desired the other to be a cross-dresser, but did not identify self as such) and gynandromorphophilic cross-dressers (desired other to be cross-dresser and identified self as a cross-dresser).

Scoptophilia

Scoptophilia (from the Greek, *skopein*, to view; *philia*, love, Money, 1986), which is also referred to as scopophilia and scoptolagnia, involves deriving sexual pleasure from viewing sexual activity. A special case of scoptophilia is mixoscopia, which involves the viewing of a couple having intercourse.

Historically, scoptophilia (Karpman, 1954), scopophilia (Hirschfeld, 1948), peepers (Gebhard, Gagnon, Pomeroy, & Christenson, 1965), inspectionalism (Coleman, 1964) and voyeurism have been used to describe sexual viewing. Smith (1976) questioned whether certain types of sexual viewing warrant categories of their own. However, as currently defined, scoptophilia is differentiated from voyeurism. In voyeurism the paraphilic focus "involves the act of observing unsuspecting individuals, usually strangers, who are naked, in the process of disrobing, or engaging in sexual activity" (DSM-IV; American Psychiatric Association, 1994, p. 532). Because voyeurism criteria require that the observed individuals are unsuspecting, when the sexual viewing involves an individual or individuals who are aware that they are being viewed, a diagnosis of scoptophilia (or mixoscopia) is warranted.

Mixoscopia

Mixoscopia (from the Greek, *mixis*, intercourse; *skopein*, to examine; *philia*, love; Money, 1986) refers to a sexual focus which involves the observation of other individuals engaging in coitus. Mixoscopia is applicable in cases where the individuals being viewed are willing participants, whereas voyeurism is diagnosed in cases involving an "unsuspecting individual" (DSM-IV; American Psychiatric Association, 1994). The reciprocal paraphilia NOS category is autagonistophilia.

Triolism

In triolism (troilism; from the French, *trois*, three), the paraphilic focus is an activity that involves the "sharing of a sexual partner with another person while one looks on, after which the onlooker may or may not share the sexual partner" (Smith, 1976, p. 586). It has also been defined as "observing one's partner on hire or loan to a third person while engaging in sexual activities, including intercourse, with that person" (Money, 1986, p. 272). Allen (1969) indicated that triolism involves not only the man who desires his wife to have sex with another partner while he is present, but also the father who arranges to observe "his grown-up daughter" and her partner engage in sexual behavior (p. 179).

Although historically triolism has been conceptualized as a form of voyeurism, DSM-IV criteria require that the paraphilic focus in voyeurism "involves the act of observing unsuspecting individuals, usually strangers, who are naked, in the process of disrobing, or engaging in sexual activity" (DSM-IV; American Psychiatric Association, 1994, p. 532). In cases of triolism, the sexual partners are typically aware that they are being observed. However, the literature does not provide information on the possibility that triolism is a special case of scoptophilia, nor is information available on the degree of overlap between triolism and mixoscopia. Although triolism is usually reported to be a male activity (Chesser, 1971; McCary, 1967), female involvement in triolistic activities has been described (Reinhardt, 1957).

In attempts to explain triolism, authors have speculated about different motivational factors. For example, Allen (1969) suggested that viewing of another couple represents an attempt to reenact the primal scene. Yalom (1960) suggested that there is incestuous identification whereby the observer can have sex vicariously with a mother, sister, or daughter. Coleman (1964) proposed that, in males, the motivation is heterosexual identification with the man performing the sexual activity.

Pictophilia

In pictophilia (from the Latin, *pictura*, picture; *philia*, love), the erotic focus involves viewing obscene or pornographic pictures, movies, or videos of sexual activities alone or with a partner (Money, 1986). Pictophilia can be differentiated from voyeurism because, in most cases, it does not involve the observation of unsuspecting individuals, as the participants in pornographic pictures and movies are usually aware of the erotic nature of their activities and know that they will be observed (erotically) by others. However, data are lacking on the degree of overlap between pictophilia and voyeurism.

Autagonistophilia

In autagonistophilia (from the Greek, *autos,* self; *agonistes,* principal actor; *philia,* love; Money, 1986), the erotic focus involves being observed by an audience. The observation may involve being seen on stage or on camera (Money, 1986). Autagonistophilia is applicable in cases wherein the viewers are willing participants, whereas exhibitionism is diagnosed in cases involving an "unsuspecting stranger" (DSM-IV; American Psychiatric Association, 1994). The reciprocal paraphilia NOS category is mixoscopia.

Hybristophilia

In hybristophilia (from the Greek, *hybridzein,* to commit an outrage against someone; *philia,* love; Money, 1986), the sexual focus is on having a sexual partner who is known to have "committed an outrage or crime, such as rape, murder, or armed robbery" (p. 263). The sexual focus may be on a sexual partner who has been incarcerated for criminal activity. On some occasions the hybristophiliac may urge their sexual partner to commit a crime and thus be convicted. Some cases involve women who marry men (including murderers) who are in prison.

Kleptophilia

In kleptophilia (from the Greek, *kleptein,* to steal; *philia,* love; Money, 1986), or klepto-lagnia, the sexual focus involves "illicitly entering and stealing from the dwelling of a stranger or potential partner" (Money, 1986, p. 264; Revitch, 1983; Zavitzianos, 1983). If objects (e.g., clothing) are the focus, then fetishism may be the appropriate diagnosis. If the act (e.g., entering or stealing) and not the object taken is the focus, then a diagnosis of kleptophilia is appropriate. In some instances, kleptophilia may be associated with sexual sadism. For example, Boglioli et al. (1991) indicated that in some cases the kleptophiliac may force sexual intercourse (i.e., biastophilia).

FUTURE DIRECTIONS

In many of the paraphilia NOS categories, there is disagreement regarding what constitutes the paraphilia. However, adequate definitions are needed before any progress can be made in our understanding of residual paraphilias (e.g., even the collection of descriptive data requires consensus regarding definitions). Beyond a refinement of definitions, there is the need for additional model development. Models are needed to generate *a priori* predictions so that research can be hypothesis driven. Paraphilic models need to move from the extant, single-focus models (e.g., psychoanalytic and learning) to multiple-level (e.g., biological, personality, familial, and cultural), interactional models. Not only should the interrelationships among putative causal variables be examined, but also the possibility that the same paraphilic behavior may result from different conditions should be explored. Ultimately, to properly inform intervention efforts, models are needed which contain a series of conditional statements which indicate how the disorder develops.

The present literature on the residual paraphilias is plagued by inadequate sampling procedures and a general lack of matched comparison groups. Source- and setting-related biases (data are primarily from mental health and forensic settings) limit the representativeness of findings. In addition, setting confounds may produce associated factors that are artifacts of the setting and are not causally related to the residual paraphilias. Extant descriptive and correlational studies are also limited because it is impossible to separate causal variables from marker variables. Finally, there is little information on ethnic and social class differences in the residual paraphilias, and few data are available on the incidence of female participation.

Admittedly, research problems in the area of residual paraphilias present formidable challenges. For example, the development of discrete definitions of the paraphilia categories is complicated by the fact that the paraphilia categories frequently overlap (e.g., many reported cases of paraphilia involve more than one type of paraphilia). Whereas more representative and larger samples are needed, we recognize that sample sizes are affected by a number of factors, including the fact most paraphilic behaviors are low base-rate phenomena, deal with socially and legally sensitive issues, and occur in populations that are difficult to engage in research.

Beyond the definitional, theoretical, and empirical shortcomings in our understanding of the paraphilias, several authors have questioned the inclusion of paraphilias, including the residual paraphilias, in a taxonomy of mental disorders. Some have argued that statistical and ideal behavior definitions of abnormality, upon which the general category of paraphilias appears to be based, should not apply to sexual behavior (e.g., Tallent, 1977; Silverstein, 1984). Further, problems can arise when the current distress criteria are used to define paraphilic behavior.

First, there is evidence that people routinely engage in a wide array of sexual fantasies and behaviors, thus bringing into question issues of statistical rarity in some cases of paraphilia. In addition, precisely what constitutes normal and abnormal sexual behavior has varied as a function of culture and time. Tallent (1977) noted that diagnosing sexual deviations is based upon dominant cultural values and efforts to produce conformity. In discussing the paraphilias, Davis and Whitten (1987) write that "by comparison with many other societies, Western cultures appear to be particularly concerned with sexual norms and variation, and have taken extreme measures to enforce normality" (p. 76). Silverstein (1984) suggested that moral reasoning is the principal criterion in the diagnosis of sexual deviations. He argued that such behaviors are labeled pathological, in part, because they appear "kinky" and are offensive to some. Obfuscating moral values and psychological determinations makes the contributions of each to our defining and understanding paraphilias unclear.

Second, DSM-IV states that for a diagnosis of paraphilia to be made, the individual must suffer distress or impairment. It is often unclear, however, whether distress associated with paraphilic behavior represents a disturbance due to the paraphilia or merely a conflict with society. In the latter case, DSM-IV states that "Neither deviant behavior (e.g., political, religious, or sexual) nor conflicts that are primarily between the individuals and society are mental disorders unless the deviance or conflict is a symptom of a dysfunction in the individual" (American Psychiatric Association, 1994, p. xxii). Further, much of the research, at least in the paraphilia NOS categories, has focused solely on the behavioral manifestations of individuals (e.g., sexual contact with animals, sexual asphyxia) and have *not* assessed distress or impairment. Thus, the research base for paraphilias NOS provides little information to clarify the relevance of distress or impairment to variations in sexual behavior.

Finally, in line with the removal of homosexuality from the DSM, Tallent (1977) and Silverstein (1984) proposed that the general category of paraphilias should be eliminated. At this time, additional consideration of this suggestion appears warranted. Although it is impossible to remove values from a diagnostic system, the bases for inclusion in and exclusion of categories from the nosology of mental disorders should be clearly defined and followed. As previously discussed, this has not been the case for the paraphilias. If most or all of the paraphilias, including paraphilia NOS, were removed from the DSM system, the study of sexual variety would remain a moral, legal, and scientific endeavor, but would generally be separated from the study of psychopathology.

REFERENCES

Abel, G. G., Becker, J. V., Cunningham-Rathner, J., Mittelman, M., & Rouleau, J. L. (1988). Multiple paraphilic diagnoses among sex offenders. *Bulletin of the American Academy of Psychiatry and Law, 16,* 153–168.

Abel, G. G., Becker, J. V., Mittelman, M., Cunningham-Rathner, J., Rouleau, J. L., & Murphy, W. D. (1987). Self-reported sex crimes of nonincarcerated paraphiliacs. *Journal of Interpersonal Violence, 2,* 3–25.

Abel, G. G., & Osborn, C. (1992). The paraphilias: The extent and nature of sexually deviant and criminal behavior. *Psychiatric Clinics of North America, 15,* 675–687.

Agnew, J. (1982). Klismaphilia: A physiological perspective. *American Journal of Psychotherapy, 36,* 554–566.

Allen, C. (1969). *A textbook of psychosexual disorders* (2nd ed.). London: Oxford University Press.

Allgeier, A. R, & Allgeier, E. R. (1995). *Sexual Interactions* (4th ed.). Lexington, MA: D. C. Heath.

Alvarez, W. A., & Freinhar, J. P. (1991). A prevalence study of bestiality (zoophilia) in psychiatric in-patients, medical in-patients, and psychiatric staff. *International Journal of Psychosomatics, 38,* 45–47.

American Psychiatric Association. (1952). *Diagnostic and statistical manual of mental disorders.* Washington, DC: Author.

American Psychiatric Association. (1968). *Diagnostic and statistical manual of mental disorders* (2nd ed.). Washington, DC: Author.

American Psychiatric Association. (1980). *Diagnostic and statistical manual of mental disorders* (3rd ed.). Washington, DC: Author.

American Psychiatric Association. (1987). *Diagnostic and statistical manual of mental disorders* (3rd ed., rev.). Washington, DC: Author.

American Psychiatric Association. (1994). *Diagnostic and statistical manual of mental disorders* (4th ed.). Washington, DC: Author.

Arndt, W. B., Jr. (1991). *Gender disorders and the paraphilias.* Madison, CT: International Universities Press.

Baker, R. (1984). Some considerations arising from the treatment of a patient with necrophilic fantasies in late adolescence and young adulthood. *International Journal of Psycho-Analysis, 65,* 283–294.

Balint, M. (1956). Perversions and genitality. In S. Lorand & M. Balint (Eds.), *Perversions: Psychodynamics and therapy* (pp. 16–27). New York: Random House.

Bartholomew, A. A., Milte, K. L., & Galbally, F. (1978). Homosexual necrophilia. *Medical Science and Law, 18,* 29–35.

Berest, J. J. (1971). Fetishism: Three case histories. *Journal of Sex Research, 7,* 237–239.

Blanchard, R. (1989). The classification and labeling of nonhomosexual gender dysphorias. *Archives of Sexual Behavior, 18,* 315–334.

Blanchard, R. (1991). Clinical observations and systematic studies of autogynephilia. *Journal of Sex and Marital Therapy, 17,* 235–251.

Blanchard, R. (1993a). Partial versus complete autogynephilia and gender dysphoria. *Journal of Sex and Marital Therapy, 19,* 301–307.

Blanchard, R. (1993b). The she-male phenomenon and the concept of partial autogynephilia. *Journal of Sex and Marital Therapy, 19,* 69–76.

Blanchard, R., & Collins, P. I. (1993). Men with sexual interest in transvestites, transsexuals, and she-males. *Journal of Nervous and Mental Disease, 181,* 570–575.

Blanchard, R., & Hucker, S. J. (1991). Age, transvestism, bondage, and concurrent paraphilic activities in 117 fatal cases of autoerotic asphyxia. *British Journal of Psychiatry, 159,* 371–377.

Boglioli, L. R., Taff, M. L., Stephens, P. J., & Money, J. (1991). A case of autoerotic asphyxia associated with multiplex paraphilia. *American Journal of Forensic Medicine and Pathology, 12,* 64–73.

Brill, A. A. (1941). Necrophilia. *Journal of Criminal Psychopathology, 2,* 433–443.

Burg, B. R. (1982). The sick and the dead: The development of psychological theory on necrophilia from Krafft-Ebing to the present. *Journal of the History of the Behavioral Sciences, 18,* 242–254.

Burgess, A. W., & Hazelwood, R. R. (1983). Autoerotic asphyxial deaths and social network response. *American Journal of Orthopsychiatry, 53,* 166–170.

Byard, R. W., & Bramwell, N. H. (1988). Autoerotic death in females: An underdiagnosed syndrome? *American Journal of Forensic Medicine and Pathology, 9,* 252–254.

Byard, R. W., Hucker, S. J., & Hazelwood, R. R. (1990). A comparison of typical death scene features in cases of fatal male and female autoerotic asphyxia with a review of the literature. *Forensic Science International, 48,* 113–121.

Byard, R. W., Hucker, S. J., & Hazelwood, R. R. (1993). Fatal and near-fatal autoerotic asphyxial episodes in women: Characteristic features based on a review of nine cases. *American Journal of Forensic Medicine and Pathology, 14,* 70–73.

Calef, V., & Weinshel, E. M. (1972). On certain neurotic equivalents of necrophilia. *International Journal of Psychoanalysis, 53,* 67–75.

Cerrone, G. H. (1991). Zoophilia in a rural population: Two case studies. *Journal of Rural Community Psychology, 12,* 29–39.

Chee, K. T. (1974). A case of bestiality. *Singapore Medical Journal, 15,* 287–288.

Chesser, E. (1971). *Strange loves: The human aspect of sexual deviation.* New York: William Morrow.

Coleman, J. C. (1964). *Abnormal psychology and modern life* (3rd ed.). Chicago: Scott, Foresman.

Crepault, C., & Couture, M. (1980). Men's erotic fantasies. *Archives of Sexual Behavior, 9,* 565–581.

Dalby, J. T. (1988). Is telephone scatologia a variant of exhibitionism? *International Journal of Offender Therapy and Comparative Criminology, 32,* 45–49.

Danto, B. L. (1980). A case of female autoerotic death. *American Journal of Forensic Medicine and Pathology, 1,* 117–121.

Davis, D. L., & Whitten, R. G. (1987). The cross-cultural study of human sexuality. *Annual Review of Anthropology, 16,* 69–98.

de Boer, A. G., Moolenaar, F., de Leede, L. G. J., & Breimer, D. D. (1982). Rectal drug administration: Clinical pharmacokinetic considerations. *Clinical Pharmacokinetics, 7,* 285–311.

Denko, J. D. (1973). Klismaphilia: Enema as a sexual preference. *American Journal of Psychotherapy, 27,* 232–250.

Denko, J. D. (1976). Klismaphilia: Amplification of the erotic enema deviance. *American Journal of Psychotherapy, 30,* 236–255.

Denson, R. (1982). Undinism: The fetishization of urine. *Canadian Journal of Psychiatry, 27,* 336–338.

de Sade, M. (1966). *Justine* (H. Weaver, Trans.). New York: Putnam. (Original work published 1791)

Dewaraja, R. (1987). Formicophilia, an unusual paraphilia, treated with counseling and behavior therapy. *American Journal of Psychotherapy, 41,* 593–597.

Dewaraja, R., & Money, J. (1986). Transcultural sexology: Formicophilia, a newly named paraphilia in a young Buddhist male. *Journal of Sex and Marital Therapy, 12,* 139–145.

Diamond, M., Innala, S. M., & Ernulf, K. E. (1990). Asphyxiophilia and autoerotic death. *Hawaii Medical Journal, 49,* 11–12, 14–16, 24.

Eckert, W. G., & Katchis, S. (1989). Anorectal trauma: Medicolegal and forensic aspects. *American Journal of Forensic Medicine and Pathology, 10,* 3–9.

Edmondson, J. S. (1972). A case of sexual asphyxia without fatal termination. *British Journal of Psychiatry, 121,* 437–438.

Eisele, J. W., & Reay, D. T. (1980). Deaths related to coffee enemas. *Journal of the American Medical Association, 244,* 1608–1609.

Eriksson, A., Gezelius, C., & Bring, G. (1987). Rolled up to death: An unusual autoerotic fatality. *American Journal of Forensic Medicine and Pathology, 8,* 263–265.

Everaerd, W. (1983). A case of apotemnophilia: A handicap as sexual preference. *American Journal of Psychotherapy, 37,* 285–293.

Fleischl, M. F. (1960). A man's fantasy of a crippled girl. *American Journal of Psychotherapy, 14,* 741–748.

Foraker, A. G. (1976). The romantic necrophiliac of Key West. *Journal of the Florida Medical Association, 63,* 642–645.

Freund, K., & Blanchard, R. (1986). The concept of courtship disorder. *Journal of Sex and Marital Therapy, 12,* 79–92.

Freund, K., Scher, H., & Hucker, S. (1984). The courtship disorders: A further investigation. *Archives of Sexual Behavior, 13,* 133–139.

Friedrich, W. N., & Gerber, P. N. (1994). Autoerotic asphyxia: The development of a paraphilia. *Journal of the American Academy of Child and Adolescent Psychiatry, 33,* 970–974.

Garza-Leal, J. A., & Landron, F. J. (1991). Autoerotic asphyxial death initially misinterpreted as suicide and a review of the literature. *Journal of Forensic Sciences, 36,* 1753–1759.

Gebhard, P. H., Gagnon, J. H., Pomeroy, W. B., & Christenson, C. V. (1965). *Sex offenders: An analysis of types.* New York: Harper & Row.

Gold, S. R., Letourneau, E. J., & O'Donohue, W. (1995). Sexual interaction skills. In W. O'Donohue & L. Krasner (Eds.), *Handbook of psychological skills training: Clinical techniques and applications* (pp. 229–246). New York: Allyn & Bacon.

Gowitt, G. T., & Hanzlick, R. L. (1992). Atypical autoerotic deaths. *American Journal of Forensic Medicine and Pathology, 13,* 115–119.

Hazelwood, R. R., Burgess, A. W., & Groth, A. N. (1981). Death during dangerous autoerotic practice. *Social Science Medicine, 15,* 129–133.

Hazelwood, R. R., Dietz, P. E., & Burgess, A. W. (1983). *Autoerotic fatalities.* Lexington, MA: D.C. Heath (Lexington Books).

Herrerias, J. M., Muniain, M. A., Sanchez, S., & Garrido, M. (1983). Alcohol-induced colitis. *Endoscopy, 15,* 121–122.

Hirschfeld, M. (1948). *Sexual anomalies: The origins, nature, and treatment of sexual disorders.* New York: Emerson.

Hobson, W. F. (1983). Objective of exhibitionists. *Medical Aspects of Human Sexuality, 17,* 91–92.

Holden, T. E., & Sherline, D. M. (1973). Bestiality, with sensitization and anaphylactic reaction. *Obstetrics and Gynecology, 42,* 138–140.

Innala, S. M., & Ernulf, K. E. (1989). Asphyxiophilia in Scandinavia. *Archives of Sexual Behavior, 18,* 181–189.

Jones, E. (1931). *On the nightmare.* London: Hogarth Press.

Karpman, B. (1948). Coprophilia: A collective review. *Psychoanalytic Review, 35,* 253–272.

Karpman, B. (1949). A modern Gulliver: A study in coprophilia. *Psychoanalytic Review, 36,* 260–282.

Karpman, B. (1954). *The sexual offender and his offenses.* New York: Julian Press.

Kentsmith, D.K., & Bastani, J. B. (1974). Obscene telephoning by an exhibitionist during therapy: A case report. *International Journal of Group Psychotherapy, 24,* 352–357.

Kinsey, A. C., Pomeroy, W. B., & Martin, C. E. (1948). *Sexual behavior in the human male.* Philadelphia: W. B. Saunders.

Kinsey, A. C., Pomeroy, W. B., Martin, C. E., & Gebhard, P. H. (1953). *Sexual behavior in the human female.* Philadelphia: W. B. Saunders.

Klaf, F. S., & Brown, W. (1958). Necrophilia: Brief review and case report. *Psychiatric Quarterly, 32,* 645–652.

Kolb, L. C., & Brodie, H. K. H. (1982). *Modern clinical psychiatry* (10th ed.). Philadelphia: W. B. Saunders.

Kremer, J., & den Daas, H. P. (1990). Case report: A man with breast dysphoria. *Archives of Sexual Behavior, 19,* 179–181.

Lancaster, N. P. (1978). Necrophilia, murder and high intelligence: A case report. *British Journal of Psychiatry, 132,* 605–608.

Lee, C. (1992). On cognitive theories and causation in human behavior. *Journal of Behavior Therapy and Experimental Psychiatry, 23,* 257–268.

Litman, R. E., & Swearingen, C. (1972). Bondage and suicide. *Archives of General Psychiatry, 27,* 80–85.

London, L. S., & Caprio, F. S. (1950). *Sexual deviations.* Washington, DC: Linacre Press.

Matek, O. (1988). Obscene phone callers. *Journal of Social Work and Human Sexuality, 7,* 113–130.

McCary, J. L. (1967). *Human sexuality.* New York: Van Nostrand Reinhold.

McCary, J. L., & McCary, S. P. (1982). *McCary's human sexuality* (4th ed.). Belmont, CA: Wadsworth.

McNally, R. J., & Lukach, B. M. (1991). Behavioral treatment of zoophilic exhibitionism. *Journal of Behavior Therapy and Experimental Psychiatry, 22,* 281–284.

Mead, B. T. (1975). Coping with obscene phone calls. *Medical Aspects of Human Sexuality, 9,* 127–128.

Meyer, J. K. (1980). Paraphilias. In H. I. Kaplan, A. M. Freedman, & B. J. Sadock (Eds.), *Comprehensive textbook of psychiatry* (3rd ed., pp. 1770–1783). Baltimore: Williams & Wilkins.

Mitchell, W. M. (1968). Self-insertion of urethral foreign bodies. *Psychiatric Quarterly, 42,* 479–486.

Money, J. (1986). *Lovemaps: Clinical concepts of sexual/erotic health and pathology, paraphilia, and gender transposition in childhood, adolescence, and maturity.* New York: Irvington.

Money, J. (1990). Paraphilia in females: Fixation on amputation and lameness. Two personal accounts. *Journal of Psychology and Human Sexuality, 3,* 165–172.

Money, J., Jobaris, R., & Furth, G. (1977). Apotemnophilia: Two cases of self-demand amputation as a paraphilia. *Journal of Sex Research, 13,* 115–125.

Money, J., & Lamacz, M. (1984). Gynemimesis and gynemimetophilia: Individual and cross-cultural manifestations of a gender-coping strategy hitherto unnamed. *Comprehensive Psychiatry, 25,* 392–403.

Money, J., & Simcoe, K. W. (1984–1986). Acrotomophilia, sex and disability: New concepts and case report. *Sexuality and Disability, 7,* 43–50.

Murray, F. S. (1967). A preliminary investigation of anonymous nuisance telephone calls to females. *Psychological Record, 17,* 395–400.

Murray, F. S., & Beran, L. C. (1968). A survey of nuisance telephones calls received by males and females. *Psychological Record, 18,* 107–109.

Nadler, R. P. (1968). Approach to psychodynamics of obscene telephone calls. *New York State Journal of Medicine, 68,* 521–526.

Nagaraja, J. (1983). Sexual problems in adolescence. *Child Psychiatry Quarterly, 16,* 9–18.

O'Donohue, W. T., Letourneau, E., & Dowling, H. (1997). Development and preliminary validation of a paraphilic sexual fantasy questionnaire. *Sexual Abuse: A Journal of Research and Treatment, 9,* 167–178.

O'Halloran, R. L., & Lovell, F. W. (1988). Autoerotic asphyxial death following television broadcast. *Journal of Forensic Sciences, 33,* 1491–1492.

Peretti, P. O., & Rowan, M. (1983). Zoophilia: Factors related to its sustained practice. *Panminerva Medica, 25,* 127–131.

Prins, H. (1985). Vampirism: A clinical condition. *British Journal of Psychiatry, 146,* 666–668.

Rapoport, J. (1942). A case of necrophilia. *Journal of Criminal Psychopathology, 4,* 277–289.

Rappaport, E. A. (1968). Zoophily and zooerasty. *Psychoanalytic Quarterly, 37,* 565–587.

Reay, D. T., & Eisele, J. W. (1982). Death from law enforcement neck holds. *American Journal of Forensic Medicine and Pathology, 3,* 253–258.

Reinhardt, J. M. (1957). *Sex perversions and sex crimes.* Springfield, IL: Charles C Thomas.

Resnik, H. L. P. (1972). Erotized repetitive hangings: A form of self-destructive behavior. *American Journal of Psychotherapy, 26,* 4–21.

Revitch, E. (1983). Burglaries with sexual dynamics. In L. B. Schlesinger & E. Revitch (Eds.), *Sexual dynamics of anti-social behavior* (pp. 173–191). Springfield, IL: Charles C Thomas.

Richards, A. K. (1989). A romance with pain: A telephone perversion in a woman? *International Journal of Psychoanalysis, 70,* 153–164.

Rosenblum, S., & Faber, M. M. (1979). The adolescent sexual asphyxia syndrome. *Journal of American Academy of Child Psychiatry, 18,* 546–558.

Rosman, J. P., & Resnick, P. J. (1989). Sexual attraction to corpses: A psychiatric review of necrophilia. *Bulletin of the American Academy of Psychiatry and the Law, 17,* 153–163.

Sass, F. A. (1975). Sexual asphyxia in the female. *Journal of Forensic Sciences, 20,* 181–185.

Schneck, J. M. (1974). Zooerasty and incest fantasy. *International Journal of Clinical Experimental Hypnosis, 22,* 299–302.

Sheehan, W., & Garfinkel, B. D. (1988). Adolescent autoerotic deaths. *Journal of the American Academy of Child and Adolescent Psychiatry, 27,* 367–370.

Shenken, L. I. (1964). Some clinical and psychopathological aspects of bestiality. *Journal of Nervous and Mental Disease, 139,* 137–142.

Silverstein, C. (1984). The ethical and moral implications of sexual classification: A commentary. *Journal of Homosexuality, 9,* 29–38.

Sinn, L. E. (1993). The silver bullet. *American Journal of Forensic Medicine and Pathology, 14,* 145–147.

Smith, R. S. (1976). Voyeurism: A review of the literature. *Archives of Sexual Behavior, 5,* 585–608.

Smith, S. M., & Braun, C. (1978). Necrophilia and lust murder: Report of a rare occurrence. *Bulletin of the American Academy of Psychiatry and Law, 6,* 259–268.

Stoller, R. J. (1982). Erotic vomiting. *Archives of Sexual Behavior, 11,* 361–365.

Tallent, N. (1977). Sexual deviation as a diagnostic entity: A confused and sinister concept. *Bulletin of the Menninger Clinic, 41,* 40–60.

Taylor, B. (1976). Amputee fetishism: An exclusive journal interview with Dr. John Money of Johns Hopkins. *Maryland State Medical Journal, 25,* 35–39.

Torre, C., & Varetto, L. (1987). An exceptional case of necrophilia. *American Journal of Forensic Medicine and Pathology, 8,* 169–171.

Traub-Werner, D. (1986). The place and value of bestophilia in perversions. *Journal of the American Psychoanalytic Association, 34,* 975–992.

Vanden Bergh, R. L., & Kelly, J. F. (1964). Vampirism: A review with new observations. *Archives of General Psychiatry, 11,* 543–547.

Walsh, F. M., Stahl, C. J., Unger, H. T., Lilienstern, O. C., & Stephens, R. G., III. (1977). Autoerotic asphyxial deaths: A medicolegal analysis of forty-three cases. In C. H. Wecht (Ed.), *Legal medicine annual 1977* (pp. 155–182). New York: Appleton-Century-Crofts.

Wise, T. N. (1982). Urethral manipulation: An unusual paraphilia. *Journal of Sex and Marital Therapy, 8,* 222–227.

Wise, T. N. (1985). Fetishism—etiology and treatment: A review from multiple perspectives. *Comprehensive Psychiatry, 26,* 249–257.

Yalom, I. D. (1960). Aggression and forbiddenness in voyeurism. *Archives of General Psychiatry, 3,* 305–319.

Zavitzianos, G. (1983). The kleptomanias and female criminality. In L. B. Schlesinger & E. Revitch (Eds.), *Sexual dynamics of anti-social behavior* (pp. 132–158). Springfield, IL: Charles C Thomas.

21

PARAPHILIA NOT OTHERWISE SPECIFIED

Assessment and Treatment

Paul A. Schewe

The fourth edition of the *Diagnostic and Statistical Manual of Mental Disorders* (DSM-IV; American Psychiatric Association, 1994) provides a nonexhaustive list of sexual activities which could potentially meet the diagnostic criteria for paraphilia not otherwise specified (NOS). This category was created to aid in the classification of sexual disorders which occur either very infrequently or have not been sufficiently described in the literature to warrant a separate category (American Psychiatric Association, 1994).

CATEGORIES OF PARAPHILIA NOS AND RELEVANT LITERATURE

To begin the discussion of assessment and treatment issues regarding the minor paraphilias, the following paragraphs will describe each of the paraphilias listed in the NOS category along with any relevant literature. I must caution readers that very little literature exists addressing the assessment and treatment of the minor paraphilias. The majority of information in this chapter has been gleaned from published case reports and retrospective analyses of existing data. One limitation of case reports is that positive outcomes are often overrepresented, and therefore may present a misleading impression regarding the efficacy of treatments.

Telephone Scatologia

Telephone scatologia entails sexual arousal associated with exposing a victim to sexual and obscene language over the telephone. Frequently, the caller will masturbate while talking to the victim (Adams & McAnulty, 1993). Telephone scatologia, a relatively rare paraphilia, must be differentiated from obscene telephone calling, which is relatively common. According to DSM-IV (American Psychiatric Association, 1994), the scatologist must engage in the behavior (or have intense sexual urges or fantasies involving the behavior) for at least 6 months and must experience significant distress or impaired functioning as a result of the behavior. According to this definition, it appears that a person who engages in obscene telephone calling regularly, but who does not experience negative consequences or who does not experience difficulties in sexual, social, or occupational functioning, would not be diagnosed with paraphilia NOS.

Freund, Watson, and Rienzo (1988) found that 14.3% of a sample of paid volunteers from a Canada Employment Center and 6.2% of a sample of student volunteers admitted to making obscene telephone calls. Although it appears that a significant number people engage in obscene telephone calls, few are referred for treatment. Of 108 male adolescent sex offenders referred to the Family Court Clinic in Toronto, Ontario between 1980 and 1988, only two were known to have committed obscene telephone calling, and one had also committed exhibitionism (Saunders & Awad, 1991). The difference between incidence of the behavior and referrals for treatment may be because perpetrators of "hands-off" offenses such as obscene telephone calling might be considered less dangerous than perpetrators of rape and molestation and therefore may be less likely to be referred for treatment.

Masters, Johnson, and Kolodny (1982) distinguished between three types of telephone scatologists. The most common type involves the caller's boasting about himself and his genitalia and explicitly describing his concomitant masturbatory behavior. The second type makes sexual and aggressive threats against the victim, although the caller rarely carries out these threats. The third type of caller attempts to have the victim reveal intimate information. For example, these callers may ask questions about sexual activity, menstruation, or contraception under the guise of conducting a research survey (Skinner & Becker, 1985).

Telephone scatologia may be functionally related to exhibitionism (Alford, Webster, & Sanders, 1980; Freund et al., 1988). Nadler (1968) reported that scatologists are similar to exhibitionists in that they generally feel inadequate, are insecure, and have poorly developed social–sexual skills. Nadler (1968) suggested that scatologists differ from exhibitionists in that scatologists are more anxious and hostile in their social interactions with women. Freund et al. (1988) provided some empirical support for the relationship between exhibitionism and scatologia. The authors found that exhibitionists admitted to making obscene telephone calls at a significantly higher rate (28.7%) than did nonexhibitionist sex offenders (13.7%). Dalby (1988) questioned the hypothesized relationship between telephone scatologia and exhibitionism based on the case vignettes of four men who made indecent telephone calls without the expression of any other sexually deviant behaviors.

Published case reports of successful treatment of obscene telephone callers included psychodynamic, behavioral, and pharmacological treatments. Pearson, Marshall, Barbaree, and Southmayd (1992) reported that urges to exhibit and make obscene telephone calls gradually decreased in a 37-year-old man treated with buspirone, an antianxiety medication, within a supportive psychotherapeutic relationship. Treatment gains were reportedly maintained at 30 months following withdrawal from treatment.

Moergen, Merkel, and Brown (1990) reported the successful use of covert sensitization and social skills training in the treatment of a 34-year-old obscene telephone caller. The authors reported rapid decreases in arousal associated with obscene telephone calling, a decrease in social anxiety, and an increase in social behavior at a 1-year, posttreatment follow-up.

Alford and colleagues (1980) reported the treatment of a male with a 1-year history of obscene telephone calling and a 4-year history of exhibitionism using 10 sessions of covert sensitization targeting the obscene telephone calling. The authors reported that in posttreatment assessment the client demonstrated reduced phallometric arousal to obscene phone calls, elimination of obscene telephone calling, and a concurrent reduction in exhibitionism (Alford et al., 1980).

Goldberg and Wise (1985) reported the psychodynamic treatment of an obscene telephone caller in twice weekly visits for 1 year. The authors emphasized the need to work through the patient's masochism and unmet dependency needs as an important part of therapy. At termination, Goldberg and Wise (1985) reported that the patient was less depressed, reported no urges to make obscene telephone calls, and manifested no aberrant behavior.

Note that several of these studies did not use physiological arousal measures, but instead relied solely on self-report. Problems exist with the sole use of self-report because clients may be unwilling to report criminal and socially undesirable urges and behavior at follow-up.

Necrophilia

In this variation of fetishism, dead human bodies are the object of sexual interest. Rosman and Resnick (1989), in their review of 122 cases manifesting necrophilic acts or fantasies, differentiated between "genuine" necrophiles and "pseudo-necrophiles" based on the existence of "a persistent sexual attraction to corpses" (p. 154). Using this criterion, the authors found that most of the genuine necrophiles met the diagnostic criteria for paraphilia NOS. Rosman and Resnick (1989) further classified the cases of genuine necrophilia based on whether they murdered to obtain corpses for sexual purposes (necrophilic homicide; 14 of 50 subjects), used already-dead bodies for sexual pleasure (regular necrophiles; 21 of 50 subjects), or fantasized about sexual activity with corpses without committing necrophilic acts (necrophilic fantasy; 15 of 50). According to Rosman and Resnick (1989), the pseudonecrophile has a transient attraction to corpses but prefers sexual contact with living partners.

In Rosman and Resnick's (1989) sample, 95% were male, 26% were married, the average age at which the necrophilic activity was revealed was 34 (range = 16–65), and the sexual orientation of the sample was comparable to that of the general population. Roughly half of the sample had occupational access to corpses (e.g., hospital orderly, cemetery employee, pathologist). Finally, Rosman and Resnick (1989) found that of the cases of necrophilia for which data were available, 56% were diagnosed with personality disorders and 55% had "unusual belief systems," although only 17% were psychotic. The authors cautioned that their data were gathered retrospectively from published and unpublished case reports across several decades, countries, and languages. The percentages given were calculated according to the number of cases for which positive or explicitly negative data were available for that item. Furthermore, the problems of low base rate and gaps in the data enhance the risk of overinterpretation.

Rosman and Resnick (1989) did not make any specific recommendations regarding the assessment of necrophilia, perhaps because their data were collected retrospectively. Their data suggested that most of the information can be obtained through clinical interview, and their discussion suggested an emphasis on the specific necrophilic fantasies and behaviors to establish a diagnosis and the assessment of early developmental and interpersonal issues to facilitate treatment. The authors noted that access to corpses should not rule out the careful assessment of necrophilic homicide, as several of the homicidal necrophiles in their sample had easy access to corpses.

Recognizing that no one has treated a sufficient number of necrophiles to determine an effective treatment using a well-controlled design, Rosman and Resnick (1989) outlined a course of treatment for necrophiles. They suggested that clinicians (1) establish rapport; (2) determine whether the person has a persistent attraction to corpses based on reported fantasies or on repeated necrophilic acts; (3) treat any associated pathology (depression, personality disorders, etc.); (4) consider treatment with an antiandrogen if the client has a heightened sex drive; (5) assist the necrophile in establishing healthy sexual and social relationships; and (6) use desensitization to decrease avoidance of living partners (Rosman & Resnick, 1989).

Baker (1984) reported on 5 years of psychoanalysis with a young man who was originally referred to treatment because of "anxiety attacks" and violent behavior. When he revealed necrophilic fantasies, treatment focused on separation anxiety, sadism, and anal masturbation, all of which manifested themselves in the therapeutic relationship. Treatment outcome was not discussed in this case report.

Zoophilia

Zoophilia entails intense and repetitive urges, fantasies, or sexual activity with animals (Adams & McAnulty, 1993). Zoophilia must be differentiated from bestiality. Bestiality involves transient sexual activity with an animal which is usually the result of curiosity, a desire for novelty, or the unavailability of a human partner (Tollison & Adams, 1979). In zoophilia, animals are the preferred or exclusive objects of sexual interest (Skinner & Becker, 1985). Kinsey and his associates (Kinsey, Pomeroy, & Martin, 1948; Kinsey, Pomeroy, Martin, & Gebhard, 1953) found that 8% of the males and 3.6% of the females in their sample had engaged in bestiality and 17% of those who were raised on farms reported reaching orgasm while engaged in sexual activity with animals. More recently, Alvarez and Freinhar (1991) found that 55% of a sample of 20 psychiatric inpatients reported having sexual relations or sexual fantasies about animals, as compared with 10% and 15% of medical inpatients and psychiatric staff, respectively.

Cerrone (1991) reported on the treatment of zoophilia in two males (ages 10 and 15). The boys lived in a rural community and were treated with family therapy, social assertiveness training, and sex education. McNally and Lukach (1991) described the successful treatment of a mildly retarded man who masturbated in front of large dogs. Outpatient treatment entailed masturbatory reconditioning, covert sensitization, and stimulus control procedures over a period of 6 months. The authors reported that the client's maximum reported arousal to his most exciting, deviant scene dropped from 10 to 0 after 15 sessions of satiation therapy, and that his arousal for the nondeviant scene increased to 10 from a baseline of 5 after 12 sessions. The authors cautioned that the client's reported arousal was not verified with penile plethysmography. At a follow-up, the client reported that his masturbation fantasies involved only women, and that he was able to cope successfully with several high-risk situations (McNally and Lukach, 1991). The authors concluded that behavior therapy is a viable and less restrictive alternative to antiandrogen treatments commonly recommended for mentally retarded people with paraphilias (McNally & Lukach, 1991).

Coprophilia and Urophilia

These paraphilias involve the use of feces or urine, respectively, to obtain sexual arousal (Adams & McAnulty, 1993). Skinner and Becker (1985) noted that the activities associated with this paraphilia range from watching someone defecate or urinate to being defecated or urinated upon (in the vernacular, "golden showers"). These activities are sometimes incorporated into sadomasochistic rituals (Adams & McAnulty, 1993; Skinner & Becker, 1985).

Denson (1982) reported on the treatment of a 17-year-old male who experienced sexual excitement by drinking from unflushed toilets in women's washrooms. The young man's treatment included explanations of normal sexual behavior and the hazards of ingesting unclean substances. A 16-month follow-up indicated that the urophilic activities had ceased.

Denson (1982) further classified urophilia or urolagnia, in which urine or the act of urinating is a focus of sexual desire, into uromasochism, urosadism, undinism, and urophilia. Denson (1982) stated that in urophilia, the individual experiences a profound need to possess the consciousness or spirit of the partner, which may be satisfied, in part, by drinking the urine of that individual. Undinism refers to those cases of urolagnia in which urine constitutes a fetish. Urosadists derive sexual pleasure from urinating on their consenting or nonconsenting partner, and the uromasochist enjoys the act of being urinated upon (Denson, 1982). The author did not report on assessment or treatment issues with respect to the different subclasses of urophilia.

Partialism

Partialism is another variation of a fetish which, in its extreme form, consists of exclusive arousal to a specific body part usually not associated with sexual activity (Adams & McAnulty, 1993). Unlike most of the other paraphilias, Skinner and Becker (1985) pointed out that partialism is considered socially acceptable in its milder forms, citing the "leg man" or "breast man" as examples. No information specific to the assessment or treatment of partialism was available in the literature at the time of this writing.

Klismaphilia

This paraphilia involves giving or receiving enemas as the preferred method of sexual arousal. Adams and McAnulty (1993) noted that klismaphilia may be an adjunct to a rubber fetish or sadomasochism.

Denko (1973) reported on the 5-month outpatient treatment of a 27-year-old, married Army officer whose preferred sexual activity was receiving enemas. Detailed interviewing suggested that this behavior was the result of early learning experiences. The goal of this analytically oriented therapy was not to reduce the klismaphilic behavior, but rather to help the client better accept himself despite his condition and to teach him to better conceal his deviant behavior.

ASSESSMENT AND TREATMENT

When confronted with a client reporting paraphilic ideas or behaviors, the clinician must first understand why the client is seeking help. The minor paraphilias are rare, and it is even more uncommon for persons exhibiting minor paraphilic behavior to present themselves for therapy. Fedoroff, Hanson, McGuire, Malin, and Berlin (1992) reported case histories of patients admitted to a sexual disorders clinic who simulated or exaggerated paraphilic symptoms. Four of 20 persons admitted during a 2-month period were suspected of simulating or exaggerating paraphilic symptoms. In all of these cases the clients were without current legal charges and three of the four clients were self-referred. Of the nonsimulators, only 5 of the 16 were without legal charges and only one was self-referred. In two of the four cases of simulated paraphilias, the patients appeared to be masking pedophilic urges and behaviors with paraphilic complaints that were not subject to mandatory reporting laws. Three of the four subjects exhibited ego-dystonic homosexuality, and these same three subjects presented with requests for treatment with antiandrogens. The authors suggested that the fear of AIDS and the increase in child sexual abuse reporting laws may contribute to patients simulating unusual and nonreportable paraphilias. These patients may request treatment with antiandrogens in an attempt to get relief from their distressing sexual urges and behaviors. The authors reported further that careful assessment using penile plethysmography is "an invaluable aid in helping patients become aware of their full range of sexual response patterns" (Fedoroff et al., 1992, p. 910).

Furthermore, literature that suggests a high rate of comorbidity among the paraphilias (Abel, Becker, Cunningham-Rathner, Mittelman, & Rouleau, 1988; American Psychiatric Association, 1994) also points to the careful assessment of other paraphilic symptoms. A client presenting with one of the minor paraphilias may exhibit other paraphilic behavior that he is less willing to admit. Thorough assessment for other paraphilias (especially those involving nonconsenting partners) is prudent and may be ethically mandated, given the high potential for comorbidity.

Throughout the assessment and treatment process, the clinician should begin with the assumption that the client does not wish to give up the atypical sexual behavior and will do everything possible to conceal important information from the therapist and to resist change (Wincze, 1989). Though this assumption should certainly be subject to change in light of evidence to the contrary, Wincze (1989) argued that beginning with this assumption will create the least amount of error. Typical assessments should include physiological and behavioral responding as well as self-report (see chapters in this volume outlining assessment procedures for pedophilia [Chapter 9], voyeurism [Chapter 17], exhibitionism [Chapter 3], and rape [Chapter 19]). In addition, collateral contacts with significant others are extremely important to verify clients' reports as well as to further inform the assessment and treatment process.

Assessment devices which include items referring to minor paraphilias include the Sex Fantasy Questionnaire (SFQ; O'Donohue, Letourneau, & Dowling, 1997) and the Multiphasic Sex Inventory (MSI; Nichols & Molinder, 1984). The MSI contains four items pertaining to obscene telephone calling, and the SFQ contains six items pertaining to scatologia, necrophilia, or zoophilia. Although these instruments provide only a limited assessment of paraphilias in the NOS category, each one provides a more thorough assessment of normal and other paraphilic behavior, including normal sexual behavior, bondage, sadism, masochism, rape, pedophilia, and sexual dysfunction on the SFQ, and pedophilia, rape, exhibitionism, sexual dysfunction, sexual development, marriage development, gender identity, and sexual orientation on the MSI. Due to low base rates of the behaviors and the relatively few items assessing minor paraphilic behavior, the reliability and validity of these instruments for assessing NOS paraphilias is unknown. Unknown validity, together with the problems inherent to using self-report to assess deviant or criminal behavior, make the usefulness of these instruments for assessing minor paraphilias questionable.

Even penile plethysmography, which is perhaps the "state of the art" in sex offender assessment, must be used cautiously in cases of suspected minor paraphilic behavior because of the low base rate problem. D. R. Laws (personal communication, July 17, 1995) indicated that in 25 years of assessing sex offenders, he has assessed a person for necrophilia only once. He suggested that clinicians use clients' reported fantasies to construct audiotaped scripts of rare paraphilic activity when more standardized scripts are not available. Arousal to these scripts relative to scripts of other deviant and nondeviant sexual activity can be useful not only for the initial assessment, but also as an indicant of therapeutic change when used throughout therapy.

Once the clinician has thoroughly assessed for the presence of paraphilic behaviors other than what the client or referral source identified, other information is necessary to inform and direct the therapeutic process (see Table 21.1). Information necessary for

TABLE 21.1. Necessary Information for Treatment Techniques Commonly Used in Treating Paraphiles

Information	Treatment(s) informed
Deviant and nondeviant sexual fantasies	Covert sensitization, aversion therapy, orgasmic reconditioning
Sources of sexual anxiety	Systematic desensitization
Cognitions surrounding deviant and nondeviant behavior	Cognitive restructuring, relapse prevention, empathy training
Social–sexual skills	Social skills training
Early sexual development	Psychoanalysis
Motivation to change	All treatments

treatment includes the content of sexual fantasies, stimuli for deviant and nondeviant arousal, sources of sexual anxiety, cognitions surrounding the deviant behavior, cognitions surrounding normal sexual behavior, social–sexual skills, motivation to change, and early sexual development. Such information is necessary for most of the standard interventions such as covert sensitization, social skills training, aversion therapy, self-control techniques, systematic desensitization, positive classical conditioning, attitude change, empathy training, cognitive restructuring, orgasmic reconditioning, masturbatory satiation, pharmacotherapy, psychoanalysis, and relapse prevention (Gudjonsson, 1986; see chapters covering pedophilia [Chapter 9], exhibitionism [Chapter 3], and fetishism [Chapter 5] for detailed information on the implementation of these interventions). Whereas no controlled data exist pointing to the efficacy of any type of treatment for the minor paraphilias, data from treatment with sex offenders (Marshall & Barbaree, 1990) suggest that cognitive-behavioral treatments, including relapse prevention, should be used whenever the paraphilic behavior involves a nonconsenting partner or the potential for a nonconsenting partner.

Clinicians should consider each of the following goals when working with paraphiles. Perhaps the most obvious goal is to decrease the atypical sexual behavior and increase appropriate sexual behavior (Quinsey & Earls, 1990). Techniques to reduce deviant sexual behavior include aversion therapy, covert sensitization, stimulus control, satiation, and cognitive restructuring (Quinsey & Earls, 1990; Wincze, 1989). Techniques used to increase appropriate sexual behavior include systematic desensitization to reduce avoidance of appropriate sexual contact, orgasmic reconditioning, and social–sexual skills training (Quinsey & Earls, 1990; Wincze, 1989).

A second goal of therapy should be the client's improved awareness of all factors that potentially lead to the atypical sexual behavior. The techniques used to achieve this goal generally fall under the heading of "relapse prevention," and have been described elsewhere (see chapters on rape [Chapter 19] and pedophilia [Chapter 9], as well as Laws, 1989). In a chapter detailing the theory of relapse prevention, Laws (1995) specifically mentioned sexual addictions, sexual compulsions, fetishism, and obscene telephone calling in a rather narrow list of disorders in which relapse prevention may be specifically useful. Though a detailed account of the application of relapse prevention to the minor paraphilias is beyond the scope of this chapter, we encourage interested readers to consult Laws (1989, 1995) or an earlier text by Marlatt and Gordon (1985). As suggested by Laws (1995), all components of relapse prevention can be applied to the minor paraphilias in a very straightforward fashion.

A third goal of therapy should be to increase victim empathy if the paraphilic behavior potentially involves victims (Hildebran & Pithers, 1989; Wincze, 1989). Psychologists working with incarcerated sex offenders have suggested that empathy toward victims may play an important role in preventing recidivism (Hildebran & Pithers, 1989). Interventions designed to increase empathy for victims include education regarding the effects of sexual abuse on victims, role plays, and written exercises from the perspective of the victim (Hildebran & Pithers, 1989)

A final goal of therapy should be to improve the client's overall well-being. To achieve this goal, clinicians need to address other potential problems such as DSM-IV Axis I and Axis II disorders, self-esteem issues, coping skills, and inter- and intrapersonal conflicts (Wincze, 1989).

FUTURE DIRECTIONS

Aside from the bizarre nature of the minor paraphilias, their most notable feature is their infrequency in the literature and the rarity with which people with the disorders appear in clinical settings. Because of their rarity, it is unlikely that controlled studies to address treatment outcome will ever be available for each of the minor paraphilias. Indeed, whereas this chapter limited itself to the seven minor paraphilias listed under the NOS category in DSM-IV, Milner and Dopke (see Chapter 20, this volume) identified 39 different minor paraphilias. Instead of attempting to validate assessment and treatment techniques for each minor paraphilia, researchers are wise to identify what is common across the paraphilias. Research questions might include "Is telephone scatologia a variant of exhibitionism?" and "Are necrophilia, zoophilia, coprophilia, urophilia, partialism, and klismaphilia distinct from fetishism?" Answers to such questions would help organize and guide future research, as well as aid clinicians. If research suggests that such distinctions are not warranted, then clinicians faced with an atypical paraphilia could refer to the existing literature on exhibitionism and fetishism in implementing assessment and treatment procedures.

CONCLUSIONS

Paraphilia not otherwise specified (NOS) is included in DSM-IV to allow classification of paraphilias which are encountered very infrequently or have not been sufficiently described in the literature to warrant a separate category. These paraphilias generally involve fantasies, urges, or behaviors involving nonhuman objects or human objects with an atypical focus. Of the examples listed in DSM-IV, telephone scatologia is the only minor paraphilia wherein the target of the paraphilic behavior involves a nonconsenting, living person. Telephone scatologia also stands out from the list in that it is the only minor paraphilia closely associated with one of the specified paraphilias, namely exhibitionism (Freund et al., 1988).

When faced with the assessment of paraphilic behavior, clinicians should keep in mind the available information regarding base rates of the milder forms paraphilic behavior such as bestiality, obscene phone calling, and preferences for certain body parts. Not every individual who is referred for therapy because he was caught in some act of sexually deviant behavior may be in need of psychological services. Clinicians adhering to DSM-IV must remember that the diagnosis of paraphilia NOS is not based on how bizarre, immoral, disgusting, or criminal the sexual behavior is, but rather upon the duration of sexually deviant behavior and upon the distress or decrease in functioning experienced by the individual. Finally, with any client presenting with sexually deviant behavior, we cannot emphasize enough the need to assess for multiple paraphilias.

REFERENCES

Abel, G., Becker, J. V., Cunningham-Rathner, J., Mittelman, & Rouleau, J. (1988). Multiple paraphilic diagnoses among sex offenders. *Bulletin of American Academic Psychiatry and Law, 16,* 153–168.

Adams, H. E., & McAnulty, R. D. (1993). Sexual disorders. In P. Sutker & H. E. Adams (Eds.), *Comprehensive handbook of psychopathology* (2nd ed.). New York: Plenum Press.

Alford, G. S., Webster, J. S., & Sanders, J. H. (1980). Convert aversion of two interrelated deviant sexual practices: Obscene phone calling and exhibitionism. A single case analysis. *Behavior Therapy, 11,* 15–25.

Alvarez, W. A., & Freinhar, J. P. (1991). A prevalence study of bestiality (zoophilia) in psychiatric in-patients, medical in-patients, and psychiatric staff. *International Journal of Psychosomatics, 38,* 45–47.

American Psychiatric Association. (1994). *Diagnostic and statistical manual of mental disorders* (4th ed.). Washington, DC: Author.

Baker, R. (1984). Some considerations arising from the treatment of a patient with necrophilic fantasies in late adolescence and young adulthood. *International Journal of Psycho-Analysis, 65,* 283–2294.

Cerrone, G. H. (1991). Zoophilia in a rural population: Two case studies. *Journal of Rural Community Psychology, 12*(1), 29–39.

Dalby, J. T. (1988). Is telephone scatologia a variant of exhibitionism? *International Journal of Offender Therapy and Comparative Criminology, 32*(1), 45–49.

Denko, J. D. (1973). Klismaphilia: Enema as a sexual preference. *American Journal of Psychotherapy, 27,* 232–250.

Denson, R. (1982). Undinism: The fetishization of urine. *Canadian Journal of Psychiatry, 27,* 336–338.

Fedoroff, J. P., Hanson, A., McGuire, M., Malin, H. M., & Berlin, F. S. (1992). Simulated paraphilias: A preliminary study of patients who imitate or exaggerate paraphilic symptoms and behaviors. *Journal of Forensic Sciences, 37*(3), 902–911.

Freund, K., Watson, R. & Rienzo, D. (1988). The value of self-reports in the study of voyeurism and exhibitionism. *Annals of Sex Research, 1,* 243–262.

Goldberg, R. L., & Wise, T. N. (1985). Psychodynamic treatment for telephone scatologia. *American Journal of Psychoanalysis, 45*(3), 291–297.

Gudjonsson, G. H. (1986). Sexual variations: Assessment and treatment in clinical practice. *Journal of Sexual and Marital Therapy, 1*(2), 191–214.

Hildebran, D., & Pithers, W. (1989). Enhancing offender empathy for sexual-abuse victims. In D. R. Laws (Ed.), *Relapse prevention with sex offenders.* New York: Guilford Press.

Kinsey, A. C., Pomeroy, W. B., & Martin, C. E. (1948). *Sexual behavior in the human male.* Philadelphia: W. B. Saunders.

Kinsey, A. C., Pomeroy, W. B., Martin, C. E., & Gebhard, P. H. (1953). *Sexual behavior in the human female.* Philadelphia: W.B. Saunders.

Laws, D. R. (Ed.). (1989). *Relapse prevention with sex offenders.* New York: Guilford Press.

Laws, D. R. (1995). A theory of relapse prevention. In W. O'Donohue & L. Krasner (Eds.), *Theories of behavior therapy.* Washington: APA Books.

Marlatt, B. A., & Gordon, J. R. (Eds.). (1985). *Relapse prevention: Maintenance strategies in the treatment of addictive behaviors.* New York: Guilford Press.

Marshall, W. L., & Barbaree, H. E. (1990). Outcome of comprehensive cognitive-behavioral treatment programs. In W. L. Marshall, D. R. Laws, & H. E. Barbaree (Eds.), *Handbook of sexual assault: Issues, theories, and treatment of the offender.* New York: Plenum Press.

Masters, W., Johnson, V., & Kolodny, R. (1982). *Human sexuality.* Boston: Little, Brown.

McNally, R. J., & Lukach, B. M. (1991). Behavioral treatment of zoophilic exhibitionism. *Journal of Behavior Therapy and Experimental Psychiatry, 22*(4), 281–284.

Moergen, S. A., Merkel, W. T., & Brown, S. (1990). The use of covert sensitization and social skills training in the treatment of an obscene telephone caller. *Journal of Behavior Therapy and Experimental Psychiatry, 21*(4), 269–275.

Nadler, R. (1968). Approach to psychodynamics of obscene telephone calls. *New York Journal of Medicine, 68,* 521–526.

Nichols, H. R., & Molinder, I. (1984). *Multiphasic Sex Inventory: Manual.* Tacoma, WA: Authors.

O'Donohue, W. T., Letourneau, E. J., & Dowling, H. (1997). Development and preliminary validation of a paraphilic sexual fantasy questionnaire. *Sexual Abuse: A Journal of Research and Treatment, 9,* 167–178.

Pearson, H. J., Marshall, W. L., Barbaree, H. E., & Southmayd, S. (1992). Treatment of a compulsive paraphiliac with buspirone. *Annals of Sex Research, 5*(4), 239–246.

Quinsey, V. L., & Earls, C. M. (1990). The modification of sexual preferences. In W. L. Marshall, D. R. Laws, & H. E. Barbaree (Eds.), *Handbook of sexual assault: Issues, theories, and treatment of the offender.* New York: Plenum Press.

Rosman, J., & Resnick, P. (1989). Sexual attraction to corpses: A psychiatric review of necrophilia. *Bulletin of American Academic Psychiatry and Law, 17,* 153–163.

Saunders, E. B., & Awad, G. A. (1991). Male adolescent sexual offenders: Exhibitionism and obscene phone calls. *Child Psychiatry and Human Development, 21*(2), 169–178.

Skinner, L. J., & Becker, J. V. (1985). Sexual dysfunctions and deviations. In M. Hersen & S. M. Turner (Eds.), *Diagnostic interviewing.* New York: Plenum Press.

Tollison, C. D., & Adams, H. E. (1979). *Sexual disorders: Treatment, theory, research.* New York: Gardner Press.

Wincze, J. P. (1989). Assessment and treatment of atypical sexual behavior. In S. R. Leiblum & R. C. Rosen (Eds.), *Principles and practice of sex therapy* (2nd ed.). New York: Guilford Press.

22

MEDICAL MODELS OF SEXUAL DEVIANCE

Don Grubin
Debbie Mason

> For there is no health as such, and all attempts to define anything
> in that way have been miserable failures. Even the determination
> of what health means for your body depends on your goal, your
> horizon, your energies, your drives, your errors and above all the
> ideals and phantasms of your soul. Thus there are innumerable
> healths of the body . . . the concept of a normal health . . . and
> the normal course of an illness, [should] be abandoned by our
> physicians.
>
> —*Nietzsche (1882/1974)*

So-called medical models of sexually deviant behavior have, in recent years, become unpopular. Indeed, the whole concept of sexual deviance, with its roots in medical soil and implying as it does psychopathology and a qualitative difference from normal behavior, is now viewed with suspicion. Driven partly by feminist arguments about the "normality" of male sexual aggression and partly by the ascendance of cognitive-behavioral and learning-based models of sexual offending, medical perspectives of sexual behavior are at best seen as patronizing, and at worst, as providing a medical excuse for guilty individuals that allows them to avoid taking responsibility for their actions, substituting treatment for punishment (Herman, 1990). In the quote at the head of this chapter, Nietzsche, though not often linked either with feminist ideology or with cognitive-behaviorism, clearly anticipated these sentiments.

The problem with much of this criticism of medical models of sexual deviance is that it tends to be directed at misinterpretations of what such models actually entail. False equivalencies are often drawn between deviance and sickness, with a blurring of the boundaries between these concepts and others such as disease, mental illness, paraphilia, and sexual offending.

In the extreme, some writers have even suggested that a medical model of sexual offending cannot be right because so few sexual offenders are psychotic (Scully, 1990). From such shaky reasoning has come the conclusion that psychiatrists have little to offer in the treatment of sexually deviant individuals in general, and sexual offenders in particular. Before deciding whether or not psychiatrists do have any role to play in these areas, however, one must first be clear about what a medical model is. Only then can the implications of applying such a model to "abnormal" sexual behavior and sexual deviance be fully appreciated.

HEALTH AND DISEASE

Medical models are based on the notions of health and disease. These are elusive and complex concepts, not easily defined. Modern attempts to describe what "health" is, for example, often begin with reference to the definition of health put forward by the World Health Organization (WHO) as "a state of complete physical, mental and social well being and not merely the absence of disease or infirmity" (1990, p. 1). Viewed in this way, a healthy life has strong similarities to the alchemist's stone of the good, or at least the happy life, something which has been on the agenda of philosophers for centuries but which, fortunately, is beyond the scope of this chapter. Its relevance lies in its recognition of both positive (well being) and negative (absence of disease or infirmity) components, though it of course begs the question of what constitutes disease.

Importantly, the WHO definition also identifies physical, mental, and social factors as integral to the concept of health. Thus, it is possible for an individual to be "diseased" but to have a high level of well being, such as someone with an undetected cancer who is in no pain or discomfort. Conversely, an individual may be free from disease but have a low level of mental and social well being, as in the case of a single mother, living in disadvantaged circumstances, on a low income, unhappy but without infirmity.

The notion of health as a subjective matter can be equally applied to notions of ill health, as can its dimensional nature: there are degrees of both health and disease, with neither being an all-or-nothing matter. Furthermore, as in health, so too in ill health can a number of related but different concepts be found (Gunn & Taylor, 1993). Illness, for instance, is concerned with symptoms (and suffering) identified by a patient, while disease is viewed as a more technical, objective entity related to the identification by a doctor of abnormalities in structure or function that cause the symptoms of which a patient complains, produces signs of which an individual may be unaware, or threatens to do one, other, or both.

Thus, ill health, like health, is partly a subjective matter, with physical, mental, and social components. When the cause of so-called illness behavior is clearly, or at least strongly suspected to be, a physical one the terms "illness" and "disease" are often used interchangeably. When mental and social factors are more dominant, however, it has become popular to deny the individual a medical label, and with it the sympathy and protection that accompanies this. Instead, illness behavior is then seen as a sign of psychological or moral weakness, or as an attempt to manipulate others. In the extreme, it leads to largely sterile arguments over whether an individual is "mad" or "bad," as if these are mutually exclusive terms, and to confusion over whether offenders should be treated or punished, epitomized by the controversy over the various U.S. sexual psychopath laws (Grubin & Prentky, 1993).

Because much of what psychiatrists call "mental illness" and "mental disorder" does not have clear physical causes, psychiatry has been left open to the charge that it "medicalizes" what are in effect personal and social problems, as well as bad behavior, allowing the individual to avoid responsibility for his or her apparently self-created situation and the distress he or she may cause others. It is this essentially moral view, linked to a belief that physical causes are essential to the notion of disease, that has led some to argue that mental illness is a myth, no more than a relabeling of deviant behavior (Laing, 1965; Szasz, 1961).

To counter this sort of argument, psychiatrists tend to hold out the hope of eventually discovering the physical basis of mental illness, personality disorder, and deviant behavior in an attempt to put their discipline on an equal footing with more physically based medical specialities (Andreasen, 1985).

But is the notion of disease really any more objective than that of illness? Certainly in practice doctors tend to focus on disease rather than on health or illness, and to view disease as an objective matter associated with the detection of pathology in an organism. A pragmatic approach such as this, providing as it does an illusion of value-free objectivity, is a reasonable one for a busy physician to take in his day to day work. As Kendell (1975, p. 306) pointed out, "The practical nature of medicine is not conducive to theorizing." But it is not the presence of bacteria, abnormal cells, anomalous structures, or deviations from statistical norms that constitute disease. Rather, it is the way in which these phenomena interact with the individual who has them and the environment in which that individual lives: We do not say someone has a disease simply because he or she carries streptococcal bacteria in his throat, or has "precancerous" cells in her cervix.

The abstract nature of disease was well described by Gunn and Taylor (1993, p. 6), who observed: "Pneumonia . . . is not a thing. The pneumococcus organism is a thing, but the term 'pneumonia' is a way of describing its effect in an afflicted person. [It] cannot be touched and seen like Mrs Brown, who suffers it, or the organisms that have invaded her." Scadding (1990) put this in a different way, warning of the risk of reifying diseases as physical entities that exist in isolation. For Scadding, diseases are simply "the sum of abnormal phenomena (that place an organism) at a biological disadvantage."

The relative nature of health and disease is reflected in the way in which modern psychiatric classifications such as DSM-IV (American Psychiatric Association, 1994) and ICD-10 (World Health Organization, 1992) define mental disorder; indeed, both avoid use of the term "disease" altogether in an attempt to limit the temptation to draw one-to-one links with specific physical causes. Both classifications define mental disorders as psychological or behavioral syndromes (that is, clinically recognizable patterns of symptoms or behaviors that cluster together) in an individual that are associated with distress or disability. DSM-IV goes further than does ICD by also associating mental disorders with a risk of impairment, and by viewing them as manifestations of a "behavioural, psychological, or biological dysfunction" (p. xxi).

Thus, the way in which psychiatrists are currently told to perceive the conditions they treat does not require a physical abnormality to be identified, or even to be postulated. Instead, what matters is the extent to which an individual is able to function successfully within his or her environment. Of course, decisions about whether clusters of symptoms or behaviors are caused by some form of dysfunction, and whether they put an individual at a biological disadvantage, are neither wholly objective nor value free, and allow psychiatry to cast its net well beyond classical mental illnesses such as schizophrenia and manic depression. But how far can the net be legitimately flung? Are all socially unacceptable behaviors fair game for an ever-expanding psychiatric empire?

MEDICAL MODELS, DEVIANCE, AND PSYCHIATRY

It often comes as a surprise to those not working in psychiatry that many psychiatrists express little interest in treating individuals whom they consider to be deviant in one way or another but who do not, in their view, suffer from mental illness per se. Although said in jest, one well-known psychiatrist quoted by Grisso (1993, p. 138) summed this up neatly when he observed that "The whole history of psychiatry has been built on hallucinations and delusions. Without them—without serious mental illness—there would be no psychiatry. We'd be nothing. Why, we'd be . . . psychologists."

The issue of whether individuals who do not have symptoms of major mental illnesses come within the remit of psychiatry lies at the heart of the heated controversy over the nature of personality disorders, and in particular, whether there is such a thing as psychopathic disorder (Chiswick, 1992). Although the inevitable focus on compulsory treatment and a confusion between what is treatable and what is curable (Gunn & Taylor, 1993) do not help the argument, the fact is that psychiatrists often want little to do with individuals who are difficult to manage and potentially dangerous. It is not uncommon for a patient's diagnosis to change from something like schizophrenia to one of personality disorder after an episode of violence, with discharge from psychiatric care following soon after.

Limiting psychiatry to the strict confines of psychotic illness, however, is not without its critics. Gunn (1992, p. 210), for instance, pointed out that society has certain expectations of what psychiatrists should be doing, and that "if psychiatry gives up all its difficult patients, society will give up psychiatry." Psychiatrists are expected to have expertise in dealing with disturbed individuals, regardless of whether the disturbance is endogenous to that individual or has its roots in external, situational factors. Whereas those who are distrustful of psychiatrists might feel that abandoning of of psychiatry would be no bad thing, the resulting vacuum would likely be filled quickly by clinicians from other disciplines who may not have the training or inclination to recognize when the causes of disturbed behavior have crossed the boundary between health and illness, and who instead deal with the individual according to whatever theory underlies their approach. At its most basic level, it is the working of our brains that produces our thoughts and behaviors; like any organ in the body, brains can go wrong, and psychiatrists at least are in a position to keep this in context.

Apart from theoretical considerations of how society expects psychiatrists to function, however, in practice few psychiatrists limit their attention solely to psychotic symptoms (at least, until the patient becomes difficult to manage). Courts force them to focus on rationality (that is, did an individual know what he was doing when he committed some act?) as a defining feature of "insanity," but in general clinical practice other aspects of both brain and mind, such as affective, volitional, and cognitive components, also loom large. Toward this end, psychiatrists evaluate individuals whose mental states contain symptoms such as anxiety, low mood, difficult to resist urges, and similar features which fall well short of psychosis (and indeed may be thought of simply as part of the human condition) to determine the extent to which these symptoms interfere with an individual's functioning and compromise his or her well being. Treatment is then based on the nature of the symptoms found.

Psychiatrists become more uncomfortable when the presenting problem is one of unusual or socially deviant behavior rather than of psychological symptoms per se. They risk being drawn into areas well beyond their expertise, providing authority to what may be no more than expressions of approval or disapproval, or in the extreme, to pronounce on the presence of evil (Prins, 1994). But when deviance is used to indicate a change in an individual from one state to another, or when it is applied in a statistical sense to denote variation from a norm, then it may have more psychiatric relevance.

Terms such as deviance, of course, may be used in a number of ways which are sometimes confused, ranging from an indication of change within an individual to statistical variations from a norm to simply a statement that something is different. What all these uses have in common is their relation to what is (or should be) "usual" or "conventional." Being unusual or unconventional, of course, does not mean that someone has an illness. An individual who wears only pink shoes might be unusual, but not necessarily ill; likewise, someone who is above average in height deviates from the norm. However, excessive growth may be an indication of acromegaly (a condition caused by a tumor that produces growth hormone), whereas an exclusive predilection for pink shoes may relate to delusional beliefs about footwear in an individual with schizophrenia. Deviation is not something that should be taken at face value.

What is usual or conventional in terms of thoughts and behavior, of course, is more dependent upon cultural influences than are straightforward physical features or more objective tests of function, even when considered in the seemingly value-free context of biological disadvantage. Something as seemingly biologically disadvantageous to an individual animal as homosexuality may have important benefits for the family group if, for example, it offered a means of limiting population expansion while at the same time increasing the number of male workers and defenders. But because one must tread cautiously when using concepts such as "normality" and "deviance" does not mean that they should be excluded from the psychiatrist's diagnostic tool kit; indeed, they are so essential in the evaluation of mental functioning that even if the words were banned, new ones would almost certainly emerge to take their place.

Thus, whereas deviance itself, whether sexual or otherwise, is not a psychiatric diagnosis, it may indicate that one is present. One of the skills psychiatrists must learn is to distinguish between deviant behaviors which, though perhaps unacceptable to society are not related to underlying dysfunction and disorder, and those that are. Merely having unusual or uncommon desires is not sufficient grounds for a psychiatric diagnosis, but the reasons for having those desires might be. And while society may put pressure on psychiatrists to help control individuals who are socially deviant as a convenient way to keep them detained (Grubin & Prentky, 1993), this alone is not a reason for psychiatrists to ignore those who display deviant behaviors. In some of these cases, medical models will best explain the behavior and provide an appropriate way to modify it.

Sexual Deviance and Psychiatry

Doctors tend to view sexuality in a dimensional rather than a categorical manner, with the borders between acceptable and deviant behavior blurred; the hinterlands, however, are more easily recognized. Christie-Brown (1983), for example, described dimensions of sexual behavior relating to the gender identity of the individual, the individual's object choice (which itself can be broken down into a number of other dimensions such as age, sex, and type of object), and arousal (including frequency, rate, and final level of arousal). Any one individual may vary over each dimension independent of the others, depending upon both inherent traits and external circumstances, but if his or her behavior consistently falls at the extreme of one or more of these dimensions then the issue of sexual deviance arises. This is particularly the case when the behavior is against the law.

On the surface, the term "sexual deviance" is merely descriptive, meaning in effect that an individual's sexual thoughts or behavior are in some way unusual or unconventional. However, it carries with it the negative connotation that these thoughts or actions are not only abnormal, but undesirable; when they are also viewed in this way by the individual who has them, or when the individual feels as if he is no longer in full control of sexual thoughts and behavior, he may seek medical help. So long as his sexual deviance has not resulted in antisocial or illegal behavior this is all straightforward enough, but once these boundaries have been crossed there is a tendency for a medical presentation to be interpreted as a search for an excuse rather than for help.

From a medical point of view an individual's sexual behavior is just part of what makes up that individual's personality. As discussed above, it becomes a valid focus of medical attention only when it is associated with a more global dysfunction, related to, for instance, feelings of distress or lack of control or actual loss of control. There is no need for the behavior to be caused by a defect in rationality (most people would view sexually deviant individuals as rational) or a complete loss of volition, nor need it be part of a psychotic illness. In terms of DSM-IV, only when deviant sexual fantasies, urges, or behaviors are recurrent and intense and when they cause significant distress or impairment in functioning does sexual deviance solidify into a diagnosis of one of the paraphilias. Simply engaging in unusual but ego-syntonic sexual behavior is not enough.

As in any medical disorder, the diagnosis of a paraphlia does not require or imply the presence of organic pathology although occasional brain abnormalities have been demonstrated (Langevin et al., 1988). There have, however, been numerous attempts to demonstrate physical abnormalities which may directly and "scientifically" explain sexually deviant behavior in the belief that an organic causal link provides a stronger argument for viewing sexual deviance as a bona fide medical disorder. There have been few directly relevant studies in this area, perhaps, unsurprisingly, when one considers the highly complex nature of human sexual behavior and the combination of genetic, biological, and environmental factors which contribute to it. For example, in a series of experiments carried out in the 1960s, Delgado (1969) showed that in the case of aggression in primates it is simply not possible to disentangle social from organic influences. In these studies electrodes were implanted in the brains of free-ranging monkeys and chimpanzees. When the electrodes were stimulated, the animals made aggressive displays. These were dependent, however, on the hierarchical position of the animal within the social group, as the monkey or chimp did not behave aggressively when it was in the presence of a more dominant monkey or chimp. It is hard to get more "organic" than an implanted, discharging electrode, but social factors nonetheless clearly come between neurons and what would otherwise seem to be obligatory behavior.

Perhaps the most extreme proponent of the strict biological view is Money. In writing about sexual sadism, for example, he argues (Money, 1995, p. 48), "Like other paraphilias, sexual sadism is a brain disease. The disease affects the centers and pathways in the brain that are responsible for sexual arousal, mating behavior and reproduction of the species." He goes on to provide an account of the various mechanisms that could lead to the relevant pathology ranging from hereditary predisposition through hormonal functioning, brain damage, and behavioral insult at a critical age. Unfortunately, he supplies no evidence to support any of these theoretical possibilities, and we are again left with the tautology that mental states have underlying brain states. But is there evidence of strong links between biology and sexual deviance?

Genetic influences have often been suggested as being important in the etiology of sexual aggression. In particular, the presence of an extra Y chromosome has been postulated to increase aggressive and criminal behavior. Detailed studies, however, have failed to support this theory. Schiavi, Theilgaard, Owen, and White (1984), in a double-blind controlled study found that men with an extra Y chromosome have higher levels of testosterone than normals. They also demonstrated a link between high testosterone levels and violent offending in all men, but concluded that the chromosome abnormalities were not a mediating factor in offending behavior.

Of course, biological factors that exert a strong influence on human sexual behavior have been identified. Hormones have been the most extensively studied, driven partly by the therapeutic possibilities of hormonal manipulation. Research has been predominantly of two types: (1) measuring testosterone levels and attempting to correlate these with behavioral variables such as sexual drive, sexual deviation, or aggression, or (2) studying the effects of castration on sexual functioning.

The hormonal environment in which a fetus develops is important for later gender-specific behavior, with high testosterone levels in utero leading to a "masculine" pattern of neural connections and more aggressive and socially dominant behavior in adulthood (Dixson, 1980). However, whether testosterone levels in later life have a direct impact on sexual behavior, aggressive or otherwise, is less clear. Testosterone is produced in the testes and to a lesser extent in the adrenals and is important in a number of physiological processes, most notably the development of secondary sexual characteristics and sexual drive and functioning. Studies involving small numbers of subjects described links between elevated plasma testosterone levels and sexual violence (Rada, Laws, & Kellner, 1976), social dominance and aggression (Ehrenkranz, Bliss, & Sheard, 1974), and hostile affect (Persky, Smith, & Basu, 1971), but other workers have failed to replicate these findings; by way of contrast, Raboch, Herna, and Zemek (1987) described two cases of sexual murder in men with extremely low levels of plasma testosterone.

At present there is no reason to believe that the level of testosterone in itself is of any particular relevance to either sexual deviance or sexual offending, though changes in testosterone levels may be more important (Prentky, 1985). Although fluctuations within the normal range do not seem to be important, reduction of testosterone to prepubescent levels results in a loss of erectile potency and a reduction in sexual urges and thoughts. Such a reduction can be achieved by either surgical castration or administration of antiandrogenic drugs.

Surgical castration has a long history, performed either for religious, aesthetic, or cultural reasons or as a form of punishment for sexual offenses or adultery. Its use as treatment for sexual deviance began only this century. It is popularly supposed that castration permanently abolishes sexual drive and potency and consequently prevents sexual offending. Research on castrated sex offenders shows that in reality the effects are less absolute. Although sex drive and sexual activity are reduced after castration, the rate of fall and final level of functioning are variable. Around 70% of men lose all sexual urges and erectile potency shortly after surgery, but 10% to 30% are still capable of intercourse and ejaculation up to 10 years later (Cornu, 1973; Heim, 1981; Langeluddeke, 1963).

Published studies claim impressive, generally single-figure reconviction rates following castration. Sturup (1968), for example, in a large Danish follow-up study involving 900 castrated sex offenders, found a reoffense rate of only 2.2%. Figures from this and other follow-up studies should be viewed with caution, however, as most were uncontrolled and involved a heterogeneous group of subjects whose deviant behaviors ranged from homosexuality and indecent exposure to rape. Given the widely differing behavioral consequences of castration, the notion of a simple physiological link is difficult to sustain and this has led authors (Heim & Hursch, 1979) to conclude that castration is not an appropriate treatment for sexual deviance.

In more recent decades drugs rather than surgery have been more commonly used to reduce androgenic activity. Drugs commonly prescribed are cyproterone acetate in the United Kingdom and medroxyprogesterone acetate in the United States. Both drugs reduce testosterone levels, but in addition, cyproterone blocks the effect of testosterone on target organs. Both have been shown to reduce sexual urges, thoughts, and erectile potency reliably (Laschet & Laschet, 1978), but their effect on reconviction rates is less clear. Berlin and Meinecke (1981) reported only three relapses of offending behavior among 20 men during treatment with medroxyprogesterone acetate, but they described a high dropout rate from treatment, with all but one of those who terminated treatment against medical advice subsequently reoffending. Other authors reported variable relapse rates from zero to one third (Neumann & Kalmus, 1991).

Although antilibidinal drugs may reduce the strength of sexual urges, they have no effect on the direction of the urge. There is no evidence to suggest that they alter any preexisting chemical abnormality and their efficacy depends on being used in association with psychological therapies.

Just as care must be taken not to overvalue the contribution of organic factors to the development of sexual deviance, however, so too must we take care not to ignore them altogether. Brain injury, for example, has been postulated as a relevant factor in sexual deviance in some cases. Galski, Thornton, and Shumsky (1990) described evidence of minor brain damage in sexually deviant individuals and suggested that such damage in early childhood may lead to disturbances of personality and sexuality in later life. The hypothalamic region of the brain may be particularly important, as it exerts a regulatory function on sexual behavior; experiments in animals have demonstrated that lesions in this area abolish sexual behavior, whereas electrical stimulation or sex hormone implantation induces it (Freund, 1980).

In both mental handicap and dementia, we can detect clear links between organic disorder and sexual offending. In both cases, however, the disorder does not affect sexual behavior primarily, but rather it causes deficits in learning and socialization which then allow expression of sexually deviant behavior. In the case of mental handicap, intellectual impairment may inhibit learning and normal socialization. The frontal lobes of the brain are particularly important in socialization, and damage to these areas by dementia, tumor, or cerebrovascular disease may cause a characteristic picture of social and sexual disinhibition, lack of self-control, poor judgment, impulsivity, and emotional lability as more primitive areas of the brain are freed from higher cortical control. In such cases a clear causal link does exist between medical conditions and sexually deviant behavior, and "medicalization" of such individuals arouses little controversy. If the role of minor degrees of brain damage in personality disorders generally and sexual deviance in particular becomes more clear, the limits of such medicalization may widen.

In the absence of clear abnormalities in hormones or brain structure, other workers (Kafka & Prentky, 1992) have conceptualized sexual deviance as associated with abnormalities of serotonin metabolism, in the same family as disorders such as obsessive–compulsive disorder and bulimia. These conditions may respond to treatment with drugs that primarily affect serotonergic neurotransmissiom. Preliminary studies have suggested that fluoxetine, for example, has a specific effect on sexually deviant fantasies and behavior, leaving culturally appropriate sexuality unimpaired (Kafka, 1995).

At one level, of course, all behavior can be reduced to neurons firing in the brain, and regardless of the importance of psychological and social learning factors in the etiology of deviant sexuality, medical explanations and treatments may still have an impact upon it. It is unfortunate that some of those who treat sexual offenders have become so blinded by arguments about the social origins of sexual deviance and the fear of bringing deviant behavior into a medical context that the only treatments they will consider are those that involve difficult and often painful psychological work by the offender. Indeed, even if a drug were developed that would "cure" sexual deviance or prevent sexual offending, it is probably the case that many would be reluctant to recommend it on the grounds that it would be "cheating."

Even among those who accept that medical concepts and physical treatments may have something to offer in the treatment of some individuals with sexual deviance, there remains a worry that in embracing a medical model they are implying that the individual is not responsible for his behavior. However, just as attacks on medical models of sexual deviance are often based on a misunderstanding of what such models imply about causation and phenomenology, so too do they often rely on simplistic and confused ideas of what such models imply about responsibility. To explore the extent to which medical models may or may not absolve individuals of responsibility, it is worth looking at the application of a medical perspective to specific types of sexual aggression.

EXAMPLES: CHILD MOLESTATION AND RAPE

Sex with Children and Pedophilia

Regardless of what professionals might think about the nature of men who are sexually attracted to children, the ordinary public on the whole readily and vocally identifies such men as "sick." Sexual activity between adults and children is usually considered both immoral and illegal, and the law in most developed countries makes it impossible for a child to give valid consent to such activity. The extent to which "normal" men are sexually aroused by children, however, is unclear, but the frequency with which adults in victim surveys report having been abused as children (Peters, Wyatt, & Finkelhor, 1986), the numbers of nonoffending men who show sexual arousal to children in penile plethysmography studies (Freund, 1981), and the way in which advertisers commonly depict children in sexually provocative poses to sell their products suggest that the phenomenon is not rare. Indeed, the strength of social taboos against men having sex with children is probably a good indication of the power of the drive these taboos seek to prevent.

The extent to which different societies proscribe sexual activity between adults and children varies, with important distinctions found depending upon age, whether the child is male or female, and the context in which the sexual activity takes place. Historically, proscriptions against sex with children were mainly concerned with boys and sexual activity with girls has usually been more widely accepted (Quinsey, 1986). Indeed, definitions of when a female child reaches adulthood have been fluid over time and between cultures, and even in the West it has only been in the 20th century that childhood, and hence the period when sexual activity is discouraged, has extended beyond the early teens (Ames & Houston, 1990). In terms of males, ritualistic initiation ceremonies involving sex between men and boys are not uncommon in many undeveloped societies, and even recreational sexual contact between men and boys is accepted in many of these countries (reviewed in Grubin, 1992; Quinsey, 1986). What is common throughout, however, is that such activity is subject to strict cultural rules, and that with very few exceptions incest is almost never tolerated.

If sexual arousal toward children is not rare, why, then, is it so readily labeled as "sick"? It is always risky to speculate on the reasons behind the development of cultural proscriptions, but it is probably safe to say that strong ones such as those associated with incest and, where they exist, sex with children serve important functions within that culture. Given the plasticity of the sexual drive and the likely presence in many individuals of at least some sexual responsiveness to children, it may be that in the face of powerful cultural prohibitions individuals attempt to distance themselves from these unacceptable feelings by conceptualizing acts of sex with children as being the product of sick minds (Bancroft, 1991).

From a medical point of view, however, an individual's sexual arousal to children or his initiation of sexual behavior with a child are in themselves of limited interest. They become relevant only if they form part of a larger pattern in which the individual experiences distress, appears to have only limited control of his thoughts, urges, or behaviors, or is unable to enter into mutually satisfying sexual relationships with adults because his sexual attraction to children has become dominant or even overpowering. It is at this point that the behavior is no longer part of an integrated, healthy whole. The man for whom sex with children is preferable and acceptable and who is able to control his behavior, although immoral and potentially antisocial, is not a potential patient.

Medical assessment of an individual for whom issues of sexual activity with children are involved aims to evaluate the sexual behavior in terms of how it interacts with his beliefs, desires, and general ability to function socially. A diagnosis of pedophilia is no more than a formulation that helps focus attention on particular issues and allows these to be communicated in a simple manner to other clinicians. In addition, it provides a rationale for treatment, because one of the distinguishing features of a medical approach is that treatment is based on diagnostic hypotheses; doctors on the whole tend to be uncomfortable treating individuals with whom there is nothing wrong.

Of course, it does not follow from the fact that a medical model is used that drug treatment emerges as the most appropriate therapy; it certainly does not follow that it will be the only treatment. Known contributors to both the etiology and maintenance of pedophilic behavior, such as cognitive distortions about childhood sexuality, dysfunctional family structures, or poor impulse control, may all be part of the medical formulation and become the focus of therapy. A physical pathology need not underlie the diagnosis, as it is function rather than structure that is the main issue for the psychiatrist.

Thus, it is not the sexual arousal or the deviant behavior that are critical for the psychiatrist, but what these characteristics indicate about the individual who is sexually aroused or who behaves in a deviant manner. This does not mean that the individual must agree that there is a problem to make a diagnosis of pedophilia, as individuals have various degrees of insight into their behavior. Such agreement, however, will help determine the extent to which treatment is likely to be successful. However, whether or not an individual can be treated should not be confused with whether or not he has a disorder. There are many disorders in all branches of medicine, including many cancers, for which we do not have treatments.

The distinction between the popular view of men who have sex with children as perverted and sick and the medical formulation of trying to understand an individual's behavior in the context of biological factors associated with sexual drive as well as with personality traits and learning experiences is usually not made by those who condemn medical models. Instead, they portray medical formulations of pedophilia as "dressing up" the popular conception of perversion in biological clothes, with the implication that the behavior is therefore beyond the individual's control and hence his responsibility. In fact, however, medical models make no assumptions about the biological contribution to pedophilia other than the broad one that the sexual drive is by its nature biological and controlled by the brain. While physical treatments may modify the drive, this has little relevance to questions of biological determinism or responsibility, as I will discuss in more detail below.

Sexual Aggression toward Women

In contrast with the tendency to view sexual activity between adults and children as alien and the men who carry it out as sick, men who are sexually aggressive toward women, with the exception perhaps of those who are extremely sadistic or those who kill, are less likely to be seen as incomprehensible by the lay public. behaviors associated with rape and other forms of sexual aggression are similar to what might be considered normal male sexual behavior. There is nothing particularly psychiatric about rape. Instead, social and cultural factors are more readily accepted as the main fuel driving sexual aggression against women, with feminist writers in particular popularizing the view that such behavior is to be expected in male-dominated societies wherein high levels of interpersonal violence are the norm.

Brownmiller (1975, p. 15), for example, famously stated that "rape . . . is a conscious process of intimidation by which all men keep all women in a state of fear."

Unfortunately, we have embraced important insights about the contribution of cultural factors to sexual aggression with such enthusiasm that arguments about the nature of sexually aggressive men have become polarized. Scully (1990, p. 35), for instance, asserted that focusing on medical factors "ignores ample evidence that links sexual aggression to cultural factors. . . . The disease model has retarded efforts to arrive at a general explanation for sexual violence." The very belief that such general explanations and categorical answers exist, however, has obscured the fact that crimes like rape cover a wide range of complex behaviors, and the circumstances in which they occur and the motivation behind them vary tremendously. The debate has become personal and political, with the desire for punishment, both of individual offenders and men in general, leaving little room for more careful distinctions to be made about the causes of sexual aggression in individual men.

One of the most frequently quoted pieces of research supposedly demonstrating the overwhelming dominance of cultural factors in the genesis of sexual aggression toward women was a study that compared sexual assault and rape in about 100 tribal societies (Sanday, 1981). The incidence of rape appeared to vary in proportion to the amount of general interpersonal and intergroup violence in a culture and with the degree of male dominance in the culture (although how these two factors interact was not examined). Although there were various methodological problems with the survey, and its relevance to sexual aggression in more developed countries is less than clear because much of the sexual aggression related to interclan rivalries and warfare, it is probably safe to assume that in societies where violence of a general nature is common, sexual violence will also be found (Grubin, 1992).

Even in male-dominated, aggressive societies, however, the question remains whether sexual arousal to violence is the norm, and in addition, where such arousal exists, whether its expression in predatory attacks on unknown women is simply an extension of aggressive behavior within a relationship. It is not self-evident that the behavior of a serial rapist falls under the same explanatory cloak as that of an abusive boyfriend. In a large English study of imprisoned rapists, for example, serial rapists were notable by the large amount of sexually disturbed behavior in their backgrounds when compared with men who had raped only once or who had raped only those with whom they had previously had social interactions (Grubin & Gunn, 1990).

General statements about sexually aggressive men must be made with caution, as they are a heterogeneous group of individuals. Although attitudes and beliefs, pornography use, hormonal abnormalities, and a variety of other considerations have been offered as the basis of the behavior, the most that can be said is that some factors are important in some men. Further, while in some senses any man is a potential rapist, the fact is that not all men are aroused by coercive sex when measured, for example, in phallometric studies (Abel, Barlow, Blanchard, & Guild, 1977; Quinsey & Chaplin, 1984), nor do all men regularly fantasize about rape (Malamuth, 1981).

Some clinicians have argued that the repetitive and compulsive nature of sexually aggressive fantasies and urges in some men, together with their early age of onset and their association with other paraphilias, implies that rape behavior in these men should be viewed as a paraphilia, and that it is driven by more than simply the social forces supportive of sexual aggression (Abel, Becker, Cunningham-Rathner, Mittelman, & Rouleau, 1988; Abel & Rouleau, 1990). The extent to which sexual sadism is an indicator of a more pervasive disorder also remains to be determined, with some arguing that it may represent an abnormality in affect associated with empathy (Grubin, 1994). As with pedophilia, these types of formulations do not postulate biological abnormalities, nor do they excuse the behavior; instead, they shift the focus away from statements about society toward an examination of individuals who happen to live in that society.

Sexual aggression toward women involves both sex and violence, and mental disorder related to either of these elements may be an important contributor to sexual assault. Even if much of sexual aggression can be explained by cultural and subcultural factors, any group of sexually aggressive men is likely to contain some in whom mental disorder is present and in whom aggression is but one manifestation. This is not to say that social context is unimportant in this group, but only that its impact is likely to have different effects because of the underlying disorder. Although some societies may be more rape prone than others, it is individuals within that societies who rape. The adoption of a medical perspective in relation to sexual aggression, entailing as it does a full assessment of the individual, ensures that we do not forget this side of the equation.

IMPLICATIONS OF MEDICAL MODELS

Many of those who criticize the application of medical models to sexual deviance and sexual offending do so because of the belief that such models provide a blame-free interpretation of unacceptable behavior. Their argument is that by "medicalizing" bad behavior and social problems, psychiatrists allow sexual offenders to claim that they are not responsible for their actions, hence enabling them to avoid punishment. By apparently blurring the distinctions between deviance and offending, proponents of this view also castigate these models for focusing attention on the individual, rather than on the nature of societies and the social forces that encourage sexual aggression.

When issues relating to morality and medicine come into contact in this way, a certain amount of backward reasoning can occur. Thus, sexually deviant behavior is seen as morally blameworthy and deserving of punishment; it is inferred that a medical diagnosis will free an individual from culpability, and it is therefore rejected. But the role of a medical model is to help explain, not to excuse, and society remains free to tolerate or to condemn independent of whether a psychiatrist has identified the presence of a mental disorder; bad deeds remain bad whether or not they are the product of mental disorder. Medical models are blame free, but it does not follow that all those with a medical diagnosis are free of blame.

At one end of the spectrum, a medical condition may result in behavior occurring which otherwise might not have taken place. This might be the case in a law-abiding, sociable, and respected man who develops a brain tumor and subsequently undergoes a change in personality, exhibiting sexually deviant behavior for the first time. The clear causal link means that many would accept that the individual ought not to be held accountable for his behavior. At the other end of the spectrum is a young man with a history of parental neglect and sexual victimization who exhibits sexually deviant, impulsive, and self-destructive behavior as an adult. Although he, too, may suffer from a mental disorder, albiet not one with a clear physical pathology, we may nevertheless refuse to excuse him, as the causal link between antecedent and behavior is less strong. In between are men with with deviant sexual drives over which they may have more or less control.

A medical diagnosis of paraphilia may contribute to the explanation of why an individual behaves as he does and suggest possible treatments, but whether it will also constitute an excuse depends on matters other than purely medical ones. In most individuals inappropriate or antisocial sexual desires are not acted upon; the mere presence of a paraphilia, therefore, does not remove the notion of responsibility. An individual may exhibit violent or deviant sexual behavior for a wide range of reasons. Only by examining the individual in his unique situation can we understand the relevant factors which account for the behavior and find appropriate responses to them.

The tendency to excuse wrongdoing in the mentally disordered is not dependent on the presence or absence of a diagnosis, but on traditional legal and philosophical issues about the quality of immoral actions. In general, individuals are held accountable only for autonomous actions, that is actions which spring from rational thought, are consistent with the individual's own goals and values, are based on full and correct information, and are free from coercion (internal as well as external). Medical considerations are relevant only when they suggest that an action is not wholly autonomous, a judgment that is not in fact part of the doctor's expertise. The law clearly recognizes this; although it allows doctors to comment on questions of responsibility, it leaves it up to juries to determine the answers.

In the end, the issues for the doctor relate to prognosis and treatment, not to evil, wickedness, or responsibility. In treatment lies the essential reason for applying medical models to sexual deviance, for doctors have at their disposal a wide range of therapeutic options, including drug therapy. Their applications seek to influence behavior without necessarily curing it; symptomatic relief of this kind is common to medical intervention of all kinds.

One implication of the medical model which can create difficulties for the doctor, however, is where a sexually deviant individual is also thought to be dangerous and the issue of compulsory treatment arises. Indeed, there may be pressure on the doctor to resort to various medical interventions as a means of behavioral control, with chemical or physical castration the most obvious examples. These, however, are issues that in reality have have little to do with medicine, and are related more to the tasks that society wants medicine to take on. To the extent that they are alternative forms of detention and punishment and not attempts to provide treatment and rehabilitation, they in fact have little to do with medicine at all.

CONCLUSION

A medical model of sexual deviance and sexual offending is not in opposition to social or psychological explanations of these phenomena. However, where the latter tend to focus on global forces and influences, the medical model has the individual as its starting point. It has a biological foundation only insofar as it recognizes that initiators of behavior such as the sexual drive are influenced by a variety of factors, some of which have a physical basis. The strength of the medical model is in its ability to recognize that individuals do not always have full conscious control over their behavior, while at the same time not placing a moral judgment on this lack of control. That medical models are sometimes viewed as a threat to society's need to condone or punish is a reflection of the confusion that tends to underlie these models, even within physical medicine. The danger is that this confusion will prevent some individuals from receiving treatment that might not only benefit themselves, but may also help prevent the suffering of others.

REFERENCES

Abel, G. G., Barlow, D. H., Blanchard, E. B., & Guild, D. (1977). The components of rapist's sexual arousal. *Archives of General Psychiatry, 34,* 895–903.

Abel, G. G., Becker, J. V., Cunningham-Rathner, J., Mittelman, M. S., & Rouleau, J. L. (1988). Multiple paraphilic diagnoses among sex offenders. *Bulletin of the American Academy of Psychiatry and the Law, 16,* 153–168.

Abel, G. G., & Rouleau, J. L. (1990). The nature and extent of sexual assault. In W. L. Marshall, D. R. Laws, & H. E. Barbaree (Eds.), *Handbook of sexual assault: Issues, theories, and treatment of the offender*. New York: Plenum Press.

American Psychiatric Association. (1994). *Diagnostic and statistical manual of mental disorders* (4th ed.). Washington, DC: Author.

Ames, M. A., & Houston, D. A. (1990). Legal, social, and biological definitions of pedophilia. *Archives of Sexual Behavior, 19*, 333–342.

Andreasen, N. (1985). *The broken brain: The biological revolution in psychiatry*. London: HarperCollins.

Bancroft, J. (1991). The sexuality of sexual offending: The social dimension. *Criminal Behaviour and Mental Health, 1*, 181–192.

Berlin, F. S., & Meinecke, C. F. (1981). Treatment of sex offenders with antiandrogenic medication: Conceptualization, review of treatment modalities and preliminary findings. *American Journal of Psychiatry, 138*(5), 601–607.

Brownmiller, S. (1975). *Against our will: Men, women and rape*. London: Penguin Books.

Chiswick, D. (1992). Compulsory treatment of patients with psychopathic disorder: An abnormally aggressive or seriously irresponsible exercise? *Criminal Behaviour and Mental Health, 2*, 106–113.

Christie-Brown, J. R. W. (1983). Sadomasochism, fetishism, transvestism, and transsexuality. *British Journal of Psychiatry, 143*, 227–231.

Cornu, F. (1973). Katamnesen bei kastrierten sittlicheitsdelinquenten aus forensischpsychaitrischrn sicht. *Biblioteca Psychiatrica, 149*, 1–132.

Delgado, J. M. R. (1969). Offensive–defensive behaviour in free monkeys and chimpanzees induced by radio stimulation of the brain. In S. Garatini & E. B. Sigg (Eds.), *Aggressive behaviour: Proceedings of International Symposium on the Biology of Aggressive Behaviour*. Amsterdam: Exerpta Medica.

Dixson, A. F. (1980). Androgens and aggressive behavior in primates: A review. *Agressive Behavior, 6*, 37–67.

Ehrenkranz, J., Bliss, E., & Sheard, M. H. (1974). Plasma testosterone: Correlation with agressive behaviour and social dominance in man. *Psychosomatic Medicine, 36*(6), 469–475.

Freund, K. (1980). Therapeutic sex drive reduction. *Acta Psychiatrica Scandinavia, 287*, 5–37.

Freund, K. (1981). The assessment of pedophilia. In M. Cook & K. Howells (Eds.), *Adult sexual interest in children*. London: Academic Press.

Galski, T., Thornton, K. E., & Shumsky, D. (1990). Brain dysfunction in sex offenders. *Journal of Offender Rehabilitation, 16*, 65–80.

Grisso, T. (1993). The differences between forensic psychiatry and forensic psychology. *Bulletin of the American Academy of Psychiatry and the Law, 21*, 133–145.

Grubin, D. (1992). Sexual offending: A cross-cultural comparison. *Annual Review of Sex Research, 3*, 201–217.

Grubin, D. (1994). Sexual murder. *British Journal of Psychiatry, 165*, 624–629.

Grubin, D., & Gunn, J. (1990). *The imprisoned rapist and rape*. Unpublished manuscript.

Grubin, D., & Prentky, R. (1993). Sexual psychopath laws. *Criminal Behaviour and Mental Health, 3*, 381–393.

Gunn, J. (1992). Personality disorders and forensic psychiatry. *Criminal Behaviour and Mental Health, 2*, 202–211.

Gunn, J., & Taylor, P. J. (1993). Introduction. In J. Gunn & P. J. Taylor (Eds.), *Forensic psychiatry: Clinical, legal and ethical issues*. Oxford: Butterworth-Heinemann.

Heim, N. (1981). Sexual behaviour of castrated sex offenders. *Archives of Sexual Behavior, 10*, 11–19.

Heim, N., & Hursch, C. J. (1979). Castration for sex offenders: Treatment or punishment? A review and critique of recent European literature. *Archives of Sexual Behavior, 8*(3), 281–305.

Herman, J. L. (1990). Sex offenders: A feminist perspective. In W. L. Marshall, D. R. Laws, & H. E. Barbaree (Eds.), *Handbook of sexual assault: Issues, theories, and treatment of the offender*. New York: Plenum Press.

Kafka, M. P. (1995). Current concepts in the drug treatment of paraphilias and paraphilia related disorders. *CNS Drugs, 3,* 9–21.

Kafka, M., & Prentky, R. (1992). Fluoxetine treatment of nonparaphilic sexual addictions and paraphilias in men. *Journal of Clinical Psychiatry, 53,* 351–358.

Kendall, R. E. (1975). The concept of disease and its implications for psychiatry. *British Journal of Psychiatry, 127,* 305–315.

Laing, R. D. (1965). *The divided self.* Harmondsworth, England: Penguin Books.

Langeluddeke, A. (1963). *Die entmannung von sittlichkeitsverbrechern in Deutschland: In die entmannung von sittlichkeitsverbrechern.* Berlin: de Gruyter.

Langevin, R., Bain, J., Wortzman, G., Hucker, S., Dickey, R., & Wright, P. (1988). Sexual sadism: Brain, blood and behavior. In R. A. Prentky & V. L. Quinsey (Eds.), *Human sexual aggression: Annals of the New York Academy of Sciences* [Special issue], *528,* 163–171.

Laschet, U., & Laschet, L. (1978). Ten years: Cyproterone acetate for the modification of sexual behaviour In Men. *bga-Berichte, II,* 91–96.

Malamuth, M. R. (1981). Rape proclivity. *Journal of Social Issues, 37,* 138–147.

Money, J. (1995). Forensic sexology: Paraphilic serial rape (biastophilia) and lust murder (erotophonophilia). *Acta Sexologica, 1,* 47–62.

Neumann, F., & Kalmus, J. (1991) *Hormonal treatment of sexual deviations: Rationale, pharmacological principles and therapeutic possibilities.* Berlin: Diesbach.

Nietzsche, F. (1974). *The gay science* (W. Kaufman, Trans.). New York: Random House. (Original work published 1882)

Persky, H., Smith, K. D., & Basu, G. K. (1971). Relation of psychologic measures of aggression and hostility to testosterone production in man. *Psychosomatic Medicine, 33,* 265–277.

Peters, S. D., Wyatt, G. E., & Finkelhor, D. (1986). Prevalence. In D. Finkelhor (Ed.), *A sourcebook on child sexual abuse.* London: Sage.

Prins, H. (1984). Psychiatry and the concept of evil. *British Journal of Psychiatry, 165,* 297–300.

Prentky, R. (1985). The neurochemistry and neuroendocrinology of sexual aggression. In D. P. Farrington & J. Gunn (Eds.), *Aggression and dangerousness.* New York: Wiley.

Quinsey, V. L., & Chaplin, T. C. (1984). Stimulus control of rapists' and non-sex-offenders' sexual arousal. *Behavioral Assessment, 6,* 169–176.

Quinsey, V. L. (1986). Men who have sex with children. In D. Wesstub (Ed.), *Law and mental health: International perspectives* (Vol. 2). New York: Pergamon Press.

Raboch, J., Herna, C., & Zemek, P. (1987). Sexual aggressivity and androgens. *British Journal of Psychiatry, 151,* 398–400.

Rada, R., Laws, D., & Kellner, R. (1976). Plasma testosterone levels in the rapist. *Psychosomatic Medicine, 38,* 257–268.

Sanday, P. R. (1981). The socio-cultural context of rape: A cross-cultural study. *Journal of Social Issues, 37,* 5–27.

Scadding, J. G. (1990). The semantic problems of psychiatry. *Psychological Medicine, 20,* 243–248.

Schiavi, R. C., Theilgaard, A., Owen, D. R., & White, D. (1984). Sex chromosome abnormalities, hormones, and aggressivity. *Archives of General Psychiatry, 41,* 93–99.

Scully, D. (1990). *Understanding sexual violence.* Boston: Unwin Hyman.

Sturup, G. K. (1968). *Treating the "untreatable" chronic criminals at Herstedvester.* Baltimore: John Hopkins Press.

Szasz, T. (1961). *The myth of mental illness.* New York: Harper & Row.

World Health Organization. (1990). *Basic documents* (39th ed.). Geneva: Author.

World Health Organization. (1992). *The ICD-10 classification of mental and behavioural disorders.* Geneva: Author.

23

MEDICAL INTERVENTIONS IN SEXUAL DEVIANCE

John Bradford

The importance of medical interventions in the treatment of sexual deviance is that they can be used regardless of the type of paraphilia or how many paraphilias are present. Today, medical intervention in the treatment of sexual deviance is synonymous with the pharmacological treatment of the paraphilias. Multiple paraphilias are frequently present in any single individual who presents for the assessment and treatment of sexual deviance (Abel et al., 1987; Bradford, Boulet, & Pawlak, 1992); it follows that a treatment approach that deals simultaneously with more than one paraphilia is preferential. The pharmacological treatments have this ability; this is a distinct advantage when considering the alternative of cognitive-behavioral treatments which generally require separate treatment approaches for each co-existing paraphilia. Second, the whole issue of comorbidity of the paraphilias with other DSM-IV (American Psychiatric Association, 1994) psychiatric disorders is only now becoming clear, which also potentially gives the newer pharmacological interventions a distinct advantage in that comorbid psychiatric disorders can be treated simultaneously.

There also is a developing concept regarding the compulsive nature of both paraphilic and nonparaphilic sexual disorders. This has developed to the extent of considering the paraphilias as part of the obsessive–compulsive spectrum disorders (OCD spectrum disorders; Bradford, 1991, 1994; Stein et al., 1992). This concept is rooted in the phenomenology of OCD, the natural history of OCD, and the developing pharmacological treatment profile of serotonin reuptake inhibitors (SRIs) in a wide variety of disorders, including paraphilias. Coleman (1992) approached this from a different perspective, postulating that any sexual behavior can become compulsive; the model is more of an addiction concept. The concept of OCD spectrum disorders defines all paraphilias as having similar phenomenology to OCD in that all deviant sexual fantasies have an obsessional quality to them and all are seen as ego dystonic. Similarly, deviant sexual behavior in the sense of paraphilic urges and behavior are seen as compulsive. There are also the nonparaphilic disorders such, as hypersexuality, that are seen as compulsive. Coleman (1986) described these disorders as related to anxiety reduction, which fits the OCD model, describing these individuals as having the subjective feeling of being *sexually addicted*. Further, the serotonin hypothesis as the basis to OCD is well established empirically from pharmacological treatment studies. In DSM-IV the essential features of a paraphilia are defined as:

> recurrent, intense sexually arousing sexual urges, or behaviors involving 1) nonhuman objects, 2) the suffering or humiliation of oneself or one's partner, or 3) children or other nonconsenting persons, that occur over a period of least 6 months (Criterion A). For some individuals, paraphiliac fantasies or stimuli are obligatory for erotic arousal and are always included in sexual activity. In other cases, the paraphiliac preferences occur only episodically (e.g., perhaps during times of stress), whereas at other times the person is able to function sexually without paraphiliac fantasies or stimuli. The behavior, sexual urges, or fantasies cause clinically significant distress or impairment in social, occupational, or other important areas of functioning (Criterion B). (pp. 522–523)

This description of the phenomenology of sexually arousing fantasies and urges as causing distress is similar to Criterion C in OCD (American Psychiatric Association, 1994). The description of obsessions as "persistent ideas, thoughts, or images that are experienced as intrusive and inappropriate and that cause marked anxiety or distress" is similar to the subjective experience of deviant sexual fantasies as ego dystonic. "Sexual imagery" is included in the descriptions of the types of obsessions. The descriptions of compulsions are very similar to compulsive sexual urges, except that they are there to reduce "anxiety or distress, not to provide pleasure or gratification." It is this latter concept in terms of the ego dystonic qualities of the paraphilic experience that appears to differentiate OCD from the paraphilias, but this is open to debate. Further the expectation that all sexual acts are pleasurable and self-gratifying is erroneous and makes a false demarcation between the obsessions and compulsions in OCD and the fantasies and urges of the paraphilic disorders. Many years of researching and treating paraphilias leads me to conclude that the pleasure of gratification is physiological, whereas at a psychological level significant distress and negative emotions such as guilt prevail.

The principles behind the medical treatments of sexual deviance are based on hormonal manipulation by selected pharmacological agents, or more recently, by the use of pharmacological agents to alter neurotransmitters which have an effect on sexual behavior at an intracerebral level. Both of these interventions are based on sex as a biological drive; the aim of medical treatment is to reduce this drive by a pharmacological intervention. The theoretical construct behind this is that the reduction of sexual drive will result in a decrease in deviant sexual behavior, as there is a global reduction of sexual interest, a reduction in sexual fantasies, a reduction in physiological arousal, and the possibility that there may be a differential effect on sexual interest wherein deviant sexual interest is reduced at a higher level compared with nondeviant sexual interest. Biological treatments have been used for sexual deviance and specifically with sexual offenders to reduce deviant sexual behavior and recidivism (Bradford, 1985).

The traditional biological treatments were stereotaxic neurosurgery and surgical castration; these have been replaced by medical treatment in the form of pharmacological treatments. Stereotaxic neurosurgery was not widely used, as it was highly intrusive and irreversible. It ablated certain brain nuclei involved in sexual behavior. Surgical castration is also irreversible and intrusive and is not an intervention I wish to consider at this time. It is, however, of important theoretical interest, as its mechanism of action in reducing deviant sexual behavior is the reduction of plasma testosterone, the principal hormone for the maintenance of sexual behavior in males and the hormone involved in sexual drive in both males and females. The other reason that surgical castration is important in the study of sexual deviance is that the postcastration studies of sexual offenders provide the most extensive outcome data available on the treatment of deviant sexual males. Large numbers of subjects and very long periods of follow-up with extensive records are available. These data cannot be replicated in formal research at this time. The studies (Bremer 1959; Heim & Hursch, 1977; Le Maire, 1956; Ortmann, 1980; Sturup, 1968, 1972) provide the most extensive outcome data of the effect of a reduction of plasma testosterone on deviant sexual behavior. They show significant reductions in recidivism, ranging from more than 70% precastration to less than 5% postcastration with periods of follow-up of up to 20 years (see Table 23.1). The individuals involved were selected not only because of their high recidivism rates, but also because of the serious nature of their sexual deviance. They included mostly rapists and child molesters with significant levels of sexual violence in their offenses. In terms of the paraphilias they most likely included sexual sadists, pedophiles, and a variety of other paraphiliacs.

THE MECHANISM OF ACTION OF SURGICAL CASTRATION AND THE ROLE OF HORMONES IN MALE SEXUAL BEHAVIOR

Animal research, specifically subprimate studies, has clearly shown that testosterone is necessary for male sexual behavior. The castrated subprimate loses sexual interest in a stepwise fashion and this can be restored by testosterone replacement (Bancroft, 1989). There is, however, considerable individual variability which may be based on genetic predisposition, intrafetal androgenization, adequate socialization in the prepubertal period, and/or other factors (Bancroft, 1989; Ward, 1977). There are various sites where androgen receptors are responsible for diverse aspects of male sexual behavior. Intercerebrally, there are the limbic system sites, particularly the anterior hypothalamus and other parts of the limbic system, the spinal cord, and the penis. It is critical that these intracerebral sites are fully operational for the full sexual behavior repertoire to occur. Placebo-controlled, androgen replacement studies in hypogonadal men have shown that testosterone in essential for sexual behavior, although considerable variability exists (Bancroft, 1989; Davidson, Camango, & Smith, 1979; Luisi & Franchi, 1980; Skakkebaek, Bancroft, Davidson, & Warner, 1981). There are also relationships between mood and androgen depletion (Bradford & McLean, 1984; O'Carroll, Shapiro, & Bancroft, 1985).

There appears to be a differential relationship between androgen depletion and its effects on sexual behavior. Additionally, there appears to be a distinction between the effects on erectile responses as measured by nocturnal penile tumescence and responses to erotic stimuli (Bancroft, 1989; Bancroft & Wu, 1983; O'Carroll et al., 1985).

Testosterone is the principal androgen produced by the testes of most animal species. It also is the important hormonal influence in male sexual behavior and, to a lesser extent, female behavior (Davidson, Smith, & Damassa, 1977). The direct influence of hormones

TABLE 23.1. Recidivism Rates Following Castration

Studies	Follow-up period (years)	N	Pre rate (%)	Post rate (%)
Langeluddeke (1963)	20	1,036	84	2.3
Cornu (1973)	5	127	76.8	4.1
Bremer (1959)	5–10	216	58	2.9
Sturup[a]	30	900		2.2

Note. Data from Heim & Hursch (1977); Bradford & Pawlak (1987). Pre rate, the recidivism rate prior to castration; Post rate, the recidivism rate after castration.

[a]Mostly rapists.

on sexual behavior is inversely related to the complexity of the species under study (Bancroft, 1989). Androgens (principally testosterone [T] and dihydrotestosterone [DHT]) are responsible for intrafetal androgenization, the development of the male genitalia, the onset of puberty, spermatogenesis, the secondary sex characteristics; the secretion of ejaculate, and the maintenance of sexual behavior in males and females. (Wilson & Foster, 1983). Intracellular androgen receptors mediate the physiological responses (Liang, Tymoczko, Chan, Hung, & Liao, 1977). Testosterone levels are driven by luteinizing hormone (LH), which is the tropic hormone for testosterone production (Mainwaring, 1977). Testosterone is conjugated to estrogens in the brain and then has an influence on sexual behavior through estrogen receptors (Naftolin, Ryan, & Petro, 1972). Androgen receptors are found in the various androgen-sensitive target organs, such as in the prostate (Liang et al., 1977) and in various parts of the brain, including the limbic system and the anterior hypothalamus (Liang et al., 1977). Antiandrogen treatment of the paraphilias targets a reduction in available androgen at the receptor level through a variety of mechanisms. This is comparable to the effect of castration, which reduces the available androgen by the removal of the testes, reducing the production of testosterone by about 95% (Wilson & Foster, 1983). The mechanism of action of the antiandrogens such as cyproterone acetate (CPA) and the hormonal agents such as medroxyprogesterone acetate (MPA) and estradiol is complex. However, available androgen, principally testosterone, is reduced and sexual behavior including sexual deviance also is reduced (Davidson et al., 1977). The behavioral effects of testosterone are the result of its action on the brain, although the actual principal site of action is uncertain. The medial preoptic area of the hypothalamus is most commonly associated with sexual behavior (Davidson et al., 1977).

In animals and humans a nonsexual behavior that appears to be associated with androgens is aggression. This also appears to be specific to aggression that is sexually motivated (Bradford & Bourget, 1987; Bradford & McLean, 1984; Brown & Davis, 1975; Ehrenkranz, Bliss, & Sheard, 1974; Kreuz & Rose, 1972; Meyer-Bahlburg, Nat, Boon, Sharma, & Edwards, 1974; Monti, Brown, & Corriveau, 1977; Olweus, Mattsson, Schalling, & Low, 1980; Persky, Smith, & Basu, 1971; Rada, Laws, & Kellner, 1976; Scaramella & Brown, 1978).

THE ROLE AND MECHANISM OF ACTION
OF NEUROTRANSMITTERS ON SEXUAL BEHAVIOR
AND SPECIFICALLY ON SEXUAL AROUSAL

The role of neurotransmitters in human sexuality is not fully understood. The neuropsychopharmacology of various pharmacological agents has been helpful in providing some understanding of the roles of dopamine, serotonin, and other neurotransmitters in various aspects of sexual behavior (Bancroft, 1989; Segraves, 1989). There is a complex interrelationship between sex hormones, neurotransmitters, genetic predisposition, and sexual behavior which I will not discuss here. There basically are two types of cerebral amines: catecholamines (e.g., dopamine) and indoleamines (e.g., serotonin, or 5-hydroxytryptamine [5-HT]). As already outlined, there are androgen receptors in the medial preoptic area of the hypothalamus as well as receptors for other steroid hormones. The hypothalamus also has significant cerebral amine systems. A variety of studies have shown that dopamine effects various aspects of sexual behavior. Dopamine agonists (e.g., apomorphine), reuptake inhibitors (e.g., cocaine), and precursors (e.g., levodopa) in general stimulate sexual behavior (Segraves, 1989). In animal studies dopamine-related agents appear to be more specific in their effects on sexual behavior in males than in females (Bancroft, 1989). Human pharmacological studies using neuroleptics support of this notion. For example, Bancroft, Tennent, Loucas, and Cass (1974) showed that benperidol, a butyrophenome, suppressed sexual drive (Bancroft et al., 1974; Tennent, Bancroft, & Cass, 1974).

The adrenergic neurotransmitters also are active in sexual behavior. Clark and Smith (1986) found that castrated male rats treated with yohimbine had enhanced sexual drive beyond low levels of androgen replacement. Yohimbine has also been shown to be effective in treating erectile failure in men (Morales, Surridge, Marshall, & Fenmore, 1982, 1987).

Serotonin appears to be the most important of the neurotransmitters in manipulating sexual behavior by pharmacological methods. There is evidence that central 5-HT pathways are inhibitory to sexual behavior. Our complete understanding of the role of 5-HT in humans is complicated by the lack of pure agonists and antagonists, based partly on the fact that they act on a number of subreceptor systems (Segraves, 1989). 5-HT receptor antagonists (e.g., methysergide) stimulate sexual behavior, whereas agents that increase 5-HT levels, such as precursors and SRIs, inhibit sexual behavior.

THE ROLE OF SEROTONIN REUPTAKE INHIBITORS IN THE TREATMENT OF SEXUAL DEVIANCE

An important recent development in the pharmacological treatment of the paraphilias is the use of serotonin reuptake inhibitors (SRIs). These agents are used primarily in the treatment of depression, phobic disorder, and OCD. These drugs and others affecting serotonin metabolism are pharmacological agents familiar to the average psychiatrist. Thus, there is the potential for the average psychiatrist to become involved in treating paraphilias in the future. In contrast, most psychiatrists are uncomfortable with antiandrogens and other hormonal agents. This should reverse a trend wherein mainstream psychiatry has not been involved in the treatment of sexual deviance. In addition, the onset of the paraphilias in early adolescence has made existing pharmacological interventions problematic, whereas if the SRIs are effective they can be used safely in early adolescence. Potentially, pharmacological treatment in adolescents may act as a primary prevention intervention (Bradford, 1991, 1993, 1994).

At the present time we lack systematic studies of the efficacy of serotonergic agents in the treatment of paraphilias. There are a number of case reports and some clinical studies of a variety of drugs which look very promising (Fedoroff, 1993). These clinical studies comprise cases without the formal discipline of an open trial. The case reports involve fluoxetine, lithium, buspirone, and clomipramine and show a reduction in deviant sexual interest for a variety of paraphilias (Bianchi, 1990; Bradford, 1991; Emmanuel, Lydiard, & Ballenger, 1991; Fedoroff, 1988; Gratzer & Bradford, 1994; Kafka, 1991; Kerbeshian & Brid, 1991; Lorefice, 1991; Pearson, Marshall, Barbaree, & Southmayd, 1992; Wawrose & Sisto, 1992). The studies of paraphilic males also reveal a reduction in deviant sexual interest. Kafka (1991) treated 10 paraphilic subjects also described as having "sexual addiction" with lithium, fluoxetine, and trazodone and showed that paraphilic interest lessened. All of these agents increase levels of 5-HT intracerebrally. Kafka and Prentky (1992) studied 20 subjects (10 with a paraphilia and 10 with a nonparaphilic "sexual addiction") in an open clinical trial. Ninety-five percent of the sample met DSM-III-R (American Psychiatric Association, 1987) criteria for dysthymic disorder and 55% for major depression. The study duration was 12 weeks, with 4-week assessment intervals. There was a 20% dropout rate. Baseline measures compared with outcome at week 12 showed statistically significant improvement in mood disorder and a reduction in sexual behaviors (masturbation, sexual activity, sexual interest). Paraphilic sexual behavior was also reduced. The pharmacological treatment was fluoxetine at an average dose of approximately 40 mg per day. The high comorbidity with mood disorder may mean that it was a secondary effect as a result of the recovery from mood disorder. As the comorbidity of the paraphilias and other psychiatric disorders is poorly understood, this may reflect a normal level of comorbidity.

Stein et al. (1992) completed a retrospective review of 13 patients treated with clomipramine, fluoxetine, and fluvoxamine for a variety of sexual disorders. Five subjects had a paraphilia, five had a nonparaphilic disorder, and nine were comorbid with OCD. The results showed that the OCD was responsive to treatment, but not the paraphilic disorder. In the nonparaphilic sexual disorder group (comorbid with OCD and major depression) there was an improvement in 40% of patients. Kruesi, Fines, Valladares, Phillips, and Rapoport (1992) treated 15 paraphilic men with clomipramine versus desipramine in a double-blind, crossover design. Eight subjects completed the study and showed some improvement, although no specific difference was noted between clomipramine and desipramine; clomipramine has a more specific action on 5-HT compared with desipramine. Coleman, Cesnik, Moore, and Dwyer (1992) studied 13 sex offenders treated with lithium and fluoxetine and found some reduction in deviant sexual interest. Perilstein, Lipper, and Friedman (1991) reported an improvement in 3 paraphilic males treated with fluoxetine. Rodenburg et al. (1991) reported that oxazepam and tryptophan increased deviant sexual activity in 3 paraphilic men; the disinhibiting effects of oxazepam possibly caused this outcome.

My colleagues and I conducted an open pilot of study of sertraline in the treatment of outpatients with pedophilia (Bradford et al., 1996). This was a 12-week open-label, dose-titration pilot study, a study that is nonblind and wherein the dose of the study drug can be increased at fixed increments at fixed intervals if the investigator feels a satisfactory response has not occurred. The upper limit of the dosage range is fixed. We obtained written consent and subjects were male outpatients over 16 years of age with a DSM-III-R diagnosis of pedophilia present for at least 6 months. These individuals were not currently receiving any other psychoactive medication or antiandrogen therapy. They received an initial daily dose of 50 mg of sertraline and then, based on patient response and toleration, we increased the dose at two weekly intervals to a maximum of 200 mg daily. Summary data from 21 patients showed that 18 patients completed the study, two withdrew because of adverse effects, and one was lost to follow-up. Marked improvement was observed on almost all aspects of sexuality. Statistically significant measures included improvements in sexual preference for sex with young girls ($p < .05$), decrease in sexual activity ($p < .05$), decrease in penile tumescence to audiotape descriptions of pedophilia ($p < .05$), and decrease in obsessions on the Yale–Brown Obsessive Compulsive Scale (YBOCS; Goodman et al., 1989) ($p < .05$) as well as general decreases in sexual drive measured by self-report on masturbation. The conclusion was that sertraline was well tolerated and appeared to be an effective treatment for pedophilia.

To summarize, there is a sound pharmacological basis for the treatment of sexual deviance using agents that affect serotonin. Clearly, further research is necessary especially research on the effects of central serotonin metabolism on the various neurobiological markers. A spin-off to the study described above (Bradford et al., 1996) studied peripheral neurobiological markers of central serotonin metabolism. In a preliminary review of the data, we found a significant correlation between changes in central serotonin metabolism (as measured by peripheral biological markers such as platelet lysergic acid diethylamide uptake) and the changes in sexual behaviors over the 12-week duration of the study. The reduction in a variety of sexual behaviors (e.g., masturbation, sexual interest) as a result of the use of serotonergic agents is an enormously promising development in the treatment of the paraphilias. Hopefully, further research will establish it as a primary pharmacological treatment in both paraphilic and nonparaphilic disorders.

THE ROLE OF ANTIANDROGENS IN THE TREATMENT
OF SEXUAL DEVIANCE

An antiandrogen is defined as having a specific action on the intracellular androgen receptors in the body. The principal pharmacological antiandrogen is cyproterone acetate (CPA). CPA has antiandrogenic, antigonadotropic, and some progestational effects (Bradford, 1983). The principal mode of action of CPA is on the intracellular androgen receptors, where it blocks the receptors by competitive inhibition (Bradford, 1983, 1985; Schering, 1983; Neumann, 1977). As outlined earlier, testosterone levels have a significant impact on sexual behavior if a situation of androgen deficiency arises. The principal androgen in the body is plasma testosterone. Reductions in plasma testosterone decreases erections and ejaculation, reduces spermatogenesis, and sexual fantasies, and generally reduces sexual interest (Bradford, 1983, 1985). In addition, CPA has a strong progestational action as well as being antigonadotropic as a result of this action (Neumann & Scleusener, 1980; Schering, 1983). The progestational effect of CPA is important. In other antiandrogens which do not have progestational effects, they actually cause an increase in plasma testosterone. With CPA there is a balance between the specific antiandrogen effect due to competitive inhibition and the antigonadotropic effects, resulting in a reduction in plasma testosterone, dihydrotestosterone. In addition, CPA blocks or reduces the release of luteinizing hormone releasing hormone (LHRH; Neumann & Scleusener, 1980). CPA is a clean drug that is well absorbed by the oral route and is 100% available with a plasma half-life of approximately 38 hours. It is available in an injectable form which is given every 2 weeks and reaches maximum plasma levels in 3½ days. There are a number of theoretical risks (adverse effects) which are unlikely to occur at the dosage levels used to treat sexual deviance. These include a liver dysfunction and adrenal suppression, which could be a very serious complication if it did occur. Adrenal suppression has been described primarily in adolescents, a further contraindication to the use of antiandrogens for this population (Cremonocini, Viginati, & Libroia, 1976; Neumann, 1977).

CPA was used primarily in Germany starting with the pioneers Laschet and Laschet who in 1971 examined the clinical outcome of approximately 100 sexually deviant men treated with CPA. This was a mixed group of paraphilic males including pedophiles, sexual sadists, and exhibitionists, in an open clinical trial which varied in duration from 6 months to 4 years. In about 80% of the cases, 100 mg per day of CPA was effective in eliminating sexual drive, erections, orgasms, and subsequently the deviant sexual behavior. Fifty milligrams per day reduced libido but allowed erectile responses, raising an important point regarding how CPA is used. Depending on dosage, it can be used as a "chemical castration" agent, reducing erection and all degrees of sexual interest and asexualizing an individual, or it can be used by titrating the reduction of deviant sexual interests, reducing sexual drive and arousability but allowing erectile ability to continue as well as normal heterosexual or homosexual relationships. In this particular study, CPA was given intramuscularly at a dosage level of 300 mg every 2 weeks. In about a fifth of exhibitionists there was complete elimination of exhibitionistic behavior even after CPA treatment was discontinued. Undesirable side effects included transient mood disorder, weight gain in about 20% of cases, and some degree of feminization including reduced body hair, decreased scalp hair, and slight gynecomastia in about 20% of cases. Laschet and Laschet (1975) reported on 300 men treated for up to 8 years with minimal side effects and very good long-term outcomes. Davies (1974) reported on 50 patients (a heterogenous sample of sexually deviant and hypersexual men) treated with CPA for up to 5 years. All patients showed considerable improvement in deviant sexual behavior.

Bancroft et al. (1974) studied 12 patients comparing CPA at 100 mg per day with estradiol at 0.2 mg per day and found that both drugs reduced sexual interest, arousal, and activity. There were no significant adverse effects, although if side effects did occur they were more likely to occur with estradiol. Neither caused any specific reduction in paraphilic sexual interest or deviant sexual interest. Other studies reported (Cooper, 1981; Cooper, Ismail, Phanjoo, & Love, 1972; Davies, 1974; Mothes, Lehnert, Samimi, & Ufer, 1971; Ott & Hoffet, 1968) demonstrated that CPA is an effective agent in treating paraphilic sexual behavior. The studies by Mothes et al. (1971) and Laschet and Laschet (1975) included over 500 males treated from 2 months to 8 years with CPA. The dosage range was from 50 to 200 mg per day orally and depot CPA was given either in one or two weekly dosages ranging from 300 to 600 mg per injection. Fatigue, hypersomnia, depression, negative nitrogen balance and some weight gain was noted. The negative nitrogen balance returned to normal, as did calcium and phosphate metabolism, after a few months. In about 20% of cases there was some degree of feminization. The desired response on sexual behavior included decreases in arousability, sexual fantasies, and sex drive in 80% of cases treated with CPA orally at a dosage level of 100 mg per day. Twenty-five patients were followed for 5 years after treatment was discontinued without any further evidence of paraphilic behavior.

Bradford and Pawlak (1993a) reported on a double-blind, placebo crossover study of CPA. At the same time, they also completed another study (1993b), specifically on the effects of CPA on the sexual arousal patterns of pedophiles. The double-blind, placebo crossover study was of 19 patients, including 12 pedophilic men who were also high-recidivating sexual offenders (Bradford & Pawlak, 1993a). Each offender had a mean of 2.5 previous convictions for sexual offenses. All subjects met the DSM-III-R criteria for a paraphilia and they received CPA or placebo blindly in 3-month active treatment or placebo phases. CPA reduced testosterone compared with placebo or baseline ($p < .001$) at statistically significant levels. This was an expected pharmacological effect. Luteining hormone levels were reduced, but not at statistically significant levels, which again was anticipated because of the pharmacological actions of CPA. Follicle stimulating hormone levels were reduced at statistically significant levels ($p < .005$) by active drug phase compared with placebo or baseline. CPA reduced simplistic sexual arousal to a visual slide stimulus selected by each subject as their primary erotic preference, but not quite at statistically significant levels. Similarly, CPA reduced arousal level to sexual fantasy compared with placebo and baseline, but not at statistically significant levels. CPA significantly reduced generalized psychopathology as measured by the Brief Psychiatric Rating Scale (Overall & Gorham, 1962) compared with baseline ($p < .001$) and with placebo ($p < .05$). CPA also reduced sexual activity at statistically significant levels compared with baseline ($p < .05$) and placebo ($p < .05$), whereas no difference was noted between baseline and placebo. Most important was the significant reduction of sexual fantasy by CPA compared with baseline ($p < .05$), although there also was a placebo effect. The efficacy of CPA as a treatment for the paraphilias is supported by the reduction in sexual arousal, activity, and fantasy.

In the study on the sexual arousal patterns of pedophiles, the authors broke the sample down into high-testosterone and low-testosterone groups (Bradford & Pawlak, 1993b). The most important finding was that CPA appeared to have a differential response, reducing deviant sexual arousal to pedophilic stimuli at a higher level than it did nondeviant arousal to sex with adults. This had the effect of "normalizing" the sexual arousal patterns of pedophiles, giving them an erotic preference for consenting sex with adults. This is a highly desired outcome in the treatment of pedophilia.

Cooper, Cernovsky, and Magnus (1992) also reported a single case study of a pedophile treated with CPA which is of interest, as this person was treated for approximately 3 years.

To summarize, CPA is an important and effective agent in the treatment of sexual deviance. Cyproterone acetate can be used as a "chemical castration" agent, wherein there is a complete reduction of sexual drive and sexual arousal with the patient unable to have erections. This is best achieved by the intramuscular, injectable CPA rather than the oral form, although the oral administration also would be effective if at the right dose. Cyproterone acetate is used in relatively low dosages of 50 to 100 mg a day when the aim of treatment is not to asexualize the individual but to reduce deviant sexual fantasies and arousal as measured by penile plethysmograph. This allows the individual to continue to be sexually active at a lower level of sex drive with the opportunity to develop nondeviant sexual interest by having sex with adults if he is a pedophile, or by engaging in other nondeviant sexual activity in the case of other paraphilias. CPA can be discontinued gradually after 12 to 15 months of treatment and some individuals indefinitely show no recurrence of their sexually deviant behavior. The mechanism for this "cure" is unknown, although in my opinion it is likely due to a downgrading in the sensitivity of the androgen receptors. In the case of some individuals there may be a gradual return of deviant sexual interest over a period of time varying from 6 months to 3 years after the discontinuation of treatment. It is not possible at this time to identify those individuals who will not have any recurrence compared with those who may.

The long-term treatment strategy is for individuals to complete cognitive-behavioral treatment also including very specific instruction in terms of how CPA may act in the long term. After the discontinuation of intensive CPA treatment they would also have a month's supply of CPA available to start retreatment if at any time they felt the onset of deviant sexual fantasies or urges. Patients contact their attending physician within 48 hours of starting to use CPA again. Treatment with CPA includes periodic monitoring of liver function and sex hormones, although in the case of CPA when used principally to suppress deviant sexual interests but not to asexualize individuals, testosterone levels are important only in that they measure treatment response (but are not specific in terms of what level is necessary to suppress deviant arousal). Generally speaking, total plasma testosterone levels in the lower third of the normal range is the acceptable range for this type of treatment approach. If CPA is to be used as a chemical castration agent, then prepubertal levels of total plasma testosterone should be the aim of treatment (the range of 3 to 4 nmol per liter). The one advantage of CPA is that estrogen levels are also low because of reductions in the conjugation of testosterone to estrogen, which may also affect sexual behavior mediated through the estrogen receptors. There are a number of treatment outcome studies which show that CPA has a significant effect on sex offender recidivism, as detailed in Table 23.2.

TABLE 23.2. Recidivism Rates after CPA Treatment

Study	Follow-up period (years)	N	Pre rate (%)	Post rate (%)
Horn (1972)	1–4.5	33	100	0
Fahndrich (1974)	3	14	93	0
Davies (1974)	3	16	100	0
Appelt & Floru (1974)	1.5	6	100	16.7
Jost (1974)	4	10	100	0
Jost (1975)	3	11	54	0
Baron & Unger (1977)	1	6	50	0

Note. Data from Ortmann (1980); Braford & Pawlak (1987). Abbreviations as in Table 23.1.

THE ROLE OF HORMONAL AGENTS
IN THE TREATMENT OF SEXUAL DEVIANCE

The traditional use of hormonal agents involved estrogen to suppress sexual drive. Studies by Foote (1944), Golla and Hodge (1949), Symmers (1968), and Whittaker (1959) were the earlier studies of this approach. Estrogen use has waned because of side effects, primarily feminization. In addition, other side effects such as nausea and vomiting have limited its use (Symmers, 1968).

Medroxyprogesterone acetate (MPA) is the hormonal agent developed and traditionally used in the United States. It was first used in 1958 (Heller, Laidlaw, Harvey, & Nelson, 1958). Money (1968) described the first case of MPA used to treat sexual deviance. Other studies included Berlin and Meinecke (1981), Cooper, Sandhu, and Losztyn (1992), Gagne (1981), Gottesman and Schubert (1993), Kiersch (1990), Meyer, Collier, and Emory (1992), Langevin et al. (1979), Meyer, Walker, Emory, and Smith (1985), Money (1970), Money, Weiedeking, Walker, and Gain (1976), Walker and Meyer (1981), and Weiedeking, Money, and Walker (1979). MPA works through the induction of the liver enzyme testosterone-A-reductase, causing a reduction of testosterone by increased metabolism; plasma testosterone levels are reduced. There also is an antigonadotropic effect. The potential side effects of MPA use are similar to those seen in androgen deficiency, including fatigue and feminization. In addition, there is some evidence of blood pressure changes and a diabetogenic tendency. Some studies have shown fatigue, weight gain, hot and cold flashes, phlebitis, nausea and vomiting, and headaches as potential side effects (Gagne, 1981). Clinical studies of MPA, with few exceptions, were clinical trials. Money in 1968, 1970, and 1972 provided the first clinical studies of MPA in the treatment of sexual deviance. The dosage level of the MPA was 300 to 400 mg per week, given intramuscularly. The expected effects on sexual behavior are mediated by lower testosterone, including a decrease in sexual interest, arousal, erections, and sex drive generally.

Weiedeking et al. (1979) treated seven males with chromosome abnormalities using MPA in dosages of between 100 and 400 mg per week and found that about 30% of the patients responded positively. A study of exhibitionists treated with MPA by Langevin et al. (1979) compared MPA with assertiveness training. In this study there was a high dropout rate, limiting its validity. Berlin and Meinecke (1981) treated 20 males with a variety of sexually deviant interests with MPA and found that while on MPA, the patients did very well. However, they relapsed shortly after discontinuing MPA. A similar study by Gagne (1981) reported on MPA treatment of 48 patients. His particular treatment regimen including keeping the total plasma testosterone level at less than 250 mg per 100 ml. The MPA was given intramuscularly at dosage levels of 200 mg intramuscular injection three times per week for the first 2 weeks, then 200 mg once or twice per week for the next 4 weeks, and a maintenance level of 100 or 200 mg every 2 weeks.

Wincze, Bansal, and Malamud (1986) used MPA in the treatment of three pedophiles in a single-case, experimental design which had a double-blind component. They used penile tumescence and noted that there was a significant reduction in arousal to erotic stimulation and some overall reduction in sexual arousability. Nocturnal penile tumescence was significantly reduced when compared with the placebo phase. Kiersch (1990) studied eight subjects who were treated with MPA. There was a 64-week follow-up period which four of the eight subjects completed. MPA was given at a dose of 400 mg per week for 16 weeks, alternating with saline injections for a crossover period of 16 weeks. The results were variable; the study was flawed because of the long half-life of the depot MPA, making the placebo periods not in fact true placebo periods.

Meyer et al. (1992) treated 40 men with MPA with a variety of paraphilias, but principally pedophilia. The treatment was MPA at 400 mg per week for 6 months to 12 years. A control group of treatment refusers of 21 patients also were followed. MPA caused the side effects already described. Eighteen percent of patients re-offended while on MPA and 35% after it was discontinued, compared with 55% in the control group. Gottesman and Schubert (1993) showed for the first time that low-dose oral MPA given at dosages of 60 mg per day for 15 months on average in an open trial was a very effective treatment. Plasma testosterone levels were reduced by 50 to 75% with this type of treatment, and side effects were minimal.

More recently, luteinizing hormone releasing hormone agonists (LHRH agonists) have been used in a number of case studies in the treatment of paraphilias. The potential for their use was outlined by Bradford (1985). Rousseau, Dupont, Labrie, and Couture (1988) reported on the changes in sexual behavior in prostate carcinoma patients treated with flutamide, a nonsteroidal antiandrogen, at 750 mg per day in divided dosages. In addition, patients received a surgical castration. Some of the patients who did not undergo surgical castration were treated with flutamide and a LHRH agonist. In the posttreatment period more than 70% of subjects noted a major decline in sexual interest. Rousseau, Couture, Dupont, Labrie, and Couture (1990) reported on a single case study of a severe exhibitionist treated with an LHRH agonist. Other case studies by Dickey (1992) also involved the treatment of a paraphilic male which in this case had failed to respond to MPA and CPA treatment. Thibaut, Cordier, and Kuhn (1993) treated six paraphilic males with a LHRH agonist. Five out of six patients had one paraphilia and one had two paraphilias. CPA was used in addition to the LHRH agonist. Follow-up periods ranged from 7 months to 3 years. Treatment outcomes were a reduction of sexual interest and activity.

There are a number of pharmacological agents that have specific effects on sexual behavior and have proven successful in treating sexual deviance. A spectrum of pharmacological treatment interventions now exists. The most minimal pharmacological intervention is the use of SRIs such as fluoxetine, fluvoxamine, and sertraline, causing a reduction in deviant and nondeviant sexual interests. MPA and CPA provide a more powerful level of intervention, a reduction of sexual drive without complete suppression. Asexualization can be achieved by using either CPA or LHRH agonists. Long-term outcome studies have shown that the CPA reduces sexual offender recidivism and compares favorably with the surgical castration studies (see Tables 23.1 and 23.2). Clearly, further research in the pharmacological treatment of the paraphilias is essential and, in particular, double-blind, placebo studies are necessary. As pharmacological agents become more specific in their actions on subreceptor systems, further developments in the pharmacological treatment of sexual deviance are likely to occur. For example, subreceptors like 5-HT1C serotonin receptors appear to have very specific actions with regard to sexual behavior; these may be modified in the future by pharmacological agents active at a single receptor site.

REFERENCES

Abel, G. G., Becker, J. V., Mittleman, M. S., Cunningham–Rathner, J., Rouleau, J. L., & Murphy, W. D. (1987). Self-reported sex crimes of nonincarcerated paraphiliacs. *Journal of Interpersonal Violence, 2,* 3–25.

American Psychiatric Association. (1994). *Diagnostic and statistical manual of mental disorders* (4th ed.). Washington, DC: Author.

Appelt, M., & Floru, L. (1974). Erfahmigen überdie beemflussung der sexualital cyproteronacetat. *International Pharmaco-Psychiatry, 9,* 61–76.

Bancroft, J. (1989). *Human sexuality and its problems.* Edinburgh: Churchill Livingstone.

Bancroft, J., Tennent, G., Loucas, K., & Cass, J. (1974). The control of deviant sexual behaviour by drugs: I. Behavioural changes following oestragens and antiandrogens. *British Journal of Psychiatry, 125,* 310–315.

Bancroft, J., & Wu, F. C. W. (1983). Changes in erectile responsiveness during androgen therapy. *Archives of Sexual Behavior, 12,* 59–66.

Baron, D. P., & Unger, H. R. (1977). A clinical trial of cyproterone acetate in sexual deviancy. *New Zealand Medical Journal, 85,* 366–369.

Berlin, F. S., & Meinecke, C. F. (1981). Treatment of sex offenders with antiandrogenic medication: Conceptualization, review of treatment modalities and preliminary findings. *American Journal of Psychiatry, 138*(5), 601–607.

Bianchi, M. D. (1990). Fluoxetine treatment of exhibitionism [Letter]. *American Journal of Psychiatry, 147*(8), 1089–1090.

Blumer, D., & Migeon, C. (1975). Hormone and hormonal agents in the treatment of aggression. *Journal of Nervous and Mental Disease, 160,* 127–137.

Bradford, J. M. W. (1983). Research in sex offenders. In R. L. Sadoff (Ed.), *The psychiatric clinics of North America* (pp. 715–733). Philadelphia: Saunders.

Bradford, J. M. W. (1985). Organic treatments for the male sexual offender. *Behavioral Sciences and the Law, 3*(4), 355–375.

Bradford, J. M. W. (1988). Organic treatment for the male sexual offender. *Annals of the New York Academy of Sciences, 528,* 193–202.

Bradford, J. M. W. (1991, October). *The role of serotonin re-uptake inhibitors in forensic psychiatry.* Paper presented at the fourth Congress of European College of Neuropsychopharmacology: The Role of Serotonin in Psychiatric Illness, Monte Carlo, Monaco.

Bradford, J. M. W. (1993). The pharmacological treatment of the adolescent sex offender. In H. E. Barbaree, W. L. Marshall, & S. M. Hudson (Eds.), *The juvenile sex offender* (pp. 278–288). New York: Guilford Press.

Bradford, J. M. W. (1994). Can pedophilia be treated? *Harvard Mental Health Letter, 10,* 8.

Bradford, J. M. W., Boulet, J., & Pawlak, A. (1992). The paraphilias: A multiplicity of deviant behaviors. *Canadian Journal of Psychiatry, 37,* 104–108.

Bradford, J. M. W., & Bourget, D. (1987). Sexually aggressive men. *Psychiatric Journal of the University of Ottawa, 12*(3), 169–175.

Bradford, J. M. W., Martindale, J. J., Lane, R., Greenberg, D., Gojer, J., Curry, S., & Goldberg, M. (1996). *Sertraline in the treatment of pedophilia: An open label study.* Manuscript submitted for publication.

Bradford, J. M. W., & McLean, D. (1984). Sexual offenders, violence and testosterone: A clinical study. *Canadian Journal of Psychiatry, 29,* 335–343.

Bradford, J. M. W., & Pawlak, A. (1987). Sadistic homosexual pedophilia: Treatment with cyproterone acetate. A single case study. *Canadian Journal of Psychiatry, 32,* 22–31.

Bradford, J. M. W., & Pawlak, A. (1993a). Double-blind placebo crossover study of cyproterone acetate in the treatment of the paraphilias. *Archives of Sexual Behavior, 22,* 383–402.

Bradford, J. M. W., & Pawlak, A. (1993b). Effects of cyproterone acetate on sexual arousal patterns of pedophiles. *Archives of Sexual Behavior, 22*(6), 629–641.

Bremer, J. (1959). *Asexualization: A follow-up study of 244 cases.* New York: Macmillan.

Brown, W. A., & Davis, G. H. (1975). Serum testosterone and irritability in man. *Psychosomatic Medicine, 37,* 87.

Clark, J. T., & Smith, E. R. (1986). Failure of pimozide and metergoline to antagonize the RDS-127-induced facilitation of ejaculatory behavior. *Physiology and Behavior, 37,* 47–52.

Coleman, E. (1992). Is your patient suffering from compulsive sexual behavior. *Psychiatric Annals, 22*(6), 320–325.

Coleman, E., Cesnik, J., Moore, A. M., & Dwyer, S. M. (1992). An exploratory study of the role of psychotropic medications in treatment of sexual offenders. *Journal of Offender Rehabilitation, 18,* 75–88.

Cooper, A. J. (1981). A placebo controlled study of the antiandrogen cyproterone acetate in deviant hypersexuality. *Comprehensive Psychiatry, 22,* 458–464.

Cooper A. J., Cernovsky Z., & Magnus, J. (1992). The effects of cyproterone acetate on sleeping and waking penile erections in pedophiles: Possible implications for treatment. *Canadian Journal of Psychiatry, 37,* 33–39.

Cooper, A. J., Ismail, A. A., Phanjoo, A. L., & Love, D. L. (1972). Antiandrogen (cyproterone acetate) therapy in deviant hypersexuality. *British Journal of Psychiatry, 120,* 59–63.

Cooper, A. J., Sandhu, S., & Losztyn, S. (1992). A double-blind placebo controlled trial of medroxyprogesterone acetate and cyproterone acetate with seven pedophiles. *Canadian Journal of Psychiatry, 37,* 687–693.

Cordoba, O. A., & Chapel, J. L. (1983). Medroxyprogesterone acetate antiandrogen treatment of hypersexuality in a pedophiliac sex offender. *American Journal of Psychiatry, 140,* 1036–1039.

Cornu, F. (1973). *Katamnesen bein kastrierten sittlichkeits—dekinquenten aus forensisch—psychiatrischer sicht.* Basel, Switzerland: Karger.

Cremonocini, C., Viginati, E., & Libroia, A. (1976). Treatment of hirsutism and acne in women with two combinations of cyproterone acetate and ethinyloestradiol. *Acta European Fertility, 7,* 299–314.

Davidson, J. M., Smith, E. R., & Damassa, D. A. (1977). Comparative analysis of the roles of androgen in the feedback mechanisms and sexual behavior. In L. Martini & M. Motta (Eds.), *Androgens and antiandrogens* (pp. 137–149). New York: Raven Press.

Davidson, J. M., Carmargo, C. A., & Smith, E. R. (1979). Effects of androgens on sexual behavior of hypogonadal men. *Journal of Clinical Endocrinology and Metabolism, 48,* 955–958.

Davies, T. D. (1974). Cyproterone acetate for male hypersexuality. *Journal of International Medical Research, 2,* 159–163.

Dickey, R. (1992). The management of a case of treatment-resistant paraphilia with a long-acting LHRH agonist. *Canadian Journal of Psychiatry, 37,* 567–569.

Ehrenkranz, J., Bliss, E., & Sheard, M. H. (1974). Plasma testosterone: Correlation with aggressive behavior and social dominance in men. *Psychosomatic Medicine, 36,* 469–475.

Emmanuel, N. P., Lydiard, R. B., & Ballenger J. C. (1991). Fluoxetine treatment of voyeurism. *American Journal of Psychiatry, 148,* 950.

Fahndrich, E. (1974). Cyproteron acetat in der handlung von sexual deviationen. *Deutsche Medizinische Wochenschrift, 99,* 234–242.

Fedoroff, J. P. (1988). Buspirone in the treatment of transvestic fetishism. *Journal of Clinical Psychiatry, 48,* 408–409.

Fedoroff, J. P. (1992). Buspirone hydrochloride in the treatment of an atypical paraphilia. *Archives of Sexual Behavior, 21(4),* 401–406.

Fedoroff, J. P. (1993). Scrotonergic drug treatment of deviant sexual interests. *Annals of Sex Research, 6,* 105–121.

Fedoroff, J. P., & Fedoroff, I. C. (1992). Buspirone and paraphilic sexual behavior. *Journal of Offender Rehabilitation, 18(3/4),* 89–108.

Field, L. H. (1973). Benperidol in the treatment of sex offenders. *Medicine, Science and the Law, 13,* 195–196.

Foote, R. M. (1944). Diethystilbestrol in the management of psychopathological states in males. *Journal of Nervous and Mental Disease, 99,* 928–935.

Gagne, P. (1981). Treatment of sex offenders with medroxyprogesterone acetate. *American Journal of Psychiatry, 138(5),* 644–646.

Golla, F. L., & Hodge, S. R. (1949). Hormone treatment of sexual offenders. *Lancet,* 1006–1007.

Goodman, W. K., Price, L. H., Rasmussen, S. A., Mazurec, J., Fleischmann, R., Hill, C., Heninger, G. R., & Chamey, D. S. (1989). The Yale–Brown Obsessive Compulsive Scale (Y-BOCS) I: Development, use and reliability. *Archives of General Psychiatry, 46,* 1006–1011.

Gottesman, H. G., & Schubert, D. S. (1993). Low-dose oral medroxyprogesterone acetate in the management of the paraphilias. *Journal of Clinical Psychiatry, 54(5),* 182–188.

Gratzer, T., & Bradford, J. M. W. (1994). Brief communications: A treatment for impulse control disorders and paraphilia: A case report. *Canadian Journal of Psychiatry, 40,* 450–455.

Heim, N., & Hursch, C. J. (1977). Castration for sexual offenders: Treatment or punishment? A review and critique of recent European literature. *Archives of Sexual Behavior, 8,* 281–304.

Heller, C. G., Laidlaw, M. W., Harvey, H. T., & Nelson, D. L. (1958). The effects of the progestational compounds of the reproductive of the human male. *Annals of the New York Academy of Sciences, 71,* 649–655.

Horn, J. H. (1972). Die behandlung von sexual delinquenten mit cyproteron acetat. In G. Raspe (Ed.), *Life Sciences Monograph 2* (pp. 113–122). Oxford: Pergamon.

Hsueh, A. J., Peck, E. J., & Clark, J. H. (1976). Control of uterine receptor levels by progesterone. *Endocrinology, 98,* 438–444.

Jost, F. (1974). Klinische beobachtungen und erfahrungen in der behandlung sexueller deviationen mit den antiandrogen cyproteron-acetat (1971–1974). *Schweizerische Rundshau. Medizinische (Praxis), 63,* 1318–1325.

Jost, F. (1975). Zur behandlung abnormen sexual verhaltens mit dem antiandrigen cyproteroneacetat Der Informielte. *Arzt., 3,* 303–309.

Kafka, M. P. (1991). Successful treatment of paraphilic coercive disorder (a rapist) with fluoxetine hydrochloride. *British Journal of Psychiatry, 158,* 844–847.

Kafka, M. P., & Prentky, R. (1992). Fluoxetine treatment of nonparaphilic sexual addictions and paraphilias in men. *Journal of Clinical Psychiatry, 53,* 351–358.

Kerbeshian, J., & Bird, L. (1991). Tardive syndrome and recurrent paraphilic masturbatory fantasy. *American Journal of Psychiatry, 36,* 155–157.

Kiersch, T. A. (1990). Treatment of sex offenders with Depo-provera. *Bulletin of the American Academy of Psychiatry and Law, 18*(2), 179–187.

Kreuz, L. E., & Rose, R. M. (1972). Assessment of aggressive behavior and plasma testosterone in a young criminal population. *Psychosomatic Medicine, 34,* 321–332.

Kruesi, M. J. P., Fine, S., Valladares, L., Phillips, R. A., & Rapoport, J. L. (1992). Paraphilias: A double-blind crossover comparison of clomipramine versus desipramine. *Archives of Sexual Behavior, 21*(6), 587–594.

Langeluddeke, A. (1963). *Die entmannung von sittlich—keitsverbrecher.* Berlin: de Gruyter.

Langevin, R., Paitich, D., Hucker, S., Newman, S., Ramsay, G., Pope, S. Geller, G., & Anderson, C. (1979). The effect of assertiveness training, provera and sex of therapist in the treatment of genital exhibitionism. *Journal of Behavior Therapy and Experimental Psychiatry, 10,* 275–282.

Laschet, U., & Laschet, L. (1971). Psychopharmacotherapy of sex offenders with cyproterone acetate. *Pharmakopsychiatrie Neuropsychopharmakologic, 4,* 99–104.

Laschet, U., & Laschet, L. (1975). Antiandrogens in the treatment of sexual deviations of men. *Journal of Steroid Biochemistry, 6,* 821–826.

Le Maire, L. (1956). Danish experiences regarding the castration of sexual offenders. *Journal of Criminal Law, Criminology and Police Science, 47,* 295–310.

Liang, T., Tymoczko, J. L., Chan, K. M. B., Hung, H. C., & Liao, S. (1977). Androgen action: Receptors and rapid responses. In L. Martini & M. Motta (Eds.), *Androgens and antiandrogens* (pp. 77–89). New York: Raven Press.

Lorefice, L. S. (1991). Fluoxetine treatment of a fetish [Letter]. *Journal of Clinical Psychiatry, 52*(1), 436–437.

Luisi, M., & Franchi, F. (1980). Double-blind group comparative study of testosterone in undecanoate and mesterolone in hypogonadal male patients. *Journal of Endocrinological Investigations, 3,* 305–308.

Mainwaring, I. P. (1977). Modes of action of antiandrogens: A survey. In L. Martini & M. Motta (Eds.), *Androgens and antiandrogens* (pp. 151–161). New York: Raven Press.

Meyer, W. J., Collier, C., & Emory, E. (1992). Depo Provera treatment for sex offending behavior: An evaluation of outcome. *Bulletin of the American Academy of Psychiatry and Law, 20*(3), 249–259.

Meyer, W. J., Walker, P. J., Emory, L. E., & Smith, E. R. (1985). Physical, metabolic and hormonal effects on men of long-term therapy with medroxyprogesterone acetate. *Fertility and Sterility, 43,* 102–109.

Meyer-Bahlburg, H. F. L., Nat, R., Boon, D. A., Sharma, M., & Edwards, J. A. (1974). Aggressiveness and testosterone measures in man. *Psychosomatic Medicine, 36,* 269–274.

Money, J. (1968). Discussion of the hormonal inhibition of libido in male sex offenders. In R. Michael (Ed.), *Endocrinology and human behaviour* (p. 169). London: Oxford University Press.

Money, J. (1970). Use of androgen-depleting hormone in the treatment of male sex offenders. *Journal of Sex Research, 6,* 165–172.

Money, J. (1972). The therapeutic use of androgen-depleting hormone. *International Psychiatry Clinics, 8,* 165–174.

Money, J. M., Weiedeking, C., Walker, P. A., & Gain, D. (1976). Combined antiandrogen and counseling program for treatment of 46 XY and 47 XYY sex offenders. In E. Sachar (Ed.), *Hormones, behavior and psychopathology* (pp. 105–120). New York: Raven Press.

Monti, P. M., Brown, W. A., & Corriveau, D. D. (1977). Testosterone and components of aggressive and sexual behavior in men. *American Journal of Psychiatry, 134*(6), 692–694.

Morales, A., Surridge, D. H. C., Marshall, P. G., & Fenmore, J. (1982). Nonhormonal pharmacological treatment of organic impotence. *Journal of Urology, 128,* 45.

Mothes, C., Lehnert, J., Samimi, F., & Ufer, J. (1971). Schering symposium uber sexual deviationen und ihre medikamentose Behandlung. *Life Sciences Monograph, 2,* 65.

Murray, M. A. F., Bancroft, J. H. H., Anderson, D. C., Tennent, T. G., & Carr, P. J. (1975). Endocrine changes in male sexual deviants after treatment with antiandrogens, oestragens or tranquilizers. *Journal of Endocrinology, 67,* 179–188.

Naftolin, F., Ryan, K. J., & Petro, Z. (1972). Aromatization of androstenediol in the anterior hypothalamus of adult male and female rats. *Endocrinology, 90,* 295–298.

Neumann, F. (1977). Pharmacology and potential use of cyproterone acetate. *Hormone and Metabolic Research, 9,* 1–13.

Neumann, F., & Schleusener, A. (1980). Pharmacology of cyproterone acetate with special reference to the skin. *Proceedings of the Dianne Symposium, Brussels,* 19–51.

O'Carroll, R., Shapiro, C., & Bancroft, J. (1985). Androgens, behaviour and nocturnal erections in hypogonadal men: The effect of varying the replacement dose. *Clinical Endocrinology, 23,* 527–538.

Olweus, D., Mattsson, A., Schalling, D., & Low, H. (1980). Testosterone, aggression, physical and personality dimensions in normal adolescent males. *Psychosomatic Medicine, 42,* 253–269.

Ortmann, J. (1980). The treatment of sexual offenders, castration and antihormone therapy. *International Journal of Law and Psychiatry, 3,* 443–451.

Ortmann, J. (1984a). *How castration influences on relapsing into sexual criminality among Danish males.* Unpublished manuscript.

Ortmann, J. (1984b). *How antihormone treatment with cyproterone acetate influences on relapsing into sexual criminality in male sexual offenders.* Unpublished manuscript.

Ott, F., & Hoffet, H. (1968). The influence of antiandrogens on libido, potency and testicular function. *Schweizerische Medrzinische Wochschrift, 98,* 1812.

Overall, J., & Gorham, D. (1962). The Brief Psychiatric Rating Scale. *Psychological Reports, 10,* 799–812.

Pearson, H. J., Marshall, W. L., Barbaree, H. E., & Southmayd, S. (1992). Treatment of a compulsive paraphilic with buspirone. *Annals of Sex Research, 5,* 239–246.

Perilstein, R., Lipper, S., & Friedman, L. (1991). Three cases of paraphilia responsive to fluoxetine treatment. *Journal of Clinical Psychiatry, 52*(4), 169–170.

Persky, H., Smith, K. D., & Basu, G. K. (1971). Relation of psychologic measures of aggression and hostility to testosterone production in man. *Psychosomatic Medicine, 40,* 265–277.

Rada, R. T., Laws, D. R., & Kellner, R. (1976). Plasma testosterone levels in the rapist. *Psychosomatic Medicine, 38,* 257–268.

Rodenberg, M., Sheldon, L., & Owen, J. A. (1991). Sexual disinhibition with L-tryptophan. *Journal of Clinical Psychiatry, 52,* 169–170.

Rada, R. T. (1978). Classification of the rapist. In R. T. Rada (Ed.), *Clinical aspects of the rapist* (pp. 117–132). New York: Grune & Stratton.

Rousseau, L. R., Couture, M., Dupont, A., Labrie, F., & Couture, N. (1990). Effect of combined androgen blockade with an LHRH agonist and flutamide in one severe case of male exhibitionism. *Canadian Journal of Psychiatry, 35,* 338–341.

Rousseau, L., Dupont, A., Labrie, F., & Couture, N. (1988). Sexuality and antihormonal therapy in prostate cancer. In W. Eicher & G. Kockott (Eds.), *Sexology* (pp. 290–303). Berlin: Springer-Verlag.

Scaramella, T. J., & Brown, W. A. (1978). Serum testosterone and aggressiveness in hockey players. *Psychosomatic Medicine, 40,* 262–265.

Schering A. G. (1983). *Androcur.* Berlin/Bergkamen: Author.

Segraves, R. T. (1989). Effects on psychotropic drugs on human erection and ejaculation. *Archives of General Psychiatry, 46,* 275–284.

Skakkebaek, N. E., Bancroft, J., Davidson, D. W., & Warner, P. (1981). Androgen replacement with oral testosterone undecanoate in hypogonadal men: A double-blind controlled study. *Clinical Endocrinology, 14,* 49–67.

Stein, D. J., Hollander, E., Anthony, D. T., Schneider, F. R., Fallon, B. A., & Liebowitz, M. R. (1992). Serotonergic medications for sexual obsessions, sexual addictions, and paraphilias. *Journal of Clinical Psychiatry, 53,* 267–271.

Sterkmans, P., & Geerts, F. (1996). Is benperidol (RF 504) the specific drug for the treatment of excessive and disinhibited sexual behaviour? *Acta Neurologica Psychiatrica (Belgique), 66,* 1030–1040.

Sturup, G. K. (1968). Treatment of sexual offenders in Herstedvester, Denmark: The rapists. *Acta Psychiatrica Scandinavica, 204*(Suppl. 44), 1–62.

Sturup, G. K. (1972). Castration: The total treatment. In H. L. P. Resnik & M. E. Wolfgang (Eds.), *Sexual behavior: Social, clinical and legal aspects* (pp. 361–382). Boston: Little, Brown.

Symmers, W. S. C. (1968). Carcinoma of the breast in transsexual individuals after surgical and hormonal interference with primary and secondary sex characteristics. *British Medical Journal, 2,* 3–85.

Tennent, G., Bancroft, J., & Cass, J. (1974). The control of deviant sexual behavior by drugs: A double-blind controlled study of benperidol, chlorpromazine and placebo. *Archives of Sexual Behavior, 3,* 261–271.

Thibaut, F., Cordier, B., & Kuhn, J. M. (1993). Effect of a long-lasting gonadotrophin hormone-releasing hormone agonist in six cases of severe male paraphilia. *Acta Psychiatrica Scandinavica, 87*(6), 445–50.

Walker, P. A., & Meyer, W. J. (1981). Medroxyprogesterone acetate treatment for paraphiliac sex offenders. In J. R. Hays, T. K. Roberts, & K. S. Solway (Eds.), *Violence and the violent individual* (pp. 353–373). New York: S. P. Medical and Scientific Books.

Ward, I. L. (1977). Regulation of sexual behaviour by hormones in male non-primates. In J. Money & H. Mustaph (Eds.), *Handbook of sexology* (pp. 377–392). Amsterdam: Exceptra Medica.

Wawrose, F. E., & Sisto, T. M. (1992). Clomipramine and a case of exhibitionism. *American Journal of Psychiatry, 149,* 843.

Whittaker, L. H. (1959). Oestrogens and psychosexual disorders. *Medical Journal of Australia, 2,* 547–549.

Wiedeking, C., Money, J., & Walker, P. A. (1979). Follow up of 11 XYY males with impulsive and/or sex-offending behavior. *Psychological Medicine, 9,* 287–292.

Wilson, J. D., & Foster, D. W. (1983). Introduction. In J. D. Wilson & D. W. Foster (Eds.), *Textbook of endocrinology* (pp. 1–7). Philadelphia: W. B. Saunders.

Wincze, W. P., Bansal, S., & Malamud, M. (1986). Effects of medroxyprogesterone acetate on subjective arousal, arousal to erotic stimulation and nocturnal penile tumescence in male sex offenders. *Archives of Sexual Behavior, 15,* 293–305.

24

SEXUAL DEVIANCE IN FEMALES

John A. Hunter
Ruth Mathews

The phenomenon of female sexual offending has historically received scant attention in the clinical and research literatures on sexual assault. The neglect of this subject matter is likely commentary on not only the apparent disparity in the ratio of identified male to female sex offenders, but also on our sociocultural beliefs about females and the nature of femininity. The notion of females as sexual aggressors and exploiters of children represents an abomination in the minds of most people and is incongruent with the societal image of females as nonviolent and their traditional role in childcare. It is also inconsistent with the sociological observation that power in interpersonal relationships typically resides with males, and that females are generally the victims of violence as opposed to the perpetrators. These well-entrenched cultural attitudes and sociological patterns likely contribute to both a tendency to question the validity of reports of sexual abuse made by children of both genders and the underreporting of sexual victimization by males. In this regard, sexual contact between adolescent and adult females and younger children is often discredited or reframed as a relatively benign derivative of child care rituals as opposed to sexual deviance per se. Similarly, sexual contact between older juvenile males and adult women is frequently construed by both parties as constituting consensual sexual activity and the practice of time-honored rites of passage for newly pubescent males.

Unfortunately, the lack of public and professional cognizance of female sexual offending and its detrimental effects serves to deprive both the victims and the females who perpetrate against them of needed familial and professional support and intervention. It is to the raising of a greater consciousness of the presence of patterns of sexual offending in females, and the need for treatment services for this population, that we devote this chapter.

PSYCHOPATHOLOGY AND THEORY

As female sexual offending is a topic which has only recently begun to receive clinical and empirical attention, there are at present a dearth of published studies in the literature devoted to this subject matter. As a result, we will both review existing published works and draw upon our own clinical experiences in the formulation of a theoretical and phenomenological understanding of female sexual offending and its developmental onset.

Description of Disorder

It is now clear that females engage in a variety of sexual offending behaviors, including "hands-on" offenses such as rape and child molestation and "hands-off" offenses such as exhibitionism and obscene telephone calling (Allen, 1991; Knopp & Lackey, 1987). For purposes of clinical discussion, we define rape as forced or coerced sexual activity between an adult female and an adult victim, or between an adolescent female and a peer, which involves vaginal or anal penetration, or oral sodomy. We define child molestation as sexual contact between an adult female and a juvenile, or between two juveniles, where there exists a significant age difference between the two parties (typically defined as a difference of 3 to 5 years). Using this definition, child molestation may or may not involve coerced sexual activities, but is nonetheless nonconsensual by virtue of the discrepancy in age between the involved individuals. Although we provide discussion on the broad spectrum of sexual offending in females, the major thrust of this chapter is devoted to the exploration of female-perpetrated child sexual molestation, as this is by far the most prevalent form of sexual offending manifested by females (Finkelhor, 1984; Knopp & Lackey, 1987).

Child Molestation

In recent years, it has become clear that patterns of sexual aggression in females may have a juvenile onset and in some cases may emerge before puberty (Mathews, Hunter, & Vuz, 1997). Young children have been observed attempting to persuade or coerce other children into engaging in oral sexual activities or vaginal or anal intercourse. In one case seen by one of us (JAH), a female at the age of 6 was found by her mother orally sodomizing her 2-year-old brother, and later was found to have coerced him and other young children into engaging in sexual intercourse with her. Similar cases have been described by other clinicians treating sexually aggressive children (Johnson, 1993; Gil & Johnson, 1992). The behavior of sexually aggressive children can be differentiated from normal exploratory sexual play by the type and persistence of the behavior, the differences in age between the children involved, and the use of threats, coercion, or trickery in gaining participant compliance.

Adolescent-aged female sexual offenders have been reported in ever-growing frequency over the past several years (Fehrenbach & Monastersky, 1988; Knopp & Lackey, 1987). These females sexually molest children of both genders, although there is some discrepancy in the literature at to whether they are more likely to molest males or females. While several earlier reports on juvenile female sex offenders suggested that their victims were more often female than male (Fehrenbach & Monastersky, 1988; Knopp & Lackey, 1987), a more recent study suggested a greater preference for children of the opposite gender (Mathews et al., 1997). In general, the sexual offending patterns of juvenile sex offenders reflect less gender specificity than what is commonly found in adult sex offenders, with approximately one third of juvenile female molesters reporting having victimized a child of both genders (Mathews et al., 1997).

The child victims of juvenile female sexual offenders typically are relatives or acquaintances, with relatively few victims being strangers (fewer than 10 percent) (Fehrenbach & Monastersky, 1988; Mathews et al., 1997). Juvenile female sexual offenders appear more likely than juvenile males to molest their victims in the context of a babysitting arrangement (Fehrenbach & Monastersky, 1988; Mathews et al., 1997). Like juvenile males, the majority of their victims are young children, nearly three quarters 8 years of age or younger (Mathews et al., 1997).

A number of juvenile female sexual offenders show a repetitive pattern of sexual offending, occasionally with a progression in the severity of offending over time. Mathews et al. (1997) found that over 50% of the 67 youthful female sex offenders whom they studied had more than one victim, with some youths having over 10 victims each. In this study, over one fourth of these youthful female sexual offenders had engaged in intercourse (vaginal or anal) with the victim and nearly one half had engaged in oral sexual activities. Surprisingly, nearly the same number of juvenile female as juvenile male sex offenders acknowledged that they utilized force to commit one or more of their perpetrations (approximately one fifth of the females vs. one fourth of the males).

Patterns of sexual offending in adult females suggests that there are both similarities and differences with patterns of juvenile sexual offending. Like juvenile female sex offenders, adult females who molest children typically select children known to them; over 60% of the cases are incestuous in nature, and relatively few victims are strangers (Knopp & Lackey, 1987). Initial data suggest that adult female sex offenders may be less likely to utilize force to commit a sexual offense than their juvenile counterparts (Mathews et al., 1997; Wolfe, 1995). Furthermore, there appear to be many more adult female sex offenders who sexually act out in the context of a relationship with a male co-offender (Faller, 1988; Mathews, Matthews, & Speltz, 1989). Relatively few juvenile females have reported sexually acting out in such a fashion, with the majority reporting that they acted out alone and on their own initiative (Fehrenbach & Monastersky, 1988; Mathews et al., 1997).

Other Paraphilias and Rape

We know less about female rape, as this is a relatively rare phenomenon. The limited data available suggest that older adolescent and adult female rapists typically perpetrate against relatives who are acquaintances and, unlike male rapists, often against same-gender victims (Mathews et al., 1989). A number of adult female rapists perpetrated with a male accomplice (McCarty, 1981; Grier & Clark, 1987).

Likewise, relatively few females are identified and referred for treatment for having only engaged in "hands-off" sexual offending behaviors; however, a number of female child molesters report having also engaged in paraphiliac behavior. Mathews et al. (1997) found in their sample of juvenile female child molesters that nearly 15% had engaged in exhibitionistic behavior and 3% in obscene phone calling. There have also been reports in the juvenile and adult literatures of females who engaged in more rare forms of paraphiliac behavior such as bestiality, genital exhibitionism, public masturbation, and voyeurism (Allen, 1991; Grob, 1985; Hunter, Lexier, Goodwin, Browne, & Dennis, 1993; Wolfe, 1995).

Epidemiology

The actual prevalence of female sexual offending in its various forms is difficult to ascertain, given the aforementioned problems of underreporting, differences in definition of types of sexual assaults across studies, and discrepancies in incidence rates relative to the source of the report. In general, there has been an increase in the number of female sex offenders identified in recent years, and it is now believed that they account for a higher percentage of the cases of sexual assault against young children than previously thought.

Finkelhor (1984) estimated that adult females account for 5% of the cases of sexual molestation against young girls and 20% of the molestations of young males. His projections were based on data reported by the American Humane Association and the National Incidence Study of Child Abuse and Neglect. Females appear to account for even higher percentages of the childhood sexual victimizations reported by male college students (43–60%) and incarcerated adult male sex offenders (40–45%; Allen, 1991; Burgess, Groth, Holmstrom, & Sgroi, 1987; Fritz, Stoll, & Wagner, 1981; Risin & Koss, 1987). Female perpetrators have also been found to be relatively highly represented in the sexual victimization histories of juvenile female sexual offenders, accounting for up to 15% of their victimizations (Hunter et al., 1993). Females appear to account for fewer than 1% of the rapes committed each year (Bureau of Justice Statistics, 1989; O'Connor, 1987).

Associated Features

Juveniles

The sexual acting out of juvenile females typically occurs in the context of more pervasive emotional and behavioral disturbances. Mathews et al. (1997) found that approximately one half of the 67 juvenile female sex offenders whom they studied evidenced moderate to severe levels of individual and family psychopathology and dysfunction. Many of these youths presented with clinically significant levels of anxiety and depression and met clinical criteria for diagnosis of posttraumatic stress disorder (PTSD). The majority of the youths in the sample reported histories of extensive maltreatment, including repeated sexual and physical abuse and/or exposure to domestic violence. Those with PTSD evidenced many residual sequelae including intrusive thoughts, recurrent nightmares, and avoidance of situations and relationships which reminded them of past trauma. A number of these youths also demonstrated dissociative symptomatology and episodes of emotional and behavioral regression during times of stress. Hunter et al. (1993) found not only a high incidence of PTSD (90%) in a sample of residentially treated juvenile female sex offenders, but also high levels of associated homicidal ideation (60%) and affective disturbances (100%).

Many juvenile female sex offenders demonstrate pervasive conduct-related problems and have engaged in a variety of impulsive behaviors aside from their sexual acting out. Approximately one fourth of the Mathews et al. (1997) sample had a history of significant substance abuse, one third a history of runaway, and nearly one half a history of suicidal ideation or attempts. These investigators also found that approximately one fourth of their sample had been diagnosed as suffering from a learning disability. Many of these youth were also found to have engaged in nonsexual, antisocial behaviors such as lying, stealing, and physical assault.

Adults

An array of psychological symptomatology is also found in adult female sex offenders. Signs of emotional dependence, low self-esteem, and social isolation are frequently found in those who molest with a male co-offender (Matthews, 1993). Those women who sexually act out with teenaged males have generally not appeared as severely or pervasively emotionally maladjusted, but they have been found to have the aforementioned dependence needs and to be prone toward substance abuse (Mathews et al., 1989). More severe maladjustment has been found in women who molest prepubescent children, whether their own or others. Many of these women report long histories of childhood maltreatment and have histories of physical aggression, stealing, substance abuse, and depression (Mathews et al., 1989). A history of sexual dysfunction has also been found in a number of adult female sex offenders

(Wolfe, 1995). Relatively few female sex offenders, adults or juveniles, have histories reflective of psychosis (Condy, Templer, Brown, & Veaco, 1987; Wolfe, 1995).

Etiology

The apparent heterogeneity of the female sex offender population argues for the likelihood that there are differential etiological pathways associated with various subtypes of offenders. Furthermore, even within various subtypes of offenders it is quite likely that there are multiple etiological factors which ultimately influence the behavior of each individual. Given the potential complexity of the subject matter, these authors have chosen to summarize the most salient etiological issues associated with the majority of cases of juvenile sexual offending and three major categories of adult sexual offending.

Juveniles

There is ample evidence that the sexual acting out of the majority of prepubescent and adolescent-aged females, especially those who are more psychosexually disturbed, follows a lengthy history of maltreatment and/or exposure to interpersonal violence. Fehrenbach and Monastersky (1988) found a history of sexual abuse in 50% of the 28 female adolescent sex offenders whom they studied and a history of physical abuse in approximately 20% of the cases. Knopp and Lackey (1987), in a survey of providers of treatment services to female sex offenders, found that 100% of the prepubescent clients, and 93% of the adolescent age clients, reported a history of sexual victimization prior to the onset of their offending.

Mathews et al. (1997), in their study of juvenile female sexual offenders between the ages of 11 and 17, found that 78% of the females versus 44% of a comparison group of juvenile male sex offenders reported a prior history of sexual victimization. A history of physical abuse was reported by 60% of the females, in contrast to 45% of the males. These investigators found not only a high prevalence rate of maltreatment in the backgrounds of these females, but also that their sexual victimization experiences were far more extensive than those of the juvenile male sex offenders. In this regard, 75% of the females versus 10% of the males reported having been molested by more than one perpetrator, with the mean number of perpetrators for the females being 4.5. The above comparisons also revealed that the female sex offenders tended to be younger than the juvenile male sex offenders at the time of first sexual victimization, and that a higher percentage reported that they had been subjected to the use of force by a molester. These comparisons also revealed that a greater number of the juvenile female than male sex offenders reported having been molested by a female perpetrator (42% vs. 19%).

The manner in which maltreatment experiences can contribute to the emergence of sexual deviance has been the subject of much theoretical discussion (Hunter & Becker, 1994). One particular avenue of influence which has received considerable attention in the professional literature is the association between maltreatment and PTSD. A number of investigators have found that sexually and physically abused children often display symptomatology consistent with the clinical presentation of this disorder. Kendall-Tackett, Williams, and Finkelhor (1993), in their extensive review of studies assessing the effects sexual abuse on children, found that over 50% of child victims displayed PTSD symptomatology, particularly those youths who had experienced ritualistic abuse. Briere (1992) found evidence that sexual abuse victims frequently reported PTSD symptomatology, including intrusive thoughts, hyperarousal, and avoidance behaviors. Briere posits that sexual abuse victims defend against painful affects and memories through dissociative defenses such as disengagement, detachment and numbing, observation, and amnesia. He furthermore is of the opinion that severe PTSD leads in some cases to the development of multiple personality disorder.

Finkelhor and Browne (1985) suggested that one of the mechanisms through which sexual abuse traumatizes children is in instilling a sense of powerlessness. They theorized that powerlessness is a PTSD-type symptom that results from not being able to prevent or escape from aversive experiences. Both Briere (1992) and Finkelhor and Browne (1985) viewed PTSD-type symptomatology as closely associated with other traumatogenic responses in child sexual abuse victims, including a negative self-image, a loss of trust in others, and a fear of impending danger.

The work of van der Kolk (1987) has been very influential in explaining the PTSD effects of trauma on children from a psychobiological perspective. He theorized that there is a biphasic response to trauma, with individuals vacillating between a reaction of numbing and constriction and one of hyperarousal and intrusion. This latter response involves repeated re-exposure or trauma reenactment by the victim as an attempt to gain mastery over the events associated with the trauma, and as a means of discharging excess affect derivative of recollection of the traumatic event(s). van der Kolk related the hyperarousal of trauma victims to emergent problems in capacity to modulate intense affects, including aggressive impulses, and discussed the manner in which trauma can alter neurobiological processes.

It has been suggested that the sexual acting out of the vast majority of prepubescent children is in reaction to their own abuse histories and may be closely related to PTSD phenomenology. Johnson (1993) found that all of the sexually aggressive young females with whom she worked had been sexually victimized and that these children generally seemed anxious and confused about their sexuality. She postulated that such youths act out sexually and aggressively as a means of reducing the painful affects and sensations which they repeatedly experience as a result of inflicted childhood trauma. Gil and Johnson (1992) have also discussed the manner in which a number of sexually victimized children are prone toward repetition-compulsion phenomena and engage in behaviors reminiscent of their victimizations, attempting to gain mastery over them.

The sexual acting out of older juvenile females also appears in many cases to be closely associated with the maltreatment they experienced during their childhoods and residual PTSD-type symptomatology. One area of potential association is in the development of deviant sexual arousal and interests. Finkelhor and Browne (1985) described a syndrome of traumatic sexualization which can occur in children as a result of conditioning experiences and the adoption of faulty assumptions regarding the appropriateness of various forms of sexual behavior. A number of investigators (Gil & Johnson, 1992; Johnson, 1993; Yates, 1991) have observed that some sexually victimized children show signs of eroticization and sexual preoccupation and become aroused by physical closeness or emotional intimacy.

Mathews et al. (1997) described a subset of more highly disturbed adolescent-aged female sex offenders who appear to have developed deviant sexual interest and arousal patterns in association with an extensive history of maltreatment. The vast majority of these youths reported extensive histories of sexual victimization and a number appeared to have become aroused by one or more of their own sexual victimizations. Hunter et al. (1993) found that 9 out of 10 severely psychosexually and psychiatrically maladjusted youths being residentially treated for sexual acting out evidenced symptomatology consistent with the diagnosis of PTSD. Eight out of 10 of these youths reported having experienced sexual arousal to a victimization experience. These eight youths described arousal to one or more experiences with a male perpetrator; four of six reported arousal to molestation by a female. These youths tended to report both more intense arousal to victimizations by female perpetrators and a greater degree of subjective distress. The majority of these youths acknowledged that they engaged in deviant sexual fantasizing before acting out sexually. Two youths reported that they ultimately coupled deviant sexual fantasizing with masturbatory activities.

A number of the more psychosexually and psychiatrically disturbed juvenile female sexual offenders with histories of maltreatment and familial dysfunction evidence attachment problems (Mathews et al., 1997). Many of these youths appear wary and suspicious of others and fearful of emotional intimacy. For these youths, emotional intimacy is often psychologically associated with a sense of helplessness and vulnerability. These youths often utilize distancing and avoidance as defense mechanisms. The degree of developmental disruption in the lives of these youths, and the absence of healthy role models, appears to have contributed to characterological impairment and a diminished capacity for forming emotionally meaningful and lasting interpersonal relationships.

The impact of maltreatment experiences on sexually offending youths has also been discussed from a social learning theory perspective, particularly as it relates to the influence of modeling. Sex offenders may imitate the behavior of aggressive role models in their environment, including those who have perpetrated against them (Becker, Hunter, Stein, & Kaplan, 1989; Freeman-Longo, 1986). Support for the salience of modeling in the etiology of juvenile females' sexual offending comes from the observation that the majority of these youths were exposed to aggressive male and female role models during their formative years. Over 40% of the youths in the Mathew's et al. (1997) study reported having been molested by a female. Many more were exposed to the female modeling of interpersonal aggression via physical abuse experiences and/or witnessing female-perpetrated aggression against others. Nearly all of the females in this study had been exposed to an aggressive male role model.

While the preponderance of the more psychosexually disturbed juvenile female sex offenders report long histories of maltreatment and manifest pervasive emotional problems, Mathews et al. (1997) found that a small subgroup of youths engaging in a single or a few episodes of sexual offending against at a nonrelative child showed relatively little evidence of individual psychopathology, past maltreatment, or familial dysfunction. These youths described their sexual offending as motivated primarily by sexual curiosity.

Adults

As there appears to be considerable diversity in the manifestations of sexual offending in adult females, we discuss etiology from the perspective of three major groups of such offenders: women who co-offend with a male, women who sexually molest teenage boys, and women who sexually molest prepubescent children of both genders.

Women who sexually offend in the company of a male co-offender clinically appear to be primarily motivated by both a fear of this individual and an emotional dependence upon him. These women have been found to generally be more passive than active participants in the sexual activities, and at least initially to be acting out sexually under duress. It has been reported that whereas many of these women initially experience their sexual behaviors as ego dystonic and evocative of guilt and shame, some later derive sexual and emotional gratification and become the initiators of the sexual perpetrations (Mathews et al., 1989; Wolfe, 1995). The women in this group appear to have long-standing problems of emotional insecurity, poor self-esteem, and social isolation. Over one half of these women report having been sexually abused as a child, either incestuously or extrafamilially, and approximately one half have histories of physical abuse (Matthews et al., 1989). These women have also frequently been the recipients of emotional abuse as children, and as adults have been the victims of spousal abuse and violence (Matthews et al., 1989). Their psychological characteristics and the dynamics of their relationships with their male co-offenders are similar in many respects to the description of the compliant victims of sexual sadists provided by Hazelwood, Warren, and Dietz (1993). These researchers described the process by which psychologically vulnerable women are manipulated into participating in sadomasochistic sexual activities. As with the women who sexually act out with a dominant male co-offender, these women were viewed as being vulnerable by virtue of their fragile senses of self-esteem and exaggerated emotional dependence needs.

The index of childhood-experienced maltreatment is typically very high for those women who molest prepubescent children. These women frequently come from very dysfunctional families and have been physically and sexually abused by caregivers (Allen, 1991; Faller, 1988). It appears that many of these women are prone toward reenacting the trauma they experienced as children in a manner similar to that previously described for juvenile female sex offenders. In this regard, many of these women appear to have suffered from PTSD in the past, with a number showing residual sequelae. The sexual acting out of these women often appears to be compulsive in nature and associated with an attempt to discharge painful affects and pent-up sexual tensions (Mathews et al., 1989). In some cases, these women appear to have developed deviant sexual interest and arousal patterns and to cognitively distort the meaning of their sexual acting out in a manner similar to that commonly seen in male sex offenders (Mathews et al., 1989).

Women who sexually act out with teenage males typically manifest less ego impairment and have lower rates of childhood-experienced maltreatment, especially sexual victimization, than the two previously discussed offender groups (Matthews, 1993). These women's sexual acting out frequently is associated with expressed dissatisfaction or dysfunction in an adult relationship (e.g., marital relationship) (Mathews et al., 1989). Many of these women construe their sexual acting out as representing an "affair" as opposed to an act of sexual exploitation (Mathews et al., 1989). Their behavior often reflects an inner sense of anger that their emotional needs are not being well met, emotional immaturity and strong dependence needs, and problems with identifying and establishing interpersonal boundaries.

ASSESSMENT AND TREATMENT

Identification and Referral

As previously stated, female sexual offenders are being identified in ever-increasing numbers and referred for sex offender treatment (Knopp & Lackey, 1987). The source of the referral may be the offender herself in the context of seeking help, a concerned spouse or parent, or a public agency (e.g., social services, court, etc.). It appears that female sexual offenders are not as frequently involved with the criminal justice system as are their male counterparts. Connor, Frost, Mathews, Raymaker, and Wolsleger (1994) found significant differences between adolescent males and females with regard to adjudication. They found that 53% of the females versus 24% of the males who were referred for treatment had no criminal charges. Interestingly, they found that the adolescent females who were adjudicated on the most serious charges were not those adolescents who had committed the most heinous crimes, but those who had abused a young, unrelated child outside of the home. Likewise, Mathews et al. (1989) found that certain subtypes of adult female sexual offenders appear to be charged more frequently than others. Women abusing young teens outside of the home, and those offending in concert with a male offenders, were more likely to be criminally charged and incarcerated than were women who acted out sexually with their own children.

Methods of Assessment

The assessment of juvenile and adult female sexual offenders should be comprehensive and conducted with the cognizance that deviant sexual behavior often occurs in the context of more broad-based psychiatric disturbances and psychosocial problems. The presence of a high incidence of psychiatric comorbidity in this population argues for careful diagnostic interviewing and consideration of psychological testing when questions of more pervasive emotional behavioral problems exist. Although formal psychological testing including intelligence and personality assessment may not be indicated in every case, at least a screening of personality functioning is usually warranted. It is important to be cognizant that whereas formal psychological testing may provide the clinician with valuable data which will aid in diagnosis and treatment planning, such testing will not identify whether the assessed female is a sexual offender, and it may provide little or no information as to the nature of her sexual disturbance, per se.

We recommend that clinical evaluations of female sex offenders generally be conducted postadjudication and presentencing, when legal action is pending. Such evaluations can address issues relevant to the court, including: the nature of the referred individual's sexual and other problems, the level of risk that she appears to represent to the community, the types and levels of intervention services required, and her amenability to treatment. The court can use these reports and any associated court testimony in making a disposition. Pre-adjudication evaluations are generally more legally complicated and raise issues regarding the admissibility of the clinician's evaluation report to the court proceedings.

Before meeting with the client it is helpful for the evaluating clinician to peruse any available legal or social service investigative reports and any previously conducted psychological evaluations of the client. In particular, it is helpful to have access to police records and victim statements. Victim statements are especially valuable in clarifying the nature of the offender's behavior, as many offenders minimize the extent of their sexual acting out.

Perhaps the most valuable diagnostic tool of the clinician working with female sexual offenders of any age is the *clinical interview*. The clinical interview can be structured in such a manner as to elicit pertinent information regarding the etiology, development, and manifestation of the client's psychosexual disturbance, her attitude toward her behavior and willingness to participate in treatment, and the larger psychosocial context in which the sexual acting out occurred. Given its importance, the interview should be conducted with sensitivity to both process and content issues. It is prudent for the evaluator to be mindful that female sex offenders, like their male counterparts, are often reluctant to fully divulge information relevant to their sexual acting out for a variety of reasons, including denial, fear of legal consequences, and issues of shame and embarrassment. These latter issues appear to be particularly prominent with female sex offenders. In the creation of a supportive environment conducive to the sharing of all relevant information, it is generally helpful for the evaluator to initially explain to the client the purpose of the evaluation, who the clinician represents, how the findings will be used, and to whom a report will be issued. It may also be helpful to explain the evaluator's qualifications and experiences so as to engender a sense of confidence in her or his abilities. It is critical that all parties are aware of the limits of confidentiality and provide written consent, when appropriate, for the release of information to other relevant parties. Such thoroughness and frankness will ultimately help the client and her family develop a sense of trust in the evaluator and the ensuing treatment process.

Depending upon the setting and the specific circumstances of the client, she may or may not be accompanied in the initial interview by family members. Under most circumstances, it is desirable that the family of the juvenile female sexual offender be present for participation in the evaluation. Though the evaluator may want to meet with the juvenile female's parents both separately as well as with the youth, it is imperative that the youth also be interviewed privately. Most youths find it very uncomfortable to initially discuss the nature of their sexual acting out in the presence of their families. However, parents should be fully apprised by the evaluator, and the youth herself when appropriate, of the full extent of her problems after completion of the evaluation process. The inclusion of family members in the assessment of adult female sex offenders is dependent upon the specific circumstances of the client and her wishes regarding this matter.

We recommend that the interview include a review of the following areas and topics: early development, including history of maltreatment experiences; the nature and quality of past and present familial and peer relationships; history of academic functioning and behavior, history of employment (adults); exposure to pornography and peer or domestic violence; history of nonsexual delinquent behavior and substance abuse; and psychosexual history, including age-appropriate and -inappropriate behaviors. It is also important that the interview include a review of mental status functioning, including any history of past symptomatology suggestive of psychological dysfunction (e.g., depression, etc.).

As previously stated, the clinical interview is often supplemented by more formal psychometric assessment. Unfortunately, at the present time there are no specialized psychosexual assessment instruments standardized and normed on a female sex offender population. Furthermore, there has been relatively little use of psychophysiological assessment of sexual arousal patterns in female sex offenders. In addition to ethical considerations about the invasiveness of the procedure, there are questions about the reliability of such measurement in females (Henson, Rubin, & Henson, 1979) and the relevance of deviant sexual arousal in the majority of cases of female sexual offending. With regard to the latter, in contrast the report of many male sex offenders, relatively few females identify sexual arousal as a major motivator of their behavior (Connor et al., 1994).

Diagnosis and Treatment Planning

The evaluator needs to utilize all of the above-described sources of data in the development of a diagnostic formulation of the client and a comprehensive plan of service. The diagnostic formulation should include both a description of the type of sexual disturbance(s) displayed by the client, as well as the overall psychiatric and psychosocial context in which the sexual acting out occurred. The failure to properly identify and diagnose all of the pertinent psychiatric and psychosocial conditions of the client typically results in a treatment plan of very limited effectiveness. As previously emphasized, female sexual offenders are a heterogeneous population and present along a continuum of psychiatric and psychosexual disturbance. Although clinicians may find formal diagnostic criteria on sexual disorders as discussed in DSM-IV (American Psychiatric Association, 1994) helpful, such diagnostic conceptualizations have generally been developed through study of adult male sex offender populations and may not be fully applicable to females. Thus, we urge clinicians to be cautious in applying adult male sex offender terminology with females, and instead focus more intently on a behavioral description of the types of sexual problems which they manifest and the larger personality–familial systems contexts in which they occur. We outline pertinent issues in the assessment of female sexual offenders in the following paragraphs.

In the assessment of the nature of the psychosexual disturbance and the level of service required, attention should be given to a number of diagnostic issues, including the following:

1. Does the client acknowledge having engaged in the alleged sexual misbehavior, and what is the level of accountability displayed?

2. What is the level of insight into the problem; ...os tivations for having engaged in the sexual behavio..

3. Does the client express guilt and remorse for the beha... ...ated reasons/mo- of guilt/remorse versus shame and embarrassment? ...the degree

4. Over what period of time has the sexual acting out occurred, and has the...degree progression in the frequency or severity of the behavior since its inception?

5. How has the client gained access and control over her victim(s), and has there been the use of force or threat?

6. Has the sexual acting out occurred in concert with a male co-offender, or was the sexual activity initiated by the female who acted alone?

7. Has the client experienced sexual arousal to the behavior or thoughts of the behavior, and have the sexual urges and impulses been experienced as compulsive in nature?

Other issues germane to diagnosis and treatment planning include an assessment of the following:

1. What is the client's motivation for change and level of amenability to receiving professional help?

2. What is the client's overall capacity for utilizing sound judgment and maintaining appropriate impulse control?

3. What is the client's capacity for forming and maintaining healthy interpersonal relationships?

4. What is the degree of family and other social support available to the client to assist her in making behavioral changes?

As female sex offenders reflect a heterogeneous population with a variety of types and levels of sexual and nonsexual disturbances represented, so should there be a continuum of treatment services to meet their different needs. The types of services required by female sexual offenders range from high-intensity, structured, and specialized residential treatment programs to community-based care. The type of programming required by any particular female sex offender obviously depends upon her special characteristics and circumstances, underlining the importance of careful assessment and diagnosis.

In planning for the treatment of female sex offenders, clinicians should be conservative in their recommendations and cognizant of issues of family and community safety. Whereas final disposition may be a legal matter, the treatment plan should reflect a process of collaboration between the various agencies and professionals involved with the client, as well as the input of the client and her family. Effective treatment is predicated on the development of a uniform systemic response to the client's behavior and effective interagency coordination in service provision. For those clients with legal involvement, careful interfacing with the criminal justice system is critical.

Treatment Issues and Approaches

Historically, relatively few females have been referred to sex offender treatment programs. Those who were referred prior to the mid-1980s, were typically placed in therapy groups along with male sex offenders with little sensitivity to gender differences (Mathews et al., 1989). Advances in the treatment of female sex offenders in recent years has led to the development of more refined, gender-specific treatment approaches based upon offender subtype, etiological factors, and psychological profiles (Connor et al., 1994; Mathews et al.,

, ıurner & Turner, 1994). We discuss approaches found to be
...ent of major subtypes of juvenile and adult sexual offenders in the

1989; M₂ ₒ.aphs.

effecti-
foll

Juveniles

Mathews et al. (1997) described three preliminary subtypes of juvenile female offenders most frequently found in treatment populations. One subtype consists of young female juveniles who have engaged in a single to several isolated incidents of offending, typically against a nonrelated child for whom they had been babysitting. These youths appear inexperienced, naive, and somewhat fearful about sexuality, and describe their behavior as being motivated primarily by curiosity. These youths are quite responsive to a short-term outpatient treatment program that consists of group, individual, and family therapy components and that focuses primarily on the following: sex education, self-esteem and improving social competence, and improving family communication.

The second subtype comprises youths who sexually molest younger children, typically over a period of less than 1 year, and in a manner that parallels their own victimizations. These adolescents generally report engaging others in abusive sexual behaviors shortly after or during their own sexual victimization, following a difficult adjustment or upon entering adolescence. Although many of these youths have been observed to possess adequate social skills and exhibit a number of personality strengths, they generally seem sexually apprehensive and report few prior age-appropriate sexual experiences. A mild to moderate level of individual psychopathology has been found in this subgroup. Most prominently, approximately half of these youth suffer from depression or a disturbance of identity. The majority of these youths are responsive to longer-term, outpatient, sex-offense-specific treatment programs. Some of these youths require out-of-home placement due to the risk they represent for sexually offending within the home, and/or as a result of the high level of dysfunction in their families of origin. Of paramount importance in the treatment of these youths is addressing unresolved conflicts stemming from their prior sexual victimization and the manner in which such maltreatment contributed to their emergent sexual aggression.

The third and most disturbed subgroup of adolescent female offenders are those who engaged in more extensive and repetitive sexual offending behaviors. These youths present as more psychosexually and psychiatrically disturbed than the two previously described subgroups. The psychosexual and psychosocial problems of these youths appear to be of a long-standing nature and closely linked with having experienced a very high level of developmental trauma early in their lives (Mathews et al., 1997). The majority of these youths report histories of extensive sexual abuse and many appear to have been eroticized to one or more of their victimization experiences (Hunter et al., 1993). The families of these youths are typically quite dysfunctional and evidence high incidence rates of the following: incest (other than what the adolescent perpetrated), parental histories of childhood sexual abuse, spousal abuse, marital discord, and parental physical abuse of the children (Mathews et al., 1997).

The youths in this subgroup evidence a high level of psychiatric comorbidity, with the majority evidencing an affective disorder, a disorder of conduct, and either past or present PTSD symptomatology (Hunter et al., 1993; Mathews et al., 1997). The presence of PTSD symptomatology in this subgroup is an issue of considerable therapeutic importance. Many of these youths manifest the previously described residual sequelae of trauma, including intrusive thoughts and recurrent nightmares, dissociative symptomatology, and a propensity for emotional and behavioral regression during times of stress (Mathews et al., 1997). These youths seem quite prone toward engaging in the aforementioned repetition-compulsion phenomena. Furthermore, they frequently form negative therapeutic transferences and have difficulty forming attachments and developing trust in others (Mathews et al., 1997). The treatment of these youths is often a relatively long and arduous endeavor and requires a keen sensitivity to the above-described relational dynamics. Given the level of maladjustment that many of these youths exhibit, treatment in a structured residential environment is often necessary. The residential treatment of these youths typically involves the integration of psychological and psychiatric therapies, including individual psychotherapy, process and didactic group therapies, family therapy, milieu therapy, and adjunctive therapies. The high incidence of psychiatric comorbidity in this group also argues for consideration of psychotropic medication in the treatment of their depressive and anxiety-related symptomatology.

Connor et al. (1994) outlined major treatment goals common to working with all adolescent female sexual offenders. These goals include fostering acceptance of responsibility for the sexual acting out, developing in each youth an understanding of the consequences of her offending behavior and enhancing her capacity for empathy; identifying and resolving underlying emotional, psychological, and situational dynamics and issues leading to the offending behavior; and acquiring the skills necessary for engaging in healthy interpersonal relationships. The treatment of those juvenile female sexual offenders with lengthy histories of maltreatment requires a careful juxtaposing of victim and offender issues. In this regard, the therapy of these youths should be viewed as an interactive process of simultaneously resolving victim and offender issues, as most of these youths are not able to make significant progress on offense issues until they have achieved some personal resolution as to the same issues in their own lives (Connor et al., 1994; O'Brien & Mathews, 1994).

Adults

We provide a description of the treatment of the following three major subtypes of adult female sex offenders: females who sexually offend with a male co-offender, adult females who molest prepubescent children, and adult females who molest teenage males.

Women who sexually co-offend in concert with a male generally are involved in an abusive relationship with that individual and socially isolated from peers and family (Mathews et al., 1989; Wolfe, 1995). These women are typically responsive to therapies which focus on improving their self-esteem, promoting assertiveness skills, and increasing social supports (Mathews et al., 1989). It is important that these women understand the parallels between their involvement in abusive relationships and their sexual abuse of others. The extent to which treatment efforts are successful in altering their sexually abusive behaviors is obviously contingent upon their ability to extricate themselves from relationships wherein they are being dominated and exploited.

Women who molest prepubescent children of both genders generally are a quite psychosexually and psychiatrically disturbed subgroup of female offenders (O'Connor, 1987). The sexual offending of these females typically follows a very lengthy history of sexual and other maltreatment. The women in this subgroup evidence a high level of psychiatric comorbidity and many meet diagnostic criteria for affective disorders, PTSD, and disorders of personality (McCarty, 1987; Wolfe, 1995). Furthermore, many of these women report having been sexually aroused by their victim(s), and some evidence more pervasive paraphiliac arousal and interest patterns (Mathews et al., 1989). Treatment of these women is typically relatively long term and complicated (Mathews et al., 1989). Major areas of therapeutic focus include the following: mood stabilization, strengthening identity development, increasing empathy, enhancing ability to engage in healthy and trusting relationships with others, and diminishing deviant sexual arousal and interests (Mathews, et al., 1989). As in the treatment of juvenile female sexual offenders with extensive histories of maltreatment, therapeutic intervention with this subgroup of adult sex offenders requires the careful interfacing of victim and offender issues.

Women who sexually molest adolescent boys often are initially quite defended and in denial with regard to having committed a sexual offense (Matthews, 1993). Most of these women describe themselves as having "fallen in love" with a young, teenaged male during a time of adult relationship failure or discontent (Mathews et al., 1989). These women tend not to see their behavior as criminal or injurious to the youths involved (Mathews et al., 1989). The treatment of these women includes correcting their distorted thinking regarding the meaning of their behavior and the response of the victim (Matthews, 1993). In this regard, it is important to help these women realize that the adolescent males with whom they were involved typically were emotionally troubled adolescents who were vulnerable and responsive to the emotional attention and support of an older female (Mathews et al., 1989). It is also important to help them understand how they misused their authority over the child and how the relationship was not truly one between two consenting peers (Mathews et al., 1989). Treatment of these women often involves individual and group therapy work around the above issues, as well as attention to their dysfunctional adult relationships. In this regard, it has been our clinical observation that many of these women are later amenable to marital therapy. In spite of their initial resistance, the vast majority of these women are responsive to treatment and do not require long-term care (Matthews, 1993).

FUTURE DIRECTIONS

In contrast to a relatively long-standing professional interest in male sex offenders, the study of female sex offenders is a comparatively recent phenomenon and the field is still in its infancy. There is much to be learned with regard to the prevalence of various forms of sexual offending in females, their developmental origins, and the treatment needs of this population. Comprehensive empirical studies are needed in each of the above areas for the field to advance.

Studies should be conducted with the cognizance that diagnostic criteria employed in the classification of male sex offenders may not be appropriate for the study of females given apparent gender differences in etiology, clinical manifestation, and motivation(s) for engaging in the behavior. Research and clinical efforts would be greatly enhanced by the development of assessment devices standardized and normed on females and which accurately reflect the psychological and psychosexual constructs germane to this clinical population.

With regard to treatment, there is a need for both process and outcome studies. Such studies are vital to the development of a comprehensive array of treatment services comparable to what is now available to male sex offenders. Process studies should include an examination of the effects of past trauma on ability to form therapeutic attachments and the influence of the gender of the therapist on the degree of client comfort in addressing sexual and identity issues. These studies should also attempt to delineate critical stages in the recovery and rehabilitation of female sex offenders. Outcome research should be directed at identifying which treatment strategies are most effective for particular types of female offenders and establishing the relative risk of recidivism across diagnostic subtypes.

REFERENCES

Allen, C. (1991). *Women and men who sexually abuse children: A comparative analysis.* Orwell, VT: Safer Society Press.

American Psychiatric Association. (1994). *Diagnostic and statistical manual of mental disorders* (4th ed.). Washington, DC: Author.

Becker, J. V., Hunter, J. A., Stein, R. M., & Kaplan, M. S. (1989). Factors associated with erection in adolescent sex offenders. *Journal of Psychopathology and Behavioral Assessment, 11*(4), 353–363.

Briere, J. (1992). *Child abuse trauma: Theory and treatment of the lasting effects.* Newbury Park, CA: Sage.

Bureau of Justice Statistics. (1989). *Criminal victimization in the United States, 1987.* Washington, DC: U.S. Department of Justice.

Burgess, A. W., Groth, A. N., Holmstrom, L. L., & Sgroi, S. M. (1987). *Sexual assault of children and adolescents.* Toronto: Lexington Books.

Condy, S., Templer, D., Brown, R., & Veaco, L. (1987). Parameters of sexual contact of boys with women. *Archives of Sexual Behavior, 16*(5), 379–394.

Connor, T., Frost, M., Mathews, R., Raymaker, J., & Wolsleger, S. (1994). *Adolescent female sexual offenders: A descriptive and comparative study and treatment manual* (Report No. SP-93-0053). Saint Paul, MN: Saint Paul Foundation.

Faller, K. (1988). The spectrum of sexual abuse in daycare: An exploratory study. *Journal of Family Violence, 3*(4), 283–298.

Fehrenbach, P. A., & Monastersky, C. (1988). Characteristics of female adolescent sexual offenders. *American Journal of Orthopsychiatry, 58*(1), 148–151.

Finkelhor, D. (1984). *Child sexual abuse: New theory and research.* New York: Free Press.

Finkelhor, D., & Browne, A. (1985). The traumatic impact of child sexual abuse: A conceptualization. *American Journal of Orthopsychiatry, 55*(4), 530–541.

Freeman-Longo, R. E. (1986). The impact of sexual victimization on males. *Child Abuse and Neglect, 10,* 411–414.

Fritz, G., Stoll, K., & Wagner, N. (1981). A comparison of males and females who were sexually molested as children. *Journal of Sex and Marital Therapy, 7*(1), 54–59.

Gil, E., & Johnson, T. C. (1992). *Assessment and treatment of sexualized children and children who molest.* Rockville, MD: Launch Press.

Grier, P., & Clark, M. (1987). *Female sexual offenders in a prison setting.* Unpublished manuscript, Behavioral Science Institute, Inc., St. Louis, MO.

Grob, C. S. (1985). Female exhibitionism. *Journal of Nervous and Mental Disease, 173,* 253–256.

Hazelwood, R., Warren, J., & Dietz, P. (1993). Complaint victims of the sexual sadist. *Australian Family Physician, 22*(4), 1–5.

Henson, D. E., Rubin, H. B., & Henson, C. (1979). Analysis of the consistency of objective measures of sexual arousal in women. *Journal of Applied Behavior Analysis, 12*(4), 701–711.

Hunter, J. A. (1993). *The clinical diagnosis and treatment of juvenile sex offenders.* Unpublished manuscript prepared for use by the National Resource Center on Child Sexual Abuse (Huntsville, Alabama), under a grant from the National Center on Child Abuse and Neglect.

Hunter, J. A. & Becker, J. V. (1994). The role of deviant sexual arousal in juvenile sexual offending: Etiology, evaluation, and treatment. *Criminal Justice and Behavior, 21*(1), 132–149.

Hunter, J. A., Lexier, L. J., Goodwin, D. W., Browne, P. A., & Dennis, C. (1993). Psychosexual, attitudinal, and developmental characteristics of juvenile female sexual perpetrators in a residential treatment setting. *Journal of Child and Family Studies, 2*(4), 317–326.

Johnson, T. C. (1993). Assessment of sexual behavior problems in preschool-aged and latency-aged children. In A. Yates (Ed.), *Child and adolescent psychiatric clinics of North America: Sexual and gender identity disorders* (pp. 431–450). Philadelphia: Saunders.

Kendall-Tackett, K. A., Williams, L. M., & Finkelhor, D. (1993). Impact of sexual abuse on children: A review of synthesis of recent empirical studies. *Psychological Bulletin, 113*(1), 164–180.

Knopp, F. H., & Lackey, L. D. (1987). *Female sexual abusers: A summary of data from 44 treatment providers.* Brandon, VT: Safer Society Press.

Mathews, R., Hunter, J. A., & Vuz, J. (1997). *Juvenile female sexual offenders: Clinical characteristics and treatment issues. Sexual Abuse: A Journal of Research and Treatment, 9*(3), 187–199.

Mathews, R., Matthews, J. K., & Speltz, K. (1989). *Female sexual offenders: An exploratory study.* Orwell, VT: Safer Society Press.

Matthews, J. K. (1993). Working with female sexual abusers. In M. Elliott (Ed.), *Female sexual abuse of children: The ultimate taboo* (pp. 61–78). Essex, England: Longman.

McCarty, D. (1981). *Women who rape.* Unpublished manuscript.

McCarty, L. M. (1987). Mother–child incest: Characteristics of the offender. *Child Welfare, 65*(5), 447–458.

O'Brien, M., & Mathews, R. (1994, November). *Adolescent male and female sex offenders: Typologies and comparisons.* Presentation given at 13th annual research and treatment conference of the Association for the Treatment of Sexual Abusers, San Francisco, CA.

O'Connor, A. A. (1987). Female sex offenders. *British Journal of Psychiatry, 150,* 615–620.

Risin, L., & Koss, M. (1987). The sexual abuse of boys: Prevalence and descriptive characteristics of childhood victimizations. *Journal of Interpersonal Violence, 2,*(3), 309–323.

Turner, M. T., & Turner, T. N. (1994). *Female adolescent sexual abusers: An exploratory study of mother–daughter dynamics with implications for treatment.* Brandon, VT: Safer Society Press.

van der Kolk, B. A. (1987). The psychological consequences of overwhelming life experiences. In B. A. van der Kolk (Ed.), *Psychological trauma* (pp. 1–29). Washington, DC: American Psychiatric Press.

Wolfe, F. (1995). *Women who commit sex crimes.* Unpublished manuscript, Northwest Treatment Associates, Seattle, WA.

Yates, A. (1991). Differentiating hypererotic states in the evaluation of sexual abuse. *Journal of the American Academy of Psychiatry, 30*(5), 791–795.

25

FUTURE DIRECTIONS

Stephen M. Hudson
Tony Ward

We deliberately choose to begin this chapter with some comments about the state of etiological theories in the sexual offending area. We believe that theory construction and development, are fundamental to the progress of science and, further, that these processes have been significantly neglected in the domain of sexual deviance. We have structured the additional issues raised in this chapter under the headings of assessment and treatment. That these topics are discussed separately does not imply that they are unrelated. Indeed, in our view they must be meaningfully integrated for appropriate professional practice to result.

THEORY CONSTRUCTION AND DEVELOPMENT

The absence of an integrated approach to theory building in the area of sexual offending is a major problem. The lack of an organizing framework, or meta-theory, has resulted in the ad hoc proliferation of theories that often overlap, confuse levels of theory, and frequently neglect each others' existence (see Ward & Hudson, in press, for an extended discussion of these points). In brief, our concerns and suggestions for the future are as follows.

In an ideal world we would have access to a global theory that integrates all relevant phenomena into a rich and coherent structure. Such a global theory does not yet exist in the area of sexual deviance and, in the meantime, the most rational strategy is theoretical pluralism (Hooker, 1987). This certainly has been the case for theorizing with respect to sexual offending, with biological, behavioral, psychodynamic, systems, feminist, developmental, and social–cognitive theories all being advanced (Lanyon, 1991; Marshall & Barbaree, 1989; Schwartz, 1995). However, we suggest that these efforts, laudable as they are, lack integration.

We believe that there is utility to viewing these theoretical efforts within a two-dimensional space; according to level, on the one hand, and temporally, in terms of distal to proximal, on the other. Level I, comprehensive or multifactorial theories, aim to construct a loosely associated set of constructs that serve as a framework with which to approach empirical problems. For example, Marshall and Barbaree's (1990) integrated model essentially suggested that biology sets a major developmental challenge for young males around puberty in that they need to acquire socially required control over both sexuality and aggression. Those males who have been exposed to a variety of developmentally adverse events, such as harsh parenting and physical and sexual abuse, are unlikely to reach puberty with the requisite skills to deal adequately with the challenges involved. Poor social skills and inappropriate attitudes toward the rights of others together with loneliness and anger result in an even lower likelihood that the vulnerable young male will be able to meet his social needs in prosocial ways. In Marshall and Barbaree's model these vulnerability factors interact with transient situation factors such as, for example, drug usage, presence of a potential victim, and beliefs concerning a low probability of being reported, to produce the offense. As such, theories at this level serve to identify variables likely to be of relevance. Theories at this level are distinguished from mature, global theories insofar as the causal factors and their relationships with each other are not clearly spelled out (Hooker, 1987).

Level II, middle or single-factor theories, typically take one variable of interest, often suggested by a level I theory, and describe the relevant structures and processes and their interrelationships. Examples of theories at this level are empathy deficits (Marshall, Hudson, Jones, & Fernandez, 1995) and intimacy deficits (Marshall, 1989; Ward, Hudson, Marshall, & Siegert, 1995). In brief, we suggest that attachment style, with the explicit use of working models of both the self and others, may assist our understanding of how difficulties in forming and managing relationships might happen in sexually aggressive men. We suggest that the three insecure attachment styles, defined by negative views of self with positive views of others (preoccupied), negative self and others (fearfully avoidant), and positive self with negative others (dismissing) are likely to be involved in different types of sexual offending (rape associated with the dismissing style), and to be associated with different psychological characteristics (loneliness related to both preoccupied and fearful styles, but anger related only to fearful and dismissing styles).

Level III, microtheories, involve building descriptive models of the offense chain or relapse process (e.g., Pithers, 1990; Ward, Louden, Hudson, & Marshall, 1995). For example, Pithers's relapse prevention model focuses on factors proximal to offending, describing the process as typically beginning with negative affect (e.g., loneliness, confusion, or anger) which is often the result of interpersonal conflict (Pithers, Kashima, Cumming, & Beal, 1988). Negative affect leads to fantasies of performing sexually abusive acts, seen as learned ways of reducing negative feelings. These fantasies are often associated with a stream of dysfunctional cognitions which serves to rationalize deviant sexuality. The offender then begins to plan and carry out an assault.

Our descriptive model of the offense chain for child molesters (Ward, Louden, et al., 1995) involves at least nine discriminable steps ranging from proximal background factors through distal planning to nonsexual contact with the victim for the purpose of offending, that is, the high-risk situation. Subsequent steps involve proximal planning, that is the immediate precursors to the sexual offense involving behaviors such as getting into bed with the child, the sexual offense itself, and finally, the evaluative processes occurring after the offense has been committed, and resolutions regarding future behavior. Both of these models are illustrative of level III microtheories. This level of model typically specifies the cognitive, behavioral, motivational, and contextual factors associated with a sexual offense. These descriptions, driven as they are by what offenders tell us they actually do when they offend, provide the touchstone for the other levels of theorizing; it is these processes that need to be explained.

A second dimension to theory is the distinction between distal and proximal factors. Distal factors attempt to answer "why" questions and address vulnerability factors, such as hostile attitudes toward women or intimacy deficits, whereas proximal factors address "how" questions (Alessi, 1992), for example, how negative affect, perhaps arising from attachment difficulties (a vulnerability factor), functions to trigger disinhibition.

Work at all three levels and across the time dimension, needs to be encouraged, as any one level and temporal focus is not superior to any other. The critical issue is that the process of theory development be orderly and inclusive. For example, early behavioral models of sexual aggression were based primarily on the sexual preference hypothesis. This view suggested that assaults occurred because the man preferred, or was sexually aroused by, deviant sexual activities (Abel, Barlow, Blanchard, & Guild, 1977; Bond & Evans, 1967). The narrow focus in this explanation led others, for example, both Marshall and his colleagues (Marshall, 1971, 1973; Marshall & McKnight, 1975; Marshall & Williams, 1975) and Abel and his colleagues (Abel et al., 1984; Abel & Rouleau, 1986) to develop more complex frameworks, ultimately leading to Marshall and Barbaree's (1990) integrated theory.

However, in surveying the current major frameworks (level I), it appears that whereas Marshall and Barbaree's integrated model (1990) robustly identified a number of distal factors, other models tend to focus more on general proximal factors (Ward & Hudson, in press). For example, Hall and Hirschman's (1991) quadripartite model is based on four components, the first three of which primarily reflect proximal factors (i.e., physiological sexual arousal, cognitions justifying sexual aggression, and affective dyscontrol). Only the last factor, personality problems, contains some distal variance. Similarly, Malamuth, Heavey, and Linz's (1993) confluence model of sexual aggression, with its two pathways, hostile masculinity and sexual promiscuity, was developed using six predictor variables: sexual arousal arousal to rape, dominance as a motive for sex, hostility toward women, attitudes facilitating aggression against women, antisocial personality characteristics, and sexual experience as a measure of opportunity. The authors provided a developmental context for some of these factors, for example, how adverse developmental experiences might impact upon negative attitudes, but the primary focus remained on phenomena close to the offense.

Second, the processes suggested to be involved in the existing level I theories tend to be described only in general terms; the mechanisms are not typically explained. For example, whereas Finkelhor (1984) specified four preconditions for offending: the motivation to offend, overcoming one's own inhibitions, the child's resistance, and finally, any external constraints such as parental presence, the description of the processes involved is quite general.

Additionally, there is a tendency for theorists to ignore the work of others. For example, in a discussion of their confluence theory, Malamuth et al.'s (1993) did not mention Marshall and Barbaree's (1990) integrated model, nor Marshall's work on intimacy (e.g., Marshall, 1989). The interactive nature of the integrated model and the ability of the intimacy-deficit perspective to provide a theoretical basis for Malamuth et al.'s impersonal sex pathway are both significant oversights. This is just one illustration of what we do not believe is a malicious tendency; rather, it reflects what Staats (1989, 1991) called the "faddish" nature of theory construction, wherein researchers strive for new ideas rather than seeking to integrate their work with existing knowledge. An alternative to this approach to theory building, suggested by Kalmar and Sternberg (1988), is "theory knitting." An example of this process is the way we have used Marshall's (1989) intimacy deficit theory and Knight and Prentky's (1990) classificatory work to develop a more comprehensive model of intimacy deficits (Ward, Hudson, et al., 1995).

The future, we hope, will not be characterized by the continued proliferation of models and theories to account for sexual offending. Our suggestion is that the metatheoretical framework, involving the three levels and the orthogonal temporal dimension (distal to proximal), can assist both theory construction and development. As such we suggest that researchers ask two critical questions (Ward & Hudson, in press): "Where are the explanatory gaps?" and "What level of theory construction would be most helpful in advancing understanding at this point?" We need better integration rather than more novelty. We need better micro-level theories to provide rigorous descriptions of the regularities in offenders' behavior that constitute the phenomena we are attempting to explain. We also need more detailed level II models capable of articulating the mechanisms required by the more general overarching frameworks; good level II theories ought to be knitted dynamically and interactively into an integrated framework.

Some of the major challenges that remain for us center around the following themes. First, we do not yet know enough about how vulnerability to offending develops. Marshall and Barbaree (1990) made an excellent beginning in identifying some of the constructs likely to be involved, but much work is needed to expand on this skeleton. Our work on intimacy and attachment is just one example. Second, other than intriguing anecdotes, we know very little about the offender-specific processes that turn vulnerability into an initial offense. Additionally, these processes often occur in adolescence, arguably the most critical and poorly studied period of sexual development. The form of these triggers, despite their significance in explaining sexual aggression, remain critically underexplored. Third, while some appropriate work is beginning, for example, our work in empathy deficits, generally insufficient attention has been paid to both the temporal instability and the situational specificity of many of the factors suggested to be important in bringing about deviant sexuality. We will return to this point in an assessment context, but we raise it here because of the theoretical implications.

Fourth, there remains the issue of classification. Taxonomy critically provides a vehicle for communication for clinicians and researchers. Such devices also help structure decisions concerning the need for treatment, the risk assessment, and setting appropriate expectations regarding interventions and the reduction of risk. Although the work of Prentky and his colleagues is a good start (Knight & Prentky, 1990; Prentky & Knight, 1991), the lack of integration with risk assessment and intervention outcomes limits its application. We are left with significant unexplained heterogeneity, even in relatively well-researched areas such as rape and child molestation, let alone with respect to the other paraphilias.

Finally, we suggest that the importation of theories and models from other domains of psychopathology and mainstream psychological theory can facilitate the development of theory in our field. For example, in some of our earlier work we argued for the integration of social–cognitive methods and principles to the sexual offending area (Johnston & Ward, 1996). Additionally, the application of theories from developmental psychology and close relationship research such as attachment theory has clarified the nature of intimacy deficits in rapists and child molesters (Ward, Hudson, & Marshall, 1996).

ASSESSMENT

The single greatest challenge facing the area with respect to assessment is the relative reliance on self-report measures. This means of collecting information, to develop an adequate case formulation, is never entirely satisfactory. In addition, the factors which serve to enhance deception and other types of validity problems abound in the area of sexual deviance and must be taken seriously. The centrality of phallometry in assessment reflects the high expectations clinicians and researchers alike had for this procedure as an alternative to self-report. We thought it would give us valid and reliable access to more than just what the offender was prepared, or indeed able, to tell us. We have chosen to discuss the failure of phallometry in some detail, as it is seems that continued adherence reflects a legitimate desire for a source of information other than self-report, but this risks negative public scrutiny. We are, therefore, very much in need of alternative strategies.

We have chosen to make our comments with respect to how the field might develop, in terms of assessment, under the following headings: sexuality, interpersonal competence, and risk issues, but we begin with an overview of the general goals and procedures in clinical case formulation.

Clinical Case Formulation

In view of the fact that very few offenders reach criteria for a DSM-IV (American Psychiatric Association, 1994) diagnosis of paraphilia, it is important to develop a comprehensive case formulation. In our view the implementation of the scientist–practitioner model with sex offenders requires the direct utilization of scientific thinking in clinical problem solving, alongside the use of empirically validated therapeutic techniques. Being a local clinical scientist requires psychologists to think more systematically and critically about individual cases, in addition to integrating research with routine clinical work (Stricker & Trierweiler, 1995). The judicious use of scientific method, or systematic inquiry, in clinical work can lead to the detection of important clinical phenomena and guide the development of a case formulation.

There are parallels between the practice of science and psychological assessment (Spengler, Strohmer, Dixon, & Shivy, 1995). The scientist attempts to detect and then to explain the occurrence of phenomena, and to this latter end, develops models or theories. These explanations describe the causal mechanisms and processes that generate the phenomena and enable us to make predictions concerning their future occurrence. Similarly, in psychological assessment clinicians attempt systematically to collect data that enable them to identify a client's difficulties and the causes (Kazdin, 1993; Ward & Haig, 1997). The result of this process is the development of a conceptual model representing the client's various complaints and their relationship(s) to each other. Like science, we can construe the process of psychological assessment as systematic inquiry into a client's problems and their interrelationships.

Traditionally, the hypothetico–deductive account of scientific method, with its restricted emphasis on the testing of hypotheses, has been associated with assessment and case conceptualizations. This model has severe problems that limit its usefulness for clinicians. We have discussed these difficulties elsewhere (Ward & Haig, 1997), but to summarize: the hypothetico–deductive account of scientific method overemphasizes hypothesis testing and neglects hypothesis generation and problem formulation, it fails to distinguish between data and clinical phenomena, it neglects the role of problems in scientific enquiry, and it is unable to provide a sufficiently rich framework to guide the multitask nature of psychological assessment.

We suggest that an alternative model of scientific inquiry, known as abductive method, can address the limitations of the hypothetico-deductive method and preserve the core conception of psychological assessment as a form of scientific inquiry (Ward & Haig, 1997). Abduction is a form of inference which takes us from a description of data patterns to a plausible explanation of those patterns; the abductive method provides an integrative structure for implementing this reasoning process. At the same time it provides an appropriate integrated framework for clinical inquiry.

We can give a typical characterization of abductive inference as follows: some phenomenon, or robust pattern, is encountered that is surprising because it does not follow from any accepted hypothesis; we come to notice that this phenomena would follow as a matter of course from the truth of a new hypothesis, concerning the existence of an underlying causal mechanism in conjunction with accepted background knowledge. We therefore conclude that the new hypothesis is plausible and thus deserves to be seriously entertained and further investigated. From an initial judgment of the plausibility of such a hypothesis we make attempts to elaborate on the nature of that mechanism, frequently by way of constructing plausible models. The developed theory is evaluated on a number of dimensions in addition to empirical adequacy. These include explanatory depth, simplicity, and fertility.

We argue that the systematic use of method in clinical assessment ought to be an integral part of everyday psychological practice in the sexual offending area. As with science, method in clinical practice functions to counter (i.e., to eradicate or reduce the impact of) our various biases and helps to compensate for many of our cognitive limitations. Abductive method has the resources to regulate clinical inquiry and result in the construction of valid psychological formulations, and therefore to help us to explain why our clients' problems have developed and how they are currently maintained. In a sense, all therapists use method whether or not they acknowledge it. By making methodological reasoning explicit and dealing with it in a comprehensive manner, we will be better positioned to avoid the various methodological pitfalls that confront all clinicians, and hopefully, as a result, we can provide more effective treatment.

Sexuality

To adequately structure a customized intervention, we need information regarding sexual attitudes, beliefs, and behaviors. This information usually includes views about sexual activity with children, attitudes toward and fantasies about various sexual activities, and hostile attitudes and acceptance of violence toward women. All of the existing devices in this area, outside of phallometry, rely on self-report and additionally are quite transparent from a social desirability perspective. Indeed, as noted above, outside the sexual preference hypothesis, the avoidance of self-report remains a major attraction to using phallometry.

Sexual preference remains an integral part of all the major theoretical frameworks, so it is not surprising that significant effort has been expended in searching for appropriate, ideally objective, measures of this phenomenon. Five physiological responses have been identified as relevant to male sexuality: electrodermal, cardiovascular, respiratory, pupillary response, and phallometry (Tollison, Adams, & Tollison, 1979). The first three of these have been rejected as unsuitable, with phallometry gaining most of the research attention. An additional, but still underexplored technique, involves assessing the slow, negative-going shift in the brain's resting electrical potential that occurs when an individual anticipates a meaningful stimulus, termed "contingent negative variation" (Costell, Lunde, Kopell, & Wittner, 1972; Howard, Longmore, & Mason, 1992).

Phallometry, originally developed in the 1950s by Freund (Freund, 1963) to assess volumetric changes in the penis in the context of sexual orientation, has had a checkered history in the sexual deviance area. The early promise of phallometry to discriminate between offenders and nonoffenders (Abel et al., 1977; Barbaree, Marshall, & Lanthier, 1979; Marshall, 1973; Quinsey, Chaplin, & Varney, 1981) has generally not been sustained. Few exhibitionists demonstrate sexual arousal to exposing themes (Marshall, Payne, Barbaree, & Eccles, 1991), and they are not distinguishable from controls. Similarly, Baxter, Barbaree, and Marshall (1986) could not distinguish rapists from matched nonoffenders, with approximately one third of both groups demonstrating arousal to rape cues. Child molesters, at least those of the nonfamilial type, fare a little better (Barbaree & Marshall, 1989) but even here, less than half of this group (48%) was identified in this manner.

Reliability, the other psychometric necessity for the appropriate use of phallometry, is also dubious. Barbaree, Baxter, and Marshall (1989) rejected data from 75% of their sample of rapists and nonoffenders as unreliable. Our own work with child molesters (Hudson & Johnston, 1997) similarly inspires little confidence.

The inability to discriminate offenders from nonoffenders has led to the theoretical basis of phallometry, the sexual preference hypothesis, being seriously questioned (Marshall, 1996). However, an equally plausible, competing perspective is simply that phallometry, with its solitary focus on the penis as the *sine qua non* of sexuality and sexual preference, is conceptually flawed. First, there are multiple sources of error variance involved in any phallometric assessment, for example, recency of masturbation and ability to distract oneself from the stimuli, to name just two of many (see Hudson & Johnston, 1997, for more detail). Therefore, it is probably best to conceptualize any result as probabilistic. In ideal circumstances we would therefore carry out multiple assessments on any one individual to get a better estimate of a "true score." This remains impractical in most settings, given the resources involved. Second, the inferential step between penis responsivity in response to an arbitrary set of fixed stimuli and sexual preference also contains the capacity for noise. It is at least possible that some men find the stimulus set unrepresentative of their preferences. What we may actually be measuring in a phallometric assessment is the capacity, including a volitional component, of the individual to participate in some active, albeit imaginary, fashion with the material presented. As such, to dismiss sexual preference as a viable component in any comprehensive model of sexual assault is premature.

An alternative means of evaluating the utility of phallometry is in terms of its ability to predict reoffending. Again, there is moderate evidence for its utility with child molesters, with a recent meta-analysis (Hanson & Bussière, 1996) reporting a correlation of .32 for phallometrically assessed sexual preference for children. These authors noted that the effect was not consistent over the six studies used and suggested that this might reflect variation in the adequacy of the assessment procedures; it may also reflect the level of severity of deviance exhibited by the participants in some of the studies used. Also consistent with the literature cited above relevant to rapists, Hanson and Bussière (1996) reported a nonsignificant correlation between phallometrically assessed arousal to rape and reoffense ($r = .05$, four studies).

All of this does not negate in any way the need to assess the relevant aspects of an offender's sexuality, both deviant and appropriate, identified above; what we lack are acceptable and sensible ways of doing the job. In addition, we lack an adequate conceptualization for many of the constructs involved. For example, sexual fantasies, an integral part of sexual preferences, are usually conceived of in terms that suggest they consist of reasonably elaborate scenarios capable of being sustained over time. This way of construing fantasies is not applicable to many of the men we treat, who have reported their sexual thoughts to be fleeting and often disconnected images. Finally, while accepting that the advantages of not having to rely on self-report are great, especially in such a sensitive area as one's sexuality, at present serious alternatives remain to be developed. Possibilities include the Abel Screen (Osborn, Abel, & Warberg, 1995) based upon reaction time to various relevant stimuli, and the future use of technology such as virtual reality.

Interpersonal Competence

Of particular relevance in this area is the ability to regulate emotions, especially anger, anxiety, and depression. Often these emotions are described as if they are simply occurring states. These states are almost always measured by self-report and treated as if they were temporally stable and situationally independent. For example, the Beck Depression Inventory (Beck, Ward, Mendelson, Mock, & Erbaugh, 1961) gives an overview of the severity of relevant signs and symptoms at a particular point in time, usually at the time of completion. In a more sophisticated fashion, the Spielberger Anger (Spielberger, 1988) and Anxiety scales (Spielberger, Gorsuch, & Lushene, 1970) allow codification of both general tendencies toward experiencing these emotional states and current experience, thus allowing for some temporal instability. However, it is rare for these devices to be used to assess emotional states during the offense process. This is the important information, as it is the relationship between these transient emotional states and specific steps in the offense chain, or problem behavior process, that is clinically useful to understand.

From an intervention perspective it is possible to argue that even knowledge about emotional states during the offense chain is not all that central, except insofar as the presence of these emotions in the offense context constitute markers for the underlying interpersonal processes and implicit schema. Arguably it is these features that are by far the most interesting. For example, a man who experiences feelings of rejection, inadequacy, loneliness, and anger when his adult partner indicates her preference not to have sexual contact with him that particular night, and who then offends against his partner's daughter, is telling us much more than just that he offends when his partner "says no." Assessing his beliefs about himself, his partner, and the role sexuality plays in sustaining these (i.e., his self and relationship schema) are at least as important, if not more so, than identifying those transient emotional states that reflect changes in how well processes such as intimacy are proceeding. Core schema, particularly those controlling interpersonal behavior, are the most important things to change, as prosocial shifts here are likely to generalize (Beck & Emery, 1985). However, it is clear that we have a lot of work to do in this area. What remains less than heartening is that even in intensively researched areas, such as depression, schema have proved quite difficult to measure (Segal & Swallow, 1994).

Nevertheless, it is reasonably clear that what we are looking for, at least in general terms, are the regularities in behavior, particularly in an interpersonal domain, that predispose men to behave in sexually assaultive ways. It is on this substrate that the temporally unstable factors, such as intense negative affect (loneliness for the child molester, anger or rejection for the rapist) and alcohol, find sustenance. An example, in level II theory terms, is our use of attachment theory to relate deficiencies in emotional regulation (the primary function of attachment-related behavior) to schema (i.e., working models) of self and others (Ward, Hudson, et al., 1995). It is likely that codifying individual differences at this level, as opposed to using devices such as the Minnesota Multiphasic Personality Inventory (Hathaway & McKinley, 1943) or Millon Clinical Multiaxial Inventory (Millon, 1983, 1987) to assess personality, is likely to be more helpful, and lessens the risk that sexual deviance will be seen as related to mental illness.

Risk Assessment

The assessment of the level of risk for reoffending has become an integral task for treatment providers, particularly where legislators enact "sexual predator" laws (see Anderson, 1992). Our local experience suggests that those people responsible for making decisions about releasing men to the community are typically delighted to be given this information. However, this serves to highlight the substantial ambiguity and inherent difficulties facing therapists when working with sex offenders. The central issues are the limits of confidentiality, the need to sustain an adequate therapeutic relationship, and the need to encourage men into therapy. Informal figures from New Zealand suggests that less than a quarter of incarcerated child molesters come to our programs (L. Bakker, personal communication, July 1, 1996). There are likely many reasons for this but a perception that going to treatment means you need to be honest with therapists, and that they will then pass all information to the Parole Board, is likely to be unhelpful. However, it is also clear that treatment providers have a social duty to provide information to the community, at least when they can foresee risk. These ethical dilemmas would be significantly circumvented by robust risk assessment procedures that rely on more than just static predictors.

There is no doubting the ability of historical features of a man's presentation to predict his future offending behavior. Hanson and Bussière's (1996) meta-analysis found positive predictive relationships for history of prior sex offenses (especially if they exhibited variety), deviant sexual preferences (at least for child molesters), victim profile (interactions between gender and relationship to perpetrator, with offenders with related female children as victims less likely to reoffend than those with unrelated males as victims), age (younger) and some aspects of developmental adversity. This list is quite similar to those variables found by Quinsey, Rice, and Harris (1995) as related to sexual reoffending in men released from the Oak Ridge facility. It also parallels our own strategies, based on Barbaree's (1991) recommendations, which include offense variables (length of history, versatility, presence of violence, and victim profile) and personality variables, measured most notably by the Psychopathy Checklist—Revised (Hare, 1991).

These static predictors work, but not perfectly. If they were acceptably accurate, then permanent incarceration might be a viable solution, at least for those men with risk values over some threshold. However, in our view accuracy is not well-enough established, and given the difficulties collecting valid indicators of recidivism (see for example Furby, Weinrott, & Blackshaw, 1989) we argue that the huge human consequences of false negatives oblige us to develop and use dynamic predictors. Indeed, Quinsey, Rice, and Harris (1995) argued well for the need to identify and evaluate dynamic predictors that could be used to moderate actuarially determined risk. We use amenability for treatment (i.e., denial and minimization processes) as well as response to treatment, both assessed in terms of clinical judgment, to do this. Quinsey et al. (1995) suggested other situational issues, such as gaining or losing employment, mood changes, fluctuating criminogenic needs, and opportunity to offend (i.e., compliance with supervision) as in need of examination.

We ought not treat risk as a static variable, nor dichotomize it for the sake of legal convenience. In the absence of permanent incarceration, which may be the only option for some men, the issue finally becomes one of external supervision, and this means being sensitive to dynamic, unstable offense precursors. It is highly probable that men would need to have gone through at least part of a treatment program for these to be identified. The challenge is for these factors to be adequately investigated, particularly to develop systematic ways of using them to moderate historically determined risk estimates.

The Future

There is no doubt that the assessment of sex offenders is a complex business that requires skillfulness, subtlety, and considerable resourcefulness from clinicians (Groth & Birnbaum, 1979). Denial and minimization processes are almost inevitable, as is some degree of reluctance to be involved in the assessment and treatment process. What are required, in the first instance, are clearer conceptualizations of the constructs we are seeking to measure. For example, despite deviant sexual preferences being a core component in all of the level I theoretical frameworks (see Hudson & Ward, Chapter 18, this volume, for argument on this point), there is little clarity as to what this construct means. As we and others have argued, equating the penis becoming erect with sexual preferences, or even broadly defined sexual interests, is too narrow a conceptualization. Sexual arousal itself is at least multidimensional, with both cognitive and physiological components (Rosen & Beck, 1988). An adequate model of what sexual preference means and what the constituent processes might be has yet to be rigorously developed. The work of Anderson and Cyranowski (1994), in the area of sexual self-schema in women is promising, but remains to be applied to the sexual deviance area.

Second, we need credible alternatives to self-report. The simple reliance on self-report, often in a pencil-and-paper format, is not even remotely sensible and probably never has been. Two examples come to mind. Random surveys asking drivers how competent they are result in a positively skewed distribution; most people rate themselves as above average. This might be fine for their mental health but is of little utility from the perspective of determining reliable and valid individual differences.

Similarly, when it comes to determining intellectual ability we are not aware of anyone who has ever seriously entertained simply asking people how intelligent they are. This is not to say that on occasions an individual may not be able to accurately assess their underlying intellectual capacity, or, as is more likely to be the case, not be able to assess their specific performance on a specific task. Rather, test constructors have assumed that the more preferable strategy is to get people to perform (and rightly so) to the best of their ability. Clearly other factors such as fatigue, motivation, and so on are also involved; that is, error variance is inevitable, as data are always an inadequate reflection of the underlying phenomenon one is attempting to detect (Bogan & Woodward, 1988). The relative proportion of error variance to true variance is likely to be lower for competence or power tests compared with self-report; especially so when there are substantial social rewards to be gained or punishments to be avoided.

The implication of this perspective is that we need a new approach to test construction. An illustration of how this could work with empathy deficits was demonstrated by Hanson and his colleagues (Hanson & Scott, 1995). Their test is based upon the notion that descriptions of a series of interpersonal situations involving an adult and a child can be constructed that vary in terms of abusiveness, that is, from clearly nonabusive, to vignettes that are ambiguous, to those that are clearly abusive. It is the presence of ambiguity that gives this methodology its power, as is true for any test of this type; an item that everyone gets right or wrong has no discriminatory power and is deleted for the item pool. The extension of this approach to other assessment areas is needed.

There are some other developments that also bode well for the future. For example, program-specific skill measures have been developed in the context of relapse prevention programs (Mann, 1996; Miner, Day, & Nafpaktitis, 1989). To do this, the program providers must specify what skills and knowledge are to be acquired by offenders, and then systematically assess these. Miner et al. (1989) detected increases in relevant coping skills as a function of treatment. Similarly, situational competence tests need to be developed specifically for high-risk situations posed to individual offenders. Stermac, Glansy, and Davidson (1989) developed one based upon Annis's (1982) Inventory of Drinking Situations. However the critical questions are what constitutes a minimum level of competency (Hanson, Cox, & Woszczyna, 1991), what are the relationships between changes in skills and knowledge and future behaviors indicative of reoffense risk, and finally, how all of these factors link with motivational issues.

Finally, there needs to be a greater emphasis on information-processing strategies in assessment (see Johnston & Ward, 1996 for greater detail). There is some provisional evidence that sexually deviant men have deficits in their abilities to accurately process social information (e.g., Lipton, McDonel, & McFall, 1987; Malamuth & Brown, 1994) and that these lead to processing biases and related dysfunctional attributions (Ward, Hudson, & Marshall, 1994). An additional issue concerns the methods utilized in gathering information on cognitive distortions. Clearly, self-report scales are transparent and therefore subject to response biases (e.g., the Burt Attitudes Scale [Burt, 1980] and the Abel and Becker Cognition Scale [Abel et al., 1989]) and are relatively crude measures of deviant beliefs and attitudes. They assume a stability, generality, and accessibility of beliefs, yet these assumptions seem unlikely to be true. The future development and application of information-processing methodologies in the assessment of sexual offenders (e.g., McFall, 1990, and Marshall, Hudson, et al., 1995) will hopefully tap automatic processing and hence avoid contamination by social desirability factors. Additionally, biases in information seeking are not confined to offenders; it is, therefore, also necessary for therapists to monitor the tendency to seek confirmatory information when testing their hypotheses about clients.

TREATMENT

The issues for the future with respect to treatment seem to us to revolve around the following questions: For whom is treatment best provided? How might we encourage these men into treatment? How ought treatment best be structured? What ought to be our reasonable expectations of treatment? Finally, how might treatment best be evaluated? We deal with each of these questions in turn.

Recipients of Treatment

Only a small proportion of men who behave in sexually aggressive ways get to be treated (Marshall, Laws, & Barbaree, 1990). Thus, one of the major issues facing treatment providers is what type of client to select for inclusion in their program. Some authors have argued that entry criteria ought to be set according to who is most likely to benefit from treatment (e.g., Marques, Day, Nelson, & Miner, 1989; Pithers, 1990). Certainly, where the major consequence of a treatment failure is the possibility of the program being closed down, this strategy confers short-term advantage. However, a positive relationship between treatment providers and the media does not happen by chance alone. Additionally, taking this position to its logical conclusion, programs are at risk of taking in only those with a very low probability of reoffending, those who arguably do not deserve, in the sense of cost–benefit, the limited treatment resources available. We need to both provide policy makers with evidence that short term, safe strategies are not in anyone's best interests and be as transparent as possible with the media.

An alternative perspective suggests that we should treat as wide a range as possible, with as customized an intervention as possible, and assess the results (Marshall, Laws, & Barbaree, 1990). To do otherwise means that we are faced with substantial limitations on our ability to generalize from treatment studies. Marshall's suggestions of a tiered approach (Marshall & Eccles, 1991) provide needed structure to the customization process.

Inclusive treatment where offenders are triaged with respect to risk, and appropriate expectations of interventions driven by notions of harm reduction, are needed. We need to persuade those who purchase service in this area that the most cost-effective, but superficially risky, strategy is to work with men posing the highest risk of reoffense. This means that administrators need to be accepting of reducing harm, rather than working with low-risk offenders, for example, incest offenders, and proffering an absence of reoffending as proof of success.

Finally, assessing efficacy in the manner suggested by Marshall (1996) requires rigorous description of the interventions involved, appropriate attention to classifying those undergoing the intervention, as well as long-term evaluation, all of which are tall orders. This does not, however, detract from the importance of this work. It is only by refining the answers to the fundamental questions of "what works for whom" can we retain what credibility we have so far developed.

Motivation for Treatment

Most offenders, whether in the community or incarcerated, do not enter treatment (Marshall et al., 1990). This raises several as yet unanswered questions. For example, how do men not entering treatment differ from those who do? We do not know enough about how variables such as, for example, sentence length, presence of a history of nonsexual crimes, lower levels of intellectual functioning, and the presence of less than adequately controlled psychotic processes, all of which affect eligibility for treatment, are related to long-term outcome.

A related issue is that of motivating men for treatment. Given the arguments raised above against restrictive selection criteria, getting men into treatment and keeping them there once they have agreed to go becomes a serious issue. For example, as we have noted elsewhere in this volume (Ward, McCormack, Hudson, & Polaschek, Chapter 19), rapists are generally seen as less willing than child molesters to acknowledge the problematic consequences of their own behavior and to participate in treatment (Marques, Day, Nelson, & West, 1994; Marshall, 1993; Pithers, 1993). Thus, motivational pretreatment interventions, for example during interviewing (Miller & Rollnick, 1991) and strategies involving external contingencies such as early parole, need to be developed and assessed.

Treatment Structure

There seems to be reasonable clarity as to what constitutes offense-specific targets (Marshall, 1996) as well as the sensible suggestion that when specialist treatment providers exist for any other problem, such as substance abuse, it is best to refer. However, as our understanding of the relevant constructs develop, offense-specific treatment targets will change. For example, our staged theory of the empathy process (Marshall et al., 1995) suggested that, for some men, deficits are likely to be at the initial stage involving emotional recognition skills. These men require different interventions than do those offenders with deficits later in the process. For example, sadistic offenders have little trouble recognizing negative affect in their victims, but they clearly lack skills at the following stages of the empathy process involving perspective taking, an appropriate vicarious emotional response, and finally, a prosocial behavioral response.

Another contentious issue regarding treatment structure is the use and length of follow up. Marshall (1996) argued that follow-up is difficult to do well and consumes extensive resources, and as yet is not justified by data. This issue is an illustration of how intervention strategies can be derived from a developing theory in the absence of data, but the onus is then on the program to document efficacy. It is quite plausible to suppose that the transition from a relatively sheltered environment, at least in terms of life skills, to the outside world, will be difficult. For example, the rate of exposure to what have been sexual stimuli, such as children, is very much lower in prison that in the community. This change may challenge a man's ability to control his deviant fantasies. Similarly, adjusting to greater levels of intimacy may prove to be quite stressful for some men, despite treatment. However, having made an argument for after care, analysis of who uses it, under what conditions, for how long, and with what results needs to occur. Detailed analysis of intervention failures, as we mentioned earlier, could also provide information relevant to this debate.

A major growth point in service provision is with respect to special groups, for example, juveniles and men from indigenous, frequently nondominant cultures (Marshall, Hudson,

Ward, & Fernandez, in press). The core question facing the field here involves the degree of modification, to the accepted, basic cognitive-behavioral intervention program required for these populations. Modifications are potentially required at three levels. First, contextual features, such as community consultative processes (both during set up the program and for ongoing contact), location, and entry and farewell rituals are all important. The issues here relate to accessibility. Second, it may well be that the ways in which we proceed with interventions may need modification. Goals such as understanding the offense chain or enhancing the man's appreciation of the harm caused by sexual abuse may remain appropriate, but the processes by which the desired prosocial changes are made may differ. For example, the process we use (Hudson, Marshall, Ward, Johnston, & Jones, 1995; Marshall, 1994), while respectful of the man's dignity and mindful that self-confidence typically precedes change, is nevertheless direct and confrontational; both of these characteristics are not appropriate in some cultures and therefore they may have a deleterious effect.

Finally, our inevitably culturally bounded theories of the causes of sexual abuse, and the interventions derived from these theories, must be in competition with other models derived from alternative cultural perspectives. Interventions developed from these models of causes may differ from those we are developing, and may by virtue of how they have come about be more effective in treating men from those cultures. However, the final touchstone must still be lowered reoffense rates.

Expectations of Treatment

One of the more contentious ideas raised recently by Laws (1996) is that of harm reduction. This notion, accepted in the substance abuse area, addresses the issue of what are reasonable expectations regarding treatment or intervention goals. From this perspective, any reduction in the frequency or intensity of sexual offending is seen as a positive outcome. Any such reduction is also reflective of a perfectly legitimate aim within the goal of making society safer. Laws noted that the logical alternative to harm reduction is the zero-tolerance position, which has been a conspicuous failure in areas such as drug and alcohol addictions. Zero tolerance equates relapse with failure, which, as we have argued (Ward et al., 1994), can lead directly to escalation of offending.

The other aspect of this argument relates to limited treatment resources and acceptable outcomes. Knowing when to stop therapy is always an issue, but usually the consequences are not devastating, as is the case with reoffending. What constitute the critical variables to modify to generate acceptable outcomes is yet to be determined. For example, we have produced preliminary evidence that attachment style in close relationships is a vulnerability factor in offenders, and further, the particular style of insecure attachment may affect offense parameters such as age of victim and amount of violence used. However, providing the treatment resources needed to ameliorate these deficits may be unrealistic in terms both of the resources available and people's ability to change such fundamental characteristics. Perhaps more critically, we need to determine how much change is needed to adequately reduce reoffense risk and across what dimensions.

Relapse Prevention

The high relapse or recidivism rates in sex offenders are associated with compulsivity or addictive processes (e.g., Pithers, 1990). Within the cognitive-behavioral framework this has led to the application of effective treatment strategies from the addiction area to sex offenders. The associated view, that relapse constitutes a process or chain of behavior occurring across time (Pithers, Marques, Gibat, & Marlatt, 1983), led to the adoption of relapse prevention as a model both to guide therapy and to enhance the client's self-management skills to maintain the initial behavior change induced by therapy.

In adapting the relapse prevention approach to sex offenders, the model has undergone a number of changes, particularly with respect to defining lapse and relapse. The attributional response to the lapse, the issue of expectancies regarding the indulgent behavior, and the decision-making style in evidence at this point are all legitimate and useful foci of therapeutic interventions. Lapses are seen as inevitable and potentially profitable experiences, notwithstanding their crisis potential. However, with sex offenders, the fact of a lapse means that a criminal offense has been committed and yet another victim harmed, or the same victim harmed again. This clearly needs to be avoided. Therefore, a lapse is now defined further back in the chain, as the occurrence of a voluntarily induced risk behavior (e.g., deviant sexual fantasizing) which is said to be the first predictable sign of losing control (Pithers, 1990). A relapse is now seen as the occurrence of any sexual offense, rather than simply a return to previously high levels of the addictive behavior, as in Marlatt's (1985) original model.

The relapse prevention model has been subject to critical analysis and a number of problems have been identified (e.g., Hanson, 1996; Ward & Hudson, 1996). First, both Marlatt's original relapse prevention theory (Marlatt, 1985) and Pithers et al.'s (1983) adaptation for sex offenders relied on diverse theoretical sources leading to conceptual confusion and redundancy. We suggested that there are other ways of conceptualizing the mechanisms associated with the relapse process (e.g., the abstinence violation effect) that are simpler and more reflective of current theory in the area of social cognition (e.g., Ward et al., 1994).

Second, Marlatt's (1985) model does not cover all possibilities involved in reoffending. His three routes to high-risk situations emphasize skill deficits as the major mediators and fail to cover situations wherein individuals consciously decide to use drugs or to engage in an addictive behavior (see Allsop & Saunders, 1989). Third, this lack of scope is exacerbated by Pithers's (1990) exclusive use of the covert route at the expense of other, clinically evident pathways. In addition, this means that Pithers's model shares (with Marlatt's) the problems of unconscious thinking and desires, and it implies the unlikely prospect of offenders covertly planning to experience negative affective states (Ward & Hudson, 1996). Finally, moving the lapse and relapse points back in the offense chain has created significant conceptual and practical problems, for example, the inherent incompatibility between the problem of immediate gratification and the abstinence violation effect as transitional mediators.

We suggest that, in the future, it may be more profitable to focus on the core process underlying both the offending and relapse processes: the problem behavior process. This would allow both research and clinical interventions to proceed on the assumption that there is a core set of behaviors and vulnerability factors involved in the development and reoccurrence of sexual offending. Theoretical work on the problem behavior process constitutes level III theory and contains microtheories specifying the cognitive, behavioral, motivational, and contextual factors constituting the offense chain. The major strength in the RP model has always been its ability to focus our attention on the idea that behavior occurs in small steps over time, rather than in an all-or-none fashion. We presented a descriptive model of the offense chain that allows different offense patterns and planned and unplanned sexually deviant behavior (Ward, Louden, et al., 1995). It also includes positive and negative affective pathways and incorporates offenders' perceptions of relationships.

The problem behavior process of each individual may involve a unique combination of factors occurring over time in an offense chain. Hence, when describing sexual offending, there are a number of types of offenders with quite different offending patterns. Viewing these different problematic behavior patterns as alternative pathways to offending means that we are able to attend to the issue of scope; we can always add new pathways to the model if our clients inform us that they are needed.

Treatment Evaluation

Adequate evaluation of interventions is the cornerstone of the area advancing in any publicly credible fashion. It is imperative that we develop the ability to demonstrate incrementally that although we cannot treat every sexually abusive man in a manner that absolutely precludes his choosing to reoffend at any time in the future, we can reliably reduce the risk, to various degrees, in identified subtypes of offenders.

While there are substantial risks to arguing by analogy, the process by which complex treatment protocols develop is instructive. For example, no one would want funding for cancer treatment to be contingent upon medicine being able to cure all types of cancer and provide guarantees against future relapse. Reasonable expectations involve conceptually differing types of problems differential interventions for these, and systematic evaluation.

Persuasive arguments have been raised against traditional random assignment to intervention and control groups in an area where such decisions can lead to considerable human suffering (Marshall, 1996). California's Sex Offender Treatment and Evaluation Project (Marques, 1984) was able to use this approach without major ethical reproach because of the limited number of places within its intervention program. As such, the long-term results of this program continue to be anticipated with considerable interest. Indeed one can argue that too much interest, given so few evaluations to adequately test myriads of offender type/intervention component combinations, is clearly unwise.

Alternatives to the global "does treatment work" strategies need to be developed. As an example, intensive assessments with men who have been through a treatment program and subsequently reoffended need to be developed. This would enable us to gather information, slowly we hope, on issues such as how the identified problem behavior process (Hudson & Ward, 1996) is involved in the reoffense. Does it resemble how it was described and understood during treatment? Additionally, was the reoffense facilitated by a loss of the skills acquired during intervention, a failure to generalize, or a motivationally driven failure to apply them? We have more to learn from our failures than from our successes.

CONCLUSION

Enormous progress has been made in the last 20 or so years. However, our understanding of the processes involved in the causal chain in sexual aggression remains at a quite primitive level. Lest we feel despondent, this is not remarkably dissimilar to other areas of psychopathology. Moving the area significantly forward will require at least the following: greater attention to integration at the theoretical level, more attention to the fine-grained detail of mechanisms involved in generating sexual aggression, greater novelty with respect to how we detect and document the phenomena of interest, and finally, intervening with a wide range of clients and being transparently scientific about the results. It has become a cliché but we still owe our best efforts to the women and children whose lives are damaged, often irrevocably, by the men we attempt to understand and assist to lead more prosocial lives.

REFERENCES

Abel, G. G., Barlow, D. H., Blanchard, E. B., & Guild, D. (1977). The components of rapists' sexual arousal. *Archives of General Psychiatry, 34,* 894–903.

Abel, G. G., Gore, D. K., Holland, C. L., Camp, N., Becker, J. V., & Rathner, J. (1989). The measurement of cognitive distortions in child molesters. *Annals of Sex Research, 2,* 135–152.

Abel, G. G., Becker, J. V., Cunningham-Rathner, J., Rouleau, J. L., Kaplan, M., & Reich, J. (1984). *Treatment manual: The treatment of child molesters.* Atlanta: Emory University School of Medicine.

Abel, G. G., & Rouleau, J. L. (1986). Sexual disorders. In G. Winokur & P. Clayton (Eds.), *The medical basis of psychiatry* (pp. 246–267). Philadelphia: W. B. Saunders.

Alessi, G. (1992). Models of proximate and ultimate causation in psychology. *American Psychologist, 47,* 1359–1370.

Allsop, S., & Saunders, W. A. (1989). Relapse and alcohol problems. In M. Gossop (Ed.), *Relapse and addictive behaviour* (pp. 11–40). Beckinham, Kent: Croom Helm.

American Psychiatric Association. (1994). *Diagnostic and statistical manual of mental disorders* (4th ed.). Washington, DC: Author.

Anderson, N. W. (Ed.). (1992). Predators and politics: A symposium on Washington's Sexual Violent Predators Statute. *University of Puget Sound Law Review, 15*(3), 507–987.

Anderson, B. L., & Cyranowski, J. M. (1994). Women's sexual self-schema. *Journal of Personality and Social Psychology, 67,* 1079–1100.

Annis, H. M. (1982). *Inventory of Drinking Situations.* Toronto: Addiction Research Foundation.

Barbaree, H. E. (1991, October). *Assessment of risk in sex offenders.* Workshop presented at the Annual Research and Treatment Meeting of the Association for the Treatment of Sexual Abusers, Fort Worth, TX.

Barbaree, H. E., Baxter, D. J., & Marshall, W. L. (1989). The reliability of the rape index in a sample of rapists and nonrapists. *Violence and Victims, 4,* 299–306.

Barbaree, H. E., & Marshall, W. L. (1989). Erectile response amongst heterosexual child molesters, father–daughter incest offenders, and matched nonoffenders: Five distinct age preference profiles. *Canadian Journal of Behavioural Science, 21,* 70–82.

Barbaree, H. E., Marshall, W. L., & Lanthier, R. D. (1979). Deviant sexual arousal in rapists. *Behaviour Research and Therapy, 14,* 215–222.

Baxter, D. J., Barbaree, H. E., & Marshall, W. L. (1986). Sexual responses to consenting and forced sex in a large sample of rapists and nonrapists. *Behaviour Research and Therapy, 24,* 513–520.

Beck, A. T., & Emery, G. (1985). Restructuring a patient's assumptions and major issues. In *Anxiety disorders and phobias: A cognitive perspective* (pp. 288–312). New York: Basic Books.

Beck, A. T., Ward, C. H., Mendelson, M., Mock, J., & Erbaugh, J. (1961). An inventory for measuring depression. *Archives of General Psychiatry, 4,* 561–571.

Bogan, J., & Woodward, J. (1988). Saving the phenomena. *Philosophical Review, 97,* 303–352.

Bond, I., & Evans, D. (1967). Avoidance therapy: Its use in two cases of underwear fetishism. *Canadian Medical Association Journal, 96,* 1160–1162.

Burt, M. R. (1980). Cultural myths and support for rape. *Journal of Personality and Social Psychology, 38,* 217–230.

Costell, R. M., Lunde, D. T., Kopell, B. S., & Wittner, W. K. (1972). Contingent negative variation as an indicator of sexual object preference. *Science, 177,* 718–720.

Finkelhor, D. (1984). *Child sexual abuse: New theory and research.* New York: Free Press.

Freund, K. (1963). A laboratory method for diagnosing predominance of homo- and hetero-erotic interests in the male. *Behaviour Research and Therapy, 1,* 85–93.

Furby, L., Weinrott, M. R., & Blackshaw, L. (1989). Sex offenders recidivism: A review. *Psychological Bulletin, 105,* 3–30.

Groth, A. N., & Birnbaum, A. H. (1979). *Men who rape: The psychology of the offender.* New York: Plenum Press.

Hall, G. C. N., & Hirschman, R. (1991). Toward a theory of sexual aggression: A quadripartite model. *Journal of Consulting and Clinical Psychology, 59,* 662–669.

Hanson, R. K. (1996). Evaluating the contribution of relapse prevention theory to the treatment of sex offenders. *Sexual Abuse: A Journal of Research and Treatment, 8*, 201–208.

Hanson, R. K., & Bussière, M. T. (1996). *Predictors of sexual offender recidivism: A meta-analysis.* Ottawa: Solicitor General Canada.

Hanson, R. K., & Scott, H. (1995). Assessing perspective-taking among sexual offenders, non-sexual criminals, and nonoffenders. *Sexual Abuse: A Journal of Research and Treatment, 7*, 259–278.

Hanson, R. K., Cox, B., & Woszczyna, C. (1991). Assessing treatment outcome for sexual offenders. *Annals of Sex Research, 4*, 177–208.

Hare, R. D. (1991). *Manual for the Psychopathy Checklist—Revised.* Toronto: Multimedia.

Hathaway, S. R., & McKinley, J. C. (1943). A multiphasic personality schedule (Minnesota): III. The measurement of symptomatic depression. *Journal of Psychology, 14*, 73–84.

Hooker, C. A. (1987). *A realistic theory of science.* Albany, NY: State University of New York Press.

Howard, R., Longmore, F., & Mason, P. (1992). Contingent negative variation as an indicator of sexual object preference: Revisited. *International Journal of Psychophysiology, 13*, 185–188.

Hudson, S. M., & Johnston, P. W. (1997). *The reliability of phallometric assessment in incarcerated child molesters.* Manuscript in preparation.

Hudson, S. M., Marshall, W. L., Ward, T., Johnston, P. W., & Jones, R. L. (1995). Kia Marama: A cognitive-behavioural program for incarcerated child molesters. *Behaviour Change, 12*, 69–80.

Hudson, S. M., & Ward, T. (1996). Relapse prevention: Future directions. *Sexual abuse: A Journal of Research and Treatment, 8*, 249–256.

Johnston, L., & Ward, T. (1996). Social cognition and sexual offending: A theoretical framework. *Sexual Abuse: A Journal of Research and Treatment, 8*, 55–80.

Kalmar, D. A., & Sternberg, R. J. (1988). Theory knitting: An integrative approach to theory development. *Philosophical Psychology, 1*, 153–170.

Kazdin, A. E. (1993). Evaluation in clinical practice: Clinically sensitive and systematic methods of treatment delivery. *Behavior Therapy, 24*, 11–45.

Knight, R. A., & Prentky, R. A. (1990). Classifying sexual offenders: The development and corroboration of taxonomic models. In W. L. Marshall, D. R. Laws, & H. E. Barbaree (Eds.), *Handbook of sexual assault: Issues, theories, and treatment of the offender* (pp. 23–52). New York: Plenum Press.

Lanyon, R. I. (1991). Theories of sex offending. In C. R. Hollin & K. Howells (Eds.), *Clinical approaches to sex offenders and their victims* (pp. 35–54). Chichester: Wiley.

Laws, D. R. (1996). Relapse prevention or harm reduction? *Sexual Abuse: A Journal of Research and Treatment, 8*, 243–247.

Lipton, D. N., McDonel, E. C., & McFall, R. M. (1987). Heterosocial perception in rapists. *Journal of Consulting and Clinical Psychology, 55*, 17–21.

Malamuth, N. M., & Brown, L. M. (1994). Sexually aggressive men's perceptions of women's communications: Testing three explanations. *Journal of Personality and Social Psychology, 67*, 699–712.

Malamuth, N. M., Heavey, C. L., & Linz, D. (1993). Predicting men's antisocial behavior against women: The interactionist model of sexual aggression. In G. C. N. Hall, R. Hirschman, J. R. Graham, & M. S. Zaragoza (Eds.), *Sexual aggression: Issues in etiology, assessment and treatment* (pp. 63–97). Washington, DC: Taylor & Francis.

Mann, R. (1996, November). *Measuring the effectiveness of relapse prevention and intervention with sex offenders.* Paper presented at the 15th annual research and treatment meeting of the Association for the Treatment of Sexual Abusers, Chicago.

Marlatt, G. A. (1985). Relapse prevention: Theoretical rationale and overview of the model. In G. A. Marlatt & J. R. Gordon (Eds.), *Relapse prevention: Maintenance strategies in the treatment of addictive behaviors* (pp. 3–70). New York: Guilford Press.

Marlatt, G. A., & Gordon, J. R. (Eds.). (1985). *Relapse prevention: Maintenance strategies in the treatment of addictive behaviors.* New York: Guilford Press.

Marques, J. K. (1984). *An innovative treatment program for sex offenders: Report to the legislature.* Sacramento: California State Department of Mental Health.

Marques, J. K., Day, D. M., Nelson, C., & Miner, M. H. (1989). The Sex Offender Treatment and Evaluation Project: California's relapse prevention program. In D. R. Laws (Ed.), *Relapse prevention with sex offenders* (pp. 247–267). New York: Guilford Press.

Marques, J. K., Day, D. M., Nelson, C., & West, M. A. (1994). Effects of cognitive-behavioral treatment on sex offender recidivism: Preliminary results of a longitudinal study. *Criminal Justice and Behavior, 21*, 28–54.

Marshall, W. L. (1971). A combined treatment method for certain sexual deviations. *Behaviour Research and Therapy, 9*, 292–294.

Marshall, W. L. (1973). The modification of sexual fantasies: A combined treatment approach to the reduction of deviant sexual behaviour. *Behaviour Research and Therapy, 11,* 557–564.

Marshall, W. L. (1989). Invited essay: Intimacy, loneliness and sexual offenders. *Behaviour Research and Therapy, 27*, 491–503.

Marshall, W. L. (1993). A revised approach to the treatment of men who sexually assault adult females. In G. C. N. Hall, R. Hirschman, J. R. Graham, & M. S. Zaragoza (Eds.), *Sexual aggression: Issues in etiology, assessment, and treatment* (pp. 143–165). Washington, DC: Taylor & Francis.

Marshall, W. L. (1994). Treatment effects on denial and minimization in incarcerated sex offenders. *Behaviour Research and Therapy, 32*, 559–564.

Marshall, W. L. (1996). Assessment, treatment, and theorizing about sex offenders: Developments during the past twenty years and future directions. *Criminal Justice and Behavior, 23*, 162–199.

Marshall, W. L., & Barbaree, H. E. (1989). Sexual violence. In K. Howells & C. R. Hollin (Eds.), *Clinical approaches to violence* (pp. 205–246). New York: Wiley.

Marshall, W. L., & Barbaree, H. E. (1990). An integrated theory of the etiology of sexual offending. In W. L. Marshall, D. R. Laws, & H. E. Barbaree (Eds.), *Handbook of sexual assault: Issues, theories, and treatment of the offender* (pp. 257–275). New York: Plenum Press.

Marshall, W. L., & Eccles, A. (1991). Issues in the treatment of sex offenders. *Journal of Interpersonal Violence, 6*, 68–93.

Marshall, W. L., Hudson, S. M., Jones, R., & Fernandez, Y. M. (1995). Empathy in sex offenders. *Clinical Psychology Review, 15*, 99–113.

Marshall, W. L., Hudson, S. M., Ward, T., & Fernandez, Y. M. (Eds.). (in press). *Sourcebook of treatment programs for sexual offenders*. New York: Plenum Press.

Marshall, W. L., Laws, D. R., & Barbaree, H. E. (1990). Present status and future directions. In W. L. Marshall, D. R. Laws, & H. E. Barbaree (Eds.), *Handbook of sexual assault: Issues, theories, and treatment of the offender* (pp. 389–395). New York: Plenum Press.

Marshall, W. L., & McKnight, R. D. (1975). An integrated treatment program for sexual offenders. *Canadian Psychiatric Association Journal, 20*, 133–138.

Marshall, W. L., Payne, K., Barbaree, H. E., & Eccles, A. (1991). Exhibitionists: Sexual preferences for exposing. *Behaviour Research and Therapy, 29*, 367–340.

Marshall, W. L., & Williams, S. (1975). A behavioural approach to the modification of rape. *Quarterly Bulletin of the British Association for Behavioural Psychotherapy, 4*, 78.

McFall, R. M. (1990). The enhancement of social skills: An information processing analysis. In W. L. Marshall, D. R. Laws, & H. E. Barbaree (Eds.), *Handbook of sexual assault: Issues, theories, and treatment of the offender* (pp. 311–330). New York: Plenum Press.

Miller, W. R., & Rollnick, S. (1991). *Motivational interviewing: Preparing people to change addictive behavior*. New York: Guilford Press.

Millon, T. (1983). *Millon Clinical Multiaxial Inventory Manual* (3rd ed.). Minneapolis: National Computer Systems.

Millon, T. (1987). *Manual for the Millon Clinical Multiaxial Inventory—II*. Minneapolis: National Computer Systems.

Miner, M. H., Day, D. M., & Nafpaktitis, M. K. (1989). Assessment of coping skills: Development of a situational competency test. In D. R. Laws (Ed.), *Relapse prevention with sex offenders* (pp. 127–136). New York: Guilford Press.

Osborn, C. A., Abel, G. C., & Warberg, B. W. (1995, October). *The Abel Assessment: Its comparison to plethysmograph and resistance to falsification*. Paper presented at the 14th annual meeting of the Association for the Treatment of Sexual Abusers, New Orleans, LA.

Pithers, W. D. (1990). Relapse prevention with sexual aggressors: A method for maintaining therapeutic gains and enhancing external supervision. In W. L. Marshall, D. R. Laws, & H. E. Barbaree (Eds.), *Handbook of sexual assault: Issues, theories, and treatment of the offender* (pp. 343–362). New York: Plenum Press.

Pithers, W. D. (1993). Treatment of rapists: Reinterpretation of early outcome data and exploratory constructs to enhance therapeutic efficacy. In G. C. N. Hall, R. Hirschman, J. R. Graham, & M. S. Zaragoza (Eds.), *Sexual aggression: Issues in etiology, assessment, and treatment* (pp. 167–196). Washington, DC: Taylor & Francis.

Pithers, W. D., Kashima, K. M., Cumming, G. F., & Beal, L. S. (1988). Relapse prevention: A method of enhancing maintenance of change in sex offenders. In A. C. Salter (Ed.), *Treating child sex offenders and victims: A practical guide* (pp. 131–170). Newbury Park, CA: Sage.

Pithers, W. D., Marques, J. K., Gibat, C. C., & Marlatt, G. A. (1983). Relapse prevention with sexual aggressives: A self-control model of treatment and maintenance of change. In J. G. Greer & I. R. Stuart (Eds.), *The sexual aggressor: Current perspectives on treatment* (pp. 241–239). New York: Van Nostrand Reinhold.

Prentky, R. A., & Knight, R. A. (1991). Identifying critical dimensions for discriminating among rapists. *Journal of Consulting and Clinical Psychology, 59*, 643–661.

Quinsey, V. L., Chaplin, T. C., & Varney, G. (1981). A comparison of rapist's and non-sex offender's sexual preferences for mutually consenting sex, rape, and physical abuse of women. *Behavioral Assessment, 3*, 127–135.

Quinsey, V. L., Rice, M., & Harris, G. T. (1995). Actuarial prediction of sexual recidivism. *Journal of Interpersonal Violence, 10*, 85–105.

Rosen, R. C., & Beck, J. G. (1988). *Patterns of sexual arousal: Psychosocial processes and clinical applications.* New York: Guilford Press.

Schwartz, B. K. (1995). Theories of sexual offenses. In B. K. Schwartz & H. R. Cellini (Eds.), *The sex offender: Corrections, treatment and legal practice* (pp. 1–32). Kingston, NJ: Civic Research Institute.

Segal, Z. V., & Swallow, S. R. (1994). Cognitive assessment of unipolar depression: Measuring products, processes and structures. *Behaviour Research and Therapy, 32*, 147–158.

Spengler, P. M., Strohmer, D. C., Dixon, D. N., & Shivy, V. A. (1995). A scientist–practitioner model of psychological assessment: Implications for training, practice and research. *The Counseling Psychologist, 23*, 506–534.

Spielberger, C. D. (1988). *State–Trait Anger Expression Inventory (STAXI) professional manual.* Odessa, FL: Psychological Assessment Resources.

Spielberger, C. D., Gorsuch, R. L., & Lushene, R. E. (1970). *Manual for the State–Trait Anxiety Inventory (self-evaluation questionnaire).* Palo Alto, CA: Consulting Psychologists Press.

Staats, A. W. (1989). Unificationism: Philosophy for the modern disunified science of psychology. *Philosophical Psychology, 2*, 143–164.

Staats, A. W. (1991). Unified positivism and unification psychology: Fad or new field? *American Psychologist, 46*, 899–912.

Stermac, L. E., Glansy, G., & Davidson, A. (1989, November). *Relapse prevention for sexual aggression: Profiling risk for offenders.* Presentation at the Annual Meeting of the Association for Advancement of Behavior Therapy, Washington, DC.

Stricker, G., & Trierweiler, S. T. (1995). The local clinical scientist: A bridge between science and practice. *American Psychologist, 50*, 995–1002.

Thornton, D. (1989). *The home office treatment program of sex offenders.* London: British Home Office.

Tollison, C. D., Adams, H. E., & Tollison, J. W. (1979). Physiological measurement of sexual arousal in homosexual, bisexual, and heterosexual males. *Journal of Behavioral Assessment, 2*, 53–59.

Ward, T., & Haig, B. D. (1997). Abductive reasoning and assessment. *Australian Psychologist, 32*, 93–100.

Ward, T., & Hudson, S. M. (1996). Relapse prevention: A critical analysis. *Sexual Abuse: A Journal of Research and Treatment, 8*, 177–200.

Ward, T., & Hudson, S, M. (in press). The construction and development of theory in the sexual offending area: A metatheoretical framework. *Sexual Abuse: A Journal of Research and Treatment.*

Ward, T., Hudson, S. M., & Marshall, W. L. (1994). The abstinence violation effect in child molesters. *Behaviour Research and Therapy, 32,* 431–437.

Ward, T., Hudson, S. M., & Marshall, W. L. (1996). Attachment style in sex offenders: A preliminary study. *Journal of Sex Research, 33,* 17–26.

Ward, T., Hudson, S. M., Marshall, W. L., & Siegert, R. J. (1995). Attachment style and intimacy deficits in sexual offenders: A theoretical framework. *Sexual Abuse: A Journal of Research and Treatment, 7,* 317–334.

Ward, T., Louden, K., Hudson, S. M., & Marshall, W. L. (1995). A descriptive model of the offense chain in child molesters. *Journal of Interpersonal Violence, 10,* 452–472.

INDEX